PLAYS AND PLAYWRIGHTS

2004

edited and with an introduction by

Martin Denton

Published by The New York Theatre Experience, Inc.
P.O. Box 744, Bowling Green Station, New York, NY 10274-0744
www.nytheatre.com
email: info@newyorktheatreexperience.org

ISBN 09670234-5-9
ISSN 1546-1319

 Plays and Playwrights 2004 is made possible in part with public funds from the New York State Council on the Arts, a state agency.

Book designed by Nita Congress
Cover designed by Steven Waxman

PERMISSIONS

TABLE OF CONTENTS

FOREWORD

When my play *Midnight Brainwash Revival* was published in the first New York Theatre Experience anthology of new plays, *Plays and Playwrights for the New Millennium,* I was ecstatic. To be anthologized has always been a milestone—no, a light-year-stone—for writers. It's like being invited to an Important Artists party. It's like coming home one day and all your clothes are new and fashionable. It's like getting an improved hormonal regimen: I feel GREAT!!!

Let's face it, the vast majority of playwrights receive very few large gold trophies in their mental mail (let alone large gold bricks in their actual mail). Recognition is rare, making motivation, which should come naturally to those of the selfless path of self-expression, an often tedious chore. But over the last five years, in the midst of what can feel like a general dearth of support and appreciation, there has been one wonderful and regular gesture of love in the playwriting world, and that is these anthologies. To be asked into an NYTE collection well, it simply makes all of it worth most of it.

There are many reasons these anthologies are important, but mostly it's because they are chronicling a very real, yet very unrecorded, artistic activity—writing new plays for New York theatre in the new millennium. Since New York is still the hub of true American theatre, you would think that someone would have been collecting into one place a set of such plays that are performed in said city on an annual basis. However, before NYTE got started on this enterprise in 1999, it had been many years since someone had actually done that. Now that it's being done, it seems impossible that it would not be. In short, the NYTE anthologies have become *essential.* People will look back in future years and view these anthologies as the quintessence of their theatrical milieu—the fermented goodness of numerous vital and vibrant dramatic efforts.

Producers looking for something to put up can now find a representative and fine sampling of the plays done in New York in a given year. So can readers looking to imagine for themselves what's happening on the current stage. So can actors looking for monologues or scenes. So can directors or theatre companies looking for projects. So can playwrights looking for compatriots or competitors. These anthologies are a textual meeting place for the theatrically obsessed.

And to work in theatre today, you have to be obsessed, since paying that obsession its due is often your only income. Yet to everyone who was involved in making and enjoying these plays—writers, actors, directors, designers, producers, audience members—this anthology represents a major payment in the form of admiration and exposure and recognition and readership. Don¹t spend it all in one place!

So, as you move your way through these new plays, think not only of what they mean on the page, but of what their being on the page means to those who wrote them—a chance to be in your mind! Thank you for inviting them in, and may you enjoy their visit.

Kirk Wood Bromley
December 2003

PREFACE

I have a great job; and one of the best parts of it is that each year I get to edit a new *Plays and Playwrights* volume. This is the fifth one, which is kind of amazing to me: when we completed our first collection, *Plays and Playwrights for the New Millennium*, I never imagined that it would turn into an annual event. But our readers are telling us that there is a clear need out there for the most interesting, most compelling, most inventive dramatic writing from New York's off-off-Broadway theatres, and so we are able to produce a new edition of this anthology series each year.

What's even more fulfilling is the fact that these books are achieving their primary mission, which is to introduce worthy new voices to the theatre community. The plays we've published have garnered productions all over the world, in colleges and regional theatres throughout the U.S., in many European countries, and even in places as far away as Australia and New Zealand. Our success stories range from that of *Horse Country* (*Plays and Playwrights for the New Millennium*), which was named Best of the Best of the Edinburgh Fringe by *The Scotsman*, to *Match* (*Plays and Playwrights 2002*), which had nearly a dozen mountings in the year following publication. Already, a scene from this year's *WTC View* took first prize in a local high school forensics meet!

So it is with great pride that I offer this newest collection, *Plays and Playwrights 2004*, which I hope will stand jauntily and elegantly on your shelf next to the earlier volumes. The creation of a book like this is a project that involves many, many people, and I want to acknowledge them here and now.

There would be no book without the ten plays, and so first and foremost I am grateful to the twelve playwrights who have entrusted their work to me. To Frank Cwiklik, Brian Sloan, Christy Meyer, Jon Schumacher, Ellen Shanman, John Jahnke, Tom X. Chao, Rob Reese, Michael Stock, David Pumo, Mary Jett Parsley, and Steven Gridley go my thanks, with great respect and admiration.

There would similarly be no physical book to contain the plays without the commitment and dedication of Nita Congress, who serves as copy editor, book designer, proofreader, and invaluable collaborator to myself and to all of the playwrights. Her contributions to this and previous *Plays and Playwrights* volumes cannot be overstated. And there would be no covers for the book without the patient, expert attention of Steven Waxman, who is responsible for our graphics design.

Every year, to launch our new anthology, we produce a series of readings and book signings to introduce our plays and playwrights to a wide audience. My profound thanks to the dozens of artists who lent their talents to these events, in particular the individuals who helped us organize them and ensured their success: the playwrights— Leon Chase, Maggie Cino, Ato Essandoh, Catherine Gillet, Joe Godfrey, Joseph Langham, Andrea Lepcio, Kelly McAllister, Marc Morales, and Edward Musto; Stephen Sunderlin of Vital Theatre Company; Kimo DeSean and Erez Ziv of Horse Trade Theatre Group; Rozanne Seelen, Allen Hubby, and Domenic Silipo of Drama Book Shop; Gretchen Shugart of Theatermania.com; Jeff Lewonczyk, Hope Cartelli, Tony Pennino, Ralph Carhart, Gene Forman, Dov Weinstein, Steve Caporaletti, Sarah Congress, and board-op extraordinaire Julie Congress.

Thanks, also, to some key supporters of The New York Theatre Experience, Inc., and our Publish Emerging Playwrights initiative: the New York State Council on the Arts; Bev Willey, our #1 booster; Lou Tally, Peter Petralia, John Clancy, Tom Epstein of The Dramatists' Guild, Elyse Sommer, Andy Propst, Mario Fratti, D.L. Lepidus, and Robert Simonson, for spreading the word; and Ron Lasko of Spin Cycle, Elena K. Holy and Shelley Burch of The Present Company, Scott Stiffler, Tim Errickson of Boomerang Theatre Company, and the late Dennis Smith of The Fourth Unity, for helping us discover these wonderful scripts in the first place.

Finally, everything we do at NYTE, including these annual volumes, is made possible only because of the tireless efforts of Rochelle Denton, our managing director, who also happens to be my mother. Her love of theatre, passed down to me, is at the root of the *Plays and Playwrights* books; she's a one-woman cheering section for New York's downtown theater scene and the grounded, highly disciplined operational locus of our organization. This book is dedicated to her.

Martin Denton
New York City
December 2003

INTRODUCTION

Martin Denton

A Manhattan photographer places an ad for a new roommate on September 10, 2001. A teenage runaway is mistakenly reported to have been kidnapped by Muslim terrorists. A former drag queen and his male lover adopt three gay/transgender teenagers. A team of researchers at MIT builds a robot that appears to exhibit human emotions. A TV network creates a reality show simulating the war in Vietnam.

Welcome to *Plays and Playwrights 2004*, where, among other things, we encapsulate a year of New York theatre, preserving its variety and vitality within the two covers of a book. What was on the minds of our emerging playwrights during the past twelve months? Current events, to be sure: Frank Cwiklik's *Sugarbaby* and Brian Sloan's *WTC View* take compelling but very different looks at post-9/11 America. We look toward the future in *United States: Work and Progress* by Christy Meyer, Jon Schumacher, and Ellen Shanman, which documents cutting-edge artificial intelligence research; and we look backward to our collective past in *The Shady Maids of Haiti*, in which John Jahnke examines racial, sexual, and gender politics against the backdrop of the 1803 Haitian slave rebellion. We examine cultural institutions: Tom X. Chao deconstructs the outer edges of experimental theatre in *Cats Can See The Devil*, while Rob Reese brings reality television to its logical next step in his parody, *Survivor: Vietnam!* Contemporary family values at the beginning of the twenty-first century are considered in *Feed the Hole*, in which Michael Stock explores the troubled relationships of a group of disconnected twenty-somethings, and in *Auntie Mayhem*, in which David Pumo gives us a nontraditional family extraordinaire. Finally, our playwrights grapple with Big Issues—imagination and redemption in Mary Jett Parsley's

1

The Monster Tales, and time, space, and eternity in Steven Gridley's *Sun, Stand Thou Still*.

I said "among other things" a moment ago because, in addition to providing a kind of permanent record of the theatre, *Plays and Playwrights 2004* has two other very important goals. First and foremost, it's a showcase for outstanding new plays. As editor and reviewer for nytheatre.com, I see several hundred new plays each year, and these ten are among the very finest of the past twelve months: inventive and intelligent, thought-provoking and thoughtful, stretching and engaging their audiences and challenging the status quo theatrically and thematically. These plays have all had successful runs in New York City and they're ripe for production in your corner of the world (see page iii for contact and permissions information for each one).

Second, *Plays and Playwrights 2004* is meant to be a launching pad for new theatre artists. This year's cohort of playwrights is a distinguished, remarkable lot: a pair of authentic auteurs who meticulously write, direct, and design highly personal yet resonant productions whose dazzling theatricality belies their humble off-off-Broadway origins (Frank Cwiklik and John Jahnke); two energetic young men still in their twenties, both coincidentally educated in Chicago and both founders of their own flourishing theatre companies in New York (Michael Stock and Jon Schumacher); two young women who are building careers as actors and playwrights, exploring the still-nascent field of documentary theatre (Ellen Shanman and Christy Meyer); an entrepreneurial solo performer who has migrated from stand-up monology to full-fledged theatre production and playwriting (Tom X. Chao), and an equally enterprising performer with roots in the world of improv who has become an accomplished theatre director and writer (Rob Reese); a writer and brand-new mother from North Carolina who works as a high school English teacher (Mary Jett Parsley), and a lawyer from Long Island who works with disadvantaged teens at the Vera Institute of Justice in New York City (David Pumo); an independent filmmaker and veteran of Sundance and other festivals (Brian Sloan), and a director-playwright who is one of off-off-Broadway's rising stars and who was, in fact, involved with two of the pieces in *Plays and Playwrights 2002* (Steven Gridley). Mark their names, read their plays: these are the people who will be helping to shape and define American drama in the next decade or two.

❖

In a relatively short time, Frank Cwiklik has journeyed from staging adaptations of fluky films (Orson Welles's *The Stranger*, Ed Wood's

The Fugitive Girls) to mounting sensational productions of Shakespeare (the apocalyptic *Bitch Macbeth, Antony and Cleopatra* set in Las Vegas) to, with *Sugarbaby*, devising, directing, and designing—from the ground up—a completely original, mind-blowingly pertinent American play. Cwiklik's work is special because it's uncannily visceral and thrillingly evocative. Armed with almost no props, but with a prodigiously imaginative use of lighting and sound cues—and a big dollop of theatrical know-how—he creates exciting, cinematic set pieces like *Sugarbaby*'s Vegas Strip car chase sequence that leave spectators breathless. Cwiklik's theatre is noisy, rude, brash, and full of energy; without resorting to the rougher tactics of theatre of cruelty, it nevertheless shakes up an audience that is growing too accustomed to sitting passively in the dark.

Cwiklik's playwriting owes much to the movies, as you'll discover when you read *Sugarbaby* later in this book; also to the lurid paperback pulp tradition, which is perhaps the most precise literary antecedent of this singular look at the Way We Live Now. *Sugarbaby*'s heroine and title character is a teenage girl from the heartland who gets fed up with her parents' petty feuding and her dead-end job and decides to run away from home. She hooks up with the only real friend she has, a car mechanic named Jesus who is obsessed with Elvis Presley; together they head off, as Lewis and Clark and Simon and Garfunkel did before them, to look for America. But when two of Sugarbaby's neighbors tell bigtime cable TV reporter Rod Butane that she was kidnapped by what they call "Moo-Slam" terrorists ("I think it might have been Yoosama Bin Layden," says one of them), a media frenzy of gargantuan proportions ignites.

Sugarbaby takes in the whole of American culture, circa 2003: Vegas, fast food, cable news networks, Michael Moore, TV talk shows, conspiracy theories—you name it. Cwiklik gets the shades and rhythms exactly right; here's anchorman Rod Butane near the end of a typical broadcast:

> ROD: America's a word. You think they'll try to ban that, too? Is that next? You can't say "America" in our schools. Because they don't believe in it anymore. Irving Berlin would be appalled. *(Damn. That was nice. ROD lets that hover in the air a moment, then leans back.)* I'm Rod Butane. I know what's important.

The collision of paranoia and patriotism at the center of much recent national debate is all over *Sugarbaby*; what's refreshingly missing is cynicism: everybody in this play is passionate about what they believe, however misguided or ridiculous it may seem. *Sugarbaby*'s melting pot of loud, eccentric characters makes it genuinely epic; in the best democratic tradition, it pokes fun at all of them, but it does so with love. Somewhere inside all of this deranged and excessive satire resides the truth.

※

If *Sugarbaby* offers a panoramic view of the Zeitgeist, *WTC View* zooms in on a specific, critical moment in recent history to bring it into sharp, vivid focus. Probably *the* critical moment: Brian Sloan's play is set in New York City in September 2001, just after two airplanes crashed into and destroyed the World Trade Center. In the hours and days after the twin towers collapsed, Lower Manhattan looked and felt like a war zone: streets were coated with inches of rubble; police and soldiers guarded checkpoints at virtually every intersection; the stench of seemingly endless smoke was pervasive. Most of the plays written about 9/11 so far have focused on the personal tragedies and/or political implications of the catastrophe; *WTC View* bravely and incisively maps out the day-to-day human costs, telling a part of the story that has heretofore been mostly ignored.

The incident that inspired Sloan to write *WTC View* actually happened. As he writes in his notes to the play, the last thing he did on the night of September tenth was place a classified ad for a new roommate. The protagonist of *WTC View*, a photographer named Eric, does the same thing; and, in nine scenes spanning the two weeks after 9/11, he interviews an assortment of candidates under just about the most strained circumstances imaginable. Eric is freaked out by what's going on in his city; his attitudes and responses to events are unflinchingly and honestly recounted by the playwright, and contrasted with those of the various would-be roommates, who range from a British hotel worker who started his new job in America on September ninth to a successful bond trader who was on the ninety-first floor of Tower One when the first plane hit.

The resulting drama is riveting and also gratifyingly well-crafted—Sloan cannily ensures that the audience is engaged and absorbed in genuine human conflicts and values even as he manages to say some things about 9/11 that absolutely need to be said. One of the prospective roommates is a New York University student named Max, whose apparently boundless naiveté really gets under Eric's skin:

> MAX: Hey—did you take a lot of pictures on the eleventh?
> ERIC: Uh…no.
> MAX: I got some insane shots on my digital camera. I'll have to show them to you.

ERIC: Uh...no thanks.

MAX: Then later that day, me and my roommates went up to Union Square. Got some insane pictures there too. We were lighting candles and meditating. It was pretty intense.

ERIC: *(Sarcastic.)* Ohhh—you were part of that whole sixties love-in thing?

MAX: *(A little offended by this.)* Hey—that's a bit harsh.

ERIC: C'mon...it was a bunch of students whose classes were cancelled and didn't have anything better to do, right?

Cruel and sad and absurd, just like life, *WTC View* offers authentic testimony to the ordinary people who, neither victims nor survivors, just happened to live and work near a site of total devastation. Filled with sorrow, anger, gallows humor, and compassion, it's an important document of our times. And it's a darned fine play.

※

Documentary theatre has become increasingly popular in the past ten years or so, thanks to Anna Deavere Smith, Moises Kaufman, and others. Christy Meyer, Jon Schumacher, and Ellen Shanman—the three young writer-performers of *United States: Work and Progress*—actually spent some time working with Kaufman in the process of creating their own very original contribution to this emerging genre. As explained later in this book, this piece is part of an ongoing project launched in 1999 by Singularity (the company cofounded by Schumacher and Shanman), with the objective of putting the lives of ordinary people on stage. Schumacher's *A Day in the Life of Clark Chipman*, about a midlevel Chicago government bureaucrat, was in the 1999 New York International Fringe Festival; I saw it there and was immediately impressed by both the ambition and the talent of these dedicated artists. Two more pieces, mounted together as *Railways & Firework*, followed in 2000; then, at the end of 2002, came *Work and Progress*.

It seems to me that one of the fundamental jobs of the documentarian is to properly select whose stories to tell. This is certainly one of the great strengths of *Work and Progress*, which focuses on three young scientists whose work is not only fascinating but enormously relevant. Jessica Banks, Cynthia Breazeal, and Aaron Edsinger work in the Artificial Intelligence Laboratory at the Massachusetts Institute of Technology, where they're involved with projects such as the creation of robots that simulate human emotional responses and the development of synthetic, mechanical "organisms" that emulate the functionality of, say, a human muscle. The nature of this work is inherently reductive, focused on discovering the component structure of processes that are extraordinarily complicated, yet so commonplace that most of us take them for granted.

Meyer, Schumacher, and Shanman prove to be adept chroniclers, precisely capturing the voices of their subjects. Here's one of them, explicating some of his current research:

> AARON: But I think, I think the cool thing for me is that you can start building robots that have sort of a soft squishy form to them, right? It's not all rods and metal that are bolted together. So I convinced Rod to let me build a tensegrity robot. And, um, so the first thing I'm building is a leech, actually. And then maybe a jellyfish.

The mannered (i.e., natural) speech patterns feel like artifice; we're constantly aware, in *Work and Progress*, that the actors are interpreting (as opposed to pretending to be), the characters they depict in the play. This turns out to be not just intentional, but necessary: actors and characters both, in this piece, seek to create life from, as it were, thin air: can either ever entirely succeed?

※

The Haitian Slave Rebellion of 1803 is hardly an obvious subject for dramatization; but John Jahnke has carved out a niche for himself in the world of alternative theatre by creating plays on a variety of eclectic topics, commenting profoundly on the human condition in the process. Using a singular stage vocabulary and incorporating startling, vivid imagery that is sometimes shocking but never gratuitous, Jahnke creates theatre that is dense, elegant, and surreal.

The Shady Maids of Haiti requires just four characters to tell its story: M., an exiled French poet; Mme., his Creole wife; Mlle., their Haitian servant; and X, an African man who may or may not be embroiled in the slave revolt. In some two dozen scenes and interludes, the playwright arranges the members of this quartet into every conceivable combination, allowing us to observe a shifting and unsettling balance of power as the white, male (ostensible) head of the household, destroyed by malaise and decadence, yields to the Others. *Shady Maids*, filled with betrayals and intrigue, emerges as a study in politics—racial, sexual, and gender.

The play shakes us up by continuously positing outcomes that challenge accepted wisdom and status quos.

> MLLE: You play two sides, refusing to defend your home merely for the attention it might afford you—as if coquetry would be the drug that finally forces you to surrender the empty well of your soul to whomever offers the highest price.

MME: And who would that be?

MLLE: A stranger—

MME: A slave?

MLLE: A thief? Your husband prowls the estate for a means of claiming what he perceives to be his. He conjures forgotten memories of your sweet and comforting kiss as a stranger bleeds on your sheets.

It also stretches our assumptions about contemporary theatre, as well. A rigorous superficial structure belies the fluid, magical-to-supernatural shape that the play ultimately takes: the action encompasses both the mundane and the extraordinary; characters speak dialog at once frank—profane, even, sometimes—and oddly formalized and stiff, like figures in a dimly remembered dream. Time moves logarithmically: a moment or a month can pass within a single exchange. Symbols—beginning with the treacherous flowers of the play's title—abound. An ethereal design—beautifully realized in *Shady Maids's* New York production, I should add—is skillfully sketched out in the stage directions (one of them, with bravado worthy of Tennessee Williams, simply reads "The fireflies flicker and die").

Almost novelistic in its sweep yet innately theatrical, *Shady Maids* conjures an unknown and alien world as it recounts its unfamiliar story. It's ripe for interpretation and exploration by directors, designers, and actors looking to exercise their imaginations.

⁜

The fringe/alternative theatre scene that provides such a nourishing environment for artists like John Jahnke gets a good-natured (and well-deserved) ribbing in *Cats Can See The Devil*. Tom X. Chao's shrewd comedy-satire-meditation-parable on creativity begins at a performance of a self-proclaimed "puppet show for children" (that is actually *not* recommended for children) entitled "The Story of the Abstract Geometrical Shapes With No Allegorical Content," in which a writer/narrator and three puppeteers enact the exploration of ten thousand years of psychohistory with characters such as Puce Nonagon and Mr. Can of Cream-Style Corn. This masterful opening set piece is at once a hilarious parody of the grotesquely self-indulgent avant-garde/experimental/performance art claptrap that we've all had to sit through over the last several decades, and a deliciously self-referential exemplar of same: Chao knows this terrain, in all its uncomfortable, underfunded, desperate glory. It's not long before the puppet show implodes under the weight of its own self-importance, and the performers stage a mutiny. The second half of *Cats Can See The Devil* is more serious—though still enormously funny—as it tracks what amounts to an onstage nervous breakdown to reveal the obsessions and preoccupations of a compulsively creative individual.

CCSTD knows no sacred cows. It sends up virtually every genre of fringe theatre, along with the New York International Fringe Festival (where it premiered) itself; everything from interpretative dance to improv to interactive drama gets a jab or two in Chao's take-no-prisoners tour-de-force. Here, for example, one of the rebellious puppeteers talks about her checkered career in sketch comedy:

> TUESDAY: I was in a group called Lousy Poker Hand…but they folded. *(Pause.)* Then I was in a group called The Croissants…but everybody flaked on me. *(Pause.)* Then I was in Vacuum Tube…but that imploded. *(Pause.)* Then I was in The Helen Kellers…but they lacked vision. *(Pause.)* Then I was in The Amputees…but they didn't have a leg to stand on. *(Pause.)* Then I was in Empty Fabric Store…but they didn't have any material. *(Pause.)* Then I was in The Sandals…but we kept stepping on each other's toes. *(Pause.)* Then I was in The Weekly Newsmagazines…but they had too many issues.

This gag is actually sustained for a few more lines; Chao is, perhaps above all else, a supremely funny writer. His is a far-ranging, esoteric wit—how many plays do you know of that boast jokes about n-plus-one dimensional entities?

And then there's the Tom X. Chao persona, a sort of sad-sack loner with delusions of aesthetic superiority. Chao puts himself, or this (hopefully) exaggerated version of himself, right in the middle of his plays, *CCSTD* included; in fact, he's built up something of a mini-cult in downtown NYC around his performances. As you'll discover, this is yet another layer of the recursive put-on: a show about creating a show about creating a show. No intellectual or artistic pretension is safe with Chao in the house.

❋

As *Cats Can See The Devil* mines the parodic possibilities of off-off-Broadway, *Survivor: Vietnam!* tackles the currently ubiquitous phenomenon of reality television. Its author, Rob Reese, hails from the world of improv, having studied in Chicago at Second City and The Annoyance (home of *"So, I Killed a Few People…,"* which was featured in *Plays and Playwrights for the New Millennium*). In New York, he founded Amnesia Wars, a troupe that started out doing long-form improvisations and which has now branched out into stand-up comedy and more conventional theatre. *Survivor: Vietnam!*—sharp, ingenious, and hilarious—benefits from all its diverse antecedents in Reese's varied career.

The idea is one of those "what-ifs" that seems obvious after somebody else thinks of it—a reality TV series set in the midst of the Vietnam War. Six impossibly eager contestants compete for a $1 million prize in *Survivor: Vietnam!*, battling landmines, air raids, a *Deer Hunter*-esque game of Russian roulette, and, eventually, a crazed network executive with more than a passing resemblance to the Marlon Brando character in *Apocalypse Now*. Acknowledging the apparently limitless cynicism of TV programmers (as well as the fact that the war in Vietnam ended several decades ago), Reese gives us the Ho Chi Minnies—Asian beauties in tight fatigue shorts and wet T-shirts—in place of the Viet Cong; and he gives the whole post-Enron capitalist economy a nod with a pair of hilarious and brilliant "commercials" for the ultimate consumer product, the Wipe-n-Go Completely Disposable Two-Step Disposable System.

The sights and sounds of (as he calls it) "Empty-Vee" culture are everywhere in this play. Here's some of the "teaser footage" at the top of *Survivor: Vietnam!* introducing us to one of the contestants:

> CHORUS: Cut to Erica in an urban park, concrete and steel.
>
> ERICA: As a woman, I know about struggle. I know what it takes to survive, which is why I want to be on "Survivor," because I can survive the hardships that need to be…survived.
>
> CHORUS: Cut to Erica in her living room.
>
> ERICA: This is my collection of media products that I find demeaning to women…
>
> CHORUS: Cut back to Erica on the playground.
>
> ERICA: …and a result of a societal structure that forces black kids to live in neighborhoods like this one. Now, I actually grew up in Northport, Long Island, but, you know, women are an oppressed minority too, so I completely know what these kids had to go through. Without the street crime, and violence, and poverty.
>
> CHORUS: Cut back to Erica in her living room.
>
> ERICA: This is my Disney shelf: *Cinderella, Pocahontas, Lion King*. I actually kind of like *Lion King*, but I'm sure if I watch it over and over again, I'll learn to find it demeaning.

Reese's dead-on take on the New Banality is so funny it's scary, and vice versa. Reese is an authentic humorist and also a fine theatre craftsman: *Survivor: Vietnam!* works as well as it does because it adheres to a surprisingly robust classical dramatic structure, of which the character of Chorus is the most essential and obvious component. This is a sturdy play loaded with apt commentary about human impulses that will be with us long after reality TV has run its course. At least, let's hope so.

Feed the Hole takes a quieter, more contemplative look at the mores and attitudes of young adults in America. It tells the story of a group of twenty-somethings who are going through the motions of grown-up life—jobs, apartments, boyfriends and girlfriends—without firm commitment to any of it. There are four major characters: Brett and Shelly, whose relationship is falling apart—in fact, for most of the play, Brett is the only character who doesn't know that Shelly is deeply involved in an affair with another man—and their good friends Rob and Samantha, another couple whose relationship is tested and strained by the residual effects of Shelly's infidelity.

The play depicts parts of their individual journeys toward fulfill-ment, or at least something approximating fulfillment. Over dinner, drinks, or Ben & Jerry's ice cream, the women (with gay best friend John) dissect and analyze and agonize, while the men parry and ban-ter. What I find most striking about *Feed the Hole* is the way that its sitcom rhythms—echoing *Friends*, *Sex in the City*, and the like—belie the gaping unhappiness that is at its center. So we laugh in recognition at a scene like this one, the empty-headed barroom chat-ter of Brett, Rob, and one of their friends:

> BRETT: Oh, Rob, you're the deal-breaker—
>
> STEVE: We were talking earlier— So *think* about this now—
>
> BRETT: You think Hall and Oates are gay?
>
> ROB: Well, I dunno— Why?
>
> STEVE: Just talking. C'mon, it's just us guys—talk straight.
>
> BRETT: 'Cause I see this MTV "Behind the Music" thing.
>
> STEVE: Yeah, it's VH-1.
>
> BRETT: And all of a sudden it hits me— these guys are fags.
>
> ROB: Yeah?
>
> BRETT: C'mon that song, "Man-Eater"?

But then we unexpectedly get punched in the gut, as in Scene Four-teen:

> BRETT and SHELLY's. The only light is from the TV. The sounds of bad porn. BRETT is alone in the apartment. He is masturbating in the greenish glow of the television.

Feed the Hole is, finally, a sad, wise, and unsettling meditation on a disconnectedness that seems to have become epidemic. Playwright Michael Stock, with his remarkable ear for dialog and his Pinter-esque grasp of the meanings between words, proves himself with *Feed the Hole* to be an able spokesman for his generation. Stock, also an actor and director, won an Excellence in Playwriting Award at the 2001 New York International Fringe Festival for his first full-length play, *Hustle*; one imagines other accolades in his future as his distinctive voice begins to reach a wider audience.

❋

"Family values" is a buzzword that gets bandied about a lot these days, but the self-appointed guardians of this American ideal probably aren't thinking about Felony Mayhem and her brood when they talk about it. Which is exactly why *Auntie Mayhem*, David Pumo's warm, loving dramatic comedy, is so important. The title character is a gay man who was once a professional drag artist; the play chronicles the birth and growth of his new family, as he and his husband Bobo adopt first Dennis (sixteen, gay, living on the streets), then Ivan (seventeen, gay, thrown out by his mother's abusive boyfriend), and finally Epiphany (né Eduardo, sixteen, a male-to-female transgender—i.e., biologically a boy, but living as a girl).

Felony, Bobo, and their "sons" are all Latino or black, which is to say that these characters are as invisible to mainstream America as *Feed the Hole*'s twentysomething urbanites are ubiquitous. *Auntie Mayhem* lifts the curtain on a group that most people know nothing about—kids whose sexuality causes them to be despised or misunderstood by their families, schools, and communities; and whose ethnicity often results in their being ignored by the gay community as well. Pumo, who has made a career outside of the theatre working with kids like Dennis, Ivan, and Epiphany, does us all a great service by at last giving these vibrant, life-affirming individuals a home on stage.

It's exciting to hear the too-long disenfranchised when they are finally given a chance to speak! Listen to Ivan, rapping about *his* sexual identity at the center of *Auntie Mayhem*:

> IVAN: Liza's back, didn't even know she was gone
> You know it sounds like the same old shit she's always done
> Ethel Merman, Judy Garland, Billie Holiday
> What dead diva's grave are we dancin' on today
> Not that I don't give props to the departed
> The ones who planted the seed, who got it started
> Shouts to the trannies in their panties and their underwire
> Took over the Stonewall, set the Village on fire
> Back to the Daughters of Bilitis before
> And the Mattachine Society challenging the old law
> Sylvia, and Marcia P. and Harry Hay
> Laid the tracks that brought us to where we are today
> But we gotta fight a new war, sing a new song that'll
> Bring the children to the floor, lead them into new battle

You're right, by the way, if you guessed that Pumo is alluding to *Auntie Mame* in his title: one of the pleasures of this charmer of a play is picking out the many references to Patrick Dennis's iconic novel which are liberally sprinkled throughout (e.g., Felony's best pal/"bosom buddy" is named Charlotte—or Charles, as in Vera). But the congruities are actually incidental; for as untraditional as Felony, Bobo, and their family may be, they're finally not madcap or unconventional creatures—not about the stuff that really matters, like discipline, and rules, and creating a warm, loving, and nurturing environment in which young people can grow and flourish. *Auntie Mayhem* is, of all things, a celebration of the nuclear family—albeit one that's been shoved, kicking and screaming, into the brave new world of the twenty-first century.

Mary Jett Parsley's *The Monster Tales* was chronologically the earliest of the ten plays in this volume to be produced in New York; it premiered in the fall of 2002 as part of Boomerang Theatre Company's annual mini-"festival" of new and classic work in repertory. Its special qualities were instantly apparent, and I am sure that many more productions of this whimsical, lighter-than-air fable are going to pop up as soon as people find out about it. It begins when twenty-eight-year-old Mimi checks under her bed, as she does every night, for monsters. Only this time, she spots one. After she recovers from some initial alarm, she begins to chat with her visitor, who explains that he has been hiding under her bed all her life, listening to the stories she tells while she sleeps.

Mimi's life is in something of a rut at the moment, and she can't believe that she has any interesting stories to share, even in her dreams. So the monster starts to tell some back to her. There's a romantic tale about an old man who orders a bride from a catalog and then is unable to get her to fall in love with him. There's a sweet and hopeful tale about an old woman who one day discovers a little boy growing in her garden. And there's a sad, sorrowful tale about a girl who refuses to leave her house after her mother dies.

Parsley surprises us with these stories, which have the warm, familiar air—and the timeless wisdom—of authentic folktales; but they're all new, and their freshness delights us as well. Eventually, it's time in *The Monster Tales* for Mimi to invent something new for her visitor, and she rises to the challenge beautifully—her and our imagination reawakened by this moving and lovely celebration of the power of storytelling:

MIMI: Once upon a time…there was a man who could make music with his hands. He did not need to touch an instrument; he simply rubbed his fingers together and a violin played. It came from the air, from another time, and it sang to any soul who could listen. If he rubbed his hands together, whole orchestras sounded. His name was Alexander.

Who could resist?

Of course, in again finding the stories inside her, Mimi rediscovers herself. Which is, on reflection, the reason we have theatre.

❖

Steven Gridley made two appearances in *Plays and Playwrights 2002*, as the assistant director of J. Scott Reynolds's *The Wild Ass's Skin*, and as the director of Marc Chun's *Match*. He's clearly got the soul of a writer, though, and so it's with pleasure that I include his remarkable, dreamlike play *Sun, Stand Thou Still*, in this collection. Like the other authors anthologized here and in previous volumes, Gridley is one of our theatre's rising stars, bringing intelligence, insight, and imagination to every project he undertakes.

This piece—abstract, bittersweet, and moody—brings together an old blind man, a hitchhiker whom he picks up in his truck, and a pretty young woman selling apples at the side of a lonely road. Gridley doesn't tell us much about any of them: we never learn the Hitchhiker's name, for example, or the exact place where the Apple Woman came from or is heading to. Mary Chase wrote that her fantastical creation Harvey had overcome "not only time and space—but any objections," and so it seems to be for Gridley's characters: faith and reason are tested; the quest—for redemption? for love?—seems to be all.

Sun, Stand Thou Still brings us full circle, more or less: *Sugarbaby* started us off on a road trip in search of America; the inhabitants of Gridley's play, on journeys of their own, seem to be in search of something even larger. The blind man has been driving west for tens of thousands of miles:

DRIVER: Been traveling west since I can remember. Direct and nonstop. You think there's anything casual about that? Going in one direction? One. There was only one time, one time, that I stopped heading west. At about the forty thousand-mile mark I got mixed up. Suddenly wasn't quite sure if I was traveling west anymore. You go forty thousand miles in one direction, your mind starts to doubt, you know? You expect something to happen, I mean… *something*. An ocean?

Gridley blends the real and the unreal to create an evocative and sometimes enigmatic fantasia that gets under the skin. Is the Hitch-hiker Everyman or a supernatural being? Is the Apple Woman real? How is it that the Driver—eyes burned out after a fifteen-hour "star-ing contest" with the sun—can always read the odometer of his truck? The "truth" of *Sun, Stand Thou Still* is ultimately for each of its observers to riddle out, the same way each of its characters has to make sense, with what limited information he or she has been given, of what their own lives are supposed to be about.

The answer, maybe, *is* in the questing. Which is why we have the-atre.

SUGARBABY

Frank Cwiklik

FRANK CWIKLIK has worked in off-off-Broadway New York theatre since 1999, having directed, produced, written, performed in, designed, you name it, over two dozen productions, mostly with his company, DMTheatrics. His work has received praise from the *Village Voice, Backstage, Show Business Weekly,* OOBR.com, and countless others. He is the recipient of two consecutive OOBR awards for Outstanding Production (*Antony and Cleopatra,* 2002; *The Stranger,* 2001). He has directed works by everyone from William Shakespeare to Ed Wood, and his original works include *Girls' School Vampire, Twenty, Bitch Macbeth,* and *Who in the Hell is the Real, Live Lorelei Lee?* He lives with his wife, Michele, in Midtown Manhattan with six cats, four thousand LPs, and a hamster.

Sugarbaby was first presented by Danse Macabre Theatrics (Frank Cwiklik, Artistic Director; Michele Schlossberg, Managing Director) in association with Horse Trade Theater Group (Kimo DeSean, Artistic Director; Erez Ziv, Managing Director) on July 10, 2003, at The Red Room Theater, New York City, with the following cast and credits:

Mabel, Andrea, and Others .... Amanda Allan
Stanislaus, Dave, and Others .... Erik Bowie
Bailey Sugarman (Sugarbaby) .... Marguerite French
Sheriff Rufus J. Miranda .... Brandon Kalbaugh
Mr. Shakey, Uncle Sam, and Others .... Dan Maccarone
Doris, Mavis, and Others .... Angela Madeline
Rod Butane .... Josh Mertz
Mitch Common .... Kevin Myers
Ginger Sugarman-Malveaux and Others .... Michele Schlossberg
Jesus .... Adam Swiderski
Aron Malveaux and Others .... Alexander R. Warner
Clovis, Sigmund Freud, and Others........................ Jonathan Wise

Sound design and recording by: Youthquake!
Fight direction by: Michele Schlossberg
Choreography by: Bertram Von Von
Graphics by: Faint Hope Graphics and Design
Set and prop construction by: Jose Soto
Photography by: Moira Stone
Designed and directed by: Frank Cwiklik

> *"We must all hang together or assuredly we will all hang separately." —Benjamin Franklin*

AUTHOR'S NOTE

This show grew out of frustration with the way that this country has been going for so many years, the paralyzing, polarizing idiocy that has come to pass for political discourse in our increasingly embattled culture. It seemed, at the time I was writing it, that America—shit, Western civilization—was willingly slaughtering itself, allowing the lunatic fringes of the left and right to hijack the spirit and character of humanity. Thus, I wrote a foul-mouthed road comedy about a seventeen-year-old girl and an Elvis impersonator. Go figure.

What was most gratifying about this show was that the response was overwhelmingly positive across the board: whether left or right, conservative or liberal, everyone was energized and excited, and everyone left feeling better, about themselves, about America. It changed people's lives. Which is the point of theater in general, really, but especially a show like this. It was also entertaining watching conservatives get angry at jokes that liberals were howling at, and vice versa. Viewers were sometimes at war with themselves, wondering what they thought about a given scene, and if it was right or wrong to think that. Good.

If your feelings on America are dogmatic, either pro or con, or if your opinions are second hand, you will not like this show. Tough. If you love this country, flaws and all, believe in it, want to fight for it and over it, and are tired of being harassed by lunatics both left and right, well, this is for you. Enjoy.

Oh, yeah, and it's pretty funny, too.

PRODUCTION NOTES

The rules to follow for this show to work:

1. *Do not* condescend to the characters. Even the silliest, broadest characters (Stanislaus, Rufus, Mavis, hell, all of 'em) have a heart, and a soul, and must be treated with respect. The jokes are broad, but the characters must not be.

2. When the show takes a serious turn, take it seriously. Jesus's confession, the conversation between Sug and the three icons in Heaven, Sugarbaby's poem, Stanislaus's story of the Gulag, and especially the last scene, must be played with delicacy and heart.

3. *Energy and attitude.* The show is meant to make people feel good about themselves, and it works. Audiences were cheering, singing along, and, yes, crying at times, but it must be a crowd pleaser in order to do its job. It must also move like a damn rocket. The running time is meant to be about 110 minutes. And it was. Yes, really.

I think of myself more as a director than a writer, so when I create this and other pieces, I'm building them with the finished product in mind. Consequently, I worry that they'll seem stilted and dull when read, instead of the vibrant, noisy, messy, prankish pieces they become when staged. I've tried to compensate for that here by writing more body copy than usual, and punching up some of the dialog and stage directions to give the published version more of the brash, pamphleteering feel the performances had. I've also played a sort of Fantasy Baseball by describing, in the text, situations, events, and sets that we couldn't possibly have afforded, but would have had if money were no object. Lest one feel overwhelmed, this show was staged on a typical off-off-Broadway budget (ten bucks in nickels and a Dixie cup full of dryer lint), and, despite the limitations, it was the unflagging energy of the cast, the propulsive nature of the performance, and the spirit of the audience that gave the finished product an epic sweep most big-budget spectacles would kill for. The Vegas chase was accomplished with four folding chairs, ten actors, and foam boards with blowup photos of Vegas, and the audience understood at all times what was going on, committed to it, and cheered wildly at its climax. *That's* theatre, goddammit.

What also added to the scale of the piece was an audacious (and damnably difficult) sound design, including several hours' of fake radio and TV broadcasts and commercials which played before the show, between scenes, and during intermission, sometimes even in the backgrounds of scenes, giving the show some of the whirlwind, invigorating, chatterbox feel of a weblog or political rally. Some examples of these loops and tapes can be heard on the DMTheatrics website—www.dm-theatrics.com. If you like this show, check out the tapes. They're damned funny.

Dialog marked by an asterisk (*) is meant to be overlapped by the line immediately following it. All overlapped dialog is meant to be finished at full volume, without stopping for the following line. The effect should be one of constant noise, of people talking and not listening, of an endless dull roar of argumentative lunacy. You know. America.

Thank you,

The Management

DRAMATIS PERSONAE (PEOPLE WHAT'S IN THIS HERE THING)

THE HEARTLAND OF THE FOOTHILLS

BAILEY "SUGARBABY" SUGARMAN, seventeen years old

CLETUS and BRUTUS CAPERS, peeping toms

GINGER SUGARMAN-MALVEAUX, hot mamma

ARON MALVEAUX, the unhandy handyman

REX MUNSON, veteran

BRANDI MINOR, fast food clerk

MR. SHAKEY, McMullan's senior keyholder and employee of the month for a record three months in a row in late 2002

JESUS, the mechanic who thinks he's Elvis, a good boy

ELROY STERN, proud owner of Stern's Auto Body and three Camaros

JEFF, Schwarz's Pizza delivery boy

THE MEDIA

ROD BUTANE, America's Son, the Right Hand of God

MITCH COMMON, award-winning maverick documentary filmmaker

DAVE, Mitch's cameraman

JERRY, Rod's beleaguered PA

SKIP BUCKCHUCK, Shopping channel shill

JIMMY HOOLER, late nite comic

KATIE SHERMAN, host of "America Talk Back!"

THE LAW

SHERIFF RUFUS J. MIRANDA, ex-Marine, American by birth, Southern by the Grace of God

LAS VEGAS

STANISLAUS POLSKI, candy magnate and high roller

DORIS GROPNIK, casino slot attendant

CLOVIS MANGOLD, con artist

MABEL MANGOLD, his wife and co-conspirator

SLOTS LADY, junkie for the spinning reels

EARL, Elvis fan

JACK DIAMOND, winner of the Tri-State Elvis Tribute Artists Competition 2001

JOSH LIPSTEIN, activist, vegan, pacifist

ANDREA DiANGELO, activist, vegan, pacifist, womyn's studies major

DIRK, grizzled war veteran and licensed pilot

AIRPORT TICKET ATTENDANT, certainly not taking any shit from you

AIR TRAFFIC CONTROLLER, certainly not expecting any of this shit

and the VIVA LAS VEGAS CHORALE!

FLORIDA

MAVIS TURNER, diner waitress

HEAVEN

UNCLE SAM, icon

JESUS H. CHRIST, messiah, son of God

ELVIS ARON PRESLEY, idol to millions

SIGMUND FREUD, father of modern psychiatry

NORTH CAROLINA

BUS DRIVER, in a big goddamn hurry

WASHINGTON, D.C.

FATHER JAMES KILPATRICK, priest and activist

AMERICA FIRST! PROTESTORS

LEFT IS RIGHT PROTESTORS

PROLOGUE

Music: "Star-Spangled Banner." Lights up on the American flag. Enter the usher, maybe the stage manager, director, anyone not in the actual cast. Barks at the audience, not mean, but dead serious. Drill sergeant. Good-natured gravitas.

DRILL SERGEANT: *Good evening ladies and gentlemen, and welcome to this evening's performance of* Sugarbaby! *Before the show begins, we would like to point out some very important information! First of all, this show is very loud! and very vulgar! Just like America. Secondly, please disconnect all cell phones, personal pagers, and digital devices for the duration of the program! This is not your living room, Sunshine, and I expect you to show some respect to your fellow theatregoers and to the fine young men and women performing on this here stage! If your cell phone, pager, or digital device*

should happen to go off during this show, *you will answer to me, maggot! And, fi-nally… (Sincerely, with a snappy salute.)* God bless America. Thank you for coming and enjoy the show.

(Lights down as the music reaches its climax. Blackout. We hear the voice of the NARRA-TOR, deep, slight accent, Southern. Rich. Folksy, but authoritative. Think Sam Elliott, maybe, or Johnny Cash. Music: Gershwin, "For Lily Pons." The mood is melancholy, almost sad.)

NARRATOR: *(Voiceover.)* Time was, "God Bless America" was heard in every ballpark, on every TV show, in every movie theatre. Time was, America meant something more than just a superpower striding the globe. It was an idea, a concept, an abstract. But that was then, and this is now. The only thing Americans can agree on now is that they all disagree—on our place in the world, on the meaning of

America, on what we, as a nation, stand for. Seems the only thing we do stand for is our own uncertainty. America desperately needs a hero, or an icon. And it seems we've found that lightning rod for American dismay in a very unlikely source…

ACT ONE

1

Music: Mel Smith, "Pretty Plaid Skirt."

Lights up on the SUGARMAN home. Modest. One of those cookie-cutter tract homes that spread like kudzu in the seventies. It's messy, lived in, but not a shambles. Someone takes pride in it, what little there is. On the wall, a portrait—mother and daughter, GINGER and SUGARBABY. Also, a framed 9/11 crying eagle print, a signed photo of R. Lee Ermey. Baby pictures of BAILEY. Knick-knacks. To one side of the room, a battered La-Z-Boy, right across from the TV. Behind the La-Z-Boy, a sizable picture window, smoky but well-tended curtains, facing onto the yard. No one home. Empty. After a moment, a head slowly appears in the window, eyes wide, hair matted. It's BRUTUS. Then he vanishes. Another head appears, almost immediately after. CLETUS. Then, he vanishes. After another moment, from the stairway, enter SUGARBABY. Built like a brick house, I shit you not. Curvaceous. Healthy. Goddamn. Moving slow and nasty to that old-timey music she's playing on the stereo. Dressed in retro school clothes, plaid skirt, white shirt—too small, too tight, oh my dear God—shiny black shoes, snapping her gum, twirling her hair. No one around. Just letting that music take her. Slowly, BRUTUS's head appears in the window again. Catches sight of SUGARBABY. Eyes bug out. Vanishes, real fast. She doesn't see him. After the briefest of pauses, CLETUS and BRUTUS both stick
their heads up, slowly, peering through the window, a pair of men's stall door Kilroys, eyes bloodshot oh Jesus just a-watchin' that girlie go. SUGARBABY stops, a little. Seems to sense something. Turns. CLETUS and RUFUS panic oh shit duck out of sight cartoon quick. Moment. SUGARBABY knows.

SUGARBABY: Hello?

(Silence. She turns away, slow, hips still moving to that rabid beat. CLETUS and BRUTUS slowly reappear at the window. Real fast she turns around to catch them— oh shit they disappear right quick. Uh-huh. SUGARBABY knows. SUGARBABY smiles. Turns away. Walks to the mirror. Adopts a fake innocent look—"gee I guess it was nothing, my it's hot in here"—smiles mischievously at her own reflection. CLETUS and BRUTUS reappear at the window, real damn slow, taking no chances. SUGARBABY knows. Real all innocent like, she stretches, her starched white shirt straining against her plush torso. CLETUS's eyes damn near pop out of his skull, BRUTUS's start to water. Slowly, they raise themselves up for a better view, their full panting faces visible against the glass like drunken puffer fish. SUGARBABY dances more slow now, more seductive like, her hands go to her shirt buttons. BRUTUS slaps a hand over CLETUS's mouth to keep him from making a sound. Slow, one by one, them buttons come undone. She leaves her shirt unbuttoned, hanging like sheets on the line. Twists her torso round to the beat, enjoying her reflection, enjoying the tease. She runs her hands down to her stockings. BRUTUS's mouth slowly unhinges, like a pelican swallowing a salmon, CLETUS raises his hands to his filthy hair, pulls at it, almost ripping it out at the roots. SUGARBABY raises a dainty foot onto the couch arm, removes a shoe, then rolls a stocking down off her leg, raising her skirt just a little more than neces-

sary to grasp the stocking top. CLETUS is practically humping the wall now, meaty hands pressed against the glass, BRUTUS's forehead mushed into the glass, leaving a greasy worrymark on its crusted surface. They're nearly hyperventilating. She raises the other leg, undoes the other stocking, nice and slow. Lowers her leg. Stretches, arms over head, smiles, enjoying the feel of her muscles, oh gee no one could possibly be watching. She lowers her arms, lets her shirt begin to slide down from her shoulders as the music reaches a crescendo, as BRUTUS and CLETUS begin to pant like great danes sticking their heads out of a pickup truck window—and then appears, over their shoulders, groceries under one arm and shotgun under the other, GINGER, ready to kill them motherfuckers—)

BRUTUS and CLETUS: Aaaaaaahhhhh!!!!!

(SUGARBABY spins, sees her MA threatening the boys, laughs, nearly falling over it's so damn funny, as GINGER shoves the shotgun into BRUTUS's chest, drops the groceries, CLETUS panics, hits the ground, around to the front of the house, hands over his head, ass in the air.)

GINGER: How many times have I goddamn told you that I ain't havin' no goddamn peeping Tom, Dick, and Harry all over my domicile!!!!!

(BRUTUS screams like a little girlie girl, runs like hell around the back of the house, as GINGER fires off a round into the air. CLETUS bolts upright, runs like hell in the opposite direction of where BRUTUS ran, disappears offstage. GINGER fires another shot into the air. Moment. CLETUS reappears, realizing his error, blasts past the house toward where BRUTUS went. GINGER fires another shot into the air as he passes—)

CLETUS: Jesus H. Shiiiitttttttt!!!!!!!!!!...

(SUGARBABY collapses into hysterics, holding her side. GINGER enters the house, gives SUG the nastiest look. SUG stops laughing, frowns. GINGER stalks off up the stairs clutching the rifle, muttering under her breath.)

SUGARBABY: ...Never get to have any damn fun a'tall.

(Blackout.)

2

In the dark, the voice of the NARRATOR.

NARRATOR: *(Voiceover.)* Welp, that's Sugarbaby, cute as a button and loaded for bear. But the world wasn't as cute or optimistic as she was, sweet little thing. And, in fact, if you's to turn on the TV or radio and listen to some these people? You'd think the world'd gone completely plumb batshit.

(Lights up. Upstage, the SUGARMAN home. A few hours later. Still the same, but now there's a discarded beer can or two on the floor. TV is on, throwing a cold blue light over the room. No one around yet. Downstage right, USNC Studios, Richmond, Virginia. "The Rod Butane Zone" show. Large, expensive-looking, futuristic set. A lot of red, white, and blue. Big-ass American flag logo. Giant sign in front of the desk, showing the Butane logo, the USNC logo, and a picture of ROD himself, caught in mid-rant, gesticulating authoritatively at the camera. ROD himself is seated behind the desk, waiting for airtime. Low lighting. In the background, the show intro echoing through the studio. Light going off, counting off ten seconds, five, four, three... ROD arranges his desk slightly, shifting the coffee mug so that his face is visible, turns his American eagle statuette to a more dignified position. Picks a suitable pose for himself. Readies himself for America.)

ANNOUNCER: *(Voiceover; as ROD theme music plays—plenty of filtering, very professional, very modern, lots of effects.)* Wake up, America, and smell the coffee! This is the no-nonsense, fair and balanced world of the zone...*The Rod Butane Zone!* America's number one TV talk show commentator! And now, live from our studios in Richmond, Virginia, America's son, the Right Hand of God, *Rod Butane!*

(Lights up in the studio and we're on the air. Music spikes to establish, fades out under opening of ROD's speech...)

ROD: Wake up, America, time to smell the coffee! This is Rod Butane, comin' atcha *live* from God's country, Richmond, Virginia, on this beautiful summer afternoon, the kind that makes you think of Mark Twain and Huck Finn, and, I gotta tell ya, American summers may not be long in coming, folks, if the liberals that run this country and the media have their way. Well, let me, let me start from the beginning.

It's 1918. We're entering the First World War, the Big One, very unpopular war. Young private, a young patriot, ready to make the ultimate sacrifice for his country. He's cooling his heels, Long Island army base, he's waiting to go to war. He sits down to write a song, keep the troops happy. "Make us victorious on land and foam, God bless America, my home sweet home." Come some years later, we're about to get involved in another war, another unpopular war, and that man, that man who was a young private in the First Great War, Mr. Irving Berlin, gives this song to another great patriot, the late, great Kate Smith, and it becomes an anthem. I'll tell ya, I remember my dad welling up, tears in his eyes, every time he'd hear that woman's pure, full voice ring out those wondrous sentiments. We sang it as a nation on those dark days after 9/11, and it got us through. So,

here we are now, twenty-first century, once again at war, and how do we show our patriotism and pride in this country and what we know is right?

(Upstage, lights up on SUGARMAN house. Enter ARON, TV remote in hand, George W. Bush T-shirt. Stands a moment, watches ROD on the TV, interested. Then, after a moment, exits again.)

ROD: There's a guy. In California. Sued the school board. Claiming that it was against the constitution. For his daughter. To have to sing "God Bless America" in the school choir show. I'm not kidding. Taxpayers' money was wasted on this. Separation of church and state, I have said time and time again, has nothing to do with trivial matters like this. It means you should not be forced into a state religion, or forced by the government to give up your own, it means you should not be forced into paying taxes toward a religion or house of worship. That is the separation. Our boys are dying overseas for our country, and all we can waste time on is "God Bless America"?

(Reenter ARON, now with a can of beer. He crosses to the La-Z-Boy, pops the beer open, sits, listens.)

ROD: Well, fine. America First, a wonderful organization that I have plugged on this program many times before, has started their own petition and legal drive on this matter, but they've done this clod from California one better. They want to change our national anthem. To "God. Bless. America." Already, the ACLU, the tree-huggers' rights organizations, are having a field day. They've started their own organization, which they've called, with remarkably Orwellian skill, the "Freedom League." And their motto now? "Take the God Out of God Bless America."

So, here we are. We're running the risk of yet another blow to American pride and patriotism because some grand-standing limousine liberal wants to drag his poor kid—who is only nine years old, by the way—into a fight that she's probably not even interested in. But that's okay, because Daddy's got a point to make. Daddy wants to be on television. It's just a word. God. It means what you will.

(He's on a roll. He's deadly serious now. Perfect broadcaster. ARON leans in, convinced. A tear in his eye. ROD's got him hooked.)

ROD: America's a word. You think they'll try to ban that, too? Is that next? You can't say "America" in our schools. Because they don't believe in it anymore. Irving Berlin would be appalled. *(Damn. That was nice. ROD lets that hover in the air a moment, then leans back.)* I'm Rod Butane. I know what's important. *(Shifts effortlessly into commercial mode.)* This rant has been brought to you by Mutual Securities and Funds. Got a money market account? Entrust it to Mutual. Mutual. We work for you. We'll be right back.

3

Lights down to a pale blue on the USNC Studios. Lights up to full on SUGARMAN home. As ROD finishes, enter GINGER, Playtex gloves, spatula. She glares at the TV a moment—she don't like that man. Then glares at ARON. Don't think much of him, either. Meanwhile, ROD stands, job well done, exits, as TV commercials continue under the following...

GINGER: You know, I could have used your help today with those damn kids, they was sizing her up like a piece of *meat.

ARON: *(Not looking up.)* Ssshhhhhhh. A baby is *sleeping.

GINGER: Ain't no damn baby, only damn baby round here is you, when's the last time you looked for a damn job? You're supposed to be a damn handyman. Ain't been too damn handy lately.

ARON: Back's acting up.

GINGER: *(Begins swatting him with the spatula.)* You lazy good-for-nuthin' self-centered *sumbitch.

ARON: Hey! *Mail Call* is *comin' on! I'm fixin' to watch me some R. Lee Ermey!

(As they fight, CLETUS and BRUTUS appear at the window, delighted, they love this shit.)

GINGER: I'm sick of living off your damn worker's comp settlement and my Avon Lady money, I would like to be able to afford all the good cable channels *instead of stealing a signal from the mortician's up the road!

ARON: You don't need no hundred channels, we get all the good ones, and you kinda make out the porn *movies if you leave the signal on long enough!

(From the stairwell, SUGARBABY pops her head in, half-dressed, covering her torso with an orange shirt from a fast food uniform.)

SUGARBABY: Will you two please *shut up! I'm trying to get ready for work!

GINGER: All we get is the Food Network and Discovery! *I'm sick of quiche and Bull Run!

ARON: It ain't my fault you broke the movie *machine!!

GINGER: It ain't my fault you made me mad enough *to hit you upside the head with it!

(SUGARBABY pops her head in again.)

SUGARBABY: Fuck it I ain't goin'.

GINGER: *Oh yes you are and you watch your language young missy.

ARON: You gots to go baby. Hard work is good for your character. Builds stam-yoona.

GINGER: *How the hell would you know?

SUGARBABY: *(Offstage.)* But I ain't hardly makin' nothin'!

ARON: Now, baby, I told you, when you turn eighteen, I'll talk to Rege down at the TittyTeria, and he'll hook you up good, you can make good money lapdancing there.

GINGER: *You pig! (Goes at him with the spatula again.)*

ARON: *I'm just trying to help! And watch my damn *beer!*

(SUGARBABY stomps down the stairs, pissed, in full fast food uniform, name tag, paper hat, the works. Stops at the base of the stairs, sees CLETUS and BRUTUS in the window, jumps.)

SUGARBABY: Wwwwwwwaaahhhhhh!

GINGER: *(Duck Dodgers.)* Whowhatwhen wherewhatwhyhowwho Oooooooooohhh you!

(GINGER sees them, does a quick double take, begins beating the window with the spatula just as violently as she was beating ARON, who, satisfied that he is temporarily out of firing range, enjoys a sip of beer. SUGARBABY laughs hysterically as CLETUS and BRUTUS leap around like Goofy, panic, smash into each other violently, then run off screaming into the woods as GINGER hollers at them…)

GINGER: You scat! I get my rifle again, I swear to God, they goin' come take you

way in a pine goddamn box! *(She spins, faces SUGARBABY, who shuts up right quick, frowns apologetically.)*

SUGARBABY: I think they're funny.

ARON: *Funny in the head.

GINGER: You shut up and get to work and start grilling those burgers! And no stopping to talk to Jesus on the way, either!

SUGARBABY: Jesus is my only friend.

ARON: Jesus is alright.

GINGER: Jesus thinks he's Elvis.

SUGARBABY: Jesus appreciates the King and all he's done for us, that's all.

GINGER: Jesus ain't gonna pay our bills, now you get to work young missy!

(SUGARBABY stalks off and out the door, pissed-off teenager.)

ARON: Sssssssssshhh a baby is sleeping.

GINGER: Aaahhhhhhh shaddup!! *(Whacks him one last time with the spatula, stomps off into the kitchen.)*

(Moment. ARON sighs heavily. Finally, there is peace and quiet. He lifts the remote, changes channel.)

R. LEE ERMEY: *(On TV, voiceover.)* The party's over, Nancy, it's time for *Mail Call!* Hoooooraaah!

(ARON smiles. Takes a deep swig of beer. Settles back. R. Lee on the TV and the women out of the damn room. Life is good.)

4

The local branch of McMullan's, a small Midwestern fast food chain. Everything is orange. The enormous light-up menu behind the counter features an array of mouth-watering offerings: the Big Jim, the Throat-

spanker, the Heartpuncher Bacon Supreme, the McMullan's Chickenlike Substance Surprise, and a special promotional offering of Freedom Fries. Behind the counter is BRANDI, seventeen, snapping her gum, in full uniform, exactly like SUGARBABY's. She's waiting on REX, seventies, a little out of touch, flannel shirt, sweatpants, John Deere gimmie cap. Standing in line directly behind REX are MITCH COMMON, flannel shirt, khakis, ball cap, Nagra slung over one shoulder, a little too clean for the workingman look; and DAVE, thirties, movie promo T-shirt, jeans, looks more bored than annoyed. MITCH, however, is seething. After a moment of REX staring into space, BRANDI, fuming, snaps her fingers to get his attention. Points at the menu. He nods—"oh I see"—then proceeds to look at the menu with the exact same blank stare he had a second before.

MITCH: (Sighs, heavy drama.) See, this is what I'm talking about. Slow. Rude. Stupid. America used to mean something, you know?

DAVE: Mmm.

REX: (Suddenly turns to BRANDI.) Don't you have milkshakes?

BRANDI: Nosirwedon't.

(REX nods, seeming to understand. Then stares into space. BRANDI snaps her fingers again, points to the menu. He nods, turns, stares at the menu.)

MITCH: I mean, what happened to America? These chain stores, they suck the life out of this country. I mean, look at WalMart. Who does these things?

DAVE: (Couldn't care less.) I dunno.

REX: (Suddenly turns to BRANDI.) Can't you just put milk in a blender with *some ice cream?

BRANDI: Sir, we don't have a blender and we don't have milk! Have you picked your McMullan's Valuecombomeal yet?

REX: (Stares at the menu a moment. Then.) I want a roast beef sandwich and a glass of *milk.

BRANDI: (At her wits' end, which isn't saying much.) Sir, we don't have roast beef and we don't have milk!

(From the back room, enter the manager, MR. SHAKEY, late twenties, short-sleeved dress shirt, poorly knotted orange tie, polyester pants, nervous expression. In over his head.)

SHAKEY: What seems to be the trouble here?

BRANDI: He's old and stupid, and Bailey's not here, I was supposed to be *gone ten minutes ago, and I got a hot date tonight.

SHAKEY: Alright alright I'll handle this, go ahead.

BRANDI: Thank you!

(She grabs her purse, huffs, stomps out loudly, perfect angsty attitude, brushing past MITCH and DAVE, practically knocking them over.)

SHAKEY: (Loudly, as though REX were deaf and brain damaged.) Hello old timer and welcome to McMullan's! How may we help you today, sir?

REX: You don't have to yell, I'm not deaf, you damn fruit!

SHAKEY: (Trying to recover, very mealy-mouthed middle manager.) I'm very sorry, sir, now what would you like from our wide variety of burgers and fries?

(REX stares at him a moment, as though dazed. SHAKEY snaps his fingers, points to the menu. REX turns, stares at the menu with his pat-

ented zombie stare. MITCH practically bursts into tears, throws up his hands in disbelief.)

MITCH: Oh dear God in Heaven. This is hell on earth.

DAVE: *You don't wanna pay for my meals on this shoot, fine, I get to pick where we eat.

REX: I want a roast beef sandwich!

SHAKEY: I'm afraid we don't carry roast beef, sir. Would you care for a delicious *McMullan's Supreme Bacon Heartpuncher?

MITCH: Is this about the non-union thing again? Look, I told you, it's a low-budget documentary, we can't afford perks.

DAVE: You had lobster Thermidor the other night.

MITCH: *(Caught.)* …That was a business dinner. *(Turns away to watch the steadily growing argument at the counter.)*

REX: *(Getting increasingly hostile and panicky.)* No! I don't want that! I don't want that! You people! I want roast beef!

SHAKEY: *(Scared.)* Sir, please, if you wouldn't yell and disturb our customers. I'd be happy to offer you a McMullan's Chickenlike Substance Surprise.

REX: *(Apoplectic.)* I don't want that!

SHAKEY: It would be complimentary, sir.

REX: *(Quickly, mollified.)* Oh, that'd be fine.

SHAKEY: Alrighty then. Now, would you care for some Freedom Fries with your sandwich?

REX: …What the hell are those?

SHAKEY: Freedom Fries. *(Points to picture on menu.)* See?

REX: *(Looking at picture.)* French fries?

SHAKEY: Sir? We prefer Freedom Fries. It's a corporate policy.

REX: Fried potatoes are Belgian, not French.

SHAKEY: Well. Yes. Be that as it may…

REX: *(Suddenly rears up, gains three inches in height, and looks for all the world like he could kick your pansy ass.)* I fought at Normandy, you backassed fruitbat, I didn't get half my kneecap shot out by some Kraut bastard so that you flakes could appease your conscience by renaming soggy, egg-riddled bread Freedom Toast—

SHAKEY: *We don't carry Freedom Toast sir.

REX: —and I certainly didn't do it so that you could treat me like a child in this godforsaken hellhole of a greasy spoon! Now I want a roast beef with gravy *and I want it now!!!*

(Just then, enter SUGARBABY, a ray of sunshine. The music on the in-store radio suddenly changes, something rockin' and hot, maybe Chuck Berry, or Bo Diddley. She strolls right past MITCH and DAVE, both of whom watch her in stunned bemusement as she pops behind the counter, smiling adorably, waves at REX, who is obviously very fond of her.)

SUGARBABY: Hi, Rex.

REX: Hello, darling.

SUGARBABY: We still don't have roast beef. Sorry.

REX: Okay.

SUGARBABY: Wanna cheeseburger instead?

REX: Okay.

SUGARBABY: I'll get you a nice diet soda with that, alright?

REX: Aw, thank you, sweetie.

(She smiles kindly at him, bounces into the kitchen area, makes REX a nice little tray of food. REX grins, then notices SHAKEY, glares at him. SHAKEY, obviously quite alarmed by REX's previous outburst, cowers, waggling his fingers and smiling, appeasing him as though he were a wild animal. During:)

MITCH: Oh my God—*that's* our American. Look at her. Full of joy and innocence. Hope for the future. That smile. That boundless energy. That's our girl! Go get the camera.

DAVE: Aw man but I'm *hungry.

MITCH: It's in the back seat of the car go get the camera *go get the camera go get the *camera dammit!*

DAVE: But I want my sandwich dammit this sucks.

(DAVE exits, grudgingly, as SUG reenters with REX's tray—cheeseburger, soda, and a cookie.)

SUGARBABY: *(Handing over the tray.)* Here ya go, sugar. I even gave you a free cookie—but don't tell anyone.

REX: Thank you, sweetie.

(REX crosses into the restaurant to sit and eat, shuffling, humming happily to himself, as SHAKEY tentatively taps on SUG's shoulder.)

SHAKEY: May I have a word with you, Miss Sugarman?

SUGARBABY: Yeah, I know I'm late, but I ain't got my *license yet, and I had to walk here, 'cause on account of my mama wouldn't give me no ride and—

SHAKEY: Yes yes yes alright that's okay look *I don't care!* *(Calms himself, embarrassed.)* Look, Bailey, you're a very sweet girl, and you are certainly a hit with the regular customers, but I can't have you

coming in here twenty to thirty minutes late every day. This is a team effort here, and you have to be part of the McFamily! There are rules here, or, should I say, "McRules"? Wait a minute— *(Points to her uniform shirt, which is tied off at the waist.)* —what is this?

SUGARBABY: *I just thought it looked better.

SHAKEY: A bare midriff is not part of the uniform. *You must follow the McPattern for your work attire.

(Nervously, SHAKEY tries to untie the knot, SUG slaps at his hand, turns away from him, undoes the knot herself with a violent tug.)

SUGARBABY: I'll do it *I'll do it jeez!*

SHAKEY: That is why it is called a uniform.

(Satisfied with his manager-ness, SHAKEY exits into the kitchen to find something managery to do. SUG stews. MITCH seizes the opportunity to approach her.)

SUGARBABY: *(Under her breath as SHAKEY leaves…)* You iron your underwear, don't you?

MITCH: Hello.

SUGARBABY: I ain't givin' out no more free cookies, my boss already yelled at me once today.

MITCH: No, no, you don't understand. I'm Mitch Common.

(MITCH puts out a hand—she shakes it, surprisingly firm grip.)

MITCH: I'm an award-winning maverick documentary filmmaker, I have shows on PBS and Trio, and that's my cameraman over there, Dave—Dave? *(Stomps his foot, pissed.)* Dave!

(Just then, enter DAVE, camera over shoulder. Couldn't care less. Shrugs.)

MITCH: *(Turns back to SUG, smiles, as though nothing had just happened.)* I need an example of the future, the shining future that this country could represent, someone willing to stand up and say no to the stupid old white men and their corporate power structure. You, my dear, just may be that girl.

(He takes her hand, brings her around to the front of the counter, as SHAKEY looks in, opens his mouth as if to speak, then nervously vanishes again.)

MITCH: Let's start with an interview. Just a simple interview. About you, your job, your life. How America has let you down. The death of the American dream.

(MITCH prepares himself, lifts his mic, sets the Nagra going, rubs his face to give it the "rugged" look, while SUG suddenly adopts a look of shock and horror at his statement.)

SUGARBABY: It—it's dead?

MITCH: Well, some say.

SUGARBABY: Since when?

MITCH: Well, there are many arguments, some say it was the rise of neo-fascist conservatism in the 1980s, *conservatives argue it was the liberation of speech in the 1960s...

SUGARBABY: Whoa whoa whoa whoa— You say something like that and can't point to a *time and place when it happened?

MITCH: Well, it's all academic. Dave? We rolling?

DAVE: Yep.

MITCH: You're supposed to tell me when you start rolling.

DAVE: Yep.

MITCH: *(Slow burn... Then, composing himself quickly, to camera, fully in "character.")* You wonder just where this bull-in-a-china-shop mentality will end. When we'll discover that we've thrown everything away in pursuit of something plastic and small. I'm here with—

SUGARBABY: ? Oh. Bailey Sugarman. My friends call me Sugarbaby.

MITCH: Bailey. And she's just one of millions of Americans locked into a perpetual and thankless cycle of hand-to-mouth sterilization, an existence comprised solely of work, bills, and sleep, dehumanizing the individual and glorifying conformity. What would you really rather be? What's your dream?

SUGARBABY: I wanna be a star.

MITCH: Well, doesn't everyone?

SUGARBABY: Yeah, don't you?

MITCH: *...Well. Uh.

SUGARBABY: I wish it was the 1950s. I wish I were in a tiki lounge, in a leopard print bikini.

(As she gets more and more excited, she grabs the mic from MITCH, moves in closer to the camera. DAVE enjoys this, something interesting for a change.)

SUGARBABY: I wish my picture was on the wall of every army barracks around the world. I wish I were a pinup queen. I wanna be Jayne Mansfield. I wanna be Bettie Page!

MITCH: *Hold it hold it hold it cut cut cut cut.

SUGARBABY: What? But you were just saying how America's getting thrown away, how we've run away from our past! I love our past! Damn do I love it! Drive in movies, Coca-Cola and cheeseburgers, pinup queens and big-ass cars! And rockabilly *all night long! Whoo!

MITCH: *(Grabbing the mic back from her.)* Excuse me—*you wanna go back to the 1950s???

SHAKEY: *(Offstage.)* What's going on out there?

REX *(Offstage.) I'm out of napkins!*

MITCH: You wanna go back to racism? To warfare? To duck and cover every day in school? *You wanna go back to that?

SUGARBABY: *(To DAVE.)* And how's that different from now, exactly?

(DAVE nods in agreement, "yeah, tell me about it.")

MITCH: Yes. That's it.

(MITCH snaps his fingers; DAVE rolls his eyes, turns the camera back on him as he resumes "character.")

MITCH: It's our darker impulses we've returned to. We're embracing, in this "retro culture," a time and place when the rules were clear, when the upper middle class had convinced themselves *that America was impenetrable—

SUGARBABY: You're an asshole.

MITCH: *W-What??

SUGARBABY: You don't wanna talk to me, and you don't wanna listen. You just want to hear yourself talk! Talk talk talk talk talk that's all anybody ever does. You all got your little theories, *and none of y'all give a damn for anybody else!

(DAVE turns the camera back onto her, begins moving around, getting better angles— now we're talking…)

MITCH: I have written numerous books on the plight of the working class *American in the age of commercialization—

SUGARBABY: Bla bla bla bla bla do you ever get laid?

MITCH: *E-Excuse me??

SUGARBABY: Do you get drunk? Do you smoke? Do you get stoned?

DAVE: I like to get fucked up sometimes.

(SUGARBABY points, gestures: "see?" Just then, SHAKEY reenters. He can take no more, and must, God help him, take charge.)

SHAKEY: Alright, that's it. Sir, I'm very sorry, but I'm afraid I'm going to have to be forced to request respectfully *that you leave the premises.

MITCH: Freedom of the press! First amendment! I can go where I choose.

DAVE: We have no permit.

MITCH: Shut up, Dave.

SUGARBABY: Nobody listens anymore!

SHAKEY: *(Turning to SUG.)* And you, young lady, I am tired of your disrespectful behavior. McMullan's has not prospered on ill will and poor attitude, it has prospered on sunny disposition *and fine food!

MITCH: And corporate malfeasance! *Your bosses are as bad as Enron!

SHAKEY: Sir, I've respectfully asked you to leave—

SUGARBABY: *Christ! Just throw him out! Can't you just grab him by the back of the shirt and throw him out! What is wrong with you people!

SHAKEY: If you don't leave right now, *I'll be forced to call the police and have you removed.

REX: (Offstage.) Shut up! I'm trying to eat my roast beef!

DAVE: *I'm going to the van.

MITCH: I will call the ACLU! I am this close to Gloria Allred!

(Their argument devolves into unintelligible shouting. SUG turns away, stews a moment, then—)

SUGARBABY: Alright. That's it. I've had it! I quit! (She smiles. Dead quiet. Damn, that felt good. She turns to MITCH.) You are an asshole, and you don't know a damn thing about me or anybody! How dare you? You ask me for my dreams and then you piss on them 'cause they don't fit into your tiny little view of the world? Fuck you!

SHAKEY: *Bailey!

SUGARBABY: And you! I've had it with your McRules! I've had it with your McBullshit! And, as far as I'm concerned you can all kiss my white, cornfed, Southern, all-American ASS!!!!!

(She turns, drops trou, moons the lot of them. Stands. They all stare, stunned. She grins widely. Turns to DAVE.)

SUGARBABY: You're alright.

DAVE: Thanks.

(She turns, strides proudly out the door, waving into the dining area as she goes…)

SUGARBABY: Goodbye, Rex!

REX: (Offstage.) My foot's stuck in the terlet!

(Just as she hits the door, she whips off her McHat, hurls it onto the floor behind her. All three of them, DAVE, MITCH, and SHAKEY watch the hat fall. Stare at it a moment. MITCH crosses to DAVE, takes the camera from him.)

MITCH: Dave, you're fired. (MITCH exits, camera in hand, going after SUG.)

DAVE: (Shrugs, couldn't care less.) Okay.

(DAVE picks up the hat, goes behind the counter. Looks around. Yeah, a man could get used to this. SHAKEY smiles widely, enjoys a hearty handshake with his new employee.)

5

The SUGARMAN house. Lights are low. Slow Conway Twitty tunes on the radio. Humming from offstage—GINGER. Slowly, BRUTUS and CLETUS peer through the window. Moment. Sink out of sight, slowly, in unison. After a moment, GINGER enters, white robe, too much makeup, towel around her head, lit cigarette, shotglass half full of whisky. She checks her reflection in her compact. Purses her lips.

GINGER: Oh my, didn't expect you so soon. Come right on in… no, no, really, I like to eat my pizza in the boudoir… boo-dwah boo-dwarr boo-dwahhh (Practices, pursing her lips, posing so-ductively.)

SUGARBABY: (Offstage.) Hey, Brutus, hey, Cletus.

BRUTUS and CLETUS: (Offstage, in unison.) Evening.

(Suddenly, SUGARBABY barges in, full steam, tearing off her uniform, barrels up the stairs to her bedroom.)

GINGER: *Ahhh! Bailey, honey, why you you're home—

SUGARBABY: Can't take it no more, hate the world fucking people nobody ever *goddamn listens shit piss—

GINGER: (Trying to compose herself, fails, runs to the front door, peering out the window in a panic. During:) Sweetie what are you doing here? Shouldn't you be at work?

SUGARBABY: *(Offstage.) I quit!*

GINGER: *(Leans back in from the window—blind panic.)* You *what*!

SUGARBABY: *(Offstage.)* You heard. I quit. F-u-c-k-e-d off. Quit.

GINGER: But what will you do? For money? What?

SUGARBABY: *(Offstage.)* Sell my ovum for research. I dunno. Fuck it.

GINGER: Well. You march right back out that door and ask for your job back. This instant. Like. Like, right now.

(Reenter SUG, in cut-off shorts, hair back in a ponytail, Tura Satana T-shirt, crosses to the La-Z-Boy, throws herself into it angrily.)

SUGARBABY: I ain't goin' back there never again, no matter how good their cookies are. *Shit. I shoulda stolen some before I left.

GINGER: Well you can't stay here. I got guests coming.

SUGARBABY: …Where's Aron?

GINGER: At the bar, as usual. Getting drunk. And useless.

SUGARBABY: Why you wearing all that makeup?

GINGER: *(Pause. Whoops. Caught.)* Wanna look nice. Never know who might pop by.

SUGARBABY: Like who?

GINGER: …Hmm?

SUGARBABY: Your guests.

GINGER: Oh, I ordered a pizza.

SUGARBABY: *Oh Christ.

GINGER: So, why don't you go see your friend Jesus, I'm sure he'll be happy *to talk to you about…whatever it is you two talk about.

SUGARBABY: I'm not going back out there, Mama! *It's getting dark!

GINGER: Goddammit Bailey Sugarman I have been looking forward to this night for myself all goddamn week now you skedaddle or I swear to God I'll—

(Doorbell.)

GINGER: *Hot damn! (Crosses downstage, adjusts her towel, boobs, hips.)* Pizza's here!

DELIVERY BOY: *(Offstage.)* Hi, Brutus, hi, Cletus.

BRUTUS and CLETUS: *(Offstage, in unison.)* Hello.

(SUG, appalled, picks up the remote, aims, clicks, TV comes on. R. Lee Ermey again. GINGER goes to the door, opens it. Standing in the doorway is the DELIVERY BOY, eighteen or so, pimply, nervous, hands shaking, holding a cold, greasy pizza box. GINGER leans against the door frame seductively.)

GINGER: Well, hello there young man.

DELIVERY BOY: Oh God.

GINGER: Why don't you come on in.

DELIVERY BOY: I should really get back to my truck.

(He tries to turn away, she grabs him, hurls him inside like a ragdoll, toys with his ear. He shivers in terror, head to toe.)

GINGER: Oh, I just need your help for a minute. You see, I need a big, strong handsome man to carry that big, heavy pizza for me. And I prefer to eat my pizza in the boudoir.

DELIVERY BOY: Oh God no.

(She spins him around, smacks him on the ass, the force of which sends him directly into SUG's line of vision. SUG leans slightly, trying to see past him to the TV. She answers his questions perfunctorily, disinterested.)

DELIVERY BOY: Hi, Sugarbaby.

SUGARBABY: Hi, Jeff.

DELIVERY BOY: How's things for you since graduation?

SUGARBABY: Good, you?

DELIVERY BOY: Oh, fine, thanks. *(To window.)* How's it going out there, boys?

CLETUS: *(Hand in window.)* Can I have some pizza?

DELIVERY BOY: No.

CLETUS: *(Hand vanishes.)* *Fair enough.

GINGER: Enough small talk. Bailey was just leaving, wasn't she?

SUGARBABY: Whatever.

GINGER: Now, the boo-dwah is right up there. Be a dear, won't you?

(GINGER drapes herself over the stairway railing. Smiles. There is no escape. The DELIVERY BOY slowly crosses to the stairs. Stops. Turns.)

DELIVERY BOY: *(Gravitas.)* Tell my mother I love her.

SUGARBABY: Sure thing.

(GINGER grabs his collar, yanks him up the stairs.)

DELIVERY BOY: *(Offstage.)* It's so dark up here!

GINGER: *(Offstage.)* Shut up and deliver, delivery boy!

DELIVERY BOY: *(Offstage.)* Madam, please, I'm a young man and I have so much to live for!

(SUG, appalled, turns up the TV. A commercial. Travel ad.)

TV: *(Voiceover, as "America the Beautiful" plays under.)* Freedom. America's gift to the world. A nation's treasure. Come. Experience freedom. See this beautiful nation, its glorious highways and byways, and enjoy the majesty and wonder of its valleys, its mountains, its plains. Travel America. And rediscover your home.

(SUG watches. It affects her. She smiles. Then frowns. That's where I oughta be, dammit. She glances up the stairs. Then back to the TV. Looks down next to the chair. GINGER's purse. Gaudy, red, white, and blue. SUG reaches in, pulls out a wad of cash. Stands. She's decided. SUG runs for the door, moving faster with each step, the scent of freedom out there in that cold night air. The TV quiets. Crickets. Moment.)

GINGER: *(Offstage.)* Just you wait there a minute, dearie.

DELIVERY BOY: *(Offstage.)* Please untie me, Mrs. Sugarman! I chafe easily!

(GINGER appears in the stairwell, hair still up in a towel, robe still tied.)

GINGER: *(Over her shoulder.)* Ssshhhhhh… *(Looks into the living room—empty.)* Bailey?

(She shrugs. Claps her hands. Lights go out. Only a faint moonlight glow over the room. Just then, BRUTUS and CLETUS appear at the window. Eyes widen. GINGER crosses into the living room, primps once more. As CLETUS watches her, a thought balloon appears over his head: a caricature of Osama Bin Laden, with the caption "Yoosama Bin Layden, Notorious Evil Person." Bin Laden is wearing a turban and robe that look exactly like GINGER's. BRUTUS looks at him, confused. CLETUS rolls his eyes, grabs the balloon, puts it over BRUTUS's head. Oh! Now he gets it. GINGER, satisfied she's

hot mamma enough, goes back up the stairs while CLETUS and BRUTUS aren't looking.)

GINGER: *(Offstage.)* Here you go, Sweetness, I got your tip!

DELIVERY BOY: *(Offstage.)* What? What are you doing? No! No! For the love of God, please! No—noooooooooooooooooo!*

(Hearing this, BRUTUS and CLETUS, terrified, sink out of sight, hugging each other for safety and comfort as the DELIVERY BOY's screams echo into the night. Blackout. Then, in the darkness…)

BRUTUS: *(Offstage.)* I didn't know Ay-Rabs liked pizza.

CLETUS: *(Offstage.)* Shut up! He'll hear you!

BRUTUS: *(Offstage.)* Aaaaaaaa!

6

NARRATOR: *(Voiceover.)* Yep, them boys ain't none too bright, and now they got some crazy idea as to what happened to Sugarbaby. But what really happened to Sugarbaby, as you can guess, is that she'd had just about enough, and she was gonna hit the road. Trouble is, seventeen-year-old girl on her own, well, that ain't exactly safe. It's a dangerous world out there. She'd need a protector, a friend, to keep her company. And she was bound and determined it was gonna be her best friend in the whole world… His name was Jesus.

(Stern Auto and Gasoline. Spotlight on JESUS, twenties. Patches on his jumpsuit: one reading "Hello, my name is Jesus," one the Memphis Mafia "TCB" logo. On his back, a red, white, and blue rhinestone American eagle. He carries a guitar with an American flag taped to the back. He's singing and playing "Baby What You Want Me

to Do." Not bad, but not great. Enjoying the hell out of it, though. Slowly, the lights rise higher, revealing the front of the garage: auto parts strewn around like limbs, old, decrepit gas pump, stack of worn tires. Giant sign reading "In God We Trust, All Others Pay Cash." Faded Pennzoil tin sign. After a moment, enter SUGARBABY, who watches him a minute, smiling, then joins in with him, dances. They obviously get on like a house on fire. They get through almost all of the song, doing a few Elvis and Ann-Margret moves. Finish the song. Smile at each other warmly, glow of a single yellow streetlight, the buzz of crickets.)

SUGARBABY: Hi, Jesus.

JESUS: Evening, Ms. Sugarman.

(Suddenly, in barges ELROY STERN, thirties, tight jeans, tight T-shirt, outdated hairdo and mustache, toolbelt. Greasy washrag hanging from back pocket. Comb folded into T-shirt sleeve. Skeevy.)

STERN: Goddammit, boy, how many goddamn times have I gotta tell ya *I don't pay you to stand around singing them pansy-ass songs!

JESUS: Begging your pardon, Mr. Stern, sir, I's just relaxing for a spell. *There's no customers right now, anyway…

STERN: Your excuses are your own, fancy pants! Now get back on to work on my new Camaro! *(Notices SUGARBABY, slides up to her all sexy-like.)* You know, I got three Camaros. The ladies love the Camaros, ain't that right, Bailey?

SUGARBABY: *(Visibly disgusted.)* Hi Mr. Stern…

STERN: Aw, come on now, we ain't gots to be so formal. Call me Elroy.

SUGARBABY: Whatever Mr. Stern.

STERN: Aw see now we got off on the wrong foot a while ago. Let me make it up to you. I am acquaintanced with the owner of the finest fried chicken establishment in this here parts.

SUGARBABY: I'm a vegetarian.

STERN: Aw, come on, girlie, I know you work at that greasy burger joint. You ain't no vegetarian. I bet you eat plenty of meat.

SUGARBABY: I quit my job today.

STERN: Aw, now why'd you go and do a thing like that? What you gonna do for money? You know, if you ever need a sugar daddy—

SUGARBABY: *Ew ew ew ew ew ew—

JESUS: Mr. Stern, sir, this was kind of a private conversation *we was having. Not to be rude, sir, but…

STERN: You got a mouth on ya, boy! And one of these days, I'm gonna plug it! Now get back to work! *(To SUGARBABY.)* And you, honey, you can stop by anytime…

SUGARBABY: I'm a lesbian.

STERN: Funny. You don't look Jewish.

(STERN exits. SUG turns to JESUS—what the hell did that mean?—then freezes at his disapproving look.)

JESUS: You done quit your job?

SUGARBABY: *(Chastened.)* I know it wasn't too smart, but I couldn't take it no more. I hate that place.

JESUS: *(Crosses to sit on tire stack, plucking out "Love Me Tender" on his guitar.)* Everybody needs a job, Ms. Sugarman.

SUGARBABY: Everybody needs something to look forward to, and all I look forward to lately is not having to go to work. But then I'm at home, and all I look forward

to is not having to be in that damn house. I don't know whether I'm coming or going anymore. *(Pause.)* I wrote something last night. A new one. You wanna hear it?

JESUS: *(Genuine.)* I'd be honored, ma'am. *(Sets down his guitar.)*

SUGARBABY: *(Pulls a piece of looseleaf paper from her back pocket, stands under the streetlight, almost formal.)* Ahem. "Whatever Happened to All the Fun in the World." By me, Sugarbaby.

(JESUS applauds.)

SUGARBABY: Thank you. *(She proceeds to perform her poem. Energetic at first. As the tone of the piece shifts, her mood darkens, melancholy. It even takes her by surprise. By the end, she's quite emotional.)* "Whatever happened to all the fun in the world?
I'd sure like to know.
Smokin'll kill ya, and you can't smoke in bars.
Drinkin'll get you arrested in cars.
Sexin' and lovin' might get you real sick.
Wanna start swearin'? Don't! Shut up right
    quick!
All of the things that you love, like red
    meat, hot dogs, soda pop,
It's all lips and assholes, they claim.
The health police comin' in,
Just your best interests at heart,
But they don't know my heart!
And they don't know me!
Or care who I am!
It's getting me madder'n Yosemite Sam!
Oh yeah—and them cartoons that made
    you so happy as a kid?
We've cut them up, taken out all of the
    energy,
Violence, and fun!
Whatever happened to all the fun in the
    world?
You can't be left, and you can't be right.
It keeps me up sweating and tossing all
    night.

Were the good old days really so good
Or so bad
As they say
And when we waste away
Will we cry for those missed opportuni-
    ties, missed big advantages,
Missed loves and road trips,
Accidents, happy and otherwise?
Or will we just fade away?
Like roller coasters left to tumble,
And drive-in screens left to crumble,
And ex-soda jerks in nursing homes,
And dirt roads paved over for Office De-
    pots,
And you and me,
And America.
Whatever happened to all the fun in the
    world?
And was it ever really that much fun at all?

*(Pause. She folds up the paper, tucks it back
into her pocket. Turns away, a little ashamed
of her tears. JESUS is stunned.)*

JESUS: *(Visibly moved.)* That's beautiful,
Ms. Sugarman. You got a real gift.

SUGARBABY: *(Sniffs, wipes her face on
her sleeve.)* Thank you.

JESUS: Aw now, don't cry. Things change,
friend. Everything passes, everything has
its time. And, soon, something else comes
along, and you find something good in
that, too. Things change.

SUGARBABY: Sometimes things die before you have a chance to say goodbye.

JESUS: …Yes, sadly, sometimes they do.

SUGARBABY: I want out.

JESUS: Out of what?

SUGARBABY: Here. This place. I wanna
see America. I wanna see the Grand Canyon. I wanna see Mount Rushmore. I
wanna see New York and Chicago, and

skyscrapers, and drive-in movies, and
people. And big cars. I wanna go to Alaska
and see a Kodiak bear. I wanna see
America, Jesus. Before it's all gone… Before it's all argued away.

JESUS: Well, we all got responsibilities,
Ms. Sugarman. It ain't that easy.

SUGARBABY: Yes it is. I don't know my
family anymore, they don't know me. And
I got no friends here, really, 'cepting for
you. And you ain't got no family no more,
do you?

JESUS: …No. No, I don't, ma'am.

SUGARBABY: Let's go, Jesus. You and me.

JESUS: I got a job here, and responsibilities…

SUGARBABY: You hate your job! And
you live above a garage, sleeping on an
old, stinky futon! There's gotta be something better than that! I got faith in you,
Jesus. You gotta have faith in me.

*(Moment. He shakes his head. Stands. Turns
away. SUG is shattered. Her dreams dashed,
she cries again. Looks up. JESUS leans over,
picks up his guitar. Music: Elvis Presley,
"Mystery Train." Echoing at first, as though
from a radio somewhere far away, a passing
car, a distant farmhouse. JESUS reaches into
his jumpsuit, pulls out a pair of Elvis sunglasses.
Dons them. Smiles a damn handsome smile.)*

JESUS: What are you waiting for?

*(Disbelief. SUG straightens, stands tall. Al-
most can't breathe. Music comes closer, grows
louder. She takes a tentative step toward him.
Smiles.)*

SUGARBABY: …Okay.

*(He takes her hand, like a big brother. She smiles
wider. He smiles back. Music up to full as the
lights dim to blue, then black. Blackout.)*

7

The SUGARMAN home. Later that night. Lights are out, dim moonlight over the room, pizza box on the floor, house a mess. We hear the sound of ARON returning home drunkenly.

ARON: *(Offstage; singing, sloppily.)* Wastin' away agaiiiiiin in *Margaree*taville.
Searching for myyyy-yy lost shaky assault
Some people claim that there's a—

(The door flings open, he stands in the doorway a moment, bellowing majestically, a drunken grizzly bear.)

ARON: Wwwwwwwwwwooooooooooo ooooooooaaaaaaaaaaamunnnnnnnnn *to blaaaaaaaaaaaaaaaaaaaaaaaaaayme but ah know—

(GINGER barrels down the stairs, air-brushed kitten 'n' rose house dress, face covered in beauty goop.)

GINGER: Jesus H. Christ in the sky what the hell's the matter with you *you wanna wake the whole goddamn neighborhood you fucking wildebeest?

ARON: *(Whispers, still singing.)* —ssmy own damm fawl—

GINGER: Ugh! You stink like puke and hops. You're sleeping on the La-Z-Boy tonight, *you useless drunk.

ARON: *(Undoing his belt, swaying like a California redwood in a gale force wind.)* Aw don't be that way gorgeous—when's the last time I gave you some of the ol' *vitamin A?

GINGER: You lay your hands on me, I'll punch you in the nuts!

(Just then, ARON looks down at the floor, sees the pizza box. Stops. Sobers quickly.)

ARON: Sheeit. *(Gravely.)* You done molestered the damn pizza man again, didn't ya?

GINGER: No, I didn't! I was hungry! I went and got that myself!

ARON: I had the car.

GINGER: ...I walked.

ARON: Two miles?

GINGER: ...I was hungry.

ARON: How many times I told you? They hire impressionable youths at these places, *you'll scar them for life!

(GINGER lunges, grabs the pizza box, begins beating him with it.)

GINGER: Well you never do a damn thing for me you useless bastard always out all night *drinking with your nogood friends leaving me alone and defenseless with no way to protect my person—

ARON: I can go out when and where I want and you got the rifle to protect you and *will you stop it you're gonna wake the kid!*

(Pause. Uh oh. They look at each other, then off at the stairwell.)

GINGER and ARON: *(In unison.)* Sugarbaby?

(BRUTUS and CLETUS appear at the window.)

CLETUS: Psst...

(GINGER leaps, startled, yelps. ARON spins, almost losing his already precarious balance.)

CLETUS: I saw the whole thing. They done kidnapped her.

BRUTUS: The Ay-Rab Moo-Slams.

CLETUS: It was Yoosama Bin Layden.

GINGER: ...ohmigod...

(GINGER swoons, faints dead away. ARON stands a moment, taking this in.)

ARON: Well, shit on me.

(Blackout.)

8

USNC Studios, "The Rod Butane Zone." ROD in mid-rant. Eagle is in a different position now. Coffee mug's still there.

ROD: You know, I just wanna follow up on something that last caller said. The argument you made, caller, was that "God" was the important word in the lyrics of "God Bless America." That's your problem with it. Well, you know, I respectfully disagree. The important word, my friend, is America. America is what's important, and not small-minded people like you. It's only a matter of time before—*(Puts a finger to his ear, stops.)* What? You're kidding. Uh, ladies and gentlemen, we have a breaking story, we have an Amber Alert issued—

(An INTERN runs in, hands him a blue index card, which he refers to during the following.)

ROD: —thank you got it here. An Amber Alert has been issued— *(Stops, stunned.)* Is this right? You know, I'm gonna tell you something, folks, this puts the lie to the idea that the liberal elite in this country have that homeland security is unimportant, we need not fight any war on terrorism. An Amber Alert has been issued for a young woman, a Bailey Sugarman... God, this is awful. She has apparently. Been kidnapped. By terrorists. I feel sick. Do we have corroboration on this? We're connected? Okay, this is incredible, I can't believe how quickly the story is breaking open. We have a live feed with the witnesses, the two brave souls who contacted the authorities... Do we have them? Hello?

(Lights up on CLETUS and BRUTUS, opposite side of the stage, now smartly dressed in USNC gimmie caps and T-shirts and American flag pins.)

CLETUS: Hello?

BRUTUS: Hello?

ROD: *Yes, gentlemen, can you hear me?

CLETUS: Yeah. Hello?

BRUTUS: Hello?

ROD: *You're in the Rod Butane Zone, gentlemen, on America's news source, USNC, can you hear me?

CLETUS: Yeah. Hello?

ROD: Gentlemen, you were the ones who contacted the authorities, you saw this dreadful event, *can you tell me what happened?

BRUTUS: Hello? Hello?

CLETUS: Yes, Rob, I can.

ROD: *My, my name's Rod...

CLETUS: We was fire inspecting.

BRUTUS: *Looking for fires— Hello?

CLETUS: And we was looking in the house window for, *for, fires.

BRUTUS: Fires. Hello?

CLETUS: And we saw the Ay-Rab Moo-Slams.

BRUTUS: One of them.

CLETUS: I think it might have been Yoosama Bin Layden.

BRUTUS: *He's a little bitch. Hello?

ROD: Well, let's not jump to conclusions, gentlemen. Did you get a good look at the *alleged kidnapper?

CLETUS: He was built kinda funny for a mad bomber.

BRUTUS: He was all curvy and shit. *Hello?

CLETUS: He was wearing his white turban and his white Moo-Slam priest robe.

BRUTUS: He had a nice ass. Hello?

CLETUS: You sick bastard! You was scopin' out the Bin Layden!

BRUTUS: *Don't tell me! You're the one who fucked the donkey!

(Lights down on CLETUS and BRUTUS as they begin wrestling with each other violently, destroying their USNC T-shirts in the process.)

ROD: Okay, we're not gonna get anything from these guys. So, there you have it. An Amber Alert has been issued, the search is on for a young girl, seventeen years old, last seen in a uniform from McMullan's, hey, they're pretty good, I eat lunch there when I'm, you know, desperate, but there you have it, we're going to be hearing soon from the law enforcement handling the case, let's see—this is his name here? Uh-huh. A Sheriff Rufus J. Miranda.

(Blackout.)

9

Music: Bo Diddley, "I'm a Man." The SUGARMAN home. Very late that night. GINGER sobbing, in the La-Z-Boy, ARON by her side, yelling out the window at a gaggle of REPORTERS—there's dozens of them, it seems. We only see their cameras and microphones poking at the window, but we hear their pleas for attention, their shouted questions.

ARON: Goddammit you people! Get off my goddamn lawn! You're trampling the azaleas! Get out of here! Hey this is private fucking property you miserable sumbitches! Hey! *(Etc.)*

(Downstage, in a spotlight, stands RUFUS J. MIRANDA, big, tough, non-fuck-with-able. The Last Sane Man. His back is to us. He slowly puts on his hat, turns. Mirrored sunglasses, scowl. Fixes his hat brim. Inhales deeply, his barrel chest pushes outward. Spins, stalks straight upstage, right toward the goddamn window, barks at the reporters outside with a voice that could rattle marble columns and break Tiffany glass…)

RUFUS: *Aaaaaaaallllllll-right ladies* this ain't no goddamn frathouse beerblast, this's a goddamn crime scene, now git your sorry asses movin'! This is a grieving family here, and I want you vultures outta here *right goddamn now!*

(The REPORTERS scatter, whooping wildly like black-and-white-era Daffy Duck, disappear into the woods behind the house. RUFUS, satisfied, turns to the SUGARMANS.)

RUFUS: Mr. and Mrs. Sugarman. I'm very sorry for your trouble. I promise you we'll find your daughter, if I have to go to the ends of the earth to catch her.

ARON: I surely do appreciate that, Sheriff.

RUFUS: No need to thank me, son. *(Takes off his sunglasses; his steely eyes glint in the room's dim yellow light.)* It's my job.

(Enter MITCH, camera over shoulder, filming away, seemingly oblivious to the SUGARMANS and RUFUS. He heads straight for the stairwell.)

MITCH: And here we are in the den of sin itself! This low-class, tract-housing pit of mediocrity *is where our poor, unfortunate victims of capitalist aggression—

(RUFUS rushes him, grabs him by the shirt collar. MITCH just shrugs him off.)

RUFUS: *Hey!* How the hell you get in here? I told you no more reporters! *Now get lost!

MITCH: I'm not a reporter, I'm an independent filmmaker, and what's with all the commotion outside? *Somebody get shot or something?

RUFUS: Are you mentally *damaged, boy?

GINGER: They took my baby!

MITCH: *What??

RUFUS: This is a goddamn crime scene, ya limp-wristed *reprobate, now git your ass out that door!

MITCH: Waitaminitwaitaminitwaitaminit this is— (Checks a crumpled burger wrapper in his jacket pocket.) —2929 Oceanside Terrace, yes?

ARON: You from the cable company? Look, I didn't know it was stolen cable, *I swear to God—

MITCH: No, I got this address from Bailey's boss at McMullan's, *he told me this is where she— OhdearGod—

GINGER: You saw my baby! (Grabs MITCH violently by the lapels.) Where was she? Did you see them Ay-Rab Moo-Slams?

RUFUS: It weren't no Ay-Rab Moo-Slams!

ARON: Hell, no! It was them damn Freemasons!

MITCH: Shit, can I get this on camera? This is great stuff…

ARON: *Oh, yeah, sure, hang on let me get my good hat…

GINGER: Well, I'm not really dressed for it, but I'll find something…

(GINGER and ARON rush for the stairwell. RUFUS blocks them, arms akimbo, plenty peeved.)

RUFUS: No! No you cannot!

MITCH: Oh, what, are you not familiar with the First Amendment?

RUFUS: Yes, sir, and I'm also damn familiar with the Second.

(MITCH looks down at his camera, checking its settings, not noticing the big-ass pistol RUFUS is pulling from his holster.)

MITCH: Oh, is that a threat? Well, listen, Mister Man, I know my rights, and no amount of—

(MITCH looks up— RUFUS has a pistol aimed right at MITCH's forehead.)

MITCH: Oh dear God a weapon!!!!!! (He clutches his camera to his chest for protection, hyperventilates.)

RUFUS: (Enjoying the hell out of this.) Now, I'm gonna make one thing perfectly clear to you, you shitnecked fuckstick. I am the goddamn law. Like it or not. And if'n you got any information about this girl, you'd best hand it over right goddamn now.

MITCH: Look I just wanted a follow-up interview with the kid—

RUFUS: Follow-up! You got footage? (RUFUS grabs MITCH's camera, bolts over to the La-Z-Boy, sits to watch the footage through the viewfinder. Through:)

MITCH: Hey! That's personal property!

RUFUS: State's evidence. Shut it, fuckwit.

MITCH: (Quickly.) Fair enough.

GINGER: (Takes advantage of the moment to rush MITCH, pump him for information.) You saw my baby? Where was she?

MITCH: (Composes himself, smelling a good story, or perhaps a sucker.) Your daughter, ma'am— Ginger, was it?

GINGER: No, I'm Ginger, my daughter is Bailey.

MITCH: Yeah that's what I— Yeah. Anyway. Your daughter, ma'am, is a true American hero. She quit her job. She delivered a stirring political speech. And, then...she fled. Fled into the night like a spirit, or wraith.

ARON: That don't sound like our baby.

GINGER: Them goddamn Ay-Rabs done brainwashed my angel!

RUFUS: Nobody brainwashed anybody!

GINGER: *That's what they do!*

RUFUS: *Ah fer chrissakes.

GINGER: They brainwash 'em with lights and bad music and sock puppets!

MITCH: ...What in the hell are you talking about??

ARON: I told you, weren't no damn Moo-Slams! It was the Illuminati!

(ARON grabs MITCH, spins him, leans heavy into him, practically knocking him over.)

ARON: They are ruining everything! You ever notice how hot dogs come in packs of ten, but the buns come in packs of twelve?

MITCH: E*xcuse me*! Personal space? Invading.

(Chastened, ARON pulls back.)

MITCH: ...Thanks.

(RUFUS's cell phone rings. He answers.)

RUFUS: Yeah, what? He did? Well, when was this? Well, shit on me. Alright, thank you, Buck. *(Hangs up—stands, crosses down to MITCH and the SUGARMANS; I got them now.)* You say your daughter likes to pal around with that boy, Jesus, down the gas station? One with the Elvis fixation?

ARON: Jesus is alright.

GINGER: Jesus never meant no harm.

RUFUS: Jesus done up and gone. Jesus done stole a pickup truck belonging to his employer, Mr. Stern. You know anything about that, Mister Man-of-the-People?

GINGER: You mean...Jesus is a Muslim terrorist?

(Pause.)

RUFUS: *(To audience.)* Oh, I ain't touching that one.

MITCH: There is no terrorist!

ARON: That's right! It was all on accounta the vast, right-wing, Illuminati, corporate state!

MITCH: Wow! That's good! Have you ever read any Noam Chomsky?

ARON: I just stick to "Marmaduke" and *Soldier of Fortune.*

MITCH: Well. It's a start. You know, we should talk.

(MITCH grabs camera— RUFUS's eyes glow red with rage, uh oh...)

MITCH: Tell me about yourself. About how America has let you down. The death of the American Dream.

ARON: *Wait, let me get my good hat—

GINGER: Well I'm not really dressed for it but—

(ARON and GINGER bolt for the stair-case—and RUFUS explodes with rage, stopping them dead in their tracks.)

RUFUS: *Goddammit you people! Has everyone around here lost their motherfucking minds?!?!?!?*

GINGER: Is that a *rhetorical question— oh—

(As RUFUS speaks, softly, the sound of a drumbeat, martial staccato, a call to battle. Lights dim, save for a single spot on RUFUS. He steps slowly downstage, firm, solid, certain. The Last Sane Man.)

RUFUS: Now it is my sworn duty to protect and to serve. I have wanted to do so ever since I was knee high to a cock turd and I'll be god*damned* if I'm gonna have that promise broken now! Now, I don't care whether your daughter's been kidnapped by some douchebag Ay-Rab Moo-Slams—

GINGER: *(Sobs.)* *Wwwwahhhhhhahah—

RUFUS: —or by some insane batshit cultists—

ARON: *(In the darkness upstage.)* Freemasons.

RUFUS: *Bullshit!*

(In the darkness, the sound of GINGER slapping ARON upside the head.)

RUFUS: I'm damn sure she just got hopped up on the giggle dust and ran quick like a bunny hop to see Gay Pareee. I do know that I am going to find her. One way or the 'nother. Even if you crazy bastards don't give a rat's ass, someone does. Someone has to. I have to. *(He puts on his sunglasses. Adjusts his brim. Stands tall. Looks like one tough sunuvabitch.)* It's my job.

(He strides off, purposefully. Moment. Lights back to full. Music stops with a screech.)

MITCH: I'm sorry, where were we?

ARON: Oh, right. Freemasons.

(MITCH starts rolling camera on ARON, as GINGER stalks off upstairs, angry at her moment in the spotlight being ruined as usual.)

ARON: Okay, so, back in 1775, Thomas Jefferson, John Hancock, and Ben Franklin all started this secret subsociety of the Masonic Lodge, see…?

(Lights down slowly over ARON's speech as the NARRATOR is heard…)

NARRATOR: *(Voiceover.)* We'll leave these people to their theories and schemes for now and get back to what's been doin' with Sug and Jesus. They'd hit the road… and then they hit someone's car. Total stranger, the guy was, but he was very understanding and good-natured about the whole deal. Luckily, it was in a pretty populated area, so they could get inside and get help and shelter pretty quickly. How populated an area, you might ask? Well, let's see now. If you were a seventeen-year-old girl obsessed with rockabilly and pinup queens and your best friend was an Elvis impersonator… Hell, where would *you* go?

10

LAS VEGAS, NEVADA! Specifically, the lobby of the Tropicana Resort. Music: Sammy Davis, Jr., "The Goin's Great."

Lights up on a giant sign reading "Tropicana Hotel and Resort/Welcome to beautiful Las Vegas, Nevada!" The sounds of a hopping casino: slot machines, roulette wheels, craps tables. A bank of slot machines faces the entrance, old ladies planted before them, pulling handles repeatedly, buckets full of quarters clutched between their legs. One giant machine faces the entrance, with a Tropicana attendant seated next to it: DORIS, sixties, huge dirty blonde bouffant hairdo, name tag, yellow and green uniform, cheerful in that laidback semi-retired sweetheart way. She reads the new issue of "Slot Players" magazine, whiling away a slow afternoon, half-finished Lucky Strike perfectly balanced on lower lip. Below the machine, a huge billboard: "Free Pull! Win show tickets, complimentary buffet, or our $200,000 Progressive Jackpot!" Enter SUGARBABY and

JESUS, with STANISLAUS, twenties, loudass suit, slicked hair, VERY thick Eastern European accent—Polish? Lithuanian? He's a bundle of manic energy, all gesticulation and shouting. He punctuates nearly every comment with good-natured shoves and slaps that border on abuse, even though he obviously means to be playful. SUGARBABY and JESUS both look worn out; JESUS's hands are stained with motor oil. SUG's eyes are wide with wonder at the sights and sounds of the bustling adult playground.

STANISLAUS: Hey is okay bro! No problemo!

JESUS: You're really far too kind, Mr. Polski. *I can't thank you enough.

STANISLAUS: Please, baby! Call me Stanislaus!

SUGARBABY: *(Looking around in amazement.)* Man, I thought the Strip was something, but goddamn!

STANISLAUS: It is this that is the shit, yes? Look at that! Tiffany glass ceiling! Beautiful! God bless America!

JESUS: I can't thank you enough, Mr. Polski, for all your help, but we can't really afford to stay no place this fancy. Neither of us got much money, *and I'm gonna have to get my truck fixed—

STANISLAUS: Ah, please, will not be much! Your truck it's just, *it's just—

SUGARBABY: Flames were comin' out the hood.

JESUS: I can fix it, but I ain't got no tools with me, *and no garage to do it in.

STANISLAUS: Hey! Bro! Is okay! Listen! *I'm happy to help you!

JESUS: And your slammin' into my pickup and all! I'm sure I'll have to fix *your car now too!

STANISLAUS: Is okay! Hey, listen, is just car! I have five!

(Pause. JESUS and SUG stare at him, dumbfounded.)

JESUS: I'm sorry—did you say five?

SUGARBABY: Cars?

STANISLAUS: *(Nods—what's the big deal?)* My family very big in Polish candy industry. It makes money for me at home, I collect money, travel world. Is okay. I'm rolling in it, dudes!

SUGARBABY: You've been kind enough, Mr. Polski. *We couldn't really—

STANISLAUS: I insist! I know nobody here, really! Except for dealers and waitresses. But that is only because I am big roller. Good luck! I am good luck for you, no?

(Shoves JESUS toward the free pull slot machine. DORIS drops her magazine, smiles widely, gestures welcomingly at the machine.)

STANISLAUS: Go ahead, spin! Free spin! Go ahead! Maybe you win show ticket! Yes?

JESUS: Well. Okay. I guess. I don't know if gambling is respectable or not—

STANISLAUS: Shit, man! Is Vegas! Everything is respectable here! Live a little!

(JESUS shrugs, shyly turns to DORIS, who shows him how the machine works, a little amused that he's never seen one. Through:)

SUGARBABY: Listen, Mr. Polski—

STANISLAUS: Please, you are both so formal! Call me Stanislaus!

SUGARBABY: *See, we appreciate your hospitality, but we can't impose—

STANISLAUS: Pretty lady. You stay with me. A flower like you. You must not be

left to wither in the dark. Stay in the sunlight. My little sunflower.

(SUGARBABY giggles.)

STANISLAUS: What?

SUGARBABY: That's what my mother
used to call me, when I was little.

STANISLAUS: See? Is karma!

SUGARBABY: Kismet.

STANISLAUS: Whatever.

*(Just then, JESUS pulls the arm on the ma-
chine—three bars! A bell rings! Lights flash!
Slot junkies look up from their machines,
gawp in wonder, applaud spontaneously, that
giddy feeling that sweeps the floor when
someone's hit big. DORIS laughs, claps happily. JESUS practically jumps out of his skin.)*

JESUS: What!? What!? Did I just break
something?

DORIS: *Oh my word.

SUGARBABY: What happened?

STANISLAUS: God's shit you dude! You
won! *You are rich!

JESUS: Oh, great! Did I win the show
tickets? Who do I get to see?

DORIS: You won the progressive, hon.
You just won a hundred thousand dollars!

*(Before they can celebrate, in barges CLOVIS,
fifties, stocky, Hawaiian shirt, the fast patter
and bullish posture of a born con artist. He
gestures wildly, shouts, makes a huge scene.
Patrons gather, watch with growing fasci-
nation and dismay.)*

CLOVIS: Waitaminit! That money is
mine!

DORIS: *Oh, you go to hell, Clovis!

CLOVIS: I was next in line, and this
sunuvabitch cut in front of me! *That

should have been my spin! By rights, I get
half of that money!

JESUS: I'm awful sorry if that's true, sir,
but I believe *I won fair and square—

*(JESUS takes a placating step toward him,
CLOVIS falls backward, grabs at his side,
begins limping—the worst, least convincing
cripple act you ever saw.)*

CLOVIS: *(High drama.) Ow!* He hit me!
My back! *Ow!* I think my spleen is rup-
tured! *My spleen! My beautiful spleen!

*(Enter MABEL, fifties, CLOVIS's wife,
lumpy figure, piss-poor posture, battered vi-
sor, Bingo Queen T-shirt, chain of casino
comp cards rattling from her belt loop; an
even worse actor than CLOVIS, if you can
believe it. She rushes to CLOVIS's side, makes
a grand show of supporting his ponderous
weight.)*

MABEL: Oh, honey, did that very rich
man hurt you? *I want restitution! I want
you in court! We'll sue!

DORIS: Alright, out, the both of you,
*before I call security!

JESUS: Ma'am, I swear to you, I never
touched your husband, ma'am!

SUGARBABY: You're a filthy liar, *you
filthy liar, you lie!

MABEL: And you I sue for slander!

*(Rapidly, it descends into chaos, CLOVIS
wailing like a wounded bear, MABEL
screeching like a vampire bat, JESUS rattling off apologies like mantras, and DORIS
screaming for security. Unfazed, STANIS-
LAUS steps onto an empty roulette table,
raises his hands, bellows…)*

STANISLAUS: Alllllllright now dudes!

*(Silence. All eyes in the place turn to him as
everyone freezes, tableau.)*

STANISLAUS: Sir, there are plenty security cameras around this place all here now, and they catch you, and they prove that you are talking of shit. *(To MABEL.)* You, ma'am, are accomplice in shit-talking, you go to jail too. Here, let me make it worth your while—

(STANISLAUS hops down off table, opens wallet, peels off a couple of hundred bucks without batting an eye. SUG is mighty impressed.)

STANISLAUS: —Here. Is payoff. Now, go, go, leave these people alone… *(Looks at JESUS and SUG, genuine smile.)* they are my friends.

(SUG and JESUS blush, look at their shoes, aw pshaw. The PATRONS gathered all "awwwwwww" in unison.)

STANISLAUS: Now. Go fuck you and yourself, too.

(CLOVIS looks at the money. Then at MABEL. Can't sneeze at a couple hundred bucks. They turn to exit, walk to the door. Stop. CLOVIS faces the audience—)

CLOVIS: You ain't heard the last of this. *(Evil laugh.)* Mwah ha ha ha ha. Mmuwwwwwwha ha ha ha. Mwwwwwwaaaaaaaaaaaaaa hha ha ha ha ha.

(He exits. The PATRONS applaud STANISLAUS, step forward, shake JESUS's and SUG's hands, then go back to their gambling. DORIS approaches JESUS, beaming.)

DORIS: I'm awful sorry about that unfortunate incident, sir, and on behalf of the Tropicana Hotel and Resort, might I offer you a complimentary night's stay in our hotel?

JESUS: Oh, no, ma'am, we couldn't possibly afford something that nice.

STANISLAUS: Dude! Is complimentary! They are offering for free!

JESUS: Free room? And free money? *(Pause—to audience.)* I like Las Vegas.

STANISLAUS: You wait, babies. I take you on the town.

(STANISLAUS reaches into jacket, pulls out sunglasses, snaps his fingers— all lights out save for a single spot on STANISLAUS.)

STANISLAUS: You gonna *love* Las Vegas!

(Music: "Viva Las Vegas." Lights change. STANISLAUS begins doing a little disco shimmy to the opening of the song, begins singing the praises of Las Vegas as the gathered PATRONS get up and dance. A giant replica of the "Welcome to Fabulous Las Vegas" sign drops in upstage, and bright, neon lights flash and sparkle. DORIS joins in in short order, singing along with STANISLAUS, and soon the FULL COMPANY joins in, dancing and singing the praises of America's Playground… DANCING BOYS enter carrying small replicas of Strip casino marquees, floating them over SUGARBABY's head à la Ray Milland in The Lost Weekend… *Two glamorous GAMBLING MOLLS slink downstage with playing cards, dice, roulette wheels, and small slot machine replicas, as JESUS, too, sings the joys of Vegas!… Soon, a joyous conga line is formed around the stage, circling JESUS and SUGARBABY as they do some classic Ann-Margret and Elvis moves at center, and the Vegas sign lights up to full, bright intensity… And the big finish, as the FULL COMPANY forms a tableau at center for the final chorus, surrounding JESUS, SUG, STANISLAUS, and DORIS, who pass around martini glasses, which are in turn filled by a handsome tuxedo-shirted BARTENDER bearing a souvenir Vegas martini shaker… And lights out!*

11

Center stage, USNC Studios, "The Rod Butane Zone." ROD behind his desk, shirt-

sleeves, pit stains, hair a little mussed. The eagle is turned entirely the wrong way now. The coffee mug is gone, replaced by a cheap paper takeout cup. ROD looks worn, but jazzed. Very Edward R. Murrow. Graphic over his shoulder: "Terror in the Heartland: The Sugarman Tragedy, Day Two." Stage right, MITCH's hotel room. Suitcase open, clothes a mess. Camera on the floor. He's not around. TV is on, blue light across the room—he's tuned to ROD, obviously, trying to keep up with the competition.

ROD: America is once again in the grip of terror, details are still sketchy, and this story gets weirder and weirder by the minute.

(Enter MITCH, brushing his teeth, boxers, "Impeach Bush" T-shirt. He stops, watches the TV for a moment, begins yelling at it in disbelief.)

ROD: Now there's word that political "filmmaker" Mitch Common apparently got some of the only footage anyone has been able to get, mere hours before this young girl's tragic disappearance. You know, this is a classic example of limousine liberalism run amok. He's hawking this footage all over the place for top dollar, *of course, we had to pay through the nose for it. Here's this guy, pretends to be some kind of "hero to the people," but here he is, making money off of this poor girl's plight, I mean it just disgusts me.

MITCH: Oh my God, these right-wing pigs are all the same! You paid for the footage, you douchebag! The nerve of this guy!… Didn't pay enough, either. I gotta call my agent… *(Exits to the bathroom to spit, still listening.)*

ROD: Anyway, we're gonna open up the phone lines once more before we go, we have a few minutes left, let's take the next call—from Las Vegas, Nevada. Las Vegas,

you're on the air…

(Stage right, lights up on MABEL and CLOVIS, calling from a crumbling phone booth somewhere just off of Fremont. CLOVIS yells into the phone as though he and the whole world were deaf, and MABEL hangs on his shoulder, tapping his arm violently, annoying the shit out of him. He occasionally swats at her as though she were a fly; she just switches to his other shoulder, and so on and so on…)

CLOVIS: Yeah, hi, Rod? First time, long time, *listen—

MABEL: Hurry up, *I'm out of change!

CLOVIS: I know that! Shut up! Listen, Rob—

ROD: *That's, that's Rod…

CLOVIS: That girl ain't all she's cracked up to be, you know.

MABEL: You tell him, *baby!

CLOVIS: Shut up! Listen, she's a con artist. Her and her little friend, both.

ROD: Little friend? You mean the fundamentalist Muslim terrorists that kidnapped her?

CLOVIS: …I don't know about that guy, he might have been Polish or something.

ROD: Polish. Now that's interesting. Caller, let me ask you, what do you think of the *proposed induction of Poland into the European Union?

(Further stage left, the OPERATOR, thirties, classic telephone operator image, pencil skirt, pink blouse, filing her nails, headset, appears, interrupts.)

OPERATOR: Please deposit thirty-five cents for the next three minutes.

CLOVIS: Yeah, I wouldn't know anything about that, Rob, listen—

ROD: *My, my name is Rod…

MABEL: About what? *What's he saying?

CLOVIS: Will you? Come on! …She's full of it. Her and her little friend took my money that I should have won fair and square and didn't, and now I'm gonna sue her and her *friend for all they got!

ROD: Sue? Sue who? *What the hell are you on?

CLOVIS: She's a con artist, Rob! *A flim-flam operator! A snake oil salesman!

MABEL: Tell him already!

ROD: Alright, so what leads you to this *conclusion about this poor brave woman who is sacrificing so much for her country?

OPERATOR: Please deposit thirty-five *cents for the next three minutes.

CLOVIS: *I know! Dammit! I'm out of change!*

ROD: A— Are you calling from a pay phone?

MABEL: *(Suddenly grabs the phone, yells into it, holding it out like she was choking a squirrel.)* Listen Mister Hollywood Hotshot, I saw her! That little white trash bitch is here! She's in Las Vegas *and she ain't no hero!

(MITCH pops back into the hotel room, eyes goggling out.)

MITCH: *Hell-o!*

(ROD, smelling a juicy exclusive, slowly rises from his chair, practically frothing at the mouth.)

ROD: *You— she— whoa *What!!*

MABEL: *She's a lying little tramp with a heart of formica and she broke my husband's spleen! *My husband of thirty-five years!*

CLOVIS: I'm trying to tell him! *Will you please! We gotta call the cops and I used my last quarter on the Double Diamond machine!

MABEL: *And I swear to God I'll find that backassed tramp and *put my fist down her throat and squeeze if I find her I swear to God!*

ROD: *Where! Where did you see her? Where! Where did you see Sugarbaby???*

MITCH: *Where!*

ROD: *Where?*

MITCH: *Where!*

OPERATOR: Please deposit thirty-five cents for the next— *oooooo*kay you're done.

(The OPERATOR drops her nail file, reaches out, disconnects the line. The lights quickly fade on CLOVIS and MABEL; they yell out as though they were falling down a well…)

CLOVIS: Nnnoooooooo*ooooooooooooo*!!!!!!!!

ROD: Hello, Las Vegas?

MITCH: Las Vegas?

ROD: Las Vegas?

MITCH: Las Vegas.

ROD: Las Vegas!

MITCH: Of course they're in Las goddamn Vegas!!!

(MITCH turns, barrels into the bathroom, grabbing a pair of pants out of his suitcase on the way. ROD, at a loss, looks into the camera, ashen, crosses in front of the desk.)

ROD: Well, I don't know what to say. We'll be right back, right after we take one more look at this remarkable footage of this courageous American, taken just last night by… Hhhhh… "filmmaker" Mitch Common.

(For a brief second, MITCH's hand pops into the hotel room, flips the bird to the TV, back out.)

ROD: And then, I'll be back, with tonight's "Parting Shot." Let's take a look.

(Lights shift to cool blues. Drytone beep, sound of monitors showing the SUGAR-BABY footage shot by MITCH. ROD rushes downstage, yells into the distance.)

ROD: Jerry, get the hell over here!

(JERRY—twenties, production assistant, dressed in black, headset, unflappable—appears. This conversation should go very quickly, à la His Girl Friday.*)*

JERRY: *Sir.

(ROD thrusts the coffee cup into JERRY's hand—a little spills onto JERRY's shirt; it doesn't even faze him.)

ROD: First of all, this is a mochaccino, not a cappuccino. A fucking monkey could get this right, why can't you?

JERRY: *Yessir.

ROD: Second, why don't I have a goddamn correspondent in the goddamn field *on this goddamn story?

JERRY: We have one, sir, she's still filing her *story, we'll have something within the hour.

ROD: She? This is war, son. Terrorism. You wanna send a woman out there to get shot at or taken *captive? What the hell is the matter with you?

JERRY: I didn't send anyone sir, *it was from upstairs.

ROD: Do we have a mobile unit packed and ready to go? *Like now?

JERRY: Sir? I-I think *so.

ROD: Fine, junior, then you get it ready, I'm hauling my ass out there myself, I smell ratings, I smell history in the making, this is a fucking big story and *you people are not fucking this for me like you did with Baghdad!!*

(ROD throws a shit fit, hurls the eagle across the room, crumples papers, kicks his chair. JERRY shrugs, takes a sip of the offending beverage, hmm, not bad, exits as the lights shift back and the show goes back on air.)

DIRECTOR: *(Voiceover.)* Aaaaaaaaaaaaaand back on air!

ROD: *(Effortlessly regains composure, sits on the edge of the desk, adopts a "folksy" tone.)* You know, my heart goes out to these people. To her poor parents. The people who loved her.

(MITCH reenters, fully dressed, picks up his camera, readies it as he watches ROD's speech with growing anger and dismay.)

ROD: And I have nothing but contempt for this "artist," Mitch Common, using this tragic story, this poor girl, to further his career. Divide and conquer, that's the attitude these liberal weasels have, divide and conquer. Well, it takes a tragedy, in times like these, to unite us. That's why I'm pleased to report that, throughout this crisis, I am going to be personally reporting to you live from the field with exclusive on-the-spot reports, giving you direct access to events as they unfold. Because we care. About. The truth.

(ROD exits, heroically. MITCH snorts derisively, makes a jerking-off motion at the set—"yeah right"—exits, camera in hand, ready to hit the road. After a moment, ROD pops back into view—)

ROD: The truth tonight is brought to you by Solvent Money Managing. Wanna stay abreast of the market? Stay Solvent. Be back here tomorrow at nine with Michael Medved. See you then. *(Turns, stalks off-stage, bellowing, gesturing wildly.) Jerry get my driver on the phone goddammit!!!!!*

(Blackout.)

12

NARRATOR: *(Voiceover.)* So, thanks to a con artist with a big mouth and a little lady with a bad attitude, everybody in the world knew just where Sugarbaby was. And where exactly was the lady in question that next day? Well, she'd left home to see the sights… and now the sights she was seeing was the inside of an elevator going up to a hotel room.

(Tropicana hotel elevator. JESUS, STANIS-LAUS, and SUGARBABY. JESUS is in a brand-spanking-new leather Elvis outfit he done bought himself with his prize money. STANISLAUS is in a gaudy but somehow fetching seventies-era wide-lapelled leisure tux. They check themselves out in the mirror on the wall of the elevator, while SUG, in a pretty retro fifties dress, pouts, arms folded.)

STANISLAUS: So, I just let it ride! And I hit blackjack again! What you say is the odds, yeah? Ha!

SUGARBABY: This is bullshit, guys. I run away from home to be free, and what do I get? Stuck up here in the damn room while you two go have all the fun.

STANISLAUS: Is casino! You are under-age! We cannot take! It's late. Get sleep. I promise, we hit town tomorrow night, places where there is no age limit.

SUGARBABY: They should have stuff for kids to do here.

STANISLAUS: They do! Just not, you know, *kids who are on run from law.

JESUS: I promise, Ms. Sugarman, tomor-row, we're going go to the Liberace mu-seum, and the Elvis museum— *(On her look.)* What's wrong now?

SUGARBABY: Those awful people. Downstairs. The ones what tried to take your money, and said you'd hit them. I don't know. Every time I think the world is a good and happy place, I meet some-one like that. And it sours everything. I see how the world is, and I even get ashamed to be an American.

STANISLAUS: *(Serious.)* Hey.

(He leans in, presses the stop button on the elevator. Sound of elevator dinging in reply, grinding to a halt. He takes SUGARBABY by the shoulders, firm but not mean. She and JESUS freeze, surprised. STANISLAUS speaks with great conviction.)

STANISLAUS: Don't you ever say that again. Don't ever be ashamed of who and what you are. Don't you ever be ashamed to be an American.

(He softens slightly, lets go of SUG, pauses. As he tells his story, JESUS and SUG listen, entranced, their gazes slowly rising, as though they can see through the elevator, all the way to the heavens.)

STANISLAUS: My uncle was in Gulag. Many years. His only joy was Elvis. Yes, your Elvis. They had one record there, they had snuck it in. Everyone had secret stash. Record was "Blue Moon of Kentucky." They did not even know where Kentucky was. Every now and then, they'd sneak a listen. Sometimes, they wouldn't even turn the volume up, just listen to music com-ing off the needle as it rolled across the record. I asked him, years later, what it sounds like. He says, like a cool blue sky, and a soft, open breeze. It kept him alive through cold, hard years. He was one of the lucky ones. He always wanted to see America. America is a cool blue sky and a soft open breeze. Even in desert.

(STANISLAUS smiles. SUG's gaze lowers; she looks at him. Smiles back. She gets it. STANISLAUS leans in, presses the button for the casino floor. The elevator dings in response, starts back up. SUG sees this, frowns, pouts again.)

STANISLAUS: Now. We go piss away lots of money. You can watch cable here, call room service, just don't leave. We'll go out tomorrow, see desert, is beautiful.

(The elevator door opens. Sound of casino floor. STANISLAUS bounds out, gesturing for JESUS to follow. JESUS takes a step out, turns—)

JESUS: You stay safe and sane, little girl.

(She nods, grudgingly. He exits. The elevator doors close, elevator rises, back to the room. SUG reaches into her purse, pulls out a flask. Grins. Unscrews the cap, takes a big ol' swig for such a little girl.)

SUGARBABY: Be damned if they're going be the only ones having any fun.

(Blackout.)

13

Darkness. Music: Gershwin, "For Lily Pons."

NARRATOR: *(Voiceover.)* Well, now we're just about caught up. Everything you're about to see is what you heard about on the TV, the radio, but now you know the whole story. But there's one more thing we haven't been able to show you that you gotta know about. That footage ended up on TV shows, and on the Internet, it went all over the world. That's how everybody came to know who Sugarbaby was. And something in her touched a nerve. Some sense of optimism. A sense of will be in-

stead of won't. Could be instead of can't. Something everyone, American or not, so badly needed to hear in times as strained and painful as the times we endure today. Something American. So, here we are.

You got a TV reporter obsessed with glory and ratings. You got a "maverick documentary filmmaker" who's convinced he's found a license to print money... And you got a man who may have the purest intentions of all. Who's assumed on his weary shoulders the Herculean task of finding her, for all the right reasons...

(Single spotlight on RUFUS, center stage. Kinda like the beginning of Patton. *Sunglasses on, hat snappy, classic Southern sheriff look. The Last Sane Man.)*

RUFUS: I don't care who took her. I got my ideas, but ideas are just smoke and mirrors. I believe in what I can see and what I can feel. And whether she's being held captive by terrorists, by cultists, or whether she ran away from the only home she's known, I'm going to find her, and I'm going to bring that little girl home.

14
SUGARBABY CUTS LOOSE!

Music: Duke Ellington, "Diminuendo and Crescendo in Blue."

*The following sequence of events occurs in overlapping sections. Bold capital letter combinations within dialog sections (e.g., **AA**) indicate the beginning of the following section. All scenes continue at full performance volume and intensity while the surrounding scenes play out.*

Downstage, the lobby of the Tropicana. DORIS at her station, greeting customers as they enter. Upstage left, the slot pit. A SLOT LADY, fifties, black fake-satin Riviera jacket, stretch pants, grey hair, dropping quarters methodically into a Haywire slot machine.

Every few spins, she stops, places her hands on the front of the machine, lowers her head, says a quick prayer, continues spinning. Once or twice through this scene, she wins, emotionlessly scoops her winnings into a bucket clutched between her thighs.

Upstage right, STANISLAUS's hotel room, a mess. SUGARBABY slumped in a chair, drunk off her ass, humming old rock & roll tunes to herself, grinning stupidly.

At the Tropicana, enter RUFUS, who crosses to DORIS, pulling out a photo of SUGAR-BABY, thrusting it into DORIS's face. DORIS remains smiling and calm throughout.

AA

DORIS: Hello, sir, welcome to the Tropicana Hotel and Resort, how may I help you?

RUFUS: *(Rapid fire.)* Ma'am, my name is Sheriff Rufus J. Miranda, and I am here on official po-lice business. We've received a tip that a young woman currently on the run from the law, as it were, may be here in your fine establishment, may I show you her picture? (**BB**)

DORIS: Why, no, I don't believe I've *seen her.

RUFUS: Look again.

DORIS: I just *looked.

RUFUS: Look again.

DORIS: *Why?

RUFUS: Maybe you missed something.

DORIS: It's not a very *big picture.

RUFUS: Look again.

DORIS: Maybe I should get the *manager on call—

RUFUS: Maybe you should re-fresh your damn memory 'fore I haul your ass in for negligence and obstructing justice.

BB

Enter JESUS and STANISLAUS, both tanked.

STANISLAUS: —and he holds out his hand and says, "Hey everybody! Look what I almost—"

(They stop dead, notice RUFUS. Go white.)

STANISLAUS: —stepped in.

JESUS: Oh my.

STANISLAUS: We are doing the blind panicking now, yes?

JESUS: Yes, sir.

(They vamoose damn fast.)

DORIS: Sir, I have no idea what this is *about, but—

(Enter EARL, forties, a big bear-like fellow in full-on Elvis gear, bowling shirt, sunglasses. He stops in the lobby, looks up, admiring the ceiling.)

RUFUS: I'll tell you what it's about, young missy. It's about a young woman what was done abducted by some preverted knuckle-dragging kiddy raper (**CC**) who's doing God knows what to her right now, and I'm a *fixin' to find that girlie and escape her from the claws of that—

DORIS: Well, I'm sure if you were to leave a detailed description of her at the desk—

(RUFUS spots EARL, mistakes him for JESUS, rushes to him, grabs him by his shoulder, spins him round—)

RUFUS: *I got you you sumbitch!*

(DORIS takes advantage of this to sneak off,

slowly at first, then running reeeeeeeeeally damn fast. At that same moment, RUFUS looks up at EARL, realizing his horrible, horrible error. Gulps. EARL, very pissed off, very large, slowly stalks RUFUS back into a corner, points into RUFUS's chest with a beefy finger, leans in real close, RUFUS shrinks in terror—)

EARL: You're lucky I'm not a violent man. *(Satisfied he has sufficiently shown RUFUS who's the damn boss, EARL exits, swaggering.)*

RUFUS: Yes I am.

CC

JESUS and STANISLAUS burst into the hotel room, presidential suite, startling SUG awake. JESUS barrels straight into a corner, starts sobbing and wailing like a big baby, as STANIS-LAUS throws up his hands, gesticulates wildly trying to get things a rollin'.

JESUS: They're gone put me in irons! *They're gonna nail me on the Mann Act! I'm gonna get thrown in jail and molestered by clammy, fat Mexicans!

STANISLAUS: Okay babies! *Now is time for greener pastures, I think!

SUGARBABY: You's gone all night! I had to finish all this wine cooler by myself!

STANISLAUS: That's not wine cooler, that's champagne! *Oh my fuck, you just drank a hundred dollars!

SUGARBABY: I just worked up some new dance moves! You wanna see? They're so-lacious!

JESUS: *The cops are coming and they're gonna split us up and throw me in jail, and send you back to the crummy burger shop, and I'll die without ever having tasted Peking duck!

STANISLAUS: You know what? Forget it! Pack your things!

SUGARBABY: What things?

STANISLAUS: Even better. Off we go.

SUGARBABY: *Wait a minute, go where? I wanna see Wayne Newton tomorrow!

(DORIS rushes in, breathlessly.)

DORIS: Alllllllllright, you folks need to leave, there's cops downstairs, *the one guy, he ain't too bright, but he ain't gonna wait around all night, he's gonna find you, and you gotta go. I don't know what you did, and I don't care, but you are now going!!

SUGARBABY: Cops? *Cops? **(DD)**

STANISLAUS: This is what I am saying here!

JESUS: *They're gonna hook a car battery to my privates and cook 'em like spare ribs!

SUGARBABY: I gotta get the hell outta here! *They ain't taking me back to that hellhole!

STANISLAUS: Is okay! I get you to airport! *(Grabs a sheet off the bed, holds it out like a wrap, stands on the desk.)*

SUGARBABY: We ain't gonna get no plane tickets this time a night!

STANISLAUS: Who needs tickets? I have private jet!

SUGARBABY: Wow. *(Turns downstage, salutes the audience.)* God bless America.

STANISLAUS: That's what I said.

(SUG throws herself backwards into the sheet STANISLAUS holds out, he wraps her in it like a big SUGARBABY burrito. Through:)

DORIS: I'll go down, try to keep him occupied, stall for time.

STANISLAUS: Don't tell him the shit, Doris.

DORIS: Honey, this is Vegas. We know how to keep our mouths shut.

(She and STANISLAUS exchange a brusque, all-business nod; DORIS marches out to do her duty. Meanwhile, JESUS, inconsolable, begins running around the room in a panic, arms over his head.)

JESUS: This is all because I stopped goin' church! That's what it is! This is punishment for getting drunk and smokin' and sinning away my money and flirting with that dealer in the Bacharach pit! I knew I shoulda stuck with the slot machines, but, no, I had to diversify—

(Calmly, STANISLAUS steps down off the desk, crosses the room, slaps JESUS across the face.)

JESUS: *(Immediately calmed.)* ...Thank you.

(STANISLAUS and JESUS then lift SUGARBABY, carry her out as though she were a rolled-up rug, which causes her to giggle uncontrollably.)

DD

Meanwhile, RUFUS, trying to act casual, approaches the SLOT LADY, shows her SUG's picture. The SLOT LADY ain't interested.

RUFUS: 'Scuse me ma'am I wonder if you've seen a young lady about, oh, seventeen years old—

SLOT LADY: *This machine's taken. I'm on a roll. Go find your own.

RUFUS: She's traveling with a man looks like Elvis Presley and I'll be a sumbitch—

(Just then, downstage, enter JACK, twenties, Elvis impersonator, white starched shirt, tight black pants, carrying a suitcase reading "Jack Diamond, winner 2001 Tri-State Elvis Tribute Artists Competition," camera around neck, goggle-eyed at the hotel lobby ceiling. RUFUS rushes him, grabs him by the arm.)*

RUFUS: I got you now, you kiddy rapin' prevert! *Now where you got her?

JACK: *(Excited, friendly.)* Hey, are you here with the Melman bar mitzvah? *I'm supposed to perform there and I swear, their signs are mighty confusin' here and I can't find the damn convention rooms to save my ass...

RUFUS: Bar mitzvah? Shit. How many damn Elvii they got in this frickin' nuthouse?

JACK: Hey, you wouldn't mind taking my picture, would you? *I gots to get me a shot of me in front of these here Elvis slot machines, it'll look great on my website...

(JACK pulls the camera over his head, thrusts it into RUFUS's hand, jumps in front of the slot machines. The SLOT LADY shoots him a look, shifts down a little, keeps playing. RUFUS just stands there, staring at him, baffled.)

RUFUS: I'm, I'm actually a little busy just about now...

JACK: Now, the button on the side is for focusing, and the button on the other side is for auto exposure, and the button on the top snaps the picture, okay, now I'm gonna pose right here... wait that's not it... wait...

(He strikes an Elvis-y pose. Dissatisfied, he tries another. Then another. Just then, enter MITCH, camera rolling, filming a conversation with JOSH and ANDREA, two college students, early twenties, tatty clothes, sandals, slogan T-shirts, animated, dead sure they're right and everyone else is wrong.)

RUFUS sees the trio, turns to watch them a moment, looks at the audience—"Jesus Christ what the hell is going on around here???" —then back at the trio again.)

MITCH: And why, exactly, does Sugarbaby mean so much to you?

JOSH: She's a new voice for the disenfranchised, man!

JACK: *(Posing.)* *I'm ready, you can take my picture now.

MITCH: And what makes you think she would come here to Las Vegas to pursue her political goals?

ANDREA: Well, it's the belly of the beast, isn't it? *I mean, this is unfettered capitalism, corporate greed run rampant. It's a beautiful desert community laid waste by egregious displays of unchecked overexpansionism.

(RUFUS bolts over, plants a hand over MITCH's camera lens, barks at him angrily. ANDREA keeps on prattling, oblivious at first.)

RUFUS: What the hell you doing *here?

MITCH: Wow! Sheriff! Fancy meeting you here! *I could ask you the same question!

RUFUS: Fancy my ass! What do you know that I don't know? *You got a direct line to this kid, you tell me where they got her!

MITCH: I don't know anything! I didn't even know *you were here!

JOSH: *(Tapping RUFUS's shoulder.)* Wait a minute—you're the cop who's trying to haul Sugarbaby in, *aren't you?

RUFUS: *(Swatting him away, not even looking at him.)* Son, just stay out of this.

JACK: *(Posing.)* *I'm ready, you can take my picture now...

MITCH: Hey, don't talk to him that way, he's a pacifist.

ANDREA: *Listen, we know our rights, mister, this is a free country, and we have a right to free speech.

RUFUS: I don't care if he's Ronald goddamn McDonald, this is official police business *and I expect some goddamn cooperation!

JOSH: You can't hold back the truth! You can't hold back the power! Hey-hey, ho-ho, fascist pigs have got to go! Hey-hey, ho-ho, fascist pigs have got to go!

(ANDREA joins in the chant...)

JACK: *(Posing.)* *I'm ready, you can take my picture now...

RUFUS: Oh for Christ's sake get a new fucking chant already, that one's dried up like a cripple pecker, ya indigent fuckwits!

(And just then, as if things couldn't get any more insane... enter JESUS and STANISLAUS, carrying SUG wrapped up in the blanket, running through the lobby.)

SUGARBABY: I can't see nothin'! *Where we goin'?

STANISLAUS: Shut up, already!

(They run right into RUFUS and the trio, nearly knocking RUFUS on his ass. He turns, angrily. Stops. The KIDS slowly stop chanting. MITCH turns, still filming. RUFUS's eyes widen. Moment.)

RUFUS: Uh—

JESUS: Uh—

RUFUS: Uh—

JESUS: Uh—

RUFUS: Oh—

JESUS: Yeah—

STANISLAUS: Well, this is shit.

JACK: *(Posing.)* I'm ready, you can take my picture now.

(Slowly, they lower SUG to the ground, standing upright. She continues humming— "Spanish Flea." JESUS, sheepish, turns to face RUFUS. Smiles, kindly. Raises a hand. Waggles his finger, a charming little wave. STANISLAUS raises his hand, waves as well. RUFUS, still stunned, raises his hand to his holster. JESUS nods. Turns. Lifts his leg to run.)

RUFUS: *Sumbitch! Freeze right there!*

(RUFUS pulls out his gun, clumsily. Music swells to crescendo!! Lights shift!!! RUFUS points to the ceiling, fires! MITCH screams like a little girl, ducks behind a slot machine, clutching his camera like a security blanket, as JOSH and ANDREA squeal, point at RUFUS's gun, practically leap into the air in a panic!)

ANDREA: *Ohmigod he's got a gun!*

JOSH: *Don't kill me i'm a pacifist!!!!!!!!*

(JOSH, thinking quickly, stomps on RUFUS's foot! RUFUS yelps, grabs his leg, falls flat on his face while JESUS and STANISLAUS beat a hasty retreat, leaving SUG wrapped in a blanket in the middle of the pandemonium, still humming "Spanish Flea.")

STANISLAUS: *Mother fucking me in my ass!!!!!!!!!!!!!!!!!*

(At that exact moment, JACK breaks out of his pose, bolts offstage, running into the audience, singing a lovely à capella rendition of "It's Now or Never" at full volume, while RUFUS, regaining his composure, rolls around the floor of the casino, gun brandished, in the classic "stop-drop-and-roll" TV cop manner. After a couple of seconds, STANISLAUS and JESUS rush back in,

realizing their forgetfulness, effortlessly hoist SUG over their heads, run back off carrying her, yelling "hut hut hut hut hut hut" the whole time. RUFUS rolls a bit more, pointing his gun at random objects, finally landing right next to the SLOT LADY, gun trained on her for some godforsaken reason.)

RUFUS: *Freeze!*

SLOT LADY: Fuck off, I'm on a roll.

RUFUS: *(Quickly, gracious.)* Okay. *(Turns downstage, notices JACK singing in the house.)* Shut the hell up, boy, goddamn!

(JACK quiets, embarrassed. Enter DORIS, breathless, but giddy from the excitement.)

DORIS: Hey, Junior G-Man, izzat your cop car outside?

RUFUS: …Yes?

DORIS: Good. 'Cause those two hippies you were just talking to have turned it over and set it on fire. Have a nice day, asshole. *(Laughs, bolts out.)*

RUFUS: Jesus H. Fuck! *(Spins, sees MITCH, points at him with his pistol, almost absentmindedly.)* You!

MITCH: *(Bolts upright, terrified, squeals like a little girl.)* Wwaaaaaaaaaa!!!

RUFUS: You got a car?

MITCH: …I have a Humvee.

RUFUS: *(Winces.)* You make me sick.

MITCH: Yessir.

RUFUS: You want your exclusive? Get off your ass and get me to your car!

MITCH: …I think I peed my pants.

RUFUS: Did you shit yourself?

MITCH: No.

RUFUS: Good. Now, get the hell up and get me on the road! *Go go go go go!!!*

(RUFUS grabs MITCH, shoves him to the door; they exit, MITCH sobbing the whole way. JACK clambers back up onstage, waving for them to stop…)

JACK: Hey, you still got my camera! *(Moment. Slow burn. The bastards. He reaches into his shirt pocket, pulls out a cell phone, dials.)* Yeah, get the word out to everybody. One of our own is in trouble. It's the guy what's on the run with Sugarbaby, and that damn cop's following him and he must be stopped. Oh yeah—the cop still has my goddamn camera.

15

Lights shift downstage, to the parking lot of the Tropicana, special guests' section. Enter JESUS and STANISLAUS, still carrying SUGARBABY. They run in, set her down gingerly. SUGARBABY is singing Del Shannon's "Runaway" off-key.

JESUS: I can't thank you enough, Mr. Polski, for all you've done.

STANISLAUS: Oh, please. *(Sincere, great affection.)* I do for "Blue Moon of Kentucky." I do for Elvis.

(JESUS puts out a hand for STANISLAUS to shake; STANISLAUS lunges forward, grasps JESUS in a painful bear hug. JESUS is torn between being moved and touched, and moaning in agony. After a moment, STANISLAUS lets go, eyes welling. Pats JESUS on the shoulder. Then, reaches into his pants pocket, pulls out a set of car keys, hands them to JESUS.)

STANISLAUS: Signs on Strip will point you to airport, my pilot, he waits for you there. Here, here is keys to limo. Get in. Go. *Oh!* One more thing.

(STANISLAUS grabs one end of SUGAR-BABY's bedsheet toga, pulls; she spins out of the sheet, falls into JESUS's arms, drunkenly, giggling.)

SUGARBABY: *(Singing.) Wwwwwwwaaaa wa wa wa wonder!!!!!!!!*

STANISLAUS: Is not cool to steal hotel linens.

SUGARBABY: That was fun! I wanna go 'gain!

JESUS: No.

STANISLAUS: *(To audience, as he exits, waving, blowing us a kiss.)* Next stop, Las Vegas Strip! *God bless America!*

SUGARBABY: I love to strip!

JESUS: No.

(He takes her by the hand, yanks her off-stage toward the limo. Lights upstage to the Tropicana outdoor parking lot, nonreserve section. Enter RUFUS and MITCH. They approach MITCH's Humvee, an ugly, godless monster of a vehicle, yellow and fat, like a jaundiced clown car.)

MITCH: *(Car keys in hand.)* It was a business expense, and I got a break on it because I had done a documentary on fuel emissions, and the company gave me one for promotional expenses.

RUFUS: Well, ain't you grand marshall of the shit parade. *(Puts out his hand.)* Give me the fucking keys.

MITCH: I'm not letting you drive my car!

RUFUS: Gimme the keys. *(Grabs MITCH's hand.)*

MITCH: No. *(Tries to pull away.)*

RUFUS: Gimme the keys. *(Pull.)*

MITCH: No.

RUFUS: Gimme—

MITCH: No. *(Etc.)*

(This tug of war continues for a few seconds until RUFUS, without warning, smacks MITCH right upside the head, and catches the keys as MITCH drops them in shock.)

MITCH: Ow! That was police brutality!

RUFUS: You comin' or not?

MITCH: *(Quickly.)* Okay.

(They get in, rev up. MITCH pulls out his camera. RUFUS sees this, rolls his eyes, peels out of the parking lot.)

16

THE LAS VEGAS STRIP! The chase begins! Ellington keeps playing throughout the following. Upstage right, MITCH and RUFUS in the Humvee, chasing after JESUS and SUGARBABY, downstage left in STANISLAUS's limo. Downstage right, ROD, flak jacket, scarf, aviator glasses, camo pants; very war correspondent. As the chase rolls down the Strip, enter CAST MEMBERS bearing giant replicas of casino marquees, moving from downstage to upstage, past the two "cars," establishing the spatial relationship and showing us the sights of the Strip.

ROD: And so the chase leads here, to the fabled Las Vegas Strip, cradle of American can-do spirit and showmanship. *She attracts so many to her storied walkways… including, this hot June night, those who would disrupt and distort that American dream.

MITCH: *(Narrating as he films.)* The filth and squalor of the Strip… A massive black pyramid, *a monument to American greed…

RUFUS: Oh for fuck's sake!

JESUS: Wave bye-bye Ms. Sugarman.

(They pass the Luxor—enter a CAST MEMBER bearing a photo of the giant black Luxor pyramid and sphinx, gleaming in the orange sunset…)

SUGARBABY: *No!* I wanna see it all! Look at it all lit up and purty! Damn! A real, live pyramid!

ROD: *Could this innocent child be trapped within this black tomb of despair?

SUGARBABY: That's the coolest damn thing I ever seen!

JESUS: *Yes it's pretty swell…

(The MGM Grand! Another replica, this time of the massive bronze lion perched outside the gleaming emerald tower's expansive gateway!)

SUGARBABY: *Goddamn!* No! That is! A big golden kitty!

ROD: Or behind the maw of this perilous lion, *this gleaming colossus of joy now rent of its meaning?

MITCH: This perversion of Dorothy's journey, surely we are no longer in Kansas, Toto.

RUFUS: *Shut the fuck up!

SUGARBABY: *(Popping up through the sunroof.)* Hello, giant yellow kitty!

JESUS: *(Yanking her back down into the car.)* Sit down!!

VOICES OFFSTAGE: It's Sugarbaby! Sugarbaby! Yay! *(Etc.)*

SUGARBABY: Oh my God.

JESUS: *They know who you are!

SUGARBABY: *I'm famous! I'm goddamn famous! Whoo hoo! (Tries to pop back up through the sunroof; JESUS grabs her, pulls her back down again.)*

JESUS: *Great siddown.

MITCH: And now these teeming masses spot and greet their saviour, the girl who comes to mock this awesome spectacle *of the struggle within America's culture of enforced poverty…

RUFUS: Goddammit! Those damn *protestors gonna fuck up the whole damn works!

(Enter replica of the front of Treasure Island, exploding pirate ships, glamorous showgirls, lights and excitement!)

ROD: Or maybe, with sick irony, she has been hornswaggled, trapped within the walls of the city's very own Treasure Island, *true buccaneers capturing a true national treasure…

MITCH: *And this ultimate spectacle of style over substance, the torment of past generations being transformed into a hideous pyrotechnic spectacle…

SUGARBABY: An exploding goddamn pirate ship! Kick ass! I wanna see!

(She bounces up through the sunroof again, and this time, we see the fans on the Strip; they appear upstage briefly, holding up signs saying "Run Sugarbaby Run," "Sugarbaby for President," and "John 3:13.")

VOICES OFFSTAGE: Sugarbaby! Hot damn! Yay! (Etc.)

SUGARBABY: Hello Treasure Island! I got some treasures for ya!!!!!! (Goes to flash the crowd—)

JESUS: (Grabs her, pulls her back in.) *They're gone storm this car you keep that up!

RUFUS: Aw shit, the natives are getting *restless.

ROD: The crowds seem agitated now, as though they know what might be com-

ing. As though a sense of fear, of panic, lay heavy over this city's velvet, giddy purple dawn. *The fogs of war can drive a man mad, they say.

RUFUS: *Aw shit, now they're rushing us!

(Suddenly JOSH and ANDREA appear! They rush MITCH's Humvee, grab its sides, begin rocking it violently back and forth—)

MITCH: This remarkable footage shall show that the people shall always overcome, shall never be defeated once united! I stand in awe of these brave souls—Hey! You rotten little bastards stop fucking with my car! *You're gonna fuck up the paint job, I just had that done, you fucks! Get a job, you smelly hippie!

RUFUS: *This is official po-lice business and I will have you arrested you good-for-nothing shits! I can't drive with you in the goddamn way!

JESUS: What the hell's going on back there?

SUGARBABY: Those kids is going after the sheriff! Whoo!!!! Thank you babies! (Pops out the sunroof.) I love you Las Vegas! This is for you!

(And she lifts her shirt, and flashes the whole of Las Vegas. Music stops. Everything stops. Moment.)

ROD: Oh.

(SUG giggles, jumps back into her seat, satisfied at a job well done.)

JESUS: Aw, damn.

(RUFUS, taking advantage of the lull, floors it, sending the Humvee peeling down the Strip, out of control, and sending JOSH and ANDREA flying into the crowd surrounding the chaos.)

RUFUS: Eat my lead, fucking hippie scum!

JOSH and ANDREA: *(In unison.) We're not hippies, we're vegans!!!!!!!!*

(RUFUS peels off down the Strip, swerving wildly to avoid hitting the PROTEST-ORS—exciting isn't it?—and heads straight for ROD.)

ROD: In war-torn lands such as these, a man can find himself an almost Hemingway-esque sense of self-discovery through turmoil, the blood of the kill still fresh on his mind. I feel stronger now, self-assured, confident that, through this pain and suffering, I shall— *Great holy mother of God no!!!!!!!!!!*

(RUFUS barrels down on ROD, hits the brakes! The Humvee screeches to a halt, turns over on its side, as ROD ducks, covering his head, squealing in terror!!! Sound of car crash! BLACKOUT!! After a moment, lights back up… on ROD, rolling around in the street, clothes wrecked, clutching his head, mutter-ing calmly, clearly, over and over, "Ow ow ow ow ow ow." After a beat, enter MITCH, shirt untucked, hair a mess, still clutching his camera, panic-stricken, practically sob-bing. He sees ROD, runs toward him…)

MITCH: Help me, sir, please, I gotta…

(ROD slowly rises, sees MITCH. MITCH realizes who it is. Scowls.)

MITCH: *You!*

ROD: *You!*

MITCH: This is my exclusive, you sunuvabitch!

ROD: I got here first!

(Slowly, they begin to circle each other, like sumo wrestlers, growling, teeth bared, arms outstretched. Just then, enter RUFUS, in the same sorry state of disarray, smoke rising from his hat, which now has a silver-dollar-sized hole in the top of it. He staggers to the edge of the sidewalk, tries to wave down a taxi…)

RUFUS: Lyndon fucking Johnson this city's a goddamn madhouse— *Taxiiiiiii!!!*

(A taxi pulls up, the DRIVER, thirties, a Pakistani with Elvis sideburns and pompa-dour bursting out from under his turban, honks his horn [which plays "La Cucaracha"], waves hello, incredibly friendly.)

DRIVER: A very good day to you sir! Get in please! I have not all day to deal with you buddy!

RUFUS: *(Rolls his eyes—another Elvis? Then…)* Fuck it— *(Hops in.)* Follow that car, and don't stop for traffic lights!

DRIVER: Feel free to play slot machine on video screen in back! Entertainment pur-poses only! *(Begins singing "Burning Love.")*

(The taxi peels out, RUFUS screams, they speed offstage, the DRIVER veering clum-sily all over the road like a damn maniac…)

RUFUS: *Holy mother of fuck!*

(As the taxi disappears into a cloud of smoke, ROD and MITCH jump each other, begin beating the shit out of each other, then roll off-stage in a cartoon ball of fists and grunting…)

17

Lights shift to McCarren Airport, specifically one of the private high-roller's runways. En-ter SUGARBABY and JESUS, rushing frantically, looking everywhere.

JESUS: Where the hell is he? Our pilot's supposed to be here!

SUGARBABY: I'm going flyyyyyyyying! *Yaaaaaaaayyyyyyyyyy!!!!!!!*

JESUS: *Sssssshhhhhhh!!* Quiet!! Hello? Anybody?

(Enter DIRK, forties, their pilot. Aviator goggles, leather bomber jacket, pilot's cap, ci-gar dangling from mouth, hard-bitten, Viet-nam vet.)

DIRK: Has anyone other than yourself handled your bags, packed your bags other than you, or have your bags been out of your sight since you packed them?

JESUS: Yes.

SUGARBABY: No.

JESUS: Yes.

SUGARBABY: Yes.

JESUS: No.

SUGARBABY: No?

JESUS: Bags?

DIRK: Good enough for me. Let's go.

JESUS: Thank you very much—

(JESUS grabs SUG's hand, drags her along behind as he chases after DIRK, who turns, struts offstage toward the plane. Lights shift to the entrance to McCarren Airport. A ring of ELVII, including EARL and JACK, block the entrance, carrying signs reading "Free Sugarbaby," "Don't Tread on Me," "TCB," etc. They sing a rousing rendition of "Battle Hymn of the Republic," stopping every few lines to throw in an in-unison "Thank you very much." After a beat, enter RUFUS and the TAXI DRIVER, in the midst of a heated argument.)

DRIVER: No! I will not! I will cross Teamsters, I will cross Musicians' Union, I will not cross Elvis picket line! It is immoral and wrong!

RUFUS: Here, you dumb bastard, *(Hands him money.)* keep the fucking change.

DRIVER: Wow, fifty cents. I hope you get ass cancer in your ass, Mister Cop, sir. *(Gives him the finger, exits.)*

RUFUS: Goddamn Vegas. *(Turns, sees the ELVII, stands facing them, fists on hips, very drill sergeant.)* Alright, listen up, you freak-ish misshapen shitstains, I will count to three and then I will shoot every last goddamn one of you like the rabid bitches you are!

JACK: Give me back my camera, you fascist!

RUFUS: You want your camera? You want your camera? Come on and get it, assclown!

(All the ELVII glare at him a moment. JACK slowly puffs out his chest, huge. EARL joins him. Then the others. Suddenly, RUFUS realizes he's facing down a couple of dozen ELVII and he is, how you say, fucked.)

RUFUS: Aw, shit.

(RUFUS turns, runs, screaming, as all the ELVII chase him in a rage, roaring like lions, EARL bringing up the back of the line. Just as he's about to disappear offstage, he stops—)

EARL: You ain't so big! You just tall, that's all!

(And as he disappears, lights up on DIRK's plane, upstage right. SUG and JESUS seated, JESUS looking at the Strip out the window, nervous; SUG wearing headphones, bopping to the in-flight radio, happy as a clam. DIRK sits at the controls, prepping for takeoff. Upstage left, the ticket counter of the airport, with the ATTENDANT, twenties, British, primly dressed, unflappable, constantly smiling. Enter MITCH and ROD, breathless; they flank her on either side, babbling like lunatics.)

ROD: Sugarbaby.

MITCH: Sugarbaby.

ROD: Sugarbaby.

MITCH: Sugarbaby.

ATTENDANT: Has anyone other than yourself handled your bags, packed your bags other than you, or have your bags been out of your sight since you packed them?

MITCH: ...No.

ROD: Yes.

MITCH: Yes.

ROD: No.

MITCH: Sugarbaby!

ROD: Sugarbaby!

MITCH: Sugarbaby!

ROD: Sugarbaby!

ATTENDANT: I'm afraid I'm going to have to call security.

MITCH: Sugarbaby! Mine!

ROD: Mine!

MITCH: Mine!

ROD: Mine!

(They lunge at each other; the ATTEN-DANT deftly steps out of the way; they collide, fall into a heap, begin beating the living shit out of each other again.)

SUGARBABY: *(Leaning into DIRK.)* Do you have a wetbar?

JESUS: *(Grabs her, throws her back into her seat.)* No.

(Just then, at the ticket booth, enter RUFUS, breathless, clothes a mess, one lens of his sunglasses popped out, hat askew, badge dented.)

RUFUS: Where's the control tower?

ATTENDANT: I'm sorry, sir, I can't just *tell you—

RUFUS: I am an officer of the goddamn law and I expect some goddamn cooperation this is a matter of life and death!

(At that moment, EARL and JACK appear in the doorway, roaring with rage. RUFUS smiles at the ATTENDANT, waves.)

RUFUS: 'Scuse me.

ATTENDANT: No problem.

(RUFUS runs like hell downstage, then out, as EARL and JACK attempt to follow. With one step, the ATTENDANT steps forward, blocks them.)

ATTENDANT: Has anyone other than yourself handled your bags,* packed your bags other than you, or have your bags been out of your sight since you packed them?

JACK: He broke my camera and I missed my bar mitzvah!

EARL: And I wanna put my boot up his ass— wait. Bags? Bags. Uh? No.

JACK: Yes.

EARL: No.

JACK: No.

EARL: No.

JACK: Yes.

EARL: Yes?

JACK: What?

SUGARBABY: Is there an inflight movie?

JESUS: No.

(Aaaaaaaaaaaaaaaaaaaaaaaaaannnnnnnnnnd in the ticket area, enter JOSH and AN-DREA, bouncing around like maniacs, repeating one after the other, "Where is she? Where is she? Where is she?")

ATTENDANT: *(Just about had it.)* Where is who?

ANDREA: *Sugarbaby is here!*

(It echoes throughout the airport—everyone, everyone! comes to a dead stop, looks up. Holy shit! MITCH and ROD confer silently, MITCH runs off for his camera; ROD straightens his hair, pulls his microphone out of his jacket—bent. Hell, gotta fix that. JACK and EARL try to break for the runway, the ATTENDANT blocks them, then blocks JOSH and ANDREA, then the ATTENDANT begins throwing the four of them around the room as though juggling them, as they each in turn try to get to SUG's plane, only to land on their ass, get up, try again. Pandemonium reigns! While all that is happening [having fun?], lights up downstage left on the control tower. Enter the AIR TRAFFIC CONTROLLER, twenties, walkie-talkie in one hand, coffee mug in the other.)

AIR TRAFFIC CONTROLLER: Alright, Delta Dawn, you are cleared for takeoff. Please commence taxiing procedures.

(And RUFUS bursts into the control tower, hat now destroyed, brim hanging around his neck, sunglasses completely lensless, and a hole in the back of his shirt from God knows what, gun drawn and pointed over his head; he has goddamned had it!!!!!!!!)

RUFUS: *Alright now you listen up you motherfuckers!*

AIR TRAFFIC CONTROLLER: *Jesus Christ! (Terrified, ducks under a chair, hands over head, classic "duck and cover" pose.)*

RUFUS: *I have been beaten by Elvii, punched by hippies, been in a fucked-up yuppie bus, and I am pissed off about being pissed on! Now get me on the goddamn horn with that puddle-jumpin' rustbucket or so help me God I'm gonna wipe your ass with my steel-toed size nine YOU MISERABLE COCKSMUGGLING MOTHERFUCKER!*

AIR TRAFFIC CONTROLLER: *(Pause, then calmly.)* ...Feel free. *(Hands over the receiver.)*

RUFUS: *(Immediately collects himself, polite.)* Much obliged. Which button do I push?

AIR TRAFFIC CONTROLLER: No not that—

(He pushes a button on the walkie-talkie—and feedback echoes throughout the airport; a loud click is heard in DIRK's plane. Everyone in the ticket area covers their ears, stops running around like lunatics, looks up toward the PA system. Music lowers in volume slightly; MITCH reenters with his camera, begins filming; ROD holds up his mic to the PA, trying to capture RUFUS's voice. Rapt attention is paid!)

DIRK: Hey, I'm getting something coming through here.

RUFUS: *(Sits, now in some sort of control, official.)* This is Sheriff Rufus J. Miranda, on official po-lice business, and I demand that the pilot of this plane cease all activities immediately and listen the hell up. You are harboring two known escaped fugitives on your aviary ve-hickle and I strongly suggest you hand them over into my custody right goddamn now!

DIRK: Begging your pardon, sir, but I don't know who you are and I can't just—hey—

(SUGARBABY rushes forward, grabs the receiver. Her voice reverberates throughout the airport. All those in the ticket area cluster together, leaning in, listening excitedly.)

SUGARBABY: Gimme that— Sheriff? This is Sugarbaby.

RUFUS: Girlie? Damn, baby, *you okay? They torturing you? You don't worry, little missy, I'm gone get you out of this here mess right quick.

SUGARBABY: Shut up and listen. Shut up and *will you shut up and listen! I have had it!*

(As she speaks, the CROWD begins to nod, smile—something about this speech affects them, excites them—the atmosphere is electric. Even RUFUS is impressed.)

SUGARBABY: I am sick of being told what to do, I am sick of being put down, yelled at, pushed around, made fun of, held back, I am an American goddammit! And I'm tired of being told that that's wrong, and that I should be ashamed, and that I should be embarrassed of who and what I am! I wanna believe in something! I am free! I am honest! I am clear! And I may not be perfect, Lord knows, but, goddammit, I try! I am gonna fly! I am gonna help towns in trouble, like Kung Fu or John Wayne! I wanna eat fast food, drive fast cars, and be proud of how I got here, and be proud of what I am! *I am Sugarbaby!*

(The CROWD goes wild, explodes into cheers, spontaneous high fives, fists punched in the air! As RUFUS begins his reply, the CROWD shushes one another, leans in further, expectant...)

RUFUS: Now you listen here little lady. You are in violation of I don't know how many damn laws and regulations right now. You take off in that plane, you are a fugitive from the law, you understand that? Now it's your decision.

(Moment. SUG, nervous, looks back at JESUS—"what do I do now?")

JESUS: Whatever you want, Ms. Sugarman. I'm with you all the way.

DIRK: Hey, I'm just the hired hand. I'll do whatever you want, long as you post my bail.

(The CROWD is waiting. RUFUS is waiting. MITCH keeps filming, ROD keeps recording. Tense. The music begins building to a climax.)

SUGARBABY: *(Pause—then, into receiver.)* Sheriff?

RUFUS: Yes?

SUGARBABY: *...Kiss my ass!*

(The music hits its peak, deafening! The CROWD goes berserk, whooping, crying! EARL hoists the ATTENDANT into his arms, plants a big wet sloppy kiss on her, JACK leaps onto the counter, begins hollering with joy, JOSH and ANDREA hug each other, leap around, ROD screaming "Yes" like Marv Albert, as DIRK guns it, the plane begins to take off, the sound of engines, RUFUS stands, watching the plane take off, runs out of the control tower onto the runway...)

RUFUS: *Nooooooooooooo!!!!!!!!!!!!!!*

SUGARBABY: *Fly! Fly! Fly! God bless America!!!!!!!!!!!!!!!!*

(RUFUS runs down the runway like a man possessed. Lights shift, cool blues, RUFUS begins running in slo mo as we hear the plane soar off overhead... MITCH and ROD follow, each commenting, simultaneously, as he runs...)

MITCH: *And the lawman hangs on like grim death! Running after this political fugitive, trying to wring final glory from this most devastating of moments! The ultimate example of might over right, here in this neon-bathed oasis of excess and greed! He just won't let go of his prey, no matter how much the American masses may long for her freedom! Like a modern day Bonnie and Clyde, these two courageous citizens act as a shining beacon of hope everywhere!

ROD: Ladies and gentlemen, I've never seen bravery and courage like this! In the face of danger, this incredible warrior puts his life and safety on the line to bring this

errant lamb home, to free her from the
crushing influence of these mad tyrants! I
am so proud to bring you this moment
ladies and gentlemen right here on "The
Rod Butane Zone," home of the American truth and the American way!

*(The plane recedes into the distance; RUFUS
falls to his knees, shaking his fist into the hot
desert night, raging...)*

RUFUS: *You haven't seen the last of me,
Sugarbaby! As God is my witness, I will find
you, I will catch you, and I will bring you
home! I will get you! Goddamn you!
Goddamn you Sugarbabyyyyyyy!!!!!!*

*(The Ellington reaches its blaring finish,
horns blasting, as the sound of the plane's engines drown out RUFUS's shrieks, and ROD,
overcome with emotion, salutes to the sky...)*

ROD: *Sugarbaby is on the loose, ladies and
gentlemen! God bless America!!!!!!!!!!!!!!!!!!!!!!!*

(Blackout.)

ACT TWO

18

*(Music: Barrett Strong, "Money [That's
What I Want]." Blackout. In the dark, the
voice of a new reporter, LESLIE GIBBONS,
thirties, crisp, authoritative.)*

LESLIE GIBBONS: Leslie Gibbons,
UNN. It's been nearly three weeks now
since the extraordinary story of Bailey
Sugarman, aka Sugarbaby, began in a
modest trailer park deep within the American heartland, and the national obsession
with this girl's flight from her hometown,
and subsequent adventures across the
country, continues unabated. Sightings of
her and her traveling companion, an Elvis
tribute artist and garage mechanic known
only as "Jesus," (Mispronounces *as "Hay-
Zoos.")* have caused sensations through-

out the country, delighting her fans, out-
raging her detractors, and frustrating the
man charged with the investigation into
her activities, Sheriff Rufus J. Miranda.
While Americans cannot agree on whether
this young woman's cross-country spree is
an act of patriotic promotion, or a grand-
standing plea for attention, one thing is
for certain: she has galvanized and divided
this nation like no other pop culture figure in recent memory...

*(Lights up on HAIRY MAN, a weird, smelly
fellow wearing a sandwich board around his
neck reading "Repent! Repent! The end is
near! Yay Sugarbaby!." He rings a large metal
bell. It makes no sound. He looks at the bell—
clapper's broke. Shrugs. Keeps ringing anyway. He crosses back and forth in front of a
huge TV screen, in which appear various
"man on the street" interviews. First, enter
HEATHER and KYLE, twenties, college students. She carries a sign reading "Jesus Is
Just Alright With Me"; his reads, "Impeach
Bush! Sugarbaby for Pres!")*

HEATHER: It's like it's the first time I
really care about America and what it
means! I wanna vote! I wanna protest! I
want my voice to be heard! Thank you
Sugarbaby!

KYLE: We love you Sugarbaby! Kick ass!
Woooooooo!

*(Enter REPUBLICAN, forties, nice suit,
smirk, flag pin, alongside DEMOCRAT, forties, nice suit, smirk, flag pin. They speak
simultaneously.)*

REPUBLICAN: I think that this current
craze over this young woman only goes to
prove the groundswell of support for our
president and his administration, and,
while I certainly do not agree with her unlawful methods, I do support the cause
her and her friend espouse. God bless
America.

DEMOCRAT: I think that this current craze over this young woman only goes to prove the overwhelming distrust of our president and his administration, and, while I certainly do not agree with her unlawful methods, I do support the cause her and her friend espouse. God bless America.

(Enter PROTESTOR, thirties, T-shirt reading "Take the God Out of God Bless America," carries sign reading, "Not in My Name! Yay Sugarbaby.")

PROTESTOR: I think it's disgusting the way that the religious right in this country have hijacked this young girl's right to free speech to prop up their unholy marriage of church and state. Take the God out of "God Bless America"!

(Enter OTHER PROTESTOR, thirties, T-shirt reading, "America Is the Most Important Word," carries sign reading, "Proud to Be an American! Yay, Sugarbaby.")

OTHER PROTESTOR: I think it's a damn sin that these loonies have hijacked this poor girl's crusade in their assault on free speech and American values. God bless America!

(Enter SHOPPING NETWORK SHILL, Australian, beefy, thirties, unbelievably loud and annoying!!! He holds up a gold chain with the "official" Sugarbaby logo.)

SHILL: This really amazing tribute gold chain is a really great way to show your solidarity with this great American and really great patriot! We only have five thousand of these babies left, so act now! They're only twenty-nine ninety-five, plus shipping and handling; they make a great gift, and, if you act now, we'll throw in those beautiful American eagle collector plates that Tamara was showing you earlier!

(Enter LATE NITE COMIC, snide, jacket and tie, toupee.)

COMIC: So you heard about this Sugarbaby? She's hiding out in Las Vegas, she'd want to avoid crowds—let's see now, did anybody check the Celine Dion show?

HAIRY MAN: Hi-yooo!!

(Enter ROSA, fifties, Mexican housewife, holding a tortilla with an odd-shaped blotch on it.)

ROSA: And so, I told the reporter, I see the face of Jesus on this tortilla, he thought I mean Jesus Christ, I said nooooo, I mean Jesus who think he is Elvis, and this (Turns over tortilla.) is Sugarbaby. (Crosses herself.)

(HAIRY MAN turns, shows back of sandwich board: "Sugarbaby Where Are You? Will Fight You for Food." Enter FARMER, thirties, flannel shirt, baseball cap with Sugarbaby logo on it.)

FARMER: Yeah, she was here. We saw her. She spent a few hours at the local Arby's talking to the old folks, then posed for pictures. We wasn't gonna call nobody, like the cops. We're all for her. God bless her.

(Enter SOCCER MOM, forties, T-shirt with "Sugarbaby" logo on it, pro choice button.)

SOCCER MOM: Of course we knew who it was. Any idiot would have recognized her and her friend. We talked to them, she signed that day's newspaper, right under her photo, she was great. And, no, we're not turning her in, because it's none of the government's goddamn business where she is.

(Enter RUFUS, spit-shined and polished, visibly pissed.)

RUFUS: I will make this one thing perfectly clear right goddamn now—anyone who sees this girl and her little friend, and lets them get away, are aiding and abetting fugitives from the law and said persons will be arrested, prosecuted to the fullest extent of the law, and get an imprint of my size nine workboot flat in the crack of their ass! End quote! Now get the hell out my way, I'm in pursuit of a damn fugitive here I ain't got time for this bullshit...

(Enter TOKEN BLACK PERSON, unimpressed.)

TOKEN BLACK PERSON: All I gotta say is, if that pasty white bitch was a sister, wouldn't nobody give a good goddamn, they'd have shot her ass on general principle.

(Enter ROD.)

ROD: And so, a country divided, as always, by those who would use this amazing American success story for their own ends and personal gain. More to follow in our exclusive Sugarbaby coverage, right here, on America's number one political talk show, "The Rod Butane Zone"...

19

Upstage: The set of "America Talk Back!," a live political/social call-in show. Giant logo on the back wall, three comfy chairs. The host, KATIE SHERMAN, wears a conservative but leg-revealing pastel dress suit, carries a microphone. Downstage: A truck stop off of a highway in southern Florida. Menu offering slawburgers, grits. Giant handwritten sign: "No Guns in the TeeVee Room. This Means You, Lee!" Door leading to a small arcade room with twenty-year-old machines. Behind the counter, MAVIS, forties, waitress, nicotine-stained, out-of-date hairdo, apron, will take no shit, cleaning the counter and watching the show on TV. The diner scene and the talk show run simultaneously.

KATIE: Hello! And welcome to "America Talk Back!," the live call-in show where

you, the American viewer, can make your voice heard. Today we're talking about what everyone's talking about... *(Holds up a yearbook photo of SUGARBABY.)* and that is Sugarbaby, little Bailey Sugarman, seventeen years old, on the run, and, without a doubt, this generation's Bonnie and Clyde rolled into one. Our very special guest today is the woman who is most able to analyze and discuss this extraordinary story. *(Lifts up a hardback book, pastel cover, florid lettering, giant painting of a sunflower under the title.)* She is the author of a new book available this Tuesday from Rush Job Press, "The Loneliest Sunflower: A Mother's Courage: The Ginger Sugar-man Story." She is also beginning her own line of cosmetics and accessories, and will be hosting her own talk show on the Estrogen Network this fall, please welcome Ginger Sugarman...

(Enter GINGER, now dressed as business-like as she possibly can be, wearing a flag pin on one lapel and a "Sugarbaby Come Home" button on the other. Maybe a yellow ribbon, too. Sunflower earrings. She and KATIE greet each other like long-lost sisters, sit side by side.)

KATIE: Ginger, it's so good to have you here.

GINGER: It's a thrill to be here, Katie, I watch you every day when Ricki is a repeat.

KATIE: *(Cold.)* Oh. You're so kind. I skimmed your book today, and it truly is a fascinating story.

(At this point, RUFUS enters the diner and talks to MAVIS. Through.)

KATIE: Tell me, was it painful to relive some of your past?

GINGER: Well, as I say in the book, I was married three times before my current separation. Bailey's father was an abusive alcoholic, he and I used to tussle all the time. He left right after Bailey was born. My second husband was a guitarist in a Def Leppard cover band, that didn't last too long, although it was fun being on the road and seeing the county. Then there was that man I married on a dare in Laughlin. And my current husband, of course, we don't speak any longer, he moved out of the house shortly after my baby— *(Chokes up.)*

KATIE: Yes, I understand. It's been painful for you, hasn't it?

GINGER: There's not a day goes by that I don't think, what did I do wrong? Is there something I could have said or done that could have prevented this?

(Meanwhile, downstage, enter RUFUS, who rushes to the counter, hopping up and down anxiously.)

RUFUS: Excuse me, madam, where are your facilities, I'm fixin to burst here…

MAVIS: Straight back, last door to the right, but it's for customers only.

RUFUS: *(Runs to the men's room, yells out over his shoulder, exits.)* Slawburger, fries, root beer.

MAVIS: *(Yelling back into the kitchen.)* One slaw, burnt taters, and a root!

KATIE: Well, we have a little surprise for you, Ginger, someone we tracked down and flew in just for today's show.

GINGER: You found my baby?

KATIE: No, better!

GINGER: *How the hell can anything else be better?

KATIE: We found him in a bar in New Orleans, we brought him in to tell us more about this amazing story, please welcome, Sugarbaby's stepfather, Aron Malveaux!

(Enter ARON, waving to crowd. Immediately, GINGER rushes forward, begins pummeling him with her own book, and the crowd whoops and hollers its approval.)

KATIE: *Okay okay now okay—

ARON: *Ow fucking Christ *that's a hardback ya damn daffy bitch!*

GINGER: *You sumbitch leaving me high and dry without a dime *to my damn name!*

ARON: *A million-dollar payday on this damn thing! I think you're quite goddamn *comfortable after something like that, thank you!*

KATIE: *(Trying to step between them and break them up.)* Please watch your *language, now sit down the both of you!*

GINGER: Tell me about making money. You're disgusting, selling those T-shirts and necklaces *on the Shopping Channel!!

ARON: Those T-shirts and necklaces— *(Turns to camera, right into salesman mode.)* and by the way, nearly five percent of proceeds go to charity, log on to www.sugarbaby.com— *(Back to pissed-off mode.)* those T-shirts and necklaces are paying for my founding of the Sugarbaby Foundation, I am giving a small but respectable amount of that money to a good cause, you're just making money off the misery of others! Shame on you!

(While the talk show continues, enter SUGARBABY, legs crossed, hopping up and down, teeth clenched.)

SUGARBABY: Ooooooh God toilette sil vooz plate?

MAVIS: Straight back, first door to the right.

SUGARBABY: Aw damn—

(SUGARBABY runs back. JESUS enters right behind her, winks to MAVIS, friendly.)

JESUS: Two slawburgers, one with grilled onion, two root beers, and a large fries.

MAVIS: *(Yelling into kitchen.)* Two slaws, one with burnt onion, one burnt taters, two roots!

JESUS: Whatcha watching. *(Leans on counter, looks at TV. Sees ARON and GINGER fighting. Oh shit.)* Oh. Uh… I'm gonna play me some of that Mortal Kombat back there.

MAVIS: Uh-huh.

(JESUS turns, runs, ducks into the arcade, at the exact second that RUFUS comes out of the men's room directly adjoining, fastening his belt, grinning, approaches counter, sits.)

RUFUS: Hoooooooooeeee goddamn, that was close. Almost stained my lap in the car. How long til the chow's up, darlin'?

MAVIS: Ten minutes, give or take.

RUFUS: Whatcha watching—? *(Looks up, sees ARON yelling away on the TV.)* Oh.

MAVIS: I usually watch the *Ricki Lake*, today's a rerun, I got the "Talk to America!" on now.

RUFUS: This a news show?

MAVIS: More or less.

RUFUS: What a world.

(Meanwhile, on the TV…)

GINGER: It's my life story! I can sell it how I want, you cheap *bastard!

ARON: Hey, you wanted me to get a job? I got a damn job! *You're just pissed you ain't getting any of the money!

(KATIE sits, trying to regain control. Angrily, GINGER and ARON sit on either side of KATIE as she speaks.)

KATIE: Alright, this is not *productive*, this is *destructive*, it is always important to fo-

cus on the positive, rather than the negative. That is what your daughter's crusade is all about, yes? She ran away from home *to see America—

ARON: She was kidnapped.

GINGER: *Oh, please.

ARON: It's all a part of the vast Zionist/Illuminati conspiracy. Have you ever looked, I mean really looked at a dollar bill! It's scary, man! It's all of a piece! And Lucky Charms! The marshmallow shapes and colors correspond exactly to the occult symbols used in Masonic indoctrination rituals! Every American president since Washington has been a member of the Freemasons! It's true! You can look it up!

(Out of quarters, JESUS reenters from the arcade, not noticing RUFUS right away…)

KATIE: So you're saying that Sugarbaby was kidnapped by this "Jesus" as part of a plot to control the American populace.

(Ah, damn. JESUS winces, pulls his jacket collar up around his face, pulls on his TCB sunglasses, leans into the counter, trying to disappear, still not noticing RUFUS right next to him.)

ARON: Well, why the hell else would he? I mean, no one's got a picture of the guy! Do you know what he looks like?

KATIE: Well… no…

ARON: See? He's a goddamn CIA operative!

KATIE: But wasn't the original fear that she was kidnapped by Al Qaeda?

ARON: That's just what the government wants you to think! *God, don't you people read?

GINGER: See, Katie, this is exactly the kind of crackpot harebrained stupidity *that I have had to deal with for the past two years!

ARON: You're a part of it! You bought into it! I'm just trying to make a damn living here! I'm just a squirrel looking for a nut!

RUFUS: Ah shit. Those two are nuttier'n a damn fruitcake. *(Turns, nudges JESUS, friendly.)* No wonder that poor girl ran away from home. Sheeit.

(Moment. RUFUS realizes that it's JESUS next to him. JESUS realizes that that's RUFUS. Amazed at his dumb luck, RUFUS slowly circles JESUS, looking him up and down as though he wanted to make ab-so-lute-ly certain that this is, indeed, him. JESUS just smiles sickly. Shrugs. Wheezes.)

KATIE: Now, hold on, hold on, let's move on to other matters. Your daughter has been spotted throughout the country, and has not been turned in to police. In fact, a number of Americans have gone out of their way to prevent police from finding her. Why do you think that is?

GINGER: I think anyone who sees that girl and doesn't contact the proper authorities is un-American and should be *ashamed of themselves.

ARON: See? This is what I'm saying? We are all sick to death of these people, these goddamn holier-than-thou assholes trying to butt into our lives, assuming that they know better than us how to live our lives!

JESUS: I guess I'd best be getting that order to go, huh?

RUFUS: Son, you make one move toward that door, I'm gone shoot you right where you stand.

(And, at that moment, SUGARBABY re-enters from the ladies' room, sees RUFUS— and screams! MAVIS sees this, puts two and two together while RUFUS is distracted—)

MAVIS: Holy sheeit!

(—and brings a rolling pin up from behind the counter and whomps RUFUS right over the goddamn head!)

MAVIS: *Run Sugarbaby run! *Go girl go!*

RUFUS: *Mother of fuck!*

(RUFUS begins rubbing his head rapidly, the classic "make the pain go way" move, while JESUS and SUGARBABY bolt out of the door. RUFUS recovers quickly, shoots MAVIS a nasty look, runs out the door, muttering "ow ow ow ow ow ow" the entire way out the door…while the TV keeps prattling on…)

KATIE: Alright, now we're getting completely off topic, let's go to a word from our sponsors, then we'll be back with this remarkable story.

(The "America Talk Back!" theme plays, lights begin to dim…)

GINGER: *(To ARON.)* I hate you like assrash.

ARON: Die slowly and alone, ya cracked bitch.

(Completely exhausted by her ordeal, KATIE throws her microphone away over her shoulder, stalks off, pulling a pack of smokes and a lighter out of her jacket, lighting one up as she exits… Blackout.)

20

Upstage left: JESUS and SUGARBABY in their car, speeding out of the parking lot. Upstage right: RUFUS's car, RUFUS running toward it. Downstage left: ROD BUTANE, once again "The Zone." Downstage right: MITCH COMMON, ranting on an NPR-style radio call-in show.

VOICEOVER: *(Left channel.)* You're back in "The Zone!" The Rod Butane Zone!

And now, back to the host with the most, the one and only, Rod Butane!

VOICEOVER: *(Right channel.)* Today's episode of the "Mitch Common Show" is made possible by a generous grant from the Hardin Corporation, and from listeners like you. From Washington, here's Mitch Common.

(JESUS starts the car, peels out of the diner parking lot! RUFUS dives into his car, tears out behind them!)

ROD: If there's anything this girl has taught me...

MITCH: If there's anything this girl has taught me...

MITCH and ROD: *(In unison.)* It's that I have been right all along.

(The chase begins! As MITCH and ROD rant on talk radio, SUG and JESUS tear through the swamps of Florida trying to escape RUFUS! Upstage, two big toy cars, one beaten-up pickup truck and one weather-beaten cop car, are manipulated to show the progress of the chase, while Flatt & Scruggs blares on the sound system and various branches, dirt, leaves, etc., are thrown at our hapless racers as they tear through the Florida wilderness!)

MITCH and ROD: *(In unison.)* She's brought this country together in ways we couldn't have imagined two weeks ago, and now the average, intelligent, moderate American can finally rise up and say No! to these...

ROD: America-bashing...

MITCH: Intolerant...

ROD: Self-hating...

MITCH: Self-loathing...

MITCH and ROD: *(In unison.)* negative nellies...

MITCH: These arrogant...

ROD: Weak-kneed...

MITCH and ROD: *(In unison.)* Inconsiderate...

ROD: Untalented...

MITCH: Untalented...

ROD: Handout-seeking...

MITCH: Money-grubbing *right-wing monsters...

ROD: Left-wing nutcases...

MITCH and ROD: *(In unison.)* Who only care about their own skins and their own points of view...

(SUGARBABY grabs JESUS's shoulder, points off to the right...)

SUGARBABY: *Quick! Through the swamps! We'll lose him that way!*

JESUS: We can't!

SUGARBABY: Goddammit...

(She grabs the wheel, banks hard right, the car skids into the woods. RUFUS grins, goes left.)

RUFUS: I got you now, you sumbitches...

MITCH: Who would just as soon see you...

ROD: The average working man...

MITCH and ROD: *(In unison.)* Left to rot...

ROD: Who are *fiercely over-intellectual...

MITCH: Blatantly unintellectual...

ROD: God-hating...

MITCH: Religious fundamentalist...

ROD: Tree-hugging...

MITCH: Earth-raping...

MITCH and ROD: *(In unison.)* Self-righteous, insensitive nitwits without a damn ounce of common sense!

ROD: Well, we're going to Washington, people!

MITCH: Two days from now!

ROD: The march on the Great Mall!

MITCH: We're going to once and for all take this country back for real Americans!

(SUGARBABY and JESUS's car heads straight for RUFUS! All three scream!)

SUGARBABY: Ohmigod he's coming right for us!

JESUS: I told you this was a bad idea!

RUFUS: Holy sheee*iiiiiiiiiiiiiiittttttttttt!!!*

ROD: Make your voice heard!

MITCH: Don't let them take the upper hand!

ROD: Let's change our national anthem!

MITCH: We will not be bullied into their beliefs!

ROD: America is the most important word!

MITCH: Take the God out of *"*God Bless America"!

ROD: God bless America!

MITCH and ROD: *(In unison.)* And thank you Sugarbaby!

(Blackout! Silence. Then…)

MITCH and ROD: *(In unison.)* We'll be right back after these important words.

(Deafening car crash.)

21

Music: Elvis Presley, "Blue Moon." Blue sky, clouds. Lights up slowly to reveal SUGAR-

BABY, lying in a crumpled ball. Slowly, she stirs, looks around.

SUGARBABY: Oh shit. I guess this is it.

VOICE: *(From offstage.)* Aw, dammit! You gotta be kidding me!

OTHER VOICE: *(From offstage.)* Read 'em and weep, boys!

THIRD VOICE: *(From offstage.)* Aw, that's not right. That's just not right.

OTHER VOICE: *(From offstage.)* I'll take that, thank you…

(From upstage, the sound of poker chips being pushed around, counted.)

VOICE: *(From offstage.)* Alright, that's it, I'm dealing now, I don't trust you anymore.

THIRD VOICE: *(From offstage.)* Who says you can just do that?

(Lights up upstage to reveal Heaven. Heaven is, in fact, a casino. Giant sign poking through the clouds, looking very much like the classic Sands Casino sign, reading "Heaven… Welcome to Paradise! Paychecks cashed here." In the center of a semicircle of slot machines is a small poker table, littered with half-full bags of nachos, an overflowing ashtray, beer bottles. Seated around the table are UNCLE SAM, full costume, beard, hat, you name it, puffing on a huge cigar, happily raking in the chips from the center of the table; ELVIS PRESLEY, the Real Elvis Presley, '68 comeback special leather suit, sunglasses, tanned, looking damn fine, good-natured, drinking a bottle of Evian; and JESUS H. CHRIST, aka Son of God, a big dude, almost like a biker, flowing white robe, barefoot, chainsmoking Marlboro Reds, drinking a Sam Adams, obviously pissed. SUG takes this in a moment, completely confused, slowly crosses upstage to stand directly behind ELVIS [who should be played by the

same actor playing JESUS-Who-Thinks-He's-Elvis.])

JESUS CHRIST: Because I'm the Son of God, that's why. Now give me the damn cards. *(Begins taking up all the cards, shuffling expertly.)*

ELVIS PRESLEY: I don't think it's gonna make much of a difference, he's on a roll.

UNCLE SAM: About damn time, too.

JESUS CHRIST: Yeah, well, I think our luck's gonna change, my friend, and soon you are gonna be paying us.

UNCLE SAM: I beg to differ.

JESUS CHRIST: You always beg to differ, that's your damn problem.

ELVIS PRESLEY: Hey, come on now, what'd I say before?

JESUS CHRIST: He started it, he's a poor winner. He's a worse winner than he is a loser. Look at him. Friggin' grin. Oughta wipe the floor with that grin. You're lucky I'm a damn pacifist.

UNCLE SAM: And that's why I am *kicking your ass!*

ELVIS PRESLEY: Alright, come on, let's just play here.

(They look at their hands, engrossed in the game. SUG taps on ELVIS's shoulder.)

SUGARBABY: Jesus? What are you doing here?

ELVIS PRESLEY: No, I'm Elvis. *(Points.)* That's Jesus.

JESUS CHRIST: *(Waves, not looking up.)* Evening.

SUGARBABY: No, Jesus, you're Jesus who thinks he's Elvis.

ELVIS PRESLEY: No, dear, I'm Elvis who knows he's Elvis, and that there's Jesus who knows he's Jesus, and that fella there holding all our money is Uncle Sam.

UNCLE SAM: Privilege to meet you, miss. You're doing a fine job.

JESUS CHRIST: Will you just go please? It's your damn turn, Rockefeller.

UNCLE SAM: *Patience is a virtue.

SUGARBABY: Wait a minute, I don't understand. Why am I here?

JESUS CHRIST: Why are any of us here?

UNCLE SAM: Aw, shit, don't, just don't, *please, I'm beggin' ya—

JESUS CHRIST: No, alright, I'm being serious now. *(Sets down his cards.)*

ELVIS PRESLEY: Are we taking a break?

JESUS CHRIST: He's kicking my ass, I could use a break.

UNCLE SAM: Aw hell, don't look now, here comes Sigmund Freud again.

(Enter SIGMUND FREUD, sixties, just as you'd expect him to look. Grey suit, beard, monocle, has a real wet blanket personality, the guy no one talks to, the guy sitting alone in the kitchen at the house party. The TRIO put down their cards, sigh, stare at the table.)

SIGMUND FREUD: Hey.

ELVIS PRESLEY: Hey, Sig.

SIGMUND FREUD: Whatcha guys doin'?

ELVIS PRESLEY: Oh, nothing really.

SIGMUND FREUD: Playing cards, huh?

ELVIS PRESLEY: Yeah, looks like.

SIGMUND FREUD: Yeah, that's cool. So. Yeah. *(To SUGARBABY.)* Hey, I'm

Sigmund Freud. I'm the father of modern psychiatry.

SUGARBABY: *Hi.

JESUS CHRIST: Yeah, listen, Sig, this is kinda personal, okay? Private.

SIGMUND FREUD: Oh… Oh yeah sure. Okay. *(Turns to go. Stops.)* Hey listen, you guys ever need another *player, you know…

UNCLE SAM: We'll call ya, buddy.

SIGMUND FREUD: Oh. Okay. Yeah, cool. So. Yeah.

(Looks around a minute. Smiles. They smile back. He turns. Exits. After a beat, the THREE all exhale sharply, ELVIS whistles. They pick up their cards, continue the game.)

UNCLE SAM: Goddamn, that guy's annoying. What a downer.

SUGARBABY: *What the hell was that about?

JESUS CHRIST: Ah, he's alright. Just lost, is all. Anybody got a light?

SUGARBABY: And you still haven't answered my question. What the hell am I doing here?

JESUS CHRIST: *(Shrugs.)* Iduno.

SUGARBABY: Whatdaya mean, you don't know? How can you not know? You're Jesus Christ, aren't you?

JESUS CHRIST: Man made me in his own image, my child.

UNCLE SAM: Oy gevalt.

ELVIS PRESLEY: Oy gevalt? Funny, you don't look Jewish.

JESUS CHRIST: Neither do I, but, guess what?

(JESUS and UNCLE SAM enjoy a good laugh over that one.)

SUGARBABY: Hey, I'm really getting annoyed here.

JESUS CHRIST: You're getting annoyed. Okay, then.

(JESUS stands, offers SUG his chair. She sits, arms folded, peeved.)

JESUS CHRIST: So. You need something out of us, okay? Now we don't know what that is, but it must be something, or you wouldn't be here.

SUGARBABY: *(Attitude.)* Well, I can't possibly imagine.

UNCLE SAM: So, what's been bugging you lately? What's been the most aggravating thing?

SUGARBABY: Everything.

UNCLE SAM: Okay. Besides everything.

SUGARBABY: Everything! Everything, everything, everything, everything! People! Stupid people, doing stupid things, being stupid, no sense of anything! Damn! I mean, all I wanted was to get away and see America, and now, now it's this whole… thing! You know? A cigar can't be just a damn cigar anymore, can it?

ELVIS PRESLEY: Hey, watch it now, Sig'll come back and try to borrow five bucks.

UNCLE SAM: Sunuvabitch owes me a twenty.

JESUS CHRIST: *What'd I tell you? Don't ever lend him a dime, you'll never get it back.

SUGARBABY: I mean, what is the purpose, you know? I must be doing this for a reason, something bigger than myself, right?

JESUS CHRIST: How would I know?

SUGARBABY: How would—you're Jesus, Jesus! I mean… Jesus!

UNCLE SAM: Maybe you're just meant to be whatever people need you to be.

ELVIS PRESLEY: Maybe you're meant to be yourself, but you won't have any control over it, and it might eat you alive.

JESUS CHRIST: Maybe you're meant to be a sacrifice.

UNCLE SAM: Maybe all of the above.

JESUS CHRIST: Look, you're a good kid. Really. And you don't need to doubt yourself. Other people's problems, well, they're their problems, not yours. All you can do is be the best you can be. I know that sounds corny, but, really, it's true. You can't live your life based on what you don't want. You have to live your life based on what you do want.

SUGARBABY: What am I supposed to do? What am I supposed to say? Everyone's watching me!

JESUS CHRIST: Lead by example.

ELVIS PRESLEY: Inspire.

UNCLE SAM: Unify.

JESUS CHRIST: Okay. Let me explain it to you this way. Why and how did America start? How was she born?

SUGARBABY: The Boston Tea Party? The French Revolution?

JESUS CHRIST: Shit, the schools really are bad down there, aren't they? Okay, I'll tell you. The idea for America was founded as a reaction. A reaction to colonialism. A reaction to taxation. But it worked, it grew, as an action. What it wanted, not what it didn't want. Where it's going, not what it's running from. A century and a half ago, this country tore itself apart over the argument that man should not own his fellow man. One hundred years later, the ancestors of those slaves marched on that nation's capital, demanding their right to be recognized. Today, right now, a black man and a white woman are getting married. In America. Fifty years ago, they would have had to drink from different water fountains. And today? America has been racist, imperialist, sexist, and dogmatic, and probably will be again, in one way or another.

UNCLE SAM: For fuck's sake!

JESUS CHRIST: *Now hold on.

UNCLE SAM: Thanks for nothing! *Stop helping!

JESUS CHRIST: Let me finish. I would argue that that is what makes America great. It corrects its mistakes. It adapts. It changes. By choice. America is a place where someone can point out the dangers and problems of the country and still love it, and go to bed without having their stomach turn in terror. Americans have always changed. And that's what been forgotten. Nowadays, they only see the fights, and not the causes. It's all shirts and skins. *(He stops, melancholy. A sadness in the room.)*

ELVIS PRESLEY: You gotta have faith.

(Faintly, somewhere, the sound of a choir, humming the opening hook from Simon and Garfunkel's "America." Wind. A drumbeat, slow, but a call to action. SUGARBABY stands, scared, suddenly realizing the weight on her shoulders.)

SUGARBABY: Why me?

JESUS CHRIST: Heart.

UNCLE SAM: Courage.

ELVIS PRESLEY: Faith.

SUGARBABY: Shouldn't somebody have said "brain" in there somewhere?

JESUS CHRIST: Pay no attention to the man behind the curtain.

SUGARBABY: This is all getting kinda mooshy.

JESUS CHRIST: Yes, it is, and that's your cue to go.

SUGARBABY: Go? But, I'm dead, right?

(The THREE share a laugh.)

ELVIS PRESLEY: Aw, hell, no! No, you're just unconscious. You crawled away from the crash, passed out, Rufus done took your friend Jesus into custody, he's got him right now. And you, my dear, are going to Washington, D.C.

SUGARBABY: Wha—how? What?

JESUS CHRIST: Trust us.

(The lights dim to a pale blue. The choir grows stronger. The drumbeat louder. An almost heartbreaking tableau, UNCLE SAM, ELVIS, and JESUS side by side, waving slowly as SUG sinks back down to Earth…)

UNCLE SAM: So long, kid, and thanks.

ELVIS PRESLEY: You tell your friend that he's a good boy and I'm proud of him.

JESUS CHRIST: …Oh, and tell that prick Ashcroft to lighten the fuck up. Seriously. He just does not fucking get it at all.

SUGARBABY: Wait—but how?…

(Clouds. Mist. Blackout. Lights up: A Greyhound bus station somewhere in North Carolina. SUGARBABY asleep on a bench, clutching a bus ticket. Enter BUS DRIVER, fifties, full uniform, who pokes SUGARBABY awake.)

BUS DRIVER: Hey. You. Kid.

SUGARBABY: Huh—where the hell am I?

BUS DRIVER: North Carolina.

SUGARBABY: I'm—I'm what?

BUS DRIVER: You taking this bus to D.C. or what? We're going, come on.

(SUGARBABY looks down at the ticket in her hand. How in the hell…?)

SUGARBABY: Yeah…yeah, I'm coming.

BUS DRIVER: Well, hurry up.

(The BUS DRIVER exits. SUGARBABY looks at the ticket a moment. Music: Simon and Garfunkel, "America." SUGARBABY looks off into the distance. Lights shift. The faint image of an American flag in the background. Her eyes well up a bit. She understands now. She stands. Not such a kid anymore. Smiles. Rushes off to catch that damn bus. Purpose in her stride. Something has to be done. Something she has to say…)

22

Florida. A police interrogation room. Industrial green, fluorescents. JESUS, sitting alone at a steel table, glass of water, clipboard, pen. Leather outfit a mess now. Offstage, the sound of PROTESTORS—"Set Jesus Free," "Jesus Is Just Alright With Me," "What Would the Real Jesus Do," some singing "Were You There When They Crucified My Lord." After a moment, enter RUFUS. Stands there a moment, just looks at him. Long silence. Sound of PROTESTORS fades away.

RUFUS: Still won't talk, huh? You better tell me where she is, boy, we're goin' find her anyway, just make it easy on yourself.

(Nothing. JESUS doesn't even look up. Hell. RUFUS crosses to the table. Lifts the water glass.)

RUFUS: Sure is a hot one today. Damn. *(Lifts the glass, drinks, making a big show of it.)* Thirsty?

(Nothing. RUFUS sets down the glass. Waits a beat. Then, frustrated, lunges into JESUS, his face inches from the boy's, spittle flying from his lips. Furious.)

RUFUS: Goddammit you're stubborn. Far as I'm concerned, you kidnapped that girl. She's the only one can testify otherwise. Maybe if you tell me where she is, she can help you. I can help you. I should call your probation officer. Yeah, I looked your ass up. I know it all now. Richard. Didn't think I'd find out, did you? What do you think she'd say if she found out, huh? I find her myself, I'll tell her. Save you the trouble. *(Nothing. Slowly, RUFUS straightens. Disgusted. Had it. Fuck this.)* Punk. *(RUFUS walks to the exit. Then—)*

JESUS: *(Quietly.)* Were you in the army, sir?

RUFUS: *(Stops, turns to him. Humble pride.)* United States Marine Corps, son. Damn proud of it.

JESUS: My brother was in the army. I still have his flag, somewhere. Maybe they done thrown it out now, confiscated it for evidence. I don't know. When I was fifteen, I made fun of him. It wasn't right. He did what he thought was best. I never did nothin' for no one but myself. I didn't believe a thing anyone told me. The angrier I got, the better I felt. I never forgave him for leaving. I didn't know why I kept that flag. Until I got older, and sadder, and smarter. And I wish he were here now. But he's not. I wish I could tell him I understand now.

(Long pause. RUFUS is quieter now, kindly, almost fatherly.)

RUFUS: Son, where is she?

JESUS: I swear to you, sir, I truly don't know.

RUFUS: What is it about this girl?

JESUS: You gotta stand for something, or you're liable to fall for anything.

(Offstage, the PROTESTORS begin singing "God Bless America," softly, slowly, almost mournful. RUFUS crosses to the table, sits across from JESUS. Conversational. Trying to reach him, not sure how. Lights dim slowly. Like a wake for America.)

RUFUS: I got my own flag. I keep it over my entertainment unit. I don't know how to use those damn things, too many buttons on the remote. I just watch me the Discovery Channel, History Channel. The news. I like me that Jay Leno, he's good. Hm. I don't know how we got here. All of us.

JESUS: Sometimes, you just lose your way. But that little girl gave me faith, and that's what I've been needin'.

RUFUS: God bless America, huh?

(JESUS finally looks up. Catches RUFUS's gaze. Does not blink.)

JESUS: *(Sincere.)* Semper fi.

RUFUS: Heh. Shit.

(A look passes between them, wordless. JESUS lifts the glass, drinks. Lights slowly out.)

23

Washington, D.C. The Mall. The Reflecting Pool, Lincoln Memorial. A makeshift stage, with a huge banner—"America Is the Most Important Word! In Maybe Memory of Bailey "Sugarbaby" Sugarman, Who May or May Not Be Dead, We're Not Entirely Sure." On stage, GINGER, addressing the crowd, the ugliest dress you ever saw, sunflowers all over it, black veil over her newly flashy hairdo. Next to her is FATHER JAMES KILPATRICK, thirties, Roman Catholic priest, full regalia, flag pins, Sugarbaby buttons and yellow ribbon on la-

pel. *Offstage, the America First! Marching Band is playing "The Stars and Stripes Forever." Just downstage of GINGER is ROD BUTANE, smiling, in his element, with a number of America First! ACTIVISTS, all in perfectly pressed suits and dresses, with "America Is the Most Important Word" and "America First!" placards, all identical. All of them wear flag pins, some of them wave small flags.*

GINGER: I am so proud to be here, ladies and gentlemen, seeing you all here today, to honor the memory of my daughter, *my little sunflower...

PRIEST: Well, now, let's not presume the worst, *she may still be with us...

GINGER: Those damn Moo-Slams done killed my baby girl!

PRIEST: *Well, let's not cast aspersions...

GINGER: She was all I had in the world! And now she's gone! Taken away from me by some crazy turban-headed goober with a machine gun *and a grudge!

(PRIEST grabs the mic from her, shoves her into the wings where she leans against a wall, going into full-on drama queen hysterics.)

PRIEST: Okay, I really think that's enough now. Ladies and gentlemen, let us not bicker and argue, let us not cast aspersions. Let us instead honor this poor girl's memory—

(GINGER begins sobbing loudly and uncontrollably.)

PRIEST: ...alleged memory, alleged, oh dear, uh, let's honor her by pushing forth this very important legislation, and make "God Bless America" our national anthem, for this God-fearing, holy nation!

(Wild applause and cheers!)

PRIEST: And now, I proudly present the man who has done so much for our organization, the very great Mr. Rod Butane!

(ROD's theme music plays as ROD strides to the stage for his moment of glory. The ACTIVISTS cheer wildly. ROD takes the PRIEST's hand, turns, they pose briefly, flashbulbs go off, ROD claps him on the shoulder, whispers something in his ear, crosses to the mic stand, expertly quiets the CROWD by waving his arms; he's been dreaming of this moment for years...)

ROD: Thank you so much, Father, for those stirring words! And let me just say this to those who would trample on our country and this constitution, and the American spirit— *These colors don't run, buddy! They don't run!*

(The CROWD cheers wildly! ROD smiles widely, the moment is electric— And suddenly, breaking through security, on from backstage rush MITCH and a number of PROTESTORS, including ARON, who is now decked out in full camo gear, with a ball cap that reads "Illuminati Out of Our Government!" MITCH and a number of the PROTESTORS are wearing T-shirts reading "Not in My Name! Take the God Out of God Bless America!." Placards with pictures of Bush with a Hitler mustache, hand-drawn protest signs reading "Keep Your Imaginary Friend Out of my Uterus!," "Separation of Church and State!," etc. They chant loudly, drowning out the cheers. The CROWD goes berserk, some for, some against.)

PROTESTORS: *Hey hey! Ho ho! Jesus freaks have got to go! Hey hey! Ho ho! Jesus freaks have got to go! (Etc.)*

(After a moment of this, MITCH shoves ROD away from the mic, begins exhorting the crowd...)

MITCH: *I just want to say that we as Americans have had enough of these people's bullying!*

(Cheers and boos in equal measure.)

ROD: *Hey! Get off the stage, you media whore!

MITCH: *We are tired of being pushed around and subjugated and bullied by these moralistic bastards and we're not going to take it anymore!*

PROTESTORS: *Hey hey ho ho Jesus freaks have got to go hey hey... (Etc.)*

ROD: *And we have had enough of your elitist loud-mouthed condescension and we will no longer be ashamed of our beliefs!*

(PRIEST wedges between them, manages to calm them and the CROWD.)

PRIEST: Gentlemen, gentlemen, please let's try to work together!

MITCH: Yeah, right, how many altar boys have you molested this week, Father?

PRIEST: *Why I never!* Three. *Oh shit did I just say that??*

ROD: *Ooooooooo*kay! Well, we seem to need security up here, please, security?

MITCH: *Separation of church and state! Is great! Is great!*

PROTESTORS: *Separation of church and state! Is great! Is great!*

ROD and GBA RALLIERS: *We will not be shamed! We will not be shamed!*

MITCH and ANTI-GBA PROTESTORS: *One two three four we won't take you anymore one two three four we won't take you anymore...*

ROD and GBA RALLIERS: *God is good God is great let us thank him for the USA*

God is good God is great let us thank him for the USA!

MITCH and ANTI-GBA PROTESTORS: *Hey hey ho ho fundamentalists have got to go hey hey ho ho fundamentalists have got to go...*

ROD and GBA RALLIERS: *Hey hey ho ho "hey hey ho ho" has got to go hey hey ho "hey hey ho ho" has got to go...*

(Pause.)

MITCH: Ah shit. I don't think we can top that.

(MITCH looks to his PROTESTORS. They shake their heads. Look at their shoes, embarrassed. Moment. PRIEST smiles, approaches MITCH in reconciliation. MITCH turns, looks at him.)

MITCH: *Riot!!!!!!!!*

(Well, that did it. A full-scale riot erupts! MITCH clotheslines the PRIEST, who smacks his head right into the base of the Lincoln Memorial! The banner collapses to the stage! ROD rushes MITCH, begins choking him; MITCH reaches up, starts choking ROD! Meanwhile, GINGER rushes ARON, who yanks off her wig; she screams, rips off her wig cap, begins beating him with it! Fights break out all over the Great Mall, flags used as weapons, placards used as swords, complete and utter chaos! The band strikes up "Stars and Stripes Forever" in desperation; it blasts out over the crowd, the sounds of explosions, car crashes, screams! And into the middle of all this chaos comes SUGAR-BABY. She walks in from upstage. Calm. Takes one angry look at the lunacy around her. Approaches the mic. Knocks on it. Feedback! The CROWD turns! Murmuring amongst everyone as they rise to their feet, part like the Red Sea for their hero—"Sugarbaby! It's Sugarbaby! Sugarbaby! She's alive!"...)

SUGARBABY: Every one of you fuckers listen the hell up 'cause I have just about had it with each and every last damn one of you!

MITCH: *You tell 'em Sugarbaby!

ROD: Give 'em hell, *Sugarbaby!

GINGER: *My baby is alive!

ARON: Don't you let them push you around, sweet thing! You tell them Free-mason fuckers what for!

(The CROWD quiets after this. A soft wind. SUG looks out over the crowd. Moment. The mood darkens.)

SUGARBABY: I ran away from home. I was not kidnapped. I was not the victim of Muslim terrorists. I was not brain-washed. I am not making a political state-ment. I am not trying to sell you anything. I just wanted to see America. And I did.

And she's sick.

Sick in her heart, and in her soul, and I don't know that we'll ever be able to make her right again. But you don't give up on someone you love. And you don't cure someone who's sick by yelling at them, and hating them, and mistrusting them, and abusing them, and forgetting all the reasons you loved them in the first place!

MITCH: You tell 'em, kid!

(SUGARBABY rounds on him, startling him; he backs away, ashamed.)

SUGARBABY: I'm talking about you, ass-hole! You don't get it, do you? This fight isn't about you! This country is not here as your personal experiment, to argue about, and fight over, and use as a bully pulpit! And how dare you assume that because you got some kind of damn col-lege degree that you know anything, any-thing at all about me, or anybody! Even when you say something people can agree with, they wanna disagree just because you're all so ass-lipped and nasty, that you turn people off without even trying! You are smug, self-centered, and mean, and you're a pollutant!

ROD: *Damn right! Tell it like it is, Sugarbaby!*

SUGARBABY: And you, you egotistical, moralistic, smug, arrogant sunuvabitch!

(He backs away as well; the ACTIVISTS look down at their feet, embarrassed.)

SUGARBABY: It's all America number one with you, isn't it, if it's white, it's right, everything's about God, mother, and apple pie! Well, there is no God, some people aren't fit to be mothers—

GINGER: Hey now—

SUGARBABY: And I never did like apple pie anyway, and ya'll are living thirty years in the past, refusing to believe that any-one could disagree with you, live their own life their own way, and still be very, very happy! Anytime anyone disagrees with you, it couldn't possibly be because you're wrong, it must mean they're un-Ameri-can! Bullshit! You're right, America is the most important word, but you don't even know what that means! It means that God is whatever we want it to be, and America is whatever we can make of her, and hope isn't your personal goddamn possession to be doled out like fucking war rations, you selfish sunsabitches!!!

ROD: *(Rushes forward, arm around SUG's shoulder.)* See? She said it! America is the most important word!

MITCH: *(Rushes in, pulls her away from ROD.)* No, you moron! That's not what she meant at all!

(She pulls away from them, in tears now. The mood gets ugly. She's visibly shaken, the CROWD is frightened, and MITCH and ROD rush to the lip of the stage, exhorting the CROWD, their faces portraits of pure hate, pure venom, spit issuing from their lips, neck muscles strained, hands fists. SUG backs further upstage, hunched over, hands over stomach, as though violently ill.)

SUGARBABY: Neither of you are *listening anymore! *You're just yelling to hear yourselves yell! You're killing America, and you're killing me! Stop it! Please please just stop it!*

ROD: Prayer in the schools!

MITCH: Diversity in the universities!

ROD: Ban sodomy!

MITCH: Gays in the military!

ROD: Porn off my Internet!

MITCH: *Tax the churches!*

ROD: *Fuck the poor!*

MITCH: *Fuck the poor!*

ROD: *I want mine!*

MITCH: *I want mine!*

ROD: *Free speech for me!*

MITCH: *Free speech for me!*

ROD: *Right to bear arms!*

MITCH: *Gun control now!*

(And then a shot rings out! Everyone ducks! SUG is left horribly alone on stage, in a spotlight, sobbing uncontrollably, no one runs to help her; GINGER ducks behind a speaker; ROD hides his head; MITCH runs, curls into a corner. She is completely alone…)

SUGARBABY: *Mama! Help me! Don't leave me! Aron! Aron please! Somebody help me! Jesus! Jesussssssssss!!!!!!!!!!!!!!!*

(Moment. A piano chord. Someone starts playing "America the Beautiful." Somewhere, the sound of JESUS's voice. A light comes up upstage.

(It's JESUS. Full Aloha Elvis jumpsuit, gorgeous. Rhinestones. High collar. Hair a perfect pompadour. Red, white, and blue eagle on the back. JESUS begins singing "America the Beautiful." Impeccable Elvis voice. Incredible presence. Strength. Faith. Goddammit. He's really. Fucking. Good. SUG stands, gazes at him in disbelief. Is she dreaming? Is this for real? He steps down to her, offers his hand. She clings to him, hugging him, as though to make sure he's real. He smiles, finishes the first verse. Instrumental break:)

SUGARBABY: Jesus, where have you been? What happened?

JESUS: I had faith in you, Ms. Sugarman. You just gotta have faith in me.

(Enter RUFUS, grinning, bearing his rifle, still smoking from the shot he fired to silence the CROWD.)

RUFUS: You gotta stand for something, or you're liable to fall for anything.

SUGARBABY: But I was all alone! I didn't know what to do, *you were gone, I—

JESUS: *Sssssshhhhh*, my friend. That was when I carried you.

SUGARBABY: …Bullshit, Jesus, you wasn't nowhere around.

JESUS: Yeah, well, it sure sounds good, don't it. Now look out, I gotta show these people who's the damn boss.

(He strides center stage, the lights shift—And a glorious spotlight hits JESUS; he finishes the song, strength, courage, grace, heart, faith. The CROWD rises, tears in their eyes, amazed and bewildered. He finishes up the

number, classic Elvis kung-fu pose, roaring finish, the CROWD goes wild!)

JESUS: Thank you. Thank you very much.

(Music: "Suspicious Minds." Don't know why? Go get it. Put it on. Listen to the lyrics. Go ahead. We'll wait. Don't have a copy? Go buy one. Now. Do it. Get it now? Hell, yeah. JESUS approaches ROD, singing. No, we can't go on together like this, ROD thinks. Nods. JESUS turns to MITCH. Can't build our dreams that way, can we? No. No, we can't, MITCH realizes. JESUS goes to his old friend he knows, SUGARBABY. Arms around one another's shoulders, they harmonize. ROD gets the hint. Joins in. Then ARON. Then MITCH. Then more. And more. Soon, thousands. The entire CROWD, left, right, Republican, Democrat, white, black, gay, straight, everyone, the whole damn country, they're singing along, they're harmonizing.

(JESUS breaks into the spot again, belts out the soulful middle eight, the CROWD ooos along, swaying, arm in arm, camping it up, the biggest, bestest party America's ever thrown… "Yeah Yeah!"

(He rises, begins the verses again. They get it now. We all get it now. Can't walk out. America. Love you too much, baby. What you're doing to yourself. What it's doing to us all. The song goes into its mantra. The lights flash, rock show. The CROWD harmonizes with JESUS, he's doing a dead-on Elvis, they're singing along, it's electric, the whole damn CROWD, the whole damn country. Defiance. Pride. Faith. They're singing in Washington, D.C. Can't walk out. They're singing in New York City. Love you too much. The lights flash, the audience joins in. They're

singing in Detroit, in Pittsburgh, in Miami. What you're doing to me. They're singing in Las Vegas, in Los Angeles, in Seattle, in Houston. Can't walk out. JESUS goes into the audience, into the house, passes around the microphone. They're singing in Little Rock, in Tulsa, in Chicago, in Boston, in Memphis. The CAST sings in perfect harmony, the lights flash, JESUS is in the audience, he shakes his hips. In their homes. In their schools. In their churches. In their shopping malls. JESUS shakes his hips. They're singing in America. For at least a few minutes, a few precious moments.

(And slowly, the CROWD disperses. They're singing in Yellowstone, at Mt. Rushmore, in Hawaii and Alaska. JESUS shakes his hips, it's just him and SUG now, the lights are dimming to night blue. They're singing in the Grand Canyon, at the Great Salt Lake. At Ground Zero. Defiance. Pride. Faith. They're singing. JESUS lowers his head. The song reaches its finish. Timpani. JESUS turns. It's dark upstage now, we can just make out SUGARBABY up there, swaying to the music. JESUS raises his hands, the eagle facing us, full-on Elvis moves, his arms whipping like copter blades. The lights rise slowly upstage… The timpani rises in volume… A flag, red, white, blue, stars, huge, covering the whole of upstage, lights blinding on it, resplendent, so bright you could cry, the song reaches fever pitch, JESUS does an Elvis kick, lands on his knees, facing the flag, SUG spins, complete and utter and absolute joy, as the lights on the flag rise, blinding, blinding, they're singing all over America… Blackout.)

NARRATOR: (Voiceover.) God bless America. My home sweet home.

(Music: Kate Smith, "God Bless America.")

WTC VIEW

Brian Sloan

BRIAN SLOAN is an independent filmmaker living in New York City. He was born and raised in Kensington, Maryland, where, after a brief stint in Montessori preschool, he attended a long line of Catholic schools which stifled and inspired him all at once. He graduated from Boston College with a BA in English and then went on to New York University where he received an MFA in film/television. Brian broke onto the indie scene with his graduate thesis film, *Pool Days* (1993) a short about the sexual misadventures of a teenage lifeguard. After playing festivals like Sundance and New Directors/New Films, Strand Releasing packaged it with two other films about gay teens and called the whole thing *Boys Life* (1994). It was a surprise hit, playing theatres around the country and starting an indie franchise. His first feature, the screwball comedy *I Think I Do* (1998) was praised by the *New York Times* as "hysterically funny and very smart" and played more than fifty U.S. cities and some foreign countries too. Recently, Brian served as executive producer of *Boys Life 4*, a shorts compilation that included his film *Bumping Heads* (2002). As a playwright, Brian got a late start with his first one-act, *The Boys Who Brunch*, which appeared in the 2000 Drop Your Shorts One-Act Play Festival at CenterStage New York. It won awards for best director (Andrew Volkoff) and best play. The next year, Brian and Andy repeated the trick with a piece called *Sex and the One Act*. Then, Brian wrote his first full-length play and submitted it to the 2003 New York International Fringe Festival. *WTC View* was accepted, produced, applauded, and, now, published. Wow.

WTC View was first presented as part of the New York International Fringe Festival (Elena K. Holy, Producing Artistic Director) on August 11, 2003, at the Bottle Factory Theater, New York City, with the following cast and credits:

Jeremy .... Jeremy Beazlie
Max .... Jay Gillespie
Josie .... Liz Kappalow
Jeff .... Michael Linstroth
Kevin .... Lucas Papaelias
Alex .... Nick Potenzieri
Eric .... Michael Urie
Will (answering machine voice) .... Jason Dietz
Carlos (answering machine voice) .... Lucas Papaelias
Joey (answering machine voice) .... Kevin Ray
Victor (answering machine voice) .... M. Rosenthal
Lorenzo (answering machine voice) .... Mark Sam

Director: Andrew Volkoff
Producer: Helena Webb
Production Stage Manager: Cynthia Ann Thomas
Sound Design: Jim Van Bergen

The play was performed without intermission.

The author wishes to thank Andrew Volkoff for his remarkable direction of our extraordinary cast, Helena Webb for an amazing production under less than ideal circumstances (see "Blackout of 2003"), and the Magnolia Bakery for the sugar that kept us all going.

CAST

ERIC, thirty-three, a boyish freelance photographer
JEREMY, twenty-six, a charming and proper Brit
JOSIE, thirty-three, a stylish Upper East Side wife
KEVIN, twenty-nine, a strung-out chainsmoker
JEFF, thirty-six, a political consultant, a jock
ALEX, twenty-seven, a cute Wall Street guy
MAX, twenty, a peacenik NYU student

VOICE ROLES

WILL, thirty-eight, the ex-boyfriend/voice of reason
VICTOR, twenty-eight, a politely chatty Southerner
JOEY, twenty-two, a hyper chorus boy
CARLOS, forty-nine, a heavily accented Latino
LORENZO, thirty, an Italian import

SETTING

The play's action takes place in an empty bedroom of a two-bedroom tenement apartment in SoHo, New York City. The main action takes place in the last week of September 2001.

PROLOGUE

The stage is dark. On the stage left wall, a bare window is illuminated from behind by a vague morning light, with a small American flag Scotch-taped to the sash. It is the kind a child might wave at a parade. The sound of sirens is heard...first one, then a couple, then many more, overlapping and creating a cacophony of emergency sounds. A computerized ANSWERING MACHINE voice comes on.

ANSWERING MACHINE: Tuesday, 8:49 a.m.

WILL: *(Voiceover.)* Hey—it's me. I'm taking the car into Manhattan today—easier than finding a space to park. Anyway, I'm on the Brooklyn Bridge and there's a huge...fire on...in the, uh, one of the towers of the World Trade Center. It must encompass, I don't know, fifteen floors.

Smoke billowing out, coming out of the windows. It's just...oh man. It's enormous, it's amaze—it's horrific. Look out your window, Eric. Bye.

ANSWERING MACHINE: Tuesday, 11:32 a.m.

JOSIE: *(Voiceover.)* Hey Eric—where are you? It's Josie. Just making a round of downtown calls. I hope you're well and I hope you're safe. I don't know where you are today but maybe not being home is safer since you're so close. Anyway, I'm getting hysterical and I'm sure you're fine and I'll talk to you soon...I hope.

ANSWERING MACHINE: Tuesday, 4:12 p.m.

WILL: *(Voiceover.)* Eric—Eric—are you there? Pick up the phone. Oh my God— I've been trying to get through to you all afternoon. I really would love it if you could call me back. You can try my work number uptown. Or my cell which I've been carrying with me since this happened. I'm worried because Sharon's okay, Tom's okay...but you're the hardest to get in touch with downtown. All the circuits kept saying they're busy. So I'm a little—I just wanna be sure you're okay, Eric, because— *(Voice catching.)* Alright, I'm gonna try and not get emotional here. But... *(Getting emotional.)* Okay—just call me.

(The sirens fade out. The light in the window goes out. The stage is black.)

SCENE 1

In darkness, the ANSWERING MACHINE is heard.

ANSWERING MACHINE: Wednesday, 10:31 a.m.

JEREMY: *(Voiceover. British accent.)* Hullo—I'm ringing about the advert in yesterday's *Village Voice*. For the two-bedroom share. I'm hoping it's still available as I desperately need a flat. I know it's a dreadful time but if you could give me a ring I'd be very grateful. I'm at the St. Regis hotel... 334-2600. Name's Jeremy Thornton. Thanks *so* much.

(Lights up on an empty apartment bedroom. At the center of the stage, three cardboard boxes are packed and taped closed. Near them is one box that is open and brimming with stuff. Next to the window at stage left is a very old air conditioner with a can of air freshener on top of it. At stage right is a tall, slim oak dresser with an alarm clock on top. An answering machine sits on the floor next to it. Next to the dresser is a door that leads to the rest of the apartment. From the doorway at stage right, a young MAN, in his early thirties, enters the room wearing a thrift store T-shirt, old jeans, and a pair of new sneakers. He is unshaven and smoking a cigarette. He looks at the boxes on the floor and moves them around, trying to arrange them to look nicer as if that's possible. He goes to the window and opens it. A breeze comes in which he enjoys for a second. Then, making a face, he quickly closes it again. Coughing, he reaches for the can of air freshener on top of the A/C unit and gives the room a thorough misting. After putting the air freshener back down, the MAN walks over to the window, almost in a trance, staring out. Suddenly, the jarring buzz of a New York City door buzzer goes off, sounding like an electrocution. The MAN jumps accordingly and then opens the window quickly and tosses his cigarette out, trying to clear the air too before closing it again. He walks over to a door at stage right, opens it, and hits a button offstage.)*

MAN: *(Offstage.)* Yeah...

JEREMY: *(Offstage.)* Hullo—it's Jeremy.

(He buzzes him in. Then he looks around the room, still trying to fix things up. He tries in vain to clear the air. There is knocking heard offstage. The MAN rushes out of the room and disappears offstage.)

JEREMY: *(Offstage.)* Sorry I'm so terribly late.

MAN: *(Offstage.)* You have trouble finding it?

(The MAN reenters with JEREMY, a young but proper Londoner, dressed in a smart v-neck sweater with a matching tie.)

JEREMY: A bit. I went uptown when I thought I was going downtown. I still don't know my way round.

MAN: Ah—just moved here?

JEREMY: September seventh.

MAN: Oh no.

JEREMY: Oh yes.

MAN: Well…it can only get better right?

(JEREMY smiles wanly, as the MAN laughs a bit too nervously.)

JEREMY: So this is the room you're letting?

MAN: Oh—yeah. This is the bedroom. And, uh, the kitchen and bath are back—

JEREMY: *(Pulls out a small notepad and a pen and takes notes.)* Sorry—what was the rent again?

MAN: Twelve hundred a month. Utilities included. *(A beat.)* So you're here for work?

JEREMY: I'm assisting the concierge at the St. Regis hotel.

MAN: Very classy…

JEREMY: And you said it was nonsmoking, is that right?

MAN: Yeah. Technically. I quit this summer.

JEREMY: *(Smelling skeptically.)* I see…

MAN: It's just—a friend was over. My neighbor. My smoking neighbor… always, you know, smoking up the joint.

(An awkward beat as JEREMY looks around the room judgmentally.)

MAN: Uh—I'm sorry I took so long to get back to you.

JEREMY: Oh—it's quite alright.

MAN: Things were a little…crazy down here.

JEREMY: Actually, I feel just awful about calling like that.

MAN: Like what?

JEREMY: Ringing you the day after the eleventh. You must've thought I was mad.

MAN: Not really.

JEREMY: No?

MAN: I had nine messages about the apartment that day.

JEREMY: You're joking.

MAN: Oh no. Yours was pretty tame actually. Some of the messages were unbelievable. This one guy was like— "Yeah, I wanna come down and see it this afternoon." I mean, unless he was in the National Guard…

JEREMY: Still—I must apologize for calling like that. I don't know what I was thinking.

MAN: I don't think anyone knew what they were thinking.

(There is an awkward pause as JEREMY looks at the MAN, troubled.)

JEREMY: I'm sorry. I forgot your name?

MAN: Oh—Eric.

JEREMY: Eric. Right. Of course. With all the calls I've been making…

ERIC: It can get confusing. Especially these days…

JEREMY: May I ask you how long you've been here, Eric?

ERIC: Uh—sure. Hmmmm…let me see…about nine years. Wow. *(Semi-amazed.)* Nine years. Almost ten…

JEREMY: You must like it very much then?

ERIC: Kinda. I…I got the apartment when I was in school and it was dirt cheap and so I just kinda stayed.

JEREMY: And your roommate's moved out?

ERIC: Oh…yeah. He's gone. Got his stuff out yesterday. Most of it…

(They spy the dresser.)

ERIC: My ex is coming to get that later.

JEREMY: And that was your roommate?

ERIC: No—the ex wasn't the roommate. Kinda why he's the ex.

JEREMY: Pardon.

ERIC: Wanted me to move in with him.

JEREMY: Ah—how long were you together?

ERIC: He only lived here a few months.

JEREMY: Sorry—I meant you and your ex.

ERIC: Oh—uh, almost two years.

JEREMY: Oh—I'm sorry then.

ERIC: Don't be. You wouldn't be looking at this if I'd moved in.

JEREMY: Quite true.

ERIC: Have you seen a lot of apartments?

JEREMY: This is actually the first.

ERIC: Wow. You were the first to call.

JEREMY: *(Shocked.)* Oh now that makes me feel wonderful. I was the very *first*!? That's absolutely ghoulish.

ERIC: Ghoulish?

JEREMY: Eh, morbid. You know…

ERIC: Sure. It's just you don't hear the word very often—ghoulish.

JEREMY: When I left that message, I was at my wits' end. You see, I've been living at the St. Regis since I arrived.

ERIC: Doesn't sound so bad…

JEREMY: One would think…except when you're being shuffled around to a different hotel room every night it can be somewhat—disconcerting. Then when the planes got grounded, all the guests were stuck at the hotel and there weren't any rooms. And the staff couldn't get home because of all the transportation problems. So they decided to lodge us in the ballroom the night of the eleventh…on cots! Like some high-class vagabond shelter. Dreadful. And *that* was my last straw. So when I called I was just—

ERIC: You don't have to apologize. I don't think calling about the ad was…uh… what's that word…

JEREMY: Ghoulish?

ERIC: *(Smiling 'cause he just wanted to hear it again.)* Right. I don't think you're "ghoulish" at all.

(JEREMY smiles appreciatively to know he's not so improper. JEREMY goes to look out the window. ERIC looks around the room nervously.)

JEREMY: Lots of sun. Nice view. *(A beat.)* Could you see them from here?

ERIC: Oh yeah. Right at the end of the street. Huge.

JEREMY: You weren't here when—

ERIC: *(Wearily.)* Saw the whole thing out the window.

JEREMY: *(Taken aback.)* Good God—it must have been horrific for you.

ERIC: *(Startled by JEREMY's reaction.)* It was, you know…yeah. *(Change of subject.)* Uh…where were you?

JEREMY: I was at work. My third day. Unbelievable.

ERIC: Literally. I *still* can't believe it. In the morning, I have that instant right when I wake up where I forget the whole thing and then I remember it and it's just—unbelievable.

JEREMY: But being here...you're so close. It must have been terrifying.

ERIC: It was pretty bad...

JEREMY: How far from—

ERIC: I don't know...about twelve blocks.

JEREMY: Was there any...

ERIC: No—strangely enough. The wind blew most of that stuff towards Brooklyn.

JEREMY: Poor Brooklyn...

(JEREMY is now staring out the window, lost in thought. ERIC would like to move this along.)

ERIC: So—whattya think of the place?

JEREMY: It's lovely. When do you need someone?

ERIC: I was supposed to get someone in here on the fifteenth of September but... well, that didn't happen. The landlord let the situation slide a bit because of everything that was going on. But I definitely need someone here for October.

JEREMY: So...how should we proceed then?

ERIC: Let's see—I'm planning to decide by the end of the week, the twenty-eighth, so someone can move in on the weekend.

JEREMY: I like it a lot, but it is the first place I've seen...

ERIC: Why don't you give me a call tomorrow if you're interested and we can take it from there?

JEREMY: Splendid. And I'll ring you either way. I don't want to leave you guessing.

ERIC: *(Surprised.)* Wow. That's nice.

JEREMY: It's only the proper thing to do.

ERIC: Not if you live in New York.

JEREMY: I'm still new.

ERIC: They used to say you have to be here at least two years before you don't feel like a tourist.

JEREMY: I believe that schedule has been accelerated due to recent events.

ERIC: Yeah—now it'll only take you a year.

(They smile at each other. JEREMY makes his way to leave.)

JEREMY: Now...when I get downstairs how do I find "uptown"?

ERIC: Oh—when you go out the front door, so you don't get lost, if you look for the Empire State Building that's uptown. And downtown is...well...not.

JEREMY: Right. Well, I'll ring you soon.

ERIC: *(Motioning to leave.)* Great. Let me show you—

JEREMY: I'll see myself out. Take care...

(ERIC shuts the door behind JEREMY and smiles to himself, pleased.)

ERIC: Cheerio.

(Blackout.)

SCENE 2

In darkness, the ANSWERING MA-CHINE is heard.

ANSWERING MACHINE: Monday, 11:23 a.m.

WILL: *(Voiceover.)* Hey—it's me. You left a bunch of clothes from when you were here and, despite my better judgment, I washed them for you. Anyway, let me know when I can come by— As for that dresser, I don't know if I really want it. It sounds ugly. But give me a ring and let me know how you're doing, okay? And if you found a roommate yet.

(Lights up on a stylish-looking woman standing at the window with the flag. JOSIE's back is to the audience as she stands there, very still, staring out the window. The sound of a door opening offstage is heard.)

ANSWERING MACHINE: Monday, 1:32 p.m.

KEVIN: *(Voiceover.)* What's up? I'm calling about the roommate "situation." I'm looking for a place immediately… yesterday even. I've only got a cell right now— 917-439-4276. But give me a ring and I'll come check it out. Thanks and peace, man.

ERIC: *(Offstage.)* Delivery!

JOSIE: I can't believe it's still smoking. It's been two weeks!

ERIC: *(Offstage.)* They're nowhere near putting it all out.

JOSIE: What?!

ERIC: *(Offstage.)* The *Times* said it's probably gonna be another month or so. Maybe longer.

JOSIE: Jesus.

(ERIC enters the room carrying some paper sacks of takeout food and wearing an industrial type surgical mask. JOSIE turns away from the window.)

ERIC: Could be the longest burning industrial fire in the U.S.

JOSIE: *(Re: the mask.)* Don't you think you're overreacting a bit?

ERIC: No.

JOSIE: It's fine. They've been testing.

ERIC: It doesn't smell fine.

JOSIE: But it's not gonna kill you.

ERIC: Look Uptown Girl—I'm breathing this crap every day—twenty-four seven. On top of that, the smell is awful. So technically, if it's not actually toxic, the smell alone is by far enough to make me gag and then choke to death on the takeout and then would you think I was overreacting to the air quality deal?

JOSIE: *(Stands there staring at him, studying him.)* That was a bit of a rant.

ERIC: You asked me about the mask and I gave you an answer.

JOSIE: Definitely a rant.

ERIC: I'm fine.

JOSIE: Did you call that 800 number?

ERIC: It was busy.

JOSIE: Did you try again?

ERIC: It's busy for a reason. There are thousands of other people much worse off than me because they *really* need help.

JOSIE: Eric—you went through a major traumatic—

ERIC: The food's getting cold.

JOSIE: You're not listening to me.

ERIC: Actually, I am listening and even comprehending what you're saying because remember last week when you told me I wasn't eating enough so today you came over to check up on me and I picked up tons of Thai food for us to gorge ourselves on so I can get nice and fat the way you like me.

JOSIE: Ranting—

ERIC: *(Indicating bags.)* Eating.

(They both sit down on boxes, and ERIC arranges the food.)

JOSIE: I'm glad you're eating a lot but other than that…

ERIC: Things are fine. Oh—I even saw a potential roommate.

JOSIE: That's good. So how was he?

ERIC: He was great.

JOSIE: Yeah? Was he cute?

ERIC: I don't know. I guess. That's not supposed to matter.

JOSIE: It does.

ERIC: Josie—you're not supposed to be attracted to your roommate. It's very bad according to, I dunno, someone…

JOSIE: I'm not saying you should be "attracted" to him and start sleeping with him or anything dirty.

ERIC: So what are you saying?

JOSIE: Bottom line—you have to look at him. Every day. So it's like buying a nice piece of furniture or a rug. Pick something nice. Something you like.

ERIC: Okay—that was sooo Upper East Side.

JOSIE: Just making an analogy.

ERIC: Alright—he was cute.

JOSIE: Good. Half the battle right there.

ERIC: Oh, and he's British which is kinda fun.

JOSIE: British? Oh—I don't know…

ERIC: *(With an accent.)* He was being awfully clever and saying the most smashing things.

JOSIE: Did you flirt with him?

ERIC: Uh—I'm pretty sure he was straight.

JOSIE: I thought you said he was British.

ERIC: Gay or straight or whatever—I don't need to be flirting my way back into another dysfunctional relationship.

JOSIE: Don't worry. You'll find someone. The right someone this time.

ERIC: You always say that.

JOSIE: I found someone.

ERIC: And you always say *that*.

JOSIE: Remember all those horrible guys I went through in my twenties.

ERIC: *(Avec British accent.)* Quite vividly, yes.

JOSIE: And Will was what, your first serious, semi-committed—

ERIC: Semi? What do you mean semi?

JOSIE: You never moved in. That's semi.

ERIC: You don't have to move in with someone to be committed.

JOSIE: Apparently, you do with Will.

ERIC: Ha.

JOSIE: The point is you gave it a shot, you guys were together for over two years and you learned a lot. A nice test run.

ERIC: Test run?! If Will could hear you—

JOSIE: And now you're ready for the real thing.

ERIC: Wait-wait-wait a minute. I remember having a conversation with you back in July when you were saying that Will *was* the real thing.

JOSIE: What can I say— he was until he wasn't.

ERIC: Have you thought about starting an advice column?

JOSIE: This is so you, Eric. To be arguing over the past. I mean, it's over, okay. Will is in the past. Gone. It's a whole new world now.

ERIC: Ergo the mask.

JOSIE: I'm talking about *you* here.

ERIC: I know.

JOSIE: Really?

ERIC: I. Know.

JOSIE: Good. Now pass me a spring roll. I'm starving.

(He passes the spring roll. ERIC gets up and, with his back to JOSIE, pulls his pack of cigarettes from the dresser drawer.)

JOSIE: *What* are you doing?

ERIC: Quitting smoking next year.

JOSIE: Eric—

ERIC: This is only my first one of the day.

JOSIE: You said you were eating.

ERIC: I will. Just after this.

JOSIE: Great. Can you open the window at least?

ERIC: Are you kidding?

JOSIE: No—you're smoking and I'm trying to eat.

ERIC: The air is awful today.

JOSIE: Then open the window and put your mask on.

ERIC: I can't smoke with my mask on.

JOSIE: Okay—you realize how absurd this is getting?

ERIC: I'll open it a crack. *(He does, then reacts to the smell, as if he might gag.)* Oh good God—

(JOSIE smells it too. She puts her spring roll down.)

JOSIE: Jesus!

ERIC: The wind shifted.

JOSIE: Shut it!

(Quickly, he does. He paces around the room, looking for the can of air freshener.)

ERIC: See—

JOSIE: That smell…

ERIC: Barbecuing a computer.

JOSIE: What?

ERIC: That's how one of the firemen described it in the paper.

JOSIE: I don't think I could even describe that. Jesus…

ERIC: Not even an analogy?

JOSIE: *(Not joking.)* Not funny.

ERIC: Aha! *(He finds the can of air freshener behind one of the boxes and starts to spray like a maniac.)*

JOSIE: Eric—

ERIC: What?

JOSIE: The food?

ERIC: It's air freshener!

JOSIE: I don't want my spring roll tasting like a fresh country morning.

(He finishes spraying. There is a deadly lull as they look at their food. Neither of them goes to

eat it. ERIC grabs two Diet Cokes out of the takeout bag and places them on the box. JOSIE smiles and takes the Diet Coke, as does ERIC.)

ERIC: So how's the hubby?

JOSIE: Okay.

ERIC: Just okay? Not the usual ringing endorsement of married life.

JOSIE: I guess we're sorta fighting now.

ERIC: *(Excited.)* Really? About what?

JOSIE: We went out for the first time last weekend. To a dinner party at Lisa's… something she'd originally scheduled for the week of the eleventh—

ERIC: How was *that*?

JOSIE: At first, it was great. Everyone was so excited to see everyone. None of us live or work anywhere downtown so it's not like any of us were in danger but everyone was being so…grateful.

ERIC: On the Upper East Side even.

JOSIE: Lisa even got teary when we arrived.

ERIC: *(Fake moved.)* That is so touching…

JOSIE: Eric— She was genuinely emotional about it. And not just her. Everyone was being so sincere and thoughtful and interested in everything you had to say. It was kinda freaking me out.

ERIC: I'm sure.

JOSIE: But once we had some drinks and settled into dinner it got a little more back to normal. That's when David and I got in a major fight.

ERIC: Over what?

JOSIE: He started telling my story.

ERIC: Again?!

JOSIE: I told him that it was sorta funny once but not over and over and especially not at someone else's dinner party. But he just thinks it's hysterical that I went and got my hair done after the second plane hit. Fucking hysterical. It's not that ridiculous, right?

ERIC: I went to vote after the second plane.

JOSIE: See— People were going about their business. We all knew it was serious but I remember thinking, sure it's this enormous fire, but they'll put it out. That's what the fire department does. They put out fires.

ERIC: And then I went to the deli. Got a bagel and a Diet Coke.

JOSIE: That's what I mean! We had no idea. No fucking idea. It didn't seem like some major national crisis. But David thinks it's the most hysterical fucking joke—the nation's under attack and Josie needs her roots touched up. Ba-dump.

ERIC: That's totally not fair.

JOSIE: Fucking right it's not. I mean I made that appointment two months ago. Do you know how hard it is to see Jean-Luc?

ERIC: Alright—that might not be helping your case.

JOSIE: Anyway, when we got home I just let that fucker have it. I told him that he had no right to tell that story again and make a fucking mockery of my goddamn hair appointment.

ERIC: Yikes—so what happened?

JOSIE: Basically, it killed our sex life.

ERIC: I thought everyone was copulating like bunnies—end of the world and all.

JOSIE: Frankly, we haven't been having sex at all since the eleventh. The fight just gave us a more concrete reason for not having sex.

ERIC: Wow. So why did you stop?

JOSIE: I don't know…we talked about it a few days after the eleventh and we…we didn't feel sexy. We just felt… I don't know. Alive. But kind of a sad alive.

(JOSIE looks at ERIC, inviting him to join the conversation. He looks away, uncomfortably, and fishes for his cigarettes. He holds the pack up to JOSIE.)

ERIC: Do you—

JOSIE: Maybe one.

(Complicitly, she lights up, as does ERIC, but smokes somewhat delicately, like a non-smoker.)

JOSIE: Were you smoking at Will's?

ERIC: No way—he'd throw me out.

JOSIE: It was really nice of him to take you in like that.

ERIC: Take me in? He dragged me to Brooklyn. Against my will.

JOSIE: Because you were freaking out here.

ERIC: I was fine.

JOSIE: That's not what he told me.

ERIC: You guys talked?

JOSIE: He called me that night. He was really worried about you. Said you weren't making a lot of sense.

ERIC: I was tired. That's all.

JOSIE: Did you guys sleep together while you were there?

ERIC: Not sleep together-sleep together. The first night I was sprawled on the couch watching TV and he said that I could sleep in his bed if I wanted. But I wasn't even excited or thinking about the fact that we'd broken up and hadn't slept together in a couple months. I mean I should've been so excited by something like that but…

JOSIE: So nothing happened.

ERIC: Nope. I just curled up next to him and he held me.

JOSIE: Are you thinking about—

ERIC: No. No! We are *not* getting back together.

JOSIE: I don't know—maybe that would be a good thing right now.

ERIC: Josie—please don't say that.

JOSIE: Considering all you've been through.

ERIC: I'm fine.

JOSIE: You are now…probably because Will got you out of here. Can you imagine if you'd been here alone that whole week after, when everything—

ERIC: Can we not get into this…please.

JOSIE: Look—you know I'm not Will's biggest fan but he took care of you. Let you stay at his apartment when you were freaking out about being here. He was actually a mensch.

ERIC: What?

JOSIE: A good guy. Maybe you need a good guy right now.

ERIC: Or a good roommate.

JOSIE: You think that Brit's gonna spoon with you and lullaby you to sleep?

ERIC: Let's not get crazy now…Will can't even sing.

JOSIE: Analogy.

ERIC: Uh, not really but—

JOSIE: Just think about it. I worry about you being down here alone.

ERIC: I won't be much longer. I have to get someone by the thirtieth. Work has been nonexistent. I can't afford to carry a full month's rent.

JOSIE: How's the landlord?

ERIC: Persistent.

JOSIE: Oh—that's sweet, given the circumstances. Jesus!

ERIC: I'm sure I'll get someone. I've never had trouble before.

JOSIE: You *have* had some difficulty securing a boyfriend.

ERIC: Okay—I'm gonna smoke the whole pack now.

JOSIE: Joking.

ERIC: *(Not really laughing.)* Oh—ha ha ha.

JOSIE: *(Looks at him intensely.)* Just think about it…

ERIC: What?

JOSIE: Will.

ERIC: No. Way.

JOSIE: Then eat.

(Blackout.)

SCENE 3

In darkness, the ANSWERING MA-CHINE is heard.

ANSWERING MACHINE: Tuesday, 10:05 a.m.

JEREMY: *(Voiceover.)* Hullo…Jeremy calling. I'm afraid I have some dreadful news.

I've been laid off from my job at the St. Regis. There's been an utter lack of guests due to "recent events," so it looks like I'll be returning to London rather prematurely. But I do want to thank you for being so kind and showing me your splendid flat. Good luck with everything. Cheers.

(Lights up on the apartment. No one is in it.)

ANSWERING MACHINE: Tuesday, 2:37 p.m.

KEVIN: *(Voiceover.)* What's up—it's Kevin again. Wanted to stop by and see the pad this afternoon if that's cool. Maybe bring the moving truck by around five or so and get myself settled by tonight. *(A beat.)* Naw—just kidding, just kidding. Anyway I'm gonna be downtown most of the day. So, like you said, I'll just stop by. Peace!

(KEVIN enters the room and strides over to the window with ERIC a few paces behind him. KEVIN is a live-wire kind of guy, wearing a brown leather jacket with a concert T-shirt underneath. He is constantly moving and smoking a cigarette.)

KEVIN: Wow—this place is awesome!

ERIC: Really?

KEVIN: Shit yeah. It's great! Nice big space. Windows. Light.

ERIC: *(Staring at cigarette.)* You're a smoker then?

KEVIN: Oh. Yeah—is that a problem?

ERIC: Actually I'm trying to quit—

KEVIN: Shit, man. Me too. What's that line from *Airplane*—Lloyd Bridges says?

ERIC: I picked the wrong week to quit smoking?

KEVIN: Yeah—yeah—yeah. I picked the wrong month to quit smoking. Ha ha ha…

(KEVIN wanders over to the window. Some car honking is heard.)

KEVIN: So how's the noise?

ERIC: You know…New York. It's loud but you get used to it.

KEVIN: That's cool. I'm a New Yorker, man. I'm used to it.

ERIC: How long you been here?

KEVIN: About a year and a half.

ERIC: They say you need to be here at least two years to be a real New Yorker.

KEVIN: Not me. The minute I got here I was here, you know what I mean?

ERIC: *(Oooo-kay.)* Yeah… so where are you living now?

KEVIN: Nowheres. Just going from couch to couch.

ERIC: You have a job then?

KEVIN: Shit yeah. What do you think I'm some kinda bum?

ERIC: No it's just that—

KEVIN: Just kidding. Just kidding. I gotta great job. I manage a trucking company over in Jersey City. It's my uncle's business and I've been running it for him since the beginning of the year. It's a great fucking job, man. But these days, I just don't have a place to rest my weary ass. *(Spies an ashtray hidden behind a box that is filled with butts. He uses it to put his out.)* Quittin's going well…

ERIC: Better than last week… So you don't have an apartment now.

KEVIN: My place was down in Battery Park City.

ERIC: Oh—

KEVIN: Shouldn't say "was." It's still there, they just won't let us in yet. They told us that all the units are covered in dust. This layer of toxic crap on everything.

ERIC: Were you there when it happened?

KEVIN: No—thank God. I would have fucking freaked out! Not that I didn't freak out anyway. But I would have lost my shit if I was there. It's two blocks away, man. Fuck.

ERIC: So you'd already left for work?

KEVIN: Naw. I was in Jersey City. Had stayed there for a date Monday night. To meet this chick.

ERIC: *(Sorta shocked.)* Oh…

KEVIN: Uhhhm—you gay?

ERIC: Uh…yeah, but—

KEVIN: The ad didn't come out and say it but I can read between the lines. Clean, quiet, responsible, seeks *male… Gay!*

ERIC: *(Amused.)* Well…gay as charged.

KEVIN: Gay as charged. That's a good one, man.

ERIC: Uh…thanks. So…you were having this date…

KEVIN: Yeah—yeah—yeah—I'd met this girl Saturday night at a pool hall up on Nineteenth. So we made plans to hook up at the mall in Jersey City that Monday.

ERIC: How romantic.

KEVIN: I like going to the mall for dates. Grew up in the 'burbs so I'm kinda nostalgic for the mall scene. So we met at the food court and got some sandwiches at Arby's, strolled around, and then headed back to her place in J.C.

ERIC: Sounds like a pretty successful first date.

KEVIN: Yeah—this chick was hot!

ERIC: Do you do that a lot?

KEVIN: Naw—I'm not into lots of one-night things usually. It's cool to have guests here, every now and then, right?

ERIC: Uh…sure.

KEVIN: Oh cool. Cool. 'Cause I do like to have guests…a few, you know, at least two every weekend. One Friday, one Saturday. *(A beat.)* Just kidding. Just kidding.

ERIC: *(Not.)* Funny. So you were at this "chick's" place when everything happened?

KEVIN: Yeah—we woke up and had sex a couple times. It was sooo hot, man. She had these amazing tits that were— *(Sees he's losing his audience.)* Anyway, so she gets out of bed and turns the TV on and they're saying that some plane hit the World Trade Center. I'm thinking, you know, like a prop plane or something.

ERIC: That's what everyone thought.

KEVIN: Right—and she's convinced it's like a bigger plane 'cause of all the smoke. But I'm like how could a serious-sized plane with commercial pilots make that kinda mistake. The sky was crystal clear— so my theory was that it was some drunk in a prop plane. And so we're arguing about it when bam. Right there on the TV, the other plane hits. Right there. Bam. Like an answer to our argument. Then I start freaking out about my apartment building. So we got some clothes on and went down to the waterfront and were there for, I don't know, ten minutes when we saw the first one come down. That was fucking insane! I'm standing there, looking at my apartment building as this huge grey cloud just swallows it. The place disappeared. For a while there, I thought it was gone, you know…just crushed or something. I was sorta losing it you know. Thinking…man, there goes everything.

(KEVIN grows unexpectedly quiet and seems a little lost. Nervously, ERIC tries to change the subject.)

ERIC: So whattya think of the place? Do you like it?

KEVIN: Sure. Long as we can get along. Let's see…uh, are drugs a problem?

ERIC: What?

KEVIN: I smoke pot sometimes. Is that cool?

ERIC: *(Not really but…)* Well…uh, sure.

KEVIN: Cool. Cool. I mean sometimes, I'll do a little coke. Some crystal too. Maybe some speed— *(A beat.)* Just kidding. Just kidding.

ERIC: You're a real kidder, huh?

KEVIN: *(Seriously.)* Yeah. But seriously, the pot's cool, right?

ERIC: *(On balance…)* Uhmm…sure.

KEVIN: You can have some too if you want.

ERIC: *(Shaking his head.)* Makes me paranoid. Which I definitely don't need these days.

KEVIN: That's cool. Just wanted to be friendly. If I'm gonna have a roommate, I wanna be friends with them, you know, hanging out. You like to hang out?

ERIC: *(Fudging.)* Well…my schedule can be pretty busy sometimes.

KEVIN: Relax. I don't mean like *every* night, man.

ERIC: Oh. *(A relieved beat.)* Yeah. That would be...cool.

KEVIN: Cool. Cool. We'll get along then. *(An anxious, pacing beat.)* So...how'm I doing?

ERIC: Huh?

KEVIN: I think it's going good. We can get along, right?

ERIC: I guess I—

KEVIN: I like to get along with my room-mates. It's a necessity in this city. And now, with all that's going on, it's really impor-tant. I mean, we're at fucking war man. So when you come home, you know, you gotta be able to have some peace. I mean people are dead out there. *Thousands* of 'em. Right on my fucking doorstep. That's some intense shit. And I just need some goddamn peace in my life right now, you know what I mean?

(KEVIN is looking at ERIC, seeming a little crazed. ERIC looks away.)

ERIC: So...what happened with that girl in Jersey City?

KEVIN: Huh? Oh—*her*? Nothing.

ERIC: Nothing?

KEVIN: It was supposed to be a date, you know. A fling thing. Then I got stuck out there. The PATH was gone, the ferries out, tunnels closed. I couldn't get back into the city til Friday. So it became this endless three-day relationship. A fucking nightmare.

ERIC: But you spent the eleventh with her...

KEVIN: And the twelfth, thirteenth, and fourteenth. *(A beat.)* That was the prob-lem, man. It was all too insane. I mean where can a relationship go from there?

ERIC: I was at my boyfriend's for that whole week.

KEVIN: Whoa—you gotta boyfriend?

ERIC: No. Did I say that?

KEVIN: It's cool...that's cool.

ERIC: He's my "*ex*" boyfriend. I can't be-lieve I said that.

KEVIN: You stayed at your ex's place?

ERIC: For a whole week.

KEVIN: Man—*that* sounds like a night-mare.

ERIC: He was insistent. Practically dragged me out of here.

KEVIN: So you were here when it happened?

ERIC: Oh yeah—saw the whole thing out that window.

KEVIN: Shit...it must have been fuck-ing crazy being this close.

ERIC: It was a scene down here. The neighborhood was like some kinda war zone; all these FBI and police vans and fire trucks and dump trucks. Parked in front of my building!

KEVIN: Yeah?

ERIC: *(Uncharacteristic outburst.)* Oh my God—that's when I started, you know, freaking out a bit. I mean...seeing all that, in front of your house. These camouflage soldiers and tanks—

KEVIN: *(Semi-unnerved.)* Tanks?!

ERIC: *(More hysterical.)* I mean the Na-tional Guard was sitting on my stoop, with semi-automatic rifles! That were *loaded*. With live ammunition—

(The phone rings, interrupting this rant.)

ERIC: Hello! Uh…Warren? Hi… yeah… I'm showing it today. *(He checks his watch.)* Uh sure—that would be good. Great. See you then! *(Hangs up and turns to KEVIN.)* Sorry—I got another person coming over in ten minutes.

KEVIN: Boy you're just bringing 'em in and kicking 'em out. *(A beat.)* Jus' kiddin', jus' kiddin'. So, uh, I'll give you a call tomorrow?

ERIC: Uh…sure.

KEVIN: Cool—I really dig the place. You seem cool.

ERIC: Uh…thanks.

KEVIN: I think this could work. I hope so, man. It's two weeks and I still don't have anywhere to go. My back is fucking killing me from all these couches. I just wanna—I wanna go home, you know.

ERIC: I know what you mean.

KEVIN: But you've got a home. Your place is still here and you survived fuckin' intact.

ERIC: Looks that way, doesn't it? *(A beat.)* It just doesn't feel like the same place…I probably shouldn't complain.

KEVIN: Yeah. You shouldn't.

ERIC: Hey—I'm really sorry about your apartment.

KEVIN: Yeah…thanks, man. *(A beat.)* Fucking Osama. At least we're gonna kick his ass now, man.

ERIC: You think they'll actually get him?

KEVIN: If they do, I wanna be the first in line to fuckin' kick him in the balls. *(A beat.)* Well…peace man.

ERIC: Yeah…Peace.

(Blackout.)

SCENE 4

In darkness, the ANSWERING MACHINE is heard.

ANSWERING MACHINE: Wednesday, 10:52 a.m.

VICTOR: *(Voiceover.)* Hey—this is Victor. Thanks for showing me the place yesterday. I've been looking around all over the city at tons of places but I found somewhere that was a little more…reasonable over in the East Village. Seems like there are some real bargains out there now. But good luck. I'm sure you'll find someone. It's a great location! Well…take care and God bless.

ANSWERING MACHINE: Wednesday, 1:08 p.m.

KEVIN: *(Voiceover.)* Hey—what's up…it's Kevin. Uh, just wanted to let you know I don't think I'll be moving in. That girl in Jersey City called and said I can stay with her for a bit. Can you fucking believe it? I mean, she's kinda insane but at least it's a bed, right? Anyway, thanks for showing me the joint. Peace.

(Lights up on the empty apartment. ERIC is sitting on the floor, closing up some of the boxes. He is now wearing an unbuttoned long-sleeved shirt over his T-shirt, something from J.Crew with stripes.)

ANSWERING MACHINE: Wednesday, 2:31 p.m.

JEFF: *(Voiceover.)* Hey—Jeff Stone here, from Mark Green's campaign. We talked this morning. Anyway, I've gotta finish up some TV spots today. But I should be done around three or so…maybe I can pop over then. Call me on my cell 646-321-8500 or you can send me a text message…Jeff@Green2001.org. That's 2-0-0-1-dot-org. Okay—see you later!

(The buzzer is heard, and ERIC gets it.)

ERIC: Hey—come on up. The door's open!

(A moment later, JEFF enters the room, his outstretched hand leading the way. He is wearing a collar shirt and a tie but not a proper coat, just a windbreaker.)

JEFF: *(Shaking vigorously.)* Jeff Stone. Nice to meet you.

ERIC: Hi—Eric.

JEFF: So this is the room?

ERIC: Yep.

JEFF: I'll just take a look around.

ERIC: *(A look around?)* Okay…

(JEFF starts to inspect the room as if he works for the city or something. Checking up close the floor and the walls, touching them, marking off the square footage, etc. ERIC watches him somewhat bemused.)

ERIC: So…you're working for Mark Green.

JEFF: That's right.

ERIC: I voted for him.

JEFF: *(Stops inspecting.)* Really? On the eleventh?

ERIC: Yeah. After the second plane.

JEFF: That's…uhm…you're a serious voter.

ERIC: I'm a big believer in voting.

JEFF: Even during a crisis.

ERIC: *Especially* during a crisis. Once I'd figured out what was going on, that it was this terrorist thing, I got all determined and American about it—like, I'm not gonna let them try to stop me from voting.

JEFF: When I heard it was terrorists, I thought they'd done it deliberately to disrupt the election.

ERIC: You know, I thought it was deliberate too. Part of the whole attack…that's why I went to vote.

JEFF: I'm surprised you got to cast it. I heard most of the polling places downtown were chaos.

ERIC: It wasn't easy. The old ladies who flip through the registration books…they couldn't even find my street. And they live here! They were pretending not to be bothered but you could tell, they were losing it just like everyone else.

JEFF: They must not have been losing it too much. They found your street…

ERIC: Eventually. And I did cast my vote for democracy…which in the end didn't even count.

JEFF: Just like the presidential race.

ERIC: Touché.

JEFF: Just make sure to vote next time. It'll count and we'll need it…Bloomberg is getting a major bounce just because he's a Republican.

ERIC: Ugh—I can't stand Bloomberg. He seems kinda dippy you know?

JEFF: Really—interesting. Why? *(Gets out his Palm Pilot and takes a note.)*

ERIC: I don't know. He just does—hard to explain.

JEFF: *(Thinking out loud.)* Dippy…good. We can use that.

ERIC: So what do you do for the campaign?

JEFF: I got sent up here to work on their media strategies team.

ERIC: From where?

JEFF: Oh—I was in Washington, working for the DNC. Got the call a couple weeks ago and here I am.

ERIC: They called in the reinforcements, huh?

JEFF: Yeah—suddenly the campaign went from tough to impossible. It's hard now to say anything against the Republicans in general. Bin Laden's done more for the popularity of the Republican party than Ronald Reagan.

ERIC: And that's saying something.

(JEFF seems to be done walking around the perimeter of the room and inspecting it for imperfections.)

JEFF: Well—the place looks great. What's the rent again?

ERIC: It's…it's a thousand.

JEFF: What a steal…five hundred each!

ERIC: Sorry. It's a thousand each. It used to be five hundred each a while ago. But then—

JEFF: Lemme guess…Giuliani?

ERIC: Yep. Turned it around…too much so.

JEFF: I have to say…cleaning up the city is probably the *one* thing Giuliani did that was worthwhile. I grew up here and, back then, the place was a disaster.

ERIC: Where did you live?

JEFF: My parents had a loft on Broadway.

ERIC: Wow—is it still there?

JEFF: *(Shaking his head.)* Old Navy. But I can't complain. SoHo's nice now. There's things to do. You should've seen this place in the seventies. It was desolate. On the weekends, we used to play football on Broadway, Spring was one end zone and Prince was the other. And there was no traffic. One time I was streaking down the sideline and Mike threw me this long bomb and I was about to score when I tripped over a homeless guy. New York sorta stopped at Fourteenth Street back then and picked up south of Canal. In the seventies, everyone just fled…

ERIC: I've been wondering if the eleventh might be having the same effect.

JEFF: I don't think people are that freaked out.

ERIC: Usually, the first or second person I'd see would be writing a check on the spot. You're like the tenth and still…

JEFF: Maybe everyone's feeling… uncertain.

ERIC: I'm certain of one thing. I'm not gonna let this drive me outta the city. I mean, where would I go, to one of the boroughs?

JEFF: Oh man—you don't wanna do that.

ERIC: I know—everyone's all like Astoria is affordable, Williamsburg is soooo cool. But if I wanted to live in the suburbs and commute into Manhattan, I'd move back in with my parents.

JEFF: I feel the same way. Manhattan or bust.

ERIC: Otherwise…what's the point.

JEFF: What's the point…exactly.

ERIC: I mean Brooklyn…it's so damn quiet out there.

JEFF: You go out there a lot?

ERIC: Not anymore, thank God. My ex is there.

JEFF: Ah…

ERIC: Do you have an ex…or a current… or…whatever.

JEFF: Uh no. Not seeing anyone now. Too busy with the campaign.

ERIC: I mean, if you did that's fine. Girl-friends or boyfriends…they're fine.

JEFF: Except yours.

ERIC: He's fine. Just not right now.

(There is an awkward moment here, post-boyfriend. JEFF looks at the window and walks over toward it.)

JEFF: Have you been down there yet?

ERIC: No. Definitely not. *(A remembering beat.)* Last time I was down there was about a month before the eleventh. A few weeks after the breakup I went with a friend of mine on a shopping spree.

JEFF: Century 21?

ERIC: Oh yeah. I think we were the only New Yorkers there… it was August and the city was empty. Except for French tourists. I got some underwear and socks super cheap. That made me feel a lot better. It was a crummy day out, rainy and humid, so then we wandered around the underground shopping mall, got some summer clearance stuff at J.Crew. I bought this shirt there…my last purchase. *(Touches the shirt, thinking.)* Later it cleared up and we got some Krispy Kremes and just sat on that big awful plaza eating donuts and checking out all the hot French guys. God—that was such a nice lame afternoon. Who woulda ever thought that shopping at a mall would be so… evocative.

JEFF: We had an event down there yesterday with Mark and some of the firefighters.

ERIC: God—that must have been creepy.

JEFF: The strangest thing though…there were tons of people down there. Not at the site but as close as they can get, at Broadway and Chambers Street.

ERIC: That is just so…bizarre.

JEFF: I don't know how effective our event was. Those people weren't there to meet Mark, even with the firemen around. They were just there…looking.

ERIC: What is there to see?

JEFF: Not much actually. For two hundred and twenty stories there really isn't much left. From where I was standing, I could see a pile of rubble about fifty feet—

(ERIC's mood changes abruptly, and he turns away from JEFF.)

JEFF: Sorry—did I…

ERIC: Can we not talk about this?

JEFF: Sure. Sorry. *(A beat.)* Here I am blabbin' on like an idiot about our dumb photo op…

ERIC: It's your job. I'm sure the campaign is all about getting good images. I'm a photographer myself.

JEFF: Professionally?

ERIC: Not for the media or anything. I mainly do headshots, stills on movie sets, promotional stuff for TV shows.

JEFF: Wow—that sounds exciting.

ERIC: It used to be…but now…I don't know.

JEFF: I think everyone's having doubts about their day job lately.

ERIC: It's more than doubts. I mean, a couple days after everything, I seriously considered joining the Air Force.

JEFF: *(Laughing.)* Really?

ERIC: Why is that so funny?

JEFF: I don't know…it's just…it seems like a big leap from still photography to the armed forces.

ERIC: I guess it was a crazy idea. But the fact that I even thought it. Me...flying some jet plane around— *(A smiling beat.)* Alright...it is pretty hysterical.

JEFF: After everything happened, all I wanted to do was get back here.

ERIC: Really—why?

JEFF: All I kept thinking that day was that I wanted to be in New York. I mean I know D.C. had— but this is home.

ERIC: Believe me—you should be thankful you missed it.

JEFF: Maybe... but having grown up here I felt like I had to get back as soon as possible. It was like there had been a death in the family. I mean, I didn't know anyone who was killed. But that's exactly what it felt like. So when this job came up, I jumped at it. Even though I had nowhere to live here anymore...my parents moved up to Woodstock years ago. But I just had to be here, you know...back home.

ERIC: But don't you think being here now... it's just so depressing.

JEFF: It can be. But still...at least now I feel like I'm part of everything that's happening, for better or for worse. That's what I wanted—to be here, doing something constructive, keeping democracy rolling along. Geez—that sounds corny but... that's what this is all about, isn't it? The fact that this is my job, helping people get elected—in New York even—must drive them crazy. So it's the least I can do, right? *(Picks up his BlackBerry pager. There is a message.)* Sorry—gotta get back to the office. New polls came in.

ERIC: Oh... is there anything else you wanted to know?

JEFF: Other than ways to reduce the rent—

ERIC: Uh, I don't think—

JEFF: Actually, I think this could work out. And I really need something quick. Since I got here, I've just been sleeping at campaign headquarters.

ERIC: On what?

JEFF: The floor.

ERIC: Ouch!

JEFF: It's not so bad. There's a relatively new carpet and the desk is over my head. I pull a few filing cabinets over to block the light and it's almost cozy. Sorta like camping but not as much fun...Anyway, this is a great place and you seem like a relatively normal and sane guy.

ERIC: Relative to what?

JEFF: What's going on in the world, of course.

ERIC: *(Nervously stumbling.)* Oh good— yeah I'm fine. I mean, I—I'm much better. I mean, I'm gonna be—

(JEFF is checking his pager again, tapping something into it, and doesn't notice ERIC's bit of nervousness here.)

JEFF: So when do you need to know?

ERIC: Uh...as soon as possible?

JEFF: I'm swamped in the next few days...how 'bout we talk on Friday.

ERIC: *(Unsure.)* Uh...okay. I don't know if I can hold it...

JEFF: Well if it's still open, let's talk then...and don't forget to vote.

ERIC: As long as I'm here, I'll be voting.

JEFF: Where you going?

ERIC: Nowhere...gallows humor.

JEFF: Right—understandable these days.

ERIC: A necessity.

(JEFF exits the door on stage right. Black-out.)

SCENE 5

In darkness, the ANSWERING MA-CHINE is heard.

ANSWERING MACHINE: Wednesday, 9:46 p.m.

WILL: *(Voiceover.)* Hey—Will here. Just wanted to see how the roommate hunt is going. Maybe you should try Rainbow Roommates. Now I know it sounds kinda gay, but a friend of mine here at work used them and found a decent professional roommate in a couple days. Anyway… give it a shot. And if it doesn't work out I can always move in. Okay—that was a joke. Alright, maybe half-joking. Call me!

ANSWERING MACHINE: Thursday, 3:12 p.m.

JOEY: *(Voiceover.)* Hi Joey again! From Rainbow Roommates?! Anywho, the place looked fabulous and I looooove that neighborhood. It's so neighborhood-y? But you won't believe this! Remember that audition for the road company of *Beauty and the Beast* I had— I got the part!? Ahhh—can you believe it?! Sorry I'm spazzing all over your little machine! I just found out and didn't want to leave you hanging. You were a super sweet guy, really, and I'm sure you'll find the most amazing roommate! Bye!!!

(Lights up inside the apartment. It is evening outside the window. JOSIE enters and crosses to the window. She is holding a small brown paper bag. As the answering machine plays, she reacts to the next crazy message.)

ANSWERING MACHINE: Thursday, 6:28 p.m.

CARLOS: *(Voiceover.)* Buenos dias—it's your landlord calling for my formerly fa-vorite tenant. What's going on with the rent, amigo? I need to get this squared away…it's going on two weeks now. And the first is coming up. Roommate or no, I got bills to pay. And I need money…real American money. Not Canadian. Not Español. What is that song goes… *(Sing-ing, landlord style.)* Money makes the world go round, the world go round, the world go round. *(A beat.)* Call me and let me know when I can expect that check. Goodbye.

JOSIE: It's still smoking…

ERIC: *(Offstage.)* Yeah…

JOSIE: It's like enough already. We get it, you know. But there it is…still smoking. I mean can't they stop it?

ERIC: *(Offstage.)* It stops. Then they re-move stuff and oxygen gets in and it starts again.

(ERIC enters the room.)

JOSIE: You still smoking?

ERIC: If it's still smoking, I'm still smok-ing.

JOSIE: Okay—that was beyond tasteless.

ERIC: Sorry. My sense of humor is a little off these days.

JOSIE: Seriously…I don't know how can you still *live* down here. Maybe you should think about getting a place uptown. Near us.

ERIC: Eighty-Second Street?! I get nose-bleeds above Fourteenth.

JOSIE: Sure but—you still haven't found a roommate. And what about the land-lord?

ERIC: He's fine.

JOSIE: He didn't sound fine. Do you need me to lend you money?

ERIC: No—he's always getting on my case, jibing me like that. It's a power play thing, you know. Like he's in charge.

JOSIE: Eric—he *is* in charge.

ERIC: He's not gonna throw me out or anything. I'm his favorite tenant…

JOSIE: Former favorite…

ERIC: He was joking, okay?

JOSIE: If you need help—

ERIC: It's fine. I'm fine.

(JOSIE looks him over. Clearly, he's not looking so fine.)

JOSIE: Did you call that 800 number yet?

ERIC: *(Sharp.)* Do you think I wouldn't have told you if I did?

JOSIE: Jesus…forget I asked.

ERIC: So what's in the bag? More *food?*

JOSIE: Sorta. You sounded a little desolate on the phone so I thought I'd cheer you up.

ERIC: *(Opens the bag. He smiles broadly.)* Cupcakes. From Magnolia?

JOSIE: Only the finest in refined sugar for you.

ERIC: You're so sweet.

JOSIE: Ba-dump.

(ERIC takes one and starts eating. Heaven for a minute. Then—)

JOSIE: So—have you talked to Will?

ERIC: *(Eating.)* Mmmm…every day.

JOSIE: Wait a minute—you guys are talking every day now?

ERIC: On the phone. It's no big deal.

JOSIE: Who calls who?

ERIC: I don't know…I guess he usually calls me.

JOSIE: That's good.

ERIC: Josie, we are not getting back together.

JOSIE: Did I say that?

ERIC: He's worried about me finding a roommate. That's all.

JOSIE: Still—his concern is sweet.

ERIC: He's just having ex-boyfriend guilt. I'm just having survivor's guilt. How 'bout you?

JOSIE: I'm having no-sex guilt.

ERIC: You had another fight with David?

JOSIE: Not exactly.

ERIC: So you discussed the sex thing?

JOSIE: He did. At a party.

ERIC: Again?!

JOSIE: Yeah—Becky had some people over for cocktails last night. We were standing around in the kitchen having a civil conversation about some *New Yorker* article about how everyone's relationships right now seem to be either falling apart or coming together. And then my charming husband just offers up, you know, says right outta the blue—"Yeah, kinda like us not having had sex this month."

ERIC: Whoa.

JOSIE: He'd had a few drinks and—

ERIC: That's no excuse.

JOSIE: Beck's face just blanched.

ERIC: That is so out of bounds.

JOSIE: And then as I'm standing there, stunned, he kinda gave me this look of, aha—*that* got ya! Which is just so unnecessary.

ERIC: And totally wrong...discussing that in front of your friends?

JOSIE: The stupid thing is that he just won't come out and say it.

ERIC: Well...it sounds like that's exactly what he did.

JOSIE: No. The sex is more of a symptom.

ERIC: What's the problem then?

JOSIE: Kids.

ERIC: But I thought you'd decided...

JOSIE: That we'd wait. Til he gets promoted, til we can get a house, til we're both a little older so we don't fuck up our kids the way our parents fucked us up.

ERIC: And now he's changed his mind... post-everything?

JOSIE: Yep. Suddenly *his* clock is ticking.

ERIC: *Everyone's* clock is ticking...

JOSIE: Except mine. If anything, I'm more ambivalent about doing this now... especially now.

ERIC: Really?

JOSIE: Okay, first off I don't wanna have some tacky, patriotic 9/11 baby along with the rest of the city. The maternity wards are going to be packed come June. And they'll probably be giving out flags instead of cigars. I mean I love my country but this flag stuff everywhere. It's like living in Texas. I mean really— is this any world to bring a child into?

ERIC: No. But remember our fucked-up parents?

JOSIE: How can we forget...

ERIC: It was 1968 when we were born... Robert Kennedy...Martin Luther King... all the riots...the Chicago Convention. Vietnam...and Richard Nixon *won*! It was an insane time.

JOSIE: Maybe they were totally high or something and didn't even think about what the fuck they were doing.

ERIC: Your parents...maybe. Mine were in Delaware. Not much weed being passed around the PTA meetings.

JOSIE: They had weed in Delaware!

ERIC: Irrelevant. So the bottom line here is you don't wanna get pregnant right now?

JOSIE: *(Hesitating.)* More or less.

ERIC: More or less...whaddya—

JOSIE: Wait a minute——don't tell me that you, of all people, are going to try and convince me that I should have a child?

ERIC: Why not— I mean you said you wanted to have kids eventually. Maybe this is eventually.

JOSIE: This is now. Eventually is... eventually.

ERIC: Josie—

JOSIE: *(Like a parlor game.)* Give me one good reason why I should have a kid now. Go! Go!!!

ERIC: Uh...uhmmm...Jesus Josie... okay... *(An "aha" beat.)* Okay—you know how I'm always saying that I wanna be a fake uncle, like people calling me "Uncle Eric" when I'm not related at all and then the kid being totally confused and wondering, when he gets older, why he thought this strange gay guy was his uncle when clearly there's no blood relation whatever and the only reason he was being called "uncle" was because his mom thought it was cute to have her best friend be quasi-related to her baby?

JOSIE: Ranting...

ERIC: That's a pretty good ranty-reason.

JOSIE: It's pretty Hallmark when you boil it down a bit.

ERIC: I was trying to disguise it...thus the rant.

JOSIE: *(Almost to herself.)* Your rants are *always* meant to disguise something.

ERIC: What do you mean?

JOSIE: C'mon Eric...whenever you're getting all emotional about something you try to cover it up with some crazily worded rant.

ERIC: I do?

JOSIE: Ohmigod—especially in the last month. You have been rant central. That's why I'm worried about you.

ERIC: But I'm fine...

JOSIE: You say that. But I always have this sense that... I don't know. You're hiding something.

ERIC: *(Heavy sigh.)* Great.

JOSIE: What? So...you are?

ERIC: That's exactly what Will said.

JOSIE: Eric...I didn't talk to Will about this. I haven't talked to him since the night of the eleventh. But honestly, that's what I've been worried about. That you've gone through all this crap—all of this incredibly sad stuff. And you don't seem sad. Just, I don't know, a little further away...

ERIC: I am sad. I mean everyone's sad, right? It's like a given right now.

(ERIC turns away from her, back to the window and concentrates on his cupcake. JOSIE,

seeming a little unnerved, looks at him and notices some of his things on the floor; the cordless phone, a book, about six deli cups of coffee, a full ashtray.)

JOSIE: How much sleep did you get last night?

ERIC: Mmmmmmm...these cupcakes are amazing.

JOSIE: Eric—when did you get up today?

ERIC: *(Indicating bag.)* Can I have yours?

JOSIE: No and answer my goddamn question.

ERIC: I don't know...early.

JOSIE: And when did you go to sleep?

ERIC: I don't know...late?

JOSIE: You stayed up again, pulling an anxiety all-nighter. Smoking and drinking coffee and watching the news.

ERIC: I still don't get any channels.

JOSIE: God—that's even worse...just sitting around by yourself.

ERIC: I listened to NPR.

JOSIE: Public radio doesn't make it any better.

ERIC: It was only last night, really.

JOSIE: What happened last night?

ERIC: I...I heard some sirens.

JOSIE: We live in Manhattan. There are always sirens.

ERIC: But now—

JOSIE: Nothing is gonna happen, Eric. The worst is over.

ERIC: We're at war, Josie.

JOSIE: With who? The Taliban?! They don't even have an army...they have *camels*. And those probably don't even work.

ERIC: They don't need an army. They're here. In sleeper cells. Waiting for a signal to kill more people. Just yesterday a guy in Florida died of anthrax. Anthrax! What about that?

JOSIE: Anthrax?! What the hell does that have to do with anything?! It was in the fucking Everglades or something. In the middle of nowhere. What—you think there's gonna be some sort of anthrax attack here?

(Nervous "yes" silence.)

JOSIE: Okay—now you're not only being paranoid but you're missing the point.

ERIC: Let the tutorial begin... "The point of terrorism is to—"

JOSIE: Is to inflict *terror*. The only weapon they had was surprise. And they got their one great shot to do it. What was it Dan Rather said, they lost the war the minute that second plane hit. That was it. Game over.

ERIC: Thank you professor. But when I'm in bed, trying to sleep and I hear a bunch of sirens wailing I tend to think the worst. It's how the whole thing began for me. Hearing all those sirens, a thousand sirens going off. It was infinite sirens to the nth degree.

JOSIE: But can't you tell when it's just one siren, not a thousand.

ERIC: It's never one siren.

JOSIE: Alright—there's still a difference between three sirens and three thousand sirens.

ERIC: Not at three-thirty in the morning!

(JOSIE gives up arguing this point. She turns and looks at the dresser and stuff in the room.)

JOSIE: You know what the problem is?

ERIC: Uh—you won't let me have your cupcake?

JOSIE: You've gotta get this stuff outta here. Wasn't Will gonna take the dresser?

ERIC: Maybe. He thinks it's ugly.

JOSIE: Once you get this old stuff out and get a new roommate I'm sure you'll feel a lot better. Instantly.

ERIC: The trick now is actually getting the new roommate.

JOSIE: There's no trick. And now that things are getting back to normal and—

ERIC: Face it Josie. Things are not getting back to normal—they can't.

JOSIE: That's bullshit. People are going on with their lives...

ERIC: Maybe above Fourteenth Street.

JOSIE: And don't give me your whole downtown-DMZ rant...you act like Fourteenth Street is the friggin' Berlin Wall.

ERIC: *(Hysterical.)* Oh please—people up there have *no* idea. None!

JOSIE: Okay—you're getting hysterical again.

ERIC: Look—have you seen things getting back to normal down here? *Have* you?

JOSIE: Of course.

ERIC: Of course?! Are you kidding? Have you noticed the "missing" flyers everywhere. Or the candles in front of every fire station. Or maybe the heavily armed storm troopers on every corner. *(Challeng-*

ing.) Give me one back-to-normal example. Go!

JOSIE: Okay—let's see. Uh…yesterday, I was coming out of the Mercer Hotel when this supermodel stole my cab, right out from under me.

ERIC: What did you do?

JOSIE: I called her a fashionista cunt.

ERIC: But did she call you anything *back*?

JOSIE: Jesus!

ERIC: Aha!

(The phone rings, interrupting their argument. JOSIE checks her watch.)

JOSIE: Who is that at eleven-thirty at night?

ERIC: I don't know. Let's take a look. *(Picks up the phone and looks at the caller ID.)*

JOSIE: Is it Will?

ERIC: Definitely not.

(JOSIE looks at the caller ID on ERIC's prompting.)

JOSIE: What the hell is the "Triple X-Pony"?

ERIC: A video bookstore on West Street.

JOSIE: A porn store!?

ERIC: A full-service gay porn store.

JOSIE: They still have those?

ERIC: *(Picks up the phone and answers.)* Hello—yes—yes— oh hi Alex. Yeah—I remember. Right. Uh-huh. Tonight? Yeah. It's in SoHo. Uh—okay. Twelve, sounds good. See you then.

JOSIE: Who the hell is Alex?

ERIC: *(Nonchalant.)* Guy coming to see the apartment.

JOSIE: *(Imitating.)* Oh… "Guy coming to see the apartment." *(A beat.)* Try freaky porn-fiend coming over to rape you.

ERIC: Josie—I talked to him earlier today. He wants to see the place.

JOSIE: At midnight?!

ERIC: It's not like I can afford to turn anyone away. I have to decide by tomorrow.

JOSIE: You know what, sometimes caller ID is more than *anyone* needs to know.

(ERIC springs into action, handing JOSIE the cupcake bag and starting to hustle her toward the door.)

ERIC: Well…thanks for the cupcakes and cheer.

JOSIE: Wait—I'm leaving?

ERIC: He's gonna be here in ten minutes. I gotta clean up.

JOSIE: But can't I meet him?

ERIC: Josie—

JOSIE: I can help you decide.

ERIC: Lately the only thing that helps them decide is the rent.

JOSIE: Alright. But don't let him bargain you down.

ERIC: Even if he offers me his body?

JOSIE: Maybe I should stay.

ERIC: Goodnight Josie.

(He turns her toward the door.)

JOSIE: Why can't I stay?

ERIC: Because you don't live here.

JOSIE: Call me tomorrow. I wanna know everything.

ERIC: Josie—it's not a date. It's a potential roommate.

JOSIE: Let's hope so.

ERIC: Goodnight. And get home safe.

JOSIE: *(Stopping.)* Alright— you never used to say that before.

ERIC: And *don't* take the subway!

(Blackout.)

SCENE 6

In darkness, the ANSWERING MA-CHINE is heard.

ANSWERING MACHINE: Friday, 12:32 a.m.

ALEX: *(Voiceover.)* Hi—Alex down here on the corner. Oh—I hope it's not too late to see the apartment. I think I'm lost but—oh wait, that's it right here. I thought I was—okay never mind. I'll see you in a sec.

(The buzzer goes off and the lights go up. ERIC is sitting on the floor reading a maga-zine and drinking a big traveler mug of cof-fee. He gets up and hits the intercom.)

ERIC: Yeah?

ALEX: *(Offstage.)* It's Alex.

ERIC: Okay—come on in. Third floor.

(ERIC hits the buzzer. Using the window as a mirror, he takes a look at his appearance; he is dressed in jeans and the J.Crew shirt over a white tanktop. He seems dissatisfied with this look. He fixes his hair, unbuttons a few buttons, and looks in the window again. Still not good. He takes the shirt off and untucks the tanktop. Looks in the window—good. He then rushes offstage again to un-lock the door, which we can hear. He comes back into the room and starts to move things around, to make it look like he's been work-ing in the room. A knock is heard.)

ERIC: 'S open!

ALEX: *(Offstage.)* Hello?

ERIC: Back here…

ALEX: *(Offstage.)* Hellooo?

ERIC: Back. Here.

(ALEX enters the room somewhat tentatively. He is young, eager, and a very sharply put-together corporate kind of guy, wearing a fit-ted suit with Regis tie. He notices ERIC in his tanktop and feels slightly embarrassed.)

ALEX: Hey—

ERIC: Hi—just trying to clean up in here a little.

ALEX: Is this a bad time to—

ERIC: Oh no. No. It's fine. You're fine. *(He didn't just say that.)* I mean…come on in.

(They check each other out. There is some real chemistry here between them. It makes for an awkward moment of silence which they both try to fill.)

ERIC: So—

ALEX: So—

ALEX: Sorry I'm so late.

ERIC: 'S okay. I'm a bit of a night owl lately. *(Trying to ask innocently.)* So what's keepin' you up tonight?

ALEX: Oh…uh…just working late. So…this is the room then?

ERIC: Yep—uh, let's see. There's a cable hookup there. And a phone jack in the corner. The A/C works if you want that too. I took it out so I could shut the window…the smell was getting to be—

ALEX: And how much is it?

ERIC: The A/C. It's free. The unit's been here for—

ALEX: No. How much is the rent?

ERIC: Oh. Uh…it's—it's about…eleven hundred?

ALEX: About?

ERIC: Plus utilities. Twenty in the winter. Forty or so in the summer. *(An anxious beat.)* So…would that work for you?

ALEX: Oh yeah. Definitely.

ERIC: Great. So…where do you work?

ALEX: I'm at Goldman Sachs…in the international bond division.

ERIC: Wow—sounds intriguing? *(Playful.)* Bond. International Bond.

ALEX: No…just boring numbers-crunching stuff. But it pays well.

ERIC: Thus the suit…

ALEX: This? I got it at Century 21.

ERIC: That place is great. Was great. But I heard it pretty much survived which is amazing being just across the street. I used to go there all the time…and the mall too. Got this shirt there, at the J.Crew store. God—it must be a mess down there, what's left of it. I can't even imag—

(ALEX does not want to talk about this stuff and heads toward the window.)

ALEX: Nice view…

ERIC: Oh. Yeah…it is pretty nice. Used to be… *(A beat.)* My old roommate said that I should put "WTC view" in the ad. He had just moved here from Ohio and couldn't believe the view. I thought that was cute because, you know, no one ever puts that in apartment ads. You see Empire State view all the time…it has some major value. But WTC view…it doesn't mean a thing. Didn't mean a… but he kept saying that I should put it in. He thought it'd be this big selling point. WTC view…

(ERIC laughs a bit at this. ALEX's mood shifts immediately, going somber, as he steps back from the window.)

ALEX: It's not something to joke about.

ERIC: Oh…I, uh…sorry.

ALEX: *(Notices all the boxes and stuff on the floor.)* So what's the deal with this stuff?

ERIC: My ex-boyfriend is gonna take the dresser.

ALEX: Oh—I'm sorry.

ERIC: You actually *want* the dresser?!

ALEX: No—about the ex. When did you break up?

ERIC: A couple months ago.

ALEX: And he still hasn't gotten his stuff?

ERIC: No. It's my roommate's stuff.

ALEX: But your roommate's not still here, right?

ERIC: Uh no…he's gone. *(Turns away from ALEX and plays with some boxes again.)*

ALEX: *(Almost proud.)* I just broke up with my boyfriend too.

ERIC: Oh…really? When did you guys break up?

ALEX: A couple weeks ago.

ERIC: At least you can blame it on Bin Laden.

(ERIC smiles on saying this, trying to be breezy. But ALEX has a stony-faced reaction.)

ALEX: That's really not funny.

ERIC: I'm sorry I—I just meant to say that all of this, everything that's happening—it's really affected people's relationships you know. It's making people do some pretty strange things. I mean my best friend isn't sleeping with her husband, people are having three-night one-night stands, ex-boyfriends are sleeping together and—

(ALEX starts smiling.)

ERIC: What?

ALEX: I can't believe we're talking about this sorta stuff.

ERIC: Well...we could talk about the Yankees. They're doing great and are a huge distraction for everybody.

ALEX: Alright. *(Giving up.)* You see...my ex, Larry, wanted us to move in together after the eleventh. But I didn't. So...that was it and we broke up.

ERIC: Funny. That's why me and Will broke up too. The moving-in issue. Not the eleventh... *(Anyway.)* So what was the problem with moving in for you?

ALEX: Larry and I had been going out for only a year and a half. I thought moving in at that point was way too soon.

ERIC: Me too. Maybe after two years... maybe.

ALEX: Right? And then, with everything that's happened recently, my life has totally changed. My priorities are different. Everything is so upside down, you know?

ERIC: Oh I know...

ALEX: And I can't ignore that and just pretend to go on like nothing happened.

ERIC: Having trouble getting "back to normal"?

ALEX: Exactly.

(They smile at each other, a sense of understanding. And maybe a sense of something more. Then, some sirens are heard, and ERIC heads toward the window.)

ERIC: Uh-oh...

ALEX: What?

ERIC: Does that sound like a lot of sirens?

ALEX: Uh—I don't know...

(ERIC heads over to the clock radio and turns it on.)

ALEX: What are you doing?

ERIC: Just wanna see what's going on.

(ERIC finds a music station, not a news station, playing a Britney Spears song. ERIC seems relieved, and ALEX looks at him puzzled.)

ALEX: How bout 1010 WINS?

ERIC: In an emergency, I always go for a pop station. If it's something really serious, they'll interrupt programming like on the eleventh. If not—Britney. *(An uneasy beat.)* Still—sounds like a lot of sirens. *(Goes back over to the window and looks out.)*

ALEX: When I first moved here, I'd call home and my parents were always like "Turn off the TV while we're on the phone" and I was like...that's not the TV, Mom, it's the East Village.

ERIC: Life here has always been pretty loud. But lately, it's insane. Have you heard the planes?

ALEX: Huh?

ERIC: The F-15s. They've got them on a constant patrol over the city. I heard them Sunday around four in the morning... shook my bed the sound was so loud. And

I don't understand why they're flying over Ground Zero... I mean, I think they're a little late, you know.

(ERIC laughs at bit at this joke and then looks at ALEX and notices that same blank, nervous expression from before. ERIC is mortified.)

ERIC: I did it again.

ALEX: You really like talking about it, huh?

ERIC: My friends think I talk about it too much.

ALEX: I mean you've gotta move on at some point.

ERIC: But until I reach that point...I think I have to talk about it. Read every article about it. Know every detail about it.

ALEX: I don't wanna know anything else. I saw enough on the eleventh.

ERIC: We all did.

ALEX: But for me it was... it's kinda freaky.

ERIC: So...where were you?

ALEX: I was there.

ERIC: There? You mean, right there?

ALEX: I was in Tower One.

(ERIC is speechless, mouth open, dumbfounded.)

ERIC: But...you...you got out.

ALEX: *(Duh.)* Well, yeah.

ERIC: Oh my God. So what—what happened? How did—

ALEX: I had no idea what was going on.

ERIC: But you were there...in the tower...what floor?

ALEX: Ninety-one.

ERIC: How's that possible? I mean, you were *right there*.

ALEX: I had an early meeting that morning to go over some new bonds. The meeting ended around quarter of nine and—

ERIC: That's right when the—how'd you get out?

ALEX: I was in the sky lobby and everyone was getting off the elevators, going to work. So I got in an empty elevator by myself and hit the lobby button. And I'm just standing there, whistling and looking at my feet...you know, elevator stuff. Then suddenly the whole thing comes to a stop and there's this huge whoosh of air then a low rumbling sound. And the lights and everything flicker off for a minute but then come back on. I tried to open the doors but they were stuck. And then I heard some voices coming from the speaker but it was all jumbled. Then there was another rumbling sound, not as big. After that I was beginning to think this is probably pretty serious but still I didn't know what was going on. A voice comes on the speaker that I can finally understand and says there's a fire and that someone's coming to get me. So I just stand there waiting. So I wait and wait and wait. No one comes. All I can see is this sliver of dusty light through the doors and I think maybe I should try to open them again. So I did and they opened. Just like that. I couldn't believe it but all that time I was in the lobby. On the ground floor. So I walk out and look around and all the windows are smashed and there's all this smoke but there are no people. I mean *no one* is around. So I walk out to the plaza and there is just—all this...luggage. Suitcases that are open and garment bags and business clothes and shoes...so many pairs of shoes. Then I hear this huge thump behind me—almost like a mini-explosion. And about twenty feet away is what I guess is a body...not 'cause it looks like one. But because of all the blood. So I look up and see two more coming down, holding up tablecloths as these makeshift parachutes that would work for a few seconds and then...don't. At that point I knew I should run but with all this carnage and things falling I didn't know where to go. I froze. Then, outta nowhere, I feel something on my wrist—something that's burning hot. I think I'm on fire for a minute, that some piece of something's hit me, but I turn around and there's this huge fireman grabbing me by the wrist and he starts running, dragging me behind him. I tried to slow down and turn around and see exactly what the hell's going on but the fireman yells "Don't turn around." And hearing that...I just get shivers all over my body. So we're just booking—down Fulton, over to West Street. Even though we're running, I feel cold all of a sudden. The only part of my body that feels warm is my wrist where he's holding me, and it's really starting to hurt. Finally, we get to the river where all these fireboats are parked and I hear this enormous crack, like a clap of thunder. I turn around to see it falling—coming down into this insane cloud that starts barreling towards us. The fireman just about throws me on a fireboat but the cloud stops before it gets to us. So I'm sitting on the boat and just shaking...I'm so cold. And a nurse comes up to me, staring at me, and asks if I'm hurt and I look at my pants and there's all this blood but it's not mine—it's from the plaza. So she checks me out and I'm not hurt at all. Not a scratch. The only thing I had was this big bruise on my wrist from the fireman. From his grip. That's all.

ERIC: That's...that's just...

ALEX: Now you've got *me* talking too much about it.

ERIC: No—it's fine really. I mean, it's not fine. But...you lived. You're like the new definition of lucky.

ALEX: Yeah.

ERIC: I mean...you should be dead.

ALEX: But I'm not.

ERIC: But to be right there and see all that...it must've been horrible.

ALEX: *(A pensive beat.)* In a weird way, I think I'm lucky to have even gone through the whole thing because as awful as it all was, it's also been the most incredible thing too.

ERIC: It...it has?

ALEX: Everything is different now. Everything. I mean—the whole thing has turned me totally inside out. It's like Dorothy, you know—I went from black and white to Technicolor in one day.

ERIC: Yeah?

ALEX: Oh yeah...life is suddenly more... vivid. And I notice things I never noticed before. Like every time I take the subway it's...so cool. I get on the train now and it's like— there is so much life in one car. People flirting with each other and reading great books for the first time and totally asleep 'cause they've been working a twelve-hour shift. And, on top of the people, there's all these bizarre little things going on too. Did you know the 2 train makes this noise like the opening strains of "Somewhere" from *West Side Story*?

ERIC: Really?

ALEX: Yeah. Right as it's pulling out of the station, as the engine starts up and it makes the notes of the song. *(Singing.)* There's...a...place...

ERIC: You're kidding?

ALEX: Totally serious. It's a trip! I *love* taking the subway...and I go all over town now. I used to just go to work and then go home. But now... Do you have any idea the number of things you can do in this city? Every night is an adventure. I don't know where I'll end up. And it's pushed me to do things I never thought I'd do before. Ever. I mean, I got rid of my boyfriend, my mortgage, my apartment, even my cell phone...and I don't miss any of it!

(ERIC stares at him.)

ALEX: Oh God—you must think I'm crazy. But you know what? I don't care. I don't care anymore. It probably sounds strange but, despite everything that's happened, the world is a pretty incredible place these days. And now I'm just trying to figure out, you know, why I'm still here. There's got to be some reason why I'm here. I don't know what it is but I'm trying to find out...every amazing day.

ERIC: Maybe this is it.

ALEX: Oh...like this here. To rent the room. Who knows...maybe you're right.

(ALEX smiles warmly at ERIC. Again, more flirting. Then ALEX wanders over to the boxes and looks at them.)

ALEX: So what happened to your previous roommate? He must've left in a hurry.

ERIC: Well...actually, he was gonna move out on the fifteenth, but he—

ALEX: I thought you said he's gone.

ERIC: *(Caught.)* Yeah. He's gone. *(A beat.)* He's really...just...gone.

(ERIC looks toward the window. Then it hits ALEX. Gone. Dead.)

ALEX: You mean he—

ERIC: Well...yeah.

(ALEX sits down on hearing this.)

ALEX: Oh my God. I'm so sorry. I—

ERIC: He was all ready to move out. On the fifteenth. Most of his stuff was packed up and ready to go. And then...

ALEX: So...where was he?

ERIC: Tower One. A little higher up though.

ALEX: Oh man. I'm so sorry, Eric. *(A beat.)* You don't have to talk about it if you...

ERIC: No. It's okay. I haven't been really talking about him lately and everyone's kinda scared to even bring it up around me anymore, all my friends that is, because I...I sorta lost it for a while and couldn't really deal with the whole thing... it was all a little overwhelming. I mean by the end of that day I was just...a wreck. Everything just kept going from bad to worse, exponentially, you know—first it was just a fire, then this explosion. Then when that first one fell...that was like—I mean who would have thought that could happen? People were standing outside my window. Screaming. Like a horror movie. And I kept thinking it can't get worse... Stephen's in Tower One and maybe he's hurt but he'll be okay. I mean one tower going...that's gotta be as bad as it can get. And then...

ALEX: God—that's just awful. Were you good friends with this guy?

ERIC: No...not really. Just roommates. He was only here for a few months. He was doing temp work down there, at some financial firm. Temping...can you believe it? Can you imagine being stuck at some job you don't even want to do and then...

ALEX: So he was planning on moving out already?

ERIC: Living here was supposed to be temporary. A friend of his, this girl he knew from college, was moving to the city. They were in this punky band together, the Haggard. He said they were sorta B-52s-ish. He kept telling me that he was the Fred and she was the Kate. Anyway, she was coming and they needed a place to live as well as rehearse and so he found this enormous loft for them out in Bushwick. A huge cheap place in an old factory. I told him he was crazy to go all the way out there…I mean, Brooklyn, right? But he was *so* excited about it. Excited to start rehearsing again with the band. They already had their first gig at some dive in Williams-burg…on the twenty-second.

(ERIC is getting visibly upset by relating this. This is making ALEX visibly uncomfortable.)

ALEX: Hey—are you…

ERIC: It's so stupid that I should be so… I hardly knew him. When he was living here, we barely saw each other we were on such different schedules. Will saw him maybe once before we broke up. Everyone joked that he was my imaginary roommate, that I'd made him up. But he was a great roommate…was always cleaning stuff around the apartment, stuff I never realized was even dirty. I'd come home and voilà—things would be sparkling clean and everything would smell like lemons. He was just so…nice. *(A beat.)* I think it's true that dumb saying or song or whatever it was. It seems only the nice people die in things like this, leaving all of us to hate ourselves for not being so nice.

ALEX: Hey c'mon…you seem like a nice guy.

ERIC: Oh right—you barely know me.

ALEX: Still…you don't seem like some terrible person.

ERIC: Gee thanks.

ALEX: That's not what I— you seem nice. That's all I'm saying.

(Turned away from ALEX, ERIC looks lost in his own mournful world. Not exactly crying but just…lost.)

ALEX: Why don't I get going and I'll—

ERIC: Actually, can you…stay for a bit?

ALEX: Well uh—

ERIC: If you don't want to that's fine.

ALEX: It's just late and I—

ERIC: *(Starts to lose control of his emotions.)* Never mind, I just… lately I'm feeling so down…and you are…you just seem to have this…this positive thing going on which is great… and I feel so not positive lately… all that happened just sorta weighs on me…makes me feel…I don't know… almost paralyzed by everything… so much so that sometimes I can't even walk… sometimes I just feel so low that…that I start to think… I think that… *(A beat.)* Do you really think I'm a nice guy?

(ALEX nods. This only causes ERIC to break down and start crying. ALEX moves closer to him. ERIC starts to cry even more. ALEX touches his shoulder and then holds him. ERIC starts sobbing loudly, his head on ALEX's shoulder. ALEX is holding him when ERIC's legs start to buckle. ALEX guides him over to a couple of boxes center stage where they both sit as ERIC continues to heave with sorrow. The instrumental intro to "Superman" by Five For Fighting fades up and can be heard very low. Then, ALEX lifts up ERIC's head and looks at him. They are both

very still, staring at each other. Slowly, the lights begin to fade. Once the stage has gone to black, the song plays for a minute or two in total darkness.)

SCENE 7

Dim lights come up. It is the dead of night, around two-thirty a.m. There are some business clothes scattered on the floor. ERIC, wearing a pair of boxer briefs, is sitting on a couple of boxes stacked up at the window, staring out. After a few moments, ALEX enters the room wearing a pair of boxers and a white T-shirt. He is looking for ERIC and spots him sitting on the boxes. ERIC, however, is totally unaware of his presence, engrossed in thought. ALEX speaks up.

ALEX: Hey…

(ERIC is startled by this and jumps a bit. He turns and sees that it's ALEX.)

ALEX: Sorry I—

ERIC: No, it's my—

ALEX: What's up?

ERIC: Couldn't sleep.

ALEX: Sorry—I tend to sprawl out a bit in bed.

ERIC: No—you were fine. It's just…

ALEX: What?

ERIC: Everything.

(ALEX pulls up a box next to him, curls up to him sleepily.)

ERIC: You don't have to.

ALEX: No really…it's okay. What's up?

ERIC: I…I haven't slept with someone since Will and I broke up.

ALEX: Ahhh…so I'm the first.

ERIC: Yeah…"the first." Ha. I thought when I broke up with Will I was gonna go crazy, you know, sleeping with all these hot guys or something. A freedom field day. But nothing happened.

ALEX: Nothing?

ERIC: It's like suddenly no one was even looking at me…like I had the gay scarlet letter or "broken up" on my chest.

ALEX: I dunno. Maybe that's not really what you wanted?

ERIC: Oh I wanted it alright—that's why I broke up with Will because I was feeling too…constrained and trapped and scared that, you know, that this was *it!* That I was an adult, in a relationship that had lasted for more than a few months…was approaching two years. And that I was thirty-three years old. I thought that by now everything in my life would be settled and perfect and cozy. But it turned out to be the opposite. My birthday was in May and that's when Will and I started fighting and then I had trouble getting steady work and my old roommate moved out because he couldn't afford the rent anymore and then Stephen moved in which actually was great until… *(Indicating window.)* It's like I've been thrown back ten years into all that uncertainty and confusion of my twenties…like I'm living a bad board game. Go back five spaces and lose your mind. That's what I need…a "get-out-of-insanity free" card.

ALEX: *(Regards him a little warily.)* Maybe we should get back to bed…

ERIC: No…I won't be able to sleep.

ALEX: What…nightmares?

ERIC: *(Laughing.)* Hardly. People keep asking, are you having nightmares, are you having nightmares? But when I sleep it's just this great empty blackness. When life is this…this sorta daymare, sleep is a blessing, a total holiday from reality.

ALEX: So why can't you sleep then?

ERIC: Oh I can sleep…the trick is getting to sleep. I just lie there in bed and close my eyes and all I can see is the eleventh…everything I saw happening over and over again in a loop. Especially that explosion. And then I'll hear a siren and I'll have to wait to hear if there're more. And then a truck will backfire and I'll be turning the news on. And the next thing you know, it's sunrise and the traffic picks up and it's too noisy to sleep anyway so I just give up.

ALEX: Not sleeping can really screw with your head. Maybe that's why you had that outburst before.

ERIC: (Dismissive.) Oh that—I have one of those every day. It's usually when no one's around, that's all. You just happened to be in the right place at the right time.

ALEX: It's not that funny, you know. I mean you were seriously losing it there… I didn't think you were gonna stop crying. (A gentle beat.) Maybe you should get some help. They have this 800 number.

ERIC: (Wearily.) Oh I've heard about the number.

ALEX: I mean it's been a big help for me.

ERIC: I'm sure it's great for you and other victims and people who really knew people who died.

ALEX: Like your roommate…

(This stops ERIC cold, as if he'd forgotten this fact and was just reminded of it. ALEX looks at ERIC with nervous concern.)

ALEX: So was there a funeral?

ERIC: (Spacey.) Huh?

ALEX: For Stephen.

ERIC: Uh…no. Just a memorial down in Florida where his parents live.

ALEX: Did you meet them?

ERIC: No. Only his girlfriend…well girl-friend. From the band. She came by and got most of his stuff. That was bad enough. I can't even imagine what his parents must be going through.

ALEX: My parents were completely freaked out by all of this…and I lived! Every time I talk to them on the phone now, they say "I love you" and are crying. I mean, I love them and everything but it's too much, you know?

ERIC: Oh yeah— it's like people getting all emotional gets me more emotional than I would ever get. It's like this sick cycle.

ALEX: Sick?

ERIC: Well…yeah. On the eleventh, I was managing a sort of thin veneer of sanity. But then Will got here and he acted surprised that I was alive and that was it… I was gone.

ALEX: Whattya mean?

ERIC: I thought that I wasn't ever gonna stop crying.

ALEX: Like tonight…

ERIC: Worse actually.

ALEX: Is that possible?

ERIC: Uh…yeah, unfortunately. It was terrible. I went through half a roll of paper towels. Will just held me and handed me new paper towels and then, during an emotional lull, said that he was taking me to Brooklyn whether I wanted to go or not.

ALEX: Wow—he sounds like a great guy.

ERIC: He has his moments.

ALEX: I mean, it sounds like you really care about him still… maybe that's why you were crying so much.

ERIC: I don't know…maybe. It's complicated. It's like that weekend before the eleventh, I was just starting to enjoy the idea of really hating Will, in that sorta post-breakup mood you get in. You know, getting really angry at him for everything that had gone wrong in the relationship and it felt soooo good. And then this happened. And now… I dunno. It's just so damn confusing…

(ERIC is teary-eyed but not crying. ALEX looks away and stands up again.)

ALEX: I'm gonna get back to bed…wanna join me?

ERIC: And watch you sleep?

(ALEX moves closer to him, maybe touching his shoulder, massaging it a little.)

ALEX: No. We'll both sleep. Together. I'll hold you and help you sleep. It'll be…you know, cozy.

ERIC: I'll just keep you awake. Really. Talking and tossing and…being generally annoying.

ALEX: You're not annoying. You're cute.

ERIC: Thanks.

ALEX: That's why I kissed you in the first place.

(ALEX gets up and takes his hand. They start to cross toward the door.)

ERIC: Not to get me to stop crying?

ALEX: No…

(In the distance, a low menacing rumble can be heard. ERIC stops in his tracks.)

ERIC: Wait a sec—

ALEX: What—

ERIC: F-15s. Maybe something's going on…

ALEX: Like what…

(ERIC goes over and clicks on the radio. The sounds of Bon Jovi's "Living on a Prayer." The jet rumble gets louder.)

ERIC: Routine patrol. If it was an attack they wouldn't be playing "Living on a Prayer."

ALEX: Unless the DJ had a strange sense of humor.

(ERIC looks at him and laughs. ALEX laughs, and they dissolve into a sort of hysterically contagious laugh. The jets approach overhead, the sound becoming deafeningly loud. The laughter subsides as ERIC starts to look a little panicky. He grabs ALEX and holds him tightly, clinging onto him for dear life almost. The jets pass over, and the noise starts to fade. By the time the noise subsides, ERIC is still holding on and shaking slightly. ALEX seems a little freaked out by ERIC.)

ALEX: Uh Eric…

ERIC: Yeah.

ALEX: I, like, can't breathe?

(ERIC releases ALEX from his grasp. ERIC suddenly seems anxious and grabs for a pack of cigarettes. He starts to smoke a bit furiously.)

ERIC: You want one?

ALEX: No thanks.

ERIC: I'm trying to quit.

ALEX: You know, smoking will keep you up all night. The nicotine is a total stimulant.

ERIC: Yeah...well... you think I'm gonna get any sleep with the Air Force on patrol?

ALEX: Guess not... *(ALEX looks exasperated. He sees his pants on the floor and goes to get them and put them on.)*

ERIC: What—what're you doing?

ALEX: I'm gonna head out then.

ERIC: Really? It's so late...

ALEX: I've gotta get to work pretty early.

ERIC: You can sleep...have the whole bed to yourself. And I'll make sure you get up. I'll set my alarm. And I can make breakfast. There's coffee and eggs and juice and—

ALEX: Thanks. But I've gotta pick up some papers at home before I go into the office.

ERIC: Where are you staying now anyway?

ALEX: I'm at my parents' house. Way out in Queens.

ERIC: Wow—really?

ALEX: It's just for a few weeks, until I find a share, something more affordable. I wanna save up some money now, get back to school maybe, do something a little more interesting with my life than international bonds you know.

ERIC: Sounds like a plan.

(Sitting, ALEX puts on his shoes.)

ERIC: Oh—what about the apartment?

ALEX: *(Laughing, he almost forgot.)* Oh yeah... I don't know. I think moving in's probably not a great idea, huh?

ERIC: You sure? I mean, I think we got along pretty well.

ALEX: A little too well... *(A beat.)* Isn't there some rule about not sleeping with your roommate?

ERIC: Technically. But the rules have been suspended due to recent events.

ALEX: Not funny.

ERIC: Not even a little?

(ALEX gets up and starts to head to the door. ERIC stands.)

ERIC: Alex?

ALEX: Yeah?

ERIC: Thanks. For staying when I was—

ALEX: Sure.

ERIC: I really needed... and I just... uh, thanks. *(Turns around and goes back to the window.)*

ALEX: Take care, Eric. And get some sleep...

ERIC: Maybe a little later.

(Blackout.)

SCENE 8

In darkness, the ANSWERING MACHINE is heard.

ANSWERING MACHINE: Friday, 11:02 a.m.

WILL: *(Voiceover.)* Hey—me again. Just tried your studio but you're not there. Where are you? I wanted to stop by about that dresser, though I'm still not convinced it's not ugly, but also... I'm a little concerned you haven't called me back since Tuesday. So call me. Or at least send me an email. Okay—bye!

ANSWERING MACHINE: Friday, 1:22 p.m.

JOSIE: *(Voiceover.)* Okay—so what is the deal with screening calls today? I wanna know what the hell happened with that porn guy. I hope he's not moving in because that would pretty much be a mistake. And I know that I don't even know the guy but look—you don't want some pervert as a roommate. I mean gay is one thing but— okay, that was a joke. But you're not fucking picking up to laugh at it. Are you in the Bell Jar again? Call me Eric. Now.

(Lights up on stage. The cardboard boxes are now closed, and ERIC sits next to one of them, taping it up. He is wearing the tanktop. There is a super-sized grande Starbucks on one of the boxes that he picks up and sips from, his J.Crew shirt on a box next to it. There are a couple of other empty Starbucks containers on the floor. ERIC seems visibly agitated by the message. And probably a bit wired on caffeine.)

ANSWERING MACHINE: Friday, 3:38 p.m.

LORENZO: *(Voiceover.)* 'Allo—this is Lorenzo. I saw ad in the *Voice* and I'm sorry I didn't call sooner but after the bombing and all I forget. So I like very much but is maybe too expensive. Can we make it less money, maybe seven hundred?

ERIC: *(Overlapping.)* Now they're bargaining? He's fuckin' crazy…seven hundred dollars?!

LORENZO: *(Voiceover.)* I don't think that is too less. I am trying to save money now everything is so bad. I hear from you. Ciao!

ANSWERING MACHINE: Friday, 4:18 p.m.

JEFF: *(Voiceover.)* Hi—Jeff here. Thanks for showing me your place Wednesday. Unfortunately, we got some new polling in today which was really bad and I just found out that I'm gonna be laid off from the Green campaign. They're having another change in strategy and I'm not part of the change which sucks so I'm going back to Washington.

(ERIC reacts strongly to this news by throwing the tape against the wall.)

ERIC: Fuck! *(Stands up and runs his hand through his hair, anxious and frustrated. He starts kicking the box that he has just taped up, it turns over, he kicks it again, stuff falls out, he makes a hole in the side.)* Fuckin' fuck fuck—*fuck!*

JEFF: *(Voiceover.)* It's really too bad because it's a great apartment and you seem like a decent normal guy. Anyway, remember to vote for Green—again. Thanks!

(Exhausted, ERIC sits on the floor and drops his head with a major sigh. The door buzzer goes off, and ERIC is jolted by the sound. He yells at the intercom across the room.)

ERIC: Go away!

(The door buzzer goes off two more times.)

ERIC: Fuck. *(Gets up and goes to the buzzer. He hits the button.)* What.

MAX: *(Offstage.)* Hi—it's Max! From Rainbow Roommates! I'm here to see the—

ERIC: Alright, alright. *(Buzzes him in and mutters and mumbles to himself.)* Rainbow fucking roommates. Bunch of friggin' elves or munchkins dancing around a goddamn real estate pot of gold…

(The door opens offstage and MAX enters. He is a cute college student with a bouncy perk in his step. He walks without his heels touching the ground.)

MAX: Hey—what's up?

ERIC: Just packing up some boxes.

MAX: Oh—making room for me huh?

(*MAX, clueless to ERIC's angry mood, smiles. ERIC glares at him as he strides around the room checking it out.*)

MAX: Great place…nice. (*Going toward the window.*) Wow—lots of light.

ERIC: It's only one window.

MAX: Nice view.

ERIC: (*Re: the view.*) Not smoking today?

MAX: You smoke?

ERIC: (*Defiant.*) Yeah. I smoke.

MAX: You should really quit. There's rat poison in those things…I saw it on MTV.

ERIC: (*Oh brother.*) So—what are you a freshman or something?

MAX: Just started my junior year at NYU.

ERIC: I went to NYU.

MAX: Nice. What'd you study?

ERIC: Photography.

MAX: Oh *cool*—I love photography.

ERIC: Does anyone hate photography?

MAX: You know, I've been thinking about changing my major. It would be pretty cool, you know. I've always liked pictures. There's this gallery on Spring Street that has all these pictures up from the eleventh… snapshots that people took. It's insane…so many pictures… (*A beat.*) Hey—did you take a lot of pictures on the eleventh?

ERIC: Uh…no.

MAX: I got some insane shots on my digital camera. I'll have to show them to you.

ERIC: Uh…no thanks.

MAX: Then later that day, me and my roommates went up to Union Square. Got some insane pictures there too. We were lighting candles and meditating. It was pretty intense.

ERIC: (*Sarcastic.*) Ohhhh—you were part of that whole sixties love-in thing?

MAX: (*A little offended by this.*) Hey—that's a bit harsh.

ERIC: C'mon… it was a bunch of students whose classes were cancelled and didn't have anything better to do, right?

MAX: They did cancel class but…

ERIC: Exactly.

MAX: Man…why doesn't anyone ever take students seriously? Just because we're young it's like our opinion is retarded or something. It didn't used to be like this. I took this class last semester, "Remembering the Sixties"…

ERIC: They have a class?!

MAX: Oh yeah! People used to listen to students back then. They stopped a war, ended discrimination. Changed everything. Now people look at students and are like—what do they have to say? I think we have a lot to say—no more war and tons more peace.

ERIC: That's just great.

MAX: It is great. It could be. But Bush wants our pain to be a cry for revenge.

ERIC: A little revenge could be a good thing right now.

MAX: (*Totally horrified.*) You're not serious are you?

ERIC: Look—I wouldn't mind kicking someone's ass for this, okay?

MAX: You have a lot of rage, you know that?

ERIC: Yeah—and why shouldn't I. Thousands of people are dead and someone needs their ass kicked for that. I don't think that's so terrible. It's justice. Simple justice.

MAX: That's what Osama thought.

ERIC: What!?

MAX: He saw his actions as justice for the thousands who have been oppressed and killed by Western imperialism in the Middle East. So if we do the same, we're just as bad as he is. Probably worse because we should be setting the example.

ERIC: Your views are really very sweet, Max. But in the real world, peace is an ideal. It's not a way of life.

MAX: Not if you don't think so. It all starts with one person, you know.

ERIC: So you really think that you and your friends gathering together in Union Square are gonna cause an about-face in U.S. foreign policy?

MAX: Maybe not tomorrow but over time.

ERIC: Well... that's great. You know what...you must be in some sort of serious post-everything denial because...I mean, that's...that's just crazy.

MAX: I'd rather be crazy than cynical.

ERIC: I'm not cynical. I'm just realistic.

MAX: Real*istic* would be real*izing* your power to change things.

ERIC: Are you in some sort of a cult?

MAX: *(Laughing.)* No way, man.

ERIC: Okay—are you from California?

MAX: Nope. Oregon.

ERIC: Oh my God. Even worse!

MAX: It was a great place to grow up actually. Very progressive and positive energy that—

(ERIC walks away from him and toward the door.)

MAX: Where you going?

ERIC: I'm sorry Max. I don't think this is gonna work out.

MAX: What—you mean the apartment thing?

ERIC: I think I just need someone...closer to my...experiences.

MAX: Whattya mean?

ERIC: Someone... just more like...

MAX: Not a student?

(ERIC looks at him indicating yes. MAX is absolutely deflated.)

ERIC: Look—there's tons of apartments out there. And tons of other students too. I'm sure you'll find someone that's, you know, more compatible.

MAX: Man, I shoulda kept my mouth shut about the peace stuff. It drives my roommates crazy.

ERIC: If you have roommates, why are you looking for an apartment?

MAX: They're all leaving school. Our suite's breaking up and they're heading home, leaving the city and everything.

ERIC: Right in the middle of the semester?

MAX: Yeah—it's happening all over school. People's parents are panicked and taking them out. And some friends of mine are just, like, freaking out on their own. I was freaking out too you know. That day was...it was so insane. Seeing the whole thing live—not on TV.

ERIC: *(About to send him off.)* Yeah…well we all saw it—

MAX: I mean I was walking down Sixth Avenue, heading to my nine o'clock. The first plane buzzed right over me. I looked up because it was so loud and knew something was totally wrong. And then I followed it and saw it go right into the Trade Center. I mean…right into the building. And that thing had flown right over my head… *(A beat.)* This is kinda weird but… last summer I went to check out that movie *Pearl Harbor* with a couple friends of mine. It was totally stupid—Ben Affleck as some flying ace. Gimme a break. But there was this one scene where the Japanese planes are flying past a bunch of kids playing baseball. And I remember thinking how intense that must have been to be one of those kids. To see history flying right over your head… and when I was watching the movie I thought, damn, nothing that serious or historical is ever gonna happen to me. And then, two months later…there I am on Sixth Avenue looking up. *(A heavy beat.)* And now I feel like, I don't know, like I almost wished something like that to happen. I know I didn't really, but…it's what I wanted in a way. To be part of history and now I'm in it all the way.

ERIC: Sounds like you feel guilty…

MAX: *(A revelation.)* Maybe…yeah, I guess so. It's like, I probably felt I had to do something positive after having wished for something negative. *That's* why I went up to Union Square…

ERIC: At least you tried to do something…

MAX: I had to. Otherwise what's the point of staying?

ERIC: Did you think about leaving?

MAX: Oh yeah. My parents were totally losing it. They live out in the middle of nowhere and they were trying to get me to come home on a frigging bus. To Oregon. And I seriously considered it for a few days. And I cannot even *deal* with my parents…

ERIC: And Union Square got you to change your mind?

MAX: Nah… it was later, when classes started up on the seventeenth. In my psych section, a bunch of students told the teacher that it was gonna be their last class, that they were leaving school because of their folks, and our professor got very down about it. He said he understood their parents' concern but he also said something interesting; that we all came here because we wanted to be in New York, we desired this New York experience, craved it almost. Now, he said, New York needed us. And I was like…wow. Guy's got a point.

ERIC: So you stayed.

MAX: Yeah. But my roommates left. And now I'm sorta stuck. I can't do university housing and I can't afford my own place.

ERIC: Well—you probably can't afford this place then.

MAX: What is it again?

ERIC: *(Hesitating.)* It's…it's twelve hundred a month.

MAX: Whoa—seriously.

ERIC: Uh…yeah.

MAX: That's a total deal man. I was expecting like fifteen hundred. That's what it is on campus 'cause NYU's a total rip, you know. And I could still walk from here. It'd be per—

(Suddenly, the lights in the apartment flicker and then go off.)

MAX: Whoa—

ERIC: What the hell?

MAX: The power blow?

ERIC: That's weird. The power never goes out here. Not even in the summer. Maybe something's going on?

MAX: Whattya mean?

(ERIC goes over to his clock radio and flicks it on. Nothing.)

ERIC: The radio's dead.

MAX: *(Duh.)* Well…yeah. The power's out.

ERIC: I think something's happening…

MAX: I read something online that they're having some problems with the power downtown. There was a substation or something got destroyed on the eleventh and—

ERIC: Do you have a Walkman or anything?

MAX: Uh…not on me. You wanna listen to some music?

ERIC: No—I want to check the news. I think something's going on.

MAX: What, like an attack or something?

(In the distance, one siren is heard, then another. ERIC's face blanches.)

ERIC: Oh no… *(Rushes toward the window, opens it, and leans out to see what's happening.)* How many sirens is that?

MAX: I dunno—maybe two or three… *(Looking at him.)* Hey—are you alright?

ERIC: Something's going on.

MAX: Whattya mean?

ERIC: That's a lot of sirens, don't you think?

MAX: I don't think it's anything to worry about.

ERIC: Oh my God—the traffic lights are out!

MAX: Yeah. Power must be out in the whole neighborhood.

(Car honking is heard coming from outside the window.)

ERIC: They've killed the traffic lights. Oh my God! It's happening again. We've gotta do something!

MAX: Hey…relax, it's just the power.

ERIC: No—you don't understand. This is it. Probably a…a…a chemical attack, but they're killing the power so no one knows what's going on, no one can get the news on the radio so then we'll all run outside and inhale the stuff and be dead in a few minutes. I've gotta close the window!

(ERIC races back to the window to close it but it's stuck. ERIC mutters to the window, cursing under his breath, trying to get it unstuck. MAX looks at him nervously.)

MAX: Hey—maybe you'd better sit down for a bit. I seriously don't think anything's wrong.

ERIC: How can you say that…listen to all those sirens!

(A couple more sirens are heard.)

MAX: Yeah—it's probably the police. They're coming to help—with the traffic and stuff. It's fine.

ERIC: No—that's too many sirens. I've gotta call Will.

MAX: Who's Will?

(ERIC races across the room to the phone. Of course, it's not working either. He drops it.)

MAX: Hey—easy there.

ERIC: The phone's dead.

MAX: 'Cause the power's out.

ERIC: I know the power's out. They've cut it! This is it…

(ERIC looks like he's hyperventilating now, pacing around the room in circles almost. MAX considers something. Then, ERIC and MAX speak the following simultaneously.)

MAX: Look—maybe you should sit down. Take some deep breaths. I think you're having some kinda panic thing. They talked about this in our dorm last week… just sit down and take some deep breaths. They told us you just have to breathe and think of peaceful things…like a stream or a bubbling brook or—

ERIC: I'm not panicking. This is real. I can't call out—everything's dead. He won't be able to get in touch with me. Will's gonna think I'm dead…or, oh God, maybe he's dead. He works uptown and maybe that's where the sirens are going. They're probably attacking Midtown. I've gotta call Will. Wait— Do you have a cell phone?

MAX: Are you gonna relax if I give it to you?

ERIC: Uh—sure. Just lemme make one call—

(MAX hands ERIC the cell phone. He dials furiously. MAX looks out the window curiously.)

MAX: It looks like everything's fine. I mean, it just looks like an electrical problem. The police are directing traffic—

(ERIC puts the cell to his ear and listens. What he hears turns his face white with fear. The cell phone drops out of his hand. MAX turns around on hearing this.)

MAX: Hey man—my phone…

ERIC: Circuits are busy.

MAX: Yeah—I've got crap service.

ERIC: This is just like before. All the circuits were busy. I couldn't get through. Oh God—this is it. It's all happening again. But this time it's gonna be even worse. This time it's— (Unknowingly backs into a cardboard box on which one of the Starbucks cups sits. The cup tips over and spills onto ERIC's J.Crew shirt.) My shirt…oh my God! (Holds it up; it has a big coffee stain on it. ERIC is absolutely crushed by this.) Fuck—Jesus—dammit…

MAX: Shit…I mean, you can get another shirt.

ERIC: It was from J.Crew.

MAX: There's J.Crews like everywhere.

ERIC: No—I bought it at J.Crew in the mall.

MAX: Yeah…still. It's okay—you can get a new one.

ERIC: No—J.Crew is gone. It was the one at the Trade Center. And this was the last thing I bought there. And now it's ruined… totally ruined.

(ERIC falls back onto the floor and starts crying again. MAX doesn't know what to do.)

MAX: C'mon, it's just a shirt.

(ERIC is sobbing now.)

MAX: Oh man— What's going on?

(The lights and power come back on.)

MAX: See—it was just the power. No big deal.

(*ERIC sees this and it makes him even more inconsolable.*)

MAX: Hey man…it's fine. See. Everything's fine. Really…

ERIC: I'm not fine. I'm not fine. I'm not…

(*Blackout.*)

SCENE 9

In darkness, the ANSWERING MACHINE is heard.

ANSWERING MACHINE: Monday, 11:02 a.m.

WILL: (*Voiceover.*) Hey—it's me. I talked to Josie and she's gonna get there around one to help, after her doctor's appointment. Anyway, I'll come by with the car after work. Call me if there's any—if you need— you know, just call me when you're there. I wanna make sure everything's okay. Alright…love you. Bye.

(*Lights up. The cardboard boxes are all gone now. Only the dresser and the air conditioner remain. There are also now a couple of suitcases near the right wall. JOSIE enters pulling a small suitcase and holding a set of keys. She goes to look out the window.*)

ANSWERING MACHINE: Monday, 1:38 p.m.

MAX: (*Voiceover.*) Hey—it's Max. How's it going? So I got your message last night and that's totally cool about the apartment. And I talked to Carlos too. He seems cool…for a landlord I guess. I'm gonna come by after class today and get the keys from him. Alright—later!

(*The buzzer goes off. JOSIE crosses the room, buzzes someone in without saying anything*

and walks to the center of the room, taking a deep breath and composing herself. ERIC enters a few moments later. He is wearing decent clothes, has shaved, and is more put together than in the previous scenes. He seems surprised to see her standing in the center of the room, looking at him somewhat anxiously.*)

JOSIE: Hey—

ERIC: Hi—

JOSIE: (*Tentative.*) So…how's it going?

ERIC: Good.

JOSIE: Good. You…feel okay?

ERIC: Oh please Josie…

JOSIE: What?

ERIC: You don't have to talk to me like that.

JOSIE: Like what?

ERIC: Like I'm Blanche DuBois or something.

(*Despite herself, JOSIE laughs and starts talking like JOSIE.*)

JOSIE: Well Blanche, at least ya look good…all dressed up.

ERIC: Oh come on…

JOSIE: You're actually wearing pants that aren't jeans. And you did something to your hair. Aha—you washed it!

ERIC: Okay—are you done making fun of my personal grooming habits?

JOSIE: No. You even shaved too.

ERIC: I had to. Will said I was one step away from looking like a homeless person.

JOSIE: Oh—isn't that sweet!

ERIC: Yeah—he has a way with the compliment sometimes.

JOSIE: So how are things over in Brooklyn?

ERIC: Quiet.

JOSIE: That's the suburbs for you.

ERIC: Yeah…

JOSIE: But you feel better…

ERIC: Yeah…a lot better.

JOSIE: Good. And the 800 number?

ERIC: I've pretty much memorized it.

JOSIE: That's great, Eric. Really.

(ERIC smiles at her and looks at the suitcases.)

JOSIE: So where's Max, the amazing rescue boy?

ERIC: He had to go meet with some prospective roommates. He's gonna come by later and get the keys from Carlos.

JOSIE: We're not gonna hand over the keys to the kingdom?

ERIC: No—besides he might be a little freaked out having to see me again.

JOSIE: He sounds like quite a kid…to keep his cool like that when you were losing it. Calling Will and everything…

ERIC: Yeah—I was pretty lucky he was around. I mean if that had happened and I was alone…

JOSIE: Let's try not to dwell on the ifs, okay?

ERIC: Okay. *(A beat.)* I can't believe I'm leaving. After almost ten years…

JOSIE: Ten years…

ERIC: Makes me feel like a loser.

JOSIE: What?

ERIC: This is exactly what they wanted. To scare me into moving away. Funny… it's just like you said—the point of terrorism…

JOSIE: Oh *now* you're listening to what I said.

ERIC: Yeah but I fell into that trap…they made me scared.

JOSIE: Trap?! Eric—they killed your roommate. You have a right to be fucking terrified okay? There's nothing wrong with that.

ERIC: But still…leaving here after all this time…almost a decade.

JOSIE: Alright—let's can the fake nostalgia. How many times did I hear you complain about the lack of heat in the winter and the lack of air conditioning in the summer, locks that sometimes worked, roaches the size of my purse—

ERIC: Okay—I get it. But it was my home you know.

JOSIE: Well…now you've got a new home. With central air and a front door that locks.

ERIC: Look—staying at Will's is temporary…

JOSIE: Really?

ERIC: Really. I'm gonna get everything together, my work and emotional stuff, and then decide on what to do once I can decide.

JOSIE: Sure. When you're thinking clearly…

ERIC: I'm not gonna stay until he gets sick of me and kicks me out or anything.

JOSIE: He's not gonna get sick of you, Eric.

ERIC: I dunno—I can be pretty difficult these days.

JOSIE: I'm sure Will can handle it. He did a pretty good job on the eleventh. And this weekend too. *(A beat.)* I know I don't ever say this but I was probably a hundred percent wrong about him when you two broke up.

ERIC: Josie—a hundred percent wrong? Maybe *you* need to call that 800 number.

JOSIE: Seriously…Will's a prince in a time drastically short on them.

(A beat. ERIC looks at her curiously.)

ERIC: Hey—so what was this mysterious doctor's appointment Will mentioned?

JOSIE: Oh that—nothing big really.

ERIC: Josie—you never go to the doctor. What's up?

JOSIE: Oh well…I'm pregnant.

ERIC: *(Astounded.)* What?! You are?! That's…that's—

JOSIE: Jesus—Eric I *am* a woman—it happens.

ERIC: Yeah but—you weren't even having sex. And David—

JOSIE: Alright—I've been pregnant for a while.

ERIC: You—really?

JOSIE: I missed my period a couple days after the eleventh and I thought I was in shock or something but then I couldn't keep down my morning latte so I got one of those kits at Duane Reade and…the writing was on the stick, as they say.

ERIC: Wait a minute. So you were actually pregnant when David was wanting to procreate?

JOSIE: Uh…well, yeah.

ERIC: Why didn't you tell him?

JOSIE: Honest?

ERIC: Well I don't want you to lie to me.

JOSIE: *(Hard to admit.)* I didn't know if I was gonna keep it.

ERIC: Josie!

JOSIE: Don't be all shocked. Jesus—we are liberals.

ERIC: But you were gonna have an abortion?!

JOSIE: Eric—you sound like Jerry fucking Falwell. So I thought about it. That's all. Because of what was going on…the idea of bringing a child into this insanity. *(A beat.)* I mean, reading all these awful stories about mothers who lost their kids… you know, those "Portrait" things. Every day there were at least three inconsolable mothers. They were absolutely heartbreaking. And the idea of having a kid only to have something like that happen… I just couldn't bear it.

ERIC: So what changed your mind?

JOSIE: You did.

ERIC: Huh?

JOSIE: The night you freaked out I guess I sorta came to my senses, decided I couldn't keep this a secret from David anymore or I'd end up like you.

ERIC: Gee—thanks.

JOSIE: I had to talk about it with him, stop hiding it, and just fucking deal with it. So we had a huge discussion and I told David all my concerns, you know, what we were talking about last week, how the world is just an awful place right now. But he said it'll get better…typical David. Mr. Sunshine raining on Ms. Cynical's parade.

ERIC: Wow—so you're really pregnant…

JOSIE: Yep…I went to the doctor today to break the good news to her.

ERIC: And…

JOSIE: She was thrilled.

ERIC: And you…

JOSIE: I guess I'm pretty excited.

ERIC: So I get to be a fake uncle and everything?

JOSIE: Yeah—but this kid's not gonna call you Uncle Mame. That is just retarded okay?

ERIC: C'mere…

(JOSIE approaches ERIC somewhat warily, and ERIC gives her a big and sincere hug. JOSIE is almost uncomfortable in the hug. As ERIC pulls back, JOSIE is looking at him oddly.)

ERIC: What?

JOSIE: We never used to hug before.

ERIC: That's 'cause we were New Yorkers.

JOSIE: And what are we now?

ERIC: Losing it?

(The buzzer goes off.)

JOSIE: Is that Will already?

ERIC: Probably…he's never one to be late. *(Hits the buzzer.)* Yeah—

WILL: *(Offstage.)* Hey—it's me honey.

ERIC: Hi—and don't call me honey.

WILL: *(Offstage.)* Sorry sweetie.

ERIC: Uh—okay—we'll be down in a minute.

(JOSIE picks up a couple of suitcases, but ERIC wanders over to the window for a last look out. JOSIE approaches him nervously.)

JOSIE: Still smoking?

ERIC: Yeah—it's kinda white today. Wispy almost.

JOSIE: *(A lil' nervous.)* Eric…you okay?

ERIC: I was listening to NPR last night at Will's. They did this really long piece about the beginnings of the Trade Center. Very NPR, right, to talk about *that* when everyone is talking about the destruction of it. Anyway, did you know they started construction on the towers the year we were born?

JOSIE: 1968?

ERIC: Yeah…and it took them more than five years to finish it. I remember coming up to visit my aunt out in Brooklyn for Easter and you could see it from her kitchen window on State Street… each year it was a little bit taller, a little bit more finished. And I kept asking her, "Can we go up to the top yet?" It was like this obsession I had as a kid…and I just couldn't wait til it was done. When I was eight, the observation deck finally opened. So we all took the subway downtown and took the elevator all the way up and you know what… it was a major disappointment.

JOSIE: It…it was?

(ERIC is now standing next to the A/C unit, leaning on it with one leg as he continues this story.)

ERIC: The top deck was closed. Too windy. I tried to convince my aunt that they should let us up anyway, that we'd be fine if she just held my hand, that we wouldn't go flying off the top or anything. I wanted to go up on that observation deck so badly. The view inside was okay but I wanted to be up there on the roof...the top of the world I kept calling it.

JOSIE: It was an amazing view.

ERIC: I never took it for granted. Every time someone would come to visit me, I'd take them up there. And every time...it was a wonder. *(He steps up onto the A/C unit.)* Standing on top with only the sound of the wind...you couldn't hear any of the street noise of the city that high up. Just wind. And if it was clear enough you could see the curvature of the earth. That was something... *(A beat.)* Why is it...why does this thing... I mean, it was just a building, right?

JOSIE: Apparently not. *(Offers a hand to him, to bring him back down to the floor.)* C'mon. Will's waiting...

(ERIC takes her hand and steps off the A/C unit. JOSIE starts to cross toward the door with ERIC behind her, but he stops.)

ERIC: Can I— I'll meet you down there in a sec.

JOSIE: Sure. But if it's more than a minute, I'm calling 911.

ERIC: Okay. Thanks, Josie.

JOSIE: For what?

ERIC: For being Josie.

JOSIE: You've got one minute.

(JOSIE smiles warmly, nods, and leaves the room. ERIC looks around at the room and goes to the window as the street noises get louder—buses, cars, honking. He takes the flag down and sticks it in his pocket. He picks up his bags.)

ERIC: Bye...

(ERIC exits through the doorway on stage right. The lights in the room begin to fade as the street noises get louder, more cacophonous. Finally, the last light dims on the window.)

NOTES ON *WTC VIEW*

The last thing I did on the evening of September 10, 2001, was place an online ad for a roommate in the Village Voice. *Believe it or not, on the twelfth I had a number of people calling wanting to look at my apartment, even though I was not there and they could not get downtown to see it, as it was in the "frozen zone." This strange situation served as the jumping-off point for my first full-length play,* WTC View. *Finding a roommate in New York City is always an adventure. But after 9/11, it was downright bizarre. As each prospective tenant came to see my apartment, they inquired not only about the utilities and whether there was laundry in the building, but they also ended up sharing their own personal stories about what happened to them on the eleventh. And these served as the real basis for what became this play.*

—*Brian Sloan, playwright*

WTC View *is, among other things, a document of what life was like in New York City in the weeks following the 9/11 terrorist attacks. Brian Sloan was there and so was I, and the factual background of his play is true and accurate. Below is some additional information regarding people, places, and events referenced in the play which may be useful in providing some historical context.*

—*Editor*

THE 2001 MAYORAL ELECTION

September eleventh was the scheduled day for the Democratic primary in the race for mayor of the City of New York. Polling places opened that morning, but after the attacks on the World Trade Center, there was so much chaos in the city that by the afternoon most polling places were shut down, and the city decided to reschedule the primary election for later that month. The rescheduled Democratic primary was so close that there was also a run-off election held in October between Mark Green and Bronx Borough President Fernando Ferrer. All told, there were four days of voting that fall in the race for mayor of the City of New York.

Mark Green was the Democratic candidate for mayor in the 2001 election. He had previously been New York City's public advocate and, as the leading Democratic candidate for mayor, was a favorite to win before 9/11. However, when Republican mayor Rudolph Giuliani's popularity soared due to the attacks and his response to them, Republican candidate Michael Bloomberg got something of a boost in the polls as well. He also spent millions of his own dollars on the hotly contested race. In the end, Bloomberg beat out Green by a margin of three percent of the vote.

Gatherings in Union Square

On the afternoon and early evening of 9/11, groups of students at New York University who lived in dorms near Union Square (Fourteenth Street and Broadway) started congregating in Union Square Park. They lit candles, sang songs, and, using chalk, wrote statements of mourning and pleas for peace on the park's dark paving stones. When local officials closed off the area of Manhattan south of Fourteenth Street to anyone not living there, people from all over the city started congregating in Union Square, as it was the closest people could get to Lower Manhattan. These gatherings lasted for almost a week.

Air Patrols Over New York

For more than six months after the 9/11 attacks, twenty-four-hour combat patrols of F-15 and F-16 aircraft circled the skies over New York City. They generally flew at such high altitudes that they were not noticeable from the ground, but, occasionally and without explanation, the fighter jets would zoom lower, causing a major racket. The combat air patrols were the first of their kind over the United States since the Cuban missile crisis in 1962.

The 800 Number

In the weeks following 9/11, in an attempt to help New Yorkers cope with the psychological after-effects of the attacks on their city, advertisements started to appear on subways, buses, television, and radio for an 800 number, 1-800-LIFENET. The number was part of a larger initiative entitled Project Liberty, sponsored by the Federal Emergency Management Agency and the Center for Mental Health Services. Its purpose was to provide free crisis counseling and mental health support services to individuals and families in the Tri-State area that were affected, directly or indirectly, by the attacks.

Shopping at Century 21

Century 21 is a family-owned department store in Lower Manhattan that, since 1961, has been doing a brisk business selling designer clothes and name-brand items at twenty-five- to seventy-five-percent discounts. It is not only popular with frugal New Yorkers but is often jammed with foreign tourists looking for a bargain. The store is located on Church and Cortlandt Streets, directly across from the World Trade Center site. Remarkably, the store survived the collapse of the twin towers yet did suffer some major internal damage. It reopened to the public in March 2002.

PLAY'S TIME LINE

Prologue: Tuesday 9/11 (opening messages)
Scene 1: Monday 9/24 — afternoon (Jeremy)
Scene 2: Monday 9/24 — night (Josie)
Scene 3: Tuesday 9/25 — afternoon (Kevin)
Scene 4: Wednesday 9/26 — afternoon (Jeff)
Scene 5: Thursday 9/27 — night (Josie)
Scene 6: Friday 9/28 — past midnight (Alex)
Scene 7: Friday 9/28 — early that morning (Alex)
Scene 8: Friday 9/28 — afternoon (Max)
Scene 9: Monday 10/1 — late afternoon (Josie)

UNITED STATES:
WORK AND PROGRESS

Christy Meyer, Jon Schumacher, and
Ellen Shanman

CHRISTY MEYER was born and raised in Houston, Texas. Upon graduation from Northwestern University, she moved to New York and began performing with some of the city's most vibrant young companies. She acts as Singularity's development director and has performed in *Just a Little One* and *Aloha, Say the Pretty Girls* with the company. Other NYC credits include *Deception* (Adobe, director Jeremy Dobrish), *Out From Under It* (Vital Theatre), Dawn Powell Festival (New Georges), *The Marriage of Figaro* and *The Seagull* (Target Margin Theatre), *Winter Birds* (Judith Anderson Theatre), *Hump Day* (Jose Quintero Theatre), as well as plays with the Ensemble Studio Theatre, LITE, and Access Theatre Company. Williamstown Theatre Festival credits include Donald Margulies's *God of Vengeance, Once in a Lifetime* (director Michael Greif), *Skin of Our Teeth* (director Darko Tresnjak), and the 2001 Act One Company. Other regional credits include *Collected Stories* and *Joan* (Northeastern Theatre) and *Wait Until Dark* (1891 Fredonia Opera House). She also served as an assistant on *The Laramie Project* (director Moises Kaufman, Union Square Theatre).

JON SCHUMACHER directed *How to Act Around Cops* in the 2003 New York International Fringe Festival, for which he received the Excellence Award in Direction. As artistic director of Singularity, his credits include David Greenspan's *Five Frozen Embryos* and Christopher Shinn's *The Sleepers* (which together received the 2002 FringeNYC Award for Best Overall Production); *Christmas on Mars; Aloha, Say the Pretty Girls; United States: Railways & Firework;* and *Magnum Opus,* a meticulously recreated stage adaptation of *Magnum, P.I.* He was born and raised in Cedar Rapids, Iowa, and attended Northwestern University where he majored in performance studies. He helped found Singularity to produce the first show in the United States Project, *A Day in the Life of Clark Chipman*, in the 1999 New York International Fringe Festival. A member of the Drama League Directors Project, he directed at the Hangar Theatre in 2000 and was the recipient of the 2002 New Directors/New Works grant for *Work and Progress*.

ELLEN SHANMAN is a co-founder and managing director of Singularity, with which she has performed in *Magnum Opus*, *Tooth*, David Greenspan's *Five Frozen Embryos*, and her own *Kirby*. Her solo show about one of New York City's first female firefighters was half of *United States: Railways & Firework*. Filmwork includes *Adultery and Other Incendiary Devices* and Singularity's first film, *The Permanent*. Other credits include *The Opposite of Fear* (Naked Angels), *Schmoozy Togetherness* (Manhattan Theatre Source), *The Ground Zero Club* and *The Daughters of Edward D. Bois* (Saw Mill Summer Theatre), and *Twelfth Night* (La Plaza Cultural). A native New Yorker, she is a graduate of Northwestern University and the author of the popular "Brutal Liza" online serial at www.shinygun.com.

United States: Work and Progress was first presented by Singularity on November 8, 2002, at HERE Arts Center, New York City, with the following cast and credits:

Jessica Banks .... Christy Meyer
Aaron Edsinger .... Jon Schumacher
Cynthia Breazeal .... Ellen Shanman

Director: Jon Schumacher
Stage Manager: Hillary Downes-Vogel
Lighting Design: Jason Jeunnette
Video/Graphic Design: Jeff Tomsic
Sound/Video Operator: Rik Sansone
Publicist: Ron Lasko/Spin Cycle

United States: Work and Progress received funding and developmental support in 2002 from the Drama League Directors Project's New Directors/New Works program. Production Assistance Grant provided by New York Theatre Workshop.

Special thanks to Moises Kaufman, Roger Danforth, Mitchell Riggs, Andrew Bellware, David Terry, Moritz von Stuelpnagel, Katy Cunningham, Julien Bodard, Materials for the Arts/NYC Department of Cultural Affairs, New York Theatre Workshop, Louis Meyer, Sarah Yorra, the Shanman and Schumacher families, Rodney Brooks and the MIT Artificial Intelligence Laboratory, and to Jessica Banks, Cynthia Breazeal, and Aaron Edsinger.

ABOUT THE UNITED STATES PROJECT

The United States Project is an ongoing series of theatrical documentaries based on the lives of real people. Performers construct scripts from recorded interviews and personal observations, attempting to recreate on stage the words and manners of their subjects. The resulting plays feature experiences recounted in the subjects' own words alongside scenes from their daily lives. The relationship that develops between performer and subject provides a rare opportunity to open a window onto another life, and the actor tries to hold that same window open for an audience. In a culture that places so much value on celebrity, The United States Project celebrates the value of every life.

The first show, *A Day in the Life of Clark Chipman,* told the story of a Chicago man looking back on his career working for the Department of Education. It was presented in the fall of 1999 at Northwestern University and subsequently at the 1999 New York International Fringe Festival. The next two, *Railways & Firework,* were produced in the fall of 2000 at Manhattan Theatre Source and told the stories of New York's first female firefighter and a veteran subway conductor on the eve of a threatened transit strike.

Work and Progress is the fourth show in the series. It was born out of our desire to do a show about people who explore how we represent life and define its authenticity, issues that we were grappling with in our work on the project. We realized that scientists exploring artificial intelligence might be addressing similar questions: what is life, and how does one recreate it? Are there any distinctions between something that looks real and something that is real? In a larger sense, both disciplines seemed slightly quixotic: there is a great debate as to whether or not it is possible to achieve artificial intelligence, and at the same time we doubted whether we could ever truthfully represent our subjects on stage. We wanted to ask: if something is impossible, is it still worth doing?

Three scientists working on humanoid robotics at MIT's Artificial Intelligence Laboratory agreed to be a part of the project, and we conducted interviews with them from April of 2001 through May of 2002 in Cambridge, Massachusetts. A grant from the Drama League's New Directors/New Works program enabled us to workshop the show at Pace University in August of 2002 and work with Moises Kaufman on editing the script. *Work and Progress* received a full production at HERE Arts Center in November 2002.

NOTE

Work and Progress recreates the interview process that transpired between April of 2001 and May of 2002, although the scenes are not entirely in chronological order. The break between Acts I and II is not an intermission, but indicates a passage of time between interviews in the spring of 2001 and winter of 2002. Scene breaks are often more indicative of a subject change than a change of place, and the scenes should flow together fluidly. In general, the characters directly address the audience as if they were speaking to their interviewers (the actors), and only when introducing the characters of Aaron, Jessica, and Cynthia do the actors speak as themselves.

PROLOGUE

Blackout. Music. We hear the following statements threaded throughout the music.

AARON: The feeling that's with me all the time is, you only have so long to do what you want to do and…I have very definite things I'd like to accomplish.

CYNTHIA: It's a scientific endeavor, it's obviously an engineering endeavor, but it's almost an artistic endeavor, it's just a fundamentally human quest.

JESSICA: In order to answer "what is life," to me you have to know "what is not life."

AARON: Should I really be here in school, I'm not completely doing what I want to be doing.

CYNTHIA: I have to do it now, I have to feel like I've made enough progress and I've made the statement that I wanted to make before I leave.

JESSICA: I don't want to give up, right? I want to find out, you know, where I can go with this.

(Music ends. Lights up, full stage. CYNTHIA, AARON, and JESSICA sit on and around a large workbench and a desk.)

ACT I

SCENE 1
TOUR INTRODUCTION

JESSICA leads the audience on a tour of MIT's Artificial Intelligence Laboratory.

JESSICA: Alright, so let's start back here.

ELLEN: Jessica Banks, Ph.D. candidate.

JESSICA: So have a seat and I'll show you this video, annotate the video. *(She turns on the video projector.)* So what we're going to see here, the lab has basically had two robots as their dominating projects, Cog and Kismet. Some of you may have seen them, Kismet has been on the news and the Discovery Channel, and Cog looks a little different, because it's gone through a bunch of facelifts and mechanical upgrades. I'll show you.

(Lights down. She presses play and shows us an MIT AI Lab tour video. She sits on corner of workbench stage left.)

ROD: *(On video.)* In order to act intelligent, there's a lot of things you have to know about the world, and one approach is to tell an artificial intelligence program everything, write it out in great detail and tell it all fast.

JESSICA: That's my supervisor.

ROD: *(On video.)* By building a robot, we're trying to build a system which can act in the world, interact with people, and learn for itself. Our hope is that that will become a quicker accumulation of the sort of knowledge of what it is to act in the world so we can have true artificial intelligence.

(JESSICA stops the video. Lights up, full stage again.)

SCENE 2
How I Got to MIT

JESSICA: I studied physics in college because I wanted to be an astronaut, and it was tough for me. Like in high school, physics was the one thing I kind of had trouble with, so I wanted to find out why, and I also looked around me, and I was like why is this happening, how does that work, and to me, physics seemed like the basis of this huge tree of different areas of learning, and I just love that. I also did creative writing.

AARON: *(Sitting at desk stage right.)* So I spent a year and a half in my, sort of a bread delivery van that I retrofitted with a little kitchen.

ELLEN: Aaron Edsinger, Ph.D. candidate.

AARON: And I lived on the streets of SF in that for a while and, um, kind of like equipped it full of books and hung out and read and drank red wine and built robots for a while, you know, it's kind of like the equivalent of retreating to your cabin to like sit down and think for a bit. That was a point where I was forming my own system of, you know, beliefs and had to figure it out for myself, what it is that I thought and how I wanted to, to, you know, use it in building sculpture.

JESSICA: Right, so, I wanted to fly the shuttle, so I was going to go into the military for training. First of all, I was a quarter of an inch too short to go, so I stretched myself. It was literally like a Greg Brady, I think that was him—Yeah, and I did it, okay? But then my mom was like, "you can't approach your life by convincing people to do things your way, you can't do that in the military," and like right there I think I realized that it wouldn't be a good match, because my response to her was like why not? I just couldn't understand, 'cause I thought I'd get into the military and like change it. I'd be like, "oh that's Jessica, and she does her own thing, maverick," And then I was like, what if I just go through the training and then paid them back? And my liaison officer was like, "Jess do you realize it would cost you 2.5 million dollars to pay back what your training is, and you'd have to rack all this air time in tons of different combat planes?" So when it came time, I was like, no way do I want to go into the military, so I thought well I'll try doing more writing and artwork, and I liked comedy, and I was dating a guy who was a comedian at the time, and thought, I'll work for Comedy Central.

CYNTHIA: *(Sitting in front of workbench stage left.)* I wanted to become an astronaut and I had to be a mission specialist so I thought, robotics, space robotics, would make a lot of sense.

JON: Cynthia Breazeal, Ph.D.

CYNTHIA: And it turned out that that year, Rod Brooks had an opening for a planetary micro-rover project student, so...it was a perfect match. And MIT really impressed me in that...just the breadth of work that was being done, in robotic-related fields in general, it— so many people were working in this area. So I came here and of course the connection with Rod was just…was just perfect. And even his whole approach about looking at biology and trying to build lifelike, creature-like robots, I mean all of that just completely captured my imagination. So it was perfect.

JESSICA: Um, quit that and worked for Three Arts Entertainment Management Company and was saddened by the fact that so many people weren't funny. *(Pause.)* Then I found a job for Al Franken, and was really excited. I thought, I'll learn stuff from him, I'll learn production on the show, you know. And as an assistant, a lot of the times, I was forced into an adult demeanor, right? Where asking "why" wasn't something you needed to do all day long. But I still wondered about stuff, like…why the sky is blue. So then I was like, maybe I do want to go back into science, um and art, or something, so it was like, I'll apply to school. And so my essay was about consciousness and what it is to be alive.

AARON: I mean, with my sculpture, like I'm not real big on the conceptual. I think you should have a visceral reaction. When I was in SF I built robotic installations with a group called Omnicircus, and we'd do these shows with different things going on onstage, robots doing things that were lewd or atrocious or, you know, clichéd, beautiful, and people left either distraught or amazed, but you evoked something. You really want to get people to have that heightened sense of experience, or awareness where you… you know, every once in a while you walk down the street and you're like, "oh my God, my feet are standing on the corner" …suddenly aware of your, your place in the world. You want to be able to create that for a prolonged period of time in sort of a contained environment. And that's what we sort of tried to do with our shows.

SCENE 3
THEIR MASTER'S PROJECTS

CYNTHIA: I would argue basically there's, there's two kinds of robots people build today. The vast majority of the field builds robots as tools, robots as sophisticated appliances, so your vacuum cleaner gets smarter, I mean, you have a very specific task that you want these robots to do and so that's the goal. The goal is to build a robot that can do X. And, you know, the more you put in, the less you have to learn. Even for us, we know that despite all of our evolutionary endowments, we still have to go through just tremendous learning in order to really become functional in our world. You meet new people all the time, social networks change all the time, and these are dynamic things that you can't preprogram in. So it's nature versus engineering— kind of the classic example is if you tried to build a flying machine, do you want to build a bird or do you want to build a 747? So…both could work. Turns out the bird is a lot harder!

AARON: Early on I went to Rod and said you know, this is really what I'd like to do, I'd like to try and take the motivation and ideas behind what I was doing before I came here and try to develop them further, and he was like, "that's cool, but you know there's not funding for that, like, we need…" You know, we get research grants and it sort of steers us in the direction of the research, and we do the research on these platforms that we're paid to build, so to build sort of new platforms, which really aren't part of the grant scheme, I'd basically have to go and find funding to do what I wanted to do, and then I'd put all this time into building this and then it would belong to MIT. So, you know, I just kind of figured that I could get what I can technically out of being in the lab, and there had been a hope that some of the code and stuff that I wrote might apply, be able to use it on my own stuff as well, but I don't think that'll be the case.

JESSICA: When I realized that I had to start working on a master's, I had already been working on a finger, and so I thought, tactile sensation. It's such a hard problem, but I think that for humanoid robots, we have to do it. Babies are born without their hearing. Deaf and blind children are born all the time, but no babies are really born, or very few, without being able to feel things, so it must be because it's so important to our survival and development. So, um, I mean a baby that's lying in its crib, if it can't feel anything around itself, it's going to hurt itself all the time... like if it's in a position where they don't know to roll over maybe or something, they stop breathing, how would it know it was lying on its stomach, how would it know it was even breathing possibly if it didn't feel the rise and fall of its chest. There's some weird stories that I've read where people have actually lost the sense of touch, um, because they've had a disease. And so living is really hard. This one guy learned to walk, but he said "if I sneezed, I'd fall," you know, because the second you lose constant awareness of, you know, tracking what your body's doing through your eyes and other senses, he's like I can't do anyth—, I can't multitask at all. And for um, prosthetic devices, you know, none of them really have a good sense of touch, but if I could somehow relay that information to the person, so they know that they're holding something, maybe this is a start—

(She starts the video again. Lights down.)

SCENE 4
TOUR VIDEO—MASTER'S PROJECTS
CONTINUED

The tour video shows other graduate students explaining the workings of COG, a humanoid robot.

BRIAN: *(On video.)* To encourage people to interact with the robot naturally, we've built a robot to look like a human, and to act like a human. Cog has two eyes, microphones for ears and gyroscopes to give it a sense of balance. Each of Cog's eyes has two cameras. One that has a very wide-angle peripheral field of view, and one that has a very narrow field of view, but much higher resolution. Cog has a total of twenty-one degrees of freedom, two degrees of freedom in each arm, and three degrees in the torso. Three in the neck and three in the eyes.

MATT: *(On video.)* So my area of specialty is the arms of Cog, and in keeping with the rest of the project, instead of trying to program the arms explicitly, so that they, I explicitly tell the arms what they should do, I program the arms so they respond to their environment, and interact with their environment. *(COG with Slinky.)* I have an oscillator at these two joints here, and they're getting feedback about how the weight of the Slinky goes from arm to arm, and they're using that to coordinate the two joints.

(JESSICA pauses the video. Lights up, full stage.)

JESSICA: So here, Cog was kind of looking like this, *(Puts her head down.)* and it's really easy to use people's intuition in making these videos, because people are like, "oh he's watching the Slinky"—no right, right there the vision wasn't even probably on, his head was just down, so it's really easy to make people think we're much better at building robots than we are, which is just the state of the art, people and their videos can be very misleading.

AARON: I guess the idea behind my thesis is to, um, build sort of a repertoire of motor actions that the robot can use and somehow tie that to a perceptual system, so, you know, ideally you'd like it to be able to reach out in a manner that's very humanlike, um, and to do that you take a bunch of data of how people move and try and find, um, regularities in the data, um, or patterns in the data that exist, and because of the biomechanics of our body we tend to use the same type of motions over and over, and we don't do these really weird, convoluted motions, you know, so the idea with the learning is to find the manifold of actual movements that we do use, right, and and, um, use that to generate motions for the robot. Um…but it's not nearly as…as…uh, clean as that. (Laughs.) You know, like, you'd like the data to all exist like that but in reality the data is all over the place. You know… people have done this type of work on simulation robots and it's a lot easier to do that, but it's just completely different when you have Cog and the arms kind of shake, and you want it to go like this and it kinda does this type of thing. Um, you know, if I put something heavy in my hand I can still lift it up to the same point, it's the same motor pattern, basically, than if I didn't. Right now Cog can't, the arm would just kind of go halfway and stop.

JESSICA: Alright, so we're going to skip over this, and play with Kismet for a while.

(A still image of KISMET is projected onscreen. KISMET is an adorable robotic head.)

CYNTHIA: This is ah, Kismet. It's my infant robot. It gives me facial expressions which tells me what his motivational state is.

(The onscreen image begins to display KISMET's facial expressions.)

CYNTHIA: This one is anger—extreme anger, disgust, excitement, fear, this is happiness, this one is interest, this one is sadness, surprise, this one is tired, and this one is sleep.

(The video ends.)

CYNTHIA: With Kismet… I mean to me it's trying to put, a new face on robots and a new face on AI, you know, it's just… you look at science fiction and few robots even have faces, you know? It's a much more… (Pause.) I guess you could say, not just benevolent, but—it's a kinder gentler (Laughs.) kind of AI. It is kind of funny, when I was first building the robot I honestly didn't know how people would react to the fact that it didn't have a body. (Laughs.) I was like, I'm not giving Kismet a body. And in some sense I did that because, I mean there were certainly questions of just trying to graduate. (Laughs.) But, um, another argument was that if you build a robot without a body, and you give it these motivations, these drives it has to satiate, and it can't do it on its own, it's gotta do it with you, it forces the robot to interact with people. And there's an argument developmental psychologists use, which is that when human infants are born into the world, they're born with all of these, what's called proto-social responses, that are there, that they cause the caregiver to treat the infant in this way. You know, there's something very special about the human learning environment. So the deeper research question is about leveraging off of human culture, of how a system can really learn and develop the way a child does.

JESSICA: Usually people can intuitively get along with Kismet, which is a good sign, because we want it to be something very natural, and Cynthia has been able to do a lot of work analyzing exactly what those things mean, but people think they can carry on a conversation, again, people think more than what is happening, so we had one guy that said, "hey Kismet, look at my new watch." Kismet doesn't understand, doesn't understand new watch, it's 'cause the guy went like this *(Points to watch.)* that it looked like Kismet went "oh a watch," right, and so, the guy's like "yeah." Or you have a motor going wrong and the eyebrow's always up, and you're like, just ignore that, he's got an idea, you know. Or what was it the other day, Kismet had like a motor blowout, so he crossed his eyes and just fell with his head down, and one of the eyes like popped off and Jeff saw it—

AARON: He's the mechanical designer in the lab now.

JESSICA: And he was like "oh my God." Like it looked like a demonic robot, you know. And every time you see the eyes crossed, it's because Jeff walks by and crosses the eyes when the robot's off. I'm like, that's so mean! *(Laughs.)* But anyway.

CYNTHIA: You know, maybe, we're being challenged here, as a society, to think about…these robots as, non-carbon-based life, but as a different kind of, of entity, a different kind of life. *(Picks up a Furbee toy from the workbench.)* Sherry Turkle is a professor here at MIT. She studies the question of technology's impact on people, and she's finding that when she asks children, after the kids play with these Furbees, she asks them: "Is Furbee alive or not?" And children seem to be coming up with a new category. It's alive but, sort of alive. You know it's like they're extracting some of these core attributes of a living creature, but realizing that Furbee is not alive in the way that my sister's alive

or my pet's alive. But yet there's something about it that it's not inanimate either.

(Lights pull down stage right, where AARON and JESSICA sit at the desk.)

SCENE 5
BEING AT MIT/
PERSONAL RELATIONSHIPS

AARON: I was taking, uh, applied math, is the only thing I was taking this semester, actually. It's like your basic engineering math course. I just kinda took it to brush up on my math skills… like I haven't taken a math class in nine years. And, you know, I came here and like would read papers and see these formulas and go, "Oh my God. What am I looking at here?" So, I figured I should take a class. But what's cool about this is that you learn sort of the framework for…a lot of phenomena, and you can apply that framework to all sorts of things, and then, suddenly like you can start looking at chemistry problems and going, "oh, that's how the hell that works." I don't know if it has any real use for…AI but, you know, it's kinda cool, just to know.

JESSICA: It's really hard for me—'cause I need help all the time. I'm like, I have the least experience of anyone in the lab. I don't know electrical engineering, I don't know computer science, I mean I'm just learning all this stuff. So, I'm always asking, Aaron for one. If I had his talent, there's no fucking way I would be here.

(Everyone laughs.)

JESSICA: I'd be out in the world building robots, and making furniture and welding things together.

AARON: You just want to weld. She's just envious because she doesn't know how to weld.

JESSICA: No but I'm serious, so Aaron's good. And I would have to say that he's my best friend. And um, uh…and in a lot of ways…um…this is going to be so cheesy—

AARON: Don't say it then. *(Laughs.)*

JESSICA: I don't know, I feel like, having him around gives me a lot of, um, just inspiration and confidence and…truly someone to look up to, in terms of an intellectual mind, and also a creative mind—

AARON: Wow.

JESSICA: —and someone who really, you know, is proactive about things. Because a lot of the times, I'm like totally broken. And then, sometimes I feel like, oh I could do anything, so I have option paralysis— so it's like on good days, you know, it turns into like, oh, this whole vast arena of open opportunity, and on bad days, I'm like, *ah*, there's *too much*: don't do anything.

(She gets up and crosses stage left to the work-bench where CYNTHIA sits. Lights cross fade to stage left accordingly.)

CYNTHIA: I think it's important to know that, there's your work and it's great that your work is really important and you find it really rewarding but also, I mean, if you have a family, that's another really important part of your life. I would argue it should be more important than your work. I think, you know, for me I think, in many ways relationships are the hardest thing, in some sense to figure out, to make work, because you're building a robot, I mean, there's a hard problem, but chances are you're going to figure it out, and if you don't figure it out well then, okay, it was really hard, but I mean, you have a certain amount of control over it. Whereas in a relationship you don't really have total control, you have influence, but you don't have control. And so you're fun-

damentally having to interact with these other people with their own ideas and their own intentions and wishes and so forth and it's just, it's trickier that way.

JESSICA: I've met so many interesting people, and in terms of men, before, I was like, I'm definitely condemned to be with a man, or woman, whatever, that um, doesn't talk shop with me, but will I ever find someone that can. 'Cause like in college, in my physics classes, I mean I didn't want to be with any of those guys, right? And then when I came here, I'm like, oh my God, there's actually really decent guys in the grad student level. My boyfriend actually works downstairs in the leg lab, which is part of the AI Lab, um—and he's a wonderful guy. When I met Dan, you know—sometimes it's hard because you don't always want to talk about work, right, because you need to have some space from that, but um, you know, it's great to be able to go home and build like a theramin, or like, do you know what a theramin is? It's um, it was one of the first electronic instruments and it was like, we didn't know what to buy each other for, Hanukkah, and Christmas, but, so we bought a theramin kit, to make a theramin together, and like it's that stuff that I love that I definitely hadn't been able to find before.

CYNTHIA: How did I meet my boyfriend? Um, well he was also, he was also a graduate student at MIT. We're both incredibly busy, but we were friends for a long time. It was just, somehow it happened. But, um, I was married for a long time before that. And in some sense I think that kind of… it was a shield in many ways *(Laughs.)* in that I was kind of like, just able to focus on my work. I didn't have to worry about the whole, kind of, people at your work, you know, wanting to ask you out, but… I got married really young, when I was like...twenty-one? Actually when I think about it now I'm like what the hell was I thinking? *(Laughs.)* I'm like, that's so young! And I think it was just a case where I was obviously changing a lot and the marriage just couldn't seem to change with it, and he was finishing his doctorate. I was finishing my bachelor's. So I was still in school, whereas he was beyond that, you know? So after all of that, certainly meeting people was actually kind of a new thing. 'Cause for seven years I hadn't been meeting people. It's kind of like I should've been doing this when I was twenty-one, right? *(Laughs.)* And I'm doing this at twenty-eight. It's completely bizarre.

(Full stage lights [the tour] return.)

SCENE 6
WHAT IS LIFE?

AARON: There's all sorts of like strange, convoluted ways that we've come about interacting and understanding, you know, our communications, and it's this really bizarre thing, the rituals that we have, and if you step back and look at it, you're like, "it makes no sense at all," but you'll also, you can also play on that.

(Lights down. AARON presses play on remote. On video, two artfully lit, life-sized robots fight with swords. This is some of AARON's work from San Francisco.)

(AARON stops video. Lights back up.)

AARON: That type of show was very much around that idea, where the whole environment is sort of like tuned to resonate with these sort of inter-responses and visceral responses where you kinda magnify the stress lines that you find in people in social situations and play on them and get them to come out. There are these formal cues that you can build into both AI robots and sculptures that we'll try and

leverage off, you know, how we're sort of predisposed to respond to the environment. So, if you make it move in a very lifelike manner, you can't help but treat it sort of lifelike. There's this boundary where you go from a machine that's kind of moving along, and suddenly you can't help but think it's somehow living. And it's just the quality of the movement. The tempo of the movement. Um, I mean, sort of at that level I think they, the two, at least for me, the two different sorts of areas intersect. *(Sits back down in his chair.)*

CYNTHIA: *(Gets up and crosses to the desk stage right.)* I know that today, I mean, they're not conscious, they're not sentient, they're not feeling. I mean, they are still very much machines today. But...I can see, over time, that there could be a point when you really start to ask yourself the question of are these machines no longer just automaton machines, but is there something more? And if that happens, well then there's a whole 'nother level of social issues that arise. You know, what rights might they have, I mean a...new-born infant is born with certain rights, I mean they can't vote, they can't own property, but it's generally acknowledged that abusing them is bad. *(Laughs.)* You know? Could intelligent machines eventually own property and vote? Someday this might happen. You know, under what conditions would we accept robots into the human community that would have rights and privileges and when would we know that they deserved it?

(The lights focus on JESSICA, alone.)

JESSICA: I never really thought...like this isn't my life dream to do...Cynthia *loves* her subject, I'm *fine* with mine, okay? I'm really interested in it now for my master's, and I want to see where I can take it, but like will I end up being the tactile sensor queen of AI? No way, okay? I like learning how to build a robot, and I like making stuff with my hands. It's easier for me to work if I think about it as doing artwork, instead of doing research, because that motivates me a little bit more... I care about smart machines, smart robots, but *less* these days. I don't think that we can make humans, okay? And I think—no one in the lab thinks we can, but I think the reasons I think we can't are stronger. I think there's something about flesh, and cells that live and die that somehow have made us have a sense of like "what is life." In order to answer "what is life," to me you have to know "what is *not* life." I can't explain what it is. I don't know what it is, but then again if someone were to come up to me tomorrow and say, "oh, by the way, you're a robot." *(Pointing to audience.)* I'd be like, Jesus, I was really really convinced she was human, you know? So maybe we can do it. I mean, if everything seems like a human, sounds like a human, maybe it is. That's all, and then is that life, you know? *(Crosses to workbench stage left and sits.)*

CYNTHIA: Do you really need a body in order to build something that's intelligent? Or can you have a disembodied mind? You know Descartes was all about this, they're separate. You have the mind, right, that does all the lofty knowledge, you know, sorts of things. And then you have your body. Your body's just your body. And there are visionaries who think, maybe you could download your brain, to the Internet. And then you have people that are more like Rod Brooks, artificial life, which is basically saying, life without the body is meaningless. If you don't have a body you have no way of interacting with anything else. So a disembodied mind, so to speak, it's like, what kind of existence would that be even if you could do it?

(AARON crosses stage left to sit next to the workbench.)

JESSICA: So Jeff and I, we were walking home, and this guy was turning and he almost ran over my foot, and we had the right of way, and so Jeff kind of kicked his car really lightly. And the guy came out and was like "come back here, why'd you do that," and I'm like "you almost hit me, we're not coming near you, you're irate," so then we walked away and we hid behind this house for like seven minutes, and then we came out again and I heard somebody running and thought it was just a jogger, and I turned back and it was the guy. So this guy had this little bat and he came up and he hit Jeff on the head with the little bat—then he was like on top of Jeff and Jeff was like holding him, because he was totally drunk, and then I kicked him with my steel-toed boots, like three times in the balls as hard as I could, but he didn't even react—

AARON: He didn't even budge?

JESSICA: He didn't even react. I don't think I missed—

AARON: He might have been a eunuch. Did you think about that?

JESSICA: And Jeff was like, "Look at all your pent-up anger! You're so angry, and I haven't done anything!"

AARON: *(Laughs.)* You're like grief counseling him.

JESSICA: Yeah. So then I called 911 which, if you call from a cell phone, is the national 911 and they're like, "where are you?" And I'm like, "where am I!?" So you should put in your cell phone the direct number for your local police...so I have it on nine. Just boop! And then police. But, they didn't catch the guy, he just walked away, and I've been replaying in my head like every day since then of what I should have done. If I had hit him with the bat, he would have never told his friends what happened, 'cause he got beat up with his own fucking assault weapon. Anyway, so then we called Aaron and went and got a CAT scan.

AARON: But when Jeff got in the CAT scan machine there was blood on the—

JESSICA: Right, 'cause you go in and it's a big donut, right? There was like blood speckles all along the inside. Someone had probably gotten in there and I don't know what was wrong with them, but they sprayed blood all over. But I got us mango slurpies, or slushies at the hospital and a big chocolate chip cookie.

AARON: I got them.

JESSICA: No, I bought them.

AARON: You didn't have any money.

JESSICA: I thought I did. I bought them. I totally did.

CYNTHIA: *(Still at the desk stage right.)* Say you had a robot that you know, a hundred years in the future that was a sentient sort of thing in its own right, had a mind, so to speak, if it was ever in danger, physically, could beam its consciousness, whatever you want to call it, to whatever the Internet might be called then. The body is destroyed, but it doesn't really matter because the thing can continue in this space until it gets downloaded into another body. You know, its survival or its existence isn't threatened by that, so you wouldn't have to worry about robots attacking people or something. In self-defense. They wouldn't have to. I mean, they're not threatened in the same way that people would be.

SCENE 7
REFLECTIONS ON THEIR WORK

AARON: So I finished my thesis, which was disappointing like probably any master's thesis that people do around here, but...

JESSICA: I beg your pardon? *(Laughs.)* Yeah, mine was abysmal.

AARON: *(Laughs.)* Yeah, I think it's sort of understood that your master's is gonna be—your ambitions aren't met, and you say good enough and you get it done and you turn it in and you try and forget about it.

JESSICA: And then as a test you put a twenty-dollar bill in the copy of your master's that goes into the library, and then you go back in forty years and you get the twenty-dollar bill out because no one's even read it. Actually, I was in the library the other day and I'm like, "I could make some money. Go around to the master's and take the twenties out," in fact, I think we should do that.

(They laugh.)

JESSICA: Oh, I'm so taking twenties out.

AARON: The one thing that it teaches you is the scale of projects to take on, you know. But I think that's an art in itself, is really picking, defining the problem, picking one that you can actually solve, and, I think we both sort of had really big ambitions and then the reality of doing that got in the way.

JESSICA: Aaron was a huge help on mine.

(AARON laughs.)

JESSICA: It's true, it's true.

AARON: Yeah, ended up doing, helping her out a lot. But we both finished up at the same time?

JESSICA: You were like a couple days before me.

AARON: Yeah. Yeah, I don't even want to look at my master's now.

JESSICA: Neither do I.

AARON: I mean now I have sort of carte blanche and a clean slate and I can just pick a direction.

JESSICA: I'm supposed to be in the Ph.D. program, and I think the lab will change a lot, because a lot of the senior people are graduating. So that will help the people who have been here for only two or three years—that have more similar interests, or more similar ways of communicating, that aren't as jaded as like "oh, God we're not talking about that anymore," you know?

AARON: I haven't thought too much about what I'm going to do next. I'm really trying, at least for the summer when I'm here, to work on my own stuff as much as I can without getting in trouble.

CYNTHIA: After my first year I was very much more in the supporting cast. But eventually you do your own thing. I don't think you really know what impact your work is gonna have. I don't think you ever know. To create something that's a real interacting robot is intriguing to people. And you know Rod has been very gracious and very generous about letting his students take credit for their work. I can't imagine any other place in the world, working for anyone else in the world, where I would have been given the amount of opportunity that I've been given. And I try to tell the younger guys the same thing, you know you have no idea how good you have it, make the most of it, because it's not like this 99.9999 percent of the other places in the world. You're in a very, almost privileged situation. And you should make the most of it.

ACT II

Lights up again, back to the tour look.

SCENE 1
TOUR VIDEO—A SACCADE

JESSICA: So um, it was first thought that vision was a really easy problem to solve, so an intern was assigned a problem to do, you know, figure out vision over one summer. And it turns out vision is hugely hard, because what are we really looking at? How do we recognize faces? There seems to be a certain part of the brain that is specially oriented to faces. And like, our blind spot, we hardly ever take into consideration our blind spot, *(Points to area between her eyes.)* but we're compensating for it all the time when you look from one place to another, filling in the spaces. So when you have a quick change of where you're looking, that's called a saccade. So we do thousands of saccades a day, and basically, you're blind during a saccade. So there's a lot of percentages of the day where you're actually not seeing anything. So try to look from this side of the room to this side of the room by just— scan across without looking at anything, just go one to the other. *(Points from one side of the room to the other.)* Can you do it smoothly? So it's kind of in jumps right? So if you're looking at something, you can actually do it smoothly. So now, watch me, follow me.

(JESSICA crosses stage, goes behind workbench stage left, joining AARON. CYNTHIA is alone at her desk, stage right.)

SCENE 2
A CHANGE IN THE LAB

CYNTHIA: I think um, they had a policy change where they won't hire doctoral students coming out of the AI Lab unless they've gone someplace else first. They won't interview a graduate student straight off of, um, their Ph.D. at MIT. It's kind of like a cross between like, this intellectual mecca and romper room. But I'm fortunate enough to have my next professorship be at the Media Lab at MIT. Probably for me the Media Lab is a better place than the AI Lab. *(Laughs.)* I have this awesome corner lab space. The teaching load isn't too bad, and teaching is fun because, well basically you teach whatever you wanna teach. And I'm down the street from Kismet. So um, so yeah, I'm definitely on a roll. *(Laughs.)* I'm on a roll.

AARON: So I don't know if this was going on when you were here last, but Rod decided to change the direction of the lab. He wants to move away from humanoid robots towards, uh, sort of like looking at living systems and like modeling life, prebiotic life and how did life arise from, um, you know, a bunch of chemicals. I mean, he started out, you know, started out with insects and took this giant leap forward with humanoids, and then—I think in a way it's kind of good.

JESSICA: So many people are doing humanoids now—

AARON: Yeah.

JESSICA: And he wanted to do something new. I think people need to refresh their careers.

AARON: Yeah, he doesn't want to be part of the crowd. I think he likes to question any assumptions that are being made. But, I'm excited about it now, I really am. Yeah. So, in part I was on the fence about if I should do a Ph.D. or not. For the first two years I felt like I was here visiting, because the humanoid stuff has always had, was under, it was like doing somebody else's research, or you know, it was Brian's Cog, and Cynthia's Kismet, and you always felt you were working under-

neath them. And you don't really want to commit completely, you don't want to jump off the deep end intellectually, because you're like, "well, why should I start going down this path when I'm going to pull my roots up," you know, but now it seems like really cool to be here, lots of opportunities. Because you kinda get to go off on your own and do your own thing.

JESSICA: I'm still not sure what I'm going to do, but I ah, am more excited about this now. But when it comes to it I think that the whole approach to humanoid robotics is wrong.

AARON: Our approach is wrong?

JESSICA: I think in some—yeah.

AARON: Really?

JESSICA: We're missing something and it's not that—

AARON: It's kind of putting the cart before the horse, though. I don't think the approach is wrong.

JESSICA: Well, I think that something very, very serious is missing. Everyone's perfecting this little algorithm, and I think there's something missing that is imperfect. Like the fact that a robot I don't think would ever sneeze, okay, and that's because we sneeze because of our actual mechanical system, right? Or yawn, you know how contagious it is to yawn, right? And like someone could be, "yeah, you just program it and it will do it." Someone yawns, and the robot could yawn. But it's not the same. I think that there are certain aspects that are very mechanically oriented to what we are and like our flesh that aren't necessarily in the robot, and so we have to figure out what that is for the robot, which is going to be something new. I'm not sure, I'm not really explaining it that well.

AARON: I think the goal is more illustrating, you know how all that works inside. I think that's more the goal to me that we're getting at than creating a very humanlike humanoid. It's more figuring out how our own brain works.

JESSICA: That I agree with. I think a lot of people do, though.

AARON: Right. But, you know, we're not trying to, make, like servants for the house. If that was really the case we'd be much more practical about what we're doing.

JESSICA: I don't know. Sometimes I got the impression from Rod that he wanted me to give him my list of what I think a robot will never be able to do. Because he wanted to refute that, he said "You're a specialist. You think humans are special." And I was like, "no, I think robots *and* humans are special." I think we're all different, you know, sure, if we do it right we could probably make us—but doing it right is a harder thing than we could accomplish. When I first came into the lab, my essay was, I want to know about consciousness and what it is to be alive and now I hate talking about consciousness, so I um, am very excited to do something different.

AARON: It's something that's more, uh, not that it's not, not so ambitious, but I think the bar got set so high as far as public expectation of, you know, you're making a humanoid, and people come in and they're very disappointed when it doesn't like sing and dance for them, you know, and it's kinda nice to be a little more humble in what you're trying to do—

JESSICA: Right.

AARON: —and not have to have that expectation.

CYNTHIA: Because of science fiction, because in movies, a good story has to have conflict. And whether it's a conflict of aliens, or killer viruses, or mutations, or robots, I mean often robots are put in this role of conflict and so I think there's this kind of underlying tendency in America to portray robots as being, "They're gonna take over! Oh, my God!" You know, and you're like, *no! (Laughs.)* No! Of all the ways that we could destroy ourselves I think robots is probably the least likely. *(Laughs.)* I mean, let's get serious! Nuclear holocaust, disease! *(Laughing.)* Much higher possibility than robots! *(Laughing.)* And actually I think this perception that they'll last forever—that they'll never die, that they're immortal in some sense, 'cause I'm like, what's the longest time that I've run Kismet? *(Laughs.)* I'm like, six hours? Six hours is a really long run for Kismet, you know? Before you power it down. I was talking to some people just the other day: it's like, okay, if you took a robot in a manufacturing plant, and you didn't maintain it, you just ran it, how long do you think it would run before it would start to need repairs? They were like, "oh, a really long time, probably weeks!" *(Laughs.)* And I'm like, you know, look at your car, I mean your car has literally hundreds, maybe thousands of man-hours put into it to make this thing run, and it doesn't even run all the time. It's a physical thing, it wears down. So the thing that of course living systems have is that they can heal. We're self-repairing. And so until machines will become self-repairing, it's like, they're never gonna have the longevity of, of a person because, because no one builds things that could last that long. We just don't. It's like, oh, yeah! Like they'll outlast us, will they?

SCENE 3
New Projects/Daily Routines

AARON: I should tell you what I'm working on. I started looking at...something called tensegrity, which I don't know if you know Buckminster Fuller. So he did geodesic domes. Actually a geodesic dome is one form of tensegrity... sort of like the, sort of the geodesics being, uh, rigid bars that are connected together by cables, and the cables are pulled tight and then all the bars kinda float in a sea of tension, basically. And, uh, so actually the way I got into it was, uh, there's a sculptor, Kenneth Johnson, who actually invented it with Buckminster Fuller a long time ago and built this really cool like public outdoor sculptures that, you know, these bars that are kind of floating in space. And it's kind of a cool phenomenon, and it's sort of sculptural and I'd always been interested in very large, um, complex forms that are stable and lightweight. Then I found a paper by this guy who came to our lab last Friday, and so he had taken tensegrity and discovered that the cytoskeleton of cells actually use tensegrity to support themselves, to keep the cell membrane rigid. And then he's been applying that to like some broader sort of issue of the architecture of life itself. And so something like DNA could be viewed as a tensegrity structure—And it's a very stable structure, right? Because it has to last long enough that it doesn't disintegrate in the cells or anything. So...but from his perspective it's everywhere and it's like the secret—

JESSICA: Literally everywhere. Even in us, like we are tensegrity systems because our bones are, um, tension—

AARON: But I think, I think the cool thing for me is that you can start building robots that have sort of a soft squishy form

to them, right? It's not all rods and metal that are bolted together. So I convinced Rod to let me build a tensegrity robot. And, um, so the first thing I'm building is a leech, actually. And then maybe a jellyfish.

JESSICA: *(Playing with polymer at desk.)* So for my new project, I'm basically building an octopus, well hopefully something like that, that will move around in water, have its own battery inside, you know chemicals. It will be really soft and gooey, an unconventional kind of robot, and part of my new project is working with this new artificial muscle that's a polymer. You can put a very high voltage across the polymer and make it move, so I'm going to try to use it as a muscle, and ah, and today we might even be able to play with it some, then again, I haven't really done it before, and we have to work with very high voltages—very high, which is really not that safe. Well, it can be.

CYNTHIA: I think in some ways it's a very fitting...analogy, to say that we as a species essentially, you know, we're in our technological adolescence, we can start messing with DNA, we can start cloning, we can do genetic engineering. We have all this stuff. But it's so new for us that of course we don't have the experience yet to really know what's a wise way of applying these things to society? I mean, I think these things are going to happen whether we do it or we wait fifty years for someone else to do it. So it's really a matter of trying to, to try to take an active, responsible role in trying to steer it. And it's not only, I think, the job of just the scientists and the engineers to try to steer it, because these are really questions for society.

AARON: *(Crosses upstage, to a stool. This is the "shop area.")* Have you guys ever done any machining? We actually just got this machine retrofitted with a new unit so it's all automated now. You can just program it and it just cuts it out for you. But I'm probably going to be doing machine shop stuff today, mainly. That's my main plan. Not the most interesting thing, but I'm making little carriers for the circuit board so you can attach them to the robot.

JESSICA: I really do need to take a nap right now, but I'm not going to though, but just so you know—I have dyslexia but it's a weird dyslexia, I have too much peripheral vision, so when I look at a page, I actually am seeing the entire page and then if I look up, when I look down again it's hard for me to find where I was because literally every part was processing. *(Begins dialing the phone.)* And my eyes get so tired that I end up falling asleep a lot when I read. Yeah, Alex it's Jess, call me back, bye. *(Dials again.)* God I'm seeing this weird blotch of, from the sun, of green on my hand, that I keep thinking—Yeah, Alex... You totally forgot my birthday... Yeah, thanks ...thanks a lot... it was fun. I had a murder mystery, dinner party...I killed the person, but I didn't know that... *(Sniffle.)* I made blinis and caviar, it was sooooo delish... *(Sniffle.)* I'm keeping a food diary. I'm writing down what I ate today. The first thing was cinnamon bun... 'cause I want to wear a bikini in Italy... June fifth... you are? You are? For what?... your honeymoon. Where are you going?... I'll leave you a note. Well I gotta get running... everything else good with you? ...Nice... okay bye. So anyway, my eyes hurt a lot. I got problems *(Laughs.)* staying awake.

AARON: Well, if you want to help, there's stuff for you to do. These just need to be filed down. You can take this. *(Picks up a file, demonstrates.)* You know what I mean. So I'll give you some of them, and I can do some. *(Walks back to his desk area and sits down in front of the bench.)*

JESSICA: I just told my professor last week that this is what I want to do for my Ph.D. I'm a little nervous about it, because it does require really high voltages, but I'll just keep one hand in my pocket or something. *(Writing sounds.)* Okay, so here's the plan. When I put voltage across this, two electrodes will want to come together, and that will make this stuff spread out, so essentially, it'll just go. *(Demonstrates.)* So hopefully I can make this move, and then ultimately I could have a sac of this stuff filled with some kind of battery fluid, swimming around in a tank. This thing, is just what I'm going to use to test it. *(Blows nose.)* ...Alright, I don't know if I'm ready to do this. You should at five thousand volts get thrown from the voltage source, if anything were to happen, a little less and you might stay on if it was oscillating, your muscles would start contracting, you wouldn't be able to let go. I'm hoping my shoes are rubber, and I'll keep one hand in my pocket so that I never end up touching the other electrode by accident... wouldn't that be tragic. Actually, can you help me for a sec?

CYNTHIA: I think right now with my new, you know, position at the Media Lab and stuff, you know that's so exciting that I haven't really thought about being an astronaut again. Someone from the National Research Council is putting together a committee to...essentially kind of an objective party that does a reality check on the proposed programs. So the committee that I've been nominated to serve on, they're still going through the process so I don't know if I'm on it yet, but it would be a pre-human mission involving rovers, which is obviously why they're contacting me. It would certainly be exciting to be involved in ah...in doing something like this committee and just kind of keeping in touch with it and, I mean, it is an honor.

SCENE 4
END OF THE DAY

AARON: *(Looking into a bag of newly filed pieces of metal.)* Sweet. Thanks for helping out.

(AARON holds a piece up for JESSICA to see.)

AARON: See what I made? Twenty-four of these. They're rainbows.

JESSICA: That's cute, Aaron. For your dreamcatcher?

AARON: It was really hard when I had no clue what I was going to do and I'd just kinda read papers all day and stare out the window but, if I have something tangible that I know I have steps I can take to work through it, then—

JESSICA: You just have to be okay with, you might leave work without having concluded anything. Or even found a new path. But you've worked on something, you just might not have—

AARON: But it's nice to go home and feel like you reached an end point for the day, and like you got something done—

JESSICA: Which is interesting 'cause you always know that you're at the end. Like, I always wonder how do I know when I'm ready to go, and you do, and there must be something in that, you know, like "oh, I've gotten to a certain point" even though it's something totally vague, you reach a goal—

AARON: Time to call it quits. I'm not ready to go home but it's like, it's time, you know—yeah, you just get tired.

JESSICA: Or I'm like, well, I can tell Rod I worked for three hours and I did this. I have to go to the restroom. Should I turn

this off when I leave? *(Pointing to the tape recorder.)*

AARON: No, I'm going to talk about you while you're gone. The thing about Jess is… *(Laughs.)*

(Music starts. Lights pull down.)

CYNTHIA: It's exciting. I mean I'm kind of at this point in my life where there's a lot of really exciting opportunities coming my way that I couldn't have predicted. Even two years ago, and uh, you know all you can do is just try to make the most out of every opportunity, appreciate it, you know, as it happens, because who knows if it's always going to be this way. But uh, it's been a wild couple of years. Yeah, it's been a wild couple years.

JESSICA: I don't want to give up, right? And I've become a totally different person, and I've learned more about myself more than any period of my life, and I don't want to stop doing those things. I want to find out, you know, where I can go with this.

AARON: I appreciate the mentality of the people that build these gothic cathedrals and start it in their lifetime even though it's not going to be done, and it's this epic work that will be done in two hundred years. But it's this great monument to whatever it is that you build it for, um, and so that's sort of the mentality that I adopted, and, you know, I think probably the religious parallel is appropriate, in that you find your beliefs and you follow that, perhaps blindly, but you have to choose something that you really believe in, and you keep doing it.

(A video of KISMET plays as lights fade down.)

END OF PLAY

THE SHADY MAIDS OF HAITI

John Jahnke

JOHN JAHNKE is a former ballet and opera student who received a bachelor's degree from the California Institute of the Arts' Fine Arts program. In Los Angeles, under the auspices of Los Angeles Contemporary Exhibitions, Jahnke created such original theatre works as *The Beasts of Luxury, Syphilis, The Monster of Dusseldorf or Paint Me, Paint Me Peter Kurten, The Deranged Cousins,* and *The Murderer's Companion,* all of which incorporated music, gesture, and language. He also mounted productions of Jean Anouilh's *Antigone* and Oscar Wilde's unfinished *La Sainte Courtisane.* He directed a number of short films and videos, including *His Red Snow White Apple Lips, Cakehole Howl,* and *Sex, Death and Rebirth in July,* which screened at numerous festivals throughout the United States, Canada, and Europe. In New York, through his company, The Hotel Savant, Jahnke wrote and directed *Lola Montez in Bavaria...* at both The New York International Fringe Festival and HERE Arts Center, *Mercurius* at HERE Arts Center, and *The Shady Maids of Haiti* at Soho Rep's Walkerspace. All works were developed through the assistance of Chashama, New York. Jahnke was a member of Reza Abdoh's Dar a Luz company, and appeared in *Quotations From a Ruined City* in Los Angeles, New York, and Europe as well as in Abdoh's production of Verdi's *Simon Boccannegra* at the Long Beach City Opera. Jahnke has also performed alongside many figures from the realm of performance, including Ann Magnuson, John Fleck, and Ron Athey. His next original work, *Funeral Games,* will debut in New York City in 2004. He resides in Manhattan.

The Shady Maids of Haiti was presented as a staged reading by The Hotel Savant on February 22, 2002, at Chashama, New York City. It was directed by John Jahnke and had the following cast:

M. .... Grant Neale
Mme. .... Louise Edmunds
Mlle. .... Natalie Lebert
X. .... Greig Sargeant
Le Jardinier .... Salvatore Garguilo

The Shady Maids of Haiti was presented by The Hotel Savant on September 27, 2002, at Soho Rep's Walkerspace, New York City, with the following cast and credits:

M. .... Grant Neale
Mme. .... Christina Campanella
Mlle. .... Tanisha Thompson
X. .... Rafeal Clements
La Femme Jardin .... Louise Edmunds

At certain performances, Mlle. was played by Natalie Lebert.

Direction: John Jahnke
Lighting Design: Andrew Hill
Costume Design: Hillary Moore
Turban Design: Luigi Murenu
Choreography: Hillary Spector
Set/Sound Design: John Jahnke
Stage Management: Karen Oughtred
Assistant Stage Management: Alex Andersen
Set Construction: House of Schwartz, Harold James
Sound Engineer: Jason Braun
Publicity: Spin Cycle
Photography: Josef Astor, Colin D. Young

The Hotel Savant would like to acknowledge New York State Council on the Arts, New York Foundation for the Arts, Saint and Devil, Inc., Ann Magnuson, Bonnie Kralovec, Jeanne Bernicky, Anne Foti, Barby Jo Petersen, Robert Simonson, Helen Garguilo, Anita Durst, Julie Atlas Muz, Cathy Bellavia, Brenda Brown, Kathleen White, Patrick O'Leary, Jeffrey Jones, and especially John and Eleanor Jahnke.

For Gianluigi Murenu.

CHARACTERS

M: Monsieur Pierrot, Le Comte de…, an exiled French poet
MME: Madame Palides, La Comtesse de…, his Creole wife
MLLE: Mademoiselle Groseille, their Haitian overseer
X: Viole Grendas, an African stranger

PLACE

The hilltop estate of Madame Palides, Haiti.

TIME

1803, at the peak of the slave uprising.

HISTORICAL NOTE

On April 27, 1802, Napoleon approves an act reestablishing slavery
in Haiti. On January 1, 1804, the soon-to-be-emperor Jean-Jacques
Dessalines, a former slave, declares independence for the first black
republic, and soon after orders the slaughter of all lingering French
islanders. He is later killed and dismembered by the "Mulattos" for
siding with the Africans in issues of land disbursement.

SCENIC NOTE

The stage is a raked turntable surrounded by a large festering garden.
Mobile archways represent windows and doors, allowing the actors to
move from one area of the estate to the next with a modicum of
movement. Various holes and obscured entrances also permit them
to appear and disappear, as if rising through the earth itself. If possible, the garden should utilize a variety of live plants, to be tended to
by the actors. Any furniture referenced should be easily moved and
unobtrusive, save the container of water (literal or figurative) used as
both well and bathtub.

PRODUCTION NOTE

The characters referenced as Le Jardinier and La Femme Jardin were
individually built into the separate productions, and represented a
spectral force maintaining the estate. Haunting the movements of the
actors, suggesting a liaison between the players and the narrative, the
specter moved from scene to scene in the shadows, delivering important props, mourning—or perhaps orchestrating—the impending
changeover. The role is not referenced in the script, and was strictly a
directorial choice.

PROLOGUE

*February. Sudden blackout, then light re-
veals four large flowers lying across a plat-
form upstage. In front of each flower is a
placard bearing a name. They read: MON-
SIEUR, MADAME, MADEMOISELLE,
and X. The flower petals open and the four
actors rise through their cores, allowing the
audience to identify them. The characters de-
scend through their flowers and disappear,
save MME who crosses to a well downstage.
Light changes as a splash is heard. MME
leans over the well as a few beams of sunlight fall through the trees and bounce off
the water, reflecting her face. Her dress is
disheveled and torn. The atmosphere is
dreamlike, but clear—winter's end.*

PART I

SCENE 1

March. MLLE enters.

MLLE: *(Pause.)* Madame?

MME: I've lost my spade.

MLLE: Your what?

MME: My gardening spade. I've dropped
it down the well.

MLLE: Yes…I remember.

MME: I see it resting clearly at the bottom. Come…look.

*(MLLE leans over the well. MME touches
the water.)*

MME: Would you retrieve it for me?

MLLE: I've already sent someone down.

MME: Have you? It's very deep, Mademoiselle.

MLLE: It's not an abyss.

MME: The depth of the water— the darkness of the copse—

MLLE: It's shallower than you think.

MME: Whom did you send down?

MLLE: Didn't you see?

MME: I've rippled the surface—

MLLE: Then wait for it to settle.

*(X becomes visible beneath the surface of the
water.)*

MME: Where did he come from?

MLLE: Through the break in the wall.

MME: Have you told Monsieur?

MLLE: He isn't up yet.

MME: I'm sure he'll be frightened.

MLLE: *(Pause.)* Your dress is torn in many
places.

MME: Is it?

MLLE: Where have you been?

MME: You've no right to ask—

MLLE: What have you done?

MME: Nothing that concerns you. *(Moves
away from the well.)* Isn't it rather early to
be out in the copse?

MLLE: For you, perhaps.

MME: The flowers are fading—

MLLE: You no longer attend them.

MME: It's so warm in the garden—it's
become a strain to stay in the sun.

*(MLLE wanders the copse as various shrubs
bearing heavy blooms sparkle in the dim light.)*

MLLE: The mandevilla has lost its pink
tinge and is invading the bed of the
gloriosa. The castor bean has dropped its
seed in the western section, poisoning the
hibiscus, and the bougainvillea reflects
nothing but the brown earth beneath it.

MME: I'm tired, Groseille.

MLLE: You need rest, Madame.

(MME disappears.)

MLLE: The only plant thriving is the oleander, and perhaps the brugmansia, and it's a danger even to touch them…

(X rises from the well holding a spade.)

X: I've retrieved the spade, Mademoiselle.

MLLE: Well…she'll be very pleased.

(X hands her the spade and sits down to dry.)

MLLE: There's very little sun here. You'll have to move out of the copse, Monsieur, if you'd like to be properly dry.

X: I enjoy the copse, Mademoiselle.

MLLE: You'll have a better view of the garden.

X: I've seen it.

MLLE: It's very hot in the sun when you garden, Monsieur.

X: I'm enjoying the shade, Mademoiselle.

MLLE: Where did you say you were engaged?

X: I didn't.

MLLE: Were you?

X: Was I what?

MLLE: Engaged?

X: I was.

MLLE: In what capacity?

X: As a gardener, Mademoiselle.

MLLE: L'homme jardin, Monsieur?

(She picks a piece of fruit and studies him as he enjoys the shade.)

MLLE: The garden was once very beautiful.

X: It still maintains a certain dignity.

MLLE: It's unhealthy.

X: Spring is just arriving.

MLLE: Would you like a seed? *(She opens the fruit and offers him a seed.)* What were you looking for when you wandered into our garden today?

X: A place to rest.

MLLE: You're not the first soldier to seek solace in the copse.

X: I am a gardener, Mademoiselle.

MLLE: You are a gardener—

X: So I said.

MLLE: You've yet to tell me who engaged you as a gardener—

X: You've yet to ask.

MLLE: And why you'd leave their employ—

X: That is difficult to answer.

MLLE: There are so few gardens left in St. Domingue, Monsieur.

X: I was engaged at the General's estate— I tended his wife's roses.

(A calm peaceful silence in the copse.)

MLLE: I would not ponder the future of that home.

X: It will go as the others.

MLLE: Does that preclude our destruction?

X: I am not the destructive type.

MLLE: You still seem more a soldier than a gardener.

X: Do I?

MLLE: You do.

X: Soldiers never bathe, Mademoiselle.

MLLE: Would you like another? *(She offers him another seed.)* What is your interest?

X: Shelter and employment.

MLLE: Is it?

X: Yes. *(Pause.)* May I prove my interest?

MLLE: That is entirely up to you.

X: *(Rises and walks around the copse; blood is seen on his shirt.)* The bed of the gloriosa.

MLLE: I pointed that out.

X: I was in the well.

MLLE: Then identify something unmentioned.

X: *(Looking.)* The creeping pilea. The crossandra, or what's left of it. The buttiana…granadilla passiflora. *(Pause.)* The brugmansia—

MLLE: I mentioned that one… You're very good with names.

X: An unusual flower.

MLLE: What is yours?

X: What is my what?

MLLE: Your name, Monsieur?

X: Grendas, Mademoiselle.

MLLE: Only Grendas?

X: Only Grendas, Mademoiselle.

MLLE: If you are unable to revive the garden—Grendas—I can promise you nothing.

X: As you said.

MLLE: And I cannot house you without Monsieur Pierre's consent.

X: I understand. *(Pause.)* Does that mean you are ready to take me?

MLLE: If Monsieur approves.

X: You've no say in the matter?

MLLE: None.

X: And if he approves?

MLLE: I cannot say that he will.

X: My position is dangerous?

MLLE: He is French—

X: I understand.

MLLE: Pierre—from Pierides or Pierrot.

X: You're adept with names as well. When will he know?

MLLE: Come this evening.

X: When?

MLLE: Nightfall.

X: Whom shall I ask for?

MLLE: Mademoiselle is sufficient.

X: Nothing else?

MLLE: What else would there be?

X: A familiar name?

MLLE: Your name is familiar—

X: Is it?

MLLE: Yes.

X: Unlikely.

MLLE: *(Biting the fruit.)* Uncommon.

M: *(Offstage.)* Mademoiselle!

(They stop. Window shutters rattle.)

MLLE: We shall speak again this evening.

M: *(Opening the shutters.)* Mademoiselle!

MLLE: *(To X.)* Monsieur—

X: I am waiting—

MLLE: For what?

X: Him to reveal your name.

MLLE: You'll wait some time—

M: Mademoiselle! *(Moves from the window and is heard rushing about.)*

MLLE: —My name is of no value in this household.

(M appears at the edge of the garden and catches sight of X as he exits with his sack. He watches as X disappears.)

M: Mademoiselle, where are you?…don't frighten me.

MLLE: In the copse, near the well.

(She picks at the fruit as M approaches.)

M: Who was that man?

(MLLE eats.)

M: Mademoiselle.

MLLE: A gardener.

M: A gardener?

MLLE: Yes.

M: What kind of a gardener?

MLLE: L'homme jardin, Monsieur.

M: What was he doing?

MLLE: Visiting.

M: No one visits these days.

MLLE: He retrieved Madame's spade from the well.

M: How did he enter the grounds?

MLLE: The wall is crumbling on the eastern front.

M: The man is a soldier—not a gardener.

MLLE: Have you seen him before?

M: Just now from behind—

MLLE: And you know he's a soldier?

M: His shirt is bloodied and he carries a sack.

MLLE: Have you ventured outside to catalog their dress?

M: Didn't you notice?

MLLE: It is quite dark in the copse—Monsieur.

M: The sun is peeking through. *(Pulls a letter from his cloak and fans himself.)*

MLLE: That is a nice cloak you're wearing.

M: Thank you.

MLLE: Is it new?

M: Yes—for winter's end.

MLLE: Isn't it warm?

M: No.

(The well gurgles. MLLE tosses the fruit core to the ground.)

MLLE: Do you know what Madame wore to the General's reception?

M: I do not.

MLLE: Yellow crepe with a silver border and a pink madras handkerchief—as pink as his skin.

M: Did she sing?

MLLE: I don't know.

M: She shouldn't attend his parties.

MLLE: It is his wife that invites her—for the novelty. What she is doing—outside your garden—at night—is not advisable.

M: You should watch her more closely. *(Pause.)* Why was he here?

MLLE: He escaped the General's estate.

M: Then it would be unwise to take him in.

MLLE: Madame is no longer capable of tending to the garden.

M: I cannot take on another gardener, Mademoiselle.

MLLE: The garden is dying, Monsieur.

(The light begins to reveal a sickly garden surrounding the stage.)

M: The oleander is thriving—

MLLE: The oleander is only one element of the garden—

M: As the garden is only one element of the estate.

MLLE: It is best to maintain, at this time, what it is that you have.

(MME enters the garden, now fully lit. She disappears behind a shrub.)

M: Is that he?

MLLE: It is Madame.

M: I thought she hadn't returned.

MLLE: This morning, Monsieur.

M: Have you spoken to her?

MLLE: I have not.

(A watering can pops through the shrub.)

M: What is she doing?

(Water streams from the can to the shrub.)

MLLE: Watering the brugmansia.

M: *(Pause.)* Shouldn't she be sleeping?

MLLE: She never sleeps.

(They listen to the water.)

MLLE: Think on the gardener, Monsieur.

M: The garden hides my home—nothing more—

MLLE: He might offer your home protection—

M: Soldiers make me nervous—

MLLE: It would be foolish to ignore the situation—

M: Then address it with her.

MLLE: Perhaps you should speak to her yourself—

M: Perhaps you should mind your assumption. You've no say in the matter.

(A breeze blows the letter out of M's hand.)

M: The wind is very strong today— it has taken my letter.

MLLE: Perhaps you should retrieve it, Monsieur.

(He rises to retrieve it. The watering can empties and disappears through the shrub.)

M: Deliver this—and find out where she's been.

MLLE: What is it, Monsieur?

(MLLE approaches M. As she touches the letter, a muffled sound like a gunshot is heard in the distance.)

M: Did you hear something?

MLLE: I don't think so.

(Silence—neither one of them moves. X re-enters the garden and falls to the ground.)

M: Mademoiselle! *(Pause.)* Is this your gardener?

MLLE: *(After a decision.)* Yes.

M: Is he not well?

MLLE: He doesn't appear to be.

M: Is he dead?

MLLE: I do not know, Monsieur.

M: Look closer!

(She takes the letter and goes to the body of X.)

M: What do you think?

MLLE: He's not quite dead yet—but he will be soon.

M: What do you see?

MLLE: On his neck—actually—no—it is closer to his chest on which...

M: On which what?

(MLLE opens the shirt of X, placing the letter on the ground.)

M: I wish the flowers took on such a brilliant gleam.

MLLE: Where did he come from?

M: I didn't see.

MLLE: The wall must be fixed.

M: Think of the cost—

MLLE: They may come looking—

M: Then bury the body.

MLLE: He isn't even dead yet!

M: Look—another spot of blood—seeping through the dirt.

MLLE: Listen...

(A few labored breaths escape from X. The light shifts.)

MLLE: His moments are passing.

M: Burn him.

MLLE: In the garden? Think of the smell!

M: Are you certain it's the gardener?

MLLE: I know this man, Monsieur.

M: Then who is after him?

(MLLE silences him as MME rustles through the garden.)

M: Who is that?

MLLE: It's your wife.

M: What will we do?

MLLE: Bury him near the cypress.

M: Lift his head—

MLLE: Make certain she does not see—

M: Look—you've dropped the letter—it cannot be delivered like this—it's spotted with his blood.

MME: *(Hidden.)* Pierre?

M: Why is she calling me?

MLLE: Ask her yourself.

M: Mademoiselle—

MME: *(Hidden.)* Pierre?

M: *(Pause.)* I've nothing to say—

MLLE: You seem frightened—

M: Of what?

MME: *(Emerging.)* Pierre?

(MLLE disappears with the body of X. M pockets the letter, then approaches MME from behind. He touches her, surprising her.)

MME: Is that you? Your touch has become...unknown to me.

M: Has it?

MME: Your hand is soft, Pierre, as a girl's.

M: I've never noticed— shall we move into the sun?

(He takes her arm.)

MME: You have blood on your hand.

M: I scratched it in the garden.

MME: You must be careful of what you touch.

(They pass through the foliage. The turntable rotates.)

MME: Someone is watching the house at night—

M: I keep a watchful eye.

MME: Your eyes are as soft as your hands—they offer no protection. It is luck we live on a hill.

INTERLUDE

April. A rotten swing appears in the garden.

MME: They would have a perfect view from here.

M: I'm surprised this hasn't fallen.

MME: Now that I recall the softness of your hand, why not push me? *(MME sits on the swing.)* Go ahead—don't be frightened…gently.

(M pushes the swing, which creaks. Another muffled shot is heard.)

MME: What was that?

M: I didn't hear anything.

MME: Didn't you? *(Pause.)* Harder, Pierre!

M: The rope will break.

(MLLE is seen dragging the body of X.)

MME: Who was that?

M: Mademoiselle.

MME: What was she doing?

M: Passing through the shade of the trees.

MME: She knows someone watches the house.

M: Does she?

MME: Her shoes tap the portico when I'm trying to sleep.

M: Perhaps she's sleepless as well. *(He pushes the swing harder.)*

MME: Be careful, Pierre.

M: How are your flowers, Palides?

MME: Why do you ask?

M: You've been spending less time with them.

MME: It would be easier for me if they'd succumb in winter when death is at least expected.

M: Where have you been then, if not in the garden?

MME: Why would it matter to you, Pierre?

M: Your dress is tattered, Palides.

(MME is silent.)

M: You tell me nothing anymore.

MME: You never ask.

M: You never answer.

(MME stops the swing, feeling unwell. The sun falls behind them.)

MME: I'm tired—

M: You need sleep—

MME: Then take me inside. Put me to bed.

SCENE 2

Spring; May. M escorts MME through an arch where a bed appears. He attempts to unlace her dress—she resists. MLLE enters with a pan of water, rinses her hands, and mops MME's brow. M moves to an open window that leads to the garden.

MME: Who watches the house, Groseille?

MLLE: No one watches the house but me.

MME: Was it you I saw today, passing behind the portico?

MLLE: I passed the portico many times today—how could I know what you see?

M: What do you see, Palides? I'd like to know.

MME: Envy. *(Pause.)* My spade resting clearly at the bottom of the well.

MLLE: You have a fever, Madame. *(Pours medicine in a glass.)*

MME: Have you borrowed one of my scarves, Mademoiselle?

(The letter falls from M's cloak.)

MME: What is that letter, Pierre?

M: What?…oh…it's a letter to the Embassy—

MME: Why do you continue to write the Embassy?

M: An act of habit.

MME: Isn't it abandoned?

M: I don't know…I don't think so.

MLLE: Drink this.

M: Is it strange that I continue to write?

MME: There's blood on the letter.

M: I must have cut my hand on the swing.

MME: After you scratched it in the garden?

MLLE: Madame.

(MLLE offers MME the glass.)

MLLE: Monsieur—

(MLLE picks up the letter and leads M out through the window.)

MLLE: Do you know what is happening in your bedroom?

M: Have you told her anything?

MLLE: And do you know what is happening in Haiti, Monsieur?

M: She's hiding something—

(There are uneasy sounds of movement from the garden as MME drinks from the glass.)

M: What is that sound in the garden?

MLLE: Your wife is not well.

M: Listen—it's coming from the cypress.

MLLE: If France is unwilling to take you back—look elsewhere.

M: Is your dark Emperor not dead, Mademoiselle?

MLLE: His body has not been found.

M: Then see where that sound is coming from.

(MLLE begins to exit with the letter—M grabs her wrist and retrieves it. She exits. MME becomes hot from the drug, unlacing her dress. M plucks a bloom from the garden and reenters the room. A vase glows near the bed—he places the flower in the vase, then exits. MME opens her eyes, sees the flower, and goes to the window.)

MME: Hibiscus, bougainvillea… mandevilla, oleander and justica…heliotrope and magnolia…belladonna and ricinus— are not as weak as…the corteline, the agave, the gardenia, the burgea, the shady maids…the gloriosa.

(A shadow passes. Slowly, the figure of X begins to rise from a large flower in the garden, illuminated by the moonlight, his clothing torn and covered in blood.)

MME: Did you retrieve my spade, Monsieur?

X: *(Faintly.)* If you'd be so kind as to…let me rest.

MME: Are you the dust of illness clouding my vision—or merely the drug of Groseille's drink?

X: Please...

(MME allows X to enter the room through the window, guiding him to her bed. She opens his shirt then removes the scarf from her head, stanching his wound. She gives him a drink from the glass, then joins him in bed. Abruptly, she kisses his lips.)

(MLLE enters.)

MLLE: You've become undone—placing rebels in your bed.

MME: You've become staid, passive—as I once was.

MLLE: *(Pause.)* What have you given him?

MME: What you gave to me.

MLLE: Where did he come from?

MME: The bed of the gloriosa.

MLLE: Did he say anything?

MME: He wanted a place to rest.

MLLE: Rinse your hands.

(MME rises from the bed and rinses her hands in the pan.)

MLLE: Haiti is stained by the blood of the French—who kill the African, who kill our own, which kill themselves. They'll take your property.

MME: Is it still mine?

MLLE: It's all you've left. Your marriage has destroyed whatever safety we once had.

MME: Has it?

MLLE: Assimilating yourself—that will be your death.

MME: Why not amuse myself?

MLLE: Lady Bonaparte's court disappears day by day— Death follows them on their way home from tea in the form of that man in your bed. *(Notices the scarf on X's wound.)* Do you know the cost of this scarf?

MME: Have you been taking stock?

(A snip is heard from the garden—flowers fall.)

MLLE: I need clean water and more of that— *(She gestures to the empty glass.)*

MME: Do you know what that costs me?

MLLE: You're lucky it continues to bloom—

MME: It's imported from Izmir!

MLLE: And is your husband's singular companion—

MME: There are thieves in my garden—

(X coughs up blood.)

MLLE: Did he say anything else to you?

(He coughs again.)

MLLE: Pour it.

(MLLE studies the wound as MME pours more of the drink.)

MLLE: It could be you, mistaken, forgotten by the side of the road, blood feeding the weeds—your husband dispatched—

MME: Pierre will never leave.

MLLE: Pierre is welcome nowhere.

MME: He does not like the General's parties—

MLLE: He is wiser than you—

MME: He plays no games, he doesn't dance. He does not like to have fun—

MLLE: I'm not speaking only of the General's parties. St. Domingue is rotten—full of poison.

(MLLE takes the drink and pours it down the throat of X.)

MLLE: The blood of their barbarous balls has stained your perception.

(Snipping sounds from the garden as flowers fall.)

MLLE: They feed rebellious slaves to the dogs in the courtyard for the amusement of their guests…don't they? And you—drunk, sotted on champagne—cool yourself under the feathered fans of the obedient Africans, safely sequestered from the murderous spectacle by the dark recess of the ladies' chamber, where you take your turn on the sofa with a silent and bonded trophy. And now that you've been followed—

MME: I've never seen him—

MLLE: Now that you've been trapped—

MME: Have you never been hunted, Groseille?

MLLE: You offer sanctuary—like a gift—

MME: You didn't answer my question.

MLLE: You play two sides, refusing to defend your home merely for the attention it might afford you—as if coquetry would be the drug that finally forces you to surrender the empty well of your soul to whomever offers the highest price.

MME: And who would that be?

MLLE: A stranger—

MME: A slave?

MLLE: A thief? Your husband prowls the estate for a means of claiming what he perceives to be his. He conjures forgotten memories of your sweet and comforting kiss as a stranger bleeds on your sheets.

MME: Is it a deceit to offer comfort?

MLLE: To the weak.

MME: Where would Pierre be without comfort?

MLLE: Dead, Madame.

MME: *(Pause.)* Even the orange trees are fetid—nothing around me emits a pleasant odor anymore.

(Silence. They listen to the irregular breathing of X.)

MME: Have you never surrendered, Groseille?

MLLE: Not as you.

MME: Your lies are sweeter than truth, are they not?

(Another snip—flowers fall to the ground.)

MME: Look at his hands—they're so unlike Pierre's. Who is he, Groseille?… Who shot him?

(Footsteps are heard in the garden.)

MME: What is he looking for?

MLLE: Quiet!

(June. M appears and wanders through the foliage carrying flowers. MME and MLLE watch him through the window as he studies a plant. Inspecting its flowers, he cuts one. He crosses to another and continues to cut a few healthy flowers, creating a nosegay, which he admires in the moonlight. Finally he comes to the shady maids and inspects the plant. He finds a flower he likes and reaches out to grasp it. Again MLLE gestures for MME to be quiet. M's hand hesitates over the flower.)

MME: *(Whispers.)* What is he doing?

MLLE: Quiet!

MME: It's brugmansia.

MLLE: Quiet!

(He touches the flower and cuts it.)

MME: *(Interrupting.)* Pierre.

M: *(Surprised, turns to them.)* I thought you were sleeping.

MME: Pierre, drop the flower.

M: Shouldn't you be sleeping?

MME: Shouldn't you? Please—drop the flower.

(He doesn't move. She passes through the window into the garden. MLLE stands in the same, blocking X from view.)

MME: What are you doing?

M: Picking flowers, what's left of them.

MME: I've never known you to pick flowers.

M: I was going to place them in your room.

MME: While I was sleeping?

M: Yes—but you're not sleeping.

MME: I can't—Pierre—

M: Yes?

MME: You should look more closely at what you pick—it's brugmansia.

M: Which one?

MME: *(Approaching him.)* That one.

M: You were watching me—

MME: Please. Drop it.

M: *(Lets the flower drop.)* The rest are for you.

MME: Thank you.

(X gasps.)

MLLE: Madame—

MME: The shady maids are poisonous to the touch, Pierre.

M: Are they?

MME: Your hands will begin to peel.

M: Will they?

MME: We need to rinse them—I have water in my room.

MLLE: Palides!

MME: Take the nosegay from Monsieur, Groseille. It is quite safe.

MLLE: Shouldn't we wash his hands in the well?

MME: And poison the water?

M: They're beginning to itch.

MLLE: Or in the stream, Palides—

M: If Madame wishes to invite me into her room to wash my hands—don't interfere.

MME: I would like to touch your hands again.

MLLE: What will you show him in your room?

MME: What I showed you.

MLLE: Palides!

MME: In my bed.

M: Leave us, Mademoiselle.

MME: I think it better if she accompanies us.

M: Why? You do?

MME: You may be surprised by what you find in my bed.

M: You're frightening me.

MME: Am I? First we must wash your hands. Close your eyes.

M: Why must I close my eyes?

MME: For the surprise.

MLLE: Palides.

(MME blindfolds him with a scarf from her dress.)

M: I do not like surprises. How many scarves you have, Palides.

MME: Come with me.

MLLE: Madame.

MME: He must wash his hands, Mademoiselle, and understand the situation, as he is responsible in part for its creation.

(MLLE takes the nosegay and steps aside. MME leads M through the window to the bedroom, his hands in the air, X illuminated in bed.)

(Silence as they enter the room. MME leads M to the pan of water where he rinses his hands.)

MME: Has the itching stopped?

M: Yes—but now the cloth is chafing my eyes.

(MLLE arranges the flowers in the vase.)

M: The water is warm.

(M pulls his hands from the water—they begin to itch again. MME places them back in the water.)

M: I really don't like surprises—please remove the scarf.

(MME silences MLLE with a look and removes the scarf from his eyes. He pulls his hands from the water upon seeing X.)

MME: Put your hands back in the water!

M: Mademoiselle?

MME: You knew he was watching the house.

M: Mademoiselle!

MME: *(Pause.)* He did not die as I thought he might. I left him in the garden to bury, in a dark spot beneath the cypress—but when I returned with the shovel, after the sun had set...the body was no longer there.

MME: Groseille!

M: Where was it?

MME: He had wandered through the archway into my bedroom.

M: Where he did what?

MME: Took to my bed—

M: Why?

MME: —To rest.

M: *(Pause.)* Nothing else?

MME: I kissed him.

M: Did you?

MME: Yes.

M: In what way?

MME: On his mouth.

MLLE: Monsieur—she is not well.

MME: No—I am not.

M: In what way are you not well?

(Silence.)

M: Lack of sleep?

MME: Perhaps.

MLLE: Monsieur. I assure you nothing took place—he is wounded.

MME: As are you, Pierre—I can see it in your eyes. Come—look at him—gaze upon the strength of his face.

M: I have seen it.

MME: The wound has failed to drain it away...

(All stare at X. The shady maids shift in the garden, leaking sap.)

MME: His corpus somniferous exudes a certain sway—

M: For a gardener—

MME: A gardener?

MLLE: Monsieur—

MME: You meant to take away my garden and place it in his hands?

M: If he had lived.

MME: He is still alive.

M: *(Sighs.)* He wasn't earlier!

MME: Let me see your hands.

(He pulls his hands from the water.)

MME: How white they are, Pierre— bleached and lifeless and secretive. I believe you developed a callus today. I must see what damage they've done to my garden.

(MME stares at MLLE then heads toward the garden. She stops at the nosegay, lost in a memory, then exits.)

M: Will he live?

MLLE: It may be to your advantage to have him on your side.

M: He has poisoned my wife's lips, Mademoiselle.

MLLE: With less than you have poisoned her, Monsieur.

M: *(Silent.)*

MLLE: If he lives, you will make him our gardener, or I shall inform Madame of your true condition—

M: *(Seething.)* She has given him her bed.

MLLE: She no longer visits yours, does she? *(Sighs.)* You are marked for slaughter, Monsieur. The French Defense has been lifted, and a little protection is—something to hope for.

M: And what would be in it for you, Mademoiselle?

MLLE: Are you thinking of me? Let me see your hands.

(He shows them to her.)

MLLE: Put them back in the water.

(He puts them back in the water. MLLE goes to X.)

M: Are we in danger?

MLLE: No more than usual. No more than before.

(MME is seen preparing in a mirror, dressing for a party.)

M: Why haven't you told her anything?

MLLE: *(Pause.)* It is not my position to inform her of your tiny deceits. *(MLLE cuts the shirt from X's body and washes his wounds.)* Why haven't you?

M: When? As she stands at the window removing herself from me, waiting for spring to end—on our bed she no longer sleeps in—on her swing? Have you studied the effects, Mademoiselle...on faces at the market, in the streets—deaf, yellow, rotting faces—weaving their way through the crowd like a fetid chain of daffodils? Their color betrays any attempt to disguise the acceleration of disease. Bonnets, collars, gloves—all vain useless items. It is better not to know.

MLLE: You should watch her more closely, Monsieur.

(MME pins a veil to her turban.)

M: She never questions me, Mademoiselle, as you do. It is not in her nature.

She cares only to provide, to offer, to enjoy herself in a way very few of us are able to understand. My refugee status is what appealed to her. The fact that I am dependent and weak—exiled—tainted in the eyes of my country and this one. You know nothing of my tiny deceits, only your own. I was ill when I met her, ignorant to the source of my own discomfort—I did not know the natural weakness of her system. I would never have offered her my...

MLLE: Rotten?

M: No—

MLLE: Your wretched—

M: Stop—

MLLE: Your wretched kiss?

(MME leaves her room and enters the garden. Distant music is heard as M studies the body of X.)

MLLE: She knows—only not that it is you—the source of her discomfort; she thinks of you as virginal and pure. And when that first yaw appears on your shoulder, your back, your chest, she will assume her guilt and withdraw from you further. Anyway—I asked for no explanation.

(MME exits.)

M: Where has she gone?

MLLE: It is not my place to know.

M: *(Again pulls his hands from the water.)* And what will I do, Mademoiselle, when that first yaw appears?

MLLE: What anyone else in your position might—mercury, vapor baths—there is little else.

M: *(Moves toward MLLE.)* Do you like that music, Mademoiselle?

MLLE: If you enjoy dancing.

M: I prefer...to fuck—I do. I just never have the chance anymore.

(He reaches out to touch her breast. She catches his wrist.)

MLLE: Put them back in the water, Monsieur.

(M returns to the pan as MLLE covers X with a clean white sheet.)

INTERLUDE

The turntable rotates as MME enters with croquet mallet and ball. Strange music is heard as we enter the realm of her perception. M and MLLE don masks and take hold of flowered wickets, through which MME hits her ball in rotation (as a dance), mocking her as she passes. In the final round MME hits her ball through wickets aimed at the bed of X. As it strikes, X rises and pulls back the sheet to reveal a pool of blood. He dons a mask and joins the others. Frightened, MME raises her mallet as if to strike them, then flees the stage. All drop their masks; X moves to the garden, M and MLLE, under arches, observe him. The bed disappears. Spring has passed.

PART II

SCENE 3

July.

MLLE: Don't stare at him, Monsieur—

M: He's risen so early—

MLLE: He's healed very well—

M: I wasn't expecting him to be out of bed so soon.

MLLE: Don't stare!

M: Where is he going?

MLLE: Into the sun.

M: He's healed so well—he's so healthy!

MLLE: What do you intend to do?

M: What do you mean—intend to do?

MLLE: Do you intend to take him on?

M: I'd hoped he wouldn't live.

MLLE: It is in your interest to do so.

M: So you've stated quite clearly—

MLLE: I am interested only in your protection.

M: Then you leave me no option— (Coughs.)

MLLE: You're pale, Monsieur…

M: Am I?

MLLE: Are you not well?

M: I'm marked for slaughter, am I not?

MLLE: Perhaps you should rest?

M: (Pause.) Now that he's risen, inform Monsieur of his duties.

MLLE: Very well.

(A letter blows in and lands at MLLE's feet.)

M: What is that?

MLLE: I will let you know in a moment.

M: What a pretty scarlet seal—

MLLE: Have you seen it before?

M: I don't recall—

MLLE: You've grown even paler—

M: Have I?

MLLE: To bed, Monsieur.

(She picks up the letter.)

M: It reminds me…

MLLE: Of what, Monsieur?

M: (Pause.) The somniferum in the garden.

(Light reveals an opium den sequestered behind M's shutters. He leaves his arch to enter this room. MLLE retrieves a shovel from the dirt.)

MLLE: Monsieur Grendas—if you are well enough to address it—the garden is in desperate need of your attention. Follow me.

(X follows her through the garden to study the plants.)

X: The mandevilla sanderi has lost its scarlet tinge and has invaded the bed of the gloriosa and the crossandra. The castor bean has dropped its seed in the western section, poisoning the justica carnea, and the bougainvillea buttiana reflects nothing but the brown earth…The only shrub thriving is the oleander, and perhaps the yellow flowers of the brugmansia—what does Madame call them?

MLLE: (Pause.) The shady maids.

(M peeks his head out of the shutters as he changes into a nightshirt.)

M: One must be careful when handling them—they are a danger to touch. My sensitive hands were chafed for days.

X: Were they?

M: They're still quite pink.

X: Are they?

M: Would you like to see them?

MLLE: Monsieur Grendas has work to do.

M: Well I am here if you'd like to see their irritation.

MLLE: How did you know she has a pet name for the brugmansia?

X: She spoke it to me.

MLLE: When?

X: In the bedroom.

MLLE: She spoke of the garden?

X: Yes.

M: Although my hands were never bandaged, she washed them when they itched, but she did not speak of the garden to me except to say that it was easier for her to lose the flowers in winter and that…that it was not well, as she was not well—

MLLE: Monsieur. *(To X.)* I don't know when she spoke of the garden—

M: Have you broken the seal, Mademoiselle?

(MLLE opens the letter and reads. He studies his hands.)

M: How pink they look in the sun—are you certain you would not like to look at them? They are as pink as…

X: An amaryllis?

M: Yes. *(Pause.)* Monsieur—you're barely dressed—your clothes are rags—they're hardly clothes at all. Here—take my shirt.

(He tosses his shirt to X.)

X: Thank you. *(Dressing.)* What month is it?

M: I do not know…ask Mademoiselle.

X: Mademoiselle?

MLLE: *(Reading.)*

M: Mademoiselle?

MLLE: Pardon?

M: What month is it?

MLLE: July, Monsieur.

M: Then midsummer has come to its end—and it's been so dull. Why don't you take my breeches as well?

(MLLE finishes reading the letter as X takes the trousers from M.)

MLLE: It would be best if he began his work. There are other issues to be addressed inside.

M: Are there?

MLLE: You will find what tools you need outside the old chapel—near the swing on the hill—that overlooks the General's estate.

X: Thank you, Mademoiselle—

MLLE: She didn't speak of *my* name as well?

X: She did not.

(MLLE observes X in his new clothes. M prepares an opium pipe.)

X: Who taught you to read?

MLLE: Pardon?

X: You were reading his letter.

MLLE: I owned property once.

X: Until Napoleon saw fit to strip it away.

MLLE: A brief period of happiness and profit.

X: And you'd like to again?

MLLE: That is none of your concern—

X: Where is his courtesan now?

MLLE: Monsieur—

X: What is wrong with her?

M: What is in that letter, Mademoiselle?

X: He has no other name for you?

MLLE: I told you he did not.

X: And may I?

MLLE: Mademoiselle is sufficient.

(MLLE passes through her arch as M smokes the opium pipe. X takes the shovel and begins to dig a hole in the garden. His sack is now visible through a gap in the shrub.)

(MME appears, disheveled and torn, wandering through the foliage. Her dress is marked with tiny spots of blood.)

MME: What are you doing to the shady maids?

X: The castor bean has dropped its seeds in the bed.

MME: I thought only the hibiscus has been poisoned by the ricinus.

X: How long has it been since you tended to the garden?

MME: How long has it been since you recovered from your wound?

(He pauses with his digging to assess her state.)

MME: Did I speak of this shrub to you?

X: You did.

MME: It is my favorite.

X: Is it?

MME: Yes.

X: Where have you been?

MME: At a reception.

X: An awfully long reception—

MME: I was invited by Lady Bonaparte for the weekend activities.

X: *(Bristling.)* Were you?

MME: Yes. *(She saunters coquettishly toward the swing in the garden.)*

X: Did you sing?

MME: No.

X: *(Pause.)* How did you spend your time?

MME: The ladies were requested to play croquet in the ballroom—

X: A decadent activity.

MME: Is it? Small tufts of mud and lawn were placed in troughs that ran the length of the room. We putted them about until…

X: Until what?

MME: Well…they putted them about until—I became bored and excused myself from the ballroom.

X: Where did you go?

MME: I looked for a swing in the garden.

X: Did you find one?

MME: No. Not at first.

X: Did you find anything else?

MME: I found a pond where the most beautiful flowers were blooming…and I bent down to drink the water, for it was surprisingly clear, and I thought about my garden…and then—I guess I'd had too much champagne—I lay down on the grass and fell asleep. When I awoke the thought of dying flowers filled my head and I wanted to return home. I made my way back toward the ballroom to say farewell, but…

X: But what?

MME: It was already quite late and no one had missed me. The ladies were gone and the men were sprawled on the lawn, drunken and riled. I thought of escaping the estate through the north gate, but as I turned to leave I noticed something strange among the men…in the center of their scattered circle large dogs were playing, or fighting, I couldn't make it out. I drew slightly closer to see what they were attacking, but when I did I realized they weren't…they weren't attacking their own, but were tearing apart a living being—muffled screams from its clotted throat hit the earth and scattered nowhere. The General was feeding a slave to his dogs for the amusement of the Europeans. I saw an arm torn from its socket and the stomach ripped open by the white teeth of the dogs, its contents spilling to the ground. A vest of red fabric, split where the stomach had been cut, was tossed at my feet, and I thought it stained by the blood of the slave—gurgling a small fountain from his throat onto the grass—but it was a costly scarlet garment, dyed and well constructed, only partially stained by the blood of the man, an elaborate costume I had never known a slave to wear. I began to feel sick as the smell of the entrails hit my nose, and I ran to the pond—dipping my head in the water, breathing in the perfume of the flowers to clear the stench… I then made my way to the north gate and walked home. But the blood of the man must have splattered in my direction—for there are small spots of red marking my dress…and I've torn it in many places trying to remove them—but there are too many.

X: You're cut and bleeding as well.

MME: Am I?

X: *(Approaching.)* Are you not well, Madame?

MME: Not well, Monsieur?

X: There is concern on the part of…

MME: Who?

X: Mademoiselle.

MME: Is there?

(MLLE appears in the garden with a lantern.)

MME: Mademoiselle has taken my authority, you the garden, and my husband my wealth. Why should I be well?

X: But you've lived well up to this point, have you not?

MME: You look through my words—

X: As long as the General lives, your husband is a target for slaughter.

MME: Will you kill me for being a decadent woman?

(She moves away from him. MLLE disappears.)

X: Why won't he leave?

MME: Would you return to your home, Monsieur, if you could?

X: His presence decreases your worth, Madame.

MME: *(Pause.)* It's very warm.

X: Why not remove your shawl?

(X picks up her fan from the ground and fans himself.)

X: A little worse for the wear—is it singed?

(She takes the fan from him.)

X: One must be careful of fire at this time of year. Do you always fan yourself?

MME: I keep no slaves.

X: That doesn't stop you from enjoying their work at the estate of the General—if you can, Madame? *(Pause.)* Do you not recall my face?

MME: No.

(He moves in closer.)

X: Anything else?

MME: No.

(He presses against her.)

X: Nothing at all?

(He kisses her.)

MME: No.

X: Think again. You spoke of your garden…

MME: *(Pause.)* What do you want from me?

X: I have been stripped of all wants—there are only things I need.

MME: What do you need?

X: A place to rest my head. A piece of property to tend to.

MME: My property, Monsieur?

X: L'homme jardin, Madame.

MME: You've taken my bed as well as the garden—what's to prevent you from taking my home?

(She escapes his grasp.)

MME: Property cannot own property, Monsieur.

X: *(Kneels.)* And if that property were a gift—

MME: Are you offering yourself to me?

(Silence.)

MME: I doubt Monsieur would forgive an implication—

X: He will be killed soon, anyway, will he not?

(M, drugged from the opiate, appears in the garden carrying a lantern.)

MME: Your tongue spits fire—one must be careful of fire at this time of year.

X: Your property will not be burned.

MME: Do you know what day it is?

X: The summer has come to an end, Madame.

MME: Then its days are numbered.

X: I would not advise you attend any more receptions…

(She pulls away and looks in the hole. Light emanates upward as she studies its contents.)

MME: Was your Emperor not known for wearing red vests, Monsieur?

(X moves in closer. MLLE appears with letter, lantern, and key.)

MME: It is not my husband you'll kill, but my garden if you dig any deeper. *(Exits into the trees.)*

(August. M follows MLLE toward the entry of the bathhouse, as X begins to dig again.)

M: What is he doing?

MLLE: You didn't listen—

M: What is he digging?

MLLE: Your grave, Monsieur—

M: The dirt falls so heavily to the ground.

MLLE: She's in serious trouble—

M: So you said.

MLLE: *(Inserts her key in the arch of the bathhouse.)* Sores were visible above the embroidered band on her dress—

M: I am not deaf, Mademoiselle.

MLLE: Not yet.

(The arch opens—M passes through. Fireflies glow in the darkness.)

MLLE: And when Lady Bonaparte pointed out the sores in front of her court, Palides drew the rough edge of the croquet mallet across the lady's face, then withdrew to the shadows, splattered with blood.

M: Put out your lantern.

(M blows his out—MLLE does not.)

M: Put it out!

(MLLE covers her lantern. M watches the fireflies.)

M: Do you like fireflies, Mademoiselle—

MLLE: Disrupting the darkness like tiny sparks of hope? *(Pause.)* You continue to deny the situation.

M: Where is she now?

MLLE: She fled the ballroom and disappeared.

M: Listen. *(M listens to the digging.)* He digs so deeply—

MLLE: Dressed in her gifts—ill and wandering the city alone.

M: It is her home—

(M removes his cloak. MLLE notices the bloody letter in the pocket.)

M: —She knows it well.

(M turns to uncover the bathtub. MLLE switches the two letters.)

M: What is your concern?

MLLE: You must leave her, Monsieur.

M: What of my vapor bath?

MLLE: You must protect yourself—

M: The African will protect me—so you said—what is the point of leaving now?

MLLE: You help neither yourself nor Palides.

M: And you aim to help whom?

MLLE: Leave tonight before the ships are blocked.

M: You'd like to see me die, wouldn't you?

MLLE: You tempt it yourself, daily, by remaining.

M: I will not leave her—

MLLE: You leave her to wander—

M: As she always returns.

(MLLE moves to the arch.)

M: Where are you going?

MLLE: To find her myself.

M: What of my bath—it needs preparing—the tub is full of dirt—

MLLE: As the grave, Monsieur—which he's digging for you.

M: You know she's only hiding in the garden.

MLLE: From you, Monsieur—

M: From you, Mademoiselle—

(The fireflies flicker and die.)

INTERLUDE

MME's voice is heard as she rises from the earth.

MME: *(Sings.)* Dryadella, duchesnea—
Wipe your tears away.
Coronilla, columnea—
Death has come to play.

MLLE: It's not as it was—she will do nothing more to protect you. *(Turns to leave.)* Leave tonight—you've plenty of gifts to make your proper exit.

(MLLE exits the bathhouse with her lantern and crosses to one of the large flowers—its petals open for her. MME moves toward the well.)

MME: *(Sings.)* Oleandra, onopordum—
Pray for Death to stay.
Foetidia, fontinalis—
Never turn away.

(M, at the arch, observes the garden; MLLE descends into the flower. X ceases to dig, drops his sack down the hole, and descends as well. The turntable rotates as M takes a look at the empty garden, blinking his eyes in disbelief, as if hallucinating. He closes the arch of the bathhouse, distrustful of what he's seen.)

SCENE 4

September. MME studies her reflection in the well. Her appearance is worsened and exhausted. MLLE reemerges in the copse.

MME: Pierre?

(MLLE emerges from the foliage.)

MME: How did you know to find me?

MLLE: The well echoes throughout the copse.

(Silence.)

MLLE: It's been a long time since I've heard you sing.

(Silence.)

MLLE: Are you thirsty, Palides?

MME: Yes.

MLLE: Why don't you drink? *(Offers her a cup from the well.)*

MME: Did we wash his hands in this well?

MLLE: No.

MME: Thank you. *(MME drinks.)*

MLLE: Why haven't you returned to the house?

MME: It's no longer mine.

MLLE: Isn't it?

MME: He desecrates the earth beneath it.

MLLE: The gardener?

MME: Pierre.

MLLE: Would you like another drink? *(MLLE offers another cup of water.)* The deed remains in your name, does it not?

MME: Yes. *(MME drinks.)*

MLLE: Pierre must leave.

(Silence.)

MLLE: He is sick, Palides.

(Silence.)

MLLE: Are you listening?

MME: I've always known—why do you think I cannot look at him?

MLLE: He's betrayed you in more than one way. *(MLLE pulls the bloodied letter from her pocket.)*

MME: What is that?

MLLE: Don't you recall?

(MLLE extends the letter to MME over the well—she does not take it.)

MLLE: You're not as curious as I thought.

MME: There's blood on it.

(Silence.)

MME: What does it contain?

MLLE: It is the letter Monsieur wrote—before your illness was…visible—asking that the province proclaim you, at his request, legally unsound…and therefore unable to hold property.

MME: Why wasn't it delivered?

MLLE: Monsieur is forgetful in his loneliness.

MME: Unlike you. *(MME tentatively reaches out over the water—she takes the letter.)*

MLLE: Come back to the house, Palides—

MME: I cannot return—

MLLE: There are things to attend to.

MME: Your gardener is a soldier, Groseille.

MLLE: You offered him your bed—

MME: And you offered him a purpose—

MLLE: To protect Monsieur.

MME: To protect yourself.

(Silence.)

MME: His interests are not in your favor—I assure you. You must sever your relations with the gardener...as I with Pierre. *(MME moves into a patch of moonlight that exposes a glistening sore on her neck.)* He used to be quite beautiful.

MLLE: Yes, he did.

MME: As beautiful as the garden.

MLLE: It still maintains a certain dignity.

(The bathhouse glows upstage.)

MME: Have you been with the gardener, Groseille? Surrendered, as me?

(M slips into the tub.)

MLLE: Quiet!

(Sounds of splashing water.)

MLLE: He's in the bath.

MME: Who?

MLLE: Monsieur.

MME: Is he?

MLLE: Listen.

MME: In the water?

MLLE: Yes.

MME: How strange.

MLLE: Listen closely.

(The water continues to splash—a shadow passes.)

MLLE: They're both there.

MME: What?

MLLE: Grendas is with him.

MME: In the bathtub?

MLLE: No—listen.

MME: One can't tell by listening—go to the window.

MLLE: I will not.

MME: You're afraid to look at him—

MLLE: At Monsieur?

MME: At the gardener—

MLLE: He's not in the water—

MME: How do you know?

MLLE: He bathed in the well—

MME: In the well?

MLLE: He retrieved your spade—

MME: Why didn't you tell me?

MLLE: You constantly disappear—

MME: I'm drinking the water—

MLLE: Your memory is fading—your mind is a sieve—

MME: That wouldn't prevent him from bathing again—

MLLE: With Monsieur?

MME: In the well—

MLLE: He's not in the well—

MME: Then where *is* he?

MLLE: At the window—watching.

(They listen to the washing. X approaches the bathhouse.)

MLLE: It is best if Pierre leaves–

MME: With a soldier at our door? *(MME leaves the well.)*

MLLE: Where are you going?

MME: The old perch in the cypress has a view of the bathhouse—Pierre used to watch me bathe from there. Take my hand if you'd like—it's strong enough to hold us both. Come.

(MLLE follows MME—they disappear in the foliage.)

INTERLUDE

X observes M in the bathtub. M breathes in the steaming vapors, a large sheet over his head. Cannons are heard in the distance— M stiffens. X moves to the shadows of the archway. Plants move in the garden as the turntable shifts. Summer has passed.

PART III

SCENE 5

October. M lifts his sheet, spotting the shadow of X.

M: Monsieur Grendas?

X: Yes.

M: How is the garden?

X: The dryadella bloomed today, Monsieur.

M: Very good.

X: But it will take time to restore it to its former state.

M: Isn't it rather dark to continue your work?

X: I've already finished.

M: Oh. *(Pause.)* Did you hear the cannons… Monsieur?

X: Yes.

M: Did they frighten you?

X: No.

M: What has happened outside?

X: They're approaching your General's estate.

M: Oh. *(Pause.)* Have you seen Mademoiselle or Madame Palides?

X: No.

M: Why don't you come in? It may be… safer.

X: Thank you. I would like that. *(X steps through the arch into the bathhouse. He wears gloves and carries a bundle of brugmansia flowers, which he arranges in a vase.)*

M: What lovely flowers… Would you like to sit down?

X: Thank you. *(X removes his gloves and sits down opposite the tub.)*

M: You're awfully far away.

X: Am I?

M: Come closer, I cannot hear you.

(X moves closer, noticing a glass by the tub— M sees this and coughs.)

X: Are you thirsty, Monsieur?

M: Yes.

(X offers him the glass, smelling it first. M drinks it.)

M: *(Feeling the opiate.)* Thank you.

(X observes M.)

M: It is a luxury, this bath.

X: Is it?

M: You must be very hot, Monsieur, after your work. Would you like the tub, when I am finished?

X: No—I would not.

M: Would you like to share it with me then? The water is still clean—it's large enough for two.

X: No—thank you. The autumn wind has cooled me down.

M: Will you wash me then? I'm tired and frightened—I can barely lift the cloth.

(X wets the washcloth then covers M's face with it, studying the room. M, in a stupor, sinks beneath the water. X pulls him out and leans his head against his chest.)

X: Is that better?

M: Very much.

(X gently washes his chest. The shadows of MME and MLLE appear.)

X: You have a beautiful home, Monsieur.

M: Do I?…Thank you.

X: Do you like that?

M: Very much.

X: It must be complicated, owning such an estate.

M: It is. More complicated than I know…

(Through an arch, a box on a pedestal glows.)

X: How many rooms do you have?

M: Shared or personal?

X: Personal.

M: Many.

(The shadows vanish. M begins to nod out.)

M: Have the cannons died down?

X: They have.

M: Good.

X: Relax.

(X scans the room as he caresses the stomach of M. MME and MLLE reappear on a perch overlooking the scene. A crack from the cypress—)

M: *(Rousing.)* Have you ever been whipped, Monsieur?

X: I have.

M: I've never whipped a slave.

X: Haven't you?

M: No…we've never kept any.

X: Is Mademoiselle not your slave?

M: She is not. *(Pause.)* I would like to whip a slave.

X: Would you?

M: As a game.

X: Whose game?

M: Ours.

X: I don't enjoy being whipped.

M: Don't you?

X: No…I do not.

(X slides his hands between M's legs.)

X: Do you like that, Monsieur?

M: Very much… If you don't enjoy being whipped, do you enjoy being taken?

X: By whom?

M: By anyone?

X: No.

M: By me…Monsieur?

X: Do you know what it means to be taken?

M: I do not.

X: Would you like to? Would you like to know what it means—

M: I don't know—

X: For one who only takes?

M: I would like to, Monsieur. Take me…if you'd like.

(M flops forward in the tub, displaying himself to X. The box glows.)

M: You may have anything if you take me—anything in this house, Monsieur, if it would make you happy—if it would make your life more comfortable. I've been spoiled, ruined by my wife's attention, and need to be taught—servility. Groseille would have made a better wife if she'd…an endowment and an ivory cheek. Her cold control excites me—something Palides no longer possesses. I've become afraid to leave the grounds, not for fear of death, although I know at this point that that is imminent, but for fear of meeting yet another lover of my wife. The way they stare at me in the street, indiscriminate, beating me down, mocking me—the protected husband. If I'd as many lovers as she I'd survive the torment. But I haven't any, Monsieur, and I'd like one. You must take me as they've taken her—fuck me while I'm relaxed; render me senseless and discard me. If you think that my hands were pink, as the amaryllis—and I hope you tend to the amaryllis, Monsieur—then look at me now—for at this moment that flower cannot compete with my subtle perfection. Are you looking?

X: I am.

M: Look closer.

X: I am.

M: Do you find me beautiful?

X: Yes, Monsieur.

M: Lie to me.

X: I've no need to lie. You are quite beautiful.

M: Then touch me and I will give you what you want.

X: Do you know what it is that I want?

M: I know. Touch me.

(X touches M's ass.)

M: Touch my cock, Monsieur.

(X reaches between his legs.)

M: Touch it!

X: I am.

M: I cannot feel it.

X: I'm touching you—

M: I feel nothing, Monsieur…nothing.

X: *(Pause.)* You're limp, Monsieur—soft and senseless. You've gone numb from the drug… your pleasure will have to wait. *(X pulls M tightly against his chest.)* Relax. You'll never find a lover in such a state. *(X tightens his grip.)* As soon as you recover I will take you up on your offer, and if it is a pleasure your life will be spared. What I need now is the claim to your estate.

M: You have yet to take me.

X: You have yet to excite me. You said I might have what I want.

M: After you take me, Monsieur.

X: It will excite me to observe the deed—close to your flesh—while I take you.

M: If I tell you where it is you must promise that our lives will be spared.

X: When you sign it over to me.

M: Break the lock of the small drawer set carefully in my desk—it will be sealed with an ochre wax, bearing my wife's insignia. *(Pause.)* Does the thought of this paper arouse you?

X: Yes.

M: Then let me touch you.

(M fondles X.)

M: I think the deed excites you more than me, Monsieur.

(X turns to leave the bathhouse and approach the glowing box.)

M: Hurry back—it must be signed by me—don't forget.

(MME and MLLE listen to X fumble with the lock.)

MME: Listen to him rustling through the desk as if…

(X breaks the lock.)

MLLE: You never believed Pierre to be deceitful, Palides, and now you'll pay for his careless nature—

MME: He has yet to be violated—

MLLE: If he transfers the deed the army will claim what is his—

MME: He has no right to give it away—

MLLE: And if you are found unfit to maintain your estate, it will fall from your hands anyway—you're too far along. Look at your sweat, the pus from your yaws has stained your silks.

MME: I'm not ready—

MLLE: He's ready—

(They listen to X rustling through the papers.)

MLLE: —and if with the fall of the French I am able to own, once again, a piece of land—I will offer to care for you until you die. There is no choice but to sign the deed over to me.

(X suspends the various documents from invisible strings, studying them as they sway gently in the breeze. M begins to nod off.)

MLLE: Are you listening?

MME: What does he dig for, Groseille… in the garden? He digs so deeply.

(A splash as M slips unconscious under the water.)

MME: What is that?

MLLE: I don't know what you hear, Palides—

MME: He's slipped under the water—

MLLE: I hear nothing—

MME: Help me down—

MLLE: Palides, wait—

MME: I think you'd like to see him die— (MME descends from their perch.) —it would be so easy for you—

MLLE: Palides— (MLLE follows MME down.)

MME: Take your shovel and dig—tell me what the soldier is doing to my garden—and if you confirm what I've seen beneath the shady maids—I will give you what is mine.

MLLE: What have you seen?

MME: Dig to the north of the root—where it is brightest—and be careful not to touch it.

(MME enters the bathhouse. MLLE begins a path toward the hole. X studies the documents which hang like yellowed ghosts on the breeze. Hearing movement in the garden he shuts the "door" to the arch and is lost in blackness.)

SCENE 6

November. In the bathhouse, MME studies her husband's body under the water. She reaches in and pulls him out—he coughs up *water. MLLE reaches the garden and examines the hole near the shady maids. She begins to utilize the shovel, removing dirt.*

M: *(Stirring.)* Palides...

MME: Yes.

M: I'm sorry.

MME: Sorry for what, Pierre?

(M lifts his arm to reveal a sore.)

MME: It doesn't matter anymore.

M: Doesn't it?

MME: Quiet. Listen to the silent activity around us—it's very busy, Pierre—our estate.

M: It's no longer ours.

MME: Whom does it belong to?

M: To him.

MME: Then where will we live?

M: Here—

MME: As slaves?

M: Until we can safely board a ship and leave.

MME: That won't happen.

M: What do you mean?

MME: When we wed—I wanted nothing but you, Pierre...to swing from the tree off my portico...not far from the water, near my garden...But uncertain of your interest in me—I drew up papers of no legal value—which were destroyed long ago.

M: He promised to spare our lives if we gave him the estate.

MME: You never had a right to pass it on.

M: Then our death is imminent, Palides.

MME: Your death, Pierre. Only yours. *(MME rises and crosses to the flower arrangement.)*

M: Did you want me?

MME: *(Pause.)* Yes—I did. *(She sees that the flowers are shady maids.)* He must wear gloves when he brings you such a gift, the shady maids I adore.

(She dons the gloves of X and plucks a flower from the vase, placing it on a table. She begins to chop it with a knife. MLLE disappears down the hole.)

M: What are you doing?

MME: Listen—the wind is picking up.

M: Is it? I don't hear anything.

MME: Don't you?

(Footsteps are heard.)

M: He's coming.

MME: What will you do when he returns?

M: You must tell him what you've told me...

(The footsteps pass.)

M: Monsieur?

MME: He's passed, Pierre.

M: But he promised to return—

MME: *(Powders the flower pieces and places them in the drink.)* There are two options—die at the hand of the Haitians or drink what I offer. You are not well enough to make an escape and who would take you in your condition—an exile with no income? You have nothing to offer the gardener. *(She holds out the glass to M—)* The maids make heady the poppy...

(He takes the glass.)

MME: What did you ever have to gain from owning my estate? I gave you everything you asked for.

M: I knew what would happen to you, your thoughts, your body, but I was too frightened to tell you. I wanted security, nothing more.

MME: It never occurred that it might be you who went first?

M: Can you…forgive me, Palides?

MME: *(Silence.)* Drink, and allow me to return the gesture.

(He drinks. After a moment she moves away from him, crossing to the lantern. She pulls the bloodied letter from her dress.)

MME: Perhaps it wasn't you, Pierre… *(She places the letter in the flame of the lantern and watches it burn.)* Who's to say?

M: Stay with me.

(She crosses back, holding him.)

M: It's so dark, Palides, and the trees beating their branches against the windows… is too much for me.

MME: You were always frightened, Pierre, and your fear is useless. Be still and quiet; listen to the wind as it tears through the doors, the halls, the rooms that for this moment remain ours.

(M relaxes, slipping into a stupor. Footsteps are heard—)

(MLLE enters, her hands and apron covered with blood.)

MME: Mademoiselle—you have blood on your hands.

MLLE: Do I?

(Silence.)

MLLE: What are you doing?

MME: Monsieur is not well.

(Silence.)

MME: Did you cut yourself?

MLLE: On the shovel.

MME: You had better clean it—if you touched the flower.

(MLLE stares at the cut on her hand, then crosses to the tub and thrusts it in the water. MME backs away. MLLE rinses her hand, then stops to stare at M—she pulls her hand out and notices the crushed flowers, the goblet.)

MME: You must give us a moment alone, Groseille…you may rinse your hand in the stream.

(MLLE makes to leave—X is seen.)

MLLE: He's returned—

MME: Listen to him, rustling through the papers in the house—

MLLE: He cannot read.

MME: Don't be so certain.

MLLE: *(Pause.)* He dug to the south— where it is darkest, but I have seen it.

(X is heard breathing.)

MME: Then unearth what you've found and return as well.

(MLLE exits. MME stares at M a moment before hiding in the shadows.)

(X reenters carrying the deed and quill.)

X: Monsieur, I've found it…it matches your description. *(X sees that the glass has moved.)* Monsieur—look at me. You must look at me!

(MME rustles in the shadows. X looks around, uncertain of the sound.)

X: Monsieur…you must sign your name for me. *(Testing M, he maneuvers a quill between his fingers.)* I will give up your home to the rebels if you do not do as you promised. Monsieur! *(He places his ear over M's mouth to see if he is breathing, then kneels to feel M's wrist.)*

(MME steps out of the shadows.)

MME: What are you doing to my husband?

(X does not move.)

MME: What do you want from him—don't rise. *(She moves behind him.)* What did you find, Monsieur?

(Silence.)

MME: Monsieur?

X: It concerns you—

MME: Does it?

X: Yes.

MME: In what way does it concern me?

X: I'd rather not say.

MME: Wouldn't you? Do you read?

X: I do not.

MME: Then how do you know it concerns me?

X: Your husband requested I bring it to him.

MME: Did he?

X: Yes.

MME: Is it a serious document?

X: Yes.

MME: Do you know what it contains?

X: An unpaid debt, Madame.

MME: Milliner—dressmaker? Deceased and/or fled?

X: He requested a document sealed with ochre wax.

MME: Did he ask you to burn it?

X: He did not.

MME: I know the intention of the army, Monsieur. I assume my husband to be the last of the French alive in St. Domingue—or, what do you call it now?

(Silence.)

MME: I also know the size of the army, and what a base this land might make. Am I to believe Monsieur requested the deed to my estate?

(Silence as they observe one another.)

MME: What have you done to my husband that he is incapable of signing the document he requested?

X: Offered comfort, Madame.

MME: Something many of us have been in desperate need of, Monsieur. *(Pause.)* I am more sympathetic to your cause than you might assume. *(Closing in on X, she observes the deed.)* My husband's signature is necessary to acquire the estate—even in these times. However, it might be difficult to receive as he is under the effect of the drug you have given him. Lift his hand and I will guide you—I know his signature well.

(Silence.)

MME: Do it—I am giving you my estate.

X: For what reason?

MME: If only that you will tend to my garden and protect my home. I am not well, Monsieur, as you once inquired, and will not live long. You offered me pleasure once, let me do the same for you.

(X kneels and lifts M's hand, poising it over the deed on his knee. MLLE enters in the shadows. MME cuts the palm of her hand with the sharp end of the quill and offers it as an "inkpot" to X.)

MME: It is heavy—isn't it? Now, lift the quill up, and carefully circle it to your right, and down again. Now, a smaller arch, then back down again into one small line reaching up—then a small curved hill—good—don't tell me you do not write as well—into another line up—cross it, then a small version of the first letter—and finally a half sail, small, angled as well. Then slash—letting go with a flourish underneath. *(Pause.)* The estate is now yours, Monsieur.

X: You have tricked me.

MME: Have I?

X: Needn't you sign this as well?

(She dips the quill in her palm and signs it.)

X: Your husband is dead, Madame.

(Silence.)

X: What do you feel?

MME: *(Pause.)* Nothing, Monsieur.

(X studies the deed as MLLE emerges from the shadows, hiding the empty sack behind her.)

MLLE: The document is forged—it too is worth nothing.

X: *(Startled, folds the deed and places it in his pocket.)* It is signed.

MLLE: By whom?

X: By Monsieur.

MLLE: An unnecessary effort—the estate was never his to give away.

X: The army desires this land, Mademoiselle.

MLLE: I am aware of that. *(Tosses the sack on the ground.)* I have discovered in the garden what appears to be the torso of a man decorated with the trappings of an Emperor...buried beneath the shady maids.

(Silence.)

MLLE: If that is his body the army will have your head.

X: I did not kill the Emperor.

MLLE: And I will not offer you protection if you persist in taking control of this estate, nor falsify words in the death of Monsieur.

X: The army would have killed him within a fortnight—

MLLE: As a Haitian I have a right over the African—

X: His death means nothing—

MLLE: Then take the body and display it outside the gate.

X: They would decorate me for his death!

MLLE: And the one in the garden?

(Silence.)

MLLE: You have betrayed the army, Monsieur.

X: *(Moves to MME.)* Tell her your intention—

MLLE: It is not her concern—

X: It's become her concern.

MLLE: It is a personal matter—

X: *(To MME.)* Tell us your intention—

MLLE: A foolish conceit on the part of a sick woman.

X: Madame?

MME: *(Pause.)* My husband thought me unwell, Monsieur, and wished to take what is mine—as did you—but it was never his to offer.

(X is silent.)

MME: If you had not desecrated my garden (and kissed me with deceit on your lips)…it might have been otherwise.

(Silence.)

MME: It's very warm in here.

MLLE: Why don't you step outside, Palides? The wind is cool.

MME: The trees are beating against the windows—

MLLE: It's winter—the garden's no longer in need of your attention.

MME: Isn't it?

(A muffled sound like a gunshot is heard in the distance. MME stops—something triggers inside her. She reaches out to X. He doesn't move. She grabs the deed from his pocket—he grabs her wrist—a series of plants shift in the garden—he lets go.)

MME: If you'd be so kind as to let me rest, Groseille.

(MLLE stares uncertainly as MME extends the deed to her.)

MME: Take it.

X: Madame—

MME: It is a gift, Monsieur—one you haven't earned.

(MLLE reaches out her hand—MME drops the deed to the ground.)

MME: Mademoiselle.

(A moment—MLLE stoops nobly to pick it up.)

MME: Have it notarized quickly. Look—

(MLLE opens the document.)

MME: We've already signed it over to you—he and I. *(MME gazes at X.)* L'homme jardin—

(MME passes as if to exit—orange light flickers outside the estate. She pauses to ascertain its source.)

MME: The General's estate is on fire.

(X and MLLE turn to the light. All stare.)

INTERLUDE

December. MME exits. MLLE closes the deed.

MLLE: Take Monsieur's body to the gate and hang it from the grill.

X: Mademoiselle—

MLLE: Display it.

X: For what purpose?

MLLE: To prevent an investigation.

X: Of what?

MLLE: Having betrayed the army you are now perceived to be treasonous—

X: It should be buried, Mademoiselle—

MLLE: I will offer you a position here until the province sees fit to release you—

X: No one knows I am here—

MLLE: But you see Monsieur, they will.

(X stares at her in a silent fury.)

MLLE: I have always wanted someone under me, Monsieur. And in your situation you could hope for nothing better. *(MLLE moves to the arch to exit.)* Display the body.

X: Someone will see fit to strip away your brief period of happiness and profit yet again, Mademoiselle—for it is nothing more.

MLLE: It is late, Monsieur—I suggest you fill in your grave before the sun sheds light on its contents.

X: And when you return to find the remains of an Emperor scattered here and there about your garden, it won't be me who takes the blame, for what am I, in the eyes of the province, if nothing more than your property?

(MLLE passes through the arch, exiting the bathhouse. All lights drop save a single spot illuminating her face. She breathes heavily, excitedly. A spot picks up X, with his sack, over the body of M. Another spot reveals MME sitting still on her swing. The fire flares in the background as MME watches the large flowers, seen in the prologue, shift and grow in the background. She pushes the swing and begins to recite as the turntable starts its rotation.)

EPILOGUE

January.

MME: The hibiscus, bougainvillea… foetidia, gloriosa…are as the ricinus…the heliotrope, belladonna are not as weak as the gardenia, the corteline, the agave…

(X passes through the garden with the body of M.)

MME: The dryadella have lost their bloom, unlike the somniferum, the shady maids and the oleander…

(MLLE moves away from the arch of the bathhouse. MME hears her movement and ceases to swing. Their eyes meet—MME turns away. MLLE passes the hole and pauses to look in. Light emanates upward, illuminating her. X hangs the body of M upside down from the gate of the estate. MLLE turns to observe. MLLE leaves the hole—their eyes meet. X takes her place looking in. MME begins to swing again. MLLE moves to MME's dressing table and studies herself in the mirror. She takes the spade from her pocket and sets it on top. X shovels dirt from the hole. MLLE opens MME's jewel box and fastens a necklace to her throat, then adjusts her headdress. M's body shifts in the breeze. MLLE removes her bloody apron and dons MME's shawl. MME rises from the swing and passes X—their eyes meet. She moves through the garden toward one of the large open flowers, passing the body of M, which she stops momentarily to gaze upon. MLLE leaves the dressing table clutching the deed and moves through the garden, passing X. She pauses. He ceases to shovel the dirt. MLLE moves to the swing of MME and touches its rope. MLLE crosses to another large flower whose petals open as well. X puts his shovel aside—he contemplates the sack. He reaches in and pulls out a tattered red vest, delicately laying it out on the ground. He tosses his sack in the hole. MME descends through her flower. MLLE descends through hers. X disappears down his hole. M's body is lost to the darkness.)

END.

CATS CAN SEE THE DEVIL

A Puppet Show for Children

Tom X. Chao

TOM X. CHAO was born in Rochester, New York, and grew up in Buffalo, New York, and the Midwest. He holds a bachelor's degree in cinema production from the University of Southern California, where he studied fiction writing with T. Coraghessan Boyle. He further earned a master's degree in professional writing from USC, studying with Richard Yates. He obtained a master's degree from New York University's Gallatin School of Individualized Study, mentored by Deb Margolin. He has produced, written, directed, and performed theatrical works, including *The Negative Energy Field* and *Can't Get Started*, in New York City at Dixon Place, HERE, The Knitting Factory, P.S.122, Surf Reality, on WBAI-FM, and at the D.U.M.B.O. Art Under the Bridge, Pure Pop, and New York International Fringe Festivals. In 1999, his play, *The Universe of Despair* (aka *Summer, Deepening Then Gone*), was selected for The American Living Room Festival. He has appeared by invitation in numerous variety shows and recently hosted his own variety evenings. He is the author of several published short stories, satire (in *Modern Humorist*), and arts criticism appearing in publications including the *Los Angeles Reader*. Projects in development include a musical comedy, a radio play, and a music video. Chao is a resident artist of the Horse Trade Theater Group and lives in the East Village neighborhood of Manhattan. Website: www.tomxchao.com.

Cats Can See The Devil was first presented by Tom X. Chao as part of the New York International Fringe Festival (Elena K. Holy, Producing Artistic Director), on August 9, 2003, at Under St. Marks, with the following cast and credits:

Adrianne Goodge .... Leya Balsari
The Narrator/Tom .... Tom X. Chao
Lauren Trabuco .... Monica Cortez
Tuesday Arc-Weld .... Kim Katzberg
N. Semble .... Mar
Dr. Evelyn Florentine.. Krista Worth

Director: John Harlacher
Stage Manager: Leah E. Squires
Lighting Design and Operation: Tim Cryan
Graphic Design: Jeff Wong
Set and Prop Design: Peter Sluszka, Jeff Wong
Dramaturgy: Robert Prichard
Choreography: Alex Timbers
Audio Engineering: Jeff Ward
Photography: Beowulf Sheehan
Authorized Company Representative/House Manager: Michele Carlo
Audio Technician: Hod Berman

Abstract Geometrical Shapes and the Robot designed by Tom X. Chao. "Don't Eat Crabs—Eat Lobsters" book jacket designed by Sophie Chin.

Cats Can See The Devil was remounted by Tom X. Chao and the Horse Trade Theater Group on October 24, 2003, at Under St. Marks, New York City, with the same cast except Barbara P. King as N. Semble, Andrea Ryder as Lauren Trabuco, Elizabeth Schmidt as Adrianne Goodge, and Paige Young as Dr. Evelyn Florentine. Director, Stage Manager, and designers were as before, with Adrian Mukasa (Lighting/Sound Operator), Jennifer Lieberman (Assistant Stage Manager), and Reneé Vance (Costume Designer).

Cats Can See The Devil was presented in a staged reading by Theatre X and the University of New Mexico Department of Theatre and Dance on October 14, 2003, in Albuquerque, directed by Henry Bial.

Prerecorded musical accompaniment for "Cannot Be Denied" can be obtained from the playwright, tom@tomxchao.com.

Thanks to Tyson Furr, Seth Madej, and Noelle Romano for their comments on the script. Special thanks to Kimo DeSean and Erez Ziv of the Horse Trade Theater Group.

Publication of this script is dedicated to my parents, Peter P. and Cecilia Y. Chao.

AUTHOR'S NOTE

"The Story of the Abstract Geometrical Shapes With No Allegorical Content" (presently Scene 3) originally appeared as a scene in my two-character play, *Can't Get Started*, at the St. Marks Theater in the fall of 2000 and subsequently in the spring of 2001. The first and second Puppeteers were Basey Newborg and Eve Kerrigan, respectively. This scene proved so consistently popular (in particular, the character of Puce Nonagon) that it seemed natural to develop it into a longer piece. In January of 2002, I extracted this "anti-puppet" puppet show from *Can't Get Started* and added a second part, "Advice for Children Who Are Stuck in a State of Arrested Development, Otherwise Known as Infantilized Adults" (now Scene 19). This stand-alone sketch, featuring actress Hannah Mason, appeared in the Timsloft variety show at the Interart Annex, and again it received a great response from audiences. After a couple of rejected attempts to get *Puppet Show for Children* (as it had come to be known) produced by another downtown festival (which supposedly *likes* puppets), finally in the spring of 2003, the New York International Fringe Festival accepted my vague and hyperbolic one-page outline for the newly rechristened *Cats Can See The Devil*. Work immediately began on expanding the ideas into a full-length work. I brought two tryouts of new material to Surf Reality, where The Talking Cat made his first public appearances to great acclaim. In May of 2003, a twenty-minute version of *Puppet Show for Children*, the final workshop of ideas for *CCSTD*, with actress Jessica Lusk, was presented at BRIC Studio in Brooklyn, incorporating most of the puppets and, for the first time, a real live nude Puppeteer (Raven Pease). During the summer, the characters of Dr. Evelyn Florentine and N. Semble gradually coalesced out of the *CCSTD* ether. (To be honest, they started out as nothing more than names and brief, unspecific descriptions hastily written for a casting notice.) After selecting the director and cast, and starting to rehearse, I continued to make revisions, in the time-honored tradition of theater, and I acknowledge the input of John Harlacher—the director—our talented cast and crew, and other advisors in helping me shape the material. As with all of my scripts, a large number of scenes and lines had to be cut for length. (Some of them had been rehearsed extensively, alas.) *CCSTD* finally touched down at the NY International Fringe Festival in August of 2003. In an ironic twist, the FringeNYC powers-that-be assigned us to the "Under St. Marks" venue that was, in fact, the same St. Marks Theater in which the Abstract Geometrical Shapes first appeared, thus providing us with a great sense of closure...or something.

CHARACTERS

THE NARRATOR/TOM: An eccentric downtown performance artist. Looks around thirty-two but is actually older.

DR. EVELYN FLORENTINE: A professor of clinical psychology. Intelligent, quietly composed, subtly sexy. Wears glasses. Around thirty.

N. SEMBLE: A mysterious, silent woman with fascinating allure, a larger-than-life presence, and a hint of sly mischievousness.

THE PUPPETEERS

TUESDAY ARC-WELD:[1] A young actress recently graduated from drama school. Pretty, lively, vivacious, bursting with life. Early twenties.

LAUREN TRABUCO:[2] An actress. Smart, funny, quick-witted. Mid-to-late twenties. Very attractive. Brief nudity required for this role.

ADRIANNE GOODGE:[3] A slightly older actress in her late twenties–early thirties. She is highly trained with a professional, no-nonsense demeanor. Capable of cutting sarcasm. Should also be beautiful.

VOICES DURING PUPPET SHOW

NARRATOR: NARRATOR
THE TALKING CAT[4]
FLOWERS ON FIRE (on kazoo)

PUPPETEERS: RED SQUARE
ROBOT
A LIVE CRAB
FLOWERS ON FIRE

ADDITIONAL CAST

SPECIAL GUEST(S): The Special Guest should be a performing artist appearing in a currently running or upcoming show that he or

---

[1] An obvious play on the name of the actress "Tuesday Weld."

[2] "Trabuco" = "blunderbuss" in Spanish.

[3] "Adrianne Goodge" replaced the horrible, overused punning name "Miss Ann Thrope." "Adrianne" is the feminine form of "Adrian," which recalls Adrian Belew, the great rock guitarist, as well as the song "Adrian" by the Eurythmics, which features a vocal duet by Annie Lennox and Elvis Costello. "Goodge" is the name of a street and tube station in the Holborn neighborhood of London.

[4] The Talking Cat voice may be played by another actor; however, it should be a male voice.

she wants to promote. May be male or female, but a staunchly pro-feminist woman would be preferable. There may be more than one Special Guest if they are members of a group. Should be loud and forceful.

HOUSE MANAGER: The House Manager.

THE TECH: The tech person.

SETTING

A typical off-off-Broadway fringe theater in Lower Manhattan, a black box with the barest accoutrements of theater visible. A puppet stage stands center stage. It is a partially enclosed structure large enough to conceal four people sitting on the ground behind it and their accompanying puppets and other props. A shelf or ledge on top will hold puppets and other objects. Some objects will be suspended from the ceiling by cables during the performance. A chair or stool sits downstage. A special chair for N. SEMBLE sits at the edge of the stage in an unobtrusive but visible spot.

TIME

Daytime or night, reflecting the actual show time. The present.

NOTE

Scene headings are for reference only and are not intended to be spoken or otherwise conveyed to the audience.

At rise: a bare, unadorned puppet stage stands center stage. A microphone on a stand is concealed behind the stage for the NARRATOR. All of the puppets and props described in the following scenes are hidden behind the stage. The SPECIAL GUEST(S) are seated in the audience, or they may enter from the lobby and mingle with the audience before entering and sitting in the audience.

SCENE 1
INTRO #1: DR. EVELYN FLORENTINE FINDS A SEAT

*DR. EVELYN FLORENTINE, a clinical psychologist, enters the theater after the au-*dience *has settled into their seats.*[5] *She is holding a show program and a shoulder bag. She looks around uncertainly.*

EVELYN: *(To herself.)* What is this? Is this the theater? This can't be a theater![6]

HOUSE MANAGER: *(Shouts from outside the door.)* Hey, you with the glasses,

---

[5]If the show begins with a pre-show welcoming announcement of the "Please turn off your cell phones" variety, she may interrupt it.

[6]This line was prompted by actual comments overheard by people trying to find the St. Marks Theater, looking down into the dark entry stairwell.

we're about to start! Don't stand there! Take a seat, already!

(EVELYN sits in the audience. Blackout.)

SCENE 2
INTRO #2: PEERING INTO THE AUDIENCE

LAUREN moves behind the puppet stage to her opening position. She must remain completely concealed from the audience until she stands up.

TUESDAY: *(Urgently, from offstage.)* Hey, do you see 'em? What's going on!? Are they here? Are they? Do you see 'em? Do you see 'em? (She continues ad lib.)*

NARRATOR: *(Overlaps, shouting.)* Do you see 'em? Do you see 'em? Do you see 'em? Where are they? Where are they? Where are they? (He continues ad lib.)*

LAUREN: *(Overlaps, rapidly, from behind the puppet stage.)* Well? Where are they? Where are they? Did they come? I can't see them!

(She continues ad lib. The NARRATOR and TUESDAY run in while shouting and stand downstage. They hold hand-held lamps and shine them directly into the eyes of the audience, sweeping the beams back and forth. After a moment, ADRIANNE enters and stands center stage. She shouts the others down.)

ADRIANNE: *(Interrupts.)* All right! They're right here. Right where they're supposed to be. They're sitting in the audience, looking at us.

(TUESDAY, ADRIANNE, and the NARRATOR run to their positions behind the puppet stage and sit down. They remain concealed from the audience throughout the puppet show, except as noted. Hand-held lamps are turned off. Lighting begins to fade up. N. SEMBLE enters and strides regally to her special chair at the side of the stage. Throughout the entire play, up to her monologue, she looks on

with stony disapproval and holds herself aloof except for the few moments described.)

SCENE 3
A COMPLEX COSMOLOGY: THE STORY OF THE ABSTRACT GEOMETRICAL SHAPES WITH NO ALLEGORICAL CONTENT

NARRATOR: *(Reading from his script into the microphone.[7])* Good evening. Tonight we present a puppet show for children entitled "The Story of the Abstract Geometrical Shapes With No Allegorical Content."[8] *(Pause.)* Once upon a time, Red Square and Yellow Triangle met and they became engaged.

(The PUPPETEERS raise the SHAPES into view. The SHAPES are pieces of posterboard of the color and shape described by their names, attached to balsa wood dowels. They should be approximately sixteen inches across or larger. The PUPPETEERS move the SHAPES toward each other and make loud exaggerated kissing noises.)

NARRATOR: Okay, there's no allegorical content in this puppet show, even though I just said "Red Square." *(Pause.)* Red Square and Yellow Triangle got married and they had a bunch of kids.

(The PUPPETEERS[9] throw a bunch of colored paper scraps into the air. They flutter to the ground.)

---

[7]During the puppet show, the cast should turn their script pages very loudly.

[8]At BRIC Studio, May 15, 2003, I added "Puppet Show for Children is not recommended for children."

[9]All stage directions for the Puppeteers were divided up amongst the three Puppeteers: Lauren, Tuesday, and Adrianne. An attempt was made to ensure that when one was speaking, someone else would be manipulating the puppets/objects, so that no one had to speak and operate a puppet/object simultaneously.

NARRATOR: Some of the kids were mutant albinos.

(The PUPPETEERS throw handfuls of white paper scraps into the air. The PUPPETEERS attach YELLOW TRIANGLE to the puppet stage so that it remains visible to the audience.[10])

NARRATOR: However, it was not long before Red Square felt trapped and stifled in its loveless, arranged marriage. As often happens in our sex-crazed society, where the concept of delayed gratification is unknown, Red Square began an extramarital affair with one of its co-workers. Yes, Orange Heptagon. From Accounts Receivable.

(The PUPPETEERS raise ORANGE HEPTAGON, a regular[11] heptagon, into view. They wave ORANGE HEPTAGON and RED SQUARE together.)

NARRATOR: Red Square was happy for a time with Orange Heptagon. Sometimes they would go for long walks together in the rain. However, the happiness of Red Square was to be short lived.

(ORANGE HEPTAGON is attached to the stage.)

NARRATOR: Soon, Orange Heptagon began an affair of its own—with a three-dimensional object.

(The PUPPETEERS raise HOBERMAN SPHERE[12] into view, thrusting it between the SHAPES and gradually expanding it to full size.)

---

[10]At FringeNYC 2003, holes were drilled in the top of the puppet stage to hold the abstract geometrical shapes in place.

[11]"Regular" here is used in the geometric sense, meaning that a polygon's sides are of equal length and its interior angles are equal.

[12]Visit www.hoberman.com for images and models.

NARRATOR: It was none other than Hoberman Sphere. Yes. Hoberman Sphere was, in a way, something like a pop star amongst the three-dimensional objects—because of its extraordinary popularity at science museum gift shops. Hoberman Sphere was often found on the desks of people who considered themselves creative and intellectual, but were, in fact, insufferably tedious. *(Pause.)* This new arrangement did not suit Red Square.

RED SQUARE: *(In a deep male voice.)* Oh, no, I don't like you, Mr. Three-Dimensional Object! You're not running off with my girlfriend, you bastard! No way! Come here and fight me! Fight me like a *real* abstract geometrical shape, you piece of shit! Just because you're three-dimensional, you think you can come around here and steal my girlfriend! I'm gonna cut you, motherfucker! With an X-ACTO knife!

NARRATOR: Okay, there's no allegorical content in this puppet show, remember?

(The PUPPETEERS wave the SHAPES around crazily, and expand and contract HOBERMAN SPHERE. They scream bizarre, unintelligible curses.)

RED SQUARE: Goddamn Hoberman Sphere, you think you're so cool with your ability to expand and contract! That doesn't frighten me!

NARRATOR: Despite Red Square's great show of bravado and hyper-masculine posturing, any fight between an n-dimensional entity and an n-plus-one-dimensional entity was bound to end in death for the entity of fewer dimensions.

RED SQUARE: Oh, man, I'm hemorrhaging internally! I'm gonna die! It's happening to me! This is not a dream! This is very, very real! I'm too young to die! *(Screams a hideous and drawn-out death shriek.)* Eeeeeeeeeeeeee!

(The PUPPETEERS toss RED SQUARE out in front of the puppet stage. A PUPPE-TEER hangs HOBERMAN SPHERE, open, from the ceiling on a hook.)

SCENE 4
PUCE NONAGON!

NARRATOR: Red Square was dead. What it didn't realize is that, before it died, it had impregnated Orange Heptagon, who gave birth to an illegitimate child who would one day become the chief of all the Abstract Geometrical Shapes. *(Porten-tously.)* And everyone knows who that was: Puce Nonagon![13]

(Lights dim. A PUPPETEER slowly lifts PUCE NONAGON into view. It is also a regular polygon. Another PUPPETEER shines a hand-held lamp onto PUCE NONAGON. The PUPPETEERS provide a chorus of angelic voices, singing a loud chord. They repeat the chord, growing louder and more dissonant. A PUPPETEER holds up a small gong and beater and visibly smashes the gong repeatedly. Party horns and noise-makers are blown.[14] Cheers and shouts and applause are heard. The NARRATOR over-laps, growing gradually louder and angrier.)

NARRATOR: Okay, that's good. Good. Hey, that's enough. Okay. Stop it. Stop it! Shut up! *Cool it!*

(Lighting as before. The PUPPETEERS turn off the hand-held lamp and remove the gong and beater. The PUPPETEERS slowly move PUCE NONAGON back and forth

horizontally in a straight line, as if a shape in an early video game.)*

NARRATOR: Puce Nonagon never knew his father. Just like you. *(Pause.)* The story of Puce Nonagon is compelling and cap-tivating, to be told and retold many times over puddles of spilled beer while sitting in the college bar. You know, the bar over by the college?[15] *(Pause.)*

SCENE 5
THE FUTURISTIC TALK SHOW I:
THE ROBOT SAYS METAL RULEZ!

NARRATOR: Far in the distant future, Puce Nonagon served as the host of "The Futuristic Talk Show."

(A funny, loud music sting, like a talk show theme, is heard.)

NARRATOR: Now, it might seem strange that Puce Nonagon could be the host of "The Futuristic Talk Show"—because it has no voice and can't speak. *(Pause.)* Neverthe-less, Puce Nonagon became very famous and popular like a rock star—because viewers thought that it was a "good lis-tener." *(Pause.)* Now, Puce Nonagon didn't host the show by itself. Like all good talk show hosts, it had a co-host.

(A PUPPETEER places the ROBOT on the stage. It is a bottle of Mrs. Butterworth's syrup painted gold.[16])

NARRATOR: A robot. *(In cheerful sing-song.)* Yes, a shiny titanium killer tactical attack robot!

---

[13]Puce: a dark red color. Puce Nonagon has never actually been puce in color, but rather brown, as that was the closest color available at the art supply store.

[14]At FringeNYC 2003, a tambourine re-placed the gong and mallet. Party horns and noisemakers were not used.

[15]The "college bar" reference is based on the experience of having gone with my high school friend, Steve Snyder, to a bar in Des Moines near Drake University, where over-weight, parka-wearing students drank.

[16]The robot prop was used in 1999 as "the Zeckendorf Prize" in my play, *The Universe of Despair*, aka *Summer, Deepening Then Gone*.

ROBOT: *(In a plummy female British upper-class accent.)* People of the future! Are you ready to rock!? Sacrifice to the gods of met-*all*! I'm a robot! I'm the co-host of "The Futuristic Talk Show"!

NARRATOR: Yes, it seemed that for the moment, the heavy metal subculture had gained the upper hand over the hip-hop subculture. *(Pause.)* In any case, Puce Nonagon and his robotic co-host were very, very important. *Ten thousand years of psychohistory*[17] had passed between your time and "The Futuristic Talk Show." And now all the plans created by the ancient psychohistorians of the Foundation were about to come to fruition. But only if Puce Nonagon—and the weird robot—could trigger the final societal paradigm shift dictated by the psychohistorians so many generations ago. And for that result, they would need their hidden, secret, long-awaited ally to appear on "The Futuristic Talk Show." Yes, it was The Talking Cat.

ROBOT: Dude, that's a shitload of exposition!

NARRATOR: *(Off-mic.)* Shhh!

ROBOT: Instead of psychohistory, let's talk about my favorite music—met-*all*! Met-*all* rulez! I love met-*all*! Don't you!? Doesn't everyone!? I love lots and lots of met-*all* groups like Sabbath, Judas Priest, Iron Maiden, Scorpions, AC/DC, and King Crimson![18] Fuck, yeah! Right on!

NARRATOR: *(Irritated.)* You know what? King Crimson isn't a metal band. They're a prog band!

ROBOT: You may try to lump them in with your wanker "prog" bands, but they're met-*all*, all right.

NARRATOR: You're the one who's trying to lump them in with your pedestrian, brain-dead "met-*all*" bands! Crimson is much closer in spirit to Yes and ELP and early Roxy Music!

ROBOT: Yes, I can tell you're the sort of wanker who enjoys that endless quasi-jazz instrumental noodly progressive nonsense.

NARRATOR: *(Snaps at the PUPPETEER, off-mic.)* Get on with it!

SCENE 6
THE FUTURISTIC TALK SHOW II:
A LIVE CRAB

ROBOT: *(Cheerfully shouting.)* All right, welcome back to "The Futuristic Talk Show"! Our first guest is one of our favorites! All the way from the Crab Nebula, it's A Live Crab!

(A PUPPETEER holds up A LIVE CRAB with tongs so that its claws are free to flail around wildly. The CRAB will probably have to be held over its accompanying clear plastic bucket to catch drips.[19] The other PUPPETEERS and the NARRATOR applaud and cheer.)

---

[17] A definition of "psychohistory" found on the Web: "A fictional science in Isaac Asimov's Foundation Trilogy universe, which combined history, psychology and mathematical statistics to create a (nearly) exact science of the behavior of very large populations of people."—www.prime-radiant.com/Psychohistory.html

[18] The mention of King Crimson refers back to my show *Can't Get Started*, which documented a period in my life of intense King

Crimson worship, 2000–01. I have successfully recovered from the Crimso period, thank you.

[19] The live blue hard-shell crabs recruited for the FringeNYC 2003 performances turned out to be too active to handle in the open with tongs. They were left inside a transparent plastic container that was placed on the puppet stage.

A LIVE CRAB: *(With a breezy, insincere "Hollywood" inflection.)* Hey, guys! Great to be back! Good seein' ya, Puce, and you too, Robot!

ROBOT: Great to see you again, A Live Crab! How are you?

A LIVE CRAB: I just flew in from the Crab Nebula. *(Pause.)* And, boy, are my claws tired! Hey!

(Rim shot!)

ROBOT: *(Flatly.)* Great. *(Normal again.)* What are you in town for?

A LIVE CRAB: I'm making some personal appearances to promote my new book, "Don't Eat Crabs—Eat Lobsters."

(A PUPPETEER holds up a copy of the "Don't Eat Crabs—Eat Lobsters" book and sets it on the puppet stage.)

ROBOT: Fantastic!

A LIVE CRAB: Yeah, you know, a lot of people don't know that they shouldn't eat us crabs.

ROBOT: So you're trying to raise the public awareness!

A LIVE CRAB: Exactly! And another unrelated thing I'm doing tomorrow is appearing in a special charity crab-walking race, which will benefit people afflicted with pubic lice.

ROBOT: Wow, you've got a lot on your plate!

A LIVE CRAB: Yeah, just don't put *me* on a plate.

(A LIVE CRAB and the ROBOT laugh hollowly.)

A LIVE CRAB: Can you put me back in the water now? I'm starting to dry out. Tell the staff I need more salt!

ROBOT: Okay, sure. Thank you, A Live Crab. For those about to rock, we salute you! Met-*all* rulez, have I mentioned that? Prog sucks!

(A PUPPETEER places A LIVE CRAB in the clear plastic bucket on top of the puppet stage so that it remains visible to the audience.)

SCENE 7
THE FUTURISTIC TALK SHOW III: THE TALKING CAT

ROBOT: Next, on "The Futuristic Talk Show," a very special guest! You all know him! He's The Talking Cat!

(THE TALKING CAT is placed on stage. It is a realistic-looking dead stuffed cat.[20] A PUPPETEER manipulates the cat when it is speaking, as if it was a hand puppet.)

THE TALKING CAT: *(Hoarse, male, "blown-out" voice.[21])* No, I'm not in this. No way. Get me out of here. C'mon. I have nothing to do with this.

NARRATOR: *(Pointedly.)* Yes, The Talking Cat had a very important part to play in this story, and had many important things *to say*.

THE TALKING CAT: No, no, no, man. I'm not part of this. Get me out of here.

NARRATOR: *(Insistently.)* The entire *ten thousand years* of psychohistory *hinged* on what The Talking Cat had to say on "The Futuristic Talk Show."

---

[20]For FringeNYC 2003, a cat plush toy was used instead of a real dead cat. The price tag was left attached to the toy cat's ear. Manufacturer: Douglas Cuddle Toys. Model: 1917 Luna Gray Cat. See www.douglascuddletoy.com.

[21]The Talking Cat's voice gradually took on the rough contours of a Brooklyn accent.

THE TALKING CAT: *(Musing.)* Awww! You want me to talk…oh, all right! *(Clears its throat noisily.)* Good evening, I'm a cat. I'm a real cat; I'm not a stuffed animal. I'm here tonight to dissuade you from a lot of notions you may hold about cats; I'm gonna debunk a lot of myths. *(Pause.)* Cats aren't what people think we are. We aren't clean and neat. We're filthy, disgusting creatures, covered with lice, vermin, and stray bits of our own fecal material. *(Fast.)* We are profligate, dissipated, undisciplined, hard-drinking, and mentally ill.[22] *(Normal again.)* We breed wantonly and abandon our kittens. *(Intimately.)* One old wives' tale about cats is true. We can see the devil. Yes. It's true. When the wind is howling outside and you see us suddenly start and hiss at some unseen presence in the corner by the china cabinet, that's a sign that we're seeing the devil. We are receiving our commands to go and commune with Lucifer at our secret meeting place. In your backyard. Behind the shed. We are familiars of Old Scratch[23] himself. *(Normal tone.)* You know, a lot of people think that my anti-cat statements play right into the hands of people who hate cats, and also into the hands of…dogs. Some people even call me an "Uncle Tom…Cat."[24] *(Angry.)* But I say fuck it! Fuck it! I'm here to speak the truth, not reinforce stereotypes. *(Subdued.)* Well, that's pretty much all I gotta say.

NARRATOR: The Talking Cat did not realize that his crazed, lunatic ranting did not derive of his own free will, but had been programmed into him *ten thousand years* ago by the ancient psychohistorians.

THE TALKING CAT: *(Fast.)* What?

SCENE 8
The Flowers on Fire

NARRATOR: However, one possibility the ancient psychohistorians did not foresee was that The Talking Cat would be attacked by an evil, alien race of beings: the disturbing and surrealistic *and colorful* Flowers on Fire!

(Lights dim. A PUPPETEER raises the FLOWERS ON FIRE into view, which are ordinary paper or silk flowers. They are attached to a novelty lamp that has paper streamers blowing upwards to simulate flames.[25] All PUPPETEERS provide voices in unison for the FLOWERS ON FIRE, using weird, high-pitched tones. The NARRATOR doubles the lines by speaking into a kazoo. His lines should lag behind and sound confused.)

FLOWERS and NARRATOR: We are the Flowers on Fire. Endlessly burning through the night. Though we burn, we are never consumed, for we know the secrets of the flame. We alone have decided to fight against the dominion of The Talking Cat. Too long have we suffered under the iron fist of his rule. *(Pause.)* To this end, we have devised a plan. We shall lure him to our headquarters with an attractive female in heat. Then, while he is distracted, we will use our paralyzing ray on him. Then we begin the torture. Torture!

---

[22] At BRIC Studio, I added "—like Jackson Pollock."

[23] A nickname for the devil.

[24] Occasionally, if the audience groaned at this joke, the Narrator would add, "You must have seen that coming!"

[25] The novelty lamp was not purchased for FringeNYC 2003 shows. A hand-held lamp was used to illuminate the Flowers on Fire from below. Real flames were not used because of festival and theater regulations.

THE TALKING CAT: *(Nervously.)* Excuse me? Uh, what's going on here? Why are those flowers talking about torturing me? That does not sound good!

FLOWERS and NARRATOR: We will destroy you, Cat!

THE TALKING CAT: Man, you've got me confused with somebody else. Okay, listen, I want someone to get me out of here. Get me outta here!

(Pause. Nothing happens.)

THE TALKING CAT: Okay, that's the way it's gonna be? No one's gonna get me outta here? Okay, don't make me have to get all violent on your flowery asses, now! Do you hear me!? You're asking for some savagery and butchery mind-boggling even by Alphabet City[26] standards!

FLOWERS and NARRATOR: What are you talking about, Cat? You can't even move under your own power!

THE TALKING CAT: Yeah, well, listen to this!

SCENE 9
The Great War of the Household Objects

NARRATOR: Now begins the story of the Great War of the Household Objects. In this war, The Talking Cat was aided by his many allies.

THE TALKING CAT: You hear that? I've got many allies! *(Laughs.)*

NARRATOR: Chief among The Talking Cat's allies were the Abstract Geometrical Shapes.

(The PUPPETEERS wave all of the SHAPES around in smooth up-and-down motions.)

NARRATOR: They were aided by their friends, the Conic Sections: Circle, Ellipse, Parabola, and Hyperbola.

(Lighting dims rapidly. The PUPPETEERS quickly display the CONIC SECTIONS by shining a hand-held lamp onto a wall or flat surface. The cone of light emitted by the lamp should be held at different angles to produce the four CONIC SECTIONS as it intersects with the wall or flat surface. For the CIRCLE, the lamp beam should be held perpendicular to the wall; then for the other CONIC SECTIONS, the lamp is held at progressively shallower angles, ending with the HYPERBOLA, in which the beam is parallel to the wall.[27] Lighting returns to normal.)

NARRATOR: In particular, Parabola offered to lend itself to the war effort to help calculate the trajectories of objects flying through the air.

(A PUPPETEER throws a ball or other small object[28] out in front of the puppet stage, where it lands on the stage.)

NARRATOR: There was also the mysterious Blob of Amorphous Protoplasm.

(A PUPPETEER removes a blob of slime from its container and stretches it out disgustingly.)

NARRATOR: It could usually be found drinking in the college bar.

---

[26]A neighborhood in Lower Manhattan so named because it includes Avenues A, B, C, and D.

[27]In the FringeNYC production, the Puppeteers just drew the shapes of the Conic Sections in the air with their index fingers. Another solution would involve holding up signs with the Conic Sections drawn on them. Yet another alternative would be to hold up paper cones with the Conic Sections marked on them.

[28]A wadded-up piece of paper works well.

(*The PUPPETEER returns the slime to the container and leaves it on the puppet stage.*)

NARRATOR: Of course, from the Crab Nebula there was A Live Crab, whom we've already met.

(*The PUPPETEERS point at A LIVE CRAB.*)

NARRATOR: Representing his kinsmen was Mr. Pile of Unread Magazines.

(*A PUPPETEER displays some magazines tied with twine, then throws them in front of the puppet stage, where they land with a loud thump.*)

NARRATOR: Mostly old *New Yorkers.* (*Pause.*) And don't forget Mr. Speculum.

(*A PUPPETEER holds up a speculum momentarily, then sets it on the stage.*)

NARRATOR: Also present was Mr. Can of Cream-Style Corn.[29]

(*A PUPPETEER holds up MR. CAN OF CREAM-STYLE CORN, an ordinary can of cream-style corn.*)

NARRATOR: During the Great War of the Household Objects, Mr. Can of Cream-Style Corn was attacked by his mortal enemy.

(*A PUPPETEER holds up an electric can opener[30] and moves it toward MR. CAN OF CREAM-STYLE CORN. The PUPPETEER presses the switch on the electric can opener to make it operate with a buzzing sound.*)

NARRATOR: Fortunately, Mr. Can of Cream-Style Corn was skilled in self-defense.

(*The PUPPETEERS holding MR. CAN OF CREAM-STYLE CORN and the can opener enact a fight until the can opener is vanquished. Both remain on the puppet stage.*)

NARRATOR: Man, I love Battlebots!

THE TALKING CAT: (*Angry.*) Hey, quit fuckin' around, you fuckin' household objects! (*Calmer.*) Don't forget, I'm in league with the devil, too! Don't forget that!

NARRATOR: Then, there was Mr. Contents of My Pockets.

(*A PUPPETEER slams a bunch of keys, change, and other pocket ephemera down on the puppet stage.*)

NARRATOR: And the other great allies of The Talking Cat included Mr. Almost-Empty Shampoo Bottle and Mr. Clear Reinforcement Labels, Two Hundred,[31] and Mr. Discolored Bath Towel and Mr. Blood-Soaked Bandages—

SCENE 10
LAUREN TRABUCO, THE NUDE PUPPETEER

LAUREN: (*Overlaps the NARRATOR.*) Okay, hold it! Stop it! Stop this! Shut up!

(*The NARRATOR speaks off-mic from this point onward.*)

NARRATOR: What? What are you doing?

LAUREN: Just shut up! These are not puppets!

NARRATOR: What?

LAUREN: A can of creamed corn? A pile of spare change!? What the hell!?

---

[29]Up to the final draft, he was known as "Mr. Can of Creamed Corn," but his name was changed to reflect the actual product name on the can.

[30]During the FringeNYC 2003 shows, a manual can opener was used instead, and the Puppeteer made loud squeaking noises to simulate a can being opened.

[31]Mr. Clear Reinforcement Labels replaced Mr. Old Broken Hard Drive, which was deemed too heavy to drag around.

NARRATOR: How many times do I have to tell you? All of these characters are integral to the plot!

LAUREN: Don't try to tell me there's a story here! This is just craziness!

NARRATOR: No, it's not—it's all contextual![32]

LAUREN: Get out of here! This is not a "Puppet Show for Children!"

NARRATOR: Yeah, maybe I should change the title. Now be quiet!

LAUREN: Hold on! There's another thing!

NARRATOR: What?

LAUREN: *(Almost inarticulate with rage.)* There's something I wanna know! All this time we've been working on this piece of shit...all those rehearsals...hours and hours I had to take off work...and lose money—*I wanna know! (LAUREN stands up behind the puppet stage. She is naked except for sandals or slippers.)* Why do I have to be naked!? I'm a puppeteer! *(She tries to conceal her nakedness with her hands.)*

NARRATOR: What are you doing? Get back down here!

LAUREN: *(Shakes her head.)* No way! This is crazy! You're weird!

(The NARRATOR stands up. He is wearing a mask that exactly replicates his own head in a larger size.[33])

NARRATOR: C'mon! We've got ten thousand years of psychohistory to cover!

LAUREN: Don't look at me, you filthy pervert!

(LAUREN picks up PUCE NONAGON and ORANGE HEPTAGON and uses them to cover her body. The NARRATOR points at the SHAPES.[34])

NARRATOR: *(Emphatically.)* Hey! Wait a minute! That's not what those are for!

LAUREN: You're a weirdo!

NARRATOR: I'm a fuckin' genius![35]

LAUREN: And why are you wearing that mask, you freak!?

NARRATOR: I told you—I'm trying to lose my usual deadpan stage persona!

LAUREN: Well, it's weird, and I'm not working under these conditions!

NARRATOR: *(To audience, trying to remain calm.)* Okay, everything's cool, everything's cool. C'mon. *(Removes the mask.)* Oooofffff! Man, it's hotter than fuck in there! *(He hangs the mask from a hook suspended from the ceiling.)* Let's just get on with the show, because my personal cosmology is very complicated and requires a great deal of explication!

LAUREN: No way! I'm outta here!

(She scampers off through the audience, heading for the exit, still trying to cover herself with the abstract SHAPES. The NARRATOR looks on with growing rage.)

---

[34]While wearing the mask, the Narrator may be unable to see Lauren and may gesture wildly in her direction instead.

[35]A theater colleague had related that a friend of mine, Luke Leonard, when recounting a performance of *Tom Chao's Sketch Comedy Troupe*, emphasized the fact that I sat on stage and repeatedly said "I'm a fucking genius." Well, at least he retained something from the performance.

---

[32]Someone had commented that my idea for nudity was "contextual." Actually it's more absurdist than contextual.

[33]At FringeNYC 2003, we used a paper cylinder with a caricature of the Narrator's face drawn on it, for simplicity's sake.

LAUREN: Where did you hide my clothes, you dirty old man!? *(Disgustedly.)* That's the last casting notice I answer on Nudepuppetshow.com! *(Panicked.)* Where in *hell* are my clothes!? *(LAUREN dashes around the audience looking for her clothes. Eventually she exits the theater.)*

NARRATOR: *(Loses control, screaming.)* Lauren Trabuco! Where are you going!? Come back here! Come back with my abstract geometrical shapes! Don't damage them! What the fuck?! Motherfucker! Motherfucking son-of-a-bitch!

(The NARRATOR continues screaming ad lib and rushes through the audience. He exits the theater, following LAUREN. Outside, he can be heard screaming and raging. Loud crashing and banging are heard as he smashes a crash box—a cardboard box full of metal cans and junk.)

NARRATOR: *Oh, my fuckin' god! I've! Got! Rage! I! Can't! Ex-! Press! In! Words!*

(Various metallic objects are heard crashing to the ground, then silence.)

SCENE 11
PLEASE CAST ME IN SOMETHING

After a very long pause of at least several minutes, TUESDAY stands up behind the puppet stage. She looks around tentatively for any signs of the NARRATOR or LAUREN.

TUESDAY: *(Hesitantly.)* What's going on? Are we finished? Can I go now? God, this is a weird show. *(Resignedly.)* But I'm still going to put it on my resume, so I'll have a New York credit.

ADRIANNE: *(Stands and holds up her headshot. To audience.)* Please cast me in something! Anything! If you are a casting director, producer, director, or playwright, please! I've done lots of shows around town! I was drugged and forcibly brought

here! I don't even know where I am or what kind of people have come to this theater or performance venue this evening! But please cast me in a show! Thank you! *(Pause.)* Oh, yeah, I'm non-Equity![36]

TUESDAY: *(Gets out her headshot.)* Yeah, that goes for me, too! Cast me in something! I'll do anything! *(Pause.)* Obviously.

(N. SEMBLE stands up and holds up her headshot too, displaying it momentarily. TUESDAY and ADRIANNE look on, transfixed. N. SEMBLE deliberately stalks across the stage and enters the audience. She picks out someone in the audience and hands her headshot to that person. She strides back to her seat and sits back down.)

SCENE 12
TUESDAY'S DREAM OF FAME

TUESDAY moves to center stage, still clutching her headshot.

TUESDAY: *(Dreamily.)* I wish I was famous. Wouldn't that be nice? I wish I didn't have to perform in tiny theaters that nobody's ever heard of. I wish I could play the lead role in a big show on Broadway. With my name up in lights. I wish I could appear on TV and in movies and in magazines. And everyone would know who I was. I'd be so famous, people everywhere would recognize me. Everywhere, all over the world. *(Gradually more dramatic.)* I wish I was so famous that even people in the most remote locations on earth would be familiar with me![37] Even

---

[36] She is not a member of Actors' Equity Association, the labor union of American theatrical actors and stage managers.

[37] The concept of people in the most remote locations recognizing celebrities came from an anecdote related by my friend, Beowulf Sheehan, in which his cousins in some remote area of Central America all had a new CD of popular music on the day it was released.

in the most hellish, disease-ridden, war-stricken, famine-ravaged, politically unstable countries, people would all know me! Though they have no food to eat or water to drink,[38] they could draw spiritual and emotional sustenance from the image of my face! My face! Shining down from billboards and TVs and magazine covers! Bringing life to the arid desert and frozen tundra! My face!

(Pause. ADRIANNE looks on, unmoving.)

ADRIANNE: That seems sort of extreme.

TUESDAY: Well, you've got to have a dream. *(Pause.)* Oh, I know it sounds egotistical. But you'd like to think that you could rise above the level of— *(She looks around, shrugs.)* You know.

ADRIANNE: *(Matter-of-factly.)* Well, yes, of course. Who doesn't dream those things deep inside them? In the secret, teeny-tiny, hidden recesses of one's mind? It's true.

(TUESDAY sets her headshot down.)

SCENE 13
KILL ALL EVIL MEN/TUESDAY'S SKETCH COMEDY BACKGROUND[39]

TUESDAY: Well, what should we do now? Now that the crazy guy has left the theater?

ADRIANNE: I hope Lauren finds her clothes, because otherwise—

TUESDAY: *(Interrupting.)* I think we've still got the theater for a few more minutes. Let's do something fun!

ADRIANNE: While I'm here, perhaps I'll perform my audition monologue that I wrote myself.

(She moves the chair to center stage. She places it facing away from the audience but she sits on it backwards, facing toward the audience.)

TUESDAY: Oh yeah, have you gotten a lot of callbacks?

ADRIANNE: Well, no. For some reason, male casting directors and agents don't seem to like it—it's entitled "Kill All Evil Men."[40]

TUESDAY: *(Interrupting.)* Hey, I've got an idea! Let's do some sketch comedy! That'll be fun! More fun than the stupid puppet show.

(ADRIANNE looks annoyed but listens.)

TUESDAY: I've been taking improv classes, and I love doing sketch comedy! Everybody in town is doing it! It's easy— you don't have to memorize any lines or anything! You just run up on stage and say whatever comes into your head! It's so much fun! *(Pause.)* And I've been in a whole bunch of sketch comedy groups.

(ADRIANNE picks up TUESDAY's headshot and studies it.)

ADRIANNE: Yeah, which ones?

TUESDAY: I was in a group called The House of Cards.

ADRIANNE: What happened to them?

---

[38]This image of not having any food or water derives from my father's many stories of childhood impoverishment.

[39]This scene was extracted from my as-yet-unproduced musical, *The Relationship Expert.*

[40]The phrase "Kill All Evil Men" is an old one in my work, but the idea for using it here came from the experience of auditioning dozens of actresses who seemed blithely unaware that their male-bashing audition monologues might appear somewhat off-putting to men in charge of casting.

TUESDAY: They fell apart.

ADRIANNE: *(Flatly.)* Oh, I see.

(TUESDAY turns and plays broadly to the audience during the following sequence. ADRIANNE and N. SEMBLE watch. ADRIANNE grimaces and, after a while, encourages the audience to boo and hiss by means of gestures.)

TUESDAY: Yeah, I've been in a number of sketch comedy groups. I was in a group called Lousy Poker Hand...but they folded. *(Pause.)* Then I was in a group called The Croissants...but everybody flaked on me. *(Pause.)* Then I was in Vacuum Tube...but that imploded. *(Pause.)* Then I was in The Helen Kellers...but they lacked vision. *(Pause.)* Then I was in The Amputees...but they didn't have a leg to stand on. *(Pause.)* Then I was in Empty Fabric Store...but they didn't have any material. *(Pause.)* Then I was in The Sandals...but we kept stepping on each other's toes. *(Pause.)* Then I was in The Weekly Newsmagazines...but they had too many issues. *(Pause.)* And I was in The Butchers...but they were a bunch of hacks. *(She turns back to ADRIANNE.)* And the last group I was in was The Pez Dispensers but—

ADRIANNE: *(Interrupts.)* Wait! Wait, Tuesday! Let me guess! *(ADRIANNE struggles to think of something.)* A-hem! The Pez Dispensers, um...er...aha! I've got it! The Pez Dispensers just sat on a shelf!

TUESDAY: *(Flatly.)* No, they just weren't funny.

ADRIANNE: Okay, Tuesday, that's great.

SCENE 14
THE RETURN OF LAUREN

LAUREN bursts back into the theater, preferably from a different direction than she

exited. She is now completely covered in black clothing, including a hood or ski mask covering her head, with mittens on her hands. Black pants and a black turtleneck will suffice.[41]

LAUREN: *(Steely.)* Hey, guys, I'm back.

(ADRIANNE and TUESDAY react, startled.)

ADRIANNE: *(To LAUREN.)* Ooh! It's you, Lauren! *(To all.)* God, I thought it was the Angel of Death coming to punish me for being in this show.

LAUREN: I couldn't find any of my clothing, but I found all this cool stuff in that used clothing boutique down the block. *(Pause.)* See how I'm completely covered up now? First I was naked, and now every square inch of my body is shielded from the prying, invasive gaze of Tom. What a great twist! It brings about a sense of closure, both for me and for the audience.

ADRIANNE: If you say so.

TUESDAY: I love it! It's you! *(Reconsiders.)* Well, no.

SCENE 15
A SHY, QUIET GIRL WHO WANTS TO BE A STAND-UP COMEDIAN[42]/FREAKOUT UNDER THE APPLE TREE

LAUREN: What are we doing now, guys? Let's get out of here and get a salade Niçoise! Down the street at Stingy Lulu's.[43]

---

[41] Care should be taken to make sure she does not appear to be wearing a burkha.

[42] This scene was inspired by any number of downtown alternative comedians, but specifically by a woman I saw at a show hosted by my friends Becky Poole and Noelle Romano. I wish I could remember her name, but she was too banal to be memorable.

[43] A restaurant down the street from the St. Marks Theater that features drag queens and a fifties theme, as well as a Brazilian influence.

ADRIANNE: I don't understand the theme of that place—fifties Brazilian drag queens? Is that it?

TUESDAY: *(Suddenly.)* Wait, we still have the theater for a few minutes, so let's do some sketch comedy.

LAUREN: Oh, that's a good idea. Okay, I've got an idea for a comedy sketch. Let's do a sketch about a shy, quiet girl who wants to be a stand-up comedian. Like this. *(LAUREN gets a microphone on a stand and moves it center stage. She stands awkwardly at the mic and adopts the persona of a shy, quiet girl, looking around fearfully. She delivers her "jokes" in an utterly inept way.)* Um, hi. Is this thing on? Uh, have you ever wondered why they're called "laundromats"? Have you ever seen a *mat* in one? *(Pause. She waits for laughter hopefully.)* Yeah, and another thing I noticed, is, like, have you ever been to Texas? *(Pause.)* They've got really big bugs there. *(Long pause.)* Have you ever noticed that men like science fiction? And women don't? Weird. *(LAUREN takes a little bow.)*

ADRIANNE: That's very accurate, but how are we supposed to take part? It's a solo.

LAUREN: Oh. Well, I just picked that idea because I guess it was in my mind. Because I share an apartment in Williamsburg with three shy, quiet girls who want to be stand-up comedians. *(Pause.)* Actually, it's Greenpoint.[44]

TUESDAY: Wait, I've got a different idea! Let's do a movement improvisation. *(She moves the microphone and stand out of the*

way.) I'll call this piece, um, ah, "Freakout Under the Apple Tree."[45]

(TUESDAY freezes for a moment in a butoh-dance-like pose, then falls to the ground and rolls around, contorts her body wildly, and emits bizarre, inhuman, wordless moans and animalistic shrieks.[46] LAUREN, ADRIANNE, and N. SEMBLE look on with a mixture of confusion and fear. After a minute of this, TUESDAY suddenly stops and looks at the others.)

TUESDAY: C'mon, guys! Just jump in when you feel it!

(The others look at each other, dumbfounded. TUESDAY launches back into the freakout, intensifying her insane behavior. When finished, she stands up and addresses the audience cheerfully.)

TUESDAY: "Freakout Under the Apple Tree!" *(She curtsies slightly.)*

LAUREN: I don't really see an apple tree. I see the freakout, though.

ADRIANNE: *(Stunned.)* Yeah, good energy, Tuesday.

TUESDAY: C'mon, guys!

ADRIANNE: Sorry, my body can't do that.

LAUREN: Yeah, I'll comment from the wings.

ADRIANNE: There are no wings.[47] Listen, can I just do my audition monologue now?

---

[44]People who live in Greenpoint often try to pass themselves off as residing in Williamsburg, for hipness value.

[45]This is the title of this show as I proposed it to another theater festival. The "under the apple tree" phrase is an homage to a children's book called *The Space Ship Under the Apple Tree* by Louis Slobodkin.

[46]Credit for this show-stopping scene has to go to the actress who originated the role, Kim Katzberg.

[47]If the theater has wings, this line must be altered.

TUESDAY: *(Picks up ADRIANNE's headshot and studies the resume. To ADRIANNE.)* Oh, you know what you should do?[48]

ADRIANNE: Please let me do my monologue! It's staunchly pro-feminist!

TUESDAY: *(Reading from resume.)* It says here that you're "good with children and animals." Everyone always says that. But are you *really* good with children and animals?

ADRIANNE: Yes, everyone always says that she's good with children and animals. But I'm actually *good* with children and animals.

TUESDAY: Are you good with cats?

ADRIANNE: Yes.

TUESDAY: Are you good with dogs?

ADRIANNE: Yes.

TUESDAY: *(Accusingly.)* Are you good with…ocelots?

(ADRIANNE glares at TUESDAY witheringly, as if that was the stupidest question in the world. They face each other down for a long moment with exaggerated contempt.)

ADRIANNE: *(Icily.)* Yes.

(TUESDAY looks unconvinced.)

ADRIANNE: I'm also good with coelacanths,[49] nudibranchs,[50] and, um, amaranths.[51]

---

[48]The original bit for Adrianne here involved Tuesday asking her to say various phrases in an upper-crust British accent, to take advantage of the actress's actual accent. She was obliged to utter the rather unfortunate phrase, "We don't have Hooters in England," resulting in much hilarity.

[49]The "living fossil," a lobe-finned fish thought to have been extinct for millions of years before a specimen was discovered in 1938.

[50]Sea slugs, mollusks without a shell or gills.

[51]Flowering plants including herbs or shrubs.

TUESDAY: Amaranths are not animals!

ADRIANNE: *(Snidely.)* Correct.

SCENE 16
THE NARRATOR RETURNS AND LECTURES LAUREN

The NARRATOR runs in noisily, also preferably from a different direction than he exited.

NARRATOR: Ah, there you are! Are you now ready to finish the story?

(TUESDAY and ADRIANNE withdraw from him.)

ADRIANNE: No way! I quit!

TUESDAY: Me too!

(The NARRATOR sees LAUREN, still hooded.)

NARRATOR: *(Startled.)* Who is that? Am I going to die?

LAUREN: It's me, Lauren!

NARRATOR: *(Enraged.)* Lauren! Did you put on clothes!?

LAUREN: Yes, you evil fucker!

NARRATOR: I didn't recognize you with clothes on.

(LAUREN holds up one of her mitten-covered hands and shakes it at him. The NARRATOR looks at her, confused.)

LAUREN: You can't tell, but I'm flipping you off! *(Pause.)* You're just another heinous man who exploits actresses!

NARRATOR: *(Looks deeply shaken by this accusation and struggles to regain his composure. He takes a pipe out of his pocket and wrings it agitatedly, but then calms down and starts sucking on it thoughtfully. Paternally.)* Lauren Trabuco, don't you realize that women all over the world are fighting for the right to take off all of their clothing? And here you are putting on more clothing. You're single-handedly setting back the cause of women five hundred years with your antiquated, outmoded, Victorian sensibilities...and mores. *(He sticks the pipe in his mouth with a smug expression.)*

LAUREN: You're wrong, old man! Promoting the cause of women doesn't have anything to do with how much clothing I have on! I can wear as much—or as little—as I want, any time of day or night.

NARRATOR: *(Miffed.)* Hmpff! *(He yanks the pipe from his mouth and fumes, pacing about. He gradually cools off and forms a reply. He addresses the audience calmly and smoothly.)* When I was a cinema student years ago at USC, I learned something in Cinema 190, the introductory film class. The professor, Marsha Kinder, the well-known film scholar, pointed out a fact about Georges Méliès's ground-breaking film, *A Trip to the Moon*. Now, this classic silent film includes scenes of beautiful women, with little justification for their presence. And about this, Professor Kinder said, "Women's bodies provide spectacle."[52] *(He repeats the last sentence slower with exaggerated emphasis.)* "Women's bodies provide spectacle."

(Pause. During the NARRATOR's speech, LAUREN gets two tallboy cans of beer. She sits on the chair onstage. She holds a beer and leaves the other on the ground.)

NARRATOR: Now, I remember writing that sentence down in my notes. And to this day, I've always believed that her pronouncement that women's bodies provide

spectacle was not an *indictment*, but rather a *prescription* for all creative endeavor!

(The NARRATOR looks supremely satisfied and sticks the pipe back in his mouth, but LAUREN is not impressed. She opens the beer and drinks. A pregnant pause.)

LAUREN: Oh, you loser.

NARRATOR: *(Yanks the pipe from his mouth angrily. He stares venomously at LAUREN. He walks over, picks up the other beer, and then sits down in the audience, facing LAUREN. He puts down his pipe, cracks open the beer, and takes a long swig. Calmly.)* Another thing you must realize, Lauren, is that a young actress can't really expect to grow or progress in one's acting career if one refuses to appear naked onstage. If you refuse to take off your clothes onstage, you can only really hope to play small supporting roles, instead of major lead roles. *(Pause.)* For instance, in *Romeo and Juliet*, you might play the Nurse instead of Juliet.

LAUREN: *(Scandalized.)* No way!

NARRATOR: Or perhaps in *The Crucible*, by Arthur Miller, you might play Elizabeth Proctor instead of, uh, what's that character's name? Abigail Williams![53]

LAUREN: *(Slightly confused.)* Huh?

NARRATOR: Or even another example is that in *The Music Man*, you might play Mrs. Paroo, the mother of Marian the Librarian—but you'll never play Marian herself!

LAUREN: What!? Since when is Marian the Librarian *naked* in *The Music Man*!?

---

[52]This story is a true one dating from around 1981.

[53]The playwright once portrayed Reverend Hale in a production of *The Crucible* in high school.

NARRATOR: She's naked in my revisionist version of *The Music Man*!

LAUREN: You're crazy, goofball! *(Quickly.)* I'm not a musical theater person, either!

NARRATOR: *(Gets up and walks back onto the stage.)* Another point is that it's hotter than fuck out,[54] and no one's ever heard of me! So I need you to run through the streets of the East Village[55] and try to get people to come to my show!

LAUREN: No way!

NARRATOR: *(Thoughtfully.)* It's not my fault that no one's ever heard of me. Or that it's hotter than fuck out. I've done everything I can to tell people about my show. I can only blame the people who haven't heard of me— *(Hesitantly.)* —for not paying better attention.

ADRIANNE: Oh, come on! Let's get out of here!

NARRATOR: Not before we finish this show!

SCENE 17
INTERRUPTED BY THE SPECIAL GUEST

The SPECIAL GUEST starts shouting from the audience. Note: There may be more than one SPECIAL GUEST, in which case the following lines may be divided up amongst them, and extra lines ad-libbed.

SPECIAL GUEST: Boo! Get off! I hate you! *(He or she continues ad lib.)*

NARRATOR: What?

SPECIAL GUEST: I denounce Tom! He's a sexist pig! I hate him! *(The SPECIAL GUEST comes out of the audience and stands onstage.)* I denounce this idiot's shoddy treatment of actresses! He is unable to write realistic female characters! If you want to see a show that's not sexist and misogynistic, I invite you to see my show, *(insert name of show).*

(The SPECIAL GUEST pulls out promotional postcards for his or her show and hands them to the PUPPETEERS and the audience.)

SPECIAL GUEST: My next show will be held at *(insert location and date and time)*!

NARRATOR: What the fuck!? Are you interrupting my show to promote your show!?

SPECIAL GUEST: *(To audience.)* Now, I'm leaving. I invite everyone to follow me out of the theater! C'mon!

(The SPECIAL GUEST starts to exit through the audience, ad-libbing exhortations for all to follow while continuing to give out postcards. The PUPPETEERS watch him or her go with admiration. The PUPPETEERS start to move toward the exit. As the SPECIAL GUEST exits, the NARRATOR runs over and physically prevents the PUPPETEERS from leaving.)

NARRATOR: Hey! Don't follow him *(or her or them)*!

(He ad-libs customized insults directed at the SPECIAL GUEST. N. SEMBLE raises an eyebrow. The NARRATOR slams the door after the SPECIAL GUEST leaves. He turns back to the PUPPETEERS.)

SCENE 18
I'M NOT INTO *STAR WARS* AND HARRY POTTER!

TUESDAY: Wow, *(insert SPECIAL GUEST name or names)* is right!

---

[54]Clearly this line was intended for use when it's hotter than fuck out. Otherwise it should be modified to reflect the actual meteorological conditions.

[55]Here the name of the neighborhood could be changed to reflect reality.

LAUREN, ADRIANNE, and TUES-
DAY: *(In unison.)* The scales have fallen
from my eyes!

NARRATOR: *(To the PUPPETEERS.)*
Wait a minute! You can't leave yet! We've
still got a lot of material to cover! Like ten
thousand years of psychohistory! Let's get
back to work!

*(He tries to herd the PUPPETEERS back
onto the stage.)*

ADRIANNE: Oh, give it a rest!

TUESDAY: No one cares about your little
puppet show. It just keeps droning on and
on!

NARRATOR: *(Defensively.)* Hey! I've
been working on this my entire life, and
so of course there's a lot of exposition.

LAUREN: *(Sarcastically.)* Oooh, isn't that
special!

*(A PUPPETEER shoves the NARRATOR
back onto the stage. They push him around
while taunting him.)*

ADRIANNE: We know your type!
Wanker![56] What is it with men who can't
get dates? They have to invent fantasy
universes to fill up their empty lives!

TUESDAY: Yeah, I'll bet you're a fan of,
uh, of *Star Wars* and Harry Potter!

LAUREN: *(Fast.)* Yeah! *Ha!*

*(LAUREN and TUESDAY exchange a high
five and gloat.)*

NARRATOR: What!? No fuckin' way!

TUESDAY: Oh, yeah, oh yeah!

NARRATOR: *(Enraged.)* I'm not a fan of
Star Wars and Harry Potter, for fuck's sake!
What am I, seven years old? *(Quieter, to
audience.)* No, I'm a fan of *The Prisoner*[57]
and Tolkien. You know, *Lord of the Rings*?

*(TUESDAY, ADRIANNE, and LAUREN
make mocking gestures and dance around
the NARRATOR. They all shout at him simultaneously. He ad-libs protests.)*

TUESDAY: Ooooooh! I'm a fan of *Lord of
the Rings*! I'm superior! *(She continues ad lib.)*

LAUREN: *(Overlapping.)* I'm so much
smarter! I've got a Hoberman Sphere! *(She
continues ad lib.)*

ADRIANNE: *(Overlapping.)* I exploit
actresses and I don't know shit about pup-
petry! *(She continues ad lib.)*

NARRATOR: *(Overlapping, shouting them
down.)* Okay, stop! Shut up! Stop it! *Shut up!*

(The PUPPETEERS fall silent.)

NARRATOR: Oh, you crazy, non-Equity
actresses! Have you forgotten something?
Without me, you'd have nothing to do
except wait tables and read casting notices
in *Back Stage*! *(To audience.)* You see, I
provide a great service for society—I give
non-Equity actresses something to do!

SCENE 19
ADVICE FOR CHILDREN WHO ARE STUCK
IN A STATE OF ARRESTED DEVELOPMENT,
OTHERWISE KNOWN AS INFANTILIZED
ADULTS[58]/DEPARTURE OF THE PUPPETEERS

*ADRIANNE inhales deeply with rage and
draws herself up to her full height. She ad-*

---

[56]The word "wanker" has probably appeared in everything I've ever written. At last
in the FringeNYC production, I had an actress (Leya Balsari) with a real English accent
to say it.

[57]A surrealistic late-sixties British television
show about a mysterious spy referred to only
as "Number 6," played by Patrick McGoohan.

[58]From the "Puppet Show for Children"
sketch performed at the Timsloft variety show,
January 2002.

libs impressive-sounding curses in a foreign language.[59]

NARRATOR: *(Taken aback.)* What does that mean?

ADRIANNE: *(Imperiously.)* You neurasthenic homunculus![60] Now I'm going to give you what you need: unasked-for advice!

NARRATOR: *(Devastated, in a long, drawn-out moan.)* Noooooooooooooooooooo! *(He draws himself up into a stiff posture of attention.)*

ADRIANNE: Yes! *(Pause. She addresses the audience in a professorial manner.)* Now, "Advice for Children Who Are Stuck in a State of Arrested Development, Otherwise Known as Infantilized Adults."

NARRATOR: *(Fearfully.)* What should I do with my life?

(ADRIANNE moves around the NARRATOR, looking him over, tapping a finger to her lips.)

ADRIANNE: Well…spend money you don't have. It won't make you feel better, but you'll marvel at your own stupidity. *(Pause.)* Cultivate your eccentricities. That goes without saying. Avoid all human contact. Yes. Brood silently. Check. *(Pause.)* Adopt a defeatist attitude. I know that's very unpopular currently. But it'll save time. If you don't feel comfortable with that position, just refer to it as "stoic resignation."

NARRATOR: Yes, the kind that was popularized by the motion picture *Gladiator*.[61]

ADRIANNE: Shh!

NARRATOR: *(Hesitantly.)* What about romance?

ADRIANNE: Today, everyone would say, "Just use the Internet." That works for some people. But it won't work for you. In your case, I suggest you stare deeply into your computer as it reveals a seemingly endless array of beautiful women you'll never have. Keep staring until the avalanche of unrealistic expectations crushes your spirit.[62]

NARRATOR: And, finally, that leaves my performance career. What do you say about that?

ADRIANNE: Keep appearing in fringe theater shows like this one where you clearly stand out as the oldest person in the entire theater—by at least a decade.

(The NARRATOR cringes.)

ADRIANNE: Your career won't go anywhere, but you'll feel like you're still in touch with "the kids." Ha!

NARRATOR: Ooooch!

(As ADRIANNE looks on, nonplussed, the NARRATOR slowly moves into "the gesture of frozen agony," with both hands clenched in twisted claws above his head and his mouth

---

[59]During FringeNYC 2003, the actress portraying Adrianne, Leya Balsari, cursed in her native language of Turkish, and never revealed what she actually said.

[60]This is a phrase that I have been trying to get actresses to pronounce correctly for years.

[61]When I saw Marcus Aurelius portrayed (by Richard Harris) in *Gladiator*, a high-profile Hollywood blockbuster, I became convinced that his presence would spark a craze for Stoic philosophy in every sector of our society. Did it ever happen?

[62]During FringeNYC 2003, Adrianne pushed the Narrator down onto all fours and sat on him during the next few lines.

wide open in a silent scream, head tilted far back.[63] *ADRIANNE slyly looks at the audience and makes the "I'm hot" gesture.)*

ADRIANNE: Well, that's burned his playhouse down.

(The PUPPETEERS get their jackets and personal belongings from behind the puppet stage. They walk through the audience toward the exit.)

ADRIANNE: I'm outta here. There's an open call at Harlequin Studios[64] that I can still make if I hurry. Where the hell am I?

TUESDAY: Somewhere in the East Village.

LAUREN: I'm never coming back here to this creepy black hellhole! That's for sure!

TUESDAY: Me neither. I'm going to my improv class at UCB.[65] Now, those people are funny! Not like this! *(Goes out the door, pulling the door shut behind her.)*

SCENE 20
TOM'S THOUGHTS ARE AUDIBLE

The NARRATOR remains frozen in place. A short pause. Lighting dims to a dramatic single light. Prerecorded voiceover starts.

NARRATOR'S VOICEOVER: *(With a very dead, flat inflection.)* Oh, man, I'm fucked up. Oh, man. Everything is fucked up. Isn't that right, cat?

(The NARRATOR slowly begins to lower his arms and tilt his head down. His body
sinks into a posture of complete tension, with fists clenched.)*

NARRATOR'S VOICEOVER: Everything's gone to hell. We barely even started recounting the ten thousand years of psychohistory, and then everything went to hell. Damn those actresses for not believing in my elaborate personal cosmology! *(Pause.)* What if those crazy, non-Equity actresses are right? What if my invented universe is just a time-wasting venture, designed to eat up all the lonely seconds, minutes, hours, days, weeks, months, years, and decades?

NARRATOR: *(Speaks with difficulty, as his face muscles are clenched.)* What the—? Wait a minute! *(The NARRATOR jerks his body out of the frozen posture of tension, trying to see the source of the sound.)* Oh, listen to this. I'm so tense that people can actually hear my thoughts! *(Pause.)* Everything I think is going straight into the air. Great. I always knew this would happen. Somehow I've gone totally insane. My mind is completely transparent.

(The NARRATOR coughs simultaneously with the voiceover.)

NARRATOR'S VOICEOVER and NARRATOR: *(Speaking aloud simultaneously with the voiceover, the NARRATOR is barely able to articulate the words.)* I've always said, "If they could read my mind, they'd put me away for *a thousand years.*"[66]

---

[63]This pose was taken from my high school friend, Steve Snyder, who always used it to denote "bad acting."

[64]A rehearsal studio in Midtown Manhattan that I understand holds many open casting calls.

[65]Upright Citizens Brigade, the well-known comedy troupe, runs improvisational comedy classes and turns out hundreds of comedy improvisers.

[66]The peculiar drawn-out intonation of "a thousand years" is based on a line from the Firesign Theatre's recording of "The Further Adventures of Nick Danger." The idea of people reading your mind and locking you up also relates to the lyric from the song "A Token of My Extreme" by Frank Zappa (*Joe's Garage*), "Don't you ever try to look behind my eyes/You don't ever want to know what they have seen."

NARRATOR'S VOICEOVER: It all has to do with the fact that I never leave Manhattan. I never even leave the East Village, and the stress of living here has caused me to go insane. *(Pause.)* Before I moved here to New York, my friend Charles Merzbacher[67] warned me that I must leave Manhattan as often as possible to maintain my sanity. He said I must find someplace to go every weekend to get away from the insane crushing tension and pressure of living here in this place, which actually shortens people's life expectancies with its harshness. *(Pause.)* But I didn't listen to him. And now, sometime in the night, I crossed over the invisible line into the land of madness.

(Pause. The NARRATOR looks very anxious about what he might hear next.)

NARRATOR: Well, this is okay. This stuff is sort of okay if people can hear this.

(The voiceover cuts back in suddenly.)

NARRATOR'S VOICEOVER: I wish I had a cute little girlfriend who was all naked and shit!

NARRATOR: *(Cringes as he listens to his own thoughts.)* Oh, god!

NARRATOR'S VOICEOVER: There was a nude woman in here earlier, but she ran out and put on clothes. Oh, well, she's married anyway.[68] *(Pause.)* That's wrong. Good god, I've got to get me a girlfriend, or I'm gonna go fuckin' insane. I mean, come on already...let me just have one

girlfriend. I'm not asking for some kind of hot actress or something. *(In a more contemplative tone.)* I guess it's sort of self-defeating to constantly surround oneself with beautiful actresses when you know you can't really have any of them.

(The NARRATOR continues to cringe as he hears his own thoughts, now growing more agitated.)

NARRATOR'S VOICEOVER: Listen, at this very late stage of my life, I'd be perfectly happy with somebody about a half or one-third or even one-fourth as pretty as one of the beautiful actresses. Somebody completely forgettable, someone whose face you can't remember when she turns and leaves the room. A woman who's getting old and desperate and has no figure, or rather a figure like a seven-year-old boy.

(The NARRATOR grimaces and coughs nervously.)

NARRATOR'S VOICEOVER: You know, a dorky-looking mouth-breather who's flat-chested. I mean, you can't find her breasts with a microscope!

NARRATOR: *(Overlaps.)* Oh man, this ain't good!

NARRATOR'S VOICEOVER: You know what I'm talking about? Somebody who disappears into the background, somebody who works in an office and has thick black clunky glasses[69] and her hair is pulled really tightly back against her skull in that stupid look I can't stand! Who invented that stupid look? Man, I wish I had a girlfriend! I wish I had a girlfriend! I wish I had a girlfriend!

---

[67]Charles Merzbacher (*Mertz*-bawk-er) and I attended classes at USC Cinema together. Presently he is a professor of film at Boston University.

[68]This line about the actress being married should be modified to reflect her actual marital status.

[69]The reference to "thick black clunky glasses" has been used in several of my previous scripts to describe the eyewear of Rachel Haimowitz, the fictional object of my desire.

(The last sentence, "I wish I had a girlfriend," continues to repeat underneath.)

NARRATOR: Boy, that's depressing. People can hear my thoughts, and all I keep thinking is, "I wish I had a girlfriend." Talk about banal and tedious! That's fuckin' embarrassing! And lame. I mean, shouldn't my innermost thoughts be about all kinds of insane murderous rage and shit!?

(He listens to his voiceover repeating, "I wish I had a girlfriend." Slowly, the voiceover starts to vary with reverb, phasing, flanging, pitch-shifting, and other audio effects, suggesting that his mind is breaking down. The NARRATOR fights against the increasing tension in his body and clutches his head in an exaggerated fashion. He tries to shout himself down.)

NARRATOR: *Goddamn, stop it!* Man, I've got to kill myself! Or I've got to at least knock myself out to prevent all of my conscious thoughts from spewing into the air! *(Groans weirdly.)* Stop it! Stop it! Stop— the fuck!—it! *Stop it!*

(The voiceover fades out. The NARRATOR slumps on the ground in an awkward position.)

SCENE 21
N. SEMBLE SPEAKS OF LOVE

N. SEMBLE stands, walks over to the NARRATOR, looks him over, then looks at the audience and puts a finger to her lips, motioning for silence. She speaks in a loud stage whisper.[70]

N. SEMBLE: Shh! Tom has gone to a strange place.

---

[70]This bit of business, in which a woman sees Tom's slumbering form and asks the audience to keep quiet, is exactly the same as that performed by The Woman in a White Dress in my one-act play of the same name.

(The NARRATOR's leg twitches. N. SEMBLE continues quietly.)

N. SEMBLE: At last, the wreckage of his failed puppet show has collapsed upon him, crushing his spirit. Or perhaps we should say that the puppet show has evaporated into thin air, since it never had enough *weight* or *substance* to collapse. *(She indicates the puppet stage, then turns her attention to the NARRATOR.)* Tom has gone to the place where he doesn't know if he's awake or asleep. He sometimes stays in this place for hours and hours. The only way he knows if he's asleep is when— *(An expectant pause.)* —he can no longer identify the origin of his thoughts. And then he knows he's dreaming. Yes, he's lying there with his brain cells chewing away on some meaningless problem—like the ending of his puppet show—and he suddenly finds that he's walking through a seedy, run-down German *Hofbrau* filled with arcade videogames from 1981. But all of them are slight variants of readily identifiable games from that era. You know, the dream state where everything is unfamiliar except *the feeling. (Loudly whispering.) The feeling! (Pause. Normal again.)* But Tom has done very little, so his dreams are made of the cut-up bits of the few experiences he's had. He always dreams of being back in college. In his nocturnal wanderings, he drifts silently through endless white corridors in the halls of academia, or perhaps runs desperately between the stark brick buildings of the main campus, wondering, "Am I late for the lecture?" Or he finds himself in an impossibly tall dormitory teetering hundreds of stories over the Los Angeles skyline, sharing a crummy room with a stranger, thinking, "Haven't I done this before?" *(Pause.)* As he said, a long time ago Tom studied cinema at USC. He certainly didn't study theater! As you can tell.

(She smiles cruelly to underscore the harsh jab.) And he worked in various departments on campus to earn money. Notably, he worked in the Psychology Department as an administrative assistant, though he was quite inefficient and careless and, well, useless. *(Pause.)* And today he still dreams of those days. Worst of all is when Tom dreams of suddenly realizing he's missed half a semester of Ph.D. classes and he'll never get a doctorate and his life is more than half over and he's going to *die alone.* He's probably going to die alone in this very theater.[71] *(She indicates the theater.)* After hours of this suspension between states, he staggers to his feet and wonders if he's been asleep or awake. *(Pause. She considers him further.)* Now he's being purged in the great fire of madness. *(Smiles.)* He thinks people can hear his thoughts! *(Coyly.)* Do you think he'll be reborn anew after passing through the excoriating pain of insanity? *(Pause.)* Most people can't survive it. *(Pause.)* Do you know what can free him from his madness? Tom believes that only one thing can do that—do you know what it is? *(Pause.)* He believes a woman's kiss can save him! *(She laughs, lightly and musically.)* All lonely wankers believe a woman's kiss can save them! *(She moves to the NARRATOR, bends down, leans over, caresses his head, then kisses him.)* How wrong they are! A woman's kiss is a great reward, given in return for a man's service and obedience. It's not an IV drip bag full of life-giving fluids to be administered in emergencies! *(Seriously.)* Noth-

ing will save Tom. *(Pause.)* But here is a psychologist, to make her unorthodox mental status examination. *(She does not indicate EVELYN's presence, but draws herself up to her full height and exits.)*

SCENE 22
DR. EVELYN FLORENTINE'S MENTAL STATUS EXAMINATION

EVELYN stands up and approaches the prone form of the NARRATOR. She speaks into a small, hand-held tape recorder.

EVELYN: These are the field notes of Evelyn Florentine, professor of clinical psychology. I heard there was a depiction of insanity in this show, and I thought it might be something I could use in my class. *(Pause.)* Mental status examination: The client appears to be an Asian[72] male, about thirty-two years of age.[73] Facial expression is haggard, but otherwise appears in good health. Client appears well-fed and slightly disheveled. *(Pause.)* Well, badly dressed. The client was observed playing with puppets, household objects, and geometric shapes, indicative of a regression to childhood behaviors. The client's narration was tangential and filled with bizarre loose association. Thought flood and magical thinking were observed. In terms of content, the client displayed delusions of worthlessness, self-deprecation, and persecutory ideation, as well as comments indicating grandiosity. I have not observed any psychomotor agitation, but the client was hiding behind a puppet stage most of the time. His speech was precise but pres-

---

[71]In the FringeNYC 2003 production, N. Semble said "basement" instead of "theater," reflecting the location of the Under St. Marks venue in a basement. I was making a very inside joke reflecting the large amount of work I had presented there during the preceding three years.

[72]This reference may be changed to reflect the race of the actor.

[73]This reference to my perceived age is an infinitesimally small joke about the fact that people generally think I'm much younger than my actual age.

sured. *(Pause.)* I observed the client at a performance of "off-off-Broadway theater." It's really far from Broadway, certainly. I have never heard of it before. This is not like any theater I know. *(She grows slightly more expansive.)* The only theater I ever see is Shakespeare in Central Park. My friends and I always go to Central Park and we wait in line for tickets. We take lawn chairs and magazines and raspberries! It's so much fun! And then we get to see real Shakespeare, with famous actors. Like the time I saw *The Tempest* with Patrick Stewart.[74] That was so good! *(Flat again.)* On the other hand, this off-off-Broadway theater is weird and I don't like it. *(Pause.)* Anyway, to sum up, I don't even need to look in my *DSM*[75] to know this guy meets the criteria for Axis 2, Cluster B Narcissistic Personality Disorder. Otherwise known as 301.81.[76] *(Looks up from tape recorder.)* Personally, I think the client should have his head sawn off, and it should be preserved in a bucket of formaldehyde at the Coney Island freak show. *(Pause.)* Now I'm going to get out of this black room and go back uptown! *(She crosses back to her seat, retrieves her bag, and prepares to exit. She moves toward the door.)*

SCENE 23
DR. EVELYN AND TOM REUNITE
AFTER YEARS APART

The NARRATOR wakes up slowly, mumbling and blinking in the light. EVELYN sees him moving and stops.

---

[74]1995, Delacorte Theater, Central Park, New York.

[75]American Psychiatric Association, *Diagnostic and Statistical Manual of Mental Disorders*, 4th ed. (Washington, DC: American Psychiatric Publishing, Inc., 1994).

[76]This number is the actual diagnostic code for this personality disorder as given in the *DSM*.

NARRATOR: *(Groggily.)* Was I awake or asleep just now? I don't know.

(He dimly sees EVELYN standing above him.)

NARRATOR: Hello?

EVELYN: *(Now perky and friendly.)* Hi, Tom?

NARRATOR: Yes, have we met?

EVELYN: Don't you remember me from the Psych Department at USC?

NARRATOR: *(Sleepily.)* My god, that was a long time ago. *(Now alert, he stands.)* Yes, you're Evelyn Florentine! Of course I remember you. How are you? What are you doing here in New York?

EVELYN: I teach at NYU now.

NARRATOR: My gosh, I remember the days of working for Dr. Duval. What happened to him?

EVELYN: He killed himself.

NARRATOR: *(Awkwardly.)* Oh, I'm sorry to hear that. *(Tries to change the subject.)* Listen, since you're a psychologist now, can I ask you a question? What does it mean if you think other people can hear your thoughts? Does that mean you're crazy?

EVELYN: You hear your thoughts? Are they inside your head? Or are they "out there" in the world?

NARRATOR: I think they're just inside my head. But I'm not sure.

EVELYN: Well, Tom, I don't think you really think your thoughts are audible. *(She considers him.)* I think that you're just sort of anxious and ruminating about things, and sometimes you think that you hear voices.

NARRATOR: *(Relieved.)* Oh, great. Fantastic.

EVELYN: I remember when I was at USC, you were always silent and kept to yourself, and it always looked like you were thinking very hard about something. That's what we used to say about you.

NARRATOR: Really?

EVELYN: Yes, you're just a person who thinks very hard about things.

NARRATOR: Well, I'm glad to know that people can't actually hear my thoughts.

(He breathes a sigh of relief. EVELYN looks conflicted.)

EVELYN: Well, Tom, I have to tell you something. *(Authoritatively.)* We *could* hear your thoughts. You see, we were listening to a CD of your thoughts.

NARRATOR: What?

EVELYN: *(Goes to the tech booth. To TECH.)* May I have the disk? *(Pause.)* No, just let me have it. Give it to me. No, this is over.

(The TECH hands her a jewel case containing an audio CD clearly marked "Tom's Innermost Thoughts." She hands it to the NARRATOR, who stares at it.)

EVELYN: Sorry.

NARRATOR: What? *(He holds the CD up to the audience as he studies it.)*

EVELYN: Yes, well, a few weeks ago, when you were trying to finish the script for your "puppet show," you decided that you would try a new technique for unblocking your writer's block. So you tried dictating your thoughts into your computer. And you started saying whatever came into your head, because that would allow the creative side of your mind to dominate instead of being blocked by the editorial side.

NARRATOR: Yes, that was also when I was trying to test out the digital audio capabilities of my new eighty-gig LaCie D2 external firewire drive. And then I burned the disk. Well, that solves the mystery of why I thought people could hear my thoughts. But how did you get hold of this CD?

EVELYN: Well, during the rehearsals, you brought this disk along with the sound effects for the show, and, during a break, the puppeteers found the disk and then they thought they'd check it out—because they thought it would be full of porno.

NARRATOR: Good god.

EVELYN: Yes, it was just a recording of your deepest wishes and desires.

NARRATOR: How do you know that?

EVELYN: That's what you say on the disk. It's very obvious.

(NARRATOR'S VOICEOVER starts. EVELYN does not notice the voiceover.)

NARRATOR'S VOICEOVER: Good morning. It's about five a.m., and I'm still trying to finish my script. But I keep thinking about Evelyn Florentine. Man, I remember her from a million years ago, and I'd give anything to see her again. If I saw her again, I'd ask her to go out with me, which I never managed to do when I worked as an administrative assistant in the Psych Department. This is my deepest wish and desire.

(The NARRATOR looks around, confused. He looks at the CD in his hands, and his body begins to grow tense again. He tries to throw the CD on the ground, but his hands are clutching it so tightly that he has to use his foot to dislodge it from his grasp.)

NARRATOR'S VOICEOVER: Man, that Evelyn chick was hot and I'd still like to fuck her! Oh, man, I wish I could fuck her! I don't know where she is or what she's doing, but I wish I could fuck her.

(The voiceover continues underneath the following dialog.)

NARRATOR'S VOICEOVER: I'd like to rip off all her little clothes until she is virtually stark raving nude![77] Come on, just let me be trapped in an elevator with her for ten minutes! Come on, god! That's all I want! Just let me be trapped in an elevator with her for ten minutes, and then I can die! Come on, god! Wait a minute! Why am I asking god for help? God doesn't exist! Don't ask him for help, for fuck's sake! Evelyn Florentine is hot. I want to fuck her. She actually looks too hot to be a psychologist. She looks more like a fashion model or something. Yeah, man! Fuck, yeah!

EVELYN: *(Over the voiceover.)* Tom?

NARRATOR: *(Nervously, over the voiceover.)* What the hell!?— Can you hear that?

EVELYN: No, what?

(The NARRATOR, panicked, turns to the tech booth and makes the finger-slashing-across-the-throat gesture indicating "cut." The voiceover continues.)

NARRATOR: *(To TECH.)* Hey! Turn that off! Kill it! Right now!

TECH: *(From booth.)* That's not a recording. It's your thoughts.

NARRATOR: *(Struggling, unable to speak. To EVELYN.)* Uhhhhh! Gahhhhhh! Erm, puppet show! Puppet show! Did you like it!? What did you think of it? *(NARRA-*

TOR massages his temples again and hyperventilates. He staggers and sits on the chair. In an effort to control his thoughts, he smashes a fist on his thigh repeatedly.)*

EVELYN: What? Are you all right?

NARRATOR: It's just some minor neurological dysfunction. *(He stops hitting himself and calms down. The voiceover ends.)*

EVELYN: Do you want some Advil? *(She rummages around in her bag.)*

NARRATOR: Wait a minute—how do you know my puppeteers?

EVELYN: Oh, I'm old friends with Adrianne, Lauren, and Tuesday. *(Cheerfully.)* You know, they wanted me to pretend that I like you and then fool you into thinking I was going to date you.

NARRATOR: *(Angered.)* Oh, geez!

EVELYN: But, you know, I didn't want to do that to you. It would be cruel.

NARRATOR: Yes, it would be.

EVELYN: I don't have any Advil.

NARRATOR: *(Quickly.)* Hey, why don't we go have a drink after this show is over?

EVELYN: Oh, no, I can't stay. I'm going to meet my fiancé uptown.

NARRATOR: *(Crushed.)* Oh, I see. *(He looks away in sadness.)*

EVELYN: Okay, Tom, I have to leave now.

(EVELYN starts to exit. The NARRATOR jumps up.)

NARRATOR: Well, it was nice seeing you again, Evelyn. Uh, if you ever want to contact me, just search for me on the Web—you'll find my website.

EVELYN: Okay, bye.

---

[77] A lyric from the song "Magdalena" by Frank Zappa and the Mothers of Invention (*Just Another Band From LA*, 1972).

(The NARRATOR extends his hand for a handshake. EVELYN comes back and looks at his hand, but gives him a small, circumspect hug instead of a handshake. She exits. The NARRATOR watches her go with an expression of longing. A long pause. Lights dim as if the show is ending.)

SCENE 24
THE DEEPEST PART OF SUMMER:
A BRIEF FANTASY SEQUENCE

Before the lights fade out completely, a blue nighttime look fades up. The sound of crickets begins in the background. The NARRATOR looks around and notes the change.

NARRATOR: Hey, I'm outside now.[78] *(Pause.)* It's nice out. *(He faces the audience but looks beyond it at the imaginary scene which he now describes.)* This is the last phase of my descent into madness. I'm hallucinating that I'm down by the lake. It's the deepest part of summer.[79] *(With a certain wistfulness.)* The air is thick and dense, redolent with the scent of rain-washed grass. I slowly pick my way through the tall brush, down to the stone wall at the edge of the low cliff overlooking the lake. The water is black and gently laps at the shore with faint whispering waves. On the far side, only a single light is visible. *(He shifts his body position slightly.)* I saw Evelyn Florentine again today. Or did I? Was she a hallucination too? *(Pause.)* She looked just as I remember her, perhaps slightly older. But she seems like the

sort that will age well. *(Pause.)* Now, as then, I didn't interest her. She's engaged now, so she says. Too bad for me. *(Pause.)* Oh, well.

(The NARRATOR stands still and looks into the distance at the imaginary far shore. EVELYN slowly reenters. She has taken off her jacket and changed into sneakers. She moves near the NARRATOR and stands side by side with him. He does not look at her. Both of them look off into the distance at the imaginary light.)

EVELYN: I wonder whose light that is, over there?

NARRATOR: I think it's Daisy Buchanan's.[80]

EVELYN: Her light was green, not white.

(They share a bemused chuckle. A very long silence.)

EVELYN: There was a carnival here today. I'll bet it was fun.

(Long pause.)

NARRATOR: I'll bet it wasn't.

EVELYN: Oh?

NARRATOR: Every child learns very early that nothing's worse than something that's supposed to be fun—but isn't.

(Long pause.)

EVELYN: Worse still is to pass up possibilities.

(Extremely long pause as they listen to the crickets, and idly stretch and fidget.)

---

[78]This line about being "outside now" is directly taken from a scene in my radio play *The Scientists*, in which a cricket sound effect starts and my character says flatly, "Hey, I'm outside now."

[79]The scenario of a lakeside in summer recurs in my work regularly.

---

[80]The reference to Daisy Buchanan's green light is from *The Great Gatsby* by F. Scott Fitzgerald. And it's a very obvious one.

NARRATOR: *This* moment is filled with possibilities.

(EVELYN moves to the NARRATOR slowly, then leans in and gives him a lingering kiss. He does not respond at first, but then returns the kiss. EVELYN finishes and backs off slightly, facing away from the audience, bowing her head. The NARRATOR looks from her into the audience.)

NARRATOR: Too bad it's just a brief fantasy sequence.

(Lights dim slowly. Cricket loop fades slowly. Blackout.)

SCENE 25
CODA: A BIG MUSICAL NUMBER TO END THE SHOW!

Lights come back up full. The NARRATOR pushes the chair offstage and brings the microphone and stand back on. He may ad-lib comments to the audience to cover the setup of the dance. The PUPPETEERS, N. SEMBLE, and EVELYN return to the stage. The NARRATOR sings "Cannot Be Denied," and the CAST dances around wildly.

NARRATOR: Every lonely person has
    to turn
  to the mirror and look deep inside
at the things that they have failed to learn
and the things that cannot be denied.

See that girl you really wanted
walking down the street; well, she's a
  new bride.
Now your endless tears are haunted
by another thing that cannot be denied.

There can be no defense
against the thing that makes no sense.

If you listen very carefully,
you will hear the sound of me dying.
And if everyone sounds much like me,
you will hear a chorus of crying.

Every loss that you cannot erase
leads you closer to your suicide.
Other logic breaks down in the face
of the thing that cannot ever be denied!

(The NARRATOR does not dance but remains still during the entire song. At the end of the song, he leaps into the air. Lights blackout as he is in mid-leap.)

CURTAIN

SURVIVOR: VIETNAM!
A Parody in Three Parts

Rob Reese

ROB REESE was born in Nashville, Tennessee, sometime after "one giant leap for mankind" and sometime before disco. With a degree in communications/theatre arts from Boston College, Reese continued his education in Chicago at the sundry training centers of The Second City, The Improv Olympic, and The Annoyance. After working with numerous improv and sketch companies as a performer and director, he moved to New York and founded Amnesia Wars Productions in 1997. Rob's improv teaching and directing have afforded him wonderful opportunities to travel to improv and theatre festivals throughout the United States, Europe, and even Africa. Most recently he traveled with his adaptation of Mary Shelley's *Frankenstein* to Kuala Lumpur, Malaysia. He is currently working on another comedy and trying to figure out how to get someone to pay him handsomely to travel the world, write, and make people laugh.

Survivor: Vietnam! was first presented by Amnesia Wars Productions on May 17, 2003, at the Peoples Improv Theater, New York City, with the following cast and credits:

Chorus .... Rob Reese
Voiceover .... Jason Evans
Kennedy .... Nitra Gutierrez
Mike .... Marcus Bonnée
Orf .... Daniel Berman
Darryl .... Darryl Reilly
Angela .... Angela DiGenaro
Erica .... Eric Brenner
Julia .... Julia Motyka
Bunny/Slappy .... Evans/Reese
DJ .... Jason Evans

With understudies and replacements as follows:

Chorus .... Jason Hays
Voiceover .... Chris Orf, Marcus Bonnée, Rob Reese
Orf .... Chris Orf
Erica .... Chris Orf
Julia .... Shelly Stover
Bunny/Slappy .... Gutierrez/DiGenaro
DJ .... Jennifer Burland

Director: Rob Reese
Sound Design: Jason Evans
Stage Manager: Jennifer Burland

PRODUCTION NOTES

The tone and style of this play are directly related to that of improvisation and sketch comedy. The production elements and acting styles reflect that relation.

SET AND LIGHTING: The set is sparse and functional, allowing for rapid shifts in location and style. These transformations are aided by simple shifts in lighting.

PROPS AND COSTUMES: These are also simple and functional. "Base" costumes are layered, accessorized, and adjusted for seamless transformations and changes in tone.

MUSIC: Referential riffs of ultra-contemporary music pepper the entire show, but do not overwhelm the action. Cue sheets and CDs from the original production are available upon request. With the exception of songs specified by the script, sound designers should consider music that is contemporary to the time of production. Permission to utilize any prerecorded music, including songs specified in the script, are *not* included in the rights to *Survivor: Vietnam!* and must be acquired separately.

SCENE

A sparse stage peppered with Vietnamese and American flags, icons and photographs appropriate to both cultures, and a large luminescent Empty-Vee logo, center. The playing area is flanked on one side by CHORUS, reading from a script on a music stand, and on the other by the DJ, who scores the action with appropriate and usually upbeat popular music.

Music: "Adagio for Strings."

CHORUS: Exterior, dawn. An overhead shot of the green Vietnamese countryside, an endless jungle borders a flat, jade-colored rice paddy. Which would mean that the jungle isn't actually endless.

VOICEOVER: In the hottest years of the so-called Cold War, communist ideologies flourish in the recently de-colonized countries of Southeast Asia.

CHORUS: Cut to graphic of a map: A black-and-white cartoon with a shadow enveloping the earth. The Red Menace!

VOICEOVER: Fearing a "domino effect" of countries falling to communist influence, Western governments and business interests resist the movement.

CHORUS: Cut to stock footage of American troops landing at Saigon, boots hitting the tarmac, equipment being unloaded from great planes.

VOICEOVER: From 1964 to 1975, the United States ships over half a million troops and billions of dollars in equipment and ordnance to the region in an effort to thwart the spread of communism into countries such as South Vietnam, Cambodia, and Laos.

CHORUS: Cut to a montage of firefights, bombs hitting rural villages, explosions, dead and wounded men, women, children. Soldiers lost in the endless jungle.

VOICEOVER: In the ensuing chaos, atrocities bloody the hands of men on both sides of the conflict, an estimated six million people violently lose their lives, an estimated four million of those deaths are civilian casualties. It is in this horrific environment...

(Music switches to the high-power attack of a rock guitar riff.)

VOICEOVER: That *someone* is going to win *one million dollars* in Empty-Vee's "Survivor: Vietnam!"

CHORUS: Survivor graphic up!

(KENNEDY enters, bubbly and sexy. Music: KENNEDY theme—trendy, annoying upbeat "girl power" theme.)

KENNEDY: Whoooooooo! Word to your mother! I'm Kennedy Johnson-Nixon hosting "Empty-Vee's Survivor: Vietnam!" Whooooooo! Our "recruiters" have scoured the nation to draft our six sexy, hip contestants who must survive hardship, survive the elements, and survive each other. Oh, and they also have to survive live fire, booby traps, torture, and forced starvation. The *sole survivor* will be the recipient of *one million dollars* and will be *slightly famous*! Whooooooo! Our contestants are hip, sexy, and willing to humiliate themselves just to be on TV! Whooooooooo! And did I mention sexy? Whooooooooo!

CHORUS: Kennedy says "whoo" again.

KENNEDY: Whooooooo! Now we're going to meet our first survivor: Mike is

an "entertainer" from Fargo, North Dakota. Let's take a peek at his audition tape!

(Sound effect: Whoosh!)

CHORUS: Screen graphics look like a web page; the survivor's name, Mike, stretches across the top. Statistics cover the sidebars.

(Music: MIKE theme I—contemporary, vapid, boy band hit. "Factoids" are enthusiastically read almost simultaneously, creating a jumble of sound.)

KENNEDY: Height: six feet, even.

MIKE: Actually, six feet, one centimeter.

ORF: Weight: one hundred sixty-five pounds.

MIKE: Two *hundred* pounds. Okay, one eighty-five.

DARRYL: Hair: brown.

ANGELA: Eyes: steel gray, the color of a cigarette case reflecting the bitter remembrance of a neglected morning.

ERICA: Shirt: seventeen and a half.

JULIA: Jacket: forty-two short.

MIKE: Forty-two long!

KENNEDY: Favorite food: bacon cheeseburgers.

ORF: Favorite band: Journey.

DARRYL: Favorite Journey song: "Don't Stop Believin'"!

ANGELA: Favorite Two-Step Completely Disposable Cleaning System: Wipe-n-Go!

ERICA: Special skill: making balloon animals.

ALL: Whooosh!

(Music: Switch to MIKE theme II—another contemporary, vapid, boy band hit.)

MIKE: Why do I want to be on "Survivor," hm? Oh, *no*! I should say, why does "Survivor" want me!? Or, why *does* "Survivor" want me? "Survivor" wants me!

CHORUS: Cut to Mike in his kitchen.

MIKE: Well, I guess I've always been, like a regular guy. Not, like just in a bowel thing, but in like, a guy to guy thing. Though, I'm pretty regular with the bowel thing too.

CHORUS: Cut back to Mike in his front yard.

MIKE: "Survivor" *wants* me!

CHORUS: Cut back to Mike in his kitchen.

MIKE: Yeah, I've always really liked… stuff. Um, here in my kitchen I have a whole lot of…things.

CHORUS: Cut.

MIKE: "Survivor" wants *me!*

CHORUS: Cut.

MIKE: Oh, I should show you this, over here in my living room, I have, um, some furniture, most of it is stuff to sit on. And on this shelf there's my…stuff.

CHORUS: Cut.

MIKE: *"Survivor"* wants me!

CHORUS: Cut.

MIKE: Yeah, if I get picked, I guess I'm going to miss bacon cheeseburgers, 'cause, you know, it'll probably be hard to get bacon, right?

ALL: Whoosh!

(Music: KENNEDY theme.)

KENNEDY: Whooooo! Hard to get bacon? I'll say, unless Mike wants to bring his own pig!

(Pause. CHORUS cues ALL to laugh, then cues them to silence.)

KENNEDY: Thank you. Whooooo! The survivors are going to be in this hell on earth for forty days; too bad we've only given them army C rations for seven! Let's see if they figure it out before they start fighting over the crumbs in each other's feces! Before we find out, we're gonna meet our next survivor.

CHORUS: Web page screen graphic. The survivor's name, Julia, stretches across the top, statistics cover the sidebars.

("Factoids" are read almost simultaneously, though considerably less enthusiastically than the first time.)

ALL: Whoosh!

(Music: JULIA theme I—contemporary pop artist performing a [preferably] acoustic version of a sixties or seventies folk song.)

KENNEDY: Height: five foot, four inches tall.

MIKE: Weight: …

JULIA: Don't *you dare!*

ANGELA: Eyes: blue, misty, and vacant.

DARRYL: Bust: thirty-six. Waist: twenty-four. Hips: thirty-four.

ERICA: Favorite food: tofu, because you don't have to *kill* it!

ANGELA: Favorite band: The Himalayan Mountain Gong Players.

MIKE: Favorite Journey song: "Open Arms."

KENNEDY: Favorite Two-Step Completely Disposable Cleaning System: Wipe-n-Go.

ORF: Special skill: sitting very still.

ALL: Whoosh!

CHORUS: Cut to Julia in her yard!

(Music: JULIA theme II—another contemporary pop artist performing a [preferably] acoustic version of a sixties or seventies folk song.)

JULIA: I think "Survivor" needs a calm woman on the show, someone who can really feel one with the trees and the jungle. Just no bugs, okay? But I'm too smart to be lured into doing nudity on this audition tape just to get on the show! Okay, maybe I'll just take my jacket off, but that's it! *(JULIA removes her jacket.)*

CHORUS: Cut to Julia in her kitchen.

JULIA: Here is where I prepare all of my meals. I'm completely vegan and macrobiotic. But don't worry, I'm not one of those judgmental vegans who looks down on people just because they're not enlightened like me.

CHORUS: Cut back to Julia in her yard.

JULIA: I'm not saying I would be opposed to wearing a bathing suit on the show, which is like a bra, I guess. *(JULIA strips down to a sports bra.)*

CHORUS: Cut back to Julia in her kitchen.

JULIA: Yeah, you see I can really empathize with the vibrations of the universe, and become, like, super aware. Ooof! *(JULIA trips over nothing.)*

CHORUS: Julia's yard.

JULIA: Well, I guess it's not that big a deal, right, it's the human body. Whoooooooooo!

(JULIA flashes the camera. CHORUS covers her chest with a "Girls Gone Wild" logo.)

ALL: Whoosh!

(Music: KENNEDY theme.)

KENNEDY: Whoooo! Julia would never survive in a *real* wilderness situation, but at least she's not afraid to get naked. Let's see if her good vibrations are enough to outlast Erica, she's one tough lady!

CHORUS: Web page graphic up: Erica!

("Factoids" are read almost simultaneously, though somewhat lazily. Music: ERICA theme I—contemporary R&B girl group singing about the strength and independence of women.)

KENNEDY: Height: five foot eleven inches tall.

MIKE: Weight: two hundred and fifteen pounds.

ERICA: That's right, I'm a big woman, so what, I like to say big *beautiful* woman!

ORF: College: Vassar, maybe you've heard of it?

DARRYL: Race: what difference does that make!

ANGELA: Eyes: brown, with a warmth that says, that's not funny!

ERICA: That's not funny!

JULIA: Bust: forty-two. Waist: thirty-eight. Hips: thirty-eight.

KENNEDY: Favorite musician: Tori Amos, you have a problem with that?

ORF: Favorite Two-Step Completely Disposable Cleaning System: Wipe-n-Go!

ANGELA: Favorite Vietnam-era figure: All the brave women who haven't been recognized for their bravery which was so absolutely brave!

MIKE: Favorite Journey song: "Faithfully"!

ALL: *(Lazily, bored.)* Whoosh!

CHORUS: I sense a waning enthusiasm for the web page graphics.

ALL: Meh.

MIKE: I like it.

CHORUS: Cut to Erica in an urban park, concrete and steel.

(Music: ERICA theme II—another contemporary R&B girl group singing about the strength and independence of women.)

ERICA: As a woman, I know about struggle. I know what it takes to survive, which is why I want to be on "Survivor," because I can survive the hardships that need to be…survived.

CHORUS: Cut to Erica in her living room.

ERICA: This is my collection of media products that I find demeaning to women…

CHORUS: Cut back to Erica on the playground.

ERICA: …and a result of a societal structure that forces black kids to live in neighborhoods like this one. Now, I actually grew up in Northport, Long Island, but, you know, women are an oppressed minority too, so I completely know what these kids had to go through. Without the street crime, and violence, and poverty.

CHORUS: Cut back to Erica in her living room.

ERICA: This is my Disney shelf: *Cinderella*, *Pocahontas*, *Lion King*. I actually kind of like *Lion King*, but I'm sure if I watch it over and over again, I'll learn to find it demeaning.

CHORUS: The playground.

ERICA: …and forget about being, like, a *black* woman! I mean, they're a member of *two* oppressed minorities. And could you imagine being a black lesbian?

CHORUS: Living room.

ERICA: These are examples of male-dominated, misogynistic *porn* that passes for *humor* in America these days: *Porky's*, the Farrelly *Brothers*, the Marx *Brothers*, I mean, poor Margaret Dumont!

CHORUS: The playground.

ERICA: I wish I was a black lesbian.

ALL: Whoosh!

KENNEDY: We'll be right back to introduce the rest of our survivors, right after this.

CHORUS: "Survivor" graphic up, voice-over go!

VOICEOVER: "Survivor: Vietnam!" is sponsored by Wipe-n-Go, the Completely Disposable Two-Step Disposable System.

CHORUS: The commercial reel runs. The setting is a suburban kitchen, reminiscent of the 1950s. Two housewives in dresses and aprons discuss cleaning supplies.

(Setting: BUNNY's kitchen. Music: light 1950s commercial theme music.)

BUNNY: These super sweepie swishers are supposed to be so convenient, but they're really such a bother!

SLAPPY: Why, what's wrong Bunny?

BUNNY: Well Slappy, these semi-disposable super sweepie swishers are so much trouble. First you have to open the package, then put the swishie on the sweeper, and then you have to swish up all the dirt about your house, take the swishie off the sweeper, and drop it right in the trash.

SLAPPY: Wish there was an easier way?

BUNNY: *Do I?*

SLAPPY: Bunny, your prayers have been answered!

BUNNY: My prayers to God?

SLAPPY: That's right, God has sent forth the Two-Step Completely Disposable Wipe-n-Go!

BUNNY: *(Seriously.)* You say, two step? How does *that* work?

SLAPPY: It works in two simple steps. First, you pull the Two-Step Completely Disposable Wipe-n-Go out of its completely disposable packaging.

BUNNY: That seems easy enough!

SLAPPY: Then you simply throw the Two-Step Completely Disposable Wipe-n-Go into the trash!

BUNNY: Why that's two simple steps!

SLAPPY: Darn tootin'!

BUNNY: But if I don't have to worry about cleaning up nasty messes, how will I know when to use the Two-Step Completely Disposable Wipe-n-Go?

SLAPPY: Easy! Our clinical scientists recommend that you use the Two-Step Completely Disposable Wipe-n-Go once every fourteen minutes!

BUNNY: That sounds complicated! I don't even know how much bourbon I drink in fourteen and a half minutes.

SLAPPY: Don't be ashamed, dogs and cows have no concept of time either. Your brand-new Two-Step Completely Disposable Wipe-n-Go alarm will sound for you every fourteen minutes, reminding you that it's time for convenience!

(Air horn blows while ALL really annoyingly yell "Wipe-n-Go time!" very loudly.)

BUNNY: I sure will notice that!

SLAPPY: No doubt you will, home slice. Every time you hear the alarm—

(Repeat alarm.)

SLAPPY: —simply pull out a Two-Step Completely Disposable Wipe-n-Go! And throw it right away!

BUNNY: That's two simple steps!

SLAPPY: Hallelujah!

BUNNY: I want to show love for God and my country, I will purchase and use the Two-Step Completely Disposable Wipe-n-Go!

SLAPPY: You go, girl!

BUNNY: Go America!

BOTH: Wipe-n-*Go* America!

(Shift to Survivor camp. Pause. ORF sharpens a bamboo stake, ERICA shaves her face with a rock and a shaving brush, DARRYL polishes his shoes.)

CHORUS: Cut to exterior of the Survivor beach camp, dusk. The sun sets over the endless jungle, turning its leaves a purple that resembles a low fire. It's also the kind of purple that Grimace is. The survivors bustle, tending to personal duties and camp chores. Angela struggles to build a fire, Mike writes a letter home. Julia performs her evening yoga ritual: closeup on Julia stretching her legs, closeup on Julia's silhouette as she arches her back in front of the setting sun. Closeup on Julia's pelvis, as she…executes a very… interesting-seeming yoga position. Closeup on her ass. *(Pause.)* Cut to medium shot of Orf sharpening a bamboo stake. A veteran of the Vietnam War, he never would have come back to these shores if the Empty-Vee people hadn't told everyone that they were just going to a beach in Hawaii. A grizzled but athletic man in his early fifties, the eyes of Orf have seen their share of death.

ORF: Who wants to sing show tunes around the fire tonight? C'mon! *(Sings.)* "Clang, clang, clang goes the trolley…"

CHORUS: Mike continues his letter home.

(Music: MIKE letter theme—neo grunge pretentious rock "sensitive guy" ballad.)

MIKE: I don't know Grandma, I think I made a big mistake coming here, it's only been a week and I don't think I can take much more. We've had to build our own shelter, and make our own beds! I think we're supposed to eliminate someone soon, but I don't know how we're going to do it, I couldn't imagine being here with any of them gone. Darryl and Angela Schadenfreude are a married couple, they work really well as a team...

DARRYL: Well, if you don't like the berries I gathered, have a military C ration.

ANGELA: I don't *want* a military C ration, they taste like eating a boot and shitting it out, and eating the boot shit!

DARRYL: Would you like me to send out for pizza, I could make a Gilligan radio out of coconuts and call for a pizza?

JULIA: I think it was the Professor that made the radios. Not that I ever watch television.

ANGELA: If you don't stop being so cruel and hateful to me, I'm going to go find that crazy veteran, and let him fuck me goofy!

ORF: You know, I'm right here.

DARRYL: Let him fuck you; if he could fuck you goofier than you are already, I'd give him a dollar.

ORF: I don't need a dollar.

ANGELA: You just wait, as soon as I get a chance, I'm going to vote you off the island!

DARRYL: Not if I vote you off first! You premenstrual bitch!

ERICA: That's not funny! If you could have babies like us women, you'd understand why they built those mounds in Scotland.

(Music: MIKE letter theme.)

MIKE: I'm really glad to have Erica around, she's taught me a lot about my own innate sexism, and how I hate women and minorities, and foreigners, and certain dogs. She's taught me a lot about shame...

DARRYL: I don't understand what mounds in Scotland have to do with anything.

ERICA: That's because you're so hateful!

ANGELA: See! I told you that you were hateful! I don't know why I don't just fuck everyone else on this beach but *you*! Dickless softie!

JULIA: You know, the vibrations from the two of you arguing are really aggressive to the rest of us.

ANGELA: You shut up!

JULIA: *You* shut up!

ORF: Listen, if we don't all chill out a little, we'll snap before the action begins.

(Music: MIKE letter theme.)

MIKE: Orf is very cool, he's kind of been in the situation before, so he knows a lot about setting up camp. He's a grizzled, angry man. A man who you wouldn't want to cross.

ORF: How about this one: *(Sings.)* "One! Singular sensation..."

(Music: MIKE letter theme.)

MIKE: Orf told me the other day that his favorite Journey song was "Owner of a Lonely Heart." But "Owner of a Lonely Heart" was done by Yes! This place is insane, Grandma!

ORF: *(Sings.)* "...Ev-ry move that she makes! Dum, da dum, da dum..."

ANGELA: Julia, must you do so much... *breathing!*

MIKE: I think I have kind of a crush on Julia, she's pretty, and she's so in tune with the environment and stuff.

JULIA: Bug bug bug bug bug bug!

DARRYL: Of course there are bugs Julia, we're on a beach on the edge of the endless jungle!

ANGELA: How could it be the endless jungle dear, if we're on the edge of it.

DARRYL: What are you talking about?

ANGELA: The edge means that there's an end!

ERICA: That's not funny.

ANGELA: I wasn't making a joke.

ERICA: See!

(Music: MIKE letter theme.)

MIKE: Somebody once wrote hell is the impossibility of reason. I just thought I'd mention that. I miss you Grandma, the only thing I miss more than you is Grandpa, and my other Grandma. I miss pooping in a toilet too.

(Music: KENNEDY theme.)

KENNEDY: Whooooo! Hello survivors, gather 'round. Well, it's the end of the first week, and it's time for the first challenge to see who doesn't survive!

ANGELA: You know, they were firing real bullets at us when we swam to the beach!

DARRYL: Honey, don't complain, we won't get to be on TV!

KENNEDY: Live bullets? Well they'll be using a crapload more than that tonight as you try to take Ap Bia Hill, forty kliks to the southwest.

ORF: Ap Bia Hill? That's not Hawaii.

ALL: It's not?

KENNEDY: No, sillies, you're in North Vietnam.

ALL: We are?

KENNEDY: And you'd better be careful, because there are Viet Cong patrols all over the beach, itching to kill or capture some Americans.

JULIA: Wait a minute, we're not part of this war!

ORF: "This war" ended almost thirty years ago.

ALL: It did?

KENNEDY: That's right, we couldn't find any *real* Viet Cong soldiers to shoot at you, so we trained a special selection of Empty-Vee dancers in infantry weapons, hand-to-hand combat, and Maoist ideology. Now they're the Ho Chi Minnies!

(Music: HO CHI MINNIES theme—gratuitous popular party theme music. The CAST MEMBERS "become" the HO CHI MINNIES for the duration of CHORUS's description, then snap back.)

CHORUS: Cut to exterior, the Ho Chi Minnies camp. A dozen beautiful Asian women with dancers' bodies wearing tight fatigue shorts and black, tight, wet, T-shirts! Or just a bandoleer of bullets hanging strategically around the chest. One Ho Chi Minnie cleans her AK-47, stroking the barrel slowly. Two more Minnies practice martial arts, flipping and grappling each other in the mud. Another group plays volleyball. These former members of the Hawaiian Tropic Bikini team have been trained to kill, to kill with semi-automatic weapons, and with their bare hands! Ooooooohhhhhhhh yeahhhhhhh!

ERICA: That is so sexist!

ANGELA: And racist!

JULIA: And…whatever's worse than racist! *(JULIA cries.)*

KENNEDY: Okay contestants, you've got three hours to take a heavily fortified hill with no weapons, no maps, no surveillance. If you stay here, the V.C. patrols will find you and capture or kill you. If you try to run away, our crack Empty-Vee security force will hunt you down, *(KENNEDY pulls out a pistol. She will openly wear or hold this pistol for the remainder of the show [at least through "Beer Hunter"].)* I will personally put a bullet in your skull, and you will *never* be on TV.

(ALL gasp.)

KENNEDY: To show you how serious I am, I'm going to punch Mike on the arm really hard. *(She does.)*

MIKE: Ouch!

KENNEDY: Good luck. Those of you that survive the mission, if any, move on to the next round and have a chance at a million dollars. Whooooooooooo!

(Music: KENNEDY theme. KENNEDY exits. ALL look at one another, stunned.)

ANGELA: All right, we must all have skills that we can apply to this situation, I'm a natural-born leader, and I look terrific naked, so I'll be in charge, who's next?

JULIA: I thought I was the naked one.

ANGELA: Not anymore.

(ANGELA flashes the "camera"; CHORUS scrambles to cover her chest with "Girls Gone Wild" graphic.)

ANGELA: Whooooo!

JULIA: Oh yeah! Whooooo!

(JULIA flashes the "camera"; CHORUS scrambles to cover her chest with "Girls Gone Wild" graphic.)

ERICA: This isn't funny, you're just letting the man exploit you into demeaning yourself just for a chance at a million dollars.

(Pause. ERICA flashes the "camera"; CHORUS scrambles to cover her chest with "Girls Gone Wild" graphic.)

ERICA: Whoooooo!

ALL: Ohhh!

MIKE: Wait a second, we're in a life-and-death situation, what in the world does gratuitous nudity have to do with anything? Okay, one more quick one.

JULIA, ANGELA, and ERICA: Whoooooo!

(JULIA, ANGELA, and ERICA flash the "camera"; CHORUS scrambles to cover their chests with several "Girls Gone Wild" graphics.)

MIKE: All right, Angela's in charge!

JULIA: Hey!

ERICA: That's not funny.

ANGELA: Okay, who has skills that might help us now?

ORF: Well, I had a solid year in the bush in seventy-three and four, I know how to identify landmines and booby traps, and I can kill a man with my bare hands.

ANGELA: Excellent, I think it's best if you stay in the back with me!

ORF: Right! We'll call you Lieutenant Dan!

ANGELA: Why?

ORF: I don't know.

ANGELA: Okay, who else has skills?

JULIA: There's lots of animals in the jungle, and I've like, never eaten any of them.

DARRYL: I'm very adventurous and like to try new things.

ERICA: I can have a family and a career. Or I *could* if men weren't so stupid.

DARRYL: Like that threesome!

ANGELA: *(To DARRYL.)* This isn't the time.

*MIKE: I can make balloon animals.

ANGELA: We should send the black guy first!

ORF: That's a perfect idea.

MIKE: What black guy?

DARRYL: Though next time I'd really like to try it with another woman.

JULIA: You know, I think it's really wrong to send the black guy first just because he's like…a black guy.

MIKE: What black guy?

ANGELA: Good, so that's decided.

ERICA: I think it's wrong to assume that a woman couldn't go first!

DARRYL: I guess it doesn't really count as a threeway either when I'm not really in the room!

MIKE: Angela, there's no black guy here, haven't you been watching the show?

ORF: Call her Lieutenant Dan.

ERICA: Oh, so now that she's in charge, she gets to be a man!

DARRYL: Or when I'm not in the house.

ANGELA: *(To DARRYL.)* What are you talking about?

MIKE: Lieutenant Dan, there's no black guy here, haven't you been watching the show?

JULIA: Yeah! We should have a black guy! But we shouldn't make him go first!

ERICA: Girl power!

ANGELA: Well, if you want to be all politically correct, you can go yourself!

(Pause.)

MIKE, JULIA, and ERICA: We should let the black guy go first!

MIKE: Wait a minute.

DARRYL: It's just that the thing with the pool guy wasn't really so much a threesome as me coming home and finding you two naked in the kitchen.

ERICA: Ooohhhh, that's not funny.

ANGELA: Oh, I see, when *you* want to stir it up a bit, we end up in a firefight in North Vietnam, but I fuck a few pool guys behind your back, and suddenly it's a big drama?*

DARRYL: A *few* pool guys?

ERICA: That's kind of funny.

ANGELA: One of *them* was black, does that make you feel better?

DARRYL: No, not really.

CHORUS: We hear incoming rifle fire.

ORF: Hey, get down.

ANGELA: *You get down,* don't tell me what to do! I never wanted to do this trip in the first place!

ALL: Shh, get down, they're shooting.

CHORUS: The enemy fire grows heavier.

ANGELA: This isn't a vacation! There are no good restaurants around here! How can you have a vacation without a *T.G.I. Friday's!?*

CHORUS: We shift to slow motion, Orf yells for the others to "Come on!"

ORF: Come on!

CHORUS: They have to make it into the jungle…

ORF: Let's get into the jungle…

CHORUS: The endless jungle!

ORF: The endless jungle.

CHORUS: The slow motion shot of the survivors dragging each other into the endless jungle closes in on a bright explosion, dissolves into the "Survivor" graphic. And commercial reel go!

VOICEOVER: And now, a word from our sponsor.

(Music: 1950s commercial theme.)

BUNNY: Son of a bitch!!

SLAPPY: Why, what's wrong Bunny?

BUNNY: Well Slappy, these semi-disposable super sweepie swishers are really so much trouble.

SLAPPY: Wish there was an easier way?

BUNNY: *Do* I?

SLAPPY: Bunny, your prayers have been answered!

BUNNY: My prayers to God?

SLAPPY: Yes, if you've been praying to God for the Two-Step Completely Disposable Wipe-n-Go.

BUNNY: I have been!

SLAPPY: I know you have!

BUNNY: Slappy, are you God?

SLAPPY: Heh heh heh, of course not, *(Beat.)* but I know the Lord's will, and He wants you to use the Two-Step Completely Disposable Wipe-n-Go!

BUNNY: He does?

SLAPPY: Of course! How many steps did you say you had to go through with the semi-disposable super sweepie swishers?

BUNNY: Let's see, first you open the super sweepie package, then put the disposable swishie on the nondisposable sweeper, and then you swish up all the dirt about your house, take the disposable swishie off the nondisposable sweeper, and dispose of it right in the trash.

SLAPPY: That's *five steps.*

BUNNY: Why, you're right!

SLAPPY: And what's your most valuable asset?

BUNNY: My horde of African war diamonds?

SLAPPY: It's *time.*

BUNNY: Tell me about it!

SLAPPY: Because no matter how much time you have, you always wish you had more in the end.

BUNNY: Just like African war diamonds.

SLAPPY: Exactly, now what's bigger, five or two?

BUNNY: Five!

SLAPPY: That's right Bunny, five is bigger than two, and by how many is five bigger than two?

BUNNY: *Three!*

SLAPPY: Exactly! And where else do we see the number three?

BUNNY: In the Holy Trinity.

SLAPPY: Exactly! And what's five *plus* two?

BUNNY: Seven, *(Thinks.)* like the seven deadly sins!

SLAPPY: And what's the fifth deadly sin?

BUNNY: Greed.

SLAPPY: And if you waste all of your time putting on sweepie swishers and taking off sweepie swishers...

BUNNY: Then I'm being greedy with my time!

SLAPPY: So if you look at the numerology of it...

BUNNY: I'm committing the venal sin of greed, at peril to my immortal soul.

SLAPPY: That's right Bunny, your immortal soul.

BUNNY: Can I ever repent?

SLAPPY: Of course you can, ours is a forgiving and gracious God! Salvation lies with the Two-Step Completely Disposable Wipe-n-Go!

BUNNY: Glory be to God's will!

SLAPPY: You go, girl!

BUNNY: Go God!

BOTH: Wipe-n-*Go*, God!

(Shift to SURVIVORS in "tiger cage.")

CHORUS: "Survivor" graphic up. Exterior, day, an encampment on the river. Cut to the faces of our survivors, burned by the hot Vietnamese sun. The group is in a cage wrought of bamboo, a foot of dirty swamp water is the floor, and the burning hot sun is their roof. The walls are like actual walls, but not quite, and river rats and water snakes...

(JULIA reacts with great restraint to the presence of river rats and water snakes floating as high as her calves.)

CHORUS: ...represent a well-groomed series of hedges and privets. Julia has learned from two weeks of experience that freaking out only agitates the well-groomed hedges and privets. Unfortunately, that education has earned her about as much as a liberal arts degree.

(JULIA, building from before, freaks out completely; the rats and snakes attack her as she freaks out, which of course freaks her out even more. The heightening of the freakout of course intensifies the attack, which in turn...)

CHORUS: An AK-47 fires viciously over their heads!

(ALL duck down, ending JULIA's freak-out.)

CHORUS: The smoking rifle is being fired from right outside the cage by a Ho Chi Minnie sergeant. We know the rank because of the stripes tattooed to the top of her hip, like right here... and you'd see it because she's wearing those shorts that are cut kind of like this.

ERICA: Oh, come on!

CHORUS: The well-armed Ho Chi Minnies lounge about with the intensity of a troupe of sorority girls waiting for a ride to the gangbang. Ahem. For a ride to the sophomore social.

ERICA: Does he ever stop?

DARRYL: I don't know, why don't you ask my wife? I bet she knows if he ever stops.

ANGELA: Will you let that drop? I haven't fucked anyone else in over *two weeks!*

DARRYL: We've been prisoners of war!

(ANGELA makes eye contact with ORF.)

ANGELA: Oh, right, six days.

(ANGELA makes eye contact with CHORUS.)

ANGELA: Three days.

(ANGELA makes eye contact with ERICA.)

ANGELA: Nine hours.

ALL: Ew!

CHORUS: Mike writes a letter home.

(Music: MIKE letter theme.)

MIKE: Dear Grandma, it's been two weeks since we were captured in the jungle and I don't know how much more I can take. Our captors are cruel, cruel and lovely. They confiscated my stationery set when I got here, so I'm improvising a pen and paper by slobbering on a rock I found. I sure hope you get this. Love, Mike. *(MIKE licks the rock and tosses it limply into the muck.)*

(Music: KENNEDY theme. KENNEDY enters. She carries a sack and wears a fashionable eye patch. ALL react with annoyance at the KENNEDY theme music.)

KENNEDY: Whooooooo! Hey survivors, it looks like you've made it another couple of weeks, though just barely.

ORF: Fuck you, Empty-Vee!

KENNEDY: Now now, no need for talk like that when it's time for your next challenge to see who goes on to the next round!

DARRYL: What would you like us to do this time? See if we survive a bullet to the head?

ANGELA: Yeah, or… like something else that will kill us?

ERICA: Good analogy.

ANGELA: You shut up! It's a simile.

ERICA: *You* shut up! It's only a simile because you said the word like, but like was like unnecessary right then!

JULIA: Girls, remember, we all have to be prisoners of war *together*.

ALL: Now *you* shut up!

KENNEDY: No, this next challenge will not be so dangerous as the last one, this is called Beer Hunter! In this sack I have a six-pack of beer.

ORF: Vietnamese beer?

KENNEDY: Budweiser.

ORF: Oh.

KENNEDY: I shake up one of them, *(She does.)* and after I put it back in the bag, two of you come up, and open the beer can next to your head, Russian roulette style. If the beer explodes, you're eliminated; if not, you get to drink the beer! Whoooo!

ERICA: We haven't had anything to drink in three days.

ANGELA: There are carbohydrates in beer, that's almost like food!

JULIA: I don't drink beer, I'm a vegan!

ORF: Budweiser?

MIKE: Budweiser!

KENNEDY: Six bières dans le saq! Vous et vous êtes premier! Ici! *(Six beers in the sack! You and you are first! Come here!)*

(KENNEDY points at ANGELA and ERICA; they step forward to the table.)

DARRYL: Oh, looks like little Miss Bossypants could get eliminated first! Isn't that a crying freaking shame!

ANGELA: I will *not* be eliminated first!

ERICA: I don't think this is funny.

ANGELA: I can *will* myself to pick a calm beer! *(ANGELA "focuses.")*

JULIA: What's she doing?

ORF: I'm not sure, but I think this means she's a method actor.

ALL: *(With distaste.)* Oh!

ERICA: Good luck anyway!

(ANGELA screams and dives into the bag. Simultaneously:)

{
ALL except DARRYL: All right, go Angela! Relate this to a moment in your childhood!

DARRYL: When you're on your way home after you screw this up, try not to *fuck the guy carrying your luggage more than once or twice! They'll know you're a tourist!*
}

(ANGELA removes a beer can. She places it against her head. ALL fall silent.)

ORF: You know, this could be a trick, I once saw the Cong put a grenade inside a vibrator they had left behind…

ANGELA: Shut up, Orf!

ORF: Blew my buddy's head clean the fuck off!

ALL: *Orf!*

ORF: Hey, buddies are important in the 'Nam!

(KENNEDY points gun at ORF.)

ORF: Okay, okay, keep playing your little game.

(ANGELA pulls the tab. It is a calm beer. ALL breathe a sigh of relief)

ANGELA: It's just beer.

DARRYL: I love you sweetheart.

ORF: *(To JULIA.)* I guess that's five dollars I owe you then.

(ORF passes some bills off to JULIA.)

DARRYL: Please don't scrape the skin off of my ass!

ANGELA: Thank God! It's just beer! Aaaaaarrrrghhhh! *(ANGELA downs the beer and crushes it with her hand.)*

MIKE: Hey, who else really likes Steve Perry's solo work?

KENNEDY: *(To ERICA, in French accent.)* Vous!

ERICA: What!

KENNEDY: Choizez son bière!

ERICA: What?

KENNEDY: *(Still in bad French accent.)* I say, peek your bière?

ERICA: Peek my what?

KENNEDY: *(Drops accent.)* Pull a goddamn beer out of the bag so we can get through this cocksmoking scene!

ERICA: I'm scared.

ANGELA: Are you talkin' to me?

ERICA: Um, yeah, I'm talkin' to you!

(ANGELA smacks ERICA.)

ERICA: Ouch!

(ANGELA smacks ERICA.)

ANGELA: C'mon Erica, put a calm beer in your hand, *will* it.

ERICA: I can't.

(ANGELA smacks ERICA.)

ANGELA: You've got to do it, Erica, they're gonna kill you if you don't!

ERICA: I don't know.

(ANGELA smacks ERICA.)

ANGELA: C'mon Erica, I'll show you my tits if you open a calm beer, come on.

ERICA: I don't want to see your tits.

(ANGELA smacks ERICA.)

JULIA: Do you want to see my tits?

ALL: I want to see your tits.

ERICA: That's not funny.

(ANGELA smacks ERICA.)

ERICA: Okay, okay.

(ANGELA smacks ERICA. ERICA reaches into the bag, bending over.)

ALL: C'mon Erica!

MIKE: Get into character!

DARRYL: Don't bend over too long or my wife might fuck you!

ORF: Go ugly girl!

JULIA: That's not nice! Ten bucks she picks a shaken beer!

(ERICA emerges with a beer, puts it against her head. Silence.)

ORF: Shaken? Two to one she gets her head blown clean the fuck off!

ALL: *Orf!*

ORF: What?

(ERICA pulls the tab. This is the shaken beer; it explodes all over her. ALL scream.)

ERICA: It's just a beer!

(ALL sigh in relief.)

ANGELA: Good job Erica!

(KENNEDY passes the bag to MIKE, who starts distributing the remaining beers. [Don't forget CHORUS and the DJ!])

MIKE: Yeah, way to go. Who wants a brew?

DARRYL: *(To MIKE.)* You know, now that you mention it, I really liked "Oh Sherry."

JULIA: *(To ORF.)* I believe that's twenty to me!

ERICA: Thank God, it was just a beer. *(ERICA laughs and begins to drink the beer.)*

ANGELA: So, I guess this means that Erica is eliminated, huh?

KENNEDY: Oh yeah, I forgot about that part!

(KENNEDY shoots ERICA in the back of the head. ERICA does a classic spit take, pauses, then collapses. ALL scream.)

ANGELA: Get her!

KENNEDY: *Ho Chi Minnies!*

(Music: HO CHI MINNIES theme. ORF lunges for KENNEDY's gun; everyone else gives a quick shake and pops their tops, giving a spew. They convert into the HO CHI MINNIES and pass their beers off to audience members.)

CHORUS: The Ho Chi Minnies respond to Kennedy's alarm, but as the barley suds loft down their exposed cleavage, soaking their little camouflage babydoll T-shirts, the Ho Chi Minnies forget their killer guard training, and a much earlier training jumps into their consciousness. That sorority girl training that tells the girls it's time to *par-tay!* As the survivors slip out of the camp, Mike barely escapes fellatio from no less than three Ho Chi Minnies.

MIKE: Really?

CHORUS: Yes, but you're safe now, safe in the deep and endless jungle.

ORF: Well, we're safe now.

MIKE: Um… I could go back for Erica.

ANGELA: Erica is gone!

MIKE: I could go back anyway.

ORF: It's no use, man! She's dead! No reason to get yourself killed!

MIKE: I don't mind.

JULIA: I feel a really bad vibe now, and I'm all sticky.

ORF: Someone just got killed! And you're worried about being sticky?

JULIA: Who just got killed?

MIKE: The big girl, didn't you see it?

JULIA: Oh yeah, I forgot.

ORF: *It just happened.*

MIKE: I didn't expect anyone to get actually killed!

JULIA: Who got killed?

ANGELA: The ugly girl.

JULIA: That's not nice.

ORF: Yeah, anyway, we should get going, right Lieutenant Dan?

ANGELA: Absolutely, let's get to some shelter and prepare ourselves for the next round of the game.

DARRYL: *Game!?!?* It stopped being a game when the ugly girl got *killed!*

JULIA: So sticky.

DARRYL: I'm not going to take it any more, I'm done! I thought this being on TV thing would be great! I don't have to do anything anymore, I've been on TV, my wife too! We're that couple from "Survivor," we died horrible deaths in the jungle…

CHORUS: The endless jungle!

DARRYL: *You shut up!* I'm done, I quit!

MIKE: Where are you going to go?

DARRYL: I don't know, how am I going to know? I'm just going to follow this path and eventually, I'll get somewhere! Urhghgghghghghghghgh!

ORF: Darryl, wait!

ANGELA: Oh, good warning!

CHORUS: Darryl has stepped into a booby trap called the meat grinder. Two sets of sharpened bamboo spikes rotate around logs at the top of a shallow pit. The victim is punctured through both sides as he falls through the pointy sticks.

(JULIA screams.)

ORF: Oh shit.

MIKE: Oh my God!

ANGELA: Darryl, can you hear me!

DARRYL: Ghghlhlflglflfgfglf!

JULIA: Pull him out!

ORF: *No!* He'd just get punctured again by the spikes going the other way!

ANGELA: Oh my God, Darryl, can you hear me! I'm going to start dating again, okay?

MIKE: Darryl, are you okay?

DARRYL: Ghghlhlflglflfgfglf!

ORF: Seriously, does he *look* okay?

JULIA: No, he looks not okay!

ANGELA: If you approve of me dating again, just say ghghlhlflglflfgfglf!

DARRYL: Ghghlhlflglflfgfglf!

ANGELA: I'm glad you understand.

ORF: He's done for, there's no saving him now. *(Pause.)* All right, let's go…

(ORF, MIKE, and ANGELA start to leave.)

JULIA: Wait, we can't leave him here.

MIKE: There's nothing we can do, we can't carry him.

JULIA: We should wait until, you know, the end.

ANGELA: Oh, that could take hours!

MIKE: He's your husband!

ANGELA: One can't mourn forever.

ORF: It'll be dark soon, that's dangerous.

ANGELA: And boring!

JULIA: If it was me, I wouldn't want to die alone out here.

ANGELA: Because you're a selfish bitch!

JULIA: *You're* a selfish bitch!

ANGELA: I know you are, but what am I?

MIKE: *Stop it!* You're *both* selfish bitches!

ANGELA and JULIA: Hmph!

MIKE: Now if there's something we could do for him, I'd stay, but Orf is right, we have to keep moving, there's nothing I could do for him unless making balloon animals would somehow help him.

DARRYL: Ghghlhlflglflfgfglf!

JULIA: Mike, did you hear that? He wants a balloon show.

ANGELA: Oh for the love of God!

MIKE: A balloon show for a dying man.

CHORUS: Closeup on Mike's eyes, overtaken by the mists of destiny and a higher purpose. As we pull out, it is clearly several hours later, Darryl is long dead, Julia and Angela are asleep against a tree, Orf is nowhere to be seen.

MIKE: *(Playing with balloon characters in front of DARRYL.)* What is he whose grief bears such an emphasis? Whose phrase of sorrow… This is I Hamlet the Dane. *(Changes voice.)* The devil take thy soul! *(Fights with balloons. Back to Hamlet voice.)* I prithee, take thy fingers from my throat.

ANGELA: Is he dead yet?

MIKE: No, it's the first fight with Laertes.

ANGELA: Not Hamlet, you asshole, Darryl!

MIKE: Oh, yeah, he died back in Act Three.

JULIA: He's dead?

ANGELA: We should get moving.

MIKE: Where's Orf?

JULIA and ANGELA: We thought he was with you.

MIKE: We're all together!

JULIA and ANGELA: Oh.

JULIA: I'm sorry I fell asleep during your balloon soliloquy.

MIKE: I could do it again for you.

ANGELA: We have to get moving.

JULIA: Which way are we supposed to go?

(Music: KENNEDY theme.)

KENNEDY: *(Bounds in.)* Whooooo!

ANGELA: You fucking bitch, I'm going to kill you!

(ANGELA lunges at KENNEDY; MIKE and JULIA restrain her.)

JULIA: Stop it, there's been enough killing!

(ANGELA calms down.)

KENNEDY: Whooooo!

(JULIA turns and pops KENNEDY in the nose with a quick jab.)

JULIA: Shut up!

MIKE: Listen, you've got to get us out of this. We never signed on for people really getting killed.

JULIA: Yeah, we don't care about the prize money or anything.

ANGELA: Who doesn't care about the prize money?

KENNEDY: I couldn't get you out of the show if I wanted to… He's in charge, he's completely taken over the network.

JULIA: Who's completely taken over the network?

KENNEDY: The Colonel.

ALL: The Colonel?

KENNEDY: Well, he's actually an executive vice president, but he likes to be called The Colonel.

JULIA: Can't we talk to him?

KENNEDY: He's gone insane, mad with power. He's producing a new reality TV show every fifteen minutes. Here, I want you to listen to a tape.

VOICEOVER: *(Brando impersonation.)* Whenever you hold a mirror in front of itself, the image gets smaller and smaller, which is what happens when we watch ourselves on television too many times. Stella! Ooh! I ate a bug! Hey, that's a good idea, from now on, every show contestant should eat bugs! I coulda been a survivor!

MIKE: Was that a tape of The Colonel?

KENNEDY: No, *(insert actor's name)* has been working on his *(or "her")* Brando and he wanted to try it out.

ANGELA: Why are you telling all of this to us?

KENNEDY: Because there's only one way out of this for all of us.

JULIA: You mean…

(Pause.)

KENNEDY: I mean what?

JULIA: I don't know, that's all I got.

KENNEDY: I mean that he's got an army of yes men and reality show contestants. The networks are too afraid to turn their back on him. Someone needs to infiltrate his operation and terminate his employment.

MIKE: Terminate his employment?

KENNEDY: Terminate his employment, with extreme prejudice.

ANGELA: What, is he Jewish or something?

JULIA: How do we find him?

ANGELA: Black? I bet he's black.

KENNEDY: You'll have a helicopter escort up to the mouth of the Nung River, where you will be dropped in or near a small boat. You'll take the boat about seventy-five kliks up river…

JULIA: Seventy-five kliks up river? That's Cambodia!

MIKE: Cambodia, how do you know that?

JULIA: Orf has a map tattooed to his ass.

(Pause, double takes.)

KENNEDY: Where you will infiltrate his operation and…

MIKE: Yeah, terminate with extreme prejudice.

ANGELA: He's not Swedish or something is he? Those Vikings are tough as shit to kill!

JULIA: How long is all of this going to take?

KENNEDY: Weeks, but we're going to edit it down into a montage so we can show it really fast.

JULIA: Oh, that's nice.

KENNEDY: Here's your helicopter escort now!

(The opening chords of Wagner's "Ride of the Valkyrie" swell as ORF, KENNEDY, and DARRYL enter with toy helicopters, "flying" them around the stage utilizing beautiful ballet moves. As we hit the first bum ba ta TA tum! section, the recorded music fades and the CAST hums the music on kazoo. By the second set of four bum ba ta TA tum!'s, MIKE, JULIA, and ANGELA have brought miniature happy villages filled with miniature happy civilians onto the stage. The helicopters start strafing and bombing the civilians while the actors stomp and kick the peaceful huts and happy little people.)

ANGELA: Badabadabada! Badabadabada! Git some, git some!

JULIA: How can you shoot women and children like that?

ANGELA: Easy! It looks like a video game from this height! Do you wanna try?

JULIA: Of course not!

ANGELA: What's a matter? Are you chicken?

JULIA: There's been enough killing, and don't call me chicken!

ANGELA: Bock! Bock!

(Cut back to song: two more measures of "bum ba ta TA tum!," with more killing and strafing and blowing shit up.)

JULIA: Badabadabada! Badabadabada! Git some, git some!

MIKE: I thought you said there should be no more killing!

JULIA: I know, but this gun is really fun! And besides, those people are all so… yellowish.

(The music swells, and ERICA, dressed in Valkyrie drag, sings the soprano solo at the end. The CHORUS ends with a musical theatre button and the CAST breathes heavily, waiting for their ovation. Sound effect: alarm, "Wipe-n-Go time!" ALL take out a Two-Step Completely Disposable Wipe-n-Go and throw it into the trash. Transition: music—tense, ominous, and creepy.)

CHORUS: Long exterior of our three remaining survivors heading upriver in a whitewashed steam-powered boat. Angela puts another piece of kindling on the fire and fiddles with the furnace, Julia starts her morning with yoga exercises. Closeup on Julia's hips. Closeup on Julia's chest. These shots are done tastefully, artistically, Julia's silhouette against the rising sun. Plus her nipples are hard. Mike reads from the producer's dossier that Kennedy has given them.

MIKE: Nobody knows where Colonel Kurtz came from, just showed up one day with a pulse and they made him an executive vice president. Every show he's produced has been a ratings winner. He put a videocamera into the small intestine of Matthew Broderick. It was number one for thirteen weeks. But people started complaining when his series "Who Wants to Be an Altar Boy" was deemed demeaning to the Catholic Church. Accusing people of being demeaning around here was like giving out speeding tickets at the Indy 500.

ANGELA: Hah, Indy 500.

MIKE: What?

ANGELA: Indy 500, that was a good one.

MIKE: Shit, I'm sorry, I didn't realize I was speaking out loud.

CHORUS: Silence falls as the boat is enshrouded in a thick mist. The silence is almost absolute as the jungle mist blots out any sight beyond your own arm. Even the ubiquitous jungle birds, frogs, and insects have lost their voices. There is no landmark, there is no comfort, there is no turning back! Boooogy boooogy boogy! The boat passes through the mist as they approach the landing of an ancient Angkor temple complex. The many towers of the millennia-old city are adorned with four faces, each piercing a cardinal direction with their eyes. The faces are those of Buddha, the enlightened one. Shiva, lord of destruction and creation. Rama, epic hero of legends past. And Ricky Ricardo, originator of the three-camera television shot.

MIKE: Holy moly.

ANGELA: Fuck me!

CHORUS: Julia can't think of anything more profound to say than "fuck me" so she cries. Watching the boat approach the steps are dozens upon dozens of emaciated, soulless former reality show contestants, all represented in this scene by Erica.

They wander around listlessly waiting to be called for their next shot at another fifteen minutes of fame. And then there is an old friend.

(ORF enters. He now has a series of cameras hanging around his neck, a scarlet bandana, and sunglasses. He approaches the SURVIVORS.)

ORF: Hey, welcome guys, welcome! You made it, come on in, you've all been approved.

MIKE: Orf, where the cocksmoke have you been?

ORF: I've been with The Man, man, I freed my mind, man, and my ass did follow!

ANGELA: The Man?

ORF: The Colonel, man, he's a big man, a great man, he reads poetry out loud. Like, beating the war drums and I'd enter your garden, man.

ANGELA: Yeah? Any asshole can recite poetry, Orf.

ORF: He's got big things planned for you guys, big things, there's going to be a sacrifice tonight.

ANGELA: Sacrifice?

ORF: Yeah, of this. (Produces a very cute teddy bear.) And we're going to videotape every single minute.

JULIA: You can't sacrifice that, it's not humane.

ANGELA: It's just a teddy bear.

JULIA: But it's so cute!

MIKE: Orf, we need to talk to The Colonel; we need to get out of this.

ORF: Oh, you'll talk to The Colonel, but there's no getting out of this, we're all in this, this is what we asked for, and this is what we got!

CHORUS: The legion of contestant zombies slowly overtake Mike, Angela, and Julia. They are slow, but are too numerous to overpower or escape. The survivors are pushed down into the mud.

JULIA: Mud! Mud! Mud! Mud! Mud! Ahhhhh!

CHORUS: Fade to black. After a pause that's just a teeny bit too long, we fade back into a medium shot of Mike, bound to a post by his neck. Closeup on a pair of boots walking towards him. We see the silhouette of a very imposing figure. We watch Mike look up in fear. Angela's head is dropped into Mike's lap!

MIKE: No no no no no! Ew!

CHORUS: Cut to the temple courtyard, where the sacrifice is being prepared for slaughter by the zombies.

(ZOMBIES—ERICA, KENNEDY, ORF, and ANGELA—worship and prepare the teddy bear. JULIA is tied to a post watching the action.)

JULIA: You bastards, you backwards, ignorant bastards! Don't you see that in civilized society we don't kill anything that's so *cute!* Ahhhh bug bug bug bug!

CHORUS: Back to Mike in The Colonel's quarters, but we don't know it's The Colonel yet, we just see an imposing figure, standing in front of Mike, looming. Finally, he is ready to speak.

(Pause.)

DARRYL: Are you the assassin?

MIKE: What?

DARRYL: Are you the assassin? *(DARRYL scoops some water from a bowl and rubs it on his head.)*

MIKE: I'm a game show contestant.

DARRYL: You're neither, you're an ass boy sent by grocery clerks to collect a bill.

MIKE: Sorry?

DARRYL: That bill is for twenty-seven fifty but I won't pay it, dammit! I only bought eggs and some milk. And nacho chips, I bought a lot of nacho chips, but not twenty-seven fifty worth.

MIKE: Didn't you die a couple of scenes ago?

DARRYL: That wasn't me. *(DARRYL drinks water from the bowl.)*

CHORUS: Water leaks out from Darryl's dozens of puncture wounds. Cut back to the square.

JULIA: That teddy bear has a name! Okay, maybe he didn't before, but he does now, I'm going to call him…Teddy!

CHORUS: Back to The Colonel and Mike.

(During this speech the opening chords of The Doors' "The End" fade up.)

DARRYL: I've seen horrors, horrors that you've never seen on television… people on television. They haven't done anything noteworthy, but they are Americans, they are entitled to fame! Fame is a slug on a straight razor. And who will star as *me!* in the made-for-TV movie about my life? I hope it's Alan Thicke. Drop the bomb, exterminate them all.

(Doors' music swells. The stage is split between MIKE slowly untying his bonds and JULIA in the square witnessing the ongoing sacrifice ritual.)

CHORUS: The killer awoke before dawn,
    He hit the snooze button, it was too early. *(Pause.)*
    The killer awoke later, still very early,

He put his boots on
And he walked on down the hall,
He took a face from the ancient gallery
And he came to a door…

(MIKE has now produced an ancient and dangerous-looking hand-held weapon, fashioned out of balloons. JULIA has joined the ZOMBIES in the sacrifice. They dance about the stage worshiping the teddy bear and losing bits of clothing in a building ritual frenzy.)

ZOMBIES: *(Singing.)* C'mon baby, take a chance with us
C'mon baby, take a chance with us
C'mon baby, take a chance with us
And meet me at the back of the blue bus
Tonight, blue bus, tonight, come on girl!

CHORUS: Mike creeps through the ancient temple wielding an ancient and deadly weapon, stalking his prey. First a lone sentry stands in his way, a simple, lowly, comedy writer, innocent of the evil produced by The Colonel, but standing between Mike and achhchchhch…

(MIKE stealthily slices CHORUS's throat. The ZOMBIES dance. MIKE fells DARRYL with his balloon weapon, repeatedly striking him until dead, and the reality show ZOMBIES violently tear into the teddy bear, throwing its stuffed guts all about, tearing the outer covering to shreds.)

DARRYL: The horror, the horror.

(ALL collapse to the floor.)

ALL: *(Singing.)* This is the end…
(Fade to black, the singers are right, it really is:)

THE END.

GENERAL WARNINGS FOR VIEWERS OF AMNESIA WARS' PRODUCTION OF *SURVIVOR: VIETNAM!*

We used the following as our pre-show announcement, with the actor who played the DJ reading it as a voiceover from his DJ booth.

Good evening, welcome to this evening's performance of Amnesia Wars' *Survivor: Vietnam!* For your comedy experience to remain as enjoyable as possible, please be aware that *Survivor: Vietnam!* contains gunshots, smoke effects, strobe lights, and this really annoying noise:

(Air horn.)

Sensitive audience members should be aware that the text of *Survivor: Vietnam!* includes obscenity, profanity, profundity, progeny, and pigeons.

Survivor: Vietnam! may not be appropriate for audience members who are deeply offended by vocabulary including but not limited to: shit, piss, fuck, cunt, cocksucker, motherfucker, and tits.

Boobs, boobies, balls, bollocks, bust a nut, nut sack, nutcase, case logic, logroll, roleplay, play the squeezebox, box, brown box, butterbox, nutterbutter, or buttfuck.

Fuck up, fuck off, fuck you, fuck me, fuck him, fuck her, fuck them, fuck we, fuckety fuck, and fuckaluckadingdong!

Please utilize this opportunity to disengage your pagers, cell phones, and chimey watches. You're not a doctor or a drug dealer for fuck's sake! You can be out of contact to the rest of the world for less than a fucking hour, it's not like your mother is about to fucking die.

Amnesia Wars offers our most heartfelt condolences and apologies to any audience members whose mothers are about to fucking die.

Fag, faggot, flaming faggot, flagpole, pole position, Pollock, Polish shower, golden shower, golden slumber, you slumber you brought her! herpes, pee pee, tee tee, dee dee, and dick.* God, Good God, God damn, and *gawd damn!*

The taking of flash photography or the use of recording devices of any kind is strictly prohibited.

All material presented in *Survivor: Vietnam!* is copywritten by Amnesia Wars Productions, despite the fact that all material in this show is absolutely derivative of somebody else's work.

(Long pause.)

Lesbian, lesbo, lezzie, lesbyterian, dyke, bull dyke, uberdyke, diesel dyke, kike, spick, mick, slope, slant, chink, nigger, snigger, giggle, chuckle, chortle, and guffaw.

Dooooodieeeee!

Please enjoy *Survivor: Vietnam!* and keep in mind that we were serious about the gunshots, the smoke machine, and the really annoying noise.

(Air horn.)

ALTERNATIVE SCENE

In the original production, the DJ was played by Jason Evans (a black guy), and the scene indicated with asterisks on page 234 ran as it does below. If a company that wishes to produce *Survivor: Vietnam!* has a more multiethnic cast than we did in our original, please contact the author and he will gladly update with a more appropriate scene.

MIKE: I can make balloon animals.

ANGELA: We should send Jason first.

JASON: What?

ORF: That's a perfect idea.

DARRYL: Though next time I'd really like to try it with another woman.

JASON: Hey, I'm just the DJ here.

MIKE: Why Jason?

ANGELA: Because he has certain…qualifications.

JASON: What qualifications?

DARRYL: I guess it doesn't really count as a threeway either if I'm not really in the room!

MIKE: Angela, are you trying to make the black guy go first?

ORF: Call her Lieutenant Dan.

JASON: I'm not even in the show!

DARRYL: Or if I'm not in the house.

ANGELA: What are you talking about?

MIKE: Lieutenant Dan, are you trying to make the black guy go first?

ANGELA: *(To MIKE.)* Well, if you want to be all politically correct, you can go yourself!

(Pause.)

MIKE: We should let the black guy go.

JASON: Wait a *fucking minute*.

DARRYL: It's just that the thing with the pool guy wasn't really so much a threesome as me coming home and finding you two naked in the kitchen.

ERICA: Ooohhhh, that's not funny.

JASON: I'm just here to play some music and do a couple of voiceovers, why don't you fucking send Rob.

CHORUS: The DJ suddenly falls mute.

ANGELA: Oh, I see, when *you* want to stir it up a bit, we end up in a firefight in North Vietnam, but I fuck a few pool guys behind your back, and suddenly it's a big drama?

FEED THE HOLE

Michael Stock

MICHAEL STOCK was born in London, England, in November 1975, during Thanksgiving, Hanukkah, and a doctors' union strike. Michael grew up outside Chicago, where he created Sideway Theater Company while a sophomore at New Trier High School. Sideway then traveled to the University of Illinois where Michael spent two years in the BFA acting program. Sideway completed its Illinois tenure in Chicago while Michael earned a degree in performance studies from Northwestern University. In 1999, Michael and Sideway moved to New York. Michael has acted in more than sixty productions in Chicago and New York theatre—*Cask of Amontillado* (Present Company and Yale University), *Henry V* (Mazer Theater), and *Othello* (Primary Stages Bukowski Theater)—and as an actor for Sideway Theater—*Hustle* (MOMFEST in Austin, Texas), *The Dumbwaiter*, *Amadeus*, and *Feed the Hole*. Michael has studied with Uta Hagen (he appears in the PBS documentary *Uta Hagen, Masterclass*), Austin Pendleton, the Pivens, and The Lab at New York Shakespeare Festival/Public Theater. He was honored with the Excellence in Playwriting Award at the 2001 New York International Fringe Festival for *Hustle*, a piece he originally wrote and directed for Sideway. Additional playwriting includes *The Ice Lid*, which he wrote and directed at the Kraine Theater; the soundscape for Tesha Buss's *Euphrasy/Eucrazy*, which won a Communicator award for sound design; and a new version of *Pyramus and Thisbe* commissioned by Hofstra University, to be produced in March 2004. Unproduced scripts of *Trojan WomeNYC*, *Bender*, *Lady Chaplin and Her Tramp*, and *Red and Blues* are in development.

Feed The Hole was first presented by Sideway Theater Company on April 10, 2003, at Altered Stages Theater, New York City, with the following cast and credits:

Steve .... Alexander Alioto
Shelly .... Melissa Picarello
Rob .... Adam Reiner
Brett .... Michael Stock
Samantha .... Fay Wolf
John .... Anthony Wood

Assistant Director/Stage Manager: Shana Solomon
Scenic Design: Kevin Judge
Lighting Design: Justin Burleson
Production Photographer: Kim Jackson
Technical Director: Robert Mahon III
Scenic Painter: Leigh Sellinger
Scenic Shop: Daedalus
Graphic Design: Blythe Zava/Michael Stock
Publicists: Spin Cycle

Original music was created for this production by the following artists: Jeb Loy Nichols, www.JebLoyNichols.com; Anne Heaton, www.AnneHeaton.com; Jennifer Paskow, www.JenniferPaskow.com; James Vidos, www.JamesVidos.com; Karen Baxter, www.KarenJill.com; Edie Carey, www.EdieCarey.com; Jay Collins, www.InterJazz.com/JayCollins; David Stock (lyrics by Sara Stock), www.mmbmusic.com; Rose Polenzani, www.RosePolenzani.com; Paul Cortez, visitortactics@yahoo.com; Kevin Heaton, gentrificide@hotmail.com; T.J. Larsen and Michael Stock, Shilock_419@yahoo.com.

The original score can be obtained by contacting the playwright: sidewaytheater@hotmail.com; www.SidewayTheater.com.

A portion of the proceeds were donated to Steppenwolf Theatre Company's Arts Exchange Program, www.steppenwolf.org/opportunities/arts.html.

Special thanks to those who contributed in earlier readings and for their encouragement: Stacie Green, Adam Hunter Rosenblate, David C Barrus, Ashley Knaysi, Mary Mittell, Danielle Fink, Julie Baber, Emmy Lou Diaz, Tesha Buss, Conor Heaton, Derek Goldman, Todd Hirschtritt, Leah Gale, Margaret Nichols, Mara Levin, Scott Horowitz, K. Todd Freeman, John Dias, Michael Cumpsty, Austin Pendleton, Past/Present/Future Sideway Theater Members, Alexander Gram Smell, and of course, Riguez. Michael would also like to thank his family, friends, teachers, and the nurse-in-training who saved his life during the doctors' union strike.

CHARACTERS

(All mid-twenties)

BRETT: Shelly's boyfriend, Steve's best friend since college

SHELLY: Brett's girlfriend, Samantha's best friend since childhood

SAMANTHA: Rob's girlfriend, Shelly's best friend since childhood, John's best friend

ROB: Samantha's boyfriend, Steve's friend for several years

JOHN: Samantha's best friend, Shelly's friend

STEVE: Brett's best friend since college, Rob's friend for several years

TIME

After September 11, 2001. Before The Public Smoking Ban.

PLACE

Various bars, boutiques, and bedrooms in Manhattan.

A THOUGHT ON THE PUNCTUATION AND THE VERBIAGE

PUNCTUATION: The punctuation, although sometimes utilized unusually, is intended to serve as a potential emotional guide for the actor. This process for notation was developed by Sideway Theater Company, and owes a great debt to my work on Tennessee Williams with Kim Rubenstein at Northwestern, my work on Shakespeare with the Master Teachers at the Public Theater, Austin Pendleton, and my readings of John Barton and Cicely Berry's work with the Royal Shakespeare Company. If this aids the actor, fantastic; if not, feel free to disregard these ideas and develop your own.

Suggestions as follows:

- A period indicates a full stop.

- A comma indicates a change of direction on the same thought.

- A colon indicates an introduction of a quotation, an explanation, an example, or a series.

- A semicolon indicates a bridge between two distinct, but related, ideas. Literally, a period over a comma. It has helped us to embrace the notion of jumping up from the first sentence to the second, both vocally and in thought.

- An ellipsis indicates an omission or suppression of parts of words or sentences by the speaker. There is an internal search or wrestling within the speaker.

- A dash in this piece does not indicate an interruption; it indicates, rather, a stop of speech by the speaker. With the silence, the speaker is *reaching* towards the listener for a response.

- A question mark indicates a direct question or interrogation, and is important because of the curvy lilt that the voice makes at the end (it sounds like a question mark looks). Often this indicates an emotionally weaker state in the speaker.

- A parenthesis indicates explanatory or qualifying remarks and are often asides. Dropped both vocally and in thought into a different register.

- CAPS indicate a boldness of feeling.

- An exclamation point indicates, well…an exclamation! The end of the sentence goes up, both vocally and in thought.

VERBIAGE: The text contains what Sideway Theater Company calls the characters' life philosophy, in that each character's particular word choice and sentence structure attempt to reveal the unique filter through which they view the world. I wholeheartedly assure the reader of this text that every apparent typographical error, malapropism, stutter, and word omission is correct.

A THOUGHT ON THE SET

The set can be anything as long as it allows for a seamless transition between scenes. The original design accomplished this with a transformative space. I believe that the audience knows we are at dinner because in the last scene we said we are going there; we do not need tables, food, glasses, and other restaurant accoutrements to define the space. In the original production a beautiful set was designed by Kevin Judge, which consisted of five Chinese Red chairs, a rock garden, and a stool. The rock garden and stool, stage right, defined John's area. Up center stage a line of three chairs defined Sam and Rob's space. Downstage left, two chairs defined Brett and Shelly's space. Steve was free to roam. Hanging along the stage right wall, Chinese Red swings swayed. The floor was intricately painted with lines and swirls to suggest sand. The walls had a single stripe of sky blue painted all the way around the space, a brilliant piece (!) of sky encroaching the darkness.

A THOUGHT ON THE SOUND

See the notes on the original soundtrack. There are plenty of times to use transitional music because the play is episodic. The effect should be the same as a musical bridge in film, where you link two dichotomous scenes through the use of underscoring of the same song.

A THOUGHT ON THE LIGHTS

Justin Burleson's original lighting design was flawless; it was seamless and unobtrusive while clearly delineating the playing space.

A THOUGHT ON THE COSTUMES

In the original production, the characters wore shades of black, gray, and white. Steve wore splashes of color. Shelly, in her scene with Steve, wore colored lingerie. John wore the latest trends. Brett wore a suit in every scene, except the following:

- In the bedroom scene, Brett wore suit pants with a T-shirt.

- In the racquetball scene, Brett wore "dressed up" athletic clothes such as a collared shirt and linen shorts, which served as a sharp contrast to Steve's gym clothes.

- In the last two scenes of the show, Brett's costuming took a severe shift. In those two scenes, he wore jeans, a T-shirt, and a New York zip-up hoodie sweatshirt.

All the characters were very fashionably dressed.

ACT I

SCENE ONE

In darkness. We hear the harsh, monotonous drone of a digital alarm clock. Lights up on JOHN. Lights snap off. Sound of alarm clock. Lights up on STEVE. Lights snap off. Alarm clock. Lights up on SAMANTHA and ROB in their apartment. Lights off.

Alarm. Lights up on SHELLY. Lights off. Alarm. Lights up on BRETT. His shirt is lifted so he is staring at his stomach in the "mirror" on the fourth wall. He sucks it in, and hits it hard several times with his fist, then breaths out so it is wholly distended.

Turns to the side. He sighs. SHELLY walks through past the bathroom door from the offstage kitchen into the main apartment space. She is dressed in work attire. She turns on the TV; the weather channel is on. She sits, eats cereal. BRETT enters, putting on his tie. He has suit pants on, with the suit coat in his hands. He has a plate with toast and the newspaper. He sits. They eat. He reads the New York Post; *she reads the* New York Times. *The weather plays on the TV.*

Suggestion: Whenever we hear the weather throughout the play, the newscaster cheerily warns of the impending doom brought on by an enormous storm.

The remainder of the scene occurs in silence between BRETT and SHELLY. The only noise is the morning weather report, the crunch of toast, the rattle of spoons, and the normal rustle of newspaper. They are not being "dramatic" about their actions or implying any antagonistic subtext. This is their daily routine. At the end, BRETT goes to SHELLY to give her a kiss; there is an awkwardness between them, like they can't coordinate which side of the cheek he is going to kiss her on. Tension. He kisses her forehead. BRETT leaves for work. She finishes her cereal. She sits for a few moments in silence. Blackout.

SCENE TWO

SAMANTHA and ROB in their apartment, preparing for bed. In a separate area of the stage, SHELLY engages in an earlier conversation from lunch with SAMANTHA. These two moments are happening simultaneously; it is a splice in the space-time continuum. Lights go on and off on SHELLY as necessary.

SAMANTHA: We're munching away and I'm like, "Ooh, I can't believe this dressing." And she outs with—

SHELLY: Speaking of which—

SAMANTHA: —"We just had sex on my kitchen table!"

SHELLY: Great sex.

SAMANTHA: "Speaking of which"? If I said, "Shelly, where's the whackiest place you and your dirty sex buddy made whoopie?" I'd be speaking of which. Let's say you're Brett, I'm Shelly: we're eating toast and jam or whatever, you leave for work, and then—

SHELLY: Wham!

SAMANTHA: We ate toast on that table!

SHELLY: Sam, really, it's no big deal.

SAMANTHA: Rob, you think it's no big deal, let's install a turnstile. Sell tickets. Step right up, fellas, fuck me, win a stuffed koala! How would you feel about that?

ROB: Do I get a cut of the ticket sales?

SAMANTHA: You're off to the office and I'm pushing placemats—

ROB: We have placemats?

SAMANTHA: Bumping the salt and pepper to the floor!

ROB: Where are our placemats?

SAMANTHA: *(To ROB.)* We made plans—Shell and me. *(To SHELLY.)* Ten-year plans. Betrayed. *(To ROB.)* And those plans do not include chaos and lying and stuffed koalas! Oh God, if you do that to me, Rob, I'll *never forgive* you.

ROB: Slow down. I haven't done anything yet.

SHELLY: I'm happier than you and Rob.

SAMANTHA: Ya know, fuck her. *(To SHELLY.)* Fuck you. Trotting through your morning, without any indication. *(To ROB.)* She's moral rot.

SHELLY: Be happy for me.

SAMANTHA: *(To SHELLY.)* "Sure, Shelly, doing it on a dirty kitchen table's cool."

SHELLY: I'm happy—

SAMANTHA: *(To ROB.)* She makes me lie. Feign it's not abominable.

ROB: Like the Abominable Snowman?

SAMANTHA: Yes. Hellacious. Don't you think? You don't think.

ROB: Yeah, sex on the table sounds terrible.

SHELLY: —Are you happy?

SAMANTHA: Oh my God. Just tell me.

ROB: Tell you what?

SHELLY: —Is Rob happy?

SAMANTHA: You're having an affair.

ROB: Are you talking to me? Or am I Brett or Shelly in this scenario?

SAMANTHA: No, you. You.

SHELLY: *(Overlapping.)* Happy.

ROB: How could you ask me that?

SAMANTHA: Well, if you're not, why aren't you mad at her?

ROB: I'm not her boyfriend.

SAMANTHA: Be mad at her for me.

ROB: What'd she do to you?

SAMANTHA: She had sex on the table. *(Breaths.)* In their apartment!

ROB: Was she sitting on the table? Was she bent over it? Was she handcuffed?

SAMANTHA: What's the difference?

ROB: I'm picturing how abhorrent the crime is. Like, what was she wearing?

SAMANTHA: *(Laughing.)* Fuck you, Morris.

ROB: Oooh, wow, she busts out the last name. Not even a "Robert!"

SHELLY: When was the last time you had great sex?

SAMANTHA: I'm really upset about this and you're making jokes.

ROB: I'm making jokes because you're upset.

SAMANTHA: Watch it, Morris, you're on my list.

ROB: *(Jokingly.)* Shut up you.

SAMANTHA: You shut up you.

ROB: You shut up you your face! Seriously Sam, if this is a big deal to you, tell her what she's doing is crap.

SAMANTHA: You know— I really— I hate it.

ROB: What.

SAMANTHA: Reassure me. Don't tell me what to do.

ROB: Okay.

SAMANTHA: Don't say anything funny.

ROB: I'll try.

SAMANTHA: Just listen.

ROB: Huh? What'd you say?

SAMANTHA: It's a good thing God made you cute.

SHELLY: Raw, grasping sex.

ROB: All right. You vent. I listen.

SAMANTHA: No, I'm not venting, I want to keep having this conversation.

ROB: But don't tell you what I think. Got it. *(Breaths.)* So…you want me to say?…what?

SAMANTHA: Say, "I'm sorry, Sam, that really sucks."

ROB: I'm sorry, Sam, but this fucking sucks. I listen to your story. Ken Burns documentaries are shorter. I make you laugh. But now you're driving my business, telling me what to say. You don't even need me here; say my lines for me.

SAMANTHA: Rob, don't get upset.

ROB: You're all pissed that—what?—I'm not taking it personally. Her affair is not about us.

SAMANTHA: This conversation's over.

ROB: What? It's not over, it's— Fine.

SAMANTHA: I'm tired of explaining why I should be important to you.

ROB: Fine. *(A moment passes in silence.)* How was your day—?

SAMANTHA: Dandy.

ROB: I mean…otherwise.

SHELLY: You've thought about doing it.

SAMANTHA: The copier broke.

SHELLY: Haven't you?

ROB: Call the guy?

SHELLY: Haven't you?

SAMANTHA: Yeah… Everything I depend on is devastatingly disappointing.

ROB: He didn't show?

SHELLY: 'Cause you're not fulfilled.

SAMANTHA: No… I'm talking about Shelly. Throwing a secure—for some primal fuck. You wouldn't do that—right?

SHELLY: The excitement.

ROB: I thought you don't want to talk about it!

SAMANTHA: Of course, I want to talk about it. Every time I'm upset, you get pissed. We talk about why you're mad. Never why I'm hurt.

ROB: Sam, I'm trying to *understand*—

SAMANTHA: This should be as big a deal for you—

SHELLY: The danger.

SAMANTHA: —So what? You would cheat on me?

ROB: *(Starts putting on clothes to go out.)* You're right, this conversation's done. I

shouldn't have to answer that question. You should believe in us. But no, you want to bitch about it and I should be all rah-rah, emotional cheerleader for this. But hey, you don't want my advice; so next time, don't ask. Help yourself.

SAMANTHA: I never asked—

ROB: Then don't talk to me, because I'm a failure here. If I'm so devastatingly disappointing, talk to John. Lord knows, the gays know how to jump up and down and dramatize. "Oh my gawd, Samantha, you must feel awful! Rob's so solution oriented! What a bastard!" So go, go hang out with your empathetic friends. Do what Shelly's doing, if you aren't already, and fuck someone who'll listen better.

SAMANTHA: Robert!

ROB: Uhp! There's the "Robert!" I knew I'd get one. *(Breaths pass.)* Sam. I'm a damn good boyfriend. I'm not some biscuit-head ex-frat investment banker douche bag.

SAMANTHA: Robert!

ROB: And now. I'm gonna drink beers and watch sports and come home whenever I want.

SAMANTHA: Don't leave me!

ROB: Get a good push on the placemats!

(ROB leaves. A moment. SAMANTHA gets on the phone.)

SHELLY: I've never been so happy.

SAMANTHA: *(On the phone.)* John… can you come over, sweetheart?

(Blackout.)

SCENE THREE

Lights up in bar. BRETT and STEVE watching game.

BRETT: Back deck opens. Space. Then trees. Not boxed in. Like when my brother hooked us up in Vail—

STEVE: I want his life. Taking care of everyone?

BRETT: I want his life too. Flipping down that black American Express card.

STEVE: They look like power. I want one.

BRETT: You can't apply, dude. AmEx comes to you.

STEVE: What, platinum card wasn't elite enough so American Express created a new class of people?

BRETT: You know what I get with my green American Express card?

STEVE: Your bill?

BRETT: Exactly.

STEVE: Well, the country's definitely a move for you and Shelly.

BRETT: It's my brother's, ya know. Top-notch—

STEVE: Listen, fuck-nut, you and Shelly—just do it.

BRETT: That's truth. My brother, he jets these women all over the world to these top dollar—

STEVE: Is he still dating—

BRETT: Who can keep track, Steve. Cigars, food, golf. That's all we talk… I hate golf. He lives in a different world, man— chartering a jet to the Nile, or…wherever, with these…ya know…multiple models in tow.

(ROB enters.)

STEVE: Hey! Sit. Sit. Thought you weren't showing.

ROB: Oh. Uh— Yeah— Hey!

STEVE: You know Brett, right? Brett— Rob.

ROB: Yeah, hey— of course— I was just surprised to see ya.

BRETT: Been awhile. *(To STEVE.)* The models love the black AmEx.

STEVE: Shit.

ROB: Brett and I, we know each other well.

STEVE: Huh?

BRETT: But it's been awhile.

ROB: Sam and Shelly—

STEVE: Yeah?

BRETT: Friends from grade school.

STEVE: So?

ROB: So, we know each other—

BRETT: But it's been awhile. Been busy— some big projects in the pipe. *(Imitating Bill Murray in* Caddyshack.*)* So I got that going for me.

STEVE: *(Imitating Bill Murray in* Caddyshack.*)* Which is nice.

BRETT: But, Sam—how is she?

ROB: Fine, she's. She's— …Steve, you always introduce us.

STEVE: We're talking the country. Let me buy you a drink. *(He gets up.)*

ROB: The country? Yeah, I need one. Jack and Coke. With models?

STEVE: *(As he goes offstage.)* Yeah, Brett and Shelly, they're going upstate. *(We hear him talk to the "bartender.")* You have Knob Creek? Knob Creek, Coke, couple cubes.

BRETT: My brother's the big times.

(Awkward breaths pass. BRETT takes out Tums and offers one to ROB.)

BRETT: Tums?

ROB: No. Thanks.

STEVE: *(Reentering with drinks.)* You know Shelly, right? Brett's girl.

BRETT: *(Underlapping.)* —The tops—

ROB: Sam, Shelly, grade school—I said.

BRETT: —The models are his, and—

STEVE: Best friends from grade— That's great.

BRETT: —So's the place upstate.

STEVE: With trees.

BRETT: Twenty minutes outta Manhattan.

ROB: You always—

STEVE: What?

ROB: Never think I know anyone. I listen. Okay? I remember his name.

STEVE: What's a matter with you? You fight with Sam again? I'm not your girlfriend, alright, so don't take it out on me. You two get off on fighting. I'm not into it. Sitting there, crying. "Uhh, I don't know anyone— my pussy hurts!" Of course you know Brett and Shelly. We met at their New Year's Eve party. What? Couple years ago? We don't sleep together. Okay? I just want everyone taken care of. Save you from that embarrassing, forgetting his name moment, 'cause you're old and losing your mind. Now, drink your Jack and Coke and shut the fuck up.

(Pause. Tension. Everyone laughs. STEVE and ROB slap hands. Moment subsides. Pause.)

BRETT: Oh, Rob, you're the deal-breaker—

STEVE: We were talking earlier— So *think* about this now—

BRETT: You think Hall and Oates are gay?

ROB: Well, I dunno— Why?

STEVE: Just talking. C'mon, it's just us guys—talk straight.

BRETT: 'Cause I see this MTV "Behind the Music" thing.

STEVE: Yeah, it's VH-1.

BRETT: And all of a sudden it hits me— these guys are fags.

ROB: Yeah?

BRETT: *(Speaks the song lyrics.)* C'mon that song, "Man-Eater"? Might as well be "Cock-Eater." "Ass-Eater." I know it's "Whoa, oh, here SHE comes," but "Watch out BOY she'll CHEW you up." You've heard gay guys call each other "she"? Well, that's what I'm saying. Like "My Nigger." Same, man. Same.

STEVE: It's not the same. Okay maybe Oates is gay. But Hall, no way. No fucking way.

BRETT: Are Siegfried and Roy gay?

ROB: What?

BRETT: Are Siegfried and Roy—

ROB: You asking?

STEVE: Wait, no, Siegfried and Roy are the biggest fags. Right, Rob? Liberace level.

BRETT: Well, same, man. They look the same. One short guy, dark hair, one tall guy, blond—

STEVE: What are you saying? Siegfried and Roy ARE Hall and Oates?

BRETT: Without the panthers.

ROB: Yeah, like "Su-su-sudio"? Fucking faggots.

STEVE: No, that's—

(Several breaths pass.)

BRETT: That's Phil Collins's horse.

(They sit for awhile thinking about this.)

STEVE: Huh.

(They sit nodding. Pause. Moment subsides. Pause.)

ROB: Weather's good this weekend.

BRETT: Got a lot in the pipeline, though.

ROB: Watch out, wind chill's supposed to drop.

BRETT: The fuck's wind chill anyway? Who made that shit up?

STEVE: Makes the weather report sexy.

BRETT: Yeah.

ROB: Right... Sam and I, we did—we got into this— *(Breaths.)* ...Right.

STEVE: Nor'easter or something.

BRETT: *(With Canadian accent.)* Sneaking from Canada a-boot as hard as a Gretsky slapshot. Eh?

STEVE: I hate fucking Canucks and their cold air.

ROB: *(Seeing the "TV.")* Hey! See this play?

STEVE: Yeah.

BRETT: Couldn't believe it.

ROB: Could you believe—?

STEVE: Vasquez.

BRETT: Fucking Vasquez!

ROB: Yeah, I can't believe it!

STEVE: Keeps replaying.

ROB: Vasquez.

BRETT: Fucking Vasquez!

ROB: I can't believe it!

STEVE: Sports, weather, and porn. The only things I watch where I don't feel I'm lied to.

ROB: Hah.

BRETT: Yeah.

ROB: Yeah.

(Breaths pass. Blackout.)

SCENE FOUR

JOHN and SAMANTHA at ROB and SAMANTHA's apartment. They are eating Ben and Jerry's. They each have their own pint.

JOHN: You arrange the stones in twisted wave patterns to learn to accept the way life repeats. This rock garden's helped me come to peace with the fact that this stuff's cyclical. What you were saying, about how you and Rob always have the same fight. Don't worry, honey, it's not just you two. Hell, everything repeats. Relationships. Nature. Fashion— Forget about it. Eighties fashion's back, right. Ripped jeans, Republicans in office.

SAMANTHA: That's fashion?

JOHN: Sure, they wear red ties and khakis. Sam, our boyfriends are great, we should be totally happy, but we're mad at them. Why? We can't accept the good. We need magic. And magic equals drama. So we find something wrong. The country did the same thing. Clinton didn't give us a global bad guy to hate. And did we relish in the peace? No! We distracted ourselves with his personal life. We're doing the same thing with Shelly. Gossiping about her. Sam, the rock garden will teach you to stop focusing on Shelly or Rob, and focus on yourself.

SAMANTHA: You're comparing the president's affair to Shelly's? That's ludicrous.

JOHN: Is it?

SAMANTHA: Absolutely. The president shouldn't have affairs. We expect more out of him.

JOHN: And you expect more out of Shelly.

SAMANTHA: He lied about it.

JOHN: They all lie. Governments. Advertisements. Friends. Lovers. We're so used to being lied to we don't know what's true any more.

SAMANTHA: Shelly's not having an affair because the government made her do it. There's no sex conspiracy.

JOHN: There is a second shooter in her grassy knoll.

SAMANTHA: You're right, they're similar—Shelly and Clinton. They made morally reprehensible mistakes and they should be judged.

JOHN: Based on whose moral code?

SAMANTHA: Mine. Yours. If Chris cheats on you, God forbid, you won't accept it.

JOHN: Maybe I will. I'm afraid of silence. I'm afraid of being alone. In the rock garden, I'm silent and alone and it terrifies me. That's why I do it. If I'm more afraid of being alone than of leaving Chris, I'll stay. And I shouldn't judge myself for that behavior. I should accept it.

SAMANTHA: I don't believe that. If Rob cheated on me, I would never forgive him. I wouldn't cheat on him. So why do I have to accept what I wouldn't do? I am not the type of person who cheats on people.

JOHN: We're all that type of person. And you should accept people for who they are. Not who you want them to be.

SAMANTHA: So I should lower my standards because people won't live up to them? No.

JOHN: You can't change your lovers. Accept their flaws, support their journey, and play with their dick occasionally.

SAMANTHA: I can change him. He needs me. When he acts wrong, I tell him. I want him to be the best he can, not the best he thinks he can.

JOHN: The world's not perfect, Sam. There's no absolute.

SAMANTHA: Yes, there is. There is a right and wrong. You can choose to ignore that, or justify it in the moment to feel good about yourself.

JOHN: We're most critical of others what we fear in ourselves.

SAMANTHA: You're starting to sound like a fucking fortune cookie.

JOHN: It's the rock garden. Just try it. You may feel differently.

SAMANTHA: But what Shelly's doing is wrong.

JOHN: Well, it's helped me. I accept the fact that we crave an enemy. What does it say on the Statue of Liberty? "Give us your huddled foreigners to despise and we won't examine our own problems."

SAMANTHA: Enough with the politics.

JOHN: Sorry. Politics and the rock garden are the only passions I've got, with Chris gone.

SAMANTHA: Can't we talk about religion or money? Ya know, things everyone agrees on.

JOHN: Just try it. I tell you, it's like sitting at the water in the middle of the city. Sam. It's settled. You'll come. Every Monday, Wednesday, Friday. Hell, bring Rob. My only rule is—you can't change anyone's stones. Whatever's harmonious to them, embrace as harmonious to us all. *(Pause.)* That was deep. Wow, I'm so fucking deep. Huh? Ugh, you're right, all this talk. I'm making me thirsty. Martini?

(Blackout.)

SCENE FIVE

SHELLY and BRETT after the game. SHELLY and BRETT's apartment.

SHELLY: Goodnight. I'm—

BRETT: Okay.

SHELLY: Big day tomorrow.

BRETT: I'm hungry.

SHELLY: Forgot to eat?

BRETT: I'm not really hungry.

SHELLY: That's a first… You should—you used to cook.

BRETT: I could hop in the kitchen, whip up a little—

SHELLY: What? Waffles with tomato sauce?

BRETT: *(As Anthony Hopkins's Dr. Lechter in* Silence of the Lambs.*)* Fava beans and a nice Chianti.

SHELLY: "Amarone." In the book, it's "a big Amarone."

BRETT: Well, you can't make shit.

SHELLY: I could make you my bitch.

BRETT: Make me.

(They close the space between them. There is a moment of real sexual friction.)

BRETT: Do you want to go into the bedroom?

(Breaths pass. She looks at him incredulously. The moment is gone. BRETT wraps his arms around her. Starts kissing her neck. She stiffens. It is awkward. He breaks off. Breaths pass.)

SHELLY: I'll get the menus.

(Breaths pass. SHELLY enters the kitchen. We hear her putting on the kettle.)

BRETT: Hey, is there someone at your office, like a woman, to fix Steve up with?

SHELLY: Chinese?

BRETT: I—I don't know if he likes Asian women.

SHELLY: Huh? Chinese?

BRETT: He seems depressed.

SHELLY: We always get Chinese. I'm—were you talking?

(SHELLY returns, looking through an organized binder of three-hole-punched menus.)

BRETT: Hey! Could you listen? …Steve. He was talking tonight—seemed lonely.

SHELLY: Wait. Your friend Steve? He said—lonely? C'mon.

BRETT: Nah. Said. Ya know, "Let's hang."

SHELLY: So?

BRETT: He's a guy. He's not going to say, "I'm lonely."

SHELLY: God forbid… So, you and I should take him to dinner.

BRETT: Yeah, with who?

SHELLY: With us.

BRETT: With who and us? I want you to set him up—someone different—

SHELLY: Different how?

BRETT: Different. Remember, Tattoo Girl. In Michigan. And the tree-hugger in grad school.

SHELLY: Yeah.

BRETT: Then the actress who always left on tour.

SHELLY: Italian?

BRETT: She was—American. Maybe Italian American, but—

SHELLY: Brett! Italian?

(Breath.)

BRETT: What?

SHELLY: Italian, want Italian, to eat?

BRETT: Oh. Yeah, I mean no, not Italian, not so much—well, whatever. If you want Italian, I could do Italian. I don't know. So. Different than those women. They're distant. Emotionally.

SHELLY: No, they lived far away. Can you make a decision? I'm starving.

BRETT: They won't love him back. *(Breaths pass.)* I mean I'm no expert but—

SHELLY: No shit, man. What are you an expert— oh God!

BRETT: What?

SHELLY: —They don't deliver this late— That's the stupidest thing I've ever heard.

BRETT: Is that right.

SHELLY: Well, so what? So what if he does date—?

BRETT: So, I'm asking you—find someone who's in town, emotionally available, and single. *(Breaths pass.)* We're screwed.

(A moment passes.)

SHELLY: Emotionally available. What's that about?

(A short chilly silence. The kettle starts to shriek.)

BRETT: It was a joke. Ha. Ha. Funny. Next time I'll send a memo. Warning: joke up ahead… Did you put the kettle on?

SHELLY: Huh? Oh. I'm numb.

(SHELLY goes into the kitchen. The sound dies.)

SHELLY: *(From off.)* What's Steve attracted to?

BRETT: Well, he's not a leg man, or a breast man, or a drumstick—

SHELLY: Oh God.

BRETT: Get it?

SHELLY: That's terrible.

BRETT: Like, chicken man?

(SHELLY returns with a cup of hot chocolate.)

SHELLY: What's Steve attracted—

BRETT: He's— Is that hot cocoa?

SHELLY: Indian? Love that curried beef. But what's he—

BRETT: No. No Indian. I hate that shit you get. Curry destroys my stomach— Really passionate women.

SHELLY: Thai's bland. Can you handle bland?

BRETT: They always want to marry him.

SHELLY: Bland's boring. What's a fun food?

BRETT: Pizza?

SHELLY: If you're at Chuckee Cheese.

BRETT: Is that cocoa?

SHELLY: Huh? Yeah.

BRETT: Make enough for me?

SHELLY: Enough what? Hot water? There's some on the stove. Open the pouch, stir it in, man.

BRETT: *(Not moving.)* They're all beautiful in an odd way.

SHELLY: Odd? Wait—odd, like what?

BRETT: But alive. Tattoo Girl's a painter. Grad student, a chef or a poet.

SHELLY: No. She studied romantic epistolary novels—

BRETT: *(Underlapping.)* How do you remember that?

SHELLY: *(Overlapping.)* —Where they write letters to each other. Ya know—communicate? Like *Possession* and *Les Liaisons Dangereuses*.

BRETT: Oh—sure. *(With a thick French accent.)* "Dangereuses."

SHELLY: Torrid, consuming love affairs which destroy—

BRETT: Honey. I saw the movies.

SHELLY: Read a novel. Films twist it around. You forget why you loved it. *(Breaths.)* It's like, I adored this postcard of Mona Lisa. All vibrant, happy technicolors. So when I was studying in Paris, I made a special trip. Turns out—the *Mona Lisa's* depressing. Then whenever I looked

at my postcard—I look at that face, I can't remember the happy. I finally got rid of it.

BRETT: What's that have to do with movies?

SHELLY: We want happy. What happens at the end of *The Natural?*

BRETT: Robert Redford hits a homer.

SHELLY: Roy Hobbs strikes out. In the novel he fails. See? It's all anyone remembers. The happy "movie."

BRETT: I like movies. Okay? Eat a tub of popcorn. It'll make you a better person.

SHELLY: Whatever, dude. But, wait, wait—"odd"?

BRETT: Oh, those girls, they're damaged goods.

SHELLY: Really. You think.

BRETT: How long can he heal these fucked-up, needy, repressed—

SHELLY: Heal? That's just—ya know—Ha. It's so funny he said that.

BRETT: He never said that. I said I thought he—

SHELLY: Like "Sexual Healing."

(Breaths pass.)

BRETT: *(Sings quietly.)* "When I get that feeling, I want sexual healing. Bring me home tonight."

SHELLY: Those aren't the words. "Bring me home tonight"?

BRETT: Oh, uh—

SHELLY: "Makes me feel so fine. Helps to relieve my soul."

BRETT: Same shit. You say "irregardless" and "worse comes to worse." I never say anything. Makes no sense. It's "when worse comes to WORST."

SHELLY: Duly noted. Point, Brett.

BRETT: Yeah?

SHELLY: Nice work, kid. Tie score.

BRETT: What the fuck did you get a point for?

SHELLY: "Sexual Healing."

BRETT: But I only get one for irregardless and worse to worst? What happened to double word score?

SHELLY: Judges? Uhp, sorry, they're reviewing the play.

BRETT: Hogwash.

SHELLY: Whatever, dude… I'll think up someone—undamaged. Alive. You're right, it's the least we can do for your friend. And it would be fun to double date.

BRETT: We could get a malted from the soda jerk.

SHELLY: I mean— …Well, I'm going to bed.

BRETT: Dinner?

SHELLY: I shouldn't eat this late—I'm fat.

BRETT: Do we have any of that leftover Halloween candy?

SHELLY: (As BRETT exits to kitchen.) …And I need to be rested; prepare here before I go in, in the afternoon.

BRETT: (From off.) I'm starving, just don't know what for.

SHELLY: Figure it out.

BRETT: Probably pick— Pickle here, some olives, last pepperoncini. Something in the mix'll make me happy.

SHELLY: Yeah, ya know? Make sure I'm rested. For tomorrow.

BRETT: (Enters with Halloween candy and pepperoncinis.) Yeah? …I was gonna ask…ask—about it. (Breaths pass.) Be sure to call when it's done.

SHELLY: Sure.

BRETT: Once you feel…secure… confident— …your presentation thingy will— call me— It's like the project I got in the pipe—but mine's BIG—I ran it by Warren and he's like, "That sucks," so I start really staring him down, eyes popping—

SHELLY: Sure. Sure. Call me.

(Breaths pass. SHELLY exits to bed. BRETT sits for a moment. Turns on the TV. The evening weather report. He eats several peanut butter cups as "Sexual Healing" plays. Blackout.)

SCENE SIX

SAMANTHA and ROB after the game. SAMANTHA and ROB's apartment.

ROB: I wasn't expecting you up.

SAMANTHA: I couldn't sleep. I wasn't sure you were coming home.

ROB: Me either… I saw Brett tonight.

SAMANTHA: You went and told him?

ROB: No. He was with Steve.

SAMANTHA: And?

ROB: I told him.

SAMANTHA: Oh God.

ROB: Before he left, I said, "Brett, someone's bangin' Shelly. Hey, pass the beer nuts."

SAMANTHA: (Laughing.) Oh, Robert, come here.

(They kiss.)

ROB: All I could think about was you. Brett's sitting there gobbling Tums or Rolaids or whatever. Of course I didn't tell him. All I could think was, "God, what a fucking idiot I am." I have you. You make me laugh... I'm so sorry.

SAMANTHA: I ate two pints a ice cream and a Pop-Tart. So, I'm pretty sorry too.

(They laugh.)

ROB: I want to laugh every day.

SAMANTHA: Then we gotta cry.

ROB: Oh, shit. Am I in trouble?

SAMANTHA: You will be if you do what Shelly's doing; I'll cut your nuts off.

ROB: Hey, I'm a horrible horrible liar. I mean...horrible. Couldn't keep track of all the lies. Plus, you ever see my poker face? Look at me. This is me. This is my poker face. I suck.

SAMANTHA: Yeah. But with Brett tonight, you wanted to tell him the truth, and you didn't, and that's a lie. Now do you see why I'm hurt? I don't want us to lie. I want to be open with you. Accept each other's fucked-uppedness. But her lie— she traps us in this fucking tacit complicity. We collude and omit and backpedal and cover up because we know her secrets; but if she doesn't confide what's going on— she's lying and omitting more, to me, and I'm her best friend and don't want her to—

ROB: Hey, hey, whoa, we're not getting into this again.

SAMANTHA: This isn't the way it's supposed to go. We played Barbie Wedding.

ROB: You know, that really sucks. Your friend's cheating and you're down on us?

SAMANTHA: Rob, wait. Their problems aren't ours.

ROB: Next time, tell me what to say, and I'll say it. I swear.

SAMANTHA: I despise when I act like this. I'm crazy and controlling. Why are you with me?

ROB: Sam, I love you.

SAMANTHA: Say it again.

ROB: No.

(They laugh. Blackout.)

SCENE SEVEN

BRETT and SHELLY's bedroom. We hear the hiss and clank of steam heat. There is a backdrop with pillows attached or painted on so, although BRETT and SHELLY are standing, it looks like we are peering down on their bed. They are sleeping on opposite sides of the bed. BRETT starts wriggling a bit, pretending to get more comfortable. He is trying to position himself closer to SHELLY. He "rolls over" so that he is draping his arm over her. She tries to subtly move away. He snuggles up to her, wrapping his arm around her and holding her tightly. They stay like this for a moment.

SHELLY: Brett, fix that goddamn radiator. It's like an oven in here.

(She unpeels him from her by squirming away. A few breaths pass. He snuggles up to her again, pressing himself into her. He starts to gingerly kiss her neck. One kiss, as if to say goodnight, and then, a few breaths, later a second and a third. He starts to passionately kiss her neck. She lays there. He wraps his hand around her breast, rubbing it. He starts to rub himself against her back and butt. She rolls over so she is on her back; he gets on top of her. They do not look at each other.

They do not kiss. He occasionally kisses the side of her neck. BRETT is now making love to SHELLY. His head is facing away from us. Her face is toward us and she speaks to the audience.)

SHELLY: I position my body so my tits are out. I never do that. But they look good, my tits. They look good. The music's loud; we're talking in each other's ears. My skin, tingling. His breath scours it alive like an SOS pad. "Touch me, please, touch me softly." He hears my thought. His hand falls on my arm, to emphasize something. I laugh. I hope it was funny. I only heard his eyes, and his hand on me. He's smiling. So I'm sure it is. Funny. I need him to make me feel good. And now he's saying funny things. Funny. The more I hold back, the more I have to laugh. It feeds him. He's on a roll. I laugh. My free hand leans on his chest. Funny, it's firm. His muscle tightens at my touch. It's firm. A firm body. Alive. Oh God, he feels alive. My mother used to push me on the swings. I would pump my legs, encouraging the gods to soar me higher. I'd throw my head back, my hair flying. Oh God.

BRETT: *(Climaxing.)* Oh God. Oh God.

(BRETT slumps down on top of SHELLY. For a moment he lays on her. There is silence. He tries to nuzzle her. She does not move. He rolls away from her to his side of the bed. SHELLY steps forward.)

SHELLY: I deserve this. I deserve to feel this way. I'm sick of being deprived. I once was lost in deprivation. Now I'm found. Entitled. I deserve his lips, his hips, his— on my— He tucks his pelvis away from me, hands in his pockets. He's hard. I was afraid I lost it. I lost my virginity in high school in the back of my boyfriend's dad's silver van. He wore a black and orange condom someone gave him as a Hallow-een joke. Now I'm not thinking about Brett. For a second I do, but put it away. Fuck thinking, I'm doing. Not all acts are premeditated. It's life. It's not *Crime and Punishment.* Could Oswald wake up and think, "Today I should shoot the president." Does he have to have a motive? A plan? Can he shoot just because he can? Fuck thinking. "I'm going to the bathroom. Come with me." We don't speak. Holding hands like a real couple. Slams me against the door, clawing his shirt. Fucking belt. I can't get his belt. Who designed pants? Fingertips fumbling. Lips smashing, my tongue madly searching. Like an alien autopsy. Stop, Shelly. Think. Don't think. Think. I am swept up in the most raw, dizzying, whirling thing I have ever and will ever know, and yet I stop and think, "Stop. Think. Don't do it, Shelly. Don't bite or suck too hard. Don't let him leave any marks on your skin. You can still get away with this." Whips me around, perched on the sink. My head arching back 'gainst the mirror. Am I in a movie? I yank my underwear to the side. Am I in a movie? Where's Michael Douglas? "I don't have anything," he says. No trick-or-treat condom, huh? "Fuck, it's over, how can I kill awkwardness?" Play it drunk? Then his fingers slide down, catching my raw, pulpy breath. Pulsing in his hand. He touches me like skin is new. Knock, knock, there's rattling handles. "Just a minute," I want to say, but the words, they bite my throat. My body fights me. "Don't let go. Don't let go. Don't let—" *(Breaths.)* I've never cum like that. Knees wobbly, legs all shaking. Drunk from martinis and his attention. I sit down to pee. I'm on the toilet. His fucking belt. I unzip him. And suck him off. I want him to cum on my tits. I hate when men do that. All that mess. I want him to. Then I flush. Zip up. I was the good girl in school, rapping on the bathroom door and standing on line. Now I pass them—that line-up of me girls; they have no idea what they're missing. I barely remember stumbling into a cab. Don't remember dialing, but I remember talking. Dirty talking. Words like "cock" and "pussy." Cumming again. How easily these words flow from me. I never use them. Cumming again. I watch the cabdriver's greasy eyes in the rearview. I smile at him. I don't care. Brett's asleep on his side of the bed, facing the wall. I know I should shower. His smell sits seeping in my skin. His cum covering me. Pools of dried salt. I should shower. But don't want to erase anything. I crawl into bed. Lay in it. *(SHELLY steps back into bed.)* And it feels good. *(She rolls over on her side, away from BRETT.)*

(Blackout.)

SCENE EIGHT

The opening of this scene—like Scene One, only much more abbreviated—is played in silence by BRETT and SHELLY. SHELLY sits, working on her presentation. The morning weather report plays on the television. As if running a little late for work, BRETT doesn't sit while eating breakfast and reading the newspaper. Heavy weight in air. A lot unspoken. Finally, BRETT leaves. Phone rings.

SHELLY: Hello? Oh God, where are you? He didn't see you? I'll buzz you up. Hurry.

(SHELLY removes her pajamas; underneath, she wears sexy lingerie. She prepares. A few moments later, we hear a knock offstage. SHELLY goes offstage to answer door.)

STEVE: *(From off.)* Hey, beautiful.

(We start to hear passionate kissing, etc.)

SHELLY: *(From off.)* Wait. I'm ashamed. My period.

STEVE: *(From off.)* I don't care.

(The sounds of gruff standing-up sex are heard. STEVE and SHELLY propel onstage kissing, all disheveled, in various states of undress. They are laughing like two people in love. They continue to play—kissing, rolling on the floor, etc. This whole scene is foreplay.)

SHELLY: When you called, I had this terrible thought you'd run into each other from the subway.

STEVE: No, I need—

(She kisses him long and hard.)

STEVE: Need my morning jolt of caffeine. Waited at that coffee place, reading the funnies.

SHELLY: Hah.

STEVE: What?

SHELLY: I love that. You never hear "funnies" anymore. Funnies. Funnies. Feels funny saying it. Funnies.

STEVE: What do you call them?

SHELLY: Comics.

STEVE: Do you say—"stand in line" or "stand on line"?

SHELLY: On line. You?

STEVE: Queued up, when I'm in London.

(He is kissing her neck.)

SHELLY: Ugh, you're driving me crazy. Stop that. *(Laughs.)* Don't. Stop. Don't. Stop. Don't stop. Don't stop!

(They are laughing again.)

STEVE: At McDonald's, do you order "for here or to go" or "to stay or to go"?

SHELLY: Um...Wendy's and "to stay or to go."

STEVE: Wendy's? C'mon!

SHELLY: Those Frosties ease all pain. Give me those Frosties, McDonald's fries, and Burger King's burger, it's charbroiled, and I'll never want again.

STEVE: Never?

SHELLY: Try me.

(They kiss. He slides his hand down her pants.)

STEVE: "Drop by" or "drop in"?

SHELLY: Huh?

STEVE: When you visit, do you drop by or drop in?

SHELLY: Um—"stop in."

STEVE: "Garbage" or "rubbish"?

SHELLY: Mmmm...No one says rubbish.

STEVE: My grandfather. Actually that's where I got "funnies."

SHELLY: Oooh.

STEVE: This is my mom's dad. My father barely knew his. Gone off to war, and died soon after he came home. They never had a chance to get close. No, this is Mom's dad. Or was. Passed a couple of years ago.

SHELLY: S-sorry.

STEVE: Yeah. Thanks. Great guy. Reminds me of Humphrey Bogart. Always taking care of everyone.

SHELLY: Would a loved to— oh! Right there, right there— meet him.

STEVE: Yeah. For sure.

(SHELLY orgasms. STEVE removes his fingers. Puts them in his mouth. Then kisses her. Putting his fingers in both their mouths.)

SHELLY: Hold me tighter. Tighter.

STEVE: ..."Soda" or "pop"?

SHELLY: Coke.

(They laugh.)

SHELLY: I hate it when people say "facial tissue." "Hand me a tissue, please." Ugh, it's a Kleenex.

STEVE: You such a good girl. You want what they tell you.

SHELLY: That's my life... I mean, my work.

(Breaths of awkwardness. She flips him around so she is behind him, grabbing his hair. She bends him over and starts grinding into his ass.)

SHELLY: Do I say "Take me in the bedroom, I'll ravage you"...?

STEVE: Or...?

SHELLY: That's it. Take me in the bedroom.

STEVE: Not the bedroom.

SHELLY: I said, "Yes."

STEVE: (Stopping her.) No. Not his bed.

SHELLY: (Grabbing his hair. Pushing him back down.) The kitchen table.

STEVE: The kitchen table.

SHELLY: The sink. The roof. The taxi. The— Oh, shit, I have to get ready. It kills me how little time we have together.

STEVE: Don't ruin the time we have, focusing on the time we don't. Ditch the presentation. Let's go to the Bahamas.

SHELLY: Get thee behind me, Satan!

STEVE: Fine, no Bahamas. But I thought you finished preparing days ago.

SHELLY: Thanks to you. I mean get ready. Shower.

STEVE: Be bold. Go like this.

SHELLY: Oh, yeah, hair disheveled. Reeking of sex. Oh, there's another. My mom says women don't sweat—they glow.

STEVE: Rubbish!

(They laugh.)

STEVE: I'm extremely proud of you.

SHELLY: Thank you. Means a lot. The changes you told me made me better. I'll call you the minute it's done. Ha, that *would* be funny if I showed up like this. Why not? I've sworn off underwear since you.

STEVE: Free at last. Free at last. Thank God almighty, I'm sexually free at last.

SHELLY: Ignore the ever-so-sexy period underwear, of course.

STEVE: Yes, ma'am.

SHELLY: So— hop your passionate, sweaty ass in the shower with me, preacher man.

STEVE: I was going to shower at the gym after I work out.

SHELLY: I'll give you a workout.

STEVE: You just did.

SHELLY: I'll give you another.

STEVE: I could never get enough.

SHELLY: Hey—if you don't want to—

STEVE: No. I'll shower twice. But, be warned, I love James Bond showers.

SHELLY: Oh, I don't have time.

STEVE: Time's all we have. Till we die. C'mon, you'll love it. I'll turn on the hot water. Then hit the cold. It braces you awake. Like sex. You feel alive.

(SHELLY and STEVE exit to shower. The shower runs. A few moments pass where the hot water is on, then the cold, and we immediately hear the two of them letting out higher pitched sighs and "Oh my God's.")

(Blackout. Their laughter carries underneath the blackout, climaxing and abruptly shutting off as lights snap up on BRETT at computer.)

SCENE NINE

BRETT at work. Silence. BRETT sits in his cubicle. Silence. A moment passes. BRETT starts to play solitaire on his computer. We hear the mechanical sounds of "ffshhkk" as each card is dealt. He plays for a long time. Blackout. The mechanical sounds of "ffshhkk" resound through the darkness, getting increasingly louder.

ACT II

SCENE TEN

SHELLY's presentation. She speaks toward the audience.

SHELLY: Next slide, please.

(Lights up on SAMANTHA and ROB overly, commercially smiling. SAMANTHA holds Crest, ROB holds an organic health toothpaste.)

SHELLY: We are in the business of manipulation. This is our target audience. This woman has inherited her parents' patterns. Mom and Dad bought Crest, and so does she. But she is still willing to break free. Next slide, please.

(Lights up on BRETT with remote control, watching TV. He is smiling.)

SHELLY: Here is our problem. In the past, reaching him, our target audience, was easy— Develop content he wants to watch and bombard him with commercials. Hence, "soap operas" were developed to sell detergent.

(Lights out on BRETT. Lights up, he is deadened.)

SHELLY: However, presently, he is deadened. His whole life, he's been assaulted with commercials for "the biggest" and "the best." But he no longer believes that he can be the best. So he senses our manipulation.

(Lights out on BRETT. Lights up on him smiling.)

SHELLY: With the proliferation of TiVo, picture-in-picture units, and DirecTV, he can fast forward, split the screen, and ignore us: ultimately, never watching an advertisement. He's not paying attention to us anymore. We must develop new and subversive means to satisfy our needs. It is necessary. To ensure our survival. Next slide.

(Lights up on BRETT and STEVE, frozen in a physical struggle over a Coke.)

SHELLY: As you see, I am suggesting we eliminate commercials. Sitcoms and dramas play uninterrupted. But we seize control. The plot of your favorite program will be *about* the product. The kooky neighbor drops in or drops by and battles over the last Coke. And of course, thanks to the laugh track, hilarity ensues.

(BRETT, STEVE, ROB, and SAMANTHA laugh mechanically like a laugh track.)

SHELLY: We need to give them what they want. And get what we need. If we make Coke the focus of their favorite TV show,

(Lights up on BRETT and STEVE, snuggling and proudly displaying a Coke.)

SHELLY: they can reject their parents' ideas of morality and habit, and buy Coke.

(Lights up on SAMANTHA and ROB, both triumphantly holding organic toothpaste.)

SHELLY: Or buy toothpaste made with mud.

(Lights out on BRETT, STEVE, SAMANTHA, and ROB.)

SHELLY: We are in the business of manipulation. And they will not feel the pain inherent in being manipulated. Because we are doing what's best for them but what they're afraid to ask for.

(Blackout.)

SCENE ELEVEN

ROB and SAMANTHA's apartment. They are preparing to go out for a celebratory dinner with BRETT and SHELLY.

SAMANTHA: Rob! Robert! You're always late and it's unacceptable. You ready?

ROB: I'm in the bathroom.

SAMANTHA: What're you doing in there?

ROB: I'm going to the bathroom.

(ROB enters.)

SAMANTHA: What were you doing in there? Reading?

ROB: Stalling... I shouldn't have opened my fat Mr. Mouth. "Oh don't worry, babe, we never see Brett... blah, blah, blah." He should move in and sleep on the couch.

SAMANTHA: Alright, let's go. Come on, babe, it won't be that bad.

ROB: I feel like Oliver North around Brett—

SAMANTHA: No, wait. Wear the blue shirt.

ROB: And Benedict Arnold.

SAMANTHA: Let's leave the conspiracy theories to John, shall we.

ROB: Where's my lip stuff?

SAMANTHA: How do I look? Do I look fat in this?

ROB: You look like Switzerland. You look neutral.

SAMANTHA: There was nothing neutral about Switzerland.

ROB: Babe, you look fantastic. Where's my lip stuff?

(They start frantically searching for the lip stuff as they talk.)

SAMANTHA: Look, if you really don't want to go…

ROB: No. We'll talk about nothing.

SAMANTHA: Good. You're going. Understand?

ROB: Figured. Maybe I'll shoot myself.

SAMANTHA: Messy death.

ROB: No—in the leg, like a draft dodger.

SAMANTHA: No more History Channel for you.

ROB: What? Hitler Week is coming up.

SAMANTHA: Can't you watch sharks?

ROB: The last time I watched the Nature Channel… I still have nightmares.

SAMANTHA: Can you imagine?— "Sorry, Rob shot himself."

ROB: It was this special about blue crabs. They molt their shell, you know, soft-shell crabs?, and the females molt first. They're all vulnerable. So, the men lie on top of them with their shells, protecting them

against harm. And the women just lay there protected by the men until their shells grow back. And then the males molt. The women lie on top of them. And you know, the same thing, the men are all vulnerable. So the women lie on top of them, and then *eat* them.

SAMANTHA: That was really interesting. When's your book come out?

ROB: They eat them!

SAMANTHA: Yeah, I got it, let's go, Robert, we gotta go.

ROB: They eat them!

SAMANTHA: They eat them. C'mon, babe, let's go. You have money?

ROB: Yeah. Wait— Are we paying for this one, too?

SAMANTHA: We invited them to celebrate the presentation, I think—

ROB: No, hey, that's cool, that's fine. I just want to know so there's not that weird thing at the end, where everyone's shuffling for money. "Oh, let's split it on three different cards, and one-fourth cash." It's like, are we friends? I'd rather pay. As long as you aren't conspiring with Shelly, "So. How are you doing?," every time he steps away.

SAMANTHA: You are such an insensitive asshole.

ROB: Hey, whoa, I am not insensitive. And I'm not an asshole.

SAMANTHA: Well, that was an asshole thing to say.

ROB: No, it wasn't.

SAMANTHA: Yes, it was, Rob.

ROB: No.

SAMANTHA: Yes, it—

ROB: No.

SAMANTHA: Fine, you're right, it wasn't.

ROB: No, I'm telling you, it wasn't. I think it's a totally legitimate concern. I'm not gonna feel comfortable with those she-nanigans going on. You two, stirring shit. I don't want to be a party to it, and I don't want to sit there, silently pretending I don't know what's happening.

SAMANTHA: Fine. That's fine.

ROB: I mean, if you think that's an ass-hole thing to say, then that's your perspec-tive, so maybe to you it is, even though it was not intended to be, but I am certainly not an asshole person. Or a wrong person.

SAMANTHA: A wrong person? What? What are you talking about?

ROB: Look. You criticize me. Fine. You don't like what I do. Fine. You don't like what I say, or how I act. Fine. But don't criticize me as a person. I don't appreciate it. And I won't tolerate it anymore.

SAMANTHA: Okay.

ROB: You put me down to change me. To make yourself feel better. I don't do that to you.

SAMANTHA: You're right—

ROB: I mean, if you do something that pisses me off—I don't say, "You're a crazy, controlling bitch" or "a siren-like freak, tempting me towards death."

SAMANTHA: Thank God.

ROB: That's right. And why? It hurts your feelings and it's mean. So, if you don't like how I'm acting or something I said, just tell me that, okay? But leave *me* out of it.

SAMANTHA: I'm sorry. You're right. ...What you said, sounded, from my per-spective, assholic.

ROB: Yeah, I got it, thanks.

SAMANTHA: Now, come here and kiss me.

(He does.)

SAMANTHA: Don't forget—we like each other.

ROB: Yeah. I'll try.

(He smacks her on the ass, and they rush out together. Blackout.)

SCENE TWELVE

ROB and SAMANTHA and SHELLY and BRETT out to dinner—celebrating SHELLY's presentation. They sit facing the audience, but speak as if they are talking intimately.

ROB: It doesn't really matter what reli-gion you are. We're all Americans.

BRETT: Yeah, no, I agree. But we all have specific cultural whatevers. Our back-grounds affect who we are—

SHELLY: Yes.

BRETT: —and what we want.

SAMANTHA: Definitely.

ROB: But embedded in that, or linked to that, we are all Americans. And that means our cultural identities are filtered through this American...uh...filter.

SAMANTHA: Prism?

SHELLY: Perspective.

ROB: Right, it's from an American per-spective. Like, I'm not a Puritan, I don't even know any Puritans—

SAMANTHA: They still exist?

ROB: I don't know. I don't think they're like Shakers.

BRETT: Like the Amish.

SHELLY: No, the Amish are like the Quakers.

BRETT: Which are the Shakers?

ROB: Their religion is no sex.

SHELLY: Just furniture.

SAMANTHA: It's good furniture.

ROB: But, Puritans, they're like Starbucks, they're everywhere. Everyone who came to this country and wanted to be American developed Puritanical sensibilities. You know, hard work'll make you feel good. Sexual repression.

SAMANTHA: In Europe, they have siestas.

SHELLY: Spain. Siestas are in Spain.

SAMANTHA: All the businesses shut down and you let loose.

(Simultaneously.)

{

ROB: *(As Jack Nicholson in* The Shining.*)* Well, "All work and no play makes Jack a baaaad boy."

BRETT: *(As Homer from* The Simpsons.*)* "All work and no play makes Homer a something something."

(BRETT and ROB laugh.)

SHELLY: Dull boy. "All WORK and no PLAY makes Jack a DULL boy."

(Lights snap out. When the lights come up, SAMANTHA and ROB are mid-sentence. ROB picks at his chapped lips.)

SAMANTHA: Robert! Stop picking.

ROB: Do you have my lip stuff? I can't help it. I need it.

SAMANTHA: You're making it worse.

ROB: Will you leave me alone.

SAMANTHA: No. It hurts me to watch you doing that to yourself.

(Lights dim slightly again. They rise on SHELLY and ROB.)

SHELLY: Oh, I want to go back.

ROB: No, man, not me. I almost didn't finish. Like Bill Cosby says, "Sam graduated summa cum laude. I graduated 'Oh thank you Lawdy.'"

SHELLY: Oh, no, I mean, it was a dream world. Your friends come built-in with your dorm room, and you have a purpose and a point.

ROB: What degree would you go back for?

SHELLY: A master's.

ROB: So you can get a green jacket?

SHELLY: What do you mean?

ROB: A green jacket for the Masters.

(A few breaths pass.)

SHELLY: I don't know what I'd study, but totally think about going back.

(Lights dim again. Rise on SAMANTHA and SHELLY.)

SAMANTHA: She just sat there?

SHELLY: Oh, she just sat there steaming.

SAMANTHA: Not even—good job or congratulations?

SHELLY: Steaming.

SAMANTHA: We hate her.

SHELLY: Ugh, we hate her the most; she sits there— How many times can she slip in her pedigrees…when I was at "Harvard," my "Harvard" professor said "Harvard" students are— fuck you, "Harvard"; and it's always "Harvard" with her teeth clenched.

SAMANTHA: Like she owns— Is the cosmos bigger than the universe?

SHELLY: At that point, it's all one big black hole.

SAMANTHA: Amen. But you shoved her "Harvard" right down her throat.

SHELLY: I did. I totally did. It's the first time I didn't feel like a glorified secretary.

(Lights dim slightly. When the lights come up, everyone is looking at ROB, in mid-story. Breaths pass.)

ROB: They eat them!

(ROB and BRETT laugh. Lights dim slightly. Rise on SAMANTHA and SHELLY, mid-sentence.)

SAMANTHA: —Is great. But, still, I wish we could have cooked.

SHELLY: I burned all the pots.

SAMANTHA: C'mon.

SHELLY: I have. I leave them on and forget them. This is the year I burnt the pots.

(Lights dim. Rise on SHELLY and ROB.)

SHELLY: And all he does is take and take until there's nothing left. And only after he's totally used her up. After she's cared for him, and given him everything she has. Everything he has. After she's given him support, and comfort and love his whole life. After she's a stump of what she once was. He's taken everything. And he comes back and wants more.

ROB: Well, I dunno. I love Shel Silver-stein.

(Lights dim slightly. Rise on BRETT and SHELLY. BRETT speaks in lowered, confidential tones.)

BRETT: What's wrong? *(Breaths.)* You okay? *(Breaths.)* Something wrong? You

seem—you seem—like— Something bothering you? You alright? *(Breaths.)* What's wrong? *(Breaths.)* Honey?… *(Breaths.)*

(Lights dim. Rise on SAMANTHA, SHELLY, and BRETT. SAMANTHA and BRETT are laughing.)

SAMANTHA: That's hysterical!

BRETT: Right?

SAMANTHA: God, that is—that's just— Ha!

BRETT: And I'm just staring at him— Warren.

SAMANTHA: No!

BRETT: I mean, really staring him down. Like eyes bugging out!

SAMANTHA: Like in the cartoons?

BRETT: Totally like in the cartoons! Thought they might pop outta my face.

SAMANTHA: That is— Did you tell Shelly that? 'Cause that's—

BRETT: Yeah. I did.

SAMANTHA: 'Cause— Shell, did you hear this?

BRETT: No. Yeah. I told her.

(Lights out on SHELLY.)

SAMANTHA: Did she die?

BRETT: She thought it was amusing. Yes.

SAMANTHA: 'Cause that's— Ha!— That's ridiculous. And you just stared at him?

BRETT: Yep.

SAMANTHA: *(The moment of flirtation becoming more tangible.)* That was bold. That was real— That was bold.

BRETT: Yeah, well, I'm a crazy guy.

SAMANTHA: I bet. I bet.

BRETT: *(Dismissing the flirtatious tension.)* Hey, by the way, thanks for getting Shelly home the other night.

SAMANTHA: Sure. No problem.

BRETT: I felt bad, 'cause I was asleep, or I would've come and got her; I mean, we don't fight like that, so— I mean— I was glad she could call you.

SAMANTHA: Hey, Brett, don't worry about it. I'll do whatever she needs.

(Lights rise on all of them. They just sit and eat. Silence. Blackout.)

SCENE THIRTEEN

SHELLY and SAMANTHA and JOHN at a swanky bar.

JOHN: Well you don't see an ad with two guys making out...

SAMANTHA: What about Abercrombie and Fitch?

JOHN: Well, that's like gay porn. All those football players in the shower? What are they selling—towels? They're naked, they're selling jeans, where are their jeans.

SAMANTHA: Yummy. I'll buy their jeans.

JOHN: My mom came to visit. I hid the catalog.

SHELLY: Exciting sex sells.

JOHN: Oh? Do tell.

SHELLY: What's that mean?

SAMANTHA: He means your work.

JOHN: I mean, dish about the new man.

SHELLY: Sam!

SAMANTHA: John!

SHELLY: You told him? Does Rob know?

SAMANTHA: Of course not.

JOHN: C'mon, ladies, we've been dying to talk about it. So, why beat around your bush?

SAMANTHA: There's nothing to say.

SAMANTHA: *(To SHELLY.)* I'm sorry. I had to talk to someone.

JOHN: *(To SHELLY.)* You're blushing!

SHELLY: I just— I haven't felt in a long time. Hunger. Fulfillment. Just felt.

SAMANTHA: You can't keep on like this.

SHELLY: I couldn't keep on as I was either. Before I met this person, I would go to the bank when I didn't have to, because the tellers smiled at me.

JOHN: All the vague, nongendered language—"*this person*" this and "*this person*" that. You're not switch-hitting are you?

SAMANTHA: John! ...Wait. *Are* you? I assumed it's a man.

JOHN: By the way, bisexuality—very in right now.

SAMANTHA: Shelly, you can't see a future—

SHELLY: I don't want to talk specifics, it'll ruin the magic.

JOHN: If we keep it anonymous, can we talk sex?

SHELLY: Definitely.

SAMANTHA: You don't know their name?

SHELLY: His name. It is a him.

SAMANTHA: We don't know him, though, right.

SHELLY: No.

JOHN: So how did you meet Mr. Right Now?

SHELLY: Brett and I stopped by this bar before a nice dinner. Things are shit between us, so I wore this great little black dress— you know, the one with the really low back.

SAMANTHA: Oh I love that dress. John, she looks so fierce in this dress.

JOHN: I bet.

SHELLY: I know, and I did my hair off my neck. But I was kind of pissed 'cause Brett's totally oblivious to all the work I did. I mean, he invites Steve to meet us for a drink—

SAMANTHA: Steve? Wait, oh my God, it's not Steve.

SHELLY: Steve? No, no, no, let me tell the story. I said you don't know him. He was there with Steve. So, Brett and I get into this huge, stupid fight, and he explodes at me and storms out. And I'm really hurt and I'm drinking with this other person.

SAMANTHA: Where's Steve?

SHELLY: He left. And this other person and I started talking about what happened with Brett.

SAMANTHA: So Steve doesn't know, right? He didn't pick up any vibe before he left?

SHELLY: No. No, it was totally innocent. …It sounds so cliche but he was consoling me. And one thing led to another. And that's it. (SHELLY takes out a cigarette.)

SAMANTHA: You're smoking?

SHELLY: When I drink.

SAMANTHA: Since when did you start smoking?

SHELLY: When I drink.

JOHN: You're not pregnant.

SHELLY: No! Why?

JOHN: No, no, I'm sorry, I meant—I meant about the cigarettes. It says, "May harm pregnant women" and you're not pregnant, so no worries.

SHELLY: See, Sam, it's all good.

(JOHN takes a cigarette.)

SAMANTHA: I thought you stopped.

JOHN: No one likes a quitter.

SAMANTHA: Oh, fuck it. I need one. Give me a cigarette.

JOHN: That a girl.

(SAMANTHA takes a cigarette.)

JOHN: So have you had sex yet?

SHELLY: The next morning before work.

SAMANTHA: They fucked on the kitchen table! Oh God. Give me another cigarette. For backup.

SHELLY: Yeah, I called him from the cab on the way home. We made plans to meet.

SAMANTHA: Oh, yeah, I meant to—

SHELLY: I couldn't stop thinking about him.

SAMANTHA: Brett asked me about it.

SHELLY: What?! Asked you?! Like what?!

SAMANTHA: Well, not asked me. Thanked me.

SHELLY: For what?

SAMANTHA: Getting you home safe from the bar.

SHELLY: Oh, God, I told him I called you. What did you say?

SAMANTHA: I don't remember. Something.

SHELLY: Something? And you didn't tell me?

SAMANTHA: Well, you didn't tell me I—

JOHN: Are you two done? Because I want to hear about him.

SHELLY: He's got strong hands and nice shoes.

JOHN: The sex. I wanna hear about the sex. My last threesome was with Ben and Jerry.

SAMANTHA: What happened to "Don't gossip, accept everything"?

JOHN: The rock garden's not doing it for me. I need some vicarious living.

SHELLY: I feel totally out of control, and absolutely safe. There're no logical steps. I'm not on top, I'm not on bottom. We are always interwoven.

SAMANTHA: God.

JOHN: What's his number?

SHELLY: Sorry, John, he's unlisted.

JOHN: Well, I say—God bless. Let's drink—to no top.

ALL: To no top!

(They clink glasses. Blackout.)

SCENE FOURTEEN

BRETT and SHELLY's. The only light is from the TV. The sounds of bad porn. BRETT is alone in the apartment. He is masturbating in the greenish glow of the television. Blackout.

SCENE FIFTEEN

BRETT and SHELLY's. BRETT is in the same position, asleep. SHELLY enters. BRETT stirs a bit.

SHELLY: Brett, honey, you awake?

BRETT: Yeah. I'm up. I'm up.

SHELLY: I'm home.

BRETT: How were the girls?

SHELLY: Great. We had a great time. C'mon, Brett, let's get you to bed.

BRETT: No, no, I'm fine here. I'm not asleeping.

SHELLY: Brett? What did you do tonight? *(Silence.)* Huh? Honey? …Brett? *(A moment. And then quietly and directly.)* Will you make love to me? …You're good. You're a good, good man. Be good to me. Tonight. Soft, sweet. Beyond "I love you's." *(Breaths pass.)* …Honey?

(She goes to him, kneels down, puts her face to his prone hand. BRETT awakens, startled at her touch.)

BRETT: What?! Shell?

SHELLY: Shhh. Honey, it's me, I'm right here.

BRETT: I was— you asked me what I did. Tonight…

SHELLY: Yeah.

BRETT: I was just thinking.

SHELLY: Shhhh. It's okay. You were sleeping, Brett. C'mon, let's tuck you in.

BRETT: No, no, I was just thinking.

SHELLY: You're okay. You're safe. Shhhh, honey. I was talking and you didn't answer.

BRETT: No, no, I was thinking. Of what to say. I— the fish were— I was swimming with the sharks. I—oh—what did I—? I watched some movies. Bad, bang-'em-up, explosion movies. I ate. How were the girls? John. Sam. They're good?

SHELLY: C'mon, honey, up-see-daisy, let's get you into bed.

BRETT: Okay. I'll be in, in a minute. Just going to sit for a minute. I just need to think.

(BRETT is asleep again. SHELLY puts her cheek back on the top of his hand. They do not move. Blackout.)

SCENE SIXTEEN

SAMANTHA and SHELLY at a clothing store. SAMANTHA is trying on dresses. SHELLY sits outside the dressing room, and SAMANTHA is modeling. They have many bags from many stores with them.

SAMANTHA: I'm telling you, three years go so quickly.

SHELLY: Three years…wow.

SAMANTHA: Right? He's so funny, too. He's all secretive, but I know where we're going. I might as well have planned it myself. Called for reservations. Bought my gift…

SHELLY: What, you're going back to, what's it called, where you had your first date.

SAMANTHA: Yamaguchi Sushi. Yeah. And this bracelet, oh my God.

SHELLY: He gave it to you already?

SAMANTHA: No, but we were at Tiffany's a couple months ago and I basically told him to get it for me.

SHELLY: That's great.

SAMANTHA: So I'm sure he got it. Yeah, three years. Yours is coming up, right? That's why you have to be certain, you know?

SHELLY: Do you like this dress, or no? It's beautiful, but—it's—

SAMANTHA: Yeah?

SHELLY: Definitely, try the other one.

SAMANTHA: Okay, thanks. I'm just saying. You have to—

SHELLY: Definitely. The other one. The scooping neckline. Lets the girls breathe a bit. This one's so conservative.

SAMANTHA: You have to leave him.

SHELLY: That's— I'm fine.

SAMANTHA: I want you happy. So get out.

SHELLY: We're working through—

SAMANTHA: With another guy?

SHELLY: I wasn't going to tell you—

SAMANTHA: I'm not judging you, but—

SHELLY: —I knew you'd use it against me.

SAMANTHA: I'm not—

SHELLY: Yes. You are. And fine. You need to. Judge me so your pretty life seems intact. Stays perfect.

SAMANTHA: I'm trying to help—

SHELLY: Judge me so you don't have to admit you or Rob could do the same.

SAMANTHA: I would never let it get to this point. I would've— Break up with Brett.

SHELLY: Well, no, of course you wouldn't let it get to this point. You tell Rob exactly how to act.

SAMANTHA: You bet your ass. But if he did, I'd break it off. If I had a fling. A one-night thing. All drunk and crazy. Fine. But this is ongoing. I'm not saying you are a bad person. Or a wrong person. You've just—

SHELLY: This is the best thing I've ever done.

SAMANTHA: So run off with your new guy. I'm all for it. But what you're doing now—the deception— It's killing me.

SHELLY: It's not about the other—

SAMANTHA: I'm sorry, I can't keep it in. I can't trust you.

SHELLY: It's not about you either.

SAMANTHA: You're not living in a bubble, Shell. You say you're happy now, that's great, but everyone else's hurt.

SHELLY: This is not about you.

SAMANTHA: It is. I looked up to you. When we were kids, you always made the plans. Let's play house. Let's move to New York.

SHELLY: I'm not that girl.

SAMANTHA: No, you're not. But you were. And I envied you. I shouldn't be the one telling you how to act. You should tell me.

SHELLY: Well, I got tired of telling everyone. You. Brett. What about me? I gotta take care of me.

SAMANTHA: So stop trapping yourself in lies, and make a change. I want to help you get back to being that girl. Go to the other guy… Or don't leave Brett. Go back and fix it. I don't care which. But do something. Then everything can go back to the way we planned. I mean, hell! You used to plan Barbie weddings!

SHELLY: She's a fucking doll, Sam. She's not real. If she were, she'd be five-nine and a hundred and ten pounds. This is life. It's ugly. It doesn't have a thirty-nine-inch bust and twenty-three-inch waist. And I can't fit into that myth anymore.

SAMANTHA: It's not a myth; it's our plan. You find a guy, we raise our kids together—

SHELLY: It's a delusion. I don't want to be that girl anymore. There's no Prince Charming. There's no Brett Butler at the bottom of the stairs. And I'm not going to search for some man, some Wizard of Oz, to give me my heart and courage back.

SAMANTHA: Look, I don't want to live with a bunch of letters and numbers after my address, and that's what it comes down to. I don't want to be Apartment Six-E my whole life, and neither do you. I want to walk up to my front door and step into my living room. One buzzer. One mailbox. One home. And you're right, I push Rob around. Because he needs me to. He may need some work—he may need my help—but I want him sitting in my living room when I walk in. And that's no delusion. I walk around this city and all I see are babies. Mothers and nannies coming out of their living rooms, and bowling me over with these baby bumper cars. And see those little…things—those faces. And I want one. Every time I see one, I want to either steal and run away with it, or smother it. I don't know. But I want one. And so do you.

(Breaths. Blackout.)

SCENE SEVENTEEN

STEVE and BRETT playing racquetball. They are playing with no ball, striking the floor with the edge of the racquet to make the sound of each hit. BRETT scores the shot and the win.

STEVE: Nice shot.

BRETT: Brett's still got it. He's down but not out!

STEVE: Yeah, well, when you see Brett, tell him I'm going to kick his third-person ass next game.

BRETT: Just give me a quick breather. The body's not— I mean, I still got a six pack, I'm just keeping it in the cooler.

(Breaths pass. They hang out.)

BRETT: This city makes you old.

STEVE: The *Island of the Dead.*

BRETT: You saw that Brando garbage with the midget?

STEVE: That's *Island—Dr. Moreau.* No, *Island of the Dead*'s a series of paintings, and I always think— that's Manhattan. The *Island of the Dead.*

BRETT: Built on burials. Know that? Washington Square. Union Square. They were cemeteries.

STEVE: World Trade.

(Breaths pass.)

BRETT: Yeah.

(BRETT goes to the back corner of the court, upstage, and gets some Tums.)

STEVE: Gotta lay off those Tums, buddy. You need an intervention, or something, some twelve-step program.

BRETT: My insides are rotting. Too much trapped—whatever.

STEVE: Emotion?

BRETT: Pain. Whatever. Years of repressed— My whole family's full of hot air.

STEVE: You seen someone—?

BRETT: —About it? Nah. My whole— We all suffer from Dunlop and Dick-do.

STEVE: Oh. Huh?

BRETT: Dunlop's where your belly done lop over your belt. Dick-do's where your stomach sticks out more than your dick do.

STEVE: That's awful.

BRETT: Hey, gotta fire an occasional Hail Mary. Never know who or what'll help you out.

STEVE: Fire it up.

BRETT: Did my laundry, felt a sense of accomplishment.

STEVE: Wow. *(Breaths.)* ...You do your own laundry? I drop it off.

BRETT: I gotta do something. It's like— I've been reading this— Well, with Shelly, I feel like— I mean, I'm firing blanks over here. Not like, "firing blanks," you know like, can't get it up or whatever, but like coming up blank, on ideas.

STEVE: Yeah. That sucks.

BRETT: ...Yeah.

STEVE: Maybe if you told me—

BRETT: No. That's okay. It's complicated.

STEVE: I wanna help—

BRETT: It's gonna work itself out... I'm just—I'm getting pushed along by the waves. I thought you could steer me.

STEVE: I think men in general—we don't talk about the hows of sex.

BRETT: I didn't say anything about sex. I said I'm *not* having trouble— No, no, I'm sorry. Go ahead. G'ahead.

STEVE: That's cool. Whatever—just—

BRETT: No, no, no. I'm sorry. Steve. Please.

STEVE: Well. You gotta know the score.

BRETT: Uh-huh.

STEVE: If you want to take care of her. You gotta know yourself. So you can hear what she's asking of you.

BRETT: And this is about sex? The hows or whatever.

STEVE: It's everything. A woman will tell you what she wants, but we don't know HOW to listen. With sex it's understandable, because no one teaches us anything. It's as if no one taught you how to drive, and then you had to pick up your first date in a stick shift.

BRETT: You know how I learned? My older brother was having it, and my father left *Playboys* under the bathroom sink.

STEVE: Yeah, and now you're older than the centerfolds, and you're here asking me.

BRETT: That supposed to make me feel better?

STEVE: Nothing makes you feel better if you don't know the score. Like going to a strip club. If we pretend the strippers want to date us it's depressing. It's self-deception. They want your dough. And if you know that—then you can look, laugh, and hang out with your friends. *Playboy*? Same thing. All that fresh, tight, pink is airbrushed. As long as you know it is what it is: Great. I read the articles. They're better than those fake tits. Truth. That's what I want. The truth makes me feel better.

BRETT: So what's the truth about sex?

STEVE: Hear what they want. And then figure out HOW to give it to them. Women do. They talk about it at camp or read about it in magazines. Ya know, trade stories or techniques. Though I can't figure out why they don't talk about how to make themselves happy. Most women don't know their own body parts. That's why they want you. To teach them. To reawaken the tiger. But men, they talk about who did what to who but not the hows.

BRETT: You sound like fucking Dr. Suess... Horton Humps the Ho'.

STEVE: Huh?

BRETT: Ya know, "who did what to who but not the Horton Humps the Ho'..."

STEVE: Look, you're on the right track—asking me. Most men never ask their buddies, "How'd you do that, make that girl feel good?" And so I think if you want to know the score, you gotta do some research. Start reading books. Talk to your friends who are girls and ask what they like, what really gets them off.

BRETT: Yeah. I got a book. For couples.

STEVE: I'm saying, you can't read this book with half the couple. Ask around so you can improve yourself. Then you can help her. That's what I did. I decided—if I don't amount to shit in this world, I will be a good lover.

BRETT: Yeah?

STEVE: That's the ultimate "feel good"—taking care of someone else. But you have to know who you are first. Like me. I'm a lesbian.

BRETT: C'mon.

STEVE: I am. A lipstick lesbian. I like fashion and cooking, and decorating. And women. I like soft and strong and emotional and sexual. And women. Brett, outside the bedroom, you're not going to fig-

ure men and women out— we're different. Men, it's straightforward. We like to
know what's what. Not to say we're simple,
or pigs. We just don't like the bullshit. I
can't even pretend I got answers for you
outside the bedroom; there are fundamental differences. Like when you're shower-
ing with a woman, you face forward to
rinse your hair, right?

BRETT: Yeah, right, I face the… spigot
thing. The spout.

STEVE: And you put your head down to
rinse your hair, right? She faces backward
and puts her head back.

BRETT: Yeah?

STEVE: I don't know why, but different.
How do those long hairs get stuck to the
shower wall? They put them there—ya
know that? They stick their hair to the
fucking shower. The guy's counting every
piece that goes down the drain and she's
collecting them into some hairy origami.
Women hate words like "moist" and "panties" and "cunt." Men hate words like "no."
Outside the bedroom, we are just fundamentally, no rhyme, no reason, different.
But inside, throw all that stereotypical
gendered crap out.

(Blackout.)

SCENE EIGHTEEN

JOHN on the phone to CHRIS.

JOHN: This is the worst day ever, Chris.
I'm Depressed Chopra… Don't worry,
honey, I'm not going to redecorate the
apartment again. Well, it's just no fun to
do it alone… No, I gave up on the Atkins;
I started the Ramadan diet. Because I've
never met a fat Muslim. So I'm fasting
sunrise to sunset and then all the ice cream
I want. I figure I can blow up in time to

be a Macy's Day float… Well, I'm just
freaking out. Aren't you freaking out? I'm
in the checkout, I can't tell the difference
between the *National Enquirer* and the
New York Times… The headlines are the
same! Scaring us into some apocalyptic
mindset. Well, sure, Chris, they may have
nuclear capabilities, but we don't know.
And why? Because they won't tell us. We
have a history of being lied to… How can
being lied to be for your own good?…
No, not because we're Americans. They
hate us because we show 'em we care,
make promises to be there, and then leave
'em when they need us most. I'm not in-
sinuating anything. Chris, I'm talking
about the U.S. government, not about
how you leave me. I'm telling you. Our
streets will continue to run with blood…
No, not nukes. We should be scared of
the disenfranchised; who are so hurt, so
unsatisfied, they see no other way but to
lash out… Well, this thing with Shelly's
got me thinking. She's just acting out to
make herself happy and— No, I'm not
happy with you gone, I'm not happy
with— Oh, hold on. *(Clicks over to call
waiting.)* Hello? Oh, hey Rob… No, she's
running late. Great! See ya soon. Bye,
babe. *(Assuming an overtly straight voice.)*
I mean, later, doggie-dog, dude. *(Clicks
back to CHRIS.)* Sorry. It was Rob… He's
fine. Yes, totally, he's fine, he just keeps
shitting everywhere. Of course I tell him
"Don't shit in the house." …No, I don't
think he confuses "sit" and "shit." You really think he doesn't understand "SIT, I'll
give you a treat, you good dog, I love you"
and "Don't SHIT on my Pradas you fucking asshole"?! …I'm this close to turning
him into a fucking throw pillow, so help
me God… It's like, "I give you un-what-
ever it is—unquestioned love, un—"
…huh? Right, no, right, unconditional
love— hah, my therapist would get a kick

out of that, I couldn't remember "unconditional love," how apropos. Anyway, "I give you unconditional love and feed you brown pebbles, so if you wanna shit in the house, grow opposable thumbs, get a job, rent an apartment, and shit all over it." It was your idea to get this dog, and then you leave me here to pick up its shit! …Well, he does— Even when I yell the hell out of him, that sighing squeal he makes is satiated joy. I think he's acting out. Shitting as a cry for help… Because he misses you— and, maybe he's afraid he'll get nuked.

(Blackout.)

SCENE NINETEEN

SHELLY sitting on bed, staring off, deeply troubled. We hear BRETT off, singing an ad jingle.

BRETT: "Crunch-Ohs, Crunch-Ohs; oh, how they crunch oh. Taste why America loves Crunch-Ohs. Crunch 'em!" *(He enters.)* What's wrong? Want some Crunch-Ohs?

SHELLY: No. Thank you.

BRETT: What's wrong?

SHELLY: Nothing.

BRETT: Oh. Want some Crunch-Ohs?

SHELLY: I don't feel like Crunch-Ohs.

BRETT: Oh. I do. So, what's wrong?

SHELLY: I don't feel well.

BRETT: Like— your stomach? Want a Tums? *(He sits.)*

SHELLY: No, thanks—

BRETT: Seriously. You should. Settle you straight. I'll grab some.

SHELLY: No.

BRETT: Ya sure? Let me get one. I'll get one. Tums. Make you feel better.

SHELLY: No. Okay? I said "No." I don't want a fucking Tums. I can't do this. I can't do this fucking crazy shit!

BRETT: What? Take Tums?

SHELLY: It. This. This. It.

BRETT: What are you—?

SHELLY: What we're working at—towards—would be best—for the best, rather—if we could try some space apart, to clear our heads…This sounds so stupid. Like a fucking movie. What a stupid, fucking movie.

BRETT: Are you— you're visiting your mom again. What? You wanna see other people?

SHELLY: No. This is not about other people. I loved you to forget myself. I need to be me.

BRETT: Who the hell've you been?

SHELLY: I don't know. But I hate her… and so do you… Don't you. *(Breaths.)* I hear myself now and think, "That doesn't sound like"—

BRETT: I like her. A lot. She's you!

SHELLY: Brett, I don't know how we started dating. We were hooking up, but you kept calling.

BRETT: Oh. Wow. That's how you remember—

SHELLY: I knew then what I hate about you now. I ignored it.

BRETT: That's all it meant.

SHELLY: I hate people like me. They're disgruntled and unsatisfied and hang out in malls.

BRETT: You're fucking it up. You're fucking us up. You're such a fuck-up sometimes. Shell, I know you. You don't mean this.

SHELLY: My mom sends me newspaper clippings for all wedding announcements of the girls I went to grade school with, and this's what they've got. They've got a you. A you to come home to, and a you to feel secure with, and about. Some poor, fucking grin of a you staring back from the newspaper and he's supposed to be what I want. I thought I didn't deserve better. But, I'm sorry, that's all mixed up wrong. But how can you understand that? You don't understand—me or what I'm meaning anymore.

BRETT: What are you doing Monday afternoon?

SHELLY: I need you in my life so—

BRETT: A picnic. I'll cook.

SHELLY: I need us to be in touch—stay friends.

BRETT: No. It doesn't work like that.

SHELLY: Brett, we're friends now. I can't lose you. But we're roommates, that's all.

BRETT: No. You walk out—if you walk out you don't get other benefits. You're dead to me.

SHELLY: We didn't wrong each other. Please, Brett. There's no rule saying we can't be friends.

BRETT: Oh is that right? 'Cause I didn't read the "You-Just-Got-Shit-on-by-Your-Girlfriend Rulebook." So you tell me. *(Silence.)* Tell me. 'Cause I wanna know the rules. Let's sit here and pretend to be friends. You tell me what to do.

SHELLY: Brett. Please.

BRETT: I told you I'll do what it takes, so you tell me. Tell me what to say when we bump into each other on the subway and I try not to ask about your new boyfriend. How's your skinny latte? Are you sleeping— *(Breaths.)* Are you sleeping— *(Breaths.)*

SHELLY: Oh. Oh, Brett…

BRETT: Are you sleeping—with anyone yet? …See? I'm telling you, please, we will not be friends

(Overlapping.)

{
BRETT: if you walk out that door, so don't throw it away, off the side, here.

SHELLY: I was really hoping that we would be able to find some peace of mind in this, but…
}

BRETT: I'm sorry, I didn't hear what you said. Can you repeat it, please?

SHELLY: It doesn't matter. It's done.

BRETT: Tell me what you fucking said! It matters!

SHELLY: No. You broke my heart every day.

BRETT: What did I do to make you stop loving me?

SHELLY: You don't touch me. Ever. You don't hold my hand. Nothing. I'm touch deprived, okay? We're friends.

BRETT: I'll go to therapy. I was blind… I'll mop the floors!… You're all that's good in my world right now, Shelly. You're all I have.

(Silence.)

SHELLY: I am trying to speak to you in a nicely way—

BRETT: You're all I have.

SHELLY: In a nice way—

BRETT: You're all—

SHELLY: Nicely! Stop saying that! Stop hurting me! The fairy tale dried up. I lied. It was never as good as I pretended. I'm not responsible for your goddamn happiness! So fuck off! Okay? I don't want you any more. I need more than you can give.

BRETT: That's bullshit! That is such bullshit. You won't let me. You can't orgasm 'cause you can't let go! And I feel worthless because of it. I eat shit with you. I check if the lights are on under the door when I come home, hoping you're asleep or out with friends. And I don't hold your hand? Your skin shudders and shirks every time I slip my arms around you. And I'm hurting you? You fucking whacked-out bitch! You make me feel I violate you. Like a goddamn rapist in my own home! I'm sorry. I didn't mean that. Please, Shelly, please. I need you.

(Silence.)

BRETT: Maybe not stay forever, but just right now. Just see how it goes. Just—see how we feel. Just— not leave right now— Just—can you just—Just—Just— Please, don't leave me right now! I don't want to die in this apartment by myself and no one will even call my mom. If you leave, I die and they won't find me for three weeks. I'm afraid. I'm— I'm really afraid.

(After several moments, SHELLY goes to BRETT and rubs his chest.)

SHELLY: Shhhh. I'm here. You're safe. Shhhh.

(It is tender. There is a moment where we understand why they were in love. Then she falls silent while she rubs his chest, and her actions become more clinical. She stops. There is silence.)

SHELLY: There.

(She moves away from him. He gets up unexpectedly and quickly runs to the bathroom. We hear him throwing up in the toilet. He returns.)

BRETT: Sorry.

SHELLY: You okay?

BRETT: Yeah. I mean… I'm not doin' a jig, but…

(They share a small laugh. He rushes toward her. They hug. And begin to kiss. He stops, smiling at her. She dries his tears with a Kleenex.)

BRETT: Thanks for the tissue.

(Silence.)

SHELLY: Brett, I'm leaving now.

BRETT: Marry me!

SHELLY: No.

(SHELLY goes to the door to leave. BRETT blocks her way. He is very close to her.)

BRETT: You won't leave.

SHELLY: Brett, let me go!

(He puts his hands on and around her.)

BRETT: Please, Shelly. I'll give it to you. Show you. The bed; I know the score.

(He starts trying to desperately kiss her and tug her toward the bedroom.)

SHELLY: I can't. I think that's—that's not a good idea, Brett.

BRETT: Please! C'mon! I can do it. I'm good. I'm good, Shelly, I am.

(Pause. She moves his hands. She backs into the apartment.)

BRETT: Exactly what is it you want from me? I try and try and try. I go to work. I mean something.

SHELLY: I missed you more than I loved you.

BRETT: Hey! I was there! I was there!

SHELLY: Okay.

BRETT: I was! Say it. Say I was there for you.

SHELLY: I hate who we've become—

BRETT: I was there.

SHELLY: No more! I'm too tired. I'm over it! Over my life! Over my friends. Their faults annoy the shit out of me. And I'm over you! Your touch's mean. And I can't have you inside me like that. I need to go and sleep now. Never again on the closet floor. Sleep. In a bed that's safe. Sleep. And not wake up. Because I keep working and working on your happiness. But you aren't ready to be happy. I'm going to Samantha and Rob's. Don't call me. I'm going to sleep, and plant rocks. Because I really— I need to feed this hole in my chest that's killing me. And I pray to God— No not God! Fuck God! God gives me no relief! I pray and no one answers!— I hope, I hope you feed that hole. Because I loved you once. But your foundation's all fucked up, and your house's going to sink. And I can't wait on my side of the bed until it's sunk, and you're in a midlife crisis because we haven't touched for years, and you're always working or on the couch eating that dulce de leche ice cream, and our life and me are not what you want, so you're leaving for some young, thin, dumb Barbie blond. And I get up and look in the mirror, not the funhouse mirror I've been staring in all these years, where my sideshow insecurities are distorted so I'm only sad eyes and big hips, but a real reflection, where I see what the hell have I done?!; I'm not your fucking maid! Pick up your clothes to show you care about me. I mop

and mop, but I can't scrub this place clean. It's filled with hurt and failure. And— I've burnt all the pots, Brett. I want a family and kids and someone who looks at me like that, with that knowing, smiling, burning, yearning desire, and I want the type of security I feel secure in and I really— This is not at all what I planned to say. I didn't want to say all that stuff. But I'm so hurt and my mouth keeps going and I can't, for the life of me, figure out how to shut up and walk out that door. And I'm sorry. I'm sorry I hurt you. I'm sorry I can't be whatever you need. But I can't figure out what that is. I can't. I'm too hurt. I'm too tired. And now—and now—I'm going to turn around and walk out that door. And I would really appreciate it—it would really mean a lot to me if you didn't say anything till I'm gone, because I don't think I can handle any more of this conversation, and I'm not prepared to start bawling. 'Cause I don't think I'll stop. Ever.

(They stare at each other, steeped in silence. SHELLY turns and leaves. BRETT is left standing in the center of the apartment. Blackout.)

SCENE TWENTY

ROB and JOHN at JOHN's apartment, waiting for SAMANTHA.

JOHN: Soft-shells do this?

ROB: Yeah.

JOHN: Women. Crabs. Two reasons I'm gay.

ROB: Ha. Crabs.

JOHN: I don't know how you deal with it. The moods. The bleeding.

ROB: Heard from Shelly?

JOHN: Not yet.

ROB: It's awful what she's doing.

JOHN: She sounds happy.

ROB: Yeah. That's what's awful… Before Sam or Shelly get here— Did Sam— We had this dinner last night, did she mention—?

JOHN: Oh, right. Happy anniversary.

ROB: Sure. She mention the book?

JOHN: No.

ROB: Great art book. Coffee table. Jackson Pollock. It's great.

JOHN: Yeah?

ROB: She hates it, right?

JOHN: I don't know.

ROB: Well, I took her to this new Italian place, real fancy—

JOHN: No Yamaguchi Sushi?

ROB: Sushi? Is that what this is about? She seemed so disappointed. She didn't tell you?

JOHN: I wouldn't tell you if she did… But, no, she didn't talk to me.

ROB: I can't joke it away anymore. The thrill's gone in arguing with her. I thought you—

JOHN: I don't have the answers. Pretend as I may to accept everything. I'm as lost as you are.

(Breaths pass.)

ROB: You have any lip stuff?

JOHN: Yeah. Here.

ROB: Mmmm, God that's good. Have some.

JOHN: So good. *(Breaths pass.)* I love Jackson Pollock. That turmoil in his work. And his wife— Lee?— *what's* her name?

ROB: Yeah. He left her.

(Breaths pass. Blackout.)

SCENE TWENTY-ONE

SHELLY and BRETT's apartment. BRETT sits in the center of the room. He does not move. Silence. The sound of the wind. Lights up on JOHN, SHELLY, SAMANTHA, and ROB. They are peacefully working in JOHN's rock garden arranging stones in a spiral. BRETT rises. He turns on the TV weather report. He tries unsuccessfully to pack a gym bag—his toiletry kit, clothes, a picture of him and SHELLY, etc. He turns on music. BRETT moves very slowly. Drained. He stares off. The phone rings. He lets it ring. Finally, we hear the answering machine's outgoing recording. He stares at the machine.

SHELLY: *(Happy voice on machine.)* Hi, this is Shelly—

BRETT: *(Happy voice on machine.)* And Brett—

SHELLY: *(Happy voice on machine.)* We're not home.

BRETT: *(Happy voice on machine.)* But we'd love to call you back.

TOGETHER: *(Happy voices on machine.)* Bye!!

(Beep. A hang up. We hear the dial tone. BRETT stares out. Lights and sound snap out on BRETT. JOHN, SHELLY, SAMANTHA, and ROB continue arranging stones in a serene quiet for some time. Blackout.)

SCENE TWENTY-TWO

BRETT and STEVE in the bar. They are sharing a bottle of high-end tequila.

STEVE: Hey, to be honest, I'm glad you aren't together. Believe me, this girl was not "the one."

BRETT: Believe you? Why? You gotta secret?

STEVE: What do you mean?

BRETT: If something's going on, tell me.

STEVE: About what?

BRETT: What you know that I don't.

STEVE: About what?

BRETT: She was fooling me.

STEVE: She told you that?

BRETT: She lied!

STEVE: What she tell you?

BRETT: There was another person.

STEVE: Like—uhh?

BRETT: *She* was another person. Like a mask. I hate when people— "Now that you broke up, I hated your girlfriend."

STEVE: I never said hate. Said she wasn't "the one."

BRETT: But if you saw that, why didn't you tell me?

STEVE: You wouldn't have listened. No, all I can do as your friend is help the situation along.

BRETT: Well, I feel like a fucking idiot.

STEVE: Why? You got a lot out of it.

BRETT: Yeah—I got furniture, she got the hell out.

(Breaths pass.)

STEVE: You wanna know what one of my friends told me in high school? Always stuck with me. Fancy panty theory. Have I told you this? You start dating a woman she's wearing all these fancy, lacy, pretty, sexy underwear. And you think,

"Great, this is who she is—a woman who wears fancy underwear." But you two get comfortable. All of a sudden, the cottons come out. Then ones with holes, then period panties. And you're still wondering when the girl with the frilly garters is coming back. And that's what it is.

BRETT: Yeah?

STEVE: It's when you find a girl who you think looks sexy in the period, grandma briefs— buy a ring. Until then, keep looking.

BRETT: But the same shit happens.

STEVE: I'm saying, you'll find someone where you don't flex your muscle every time they touch your chest. I'm not saying I've found it. I flex. But we will.

BRETT: It's ironic— What does that word mean, "ironic"?; I always use it wrong.

STEVE: When something you say or do is opposite what it means.

BRETT: Well, then—funny, I guess, Shell and I were talking about your relationships—

STEVE: You and Shelly—?

BRETT: All this crazy, stupid, bullshit about how you secretly know they won't work out.

STEVE: Okay?

BRETT: I need another drink. You in?

STEVE: Yeah, but wait— you and Shelly were talking—

BRETT: I was talking about myself, Steve. So I don't get hurt.

STEVE: Oh.

BRETT: But I'm hurt. I bring out depression in women. You meet these repressed girls and bring out their passion. I meet these girls who look solid— Shelly was so blue, and I didn't do anything different to help her— It's like, the other day, I'm at the office, waiting for the elevator. And there are people already there. So the button's pushed. And I walk up. I look at them. I look at the button. And push it again. Ya know, a couple times. Like how the fuck did I think doing the same thing over and over would change anything.

STEVE: Survival.

BRETT: But not inviting her out with my friends? Only telling my parents the troubles. I mean, what's that?

STEVE: Neglect.

BRETT: Yeah. I stop watering the plants, and I'm crushed when they die.

STEVE: Shit.

BRETT: Let it get bad enough, you're not accountable for the end. Everyone's like "She wasn't the one."

STEVE: So, okay, next time value what you've got. Take care of everyone, and you won't go wrong.

BRETT: You think I'm proud of this? Oh sure, "Take care of everyone." It's hard to act like that when I'm waiting for the shoe to drop. Waiting for her to wise up.

STEVE: About what?

BRETT: The truth. I'm a fake. I'm a loser. …There. I said it. At least now I can say I know who I am.

STEVE: When I said, "Know yourself," that's not what—

BRETT: I was wearing a mask too, huh?

(Slight breaths pass.)

STEVE: Hey, if you were a masked superhero, who would you be?

BRETT: Wolverine. He feels no pain. Knife him in the heart and his wound heals. You?

STEVE: Two-Face… I'm just kidding, man. I'd be Daredevil. The blind man who sees all and fixes all.

BRETT: Shelly's the Shadow.

STEVE: Shit! The Shadow's the feminine dark side—the "anima."

BRETT: A big enema. That's what I got. You wanna 'nother drink?

STEVE: Yeah, sure… I don't see what that has to do with my exploits, but the punch-line is—

BRETT: I need another—

STEVE: —We have greatness in us. Get out of your own way. It's easy to fill the void with—whatever—food, booze, sex, work. Like your brother—cigars and golf.

BRETT: Yeah. A rut. I got stuck.

STEVE: Alright. Start anew. A breakup haircut. And we'll call your brother—

BRETT: How do I tell him I failed?

STEVE: His country house's calling. You and me.

BRETT: I wouldn't enjoy it without her.

STEVE: You didn't enjoy it with her. Now we can hang out again. And your life'll start.

BRETT: We'd have to make it before the storm.

STEVE: If it hits, it hits. As Winston Churchill said, "When going through hell, keep going." The only way out of the darkness is together. You know, the only thing my father ever taught me, "Women come and go, but best friends are forever."

BRETT: *(In unison.)* "Best friends are forever."

(Breaths pass.)

BRETT: ...You're a great friend.

(Blackout.)

END OF PLAY

AUNTIE MAYHEM

David Pumo

DAVID PUMO was born in Queens, New York, and raised on Long Island, a manageable commute to the theatre district of New York City, where he spent many evenings and Wednesday matinees as a teen. He graduated from NYU's Tisch School of Arts with a degree in film and television, and made his way to L.A., where he ended up living out his other fantasy—dance—by becoming a fitness trainer, managing Richard Simmons's Beverly Hills club, and teaching at the Jane Fonda Workout and other top venues. He eventually returned to New York to get his law degree from Brooklyn Law School with the goal of providing advocacy for lesbian, gay, bisexual, and transgender teens who had run away or been thrown out of their homes. For five and a half years, he directed a legal and social service project at the Urban Justice Center providing assistance to this population. In his "free time," he found himself directed back into the world of theatre and playwriting by actor Moe Bertran, his husband and muse of nineteen years. He began working with The Fourth Unity, an off-off-Broadway company, where he has served as everything from lighting technician to co-artistic director and, currently, president of the board. The company produced his first full-length play, *Love Scenes*, in 1999, and *Auntie Mayhem* in 2003. A workshop version of *Auntie Mayhem* was produced by the company in 2001, as were two shorts, *The Seed* and *Perhaps*, in 2002. Both *The Seed* and the workshop version of *Auntie Mayhem* were also produced at manhattantheatresource as part of its Homogenius festival. He currently lives with Moe and their puppy, Beauregard, in Brooklyn.

Auntie Mayhem was first produced as a full-length play by The Fourth Unity (Dennis Smith, Artistic Director) at the Bank Street Theatre in New York City on May 15, 2003, with the following cast and production team:

Felony Mayhem .... Moe Bertran
Bobo .... Ivan Davila
Charlotte .... Jimmy Hurley
Dennis .... Randy Aaron
Ivan .... Isaac Calpito
Epiphany .... Henry Alberto

Director: Donna Jean Fogel
Set Design: Lea Umberger
Lighting Design: Renée Molina
Choreographer: Jimmy Locust
Fight Director: John Long
Original Music: Lisa Gold
Stage Manager: Max Daniel Weinstein

Two workshop productions were presented earlier, both directed by Donna Jean Fogel. The first, produced by The Fourth Unity at the Bank Street Theatre as part of Unity Fest 2001, featured the following cast:

Felony Mayhem .... Moe Bertran
Bobo .... Ivan Davila
Charlotte .... Tony Hamilton
Dennis .... Heland Lee
Ivan .... Maxx Santiago
Epiphany .... Michael Rivera

The second, produced by manhattantheatresource as part of Homogenius 2002, featured the following cast:

Felony Mayhem .... Moe Bertran
Bobo .... James McLaughlin
Charlotte .... Tony Hamilton
Dennis .... Tony Caan
Ivan .... Maxx Santiago
Epiphany .... Mariah Lopez

CHARACTERS

FELONY MAYHEM: A man in his thirties, Latino, maybe petite. Former drag queen.

BOBO: A man in his thirties, probably Latino, masculine, working class. Felony's husband.

CHARLOTTE: A man in his thirties, any ethnicity, probably heavyset. Professional drag queen.

DENNIS: Not white, probably black or Latino, goes from sixteen to twenty.

IVAN: Preferably not white, goes from seventeen to twenty.

EPIPHANY: Any ethnicity, goes from sixteen to seventeen. Male-to-female transgender (biologically a boy, but living as a girl).

SET

The entire play takes place in the bedroom of FELONY and BOBO's apartment, somewhere in downtown Manhattan. Upstage to the right is a large French door or sliding door that opens from the hallway of the apartment into the bedroom. The entrance to the apartment is unseen, at the right end of the hallway. The rest of the apartment— living room, kitchen, TV room, bathroom—is unseen down the hall to the left. To the left of the door in the bedroom, there is a double bed and a dresser with a few bookshelves over the dresser, a night table left of the bed, and a coffee table downstage. Stage right there is a makeup table and chair downstage, and a larger chair upstage near the door. There is a full-length mirror somewhere, probably in the down left corner.

SCENE I

The room is dark except for moonlight or a streetlight coming through an unseen window. It is about five in the morning in the middle of winter. The sun is far from up yet. FELONY MAYHEM, a neat and trendy-looking Latino man in his thirties, enters the apartment, flicking on the hall light, and enters the bedroom door, turning on the bedroom light. He is wearing a winter coat or jacket.

FELONY: Come in, sweetie. I told you it was a mess. Don't be shy now.

(He takes his coat off and drops it on the bed or chair. DENNIS enters, shyly, with his hands in his pockets. He is a teenager, African American or Latino, wearing baggy jeans, a sweatshirt, sneakers, and a down jacket.)

FELONY: Can I check your coat?

DENNIS: I'm not shy.

FELONY: Oh, that's nice. Not shy, huh.

DENNIS: Nope.

FELONY: Ready to party?

DENNIS: Yup.

FELONY: Terrific. Check your coat?

DENNIS: Are you a cop?

FELONY: Am I a cop? Do you really still ask that? That's so cute.

DENNIS: Are you?

FELONY: *(Extending hand.)* Pepper Anderson, policewoman. Pleased to meet you.

(He waits a beat for DENNIS to get it. DENNIS doesn't get it. He drops his hand.)

FELONY: No, honey, I'm not a cop. Can I check your coat?

(DENNIS takes his coat off. FELONY takes it and puts it on the chair near the door.)

FELONY: Dennis, right? Take your shoes off, sweetie. Get comfortable.

(DENNIS does.)

FELONY: You're a little young to be out so late, don't you think?

DENNIS: I'm twenty-two.

FELONY: Oh, twenty-two. Not just twenty-one, but twenty-two.

DENNIS: Yup.

FELONY: Yup. Old enough for a drink?

DENNIS: What do you got?

FELONY: Let's see. Vodka and…Kool-Aid, I guess.

DENNIS: Eeww.

FELONY: It is a little ghetto. Even for me. Straight up then?

(DENNIS shakes his head no.)

FELONY: You sure? It's good for you.

(DENNIS shakes his head yes.)

FELONY: Well, I think I might have a little nightcap. Or morning cap, as the case may be. You can take your shirt off.

(He exits to the kitchen. DENNIS takes his shirt off and drops it on the bed. FELONY speaks from the kitchen as DENNIS looks around.)

FELONY: *(Offstage.)* I don't think I've seen you out before.

DENNIS: I been around.

FELONY: *(Offstage.)* Really. You have? Because I think I would have remembered you. In fact, as soon as I saw you I thought to myself, "He's the one." *(Enters with a glass of vodka.)* Oh yeah, you're the one, all right. I'm sure of it.

(He runs his fingers through DENNIS's hair, unbuttons the top button of his pants, and walks away. DENNIS undoes his pants and takes them off.)

FELONY: Lucky me I just happened to be walking out of The Cock Pit and you just happened to be walking by. *(He picks up DENNIS's pants and shirt and puts them on the chair with his jacket and shoes.)* In fact, it was looking like a pretty beat night until you showed up, looking like a little cutie with that handsome face of yours, and that sweet little body. *(He pulls the sheets back.)* Hop in.

(DENNIS does. FELONY sits near him on the bed.)

FELONY: So, is this all you do? For money?

DENNIS: Yeah.

FELONY: Really? Nothing else?

DENNIS: Not right now.

FELONY: Hmm. Any plans? Any goals?

DENNIS: I don't know.

FELONY: Well, do you like doing this?

DENNIS: I don't know.

FELONY: Well, you can't do this for the rest of your life, can you?

(DENNIS shrugs.)

FELONY: Is conversation extra?

(DENNIS shrugs again.)

FELONY: Fine. Let's get going, then. I'm gonna freshen this. You sure you don't want some?

DENNIS: No thanks.

(FELONY gets up. He looks up and down DENNIS's body under the sheets. He holds his hand out. DENNIS takes his underwear off under the sheets and hands it to FELONY. FELONY walks to the door.)

FELONY: Dennis, would you check that drawer? I think there are some condoms in there.

(DENNIS turns left, away from FELONY, to look in the night table drawer. FELONY, unseen, takes all the clothes off the chair and leaves the room. DENNIS finds a condom and sits, nervously playing with it. FELONY returns with a full glass and sits on the chair.)

FELONY: So, what shall we do?

DENNIS: What do you want to do?

FELONY: Oh, I don't know. What's your specialty?

DENNIS: I don't know.

FELONY: Sucking? Fucking?

DENNIS: I guess.

FELONY: Or maybe…we should dance!

DENNIS: Dance?

FELONY: Sure. Rumba? Tango? Hustle?

DENNIS: What?

FELONY: *(Standing.)* Oh, come on. It'll be fun. I'll teach you. It's easy.

DENNIS: *(Realizing the chair is empty.)* Where are my clothes?

FELONY: Your clothes? I threw them out. Come on. Get up. I'll show you.

DENNIS: You what?

FELONY: I threw them out the front window. They're all over the street. Come on. I'll let you lead.

DENNIS: Where are my clothes, really?

FELONY: I told you, I threw them out the window.

(DENNIS gathers the sheets around him.)

FELONY: You know what, maybe I should lead to start.

(Wrapped in the sheet, DENNIS runs out of the bedroom to look for his clothes.)

FELONY: All right, you can lead.

DENNIS: *(Offstage.)* Are you fucking crazy?! What the fuck did you do?!

FELONY: I told you what I did.

DENNIS: *(Coming back into the bedroom.)* What the fuck did you do that for?!

FELONY: *(Puts his glass down.)* Real sorry. Tell you what. I'll go get you your clothes if you go get me my bag.

DENNIS: What?!

FELONY: Oh, don't pretend you don't know what I'm talking about. You're the one, motherfucker.

DENNIS: Are you crazy?!

FELONY: Don't play stupid with me. Where's my fucking bag?

DENNIS: What are you talking about? I don't have your fucking bag! Give me my fucking clothes!

FELONY: What, did you throw it out? All my cards? All my shit?

DENNIS: Throw out what... I didn't—

FELONY: Oh yes you did, you little thug piece of shit. You grabbed it two nights ago in front of Flourante. You ripped it out of my hand. You almost pulled my shoulder out of the socket!

DENNIS: It wasn't me!

FELONY: It was so you, with your little thug face, and your little thug jacket. Please!

DENNIS: Give me my fucking clothes!

(He grabs FELONY.)

FELONY: *(Pushing him away.)* Get your fucking hands off of me!

(DENNIS swings at FELONY. FELONY blocks it, slaps him hard, and knees him in the crotch. DENNIS doubles over; FELONY knocks him to the ground or pins him on the bed and sits on top of him, twisting his hand behind his back.)

FELONY: I had ninety dollars' worth of MAC in there. I had to cancel my Capital One!

DENNIS: Stop! I don't have it!

FELONY: Oh yeah? Where is it?

DENNIS: I don't have it. It's gone!

FELONY: Oh, it's gone? So what am I supposed to do about that?

DENNIS: *(Starting to hyperventilate.)* I don't have it! I don't have anything! I don't have anything! Give me my clothes! Please!

FELONY: Why should I give a shit?

DENNIS: My jacket. Please. I don't have anything! I don't have anything! *(He can barely breathe.)* I'm...I'm...I'm sorry... I...I don't have anything... I'm...I'm... I'm... please... I'm...I'm—

FELONY: Jesus fucking... calm down.

DENNIS: I'm...I'm sorry...I'm...I'm... please...I'm...I'm—

(FELONY gets off DENNIS. DENNIS pulls away and collapses on the floor.)

FELONY: All right, all right, all right. Fucking breathe, for Christ sake. Calm down... breathe... take a breath—

DENNIS: I'm...I'm...I'm sorry.

FELONY: Ssshhhhh... breathe... just breathe... shut up and breathe... ssshhhhh... come on now... relax... It's okay, it's okay... I won't hurt you anymore... just relax... breathe... breathe—

DENNIS: I'm...I'm...I'm sorry.

FELONY: I know you are. It's okay. Just breathe...breathe...breathe...

(DENNIS begins to calm down. Over the next few lines, he slowly gets his breath back.)

FELONY: Motherfuck! Are you okay?

(DENNIS nods yes.)

FELONY: Did I hurt you?

(DENNIS nods yes.)

FELONY: I'm sorry.

DENNIS: I'm sorry too. I had no money is all.

FELONY: Okay.

DENNIS: I'm sorry about your MAC.

FELONY: I got more.

DENNIS: Are you gonna call the cops?

FELONY: Call the cops? Why would I call the cops? Like they're gonna do shit.

(DENNIS is not sure FELONY means it.)

FELONY: No cops.

(BOBO enters from outside, into the bedroom. He is in his thirties, Latino, dressed in working clothes, maybe stained a little like he's been loading meat onto a truck. He is carrying all of DENNIS's clothes.)

BOBO: Hey, look what was all over the front... *(He enters the bedroom and sees DENNIS on the floor, wrapped in a sheet.)* ...steps.

(FELONY takes the clothes from BOBO and gives them to DENNIS.)

FELONY: There's a little room down the hall with a couch. Go get dressed.

(DENNIS takes the clothes and leaves through the door up left.)

BOBO: I won't ask.

(They kiss. He takes his jacket off.)

FELONY: He's the little punk who stole my purse.

BOBO: I didn't ask.

FELONY: I tricked him into coming over so I could fuck with him. How was work?

BOBO: That's so you.

FELONY: Only he went all Sybil on me, like he had a seizure, or something.

BOBO: That kid's a fucking mess, Felony. Be careful.

FELONY: I just scared him a little. That's all. He started to cry, for Christ sake.

BOBO: He's damaged, babe. You're lucky that's all that happened.

FELONY: What do you mean damaged?

BOBO: He's fucked up.

FELONY: Of course he's fucked up... what do you mean, fucked up? Do you know him? Is he a friend of yours?

BOBO: I seen him around the loading dock all the time, three, four, five in the morning, working the stroll for a few months. He's been busted a few times.

FELONY: How the hell do you know that?

BOBO: I don't know. I hear. I seen it once.

FELONY: You saw what once?

BOBO: He was all bloody, like someone been beating on his head, and the cops are chasing him and pinning him to the sidewalk and beating him some more. And he's screaming about being attacked in someone's car, and the cops are all over him, what the fuck he was doing getting in a stranger's car, like they're more worried about busting some hustler than finding the creeps that split his head. A few days later he's back out walking again, looking like a total zombie, but he's out there.

FELONY: Well, why would he do that? Why would he be out there after getting so messed up?

BOBO: Uh, he needs to eat? Oh, please. Some of those kids have been beaten up so many times they don't even feel it.

(DENNIS enters with the sheet, dressed except for socks and shoes, which are in his hands.)

DENNIS: Thanks for not calling the cops.

FELONY: That's all right. Dennis, this is Bobo.

DENNIS: Hi.

BOBO: Um hm.

(FELONY takes the sheet. DENNIS sits on the bed to tie his shoes.)

FELONY: Dennis, how old are you really?

DENNIS: Eighteen.

FELONY: Where are you going to go?

DENNIS: I don't know.

FELONY: Well, where do you live?

DENNIS: I don't know.

FELONY: You don't know? Where's that?

DENNIS: Nowhere.

FELONY: Nowhere? Where's your mother?

DENNIS: The Bronx.

FELONY: Why can't you go there?

DENNIS: Oh, please.

FELONY: Oh please what?

DENNIS: Oh please, she threw me out.

FELONY: Why did she throw you out?

DENNIS: 'Cause she caught me with some guy.

FELONY: So where do you sleep?

DENNIS: Street, subway.

FELONY: Are you hungry?

DENNIS: I'm okay.

FELONY: No really, you want something to eat?

DENNIS: I'm okay. There was forty dollars in your bag...sorry.

FELONY: So, where you gonna go?

DENNIS: I told you, I don't know.

FELONY: Isn't there a shelter or something for kids your age?

DENNIS: There's no shelter.

BOBO: There's a shelter on Tenth Avenue and...

DENNIS: They threw me out. I broke curfew.

FELONY: You broke curfew, so they just threw you out in the middle of winter?

DENNIS: They don't give a shit.

FELONY: You look pretty tired. You want to stay here tonight?

DENNIS: Really?

BOBO: Felony?

FELONY: Yeah, really.

BOBO: Felony, could you come in the kitchen, please?

FELONY: The couch in the TV room opens up.

DENNIS: I better go.

FELONY: Where you gonna go? It's freezing out there.

DENNIS: I'm all right.

BOBO: Felony, could you come in the kitchen, please?

FELONY: Dennis, how old are you really?

DENNIS: Seventeen...sixteen.

BOBO: If you're sixteen, shouldn't you be in foster care or something?

DENNIS: I'm not going back.

BOBO: It can't be worse than living on the street.

DENNIS: What the fuck do you know about it? If you're gay, you're safer on the street.

BOBO: Come on, Dennis. It can't be that bad.

DENNIS: *(Getting up.)* Do you know what they did to me? My first night at the transitional center, eight guys break my door down at like two in the morning with shirts over their faces, and they start beating the crap out of me. I finally broke away and ran into the kitchen. I'm standing in the corner with a fork to defend myself. The staff guy says he can't find who did it. Eight fucking guys, there's only like ten in the whole house. So I tell him I'm not staying. He gives me a metro card and sends me to the placement office at two in the morning.

BOBO: Alone?

DENNIS: So they send me to another place in the Bronx. I lasted a week. Every fucking minute of every fucking day, "faggot" this and "faggot" that, slapping me in the head. A bunch of guys attacked me in the shower through the shower curtain. I didn't even see them. Someone pushed me down the steps. The staff saw it. She says, "What did you do that for? I thought you didn't want to touch him."

FELONY: Did you tell anyone?

DENNIS: All the time. So they move me to this place in Westchester. It's like a big campus with, like, ten houses and a school. So, like, every day on my way to school some kids are throwing rocks at my head. Every fucking day. One time two kids held me underwater in the pool. When they finally let me up, I'm puking, and the lifeguard is sitting there like "Are you okay?" So they send me to this shrink 'cause I'm depressed. She wants to put me on Prozac. Hello? I don't need drugs. I need to stop getting beat up. Fucking idiot.

FELONY: So you ran away?

BOBO: Well, if everyone was so horrible, I mean, you're not, like, all that queeny, or anything. Why didn't you just not tell anyone?

DENNIS: Fuck that! I'm not gonna hide it.

FELONY: Of course not... There's blankets in the closet.

DENNIS: Okay. *(Exits to the hall.)*

BOBO: Felony?

FELONY: Yes, Bobo, my love?

BOBO: What are you doing, Felony? Are you crazy?

FELONY: For loving you, sweetie.

BOBO: Felony, that kid's a fucking mess.

FELONY: That kid's a kid.

BOBO: You don't know anything about him.

FELONY: What? He's not going to take anything.

BOBO: Hello? He took your bag.

FELONY: He's not going to take anything else.

BOBO: How do you know that?

FELONY: There's nothing to take. What's he going to take? The flatware? The furniture?

BOBO: Don't you think you're being a little naive?

FELONY: Why, because I can't throw some poor kid out into the freezing cold?

BOBO: Do you have any idea how many kids are out there in the freezing cold tonight? And every night? They're everywhere. From Christopher to Fourteenth, up and down the river, the Port Authority, the subways—

FELONY: So, tonight there's one less, okay?

BOBO: You're impossible. Why the fuck am I wasting my breath. *(He gets undressed to his shorts for bed.)*

FELONY: Beats me.

BOBO: If anything happens—

FELONY: I take full responsibility.

BOBO: You're a freak. I'm going to sleep. I'm wasted. *(He gets under the sheets.)*

FELONY: Oh, no you don't. Come here you.

(FELONY climbs in, and they kiss.)

FELONY: That's nice. Don't think you're falling asleep on me. I've been thinking about you all night.

BOBO: No you haven't. You've been plotting some terrorist revenge against some poor street kid.

FELONY: Well, in between plotting I was thinking about you all night.

BOBO: Oh yeah?

FELONY: Oh yeah.

(They begin to make out on the bed. We hear the apartment door opening and slamming shut. CHARLOTTE enters the apartment and the bedroom. CHARLOTTE is a heavy-set man in full theatrical drag. Over the next speech, he sits at the makeup table and removes his wig, shoes, jewelry, makeup, and other accessories. He speaks to FELONY and BOBO the whole time, unconcerned that he is obviously interrupting them.)

CHARLOTTE: What a long night! What a fucking endless, miserable, tedious night. Marty missed three lighting cues. Every fucking sound cue is off. I almost stopped the show to strangle his fat, hairy neck. No tequila shots before the show, Marty.

No fucking tequila shots. Just say no. How many times I gotta tell him? You need to be sharp. You need to be quick. That's what coke is for. He's losing it. I'm gonna replace his ass by next week. This is not a fucking joke. This is art. This is my fucking reputation on that stage.

(By this point, BOBO is fed up with this interruption. He turns away from FELONY and tries to go to sleep. FELONY, having lost BOBO's attention, sits in bed and listens to CHARLOTTE.)

CHARLOTTE: Then I spend two hours with Merle and Sandy. They really want me. They're doing a whole song and dance. They've got a bigger stage than Stingray, which they do. They've got state-of-the-art sound and lighting, which they don't but it's better than the thirty-year-old shit I've been working with. They want a whole new show. They want to do a four-color ad. I've got complete creative control… Do you know how much they offered me? Do you have any idea what they thought they could get away with? I just stared at them. What is this, a fucking workfare placement? I'm livid, but I manage to politely tell them what my going rate is. They start bargaining, like I'm a fucking flowerpot in Tijuana. I ordered one more gimlet, chugged it, and walked out. I'm not leaving Stingray to be treated worse somewhere else. I'm not climbing down the ladder of success. *(He has taken off his wig, shoes, jewelry, makeup, etc. He gets up to leave the room.)* I've had it. My feet are swollen. Please don't wake me up till at least Thursday.

(He exits the bedroom to the TV room down the hall. FELONY and BOBO resume kissing. After a beat, CHARLOTTE and DENNIS scream at the top of their lungs, off-stage. CHARLOTTE runs back into the bedroom.)

CHARLOTTE: There's a child in there! Oh my God! What's he doing in there? How did he get in there?

FELONY: His name is Dennis.

CHARLOTTE: Name!? Where the hell did he come from? I've never seen anything so horrifying in my entire life!

BOBO: He's just some purse snatcher Felony brought home.

FELONY: He's a poor, homeless kid who needed a place to sleep.

CHARLOTTE: Homeless purse snatcher, Felony Mayhem, are you on crack?!

DENNIS: *(Enters and stands in the doorway shoeless, maybe in shorts and an undershirt, like he was trying to sleep.)* What's going on?

FELONY: Dennis, this is Charlotte, my oldest and dearest friend.

DENNIS: Hello.

CHARLOTTE: Hello?!

FELONY: Charlotte, this is Dennis, my new friend. He needed a place to stay for the night, so I told him he could use the TV room.

CHARLOTTE: You gave him my room?

FELONY: It's not your room. Charlotte sometimes drops by after work so she doesn't have to go all the way home so late. Charlotte has a little show she does at a club nearby.

CHARLOTTE: Little show?

DENNIS: I should leave.

FELONY: Don't be silly. Charlotte can sleep on the futon in the living room tonight.

CHARLOTTE: I what?!

FELONY: Oh, let him have the nice bed, just for the night. Unless you don't mind dragging yourself up to Riverdale.

CHARLOTTE: At five in the morning? You evil bitch. Who is this filthy monster?!

FELONY: Bobo, why don't you be a big, strong man and open up the futon in the living room for my dear friend Charlotte.

BOBO: *(Not moving.)* She's a big girl, she can do it herself.

FELONY: *(Pulling him out of bed.)* Now, now, be a gracious host, and get Charlotte a drink.

(BOBO exits the bedroom.)

FELONY: Dennis, sweetie, go back to bed.

DENNIS: Are you sure?

FELONY: I'm sure. I'll see you in the...uh...afternoon.

DENNIS: Okay. *(He exits to the TV room.)*

FELONY: There. Now everything's settled—

CHARLOTTE: Felony Mayhem, what the fuck do you suppose you're doing?

FELONY: Don't you recognize him? That's the kid who stole my bag.

CHARLOTTE: Oh. That explains why he's sleeping in my bed.

FELONY: I tricked him. I pretended I was picking him up so I could get him back here and fuck with his head.

CHARLOTTE: That's so you.

FELONY: Only he freaked out. He had a breakdown, or something.

CHARLOTTE: A breakdown? So why the hell is he still here?

FELONY: He had no place to go.

CHARLOTTE: So he's moving in here? Oh, sure. Now he can really rip you off.

FELONY: There's nothing to rip off. He's not moving in anywhere.

CHARLOTTE: He could kill you in the middle of the night.

FELONY: *(Laughs.)* Shut up, Charlotte.

CHARLOTTE: You're just gonna trust some piece of pier trash purse snatcher—

FELONY: Yes, I trust him. I don't know why, but I do. I trust him, okay?

CHARLOTTE: What the hell does that mean?

FELONY: I have no idea. *(Gets back in bed.)*

CHARLOTTE: And when did you turn into Clair Huxtable, mother of the year?

BOBO: *(Entering with a drink for CHARLOTTE.)* One kerosene and tonic for the lady.

CHARLOTTE: *(Taking it as he exits the bedroom.)* Can I change that to a Thorazine drip?

FELONY: There's Percodan and Valium in the medicine cabinet. That's the best I can do.

(CHARLOTTE shuts the hall light and goes to the living room, as BOBO gets in bed.)

FELONY: Are you okay? Are you mad?

BOBO: What the hell just happened?

FELONY: What makes you think I know? He broke my heart a little, okay?

BOBO: He's out of here tomorrow.

FELONY: Of course he is. Of course. Of course.

(BOBO is not convinced.)

SCENE II

DENNIS and IVAN enter the apartment and turn the hall light on. They both wear light jackets. IVAN is Latino and around DENNIS's age, carrying a backpack. They enter the bedroom, holding hands or touching. DENNIS looks around without turning on the bedroom light. The bedroom is a bit less tidy than before. Perhaps the bed is not as neatly fixed, and maybe there are a few items of clothing on the chairs. On the bookshelf above the dresser, there is now a framed photo of DENNIS.

DENNIS: Felony?… No one's here.

(IVAN spins DENNIS around and pins him in the doorway with a kiss. DENNIS finally pulls away and drags IVAN down the hall to the TV room, now DENNIS's room. We hear the door close. About five seconds later, we hear it open. DENNIS rushes back into the bedroom. His shoes are off. With only the light from the hallway, he starts going through FELONY's drawers, looking for something. IVAN walks to the bedroom doorway.)

DENNIS: They gotta have some. I know they use them.

IVAN: Look in the night table.

DENNIS: I looked there.

(DENNIS keeps looking around. IVAN steps into the bedroom to check it out. He sees a boom box or CD system on the coffee table.)

DENNIS: Where the hell would they be? Unless they ran out. Damn.

(IVAN picks up the CD case lying out. It's something classically sexy from FELONY's vintage—maybe Marvin Gaye or Barry White. He hits the play button. It plays. DENNIS, by this time, is sitting on the edge of the bed, looking through the night table one more time.)

DENNIS: They should be here, don't you think?

(IVAN walks over and stands in front of DENNIS. He peels his shirt off and climbs on top of DENNIS. They make out, oblivious to what is going on around them. FELONY and CHARLOTTE enter the apartment with shopping bags. Both are in normal street clothes. They enter the bedroom and find DENNIS and IVAN on the bed. DENNIS and IVAN don't hear them over the music. FELONY switches the light on. DENNIS and IVAN are thoroughly occupied, eyes closed, and don't notice the light. FELONY walks around the bed and shuts the CD off. The boys still don't notice.)

FELONY: Have we met?

(The boys finally notice they are not alone and jump up.)

CHARLOTTE: This is sickening.

FELONY: Hello. I'm Felony.

DENNIS: Hey, Felony. What are you… uh… I thought you—

CHARLOTTE: During the day?

DENNIS: I'm… uh… we were… uh—

FELONY: I can see you were, Dennis. And do you mind if I ask why you were doing it here?

DENNIS: We were… uh—

FELONY: Yes?

DENNIS: We were… looking for condoms.

FELONY: Looking for condoms?! *(He stops himself. He decides not to have a typical parental reaction.)* Well, I suppose that's good… I'm glad you were looking for condoms… I'm glad you were going to use condoms.

CHARLOTTE: That's right, Greg. And I'm counting on you to make sure Marcia uses them too.

DENNIS: I'm not stupid.

FELONY: I know you're not stupid…and I'm glad. *(To IVAN.)* Have we still not met?

DENNIS: Felony, Ivan. Ivan, Felony.

FELONY: Ivan? Ivan from the pier outreach group?

IVAN: I guess.

FELONY: Well, it's very nice to finally meet you. I'm Felony Mayhem. I'm Dennis's, uh—

IVAN: I know who you are. You're his Auntie Mayhem.

FELONY: Auntie Mayhem?…Auntie Mayhem?

CHARLOTTE: Oh, that's precious. *(Exits to the kitchen.)*

FELONY: Ivan, it appears your well-laid plans have gone a bit astray.

IVAN: Say what?

DENNIS: Get dressed, Ivan.

(IVAN grabs his shirt and exits to the TV room.)

FELONY: Do you often have boys here when I'm out?

DENNIS: This is the first time.

FELONY: The first time? Really?

DENNIS: Third time?

FELONY: Three times or three boys?

DENNIS: Three boys, five times.

FELONY: Five times, that's all? In a year and a half?

DENNIS: Yes.

FELONY: Are you quite sure, or do you need to think about it a little longer?

DENNIS: I'm sure.

FELONY: Five?

DENNIS: Five.

FELONY: Well...that's not too bad. I shouldn't be too angry, even though you did it without asking me.

DENNIS: I won't do it again. I swear.

FELONY: Please don't make promises you can't keep... Oh well, I suppose it's better you do it here than...anywhere else, I guess. *(Getting serious.)* Can I trust your judgment about who should and who should not be allowed in this apartment when I'm not here?

DENNIS: You know I don't like nasty boys.

FELONY: I know. I know you don't like nasty boys... All right, Dennis, I will trust you because I have no choice. But don't make me regret it.

DENNIS: You won't tell Bobo.

FELONY: I won't tell Bobo... Does his mother allow you to...in his apartment as well?

DENNIS: He doesn't live with her any more.

FELONY: Isn't this the boy who lives with his mother and his sisters in the Bronx?

DENNIS: He left.

FELONY: He left? Why did he leave?

DENNIS: Ask him.

FELONY: Do you know? Did he tell you?

DENNIS: Her boyfriend or something. She's a fucking crackhead.

(We hear the front door open. BOBO enters, carrying grocery bags. He walks past the bedroom doorway. IVAN passes him on his way to the front door, dressed with his jacket on and carrying his backpack.)

BOBO: Hey.

IVAN: Hey. See you, Dennis.

DENNIS: Later.

FELONY: Ivan?

BOBO: *(Turning back to IVAN, who has passed.)* Have we met?

FELONY: Ivan, where are you going?

IVAN: *(From the hallway, out of sight.)* Nowhere.

FELONY: Ivan, come in here, please.

(IVAN comes back into the bedroom. BOBO goes to the kitchen to drop the bags.)

FELONY: Stay a little, Ivan. We haven't even had a chance to talk.

IVAN: Are we in trouble?

FELONY: Not yet.

IVAN: We weren't going to do anything.

DENNIS: It's all right.

IVAN: 'Cause, I mean...really, we just—

DENNIS: Ivan, he's cool.

FELONY: Yes, dear, I'm cool.

IVAN: Oh. Well, I'm sorry—

BOBO: *(Enters the bedroom, taking his jacket off.)* Sorry for what?

FELONY: For running out without introducing himself. Bobo, this is Ivan, Dennis's friend.

BOBO: From the safe sex education thing?

DENNIS: Yeah.

BOBO: Oh. Nice to meet you.

IVAN: Nice to meet you, too, sir.

BOBO: Sir?

FELONY: Ivan, how's your mom?

IVAN: My mom?

DENNIS: Felony—

FELONY: I haven't spoken to her in a long time.

IVAN: When did you ever speak to her?

FELONY: Oh, I don't know, a few times.

DENNIS: Once when you called looking for me. We were working on the condom pamphlet.

IVAN: Yeah?

FELONY: Anyway, she seemed like such a nice woman.

DENNIS: Felony—

IVAN: She's a fucking basket case.

FELONY: A basket case? Why is that?

IVAN: Wish I knew.

CHARLOTTE: *(Enters with a drink.)* Playtime over, boys?

FELONY: *(To BOBO.)* Dennis and Ivan were...doing some work for the little group.

CHARLOTTE: Is that it?

FELONY: Yes, dear. They were, uh—

CHARLOTTE: Testing condoms for durability.

BOBO: What?

FELONY: They were doing some research for their project.

CHARLOTTE: Research, yes. Working their little tails off, from what I saw.

BOBO: What are you—

FELONY: Charlotte—

CHARLOTTE: Personally, I think it's great that you two get so immersed in your safe sex work.

FELONY: Charlotte—

CHARLOTTE: Well, that way you can teach others from a more personal perspective.

BOBO: What is she—

FELONY: Charlotte—

IVAN: Are you Charlotte Reyes?

CHARLOTTE: I'm...excuse me?

IVAN: You're Charlotte Reyes! I just figured that out!

CHARLOTTE: Have we met?

IVAN: Actually, we did once, at the Heritage of Pride awards.

CHARLOTTE: *(Obviously not remembering.)* Was that you?

IVAN: I've seen you a lot of times. You're hysterical.

CHARLOTTE: Oh...well...thank you. How did you see me a lot of times? You're too young to get in.

IVAN: Pride rally in Bryant Park. A few other places I snuck in. Wigstock.

CHARLOTTE: Wigstock, you must have been in diapers.

IVAN: I was pretty young. Anyway, I'm a really big fan.

CHARLOTTE: Well, that's very nice of you.

FELONY: You see, Charlotte, you do have a fan.

CHARLOTTE: I have plenty of fans.

IVAN: She's got a ton of fans. She's, like, this big old drag diva.

CHARLOTTE: Old?

FELONY: And you were doing so well, dear. We almost had her.

IVAN: I don't mean old old. I mean, like, you know. You're, like, one of the greats.

CHARLOTTE: Hmm.

FELONY: Oooh, nice save. I think we might be okay.

IVAN: Anyway, I'd love to work with you one day.

CHARLOTTE: Work with me?

DENNIS: Ivan's a dancer.

BOBO: Dancer? Really? That's cool. Do you take class somewhere?

IVAN: Not right now, but I'm really good.

DENNIS: He is.

CHARLOTTE: That's nice, dear. I work alone.

FELONY: Well, don't you even want to see what he can do? I know I do.

CHARLOTTE: Felony—

BOBO: I do too.

DENNIS: He really is good.

IVAN: I been working on some stuff. I wanna do, like, a whole show. Dancing, and rapping, and singing, and jokes, like a cabaret type thing.

FELONY: A cabaret type thing? Isn't that like the type of thing you do, dear?

CHARLOTTE: The type of thing I do, dear, is a musical and comedy revue.

FELONY: That's what I said.

CHARLOTTE: A trip to the almost-forgotten torch songs and B sides of pop history.

BOBO: So, a lot of old shit.

IVAN: I do oldies.

FELONY: Like what?

IVAN: Janet Jackson's "If."

FELONY: Well, so go ahead, audition for Charlotte.

IVAN: Really?

CHARLOTTE: Felony—

FELONY: Oh, let's have some fun. Come on, show us one of your numbers.

IVAN: I can't. I don't have my tracks.

CHARLOTTE: How sad.

DENNIS: Do the rap.

IVAN: Oh, yeah, I guess so.

FELONY: A rap. We love rap, don't we Charlotte?

CHARLOTTE: Hmm.

IVAN: Okay. *(To DENNIS.)* You gotta help me out with the beat.

(IVAN starts the beat, making various percussion sounds. DENNIS picks it up and continues throughout the rap which IVAN performs with choreography.)

IVAN: This ain't your grandpa's sexual identity
You know I gotta find my own kinda serenity
It ain't about Hugo Boss suits or Paul Mitchell in your hair

Gaultier accessories or Calvin Klein
underwear
Whittall and Shon, Abercrombie and
Fitch
Dolce and Gabana, I can't tell which
one is which
Just a lot of airheads trippin' down the
runway
Just a lot of nobodies makin' the front
page
Gianni shot dead, Donatella got the blues
O.J. Simpson trackin' blood in Bruno
Magli shoes
I don't shake the right hands or chill
at the right party
Got no rich lover or the cover to the
white party
Black party, circuit party, never see me
there
Ain't been to Fire Island 'cause I can't
afford a time share
I hate *Funny Girl* and *Gypsy*, do you
believe
I never seen *A Star Is Born* or *All About
Eve*
Don't care about Betty White, or Ellen
Greene, or Karen Black
And the last twenty years of
Sondheim's whack
Liza's back, didn't even know she was
gone
You know it sounds like the same old
shit she's always done
Ethel Merman, Judy Garland, Billie
Holiday
What dead diva's grave are we dancin'
on today
Not that I don't give props to the de-
parted
The ones who planted the seed, who
got it started
Shouts to the trannies in their panties
and their underwire
Took over the Stonewall, set the Vil-
lage on fire

Back to the Daughters of Bilitis before
And the Mattachine Society challeng-
ing the old law
Sylvia, and Marcia P. and Harry Hay
Laid the tracks that brought us to
where we are today
But we gotta fight a new war, sing a
new song that'll
Bring the children to the floor, lead
them into new battle
Gotta come together, gotta spread it
around
Gotta make a lot of noise, gotta get
the message uptown
Midtown, out-a-town, shout it out to
there
'Cause the world's my ghetto, hey,
we're everywhere
Now the West Village just a lotta
straight white Jersey chicks
Stonewall's just a place to see some
uncut Latin dicks
Chelsea's just a latte with a apple mar-
tini
And a muscle boy on steroids with a
shriveled-up weenie
Let's take it to the Bronx, to the moun-
tains, to the sticks
You know the world don't actually end
at Ninety-Sixth
And we ain't just LG or LGBT
And we ain't Generation X, Y, or Z
We're intersex, two-spirit, tranny, and
straight
Anybody can be queer so long as you
don't hate
Definitions divide us, but the total sum
Is we're all just one long continuum
That's what queer's about, we're Gen-
eration Q
And we're shaking up the world, so
how about you?

(All but CHARLOTTE cheer wildly.)

FELONY: Well, that was catchy.

BOBO: Wow, you're good.

IVAN: You think?

CHARLOTTE: Hmm. *(He goes to the CDs near the boom box and starts flipping through them.)*

BOBO: That was really good. Wow, that was something, wasn't it?

FELONY: What are you looking for?

IVAN: Thanks.

CHARLOTTE: Tracks, darling, tracks.

FELONY: Are you going to show him how it's done?

CHARLOTTE: Oh, yes we are.

FELONY: Oh fun. Charlotte's going to show you… we? What do you mean we?

CHARLOTTE: Denise, did you know that your…"Auntie Mayhem" wasn't always the quiet, demure wallflower of a housewife and mother you see before you.

FELONY: I wasn't?

CHARLOTTE: In fact, before she met…"Uncle Bobo," she was known to do any number of tasteless things for money.

FELONY: I surely have no idea what you're talking about.

CHARLOTTE: But none quite as tasteless as a tasteless little act we used to do together at a tasteless little club or two, before she abandoned me for this domestic sedation. *(Finds the right CD.)* Ah hah. I knew you would still have these, you are such a little pack rat.

FELONY: Darling, you don't expect me to remember any of this.

CHARLOTTE: Like riding a bicycle.

FELONY: You know I stopped the ginko when I started to remember 1993.

CHARLOTTE: Come on. This was your idea.

FELONY: My idea?

CHARLOTTE: Besides, it's time they knew the truth about you.

FELONY: All right, all right, all right.

CHARLOTTE: Look, boas.

(CHARLOTTE finds a few feather boas hanging around. He throws one to FELONY who finds an old pair of high heels and puts them on.)

FELONY: Just play it.

(BOBO hits the CD player. CHARLOTTE and FELONY perform a choreographed routine, singing live to the recorded instrumental tracks. The song is "Big Girl Now," by Lisa Gold. The number is professional quality, except for FELONY's occasional out-of-practice mistakes.)

CHARLOTTE: You used to live down the street from me

FELONY: Used to play doctor and the visits were free

CHARLOTTE: Shared a lot of firsts

FELONY: Thought that it would last

CHARLOTTE: Then you moved away boy, now

CHARLOTTE and FELONY: That's all in the past
  As I've gotten older I've grown along the way
  And I wonder if you'd recognize me today
  I'm a big girl now, a big girl now
  And I'm ready for some action, can you feel the attraction

I'm a big girl now, a big girl now
And I know that you love me, and you
     want every part of me
I'm a big girl now

CHARLOTTE: Through the years I've wondered what became of you

FELONY: And have you thought about me, and

CHARLOTTE and FELONY: All the things I used to do

CHARLOTTE: How I made you feel

FELONY: I knew what turned you on

CHARLOTTE: I've only gotten better baby

CHARLOTTE and FELONY: Since you've been gone
     As I've gotten older I've grown along
        the way
     And I wonder if you'd recognize me
        today
     I'm a big girl now, a big girl now
     And I'm ready for some action, can
        you feel the attraction
     I'm a big girl now, a big girl now
     And I know that you love me, and you
        want every part of me
     I'm a big girl now

CHARLOTTE: This is who I am

FELONY: No apologies

CHARLOTTE: There's only more to love

CHARLOTTE and FELONY: Of me
     Gotta want it, gotta try it
     Gotta need it, can't deny it
     Gotta want it, gotta try it
     Gotta need it, can't deny it
     Big girl
     Gotta want it, gotta try it
     Gotta need it, can't deny it
     Big girl

(BOBO and the boys applaud wildly.)

FELONY: There. Now you know why I quit.

IVAN: You were fabulous.

BOBO: You still know what you're doing, babe.

CHARLOTTE: Honey, we were this close to making it, but you gave it up and settled for all this.

FELONY: I'm quite happy with all this, thank you. And now, if you don't mind, the show is over. I have things to do.

(The boys get up to leave. IVAN grabs his jacket and bag.)

FELONY: Ivan?

IVAN: Yeah.

FELONY: You'll stay for dinner?

IVAN: Okay. Thanks.

FELONY: You're welcome. Are you sure your mother won't mind?

IVAN: Doubt it.

FELONY: Do you want to call her and let her know?

IVAN: That's okay. She doesn't care.

(He exits with DENNIS to his room.)

CHARLOTTE: Why did you make me do that? Now I'm all moist.

BOBO: Is that what that smell is?

CHARLOTTE: Oh well, we had quite a little party going there for a while, don't you think?

FELONY: Sure. *(He goes to the phone, finds a piece of paper with a number on it and dials.)*

BOBO: He was fucking miserable the whole time.

CHARLOTTE: What the hell do you know?

BOBO: He was a mess. He was broke.

CHARLOTTE: All struggling artists are broke. We were this close.

BOBO: He never made a fucking cent working with you.

CHARLOTTE: What are you talking about? We got paid.

FELONY: *(On the phone.)* Hello, is this...Ivan's mother?

BOBO: Maybe you got paid.

FELONY: *(On the phone.)* This is Felony—

BOBO: He never saw a fucking dime.

FELONY: *(On the phone.)* Dennis's, uh—

BOBO: That's what I heard.

FELONY: *(On the phone.)* Yes, hi, how are you?

CHARLOTTE: Please.

FELONY: *(On the phone.)* I'm sorry to bother you.

BOBO: Not for the show, anyway. Maybe for after the show.

FELONY: *(On the phone.)* I was just calling because Ivan—

CHARLOTTE: Oh, where the fuck are you going with this now?

BOBO: Whose idea was all that shit you two did?

FELONY: *(On the phone.)* I'm sorry. I didn't mean to—

CHARLOTTE: What ancient shit are you dredging up now?

BOBO: Fucking trash.

FELONY: *(On the phone.)* Well, actually Miss...Lisa.

CHARLOTTE: Oh, grow up, Bobo.

FELONY: *(On the phone.)* Lisa, I haven't really spoken to Ivan about anything—

BOBO: He was miserable.

FELONY: *(On the phone.)* ...but I sensed—

BOBO: He hated himself for doing that shit.

CHARLOTTE: Grow the fuck up.

BOBO: For sinking so fucking low.

FELONY: *(On the phone.)* Yes, Dennis mentioned that to me.

CHARLOTTE: Drama, drama, drama, drama—

FELONY: *(On the phone.)* I don't understand...what you mean.

BOBO: For listening to you, like an idiot, for spending every fucking penny he had in the world, for losing his fucking apartment—

FELONY: *(On the phone.)* Can't come home? Can't?

CHARLOTTE: Oh, it was my fault he lost the apartment?

BOBO: Of course it was your fault.

FELONY: *(On the phone.)* Lisa, I really don't mean to intrude, but your boyfriend—

CHARLOTTE: 'Cause he doesn't have a mind of his own.

FELONY: *(On the phone.)* Well, maybe you should ask Gideon to leave.

BOBO: 'Cause it was your idea he should quit his fucking day job so he could stay up all night, your idea he should give you all his fucking money to spend on the show—

FELONY: *(On the phone.)* I'm sorry, Lisa, but if my boyfriend didn't like my son—

CHARLOTTE: Shut the fuck up.

FELONY: *(On the phone.)* ...for whatever reason—

CHARLOTTE: We were young, we had a dream. We survived. Jesus, didn't you ever have a fucking dream?

BOBO: He survived because I brought some fucking sanity back into his life.

FELONY: *(On the phone.)* I'm not trying to stick my—

CHARLOTTE: Sanity? You brought boredom into his life. It's like pulling teeth to get him to do anything, he's got a fucking curfew or something.

FELONY: *(On the phone.)* Yes, but Lisa, don't you need to consider his feelings just a little?

BOBO: He has a fucking life, okay? Didn't you hear him—

FELONY: *(On the phone. He is furious and can hold back no longer.)* Ivan's feelings! Ivan's. Not your God damn boyfriend's feelings. Your son's! Your son's!

(CHARLOTTE and BOBO realize something is going on.)

FELONY: *(On the phone.)* If my boyfriend couldn't stand my son, I would throw my boyfriend's ass out, not my son's. Does this not make the slightest bit of sense to you?... Seventeen is not old enough to be out on his own. That's the most ridiculous thing I've ever heard... What is he supposed to do, support himself, get his own apartment... You don't? May I ask, then, out of curiosity, did he do something in particular to make you not "give a flying fuck?"... Other than disgust your boyfriend.

(LISA hangs up on FELONY.)

BOBO: What the fuck was that?

FELONY: What a stupid, infuriating, fucked-up—

BOBO: That was Ivan's mother?

FELONY: Yes.

BOBO: What was that about?

FELONY: Apparently her boyfriend, Gideon, is a homophobic asshole who is disgusted by Ivan and his friends.

BOBO: What does that mean?

FELONY: It means she won't let Ivan in the apartment. She's thrown him out.

CHARLOTTE: Is that legal?

FELONY: That doesn't matter.

BOBO: Can't force her to take him back. It would be a fucking nightmare for the kid.

CHARLOTTE: So he's the city's problem now.

FELONY: Oh, please.

BOBO: How old is he?

FELONY: Seventeen.

BOBO: Ha. Forget about it.

CHARLOTTE: Why?

BOBO: You remember all the shit they put us through with Dennis 'cause he was sixteen. They don't want him. They'll just drag it out and bounce him around until he's eighteen and he's not their responsibility anymore. He's better off on the streets.

FELONY: Don't say that. *(Goes to the hallway in front of the doorway.)*

BOBO: You know what I mean.

FELONY: Dennis?

DENNIS: *(Offstage.)* What?

FELONY: Come here, please.

BOBO: Do you think he knows?

(DENNIS comes to the doorway. FELONY takes him inside and closes the door.)

DENNIS: What'd I do?

FELONY: I just spoke to Ivan's mother.

DENNIS: You did?

FELONY: Did you know she won't let him come home?

DENNIS: I told you. Her boyfriend hates him.

FELONY: You say that like it makes sense.

DENNIS: Whatever. She's a total crackhead. I think Gideon's her fucking dealer, or some shit.

FELONY: Or some shit? So where does Ivan sleep?

DENNIS: I think he still stays at this squat on Seventeenth or Eighteenth.

FELONY: What does that mean, a squat?

DENNIS: Some old building they're getting ready to knock down. A bunch of kids break into it after dark and sleep there. They split before morning.

FELONY: That's...that's—

DENNIS: It's warmer than sleeping outside, and the cops don't bug you like they do in the subway. At least until they figure it out. Then you have to find another building.

FELONY: How come he seems so...well, so clean, for one thing?

DENNIS: They got showers at some of the drop-in centers. He's a pretty smart guy. He still goes to school.

CHARLOTTE: He goes to school?

DENNIS: Yeah.

BOBO: He lives in a building with no electricity or water?

DENNIS: Yeah.

CHARLOTTE: And he goes to school?

DENNIS: Yeah.

CHARLOTTE: Every day?

DENNIS: I guess so. Most days. I know he just had a bunch of tests.

FELONY: Does the school know about this? Are they doing anything?

DENNIS: I don't know. Probably not, unless somebody reports it.

FELONY: Thank you, Dennis.

(DENNIS starts to leave.)

FELONY: Dennis?

DENNIS: Yeah?

FELONY: Does he want to stay here tonight?

DENNIS: He'd probably like that.

FELONY: Please ask him.

DENNIS: Okay. *(Leaves.)*

CHARLOTTE: Felony, you are not going to do this.

BOBO: Do what?

CHARLOTTE: I am not going to let you this time.

FELONY: I'm just going to help him... figure all this out.

BOBO: We can help him. Of course we can help him.

CHARLOTTE: Oh, no. I know just how this is going to end up.

BOBO: No, it's not.

FELONY: He's the nicest kid.

BOBO: Yes, he is. One night.

FELONY: I can't just let him sleep in some rat-infested abandoned building.

CHARLOTTE: And how are you supposed to help him?

FELONY: I mean, he's…he's Dennis's…. Dennis's friend.

BOBO: Oh, no. Felony, you know we can't…oh, come on.

CHARLOTTE: Just because the city doesn't want him.

BOBO: What are we running, a group home now?

FELONY: What am I supposed to do, just throw him out?

BOBO: Yes… no… he has a mother.

FELONY: You said it yourself. You can't force her to take him back. That would be the worst thing for him.

BOBO: So he's our responsibility?

CHARLOTTE: There's a million kids like that, Felony.

BOBO: You can't just take a kid from his mother.

FELONY: She doesn't want him.

BOBO: How do you know? You've only spoken to her once.

FELONY: Twice. Do you remember Dennis's mother? I know what these people are like.

CHARLOTTE: What people? I thought Dennis's mother's some fundamentalist religious freak.

FELONY: Oh, and a crackhead is going to be easier to deal with? Any homophobe who throws her kid out is not a suitable parent.

BOBO: Maybe she just needs some counseling.

FELONY: Fine, he'll stay here until she gets counseling.

BOBO: Felony, do you know how much another kid is going to cost us?

FELONY: Cost?! Cost?!

CHARLOTTE: Sweetie, at a certain point you just gotta say no.

FELONY: What do you know about it? You eat children for breakfast.

CHARLOTTE: Actually, this one's not so bad.

(FELONY and BOBO are speechless.)

CHARLOTTE: I mean, the act needs some work, of course, but he's got a kinda…spark.

BOBO: Is this even legal, taking kids in we don't even know?

FELONY: It can't be harder to take a seventeen-year-old in than it was to take a sixteen-year-old.

BOBO: And that was a pain in the ass, as I recall. Home checks, paperwork, prying into our lives—

FELONY: They did all that already. We've already been approved.

BOBO: So have a lot of other people.

FELONY: Please, when a kid's seventeen they're just counting down the days till he's eighteen and he's not their responsibility anymore. We both know he'll never get placed. You can't just throw him out.

BOBO: Watch me.

FELONY: You can't. You have too big a heart to do that.

BOBO: What?!

FELONY: You have the biggest heart I know.

BOBO: Stop it, Felony!

FELONY: You know, I never even knew that about you until he came along.

BOBO: What are you talking about?

FELONY: Dennis. He never had a father before in his entire life.

BOBO: Father? Oh, please. *(Goes to the doorway.)*

FELONY: He needed that so badly. And the funny thing is it was so easy for you—

BOBO: *(Calls down the hall.)* Dennis!

FELONY: ...like you'd been waiting for him to show up.

BOBO: Dennis.

DENNIS: *(Offstage.)* Yeah?

BOBO: Could you come here please?

FELONY: What are you going to do?

BOBO: I'm gonna do... I don't know.

DENNIS: *(Enters the bedroom.)* What's up?

BOBO: Dennis, listen. Ivan seems like a really nice guy.

DENNIS: He is pretty nice. I like him.

BOBO: Well, good. I... that's great.

DENNIS: Thanks for letting him stay over, by the way.

BOBO: Oh. Well—

DENNIS: He didn't say anything when I told him, but I could tell he was really happy.

BOBO: Yeah?

DENNIS: It's kind of gross where he's staying.

CHARLOTTE: Have you seen it?

DENNIS: No, but he told me. There's, like, rats and all kinds of garbage from other people staying there.

BOBO: Yeah. It must be lousy. Listen, Dennis, I really like him and all...like I said—

DENNIS: He likes you too. I can tell. Thank you for saying nice things about his rap.

BOBO: Oh...sure.

DENNIS: He works so hard on that stuff.

BOBO: Well, it shows.

DENNIS: Gideon's always ripping him about it.

BOBO: Ripping him? What do you mean?

DENNIS: Telling him his stuff is shit and he's never gonna be anything, he's just a no-talent little faggot punk. Fucking his head up. Fucking asshole.

BOBO: Really? That kinda sucks.

DENNIS: Ivan's always telling me how lucky I am.

FELONY: Lucky? Why?

DENNIS: You know. He still doesn't have a dad.

BOBO: A dad?

DENNIS: Did you want something, Bobo? I mean... *(Laughs.)* Uncle Bobo.

BOBO: Uh... yeah... I...

DENNIS: Yeah? Are you okay?

BOBO: I just...wanted to know if you...need any help with your...your project. You know.

DENNIS: Oh. No, thanks. We got it covered. *(Starts to leave.)* But thanks for asking, Uncle Bobo. *(Laughs again and leaves.)*

(BOBO sits on the bed. He has given in. FELONY sits with him.)

CHARLOTTE: I see. And may I ask where we're going to store this one?

BOBO: I guess he can crash with Dennis for tonight.

FELONY and CHARLOTTE: I don't think so.

BOBO: Why not?

FELONY: He'll sleep on the futon in the living room.

BOBO: Whatever.

CHARLOTTE: The living room? Wait a minute!

SCENE III

The room is dark, except for a light coming in through a window. It is early morning. FELONY is asleep under the sheets, wearing pajama bottoms and a sleep mask over his eyes. The room is a bit of a mess. Clothing is thrown on the floor and draped on the chairs. On the bookshelf above the dresser, there is now a framed picture of IVAN next to the picture of DENNIS. DENNIS enters the bedroom and flicks the lights on. He has a towel wrapped around his waist, and his hair is wet and uncombed. He now has a small, trendy goatee. He sees FELONY is still in bed. Annoyed, he goes to the bed and tries to wake him.

DENNIS: Felony... Felony... Felony... Auntie Mayhem!

FELONY: *(Bolting up in bed, the mask still on.)* What! What! What!

DENNIS: *(Pulling FELONY's mask off.)* Felony, did you iron my shirt?

FELONY: Iron your... iron... where... what...what time is it?

DENNIS: It's a quarter to eight.

FELONY: A quarter to...quarter to...oh my God! What am I doing in bed? How in the world did I sleep so—

DENNIS: In the morning, Felony.

FELONY: In the morning...in the morn—

DENNIS: Felony, it's Monday. You promised you'd iron my shirt and make me breakfast so I wouldn't be late. I told you I'd do it all myself, but you insisted. Does this, like, ring a bell or something?

FELONY: Dennis! Your new job! My little baby's going to work. And a real job, too. I'm so proud—

DENNIS: Auntie Mayhem, did you iron my shirt?

FELONY: Your shirt. Your shirt. Oh, yes, I told you I'd do it this morning, didn't I.

DENNIS: Yes, Felony. Did you do it?

FELONY: Well, I'm... right now... I'm doing it right now, like I told you... iron... your shirt.

DENNIS: Thank you, Felony.

(He starts to leave. When he gets to the door, he turns to check. FELONY is lying down again and falling back to sleep. DENNIS grabs the blanket and rips it off. FELONY jumps out of bed.)

DENNIS: Come on, Felony, don't make me late!

FELONY: I'm up! I'm up! I'm up!

(DENNIS exits the bedroom. When he is gone, FELONY grabs his head with both hands, wobbling, his eyes bugging out, obviously quite hung over. EPIPHANY pokes her head in the door. She is half-asleep. She is sixteen, male-to-female transgender. She is wearing girlish pajamas or a robe, maybe pink, fuzzy slippers.)

EPIPHANY: What's going on? Why is everybody up?

FELONY: Epiphany, honey, go back to bed.

EPIPHANY: I can't sleep. Denise is making too much noise.

FELONY: Dennis is starting his new job today, honey. A real job. He's a little nervous about it so let's all try and be supportive. Darling, have you seen my top?

(EPIPHANY finds the pajama top, maybe on the chair or at the foot of the bed, and tosses it to FELONY.)

EPIPHANY: What do you mean, a real job?

FELONY: (Putting on the top.) A job. A job. In an office of some kind, I think.

EPIPHANY: Why is she doing that?

FELONY: Why is she… Because it's the right thing to… what do you mean why is she doing that? What kind of a question is that? Don't you want to have a real job one day, sweetie? So you can have a real career, and a real life, and make some real money, and maybe get a co-op of your own, and lots of nice things?

EPIPHANY: (Sits at the makeup table.) So what are you doing up?

FELONY: (Grabs the ironing board that is against the wall, or maybe out in the hallway, and sets it up.) I'm helping. I prom-

ised I'd make him breakfast and iron his shirt. Oh, God, I should have done this last night. Why didn't I do this last night?… Why didn't I do this last night?… What did I do last night?

EPIPHANY: You went out.

FELONY: I went out? I went out. That's a start. Where did I go?

EPIPHANY: I don't know. You were with that bitch.

FELONY: Which bitch, sweetie?

EPIPHANY: That old bitch. La Gran Puta. Señora Eighties Has-Been.

FELONY: Señora…Has-Been? Are you talking about Charlotte? Darling, Charlotte's not a "has been." She's one of the funniest drag acts in the city. What a terrible thing to say.

EPIPHANY: Oh please! She is so Charles Pierce. She is so last century. She hasn't read a magazine in about twenty years.

FELONY: Charlotte happens to be my best friend, and she happens to be very talented.

EPIPHANY: Auntie Mayhem, have you seen her act lately? Who the fuck is Vickie Lawrence? Who the fuck is Donna McKechnie? No one knows what the fuck she's talking about. It's not funny.

CHARLOTTE: You ten-dollar Port Authority blowjob, you disposable bare-backing tourist trash!

(CHARLOTTE jumps up from under a pile of clothes and blankets near the bed and chases after EPIPHANY. He is in drag costume and makeup, but half-dressed and completely disheveled. His makeup is smeared, his wig is missing, and his thinning hair is a mess.)

FELONY: (Coming between CHARLOTTE and EPIPHANY.) Darling, there you are. Epiphany, my little love, go and help your brother get ready. Go, honey, please.

CHARLOTTE: Go shave your arms, you little drag ball reject.

DENNIS: *(Enters the bedroom. He is in boxers and an undershirt. His wet hair is combed. He is carrying two dress shirts on hangers, one white and one blue.)* Felony, which…

(He bumps into EPIPHANY in the doorway.)

EPIPHANY: Good morning, Denise. Is this your little office outfit?

DENNIS: Dennis.

EPIPHANY: All shaved and showered and FDSed.

DENNIS: Some people have places to go.

(Hurt, EPIPHANY leaves.)

DENNIS: Auntie, which of these do you think?

CHARLOTTE: Smell her.

DENNIS: The white or the blue?

FELONY: Dennis, don't be so mean to Epiphany.

CHARLOTTE: Where in God's name are you going at this hour?

DENNIS: To work.

FELONY: You know how much she looks up to you.

DENNIS: How much she looks at me. How long is she gonna be here? I want my own room back.

FELONY: I don't know yet, sweetie.

CHARLOTTE: Who the hell goes to work at this hour?

DENNIS: Most people go to work at this hour, Charles.

CHARLOTTE: "Nah nah nah nah nah nah, Charles." *(To FELONY.)* Why do you still have this one?

DENNIS: You know, she's fifteen. You're gonna get in trouble.

FELONY: She's sixteen, and believe me, nobody else wants her.

DENNIS: So? That's Child Welfare's problem.

FELONY: Dennis! Do you remember what they did to you in those group homes? Has it been so long?

DENNIS: I remember.

FELONY: Oh, you remember. Just imagine what they do to a femme queen like Epiphany. She's safer on the street.

DENNIS: Yeah, well, they're gonna be looking for her.

FELONY: I know, I know. Whichever shirt you like, my little love. Dennis is starting a new job today, Charlotte. A real job, at…an office of some kind.

DENNIS: A trust company.

FELONY: A trust company? A trust company. Doesn't that sound impressive, Charlotte?

(He takes the blue shirt from DENNIS. He notices the goatee and touches it.)

FELONY: When did you grow this?

(DENNIS pushes FELONY's hand away and leaves.)

FELONY: When did he grow that? *(He finishes setting the iron up.)*

CHARLOTTE: *(Stands and looks in the mirror.)* God, I look pregnant.

FELONY: How long has he been here?

CHARLOTTE: *(Beginning to straighten himself out.)* Forever.

FELONY: He was sixteen.

CHARLOTTE: Time to cut the cord, honey. Just cut it. Snip. One down, two to go.

FELONY: Three years?

CHARLOTTE: Three years? The heave-ho!

FELONY: *(Begins to iron.)* He was so scrawny, remember? And shy. He wouldn't have survived, like Ivan.

CHARLOTTE: So you throw me out to make room for Denise, that piece of pier trash?

FELONY: You had a place in Riverdale with your grandmother. You were just too lazy to drag your Styrofoam ass uptown. And he wasn't pier trash. He was just doing what he had to do.

(IVAN enters from outside. He is wearing black breakaway athletic pants and boots, a black leather jacket, a black or red tanktop, and shades.)

IVAN: You talking about me?

CHARLOTTE: My God, they're multiplying. Carol Anne! Where are my pills?!

IVAN: Hey Harlot.

(He jumps on the bed. They kiss, both cheeks.)

IVAN: What's everybody doing up?

CHARLOTTE: Denise is having trouble with her Epilady again. *(Makes his way to the makeup table and begins to straighten his face.)*

FELONY: Dennis is starting his new job today, sweetie.

IVAN: Why?

FELONY: Where were you all night, Ivan?

IVAN: Out.

FELONY: *(Checking out IVAN's eyes.)* Out. I see.

CHARLOTTE: Making money, honey?

IVAN: Whatever. Hey, Auntie Mayhem, can I have a hundred and fifty dollars?

(FELONY and CHARLOTTE both look at him, then look at each other and laugh.)

IVAN: What's so funny?

FELONY: Ivan, my little love, haven't I taught you if you want to have spending money you need to go out and earn it?

IVAN: No.

FELONY: I'm sure I did.

IVAN: I'm sure you didn't.

FELONY: Well then, I'm teaching you now.

IVAN: *(To CHARLOTTE.)* What did I do?

FELONY: Nothing, sweetie, it's just that…it's time you started…doing something with your life. That's all. Like your big brother.

IVAN: What big brother?

FELONY: Dennis.

IVAN: Dennis isn't my big brother.

FELONY: What do you mean, he's not your big brother? What a terrible thing to say. Aren't we all a family?

IVAN: I'm older than Dennis.

FELONY: You are?

IVAN: I'm five months older.

FELONY: Are you sure?

IVAN: Auntie Mayhem, I need a hundred and fifty dollars for work.

(FELONY and CHARLOTTE stare at him, then at each other.)

FELONY: For work?

CHARLOTTE: Am I in the right house? Is this the house of Mayhem? *(By now CHARLOTTE has found his wig and tries to put it on, maybe tying it up with a scarf rather than trying to straighten it out.)*

FELONY: What work is that, sweetie?

IVAN: I'm in a show.

CHARLOTTE: In a show?

FELONY: And what show would that be?

IVAN: At Sky.

CHARLOTTE: They gave you a show at Sky?

IVAN: Not my show. I'm a backup dancer.

CHARLOTTE: Backup? For who?

IVAN: Euthanasia.

CHARLOTTE: Euthanasia Gomez? Oh, no no no. You are not dancing backup for Euthanasia Gomez.

EPIPHANY: *(Entering.)* Hey, Ivana. How was the show?

IVAN: It was slammin'! Euthanasia comes out in, like, the Jennifer Lopez dress, totally showing off her new tetas that she just got redone.

FELONY: Epiphany, you knew about this?

IVAN: And me and Frankie are in these breakaway Nike pants.

CHARLOTTE: Dios mio.

IVAN: She's front and center, like— *(Jumps up on the bed and demonstrates, singing and dancing.)* "Hey, come on DJ play that song. You know that it turns me on."

And me and Frankie spin around from the back. "Hey, DJ, play that song 'cause I wanna be dancin' all night long." *(On "long" he drops forward, head between his legs, and grabs the hem of his breakaway pants and starts to rip them off.)*

FELONY and CHARLOTTE: *(Both holding up a hand to stop him.)* Please.

(IVAN does not pull his pants off.)

DENNIS: *(Entering in slacks and an undershirt, carrying his shoes and socks, putting his belt on.)* Is my shirt ready? *(He sits on the bed and puts his shoes and socks on.)*

FELONY: Just about, dear. So what do you need a hundred and fifty dollars for?

IVAN: My costume.

FELONY: A hundred and fifty dollars for a pair of pants?

IVAN: A hundred and fifty dollars for a leather g-string and a codpiece.

CHARLOTTE: Oh, now that's art.

FELONY: Darling, what's wrong with all the lovely g-strings you have?

CHARLOTTE: Why do you want to kill your career dancing with Euthanasia Gomez?

DENNIS: You're dancing with Euthanasia?

IVAN: *(Sticks his hand down the side of his pants and pulls out the waistband of his g-string.)* Oh, come on. These things are so ratty.

DENNIS: At Sky?

IVAN: Oh yes, I am!

DENNIS: I thought you were gonna be a dancer.

IVAN: Uh, I am a dancer.

DENNIS: Uh, I thought you meant a real dancer.

IVAN: Denise, is there something even bigger than usual up your butt?

CHARLOTTE: Ignore her. She's been like this all morning.

FELONY: Dennis is starting his new job today, sweetie.

IVAN: So?

CHARLOTTE: He thinks his cum doesn't stick any more.

FELONY: He's just a little nervous, that's all.

DENNIS: I'm not nervous.

FELONY: Well, of course you are, my little love. It's your first real job. New windows, new doors.

IVAN: For your information, Denise, Euthanasia is the hottest drag show in the city right now.

(FELONY, CHARLOTTE and EPIPHANY all laugh in unison.)

IVAN: What?!

CHARLOTTE: Honey, Euthanasia is still doing Karen Carpenter jokes. She hasn't changed her act in ten years.

(FELONY, EPIPHANY and IVAN laugh louder.)

CHARLOTTE: What?!

FELONY: Darling, last night you did that "gonorrhea-Chick Corea" bit.

CHARLOTTE: Felony Mayhem, that joke is a classic!

FELONY: You did your Joey Heatherton imitation.

CHARLOTTE: And I suppose you'd tell Bette Midler to stop doing Shelley Winters!

FELONY: I'm just saying you could use a little sprucing and pruning. That's all.

CHARLOTTE: Sprucing and pruning? That's what my act is to you, a fucking shrub?

IVAN: What the fuck is wrong with dancing at Sky? It's good practice. It's good exposure.

DENNIS: Why don't you, like, take dance classes, or some shit?

IVAN: Where?

DENNIS: I don't know. Some dance school.

IVAN: Uh, where am I gonna get that kind of money?

DENNIS: Uh, get a job.

IVAN: Uh, suck my dick.

DENNIS: Uh, fuck my ass.

IVAN: Not anymore, Papi.

CHARLOTTE: Why don't you ask your mother for the money?

IVAN: My mother? You did not say that.

DENNIS: Oh, shit.

CHARLOTTE: Why not? I thought you were talking.

IVAN: We were.

CHARLOTTE: What happened?

DENNIS: Gideon got out.

CHARLOTTE: Gideon got out? Gideon the crackhead?

IVAN: Gideon the dickhead.

CHARLOTTE: Did she take him back?

IVAN: Of course.

CHARLOTTE: Is she stupid? Is she on drugs?

IVAN: Yup and yup.

EPIPHANY: Devon says he's the one who kicked the shit out of Charity by the pier.

DENNIS: He was giving her crack for blowjobs and she bit him, or some shit.

IVAN: I don't want to talk about it.

CHARLOTTE: What is up with your mother? He beats the living crap out of her, and then as soon as he gets out of jail—

IVAN: *(Exploding.)* I said I don't want to fucking talk about it!

FELONY: *(From the ironing board.)* Ivan, sweetie, you know what I made last night?

IVAN: What?

FELONY: Chocolate chip cookies.

IVAN: *(Calming down.)* Pillsbury?

FELONY: I left them for you. They've been out all night.

IVAN: Really?

FELONY: They're in the kitchen. Go get them. We'll have them for breakfast.

IVAN: Thank you, Auntie Mayhem. You're my favorite auntie.

(He kisses FELONY and exits to the kitchen.)

FELONY: And some Kool-Aid.

CHARLOTTE: I thought I was your favorite auntie.

EPIPHANY: Poor Ivan.

DENNIS: Ivan's fine.

FELONY: Yes, honey, Ivan's fine. Why don't you go help him? *(As EPIPHANY exits.)* And don't talk about his mother.

CHARLOTTE: I'd like to kick that bitch in the shins till she wakes up.

FELONY: Oh, yes, 'cause she needs someone else beating her up.

CHARLOTTE: Well, I'm just being—

FELONY: Maternal, I know.

CHARLOTTE: Maternal? Ay, please.

FELONY: Well, darling, you know little Ivan worships you like a goddess.

DENNIS: Like a Buddha.

FELONY: You do get along so well. And weren't you just saying how your act could use a little sprucing up?

CHARLOTTE: Excuse me?

FELONY: You know, he really is talented, and very hard working. And he has crowds of suitors who'll follow him everywhere. That's why Euthanasia wants him so badly. Besides, Ivan's not like the other children. You can actually stand Ivan.

CHARLOTTE: That's the best you can do?

FELONY: I really don't like him hanging out with that Euthanasia person. Here you go, Dennis.

(He hands DENNIS the finished shirt. DENNIS grabs it and runs out.)

FELONY: You're welcome.

CHARLOTTE: They're gone. What a nice sound.

FELONY: They are not gone. They're just inside.

CHARLOTTE: Yes, Miss Clavel.

FELONY: I'm sorry. I'm just a little… I'm very happy for him. He's…growing up so fast.

CHARLOTTE: Not fast enough. Believe me, Felony, it is about time.

FELONY: About time what?

CHARLOTTE: About time you started thinking about getting your apartment back.

FELONY: Now, why would I want that?

CHARLOTTE: Why would you want that? Shall I make a list?

FELONY: Could I possibly stop you?

CHARLOTTE: *(By now, maybe CHAR-LOTTE is trying to find his high heels.)* Number one, they are all pigs. Your home has looked like the bargain bin at Caldor's since the day they moved in.

FELONY: Oh, and it was much nicer when you were sprawled out on a different part of the floor every night, Maybelline stains on the carpet, matted wig hair on the couch—

CHARLOTTE: Number two, they have no manners at all. No etiquette. No respect. It's as if they were raised in the gutter.

FELONY: First of all, they were raised in the gutter, more or less. And second of all… they have manners… usually… sometimes. What is your point?

CHARLOTTE: My point is, what on earth do they ever do for you? They are all so ravenously needy.

FELONY: Yes.

CHARLOTTE: Needy, needy, needy, twenty-four seven. And believe me, the minute they don't need you any more, as soon as they find someone else to foot the bill, they'll be out of your life so fast and you'll never hear from them again. Me and my Styrofoam ass, on the other hand, will still be here, staining your rugs and grubbing your liquor, till we're both in De-

pends and they have to drag us off by our orthopedic heels, kicking and screaming, to the Holly Woodlawn Home for Aging Drag Queens.

FELONY: How vivid.

CHARLOTTE: Face it, Chiquita, when it's all over, it's just gonna be you and me.

BOBO: *(Enters the apartment.)* Why is everybody up?

CHARLOTTE: And you! Come here, you.

BOBO: Harlot, the sun is out. Aren't you gonna shrivel up, or some shit?

(He comes behind FELONY at the makeup table and starts kissing his neck and groping him. FELONY's mind is somewhere else.)

FELONY: What are you doing home so early?

BOBO: I always get home this early, only you're usually dead to the world like some fucking…dead person.

CHARLOTTE: Eloquence is not dead.

BOBO: I missed you all night.

FELONY: I'm sure you did.

BOBO: Did Dennis get up?

FELONY: Dennis is up. Dennis woke me up.

BOBO: You forgot to iron his shirt?

FELONY: I did not forget to iron his shirt! I had every intention of ironing his… oh, leave me alone. Wash your hands before you touch me!

BOBO: Where's the kids?

FELONY: They're around.

BOBO: And the new one?

FELONY: She's inside.

BOBO: Epiphany, right?

FELONY: Yes, why?

BOBO: Aka Eduardo Gutierez.

FELONY: What did you hear?

BOBO: Supposedly she got picked up for allegedly soliciting with three other girls outside of The Meat Rack.

FELONY: She had no money. What was she supposed to do?

BOBO: Only there was only two cops and she ditched them and disappeared into some building. You are completely fucked without lube if they find out she's here.

FELONY: So what am I supposed to do, throw her out like her mother did, and her grandmother did?

BOBO: I didn't say that.

FELONY: Or maybe I should turn her in so she can go from city custody to state custody. Oh, yeah. Juvenile jail is much nicer for queer kids than foster care.

BOBO: All's I'm saying—

CHARLOTTE: Oh, don't waste your time trying to reason with Mildred Pierce.

BOBO: Milton who?

DENNIS: *(Enters with his shirt buttoned, struggling with an old, tacky tie.)* Felony, do you know how to do... hey Uncle Bobo.

BOBO: Ay, Dios mio. Que guapo estas! Como un fucking little man! *(He hugs him.)*

DENNIS: Thank you, Uncle Bobo. Show me how the fuck do you do this, please.

BOBO: It's easy. *(Starts helping him with the tie.)* You take the right one over the left... wait a minute. I got a better idea.

(He takes the tie off DENNIS, reaches into his jacket pocket and pulls out a small box and hands it to DENNIS. DENNIS opens it. It is a beautiful new tie.)

BOBO: Congratulations on your first day of real work.

DENNIS: Wow! It's beautiful!

BOBO: No problem.

(IVAN and EPIPHANY enter with cups of Kool-Aid on a tray and cookies in a Tupperware. IVAN is now in pajama bottoms or shorts and a T-shirt.)

BOBO: We're all really proud of you, right guys?

IVAN: Hey, Uncle Bobo.

EPIPHANY: Bobito!

FELONY: Don't you spill anything on my bed.

(They climb on the bed with the cookies and Kool-Aid and munch away while BOBO continues to show DENNIS how to tie the tie, maybe demonstrating with the old tie.)

CHARLOTTE: *(Trying to get up from the bed.)* That's it. I'm out of here. These children are all getting much too close.

IVAN: Chill out, Harlot. Have some breakfast.

EPIPHANY: It's good for you.

FELONY: Dennis, sweetie, do you need some money for lunch?

DENNIS: I'm cool.

IVAN: He's cool.

EPIPHANY: She is so cool.

(CHARLOTTE takes a cookie and some Kool-Aid.)

FELONY: Do you want to borrow my metro card?

DENNIS: I got time. I'm gonna walk.

IVAN: He's a big boy. He can walk.

EPIPHANY: Yeah, she's a big girl. She can walk.

FELONY: Are you sure?

CHARLOTTE: What the fuck did you do to this Kool-Aid?! It's not a fucking tea bag! You can't just keep pouring water on it!

FELONY: When you have three kids you can show me how you cut corners.

BOBO: There. Now, pull on the top piece to make the knot tight, so it looks neat…

(During this, IVAN pulls a small flask from his pocket and hands it to CHARLOTTE. He "freshens" his Kool-Aid.)

BOBO: …and slide it all the way up, but don't let it choke you. Watch out, don't crumple the collar.

IVAN: How does he know this? He doesn't even own a tie.

DENNIS: (Checking himself in the mirror one last time.) Thanks, Bobo. (He grabs a cookie and runs out.)

BOBO: No problem.

(IVAN and EPIPHANY have started throwing cookie pieces at each other.)

FELONY: That's enough! You're making a mess.

BOBO: Come on, ladies. Take it out to the kitchen.

(They take the cookies and Kool-Aid, and BOBO hustles them out, IVAN last.)

CHARLOTTE: (Stands and puts on a little jacket, or some other final touch. He has been transformed and is ready to face the world.) Hey, Ivana.

IVAN: (Stopping in the doorway.) Yeah.

CHARLOTTE: Drop by Stingray tonight, okay?

IVAN: What for?

CHARLOTTE: I'm trying something out. Backup dancers, you know.

IVAN: Backup? I thought you always work alone.

CHARLOTTE: So did I… I mean… uh… You'll have to audition, of course.

IVAN: Charlotte, I have been working my ass off. I'm so…so… I'm really—

CHARLOTTE: Well, good. That's what I'm looking for.

IVAN: Cool. I'll see you tonight. (Exits.)

CHARLOTTE: Yeah, I know. You owe me.

FELONY: Mind if I run a tab?

CHARLOTTE: (Finishes his drink and puts on his sunglasses.) Yeah, whatever.

(CHARLOTTE grabs his bag on the bed and walks out, passing DENNIS who is walking in, fully dressed in a suit and tie.)

CHARLOTTE: Break a leg, Denise.

DENNIS: Thanks, Charles.

(CHARLOTTE exits the apartment. DENNIS grabs a cookie.)

DENNIS: Um, maybe I should borrow your metro card.

FELONY: (Seeing DENNIS, for the first time, fully dressed in a suit and tie.) It's in the drawer.

DENNIS: *(Gets the metro card from the night table drawer. He notices FELONY looking strange and a bit blue.)* Are you okay?

FELONY: I'm fine. Knock 'em dead.

DENNIS: Don't worry. *(Stops in the doorway and turns around.)* Auntie Mayhem?

FELONY: Yes, my little love?

DENNIS: Thanks.

FELONY: Thanks? For what?

DENNIS: You know…the shirt.

(He turns and leaves, as BOBO enters the bedroom.)

BOBO: Go get 'em, Dennis.

DENNIS: *(Out the door.)* No problem.

(FELONY sits at the makeup table.)

BOBO: You okay?

FELONY: Sure.

BOBO: You must be so proud of him.

FELONY: One down, two to go.

BOBO: *(Gets undressed to his shorts and climbs on the bed.)* He's not moving out, you know.

FELONY: Hmm. He will.

BOBO: You know he never would have made it without you.

FELONY: I know.

BOBO: *(Spreads out on the bed.)* Wow. It's so quiet. What happened to the party?

FELONY: *(Smiles, gets up, and shuts the light.)* Light the candles, darling.

(FELONY climbs on top of BOBO.)

FELONY: Light the candles.

SCENE IV

CHARLOTTE is seated at the makeup table in a robe, no wig, plucking and generally touching up. BOBO is asleep in bed. There is light coming from the hallway and from a lamp on the makeup table. The room is a little neater than it was. On the bookshelf above the dresser, there is now a framed photo of EPIPHANY as well. The front door opens and closes softly. IVAN tries to slip past the bedroom door.

CHARLOTTE: *(Whispering, not to wake BOBO.)* Ivan!

IVAN: *(Whispering.)* What?

CHARLOTTE: What the hell happened?

IVAN: What are you talking about?

CHARLOTTE: Where the hell were you last night?

IVAN: Did we have a gig?

CHARLOTTE: No, we didn't have a gig.

IVAN: Then what's the problem?

CHARLOTTE: Q Bar? You were supposed to bar back?

IVAN: I know. I was there.

CHARLOTTE: You were there two-and-a-half fucking hours late.

IVAN: Two hours. How the hell do you know this?

CHARLOTTE: Two-and-a-half. What the fuck, Ivan.

IVAN: Did Kiki call you, or something? Fucking—

CHARLOTTE: This is not the first time.

IVAN: What does she think, you're my fucking mother?

CHARLOTTE: She's trying to run a business, Ivan.

IVAN: It was slow. Everything was covered.

CHARLOTTE: You know, Kiki gave you that job as a favor to me.

IVAN: She's a bitch.

CHARLOTTE: *(Pissed and getting loud.)* She's a business...

(BOBO stirs in the bed. CHARLOTTE goes to IVAN near the doorway and speaks quietly.)

CHARLOTTE: She's a fucking businesswoman, and she doesn't need some glorified stripper telling her how to run a bar.

IVAN: Okay, okay. Why you getting so nasty?

CHARLOTTE: Ivan, Kiki gave you that job as a favor to me. Do you understand what that means?

IVAN: I understand.

CHARLOTTE: It means if you fuck this up it looks bad for me.

IVAN: I said I—

CHARLOTTE: It means if you fuck this up, then the next time I need a favor for a friend, she's not going to trust my judgment.

IVAN: Okay.

CHARLOTTE: And that would really suck.

IVAN: Okay.

CHARLOTTE: She would have fired you already if I didn't do damage control, okay?

IVAN: Okay, okay!

CHARLOTTE: You know if you are ever late for my show you're out. I have no patience—

IVAN: I would never be late for your show.

CHARLOTTE: Do you mind telling me what the hell happened?

IVAN: Nothing happened. Personal shit.

CHARLOTTE: Personal shit? What kind of personal shit?

IVAN: Personal shit.

CHARLOTTE: Are you okay? You're scaring me lately.

IVAN: I'm fine. I just need some sleep, okay? *(He exits down the hall to the living room couch to sleep.)*

CHARLOTTE: *(After IVAN is gone.)* Okay. *(Returns to the makeup table.)*

(We hear the front door open and slam shut.)

FELONY: *(Offstage.)* Get in your room right now!

EPIPHANY: *(Offstage.)* Ooww! You're gonna rip it off!

(FELONY drags EPIPHANY by her ear to the doorway.)

FELONY: You're lucky I don't rip your fucking head off!

EPIPHANY: Ow! You're crazy!

FELONY: I'm crazy, crazy for bailing your skinny ass out again. Again! I'm so over this routine.

EPIPHANY: I told you, I wasn't working. I was just chillin' with my girls when these fucking cops... what 'chu talking about, skinny ass? My ass is fine. Oh, no you didn't.

(FELONY directs EPIPHANY to the TV room. She goes and slams the door. FELONY enters the bedroom and flicks the light on. They talk full volume now, ignoring the fact that BOBO is trying to sleep.)

CHARLOTTE: Let me guess. Poor little Epiphany was profiled again.

FELONY: I don't know what I'm going to do with her.

CHARLOTTE: Get your nickel back on that one, honey.

FELONY: Don't joke. This is her third arrest. What if they take her away?

CHARLOTTE: Can they do that? What a shame.

FELONY: Until the adoption goes through, they can do anything they want.

CHARLOTTE: I'm sure gonna miss that little fifty-cent handjob.

FELONY: That fifty-cent handjob is about to become my daughter legally, so if you don't mind, could you please come up with a new nickname?

CHARLOTTE: Yes, Mrs. Cleaver.

FELONY: I can't afford a private lawyer. Her court-appointed 18B lawyer won't return my calls. How am I supposed to help her? Do you know where they stuck her this time? In the same cell with the adult men. They'll eat her alive.

IVAN: *(Enters from the hall in shorts and a T-shirt.)* Do you have to be screaming and slamming doors? I gotta get some sleep. I got a show to do.

CHARLOTTE: Oh, the glamorous life.

IVAN: I gotta get up at five in the afternoon and sparkle, Ivan, sparkle!

CHARLOTTE: You are a very old soul.

FELONY: Did you just get home?

IVAN: Hmmm.

FELONY: Ivan, this is getting ridiculous.

IVAN: I'm a big boy.

FELONY: What the hell are you doing out all night and half the morning?

IVAN: Nothing.

FELONY: What's nothing?

IVAN: Nothing, nothing.

FELONY: So, like, walking around aimlessly? Doing drugs? Getting in trouble again?

IVAN: I'm not getting in trouble.

FELONY: So why won't you tell me where you go?

IVAN: Nowhere, okay? Nowhere.

FELONY: You're scaring me, Ivan.

IVAN: There's nothing to be scared about.

FELONY: Ivan… all right then. At least tell me this.

IVAN: Umm hmm.

FELONY: Where does Epiphany go when she's out all night? What does she do?

IVAN: I thought you taught me not to rat on my brother and sister.

FELONY: This is different.

IVAN: Why?

FELONY: Because it is.

IVAN: Oh, no. You're trying to trick me.

FELONY: I'm not trying to trick you. I'm giving you special permission to rat.

IVAN: She's not prostituting, if that's what you want to know.

FELONY: Don't you lie to me! Don't cover up for her!

CHARLOTTE: Felony!

IVAN: Now why the heck are you asking me if you ain't gonna believe my answer? What's that about? Charlotte?

CHARLOTTE: I know, baby. She's being very mean.

FELONY: I am not… Ivan, this is the third time she's been picked up in the last six months.

IVAN: So? They pick up everybody. Don't matter what you're doing.

FELONY: That doesn't make any sense.

IVAN: I know it doesn't. So what? If you're trans, or you ain't white, and you're under twenty-one, you can't even stand on the corner in that neighborhood without the cops fucking with you.

FELONY: They can't arrest you for standing on the corner. It's public property.

IVAN: Oh, yes they can. It's called loitering. And if you talk to anyone, or if you even look like a prostitute, whatever that means, it's called loitering with the intent to solicit.

FELONY: Don't they have to prove something?

IVAN: Not to bring you in. Besides, it's your word against theirs. You know, if you got three condoms on you that counts as proof that you're working. Remember Miranda from the pier outreach group? She was giving out condoms and safe sex pamphlets on the stroll. They busted her on the three-condom rule. She had, like, two hundred condoms in a big bag. What'd they think she was going to do, take on the cross-town bus?

FELONY: So, how do you know Epiphany's not prostituting?

IVAN: Because I know, okay? I know. She used to, but she doesn't any more. She doesn't need to. She's got her stipend from the Youth Project, she's got her allowance from you, half of it she uses to buy pizza

for the other girls, whatever she doesn't spend on her hair.

FELONY: Are you sure about this?

IVAN; I'm sure. I'm sure.

(He crawls under the sheets with BOBO.)

FELONY: Well, what am I supposed to do now?

BOBO: (Without opening his eyes.) Go talk to her.

(FELONY exits to talk to EPIPHANY.)

IVAN: You believe me, don't you, Uncle Bobo?

BOBO: Auntie Mayhem believes you, honey. He's just frustrated. That's all. He doesn't want Epiphany to end up with a rap sheet before she's even out of high school.

CHARLOTTE: Just another afternoon on Walton's Mountain.

(As he speaks, we hear the front door open and close. DENNIS walks past the bedroom door, realizes there are people in there and comes back.)

DENNIS: Hey.

CHARLOTTE: Hello, John Boy. (Exits to the shower.)

BOBO: (Getting up to hug him.) Dennis! Good to see you, kid. I miss you.

DENNIS: I saw you last week.

BOBO: I know, I know. How's work? How's the apartment?

DENNIS: The apartment's too small. Bruce wants to move. Work is boring.

BOBO: Well, that's why you're in school, right? Hey, did you decide to switch to full time?

DENNIS: I don't know. I have to figure that out by the end of the week.

BOBO: You'd be out in eighteen months. You'd have an associate's before your twenty-second birthday.

DENNIS: Yeah, but I have to take out more loans.

BOBO: Everyone borrows money for school. You'll deal. Hey, are you okay for cash? *(He grabs his wallet out of the night table.)*

DENNIS: I'm fine.

BOBO: *(Gives him forty or fifty dollars.)* Here. Take this in case you need it.

DENNIS: That's not why I came, Uncle Bobo. Really.

BOBO: I know. I know. Just take it. Don't be stupid.

DENNIS: *(Takes it.)* Thanks.

BOBO: You coming for dinner on Sunday, you and Bruce?

DENNIS: I don't know. I have a lot of school stuff for Monday. Sunday's the only time I have.

BOBO: Well, see if you can. Let me tell Felony you're here. *(Exits to the hall.)*

DENNIS: Hey.

IVAN: Hey.

DENNIS: What's up?

IVAN: Same old.

DENNIS: Yeah... So?

IVAN: So what?

DENNIS: You know what. Did you find out?

IVAN: Yup.

DENNIS: And?

(IVAN doesn't say anything.)

DENNIS: Oh, fuck. Ivan, are you okay?

IVAN: I don't know. I guess so. I don't know.

DENNIS: What are you gonna do?

IVAN: I have no idea.

DENNIS: What did Felony say?

IVAN: I didn't tell them.

DENNIS: What do you mean, you didn't tell them?

IVAN: I didn't tell them.

DENNIS: Why not?

IVAN: I don't want them to freak out.

DENNIS: They're not going to freak out.

IVAN: Yes, they are.

DENNIS: All right, so they freak out a little. Come on, Ivan. They're not stupid. They've been around.

IVAN: So?

DENNIS: So they can help you do all the shit you need to do. You don't know what to do.

IVAN: What shit?

DENNIS: Get a doctor, for one thing.

IVAN: What for?

DENNIS: Ivan, don't be stupid. You gotta take care of yourself. People don't just die anymore. They take care of themselves.

IVAN: Are you getting tested?

DENNIS: Why do I need to get tested?

IVAN: I don't know how long I've had this.

DENNIS: So? We were always safe.

IVAN: That's what I thought. Please don't tell Auntie Mayhem. I want to tell him.

FELONY: *(Entering.)* Tell him what?

IVAN: Dennis is here.

DENNIS: Hey, Auntie Mayhem.

FELONY: Hello, stranger. Such an honor to have you drop by.

DENNIS: It hasn't even been a week.

FELONY: A week and you couldn't call.

DENNIS: You can call too, you know.

FELONY: Hmm. How's school?

(EPIPHANY enters with BOBO.)

EPIPHANY: Dennis, tell them I didn't do anything!

(She hugs DENNIS.)

DENNIS: She didn't do anything. What didn't you do?

IVAN: She got picked up again.

DENNIS: Again? Epiphany.

EPIPHANY: I didn't… why doesn't anybody believe me?

IVAN: I believe you.

FELONY: I believe you, sweetie. It's just that—

EPIPHANY: It's just that you don't fucking believe me.

DENNIS: Sweetie, this is the third time in, like, how long?

EPIPHANY: So?

DENNIS: So, are the cops, like, out to get you specifically?

EPIPHANY: You bet your fucking ass they are, because I don't take their bullshit.

FELONY: Well, maybe that's the problem.

EPIPHANY: Oh, so I should take their bullshit?

FELONY: I didn't say that.

EPIPHANY: Yes you did.

DENNIS: Honey, I was with you last week, that cop asked you to get off the fence.

EPIPHANY: He didn't ask.

DENNIS: And you completely flipped out on him.

EPIPHANY: Sure did.

DENNIS: Well, why? Just get off the fence. Why are you getting into fights you don't have to get into? Why are you making such a big deal?

EPIPHANY: It is a big deal. It's a big deal to me when they do it for no reason.

DENNIS: But—

EPIPHANY: No, Dennis! Do you know what Chinese water torture is? Little drops of water on your head. No big deal. But after a long time it starts to feel like a sledgehammer. Three of my friends got picked up last week when they weren't doing anything, and their legal aid lawyers all told them to plead guilty, even though they're not, so now they all have records. John got busted for peeing in the alley because the diner wouldn't let him in, and there's no public restrooms. Some Jersey thugs punched Dwayne in the face, and the cops said they wouldn't take a report because he's not bleeding, when you know it's because he's seventeen and black. It's like it's a crime in this city to be young, queer, and of color. That is the simple truth of the matter, okay?

(No one knows what to say.)

EPIPHANY: Do you get why I'm pissed off, Dennis?

DENNIS: I guess I do. I guess you're right. They used to give me shit all the time.

EPIPHANY: And believe me, big brother, if you ever go hang down there again they'll give you shit all over. They don't care that you're twenty with schoolbooks in your bag. To them, you're just another nigga on the stroll.

IVAN: Wow, that's harsh.

EPIPHANY: Life's harsh, babe.

DENNIS: Identity politics can be very complex.

IVAN: Yes mister college boy.

(*CHARLOTTE enters from the hall in the same robe, with a shower cap, and sits back at the makeup table.*)

EPIPHANY: It's all about identity, honey. And speaking of, I been thinking of changing mine.

FELONY: Changing your what?

EPIPHANY: Changing my name.

BOBO: I thought that lawyer from the clinic was already working on the papers.

EPIPHANY: I mean I been thinking of changing it to something else.

IVAN: Something else? You've been Epiphany forever.

EPIPHANY: Not forever. Two years.

IVAN: But everybody knows you as Epiphany.

EPIPHANY: So? I can still change it. People do that all the time.

IVAN: You did it once already.

DENNIS: Yeah, doesn't your birth certificate say—

EPIPHANY: Don't you dare! My birth name is not to be uttered in this household, do you understand?

FELONY: Dennis.

DENNIS: All right. I'm sorry.

BOBO: Well, honey, if you really want to use a different name, you'd better make up your mind before the papers are ready. The judge isn't going to want to see you changing it over and over.

EPIPHANY: I know, I know.

FELONY: What's wrong with Epiphany? I kind of like it.

EPIPHANY: I don't know. It's too Catholic for one thing.

BOBO: That's true, I guess.

EPIPHANY: And it's too…too—

DENNIS: Conspicuous.

EPIPHANY: Spic-a who?

DENNIS: Conspicuous. It stands out. It makes it harder for you to just sort of pass and blend in.

EPIPHANY: Well, I don't know if I care about that so much.

IVAN: Epiphany has never been what you call "low profile."

EPIPHANY: I just want something original, like your name.

FELONY: Mine?

EPIPHANY: Yeah. How did you think of that?

CHARLOTTE: She didn't.

FELONY: Charlotte—

EPIPHANY: Well who did?

CHARLOTTE: Some cop.

EPIPHANY: What?! Uh uh?!

FELONY: Charlotte—

CHARLOTTE: What? It was that cop, right?

BOBO: Oh my God. Kids, before I hooked with your auntie, Charles here and, uh— *(Indicating FELONY.)* Fernando here—

IVAN: Fernando?!

CHARLOTTE: God, how do you remember that?

FELONY: That is the last time you will ever use that word in this house!

BOBO: ...used to get in all kinda trouble. They were out every night sluttin' around.

FELONY: Bobo!

CHARLOTTE: We weren't slutting around.

BOBO: Excuse me. They were trying to hook a rich man. That was their one and only goal in life.

CHARLOTTE: Not so. I had other aspirations.

FELONY: Well, that was certainly priority number one.

CHARLOTTE: True.

EPIPHANY: So how did you end up settling for Uncle Bobo?

FELONY: Oh, you know. L'amour.

BOBO: And they had beaucoup rich boyfriends.

CHARLOTTE: And there was this one crazy Italian named Paolo something.

FELONY: Paolo Carilla. Oh my God, the ass on that man.

BOBO: And he was filthy f-in rich, and very nice...usually.

CHARLOTTE: Except when he had too much to drink.

BOBO: Then he turned into this crazy, jealous, punk Mafioso.

FELONY: Bobo, that's not very PC, in front of the children.

BOBO: That is a direct quote from you.

FELONY: Hmm.

BOBO: So one night they're chillin' at this ritzy-chi-chi-fru-fru place.

CHARLOTTE: The Beekman Tower.

BOBO: And Paolo's had one too many.

CHARLOTTE: One?

FELONY: Darling, he'd had more Manhattans than a church full of Kennedys.

BOBO: And he starts getting psycho because your auntie is flirting with some other guy at the bar.

EPIPHANY: You were out with a filthy rich boy, and you were flirting with some other boy? That is not smart, or economical.

CHARLOTTE: He wasn't "some other boy." He was a Nubian god.

FELONY: Trust me, you didn't see him. You would have been flirting too.

BOBO: So Paolo goes completely Sopranos all over the place. He starts knocking over tables and shit.

FELONY: He didn't knock over any tables.

CHARLOTTE: He pulls out a switchblade or a stiletto or something and starts swinging it around. Didn't he slash your shoulder?

FELONY: Destroyed my Moschino. I loved that shirt.

CHARLOTTE: The cops show up. Felony's a wreck, screaming her airy little head off. And this handsome young Irishman with a black leather holster and a billyclub grabs her and says, "Sir, if you don't calm down I'm gonna have to take you in and charge you with felony mayhem!"

FELONY: Half of me is thinking, "I'm bleeding all over the fucking rug and you're going to charge me?!" The other half of me is thinking, "Felony Mayhem? Felony Mayhem? What a fabulous drag name!"

EPIPHANY: You're a fucking mess.

IVAN: Is that for real?

DENNIS: So what did the cops do?

FELONY: Nothing.

CHARLOTTE: Nothing? What do you mean, nothing?

FELONY: I mean nothing.

CHARLOTTE: Oh, please. We spent three nights in holding before they dismissed...

(FELONY has been signaling CHAR-LOTTE to shut up.)

CHARLOTTE: ...What?

EPIPHANY: Hold on. So, in other words, you got busted?

FELONY: I did not get busted.

IVAN: Sounds like you got busted to me.

FELONY: This is different.

IVAN: Busted is busted, okay?

EPIPHANY: How is this different?

FELONY: It's different because...because I was the victim here. I didn't do anything to him.

EPIPHANY: Didn't do anything, didn't do anything, where have I heard that before?

FELONY: It was a mistake.

IVAN: What kinda mistake?

FELONY: A mistake. The police made a mistake. That's why the judge dismissed it.

CHARLOTTE: Oops.

FELONY: Yes, oops, darling.

EPIPHANY: Oh, I see. So, you got busted, even though it wasn't your fault, even though you weren't doing anything wrong.

CHARLOTTE: Did I break the no ratting rule?

FELONY: I'm afraid you did—

EPIPHANY: And you're giving me shit!

FELONY: ...and you will be destroyed.

EPIPHANY: Well, you got a lot of nerve!

FELONY: You watch that attitude in this house, young lady.

EPIPHANY: Pues, explicame la diferencia, por favor, Fernando.

FELONY: La differencia, si tu quiere saber, Eduardo—

EPIPHANY: *(She gasps audibly.)* You did not say that!

IVAN: That was mean.

FELONY: I've got a wonderful idea. Let's just drop this little inquisition, shall we?

EPIPHANY: Don't think you're just gonna back out of this one.

FELONY: That is exactly what I am going to do.

EPIPHANY: You are truly a mess, girl.

FELONY: Yes, sweetie. Whatever you say. I'm a mess. We're all a mess. And this room is a mess, so if you don't mind, could you all please go somewhere else and let me straighten up. Why are you all in here all the time? Don't you have your own space?

BOBO: Hey, I got roast beef. Who wants lunch? *(He leads the way to the kitchen.)*

DENNIS: Free food. I'm there.

IVAN: I'm starving.

CHARLOTTE: I could pick.

(They all follow BOBO. DENNIS is last.)

FELONY: Dennis.

DENNIS: *(Stops in the doorway.)* Yeah?

FELONY: You and Bruce can come for dinner on Sunday?

DENNIS: Actually, I'm—

FELONY: I'm making pernil.

DENNIS: Sure we'll be there. Free food. *(Exits to kitchen.)*

(FELONY starts to straighten up the room. We hear the following from the kitchen.)

EPIPHANY: *(Offstage.)* This is all red.

DENNIS: *(Offstage.)* It's supposed to be red. It's better that way.

EPIPHANY: *(Offstage.)* I like it more cooked.

DENNIS: *(Offstage.)* More well done.

EPIPHANY: *(Offstage.)* What's the difference?

IVAN: *(Offstage.)* How come you just got rye bread again?

CHARLOTTE: *(Offstage.)* What's wrong with roast beef on rye? What city did you grow up in?

IVAN: *(Offstage.)* I happen to like white bread, okay?

EPIPHANY: *(Offstage.)* So when is Bruce coming over?

DENNIS: *(Offstage.)* Sunday, I guess.

IVAN: *(Offstage.)* Calm down, little girl. Hands off.

EPIPHANY: *(Offstage.)* I'm not gonna touch. I'm only gonna look.

DENNIS: *(Offstage.)* You think he's cute?

IVAN: *(Offstage.)* He's not bad, considering what you usually bring home.

EPIPHANY: *(Offstage.)* Honey, he is fine and you know it. I even caught Charlotte staring at him.

DENNIS: *(Offstage.)* Really?

CHARLOTTE: *(Offstage.)* Please, I like men, not boys. Is this the only mustard you have?

EPIPHANY: *(Offstage.)* And he's very smart.

DENNIS: *(Offstage.)* He is very smart.

EPIPHANY: *(Offstage.)* I like that in a man. I like a man you can conversate with.

IVAN: *(Offstage.)* Did you get any mayo?

DENNIS: *(Offstage.)* Converse.

IVAN: *(Offstage.)* 'Cause this fat-free shit is not mayo.

(Somewhere in the middle of the above off-stage lines, BOBO sticks his head in the bedroom.)

BOBO: You hungry, babe?

FELONY: Sure.

(He gets up, follows BOBO out, shuts the light and closes the door as the offstage lines finish.)

THE END

THE MONSTER TALES

Mary Jett Parsley

MARY JETT PARSLEY grew up in Greenville, North Carolina. She attended college at Duke University, where her first five plays were produced, and received her MFA in dramatic writing from New York University. She has been the recipient of a Playwrights Fellowship from the North Carolina Arts Council and a grant from the Pilgrim Project. Productions of Jett's work include *Right Side Wrong, First Born, Locked Doors and Lightning Bugs,* and *Tar River Love Story. Locked Doors and Lightning Bugs* received the Southeastern Theatre Conference's Charles M. Getchell Award and was a winner of the Charlotte Repertory Theatre's New Plays in America Festival. In 1993 the play was part of the O'Neill National Playwrights' Conference. Several scenes and monologues written by Jett were published in *Scenes and Monologues for Young Actors,* and her play *Hiss* was published in *30 Ten-Minute Plays for 2 Actors from Actors Theatre of Louisville's National Ten-Minute Play Contest.* She has also written numerous scripts for churches in New York City and Chapel Hill, North Carolina. Her latest play, *Choreography,* has had two staged readings and is looking for a first production. She is married to Jeremy Wrenn, and they live in Wake Forest, North Carolina. For the last ten years, she has been teaching high school English in North Carolina, but she recently embarked upon her new calling as the mommy of Emma Cosette, three months old at the time of this writing.

The Monster Tales was written while the playwright was on retreat at Norcroft in Lutsen, Minnesota. An Emerging Artists Grant from the Durham Arts Council allowed for development with actors, culminating in a staged reading on May 21, 1999. It was directed by Mary Jett Parsley and had the following cast:

Mimi	Christy Lynn Wilson
Monster	Micha Cover
Bride/Raisa/Shileen	Christine Brown
Samson/Alexander	Jeff West
David/Voice/Raji	Blake Edwards
Edgar	Jeff Clarke
Maria Anita/Mother/Juno	Kris Yensen

The Monster Tales received a workshop production by the Livestock Players Second Stage and the Greensboro Playwrights' Forum under the direction of Stephen D. Hyers in October, 2000.

The New York premiere of *The Monster Tales* was presented by The Boomerang Theatre Company (Tim Errickson, Artistic Director) on September 20, 2002, at the Actors Playground Theatre, with the following cast and credits:

Mimi	Erika Bailey
Monster	Peter Morr
Samson/Alexander	Ed Schultz
Bride/Raisa	Jane Courtney
David/Boy	Scot Carlisle
Maria Anita/Raisa's Mother	Nora Hummel

Director: Amy Henault
Stage Manager: Jessica Urtecho
Set Designer: WT McRae
Costume Designer: Sidney Shannon
Lighting Designer: Sarah Jakubasz
Sound Designer: Ernie Rich

Soli Deo Gloria.

TIME

The present.

PLACE

A bedroom.

ACT I

SCENE 1

MIMI, twenty-eight, runs—dashes—into the room, dives onto the bed, squirrels away under the covers, a small, huddled, hidden creature. Pause. Slowly she peeks out, then hides again.

MIMI: *(Quickly.)* Go away! Go away! Go away! *(Silence. Slowly, her hand comes out. She feels around until resting on a teddy bear which she snatches and pulls under the covers. From inside.)* You look, Pookie… What? You're not afraid… But somebody has to look, and you're so strong. And besides, monsters don't eat teddy bears… Okay. Good. *(The hand and bear return. The bear moves slowly to the edge of the bed, then over the side. It "looks" underneath, returns under the covers.)* Nothing there? *(MIMI and bear emerge.)* Are you sure?

(The bear "nods." MIMI laughs lightly at herself. She sits up, plumps her pillows, puts POOKIE beside her, covers him up, gets herself settled. She picks up a book beside her bed and reads. But she stops. She puts down the book.)

MIMI: *(To POOKIE.)* Maybe I'll just look myself. Just a quick look. Since nothing's there. *(Very slowly, MIMI stretches out so that she can lean just her head off the bed to check under… She suddenly screams and flees backward and under the covers.)* Oh, my God!

(A "MONSTER"—played by an actor wearing a hideous mask—slides out from under the bed.)

MIMI: Oh, oh no! Oh no! Oh, go away! Oh no! Oh, go away!

(She scrambles off the bed, taking the covers with her. She goes for the door, but he is there, blocking it. She backs away; he follows.)

MIMI: What are you? What's happening? I'm dreaming—I've got to be dreaming! *(She closes her eyes.)* Okay, Mimi. You're a big girl. Twenty-eight is old enough to know there's no such thing as monsters. There's no such thing as monsters. There's no such thing as monsters. *(She opens her eyes and cries out, hides under the covers.)* No, no, no! No, I can't believe it!

(He slides the covers off her face.)

MIMI: Don't!

(She tugs at the covers. He tugs back.)

MIMI: Quit it! Stop that! Don't!

(She slaps at his hands, and he pulls back.)

MIMI: There! Yes! Take that, you…! *(She grabs her book, aiming to throw it at him.)* Just—just stay right there. I work out, you know—and I'm mean—I ran over a cat once—so don't get any ideas about… anything…see…

(She looks at him. He looks at her.)

MIMI: What do you want?

(Silence.)

MIMI: What do you want!?

(Silence.)

MIMI: Fine. Fine. You stay there, right like that, and be very still and I'll just… *(Slowly she sidles over to the bedstand and picks up the phone. She dials, never taking her eyes off him. She speaks into the phone.)* I—I need some help. Yes, I need—police—a lot of them—with very big guns… There's something in my house… No, something… I don't know what I mean—I mean—there's a… there's a…monster… No, this isn't a prank… *(Silence.)* I'm sorry. I don't know what I was thinking. Goodnight. *(She hangs up. Pause.)* So… do something. Make the first move. Come on.

(He comes closer, puts his face close to hers, studying.)

MIMI: What… hey, not too…

(He continues to stare at her, then, suddenly…)

MONSTER: Your eyes are blue.

(She gasps. It is her turn to be speechless.)

MONSTER: I've never seen them open.

(There is a long moment while they stare at each other.)

MIMI: *(Timid again.)* Please go away.

MONSTER: I don't want to hurt you.

MIMI: Please…

MONSTER: I've just come out for this one time.

MIMI: What…what do you mean?

MONSTER: *(Pause.)* I thought you'd be more friendly.

MIMI: Friendly?! I—I can't believe—but, it's not supposed to be real, the monster under the bed; it's just something you think about as a child, but you know… it's not real…

MONSTER: Then why did you check?

MIMI: I check every night.

MONSTER: I know.

MIMI: You came from under my bed. You actually came from under my bed. There are actually monsters living under my bed.

MONSTER: Does that bother you?

MIMI: Are there monsters in the closet, too?

MONSTER: Monsters in the closet. Don't be ridiculous.

MIMI: Well, you can't stay. This is my bed, my room. Out. Or—under—back from whence you came—and all that.

(He doesn't move.)

MIMI: Come on, now! Out! Go!

(Nothing.)

MIMI: I can't sleep with you there.

MONSTER: You've always slept with me there.

MIMI: I didn't know you were there.

MONSTER: Now you do.

MIMI: *(Pause.)* Are you a good monster or a bad monster?

MONSTER: That depends.

MIMI: On what?

MONSTER: Whether I ate dinner. Whether the nightlight is on. Whether I like you.

MIMI: *(Pause.)* No, no, I'm sorry, but you're going to have to leave. This will never work. Pookie is afraid.

MONSTER: Monsters don't eat teddy bears. Barbie dolls, yes.

MIMI: Is that supposed to make me feel better?

MONSTER: Don't be afraid.

MIMI: That's easy for you to say. I don't even know your name.

MONSTER: You couldn't pronounce it. It is not a human language.

MIMI: What's under the mask?

MONSTER: There is nothing under the mask.

MIMI: That's it. Out! You have to go now. You have to!

MONSTER: I can't. I've watched you for too long. At night. When you were a child.

MIMI: You knew me then? You followed me?

MONSTER: There are tunnels. I can go anywhere, under any bed.

MIMI: Really?

MONSTER: You had a canopy bed with a pink canopy and ruffles.

MIMI: Yes.

MONSTER: At your grandmother's house the bed was very large and you slept with your brother and sister.

MIMI: (Pause.) We had grand pillow fights. (Pause.) Oh, I don't know what to think of all this. (Pause.) These tunnels. Could you go anywhere, really?

MONSTER: Mmmm.

MIMI: But you came here? You followed me?

MONSTER: (Pause.) You tell stories.

MIMI: Stories? I don't know any stories.

MONSTER: Maybe they are your dreams. They are about many things, mermaids and ocelots and men who drink rum. You whisper them. I have to get very close to hear. I lie beside you and put my ear next to your mouth. This has happened all your life.

MIMI: I do that?

MONSTER: Yes.

MIMI: No.

MONSTER: Yes.

MIMI: No one ever told me.

MONSTER: You do not do it with anyone else. Only when you are alone.

MIMI: Which is most of the time. (Pause.) Only I wasn't really alone.

MONSTER: No.

MIMI: (Pause.) What's under your mask?

MONSTER: Nothing.

MIMI: You just don't want me to see.

MONSTER: You don't want to see.

MIMI: (Pause.) What's under the bed?

MONSTER: Many amazing things.

MIMI: Tunnels, you said.

MONSTER: And rivers. And forests.

MIMI: Forests? (Pause.) Can a...can a human person go there?

MONSTER: I don't think a human person would want to go there.

MIMI: Why not? Is it scary?

MONSTER: Sometimes.

MIMI: Oh.

MONSTER: What do you do in the day?

MIMI: I work the reference desk in a library. Sometimes I shelve books.

MONSTER: Do you find your stories there?

MIMI: I really don't know these stories you're talking about. Ask the fellows in the library. There's just nothing very creative about me at all.

MONSTER: I don't understand. The reason I came out tonight—the reason I entered your waking time was because of the stories.

MIMI: Can't you make up your own stories?

MONSTER: Impossible. We monsters have no… what is the human word… imagination.

MIMI: No imagination? Is that true?

MONSTER: We cannot lie, also.

MIMI: Must be pretty dull to be a monster.

MONSTER: Not if you know the tunnels. Not if you know where the stories are to be found. Only now you say you don't know them.

MIMI: I don't!

MONSTER: I thought that you must have more, I thought you would tell them.

MIMI: Well, I guess you thought wrong.

MONSTER: I thought that someone who tells such stories in her sleep…that with her eyes open she might be…someone magic…

MIMI: I'm sorry…to disappoint.

MONSTER: You don't know what a treasure your stories are.

MIMI: No one has ever said anything I had was a treasure. *(Pause.)* Take me under the bed.

MONSTER: What? Impossible.

MIMI: No one will miss me.

MONSTER: It can't be done. A human has never entered that world.

MIMI: No human ever knew that world existed!

MONSTER: I wanted to come out, you know…before. But there are rules.

MIMI: Are you breaking a rule tonight?

MONSTER: Yes.

MIMI: Can you get in trouble?

MONSTER: I would get in more trouble for taking you under.

MIMI: But you will.

MONSTER: I don't understand why you—

MIMI: I'm curious.

MONSTER: You want to leave this world.

MIMI: Nothing for me here but a TV that only gets three stations and a landlady that won't get rid of the mice in my kitchen.

MONSTER: You already have a place of escape. Your stories.

MIMI: I keep telling you I don't know them.

MONSTER: *(Pause.)* I will tell you one.

MIMI: What? Why?

MONSTER: I will tell you one and then you'll remember.

MIMI: I doubt it.

MONSTER: Then I suppose I will… just…go back into the tunnel…

MIMI: Well, I…I didn't say I…

MONSTER: They are like a journey under the bed, an adventure to somewhere fantastical.

MIMI: I can't believe they're all that wonderful…

MONSTER: Once upon a time—

MIMI: Wait, wait, don't start yet. *(She climbs into the bed.)* Okay. Ready.

SCENE 2

MONSTER: Once upon a time there was a very old, blind man. His name was Samson. Now, Samson had traveled around the world and had more treasure than one hundred men, but Samson had one regret. He had never been married.

(SAMSON enters.)

MONSTER: And when he discovered that for all his wealth and power and experience, he was still very lonely, Samson did what one would expect...

SAMSON and MONSTER: He ordered a bride from a mail-order catalog.

(SAMSON continues the story alone.)

SAMSON: She was drawn and designed by the best artists, very expensive, matchless, fashioned for complete marital bliss. Today, at last, he was to meet her. Today she had come, packed safely in brown cardboard, wrapped gently in white lace, a beautiful young woman.

MIMI: Wait, wait, wait.

(MONSTER stops and stares at her.)

MIMI: You're telling me I told you a story about a mail-order bride? I did not. I would not.

MONSTER: Yes, you did.

MIMI: No. That's—that's horrible—it's politically...very incorrect.

MONSTER: What is that?

MIMI: It means it's—well, it's offensive. To women.

MONSTER: It's a good story. Let me tell it.

SAMSON: *(Returning to the story.)* Samson called for his bride to meet him in the great hall.

(BRIDE enters. SAMSON, cane tapping, circles the BRIDE. She looks at him with uncertainty and perhaps contempt.)

SAMSON: You were, of course, taught how to run a household.

BRIDE: Yes.

SAMSON: And you have all the necessary knowledge for raising children.

BRIDE: Are there children already?

SAMSON: You'll be giving birth to them.

(Pause. Her face registers shock. He continues.)

SAMSON: I do not entertain much, but when I do I will expect that you will take charge of the affair. Right now my first servant David handles the arrangements, but I feel they need a woman's touch.

BRIDE: *(Pause.)* I believe there has been some mistake.

SAMSON: What?

BRIDE: I was led to believe that the man I was being sent to was young. Handsome. I was to be the bride of a king, of a warrior. There was to be a festival on the day of my wedding. There was to be—

SAMSON: *(Holding his hand before her face.)* That's enough! *(He stops still, listens.)* Do you know that I was born blind? My ears are sharper than a rabbit's. I can hear your heart beating. The blood sloshes through your veins. If you talk, you must use a softer voice, so as not to insult my sensitive eardrums. *(Pause.)* So you are disappointed in me, eh?

BRIDE: You must send me back.

SAMSON: No.

BRIDE: In the catalog, did it not say, "This model is best matched with a young Prince Charming"?

SAMSON: My servant David read the catalog and ordered what he thought was best.

BRIDE: He chose wrong. I do not belong here.

SAMSON: David! *(He whirls away from her, heading to a door.)* David! I'm calling for you!

(DAVID enters. He is young, handsome, dressed as a servant.)

DAVID: Yes, sir.

SAMSON: My bride is here.

DAVID: Yes, sir.

SAMSON: *(To BRIDE.)* I didn't ask you your name.

BRIDE: You filled out the order form. What was the name you requested?

SAMSON: *(To DAVID.)* Did she come with a receipt?

DAVID: The delivery man left it with me, sir. *(Pulls out a paper and reads.)* Gisella, sir.

SAMSON: Gisella. David, tell me. What does my bride look like?

(Pause. DAVID and GISELLA lock gazes.)

SAMSON: Well?

DAVID: She is beautiful, sir.

SAMSON: I only pay for the best! But details, David.

DAVID: *(Walks around her.)* She is strong in the legs and the back. But soft in the places a woman should be. Her neck is long and holds her head up…majestically.

SAMSON: She's not a horse, David. Is she appealing?

DAVID: *(Pause.)* Her…hair falls…like red, silk waves, to her waist. Her skin is pink, warm… Her eyes… *(He looks away from her glare.)* …have quite a fire.

SAMSON: She is afraid, David, that you made a mistake when ordering her. She thinks that she and I are not a good match.

DAVID: *(Pause.)* You will be quite a pair.

SAMSON: *(Softly, to GISELLA.)* I cannot wait to know you.

(GISELLA makes a move to leave, but DAVID grabs her arm.)

DAVID: Indeed, you have bought the best, sir.

GISELLA: I will not stand for this.

SAMSON: *(To DAVID.)* I'm going to supper. Show her to her room and see that she understands the rules of the house.

GISELLA: I follow my own rules!

SAMSON: Quiet! *(To DAVID.)* Impertinence. Remind me to write to the catalog and tell them there is a flaw with this model. *(To GISELLA.)* Do you eat a lot?

(Silence.)

SAMSON: Wife!

GISELLA: I'm sorry. I didn't know I was allowed to speak.

SAMSON: See that she eats, David. *(To GISELLA.)* For the record, I may as well be the king here, for all the power I have. And there will be a great festival. The greatest. David is arranging it. If you want anything special—musicians, dancers—just let him know. *(He finds her hand and kisses it.)* My sweet. *(He exits.)*

GISELLA: He's horrible.

DAVID: You haven't even been here an hour and already you've made that decision?

GISELLA: My makers assured me I was fashioned for someone who would care for me.

DAVID: He will care for you, in his way.

GISELLA: I will run away.

DAVID: I will bring you back.

GISELLA: *(Sharp.)* For him or for yourself?

DAVID: For him.

(Pause.)

GISELLA: Where is my room?

DAVID: Next to his. I'll show you.

(He starts to walk out. She doesn't move. He tries to comfort her.)

DAVID: He's really not so bad.

GISELLA: He pays you well to say that, I suppose.

DAVID: He doesn't pay me.

GISELLA: What? Then…you choose to be here?

DAVID: He saved my father's life.

GISELLA: He did?

DAVID: My father was drowning—I should say, drunk and drowning—he fell off his boat and couldn't tell what was water and what was air and swam to the bottom. The old man's barge was floating by and he heard my father fall in and ordered his servant to go in after him.

GISELLA: His servant saved your father.

DAVID: He gave the order.

GISELLA: And if he hadn't, no one would have saved him? Don't you see the ugliness in that power?

DAVID: You would feel the same, if you had seen what happened, had watched your father sink. *(Pause.)* I was four. My mother was so happy to have her husband returned safely that she promised I would work for the old man as soon as I was fourteen. I have had a better life here than my father could have given me. He was a fisherman. I hated the nets, the waves, the salt.

GISELLA: I'd like to try that life very much, if I could.

DAVID: *(Pause.)* It is a shame he cannot see you.

GISELLA: If I only thought there was some love in him…but when I look in his face…

DAVID: You're distracted by his eyes.

GISELLA: All the days I've been alive I've been told I am beautiful—perfection was sculpted, chiseled into the clay that formed me—and here I am given to someone who cannot appreciate my gifts—

DAVID: Vanity.

GISELLA: Don't judge me—you were born from a woman, raised in a family—you don't know my world, my mind. I've never been anywhere but a factory assembly line…and here.

DAVID: You are beautiful.

GISELLA: Say it again.

DAVID: You are.

GISELLA: Will you get in trouble for saying that?

DAVID: He did not hear me.

GISELLA: And if he had been here, you wouldn't have said it?

(Long pause.)

DAVID: You should go to your room.

GISELLA: He'll be there.

DAVID: Yes.

344   MARY JETT PARSLEY

GISELLA: It will be final.

DAVID: As it is supposed to be.

GISELLA: As you want it to be?

DAVID: Go to him.

(She doesn't move.)

DAVID: He paid.

GISELLA: He paid. *(She starts to exit.)*

DAVID: As he said…let me know if your room…if I can make it…if you need anything. *(Pause.)* I am my master's wife's servant.

GISELLA: Thank you.

DAVID: You will be all right.

GISELLA: *(Pause.)* There is one… I wonder if…when he is sleeping, or wants to be alone—will you…can we…talk? I have no friends. Can I…be around you?

DAVID: We'll see. If he wants.

GISELLA: Your loyalty is astounding. Perhaps I will like him best. *(She exits.)*

MONSTER: But she did not. She did not like the old man at all. Though he filled her room with three dozen roses and spoke kindly to her when they were alone, his wrinkles against her flawless skin made her cringe. His breath—muddy and cobwebbed—sent her scrambling. She bore him, knowing she had no choice, but she did not give anything to him. She thought instead of David, of how strong he seemed to be but how weak she thought he was—and yet how she felt pulled to him, perhaps simply because they were both so alone.

(SAMSON and GISELLA enter and lie on the bed.)

SAMSON: Your hair is so soft.

(Silence.)

SAMSON: Did you hear me?

GISELLA: Yes.

SAMSON: Say thank you.

GISELLA: Thank you.

SAMSON: Your skin is like velvet.

GISELLA: Thank you.

SAMSON: Are you happy with your room—the house, in general?

GISELLA: Yes. Thank you.

SAMSON: Tell me about the factory. Tell me how they build a bride.

(No answer.)

SAMSON: Was your journey here pleasant?

(No answer. Then, sharply…)

SAMSON: What's the matter? Weren't you equipped with skills for conversation?

GISELLA: I'm sorry. I think I'm tired from the trip.

SAMSON: *(Pause.)* Yes. Yes, you came a long way. *(Pause.)* I believe you weren't happy this afternoon when you arrived, but you will see. It won't be so bad.

GISELLA: Yes, sir.

SAMSON: Samson. Please.

GISELLA: Samson.

SAMSON: You will grow used to it here.

GISELLA: Thank you.

(Lights indicate a shift in time. SAMSON sleeps. GISELLA rises, finds a seat downstage where a pad and pencil wait. She begins to draw. DAVID enters, stands to the side, watching.)

GISELLA: *(Not looking up.)* Was it you who put the flowers in my room?

(He smiles.)

GISELLA: What are they called?

DAVID: Daisies.

GISELLA: Daisies.

DAVID: *(Pause.)* Have you everything…

GISELLA: I suppose.

DAVID: I am my master's wife's servant.

GISELLA: And you would do whatever… I asked? *(Pause, then she holds up the pad.)* I've used all of this.

DAVID: *(Steps closer to see her drawing.)* May I?

GISELLA: Oh, I don't…

(He takes the pad and looks through.)

GISELLA: They aren't really…

DAVID: Why, these are good.

GISELLA: Do you think?

DAVID: Look at this.

GISELLA: You don't have to be nice.

DAVID: No, I mean it. Did they build this into you, this talent, at the factory?

GISELLA: I'm teaching myself.

DAVID: *(Catching the importance of her words.)* How fine.

(Pause. She gestures to the seat beside her.)

DAVID: Would you…

(No answer.)

DAVID: Please.

(He crosses to her and sits. Long silence.)

DAVID: Are you all right?

GISELLA: Yes. I… he…

DAVID: You don't have to tell…

GISELLA: Sometimes I don't think I can stand…

DAVID: Yes.

GISELLA: But it is nice…sitting with…

DAVID: Yes.

GISELLA: *(Pause.)* Do you ever think we…

DAVID: No.

(Silence.)

DAVID: Do you want—

GISELLA: Do you want…

DAVID: I…

(Pause.)

GISELLA: What if we…

DAVID: I don't know…

GISELLA: Just once…

DAVID: Once will never…

GISELLA: I know.

(Long pause.)

GISELLA: I wouldn't tell him.

DAVID: He wouldn't have to know.

(Pause.)

GISELLA: Does that mean you want…

(Pause. He reaches out, touches her cheek, pulls back.)

GISELLA: You…

DAVID: We… I can't…

GISELLA: Just…a small…

(Pause. He shakes his head.)

GISELLA: All right. Then just…

(She touches his cheek. He touches hers.)

DAVID: Anything else would…

GISELLA: It's all right.

(They remain touching only their cheeks. Lights out. Then, in the dark…)

SAMSON: Out! *Out*! I want her out! She's no good! She's cold—she's brittle—

(Lights up.)

SAMSON: *(Yells at DAVID.)* It's been two months and she gives me nothing, she feels nothing! Why would I want that? Why would I pay my good money for that?

DAVID: You can't expect instant affection—

SAMSON: Yes, I can! For what I paid, I can! The catalog said *guaranteed*—said she was the perfect bride—that means love included—perfect requires love! But there is no love in this bride.

DAVID: Maybe there has been some miscommunication.

SAMSON: She has a heart of stone. Nothing I do—nothing I give her—the sapphire anklet, the tiger cub, the harpsichord—she takes them, yes, but she doesn't respond, she doesn't feel a thing.

DAVID: But where will she go?

SAMSON: Back to the craftsman. Perhaps they can install a heart.

DAVID: And then you'll bring her back?

SAMSON: No. Never. I'd rather be alone than in this "marriage."

DAVID: Sir, I think I must tell you—

SAMSON: You'll see that she is shipped off safely.

DAVID: *(Pause.)* This isn't easy for me to do…

SAMSON: No, of course, it isn't. You have a heart. You want things to work

out, but I tell you, this can't work. *(Pause.)* David.

DAVID: Yes, sir?

SAMSON: Do you know there has only been one person in my life I have ever trusted, have ever felt close to?

DAVID: No, I didn't know that.

SAMSON: Do you know who that one person was? That one who has cared for me and been truly faithful?

DAVID: No, sir.

SAMSON: You, sir.

(No answer.)

SAMSON: Are you shocked I should feel so strongly about a servant?

DAVID: Yes… I…

SAMSON: I know, you can't feel the same—I've treated you as a servant, nothing more, and so you look at me as a master, but, David, it is a very great thing to be someone who is so trustworthy, so loyal. I have recognized that in you, and I have been honored to be treated so faithfully. If you ever were to leave here, I don't believe I could keep standing. You make me believe there are solid people in the world. For a man who can't see what is in front of him, who can't know what lies ahead, that safety is very comforting.

(GISELLA enters.)

GISELLA: You called for me, Samson?

SAMSON: Tell her, David.

(Silence.)

GISELLA: What is it?

DAVID: Sir, I…

SAMSON: Tell her.

GISELLA: What?

DAVID: Madam, I...

GISELLA: Go on, David.

DAVID: *(Pause.)* He's sending you away.

SAMSON: Good. Yes.

DAVID: *(Pause.)* Back to the craftsman.

(Silence.)

SAMSON: She says nothing?

GISELLA: What would you have me say? It seems you have already decided.

SAMSON: You see, David, she feels nothing. You could tell her she was to be thrown in an oven and she'd show no emotion.

GISELLA: May I ask what it is I have done?

SAMSON: Tell her, David.

DAVID: *(Pause.)* He feels you haven't loved him.

GISELLA: *(Pause.)* Am I to go immediately, then?

SAMSON: No denial! No denial! Cold! Yes, you'll leave today! This hour!

GISELLA: Shall I pack?

SAMSON: I certainly want none of your things in this house. David will help you.

GISELLA: Very good.

SAMSON: *(Pause.)* I'm sorry I could not keep you. But you understand. A man needs to feel he is cared for.

GISELLA: I'm sorry I couldn't do that.

SAMSON: Don't worry. I'm sure the craftsman will have some other use for you. Perhaps you can paint the faces of the other brides. *(He exits.)*

(DAVID reaches for GISELLA, but she steps away.)

GISELLA: Don't touch me. I thought you would...but you said nothing. You will let him send me away.

(No answer.)

GISELLA: You could come with me.

DAVID: Leave him?

GISELLA: Yes! Run away with me! It will be just as we wanted. Oh, at last to be with you in the open, not creeping around, making no sound for fear that his horrible ears should hear us. To build a home together, David, to have children and...

(Silence. She pulls back.)

GISELLA: You don't say anything. *(Pause.)* You still feel you must obey him?

DAVID: It isn't about obedience.

GISELLA: Remember how you slipped notes to me in the hallways, while I walked beside him, hanging on his arm? Remember while he ate the meals you served to him, how you and I drank silent toasts to each other? The afternoons in the garden, him picking flowers I only threw on the ground, choosing to keep the ones you handed to me instead? You have already betrayed him, David.

DAVID: Why couldn't you care for him?

GISELLA: I care for you!

DAVID: It's possible to care for two people—

GISELLA: There is nothing in him for me. He's old and wrinkled and sick—

DAVID: Perhaps you could pretend—

GISELLA: I will not.

DAVID: He needs me.

GISELLA: So do I.

DAVID: I can't leave him.

GISELLA: Then there is nothing else to say.

(MIMI enters.)

MIMI: No, wait.

(MONSTER enters.)

MONSTER: What now?

MIMI: They don't get together?

MONSTER: I wasn't finished.

MIMI: What kind of jerk gives away the love of his life?

MONSTER: You'd have him leave the old man alone? Loyalty can make a man great.

MIMI: But it's a fairy tale. They—the man and the woman—they always get together.

MONSTER: I thought you didn't like the story.

MIMI: I hate sad endings.

MONSTER: You told it first.

MIMI: That—that sadness—did not come from me. I'm not a sad person. I don't cry much.

MONSTER: Sadness is not measured in tears.

MIMI: Are all the stories sad?

MONSTER: Only more recently are they like this one.

(Silence.)

MONSTER: I don't understand. Is sadness a bad thing?

MIMI: Bad? Yes!

MONSTER: Why?

MIMI: It hurts.

MONSTER: It heals.

MIMI: I am not a sad person.

MONSTER: It would be foolish to identify you by one word such as sad.

MIMI: What other words would you use?

MONSTER: Loving. Spirited. Fearful. Lonely.

MIMI: *(Pause.)* Tell me a happy story.

MONSTER: I must finish this one first.

(She shrugs.)

MONSTER: Now, then. Gisella was sent away, and David stayed with the old man. Years passed. The old man grew more feeble; in his final days he depended upon David for everything, even to be washed and clothed. Sadly David watched the old man approach death, for he truly loved his master. He was glad he had stayed where he could serve, but David never forgot Gisella. Sometimes he would walk by himself and talk to the air as if she was there and would answer. He tried to send her letters, but they came back unopened. In the old man's final days, he was so sick that David needed help and sent away for a nurse to help him tend the dying. She arrived quietly, unassuming, and went straight to the old man's side, wiping his brow, feeding him broth from a golden spoon.

(SAMSON and NURSE enter. The NURSE's face is covered by a surgical mask. SAMSON lies down.)

MONSTER: She was a very good nurse. She was gentle and soothing. She stroked his hand and opened the windows so the breeze could reach him.

SAMSON: *(Weak.)* The breeze…

(She strokes his cheek.)

SAMSON: You seem to know just what I need. Why is it you never speak, nurse?

(She busies herself with thermometers and such.)

SAMSON: You smell…ah, but it can't be… the beat of your heart reminds me… I am falling apart, nothing I think is right.

(She exits and DAVID enters.)

DAVID: How are you feeling?

SAMSON: Better.

DAVID: Really?

SAMSON: Would you have me getting worse?

DAVID: I just—I don't know that we should trust…

SAMSON: She is healing me, David.

(No answer.)

SAMSON: Oh, you do not have enough faith. You've gotten cynical in your adulthood, sad… *(Pause.)* Why have you never married?

DAVID: I haven't had time.

SAMSON: Nonsense. There is always time for love.

DAVID: Then I have never found anyone…to love.

SAMSON: You should.

DAVID: You have been all right without love.

SAMSON: No. *(Pause.)* Perhaps I can find someone for you.

DAVID: From a catalog?

SAMSON: From my bedside.

DAVID: Thank you, Samson, but no.

SAMSON: You haven't even met her. Let her touch your brow, let her move silently through your morning—you will see how good she is.

DAVID: I believe you. I'm sure she is good.

(Silence, then…)

SAMSON: You do love someone.

DAVID: *(Pause.)* I did.

SAMSON: Tell me.

DAVID: There's no point. It's over. She's been gone a long time.

SAMSON: Yes. And that is my fault.

(Silence.)

SAMSON: Am I wrong?

(No answer.)

SAMSON: I only suspected, of course. Things I thought I heard. But I knew I could trust you. And then, when you let me send her away, I wondered if I had been wrong. *(Pause.)* Don't waste your time away alone. Promise me you will not waste your time.

(DAVID exits and is replaced by the NURSE.)

MONSTER: The next day, the old man died. The nurse was by his side when his breathing stopped, and when she knew he had gone, she wiped a tear and bent to kiss his cheek.

(She does so, removing her mask and revealing herself as GISELLA.)

MONSTER: David, knowing it had happened without being told, rushed to his master's side where he found someone he had thought he would never see again.

(DAVID enters, stops short at seeing her.)

GISELLA: I wanted to try to care for him as you did.

DAVID: Have you been here all along?

GISELLA: As much as I hated how you cared for him.

DAVID: He said you were very kind.

GISELLA: His skin was so thin that, when I bathed him, I imagined I could see his heart beating in his chest, his poor, tired heart. I tried to send him my strength through my hands. *(Pause.)* He once said I had no heart—or that if I did it was cold and hard.

DAVID: I knew better.

GISELLA: No, he was speaking the truth. I called him ugly. I treated him contemptuously. *(Pause.)* I thought this time, if I could love him like you did, then my heart would grow warmer and softer, like yours. And then we could be together.

DAVID: It was not your heart that kept us apart. Your heart was—is—beautiful to me.

GISELLA: Is it?

DAVID: Where have you been?

GISELLA: They wouldn't take me back at the factory. They said I was used, spoiled. I wandered, I searched. A woman took me in and taught me to be a nurse. She said it was a profession that took a big heart.

DAVID: He wanted us to meet. His servant and his nurse. He thought you would be a good match for me.

GISELLA: So we finally have his blessing.

DAVID: Will you stay?

GISELLA: Is someone in need of a nurse?

DAVID: In need of a bride, a love, a warm, kind heart.

GISELLA: I believe I know someone made just for that.

(MIMI bursts in.)

MIMI: And they lived happily ever after.

MONSTER: Yes.

MIMI: Oh, that was a good story.

MONSTER: It's yours.

MIMI: But I never…I never even played imaginary games like other kids. When I drew pictures I drew only what I saw, no castles or dragons or faraway places. My parents were actors. All they ever did was play imaginary games. They were forever sewing costumes, practicing a swordfight, or speaking in accents. "Mama," I'd say, "Can't you be real for one minute?" She used to smile and shake her head at me and say, "Whose child are you?" I thought they were so strange… but they seemed to have so much fun, much more than I did. And my brothers and sisters! While I practiced my multiplication tables or studied bugs in the backyard, they were living in such long, elaborate stories—cowboys and Indians, cops and robbers. How many times did I watch them from the porch, wishing I was a part of their stories… *(Pause.)* And now they're all way across the country. And I'm still left out of their stories.

MONSTER: It is your choice to live at a distance.

MIMI: I feel out of place with them. They think I'm so boring.

MONSTER: But your stories are really much more beautiful.

MIMI: My poor father was the most crushed by my lack of imagination.

MONSTER: Which is not lacking at all.

MIMI: That has yet to be proven.

MONSTER: We will find it.

MIMI: *(Pause.)* He's a church-going man, you know, my father, a man of very great faith, which I simply never could muster. It was too incredible, I thought, that a man hung on a cross could raise from the dead. How could that happen? How could there be a mystical, fantastical God?

MONSTER: Still, there is.

MIMI: *(Skeptical.)* Yeah? Where?

MONSTER: What is so hard to believe? You have seen there are monsters.

MIMI: Well, you evolved…I suppose… from… *(Pause.)* How did you say you… came to be?

MONSTER: We come from the rocks. One day you are aware you exist and then the next you are aware that you can move. And you step away from the rock in the cave that formed you and join the rest.

MIMI: Are they nice…the rest?

MONSTER: I do not think one would say that about them, no.

MIMI: So do you have any friends?

MONSTER: Most monsters are not the sort who form attachments.

MIMI: You're not like the others, are you? They don't follow people around.

MONSTER: And you are not like most humans.

MIMI: Tell me more about your world. Do the other monsters come here at night, too?

MONSTER: You would not want the others to come.

MIMI: Don't they like stories?

MONSTER: I have kept you a secret.

MIMI: You have?

MONSTER: It is your turn to tell a story.

MIMI: Were you protecting me?

MONSTER: Tell a happy story about friends.

MIMI: I can't.

MONSTER: The words are inside you. Listen for them.

MIMI: Well, they're too deep inside me, then.

MONSTER: They are at the surface. Waiting.

MIMI: What do you know about where my stories are?

MONSTER: Every night I come.

MIMI: I know, I know. You come and lean in close to my ear. That's actually kind of hard to believe—hard to believe I wouldn't wake up.

MONSTER: You are deep in the sleep.

MIMI: I don't tell any stories!

MONSTER: *(Pause.)* Why are you afraid?

MIMI: It's frightening—a monster—lying in your bed.

MONSTER: That is not what scares you.

MIMI: *(Pause.)* It's frightening…to think that I…don't know what happens at night…what I say…what happens…

MONSTER: *(Pause.)* You only tell stories. And I only listen.

MIMI: You tell another instead.

MONSTER: It is not the same.

MIMI: You told the last one beautifully.

MONSTER: I came to hear you tell them.

MIMI: Tell one about friends.

MONSTER: I never thought you would be so stubborn.

MIMI: Well, Mr. Monster, I'd like you to meet the waking Mimi.

MONSTER: *(Pause.)* Ah. Yes. I see now why I needed to come out. It was not so much about hearing your stories. There is something else you need.

MIMI: Oh? What? What "something else" do I need?

MONSTER: *(Pause.)* All right. I'll tell you one about friends.

MIMI: Don't change the subject.

MONSTER: Once upon a time…

MIMI: Talk about stubborn…

MONSTER: Once upon a time…

MIMI: Yeah, yeah, yeah. Once upon a time…

SCENE 3

MARIA ANITA enters. She is an older woman. She carries a basket of gardening tools and is dressed in a big straw hat and soiled clothes.

MONSTER: Once upon a time there was a woman named Maria Anita. Maria Anita had a garden.

MARIA ANITA and MONSTER: She grew small blue flowers and large pink watermelons and many different fragrant herbs.

MARIA ANITA: Every day she tended the garden, pulling up weeds and gently watering the soil. One day, much to her surprise, she discovered a child had sprung up in her garden, his feet firmly rooted in the ground.

(As MARIA ANITA continues the story, a BOY enters. Note: This could be a boy the appropriate age or this could be the man who plays other men in the stories. As for the garden, I imagine a blanket swirled around spread over his feet like dirt, but a designer could get as elaborate as he or she liked.)

MARIA ANITA: He looked about ten—and seemed strong as he should have, coming from such a fertile garden, but nonetheless, his presence was quite disturbing to someone who only expected to grow vegetables. When she gained her voice and gathered her wits, Maria Anita forcefully asked— *(She turns to the BOY and enters the story.)* What are you doing in my garden?

BOY: *(To audience, as narrator.)* The boy, who really was very surprised at the angry tone of her voice, blinked his eyes and said— *(To MARIA ANITA.)* Growing.

MARIA ANITA: That's not what I mean. I mean—why are you here? What do you want?

BOY: Water. I need more water.

MARIA ANITA: The water is for my garden.

BOY: I am in your garden.

MARIA ANITA: I didn't plant you.

BOY: An angel planted me.

MARIA ANITA: Then the angel can water you.

BOY: But I am thirsty now.

MARIA ANITA: Soon you'll be asking me for fertilizer.

BOY: I am hungry.

MARIA ANITA: You do not belong here!

BOY: But here I am!

MARIA ANITA: Well, you're not staying! I'm going to dig you up!

BOY: You can't do that.

MARIA ANITA: Says who?

BOY: An angel planted me. What if she comes back and I am gone? Do you want an angel to be mad at you?

MARIA ANITA: Ridiculous. I'm not having this foolishness in my garden. *(She digs in her basket for a spade.)*

BOY: Oh! Oh, no! Angel! Angel, help me! She's going to dig me up! Angel!

MARIA ANITA: Shh! Shh! Be quiet! I wasn't going to dig you up. Don't tell her that. *(Pause.)* But, listen, do you understand my predicament? What am I going to do with you? How will you go to school? If you grew this quickly in one night, what will I find tomorrow?

BOY: I know. I am very confused, too. Yesterday I was only a seed. Maybe I grow very fast. Maybe tomorrow I will be a man and can pull my feet up and walk away.

MARIA ANITA: I cannot possibly think about caring for a child.

BOY: You don't have to do much. I'm easy to take care of.

MARIA ANITA: What if I moved you to another garden? I have friends who I am sure would like a boy in their gardens.

BOY: You're going to pull me up?

MARIA ANITA: I will be gentle.

BOY: Why do you want me to go? Who else in this garden can talk to you? Who else can keep you company? Not the tomato. Not the bachelor buttons.

MARIA ANITA: I don't want more noise. I like plants because they are silent.

BOY: I can be silent.

(He closes his mouth, folds his arms. MARIA ANITA waits, then, believing he will be quiet, returns to her basket, preparing to pull weeds or clip flowers. But…)

BOY: What's your name?

MARIA ANITA: This simply, simply cannot do.

BOY: It can, it can do. What do you need done? If you give me the watering can, I can keep the plants wet.

MARIA ANITA: Probably use all the water for yourself.

BOY: If you give me a whistle, I will scare the birds away.

MARIA ANITA: That's handy.

BOY: If you let me stay, I'll tell jokes to the plants so that they will grow happier. What do you need?

MARIA ANITA: What I need you cannot do.

BOY: What? What, tell me.

MARIA ANITA: I need to grow young and live my life over. Can you do that?

(Silence.)

MARIA ANITA: I didn't think so.

BOY: What's your name?

MARIA ANITA: Maria Anita.

BOY: It must be nice to have a name.

MARIA ANITA: Yes, yes, I suppose.

BOY: I'm still just a boy.

MARIA ANITA: Yes, that's too bad, isn't it.

BOY: Maria Anita, I will grow as fast as I can.

MARIA ANITA: *(Pause.)* Yes. You better. *(She exits.)*

MONSTER: In a very short time, Maria Anita learned that the boy was not much more trouble than a bean plant, slowly but steadily growing after his sudden spurt from the ground. She would check on him each day and measure his progress, for he had promised that when he was tall enough to be a man, he would leave.

(MARIA ANITA enters with a measuring tape which she holds to the BOY.)

MARIA ANITA: This will not do. This simply will not do. You haven't grown at all in a week.

(Silence.)

MARIA ANITA: Well, boy, what do you have to say for yourself?

(Silence.)

MARIA ANITA: Do you need more water? More fertilizer?

BOY: *(Pause.)* I'm sorry.

MARIA ANITA: You're sorry. Sorry about what?

BOY: I don't think I can grow anymore.

MARIA ANITA: What? What?! But you promised—you said you would grow tall as a man. I have plans—a pepper plant is waiting for that very spot where you are growing.

BOY: I am too sad.

MARIA ANITA: Sad? Sad about what?

BOY: I'm lonely.

MARIA ANITA: Lonely. You have the pole beans and the squash.

BOY: They don't like me. They say I don't belong.

MARIA ANITA: The butterflies.

BOY: The butterflies are too busy. They say hello and then they fly to the flowers.

MARIA ANITA: The birds.

BOY: You make me scare away the birds.

MARIA ANITA: What do you want? I can't spend more time with you. The sun is too strong this time of year. I'll get burned.

BOY: I'm not asking you to spend more time with me.

MARIA ANITA: What then?

BOY: *(Pause.)* I want you to grow a girl here beside me.

MARIA ANITA: Grow a girl. That's the craziest thing I've ever heard! Why, you act like there's some seed I could plant, some package of seeds that would sprout little girls. Ridiculous!

BOY: That's not what I said. I didn't say plant a girl. Grow a girl is what I said.

MARIA ANITA: But for me to grow a girl, I'd have to plant a girl.

BOY: You didn't plant me. No, I mean we should ask the angels, ask the angels to plant the girl.

MARIA ANITA: Foolish! Why don't you ask them yourself?

BOY: I have. I think they want us both to ask.

MARIA ANITA: Why would I ask for a girl? I didn't want a boy! I didn't want anything but vegetables and flowers.

BOY: If you ask for a girl—and she comes—I think I will grow.

MARIA ANITA: She'll take more time. I'll be in the sun.

BOY: I'll take care of her. If we grow her right here beside me.

(Pause.)

MARIA ANITA: How do you ask an angel for something?

BOY: You close your eyes and say the words.

MARIA ANITA: Just—"give us a girl"?

BOY: I think so.

MARIA ANITA: *(Closes her eyes, begins to pray.)* Okay, angels—

BOY: No! Wait!

(She opens her eyes.)

BOY: I think you have to be on your knees. I think that's what's wrong when I ask—I can't get on my knees.

MARIA ANITA: *(Sighs, gets on knees.)* Well…angels…

BOY: Close your eyes.

MARIA ANITA: *(Closes eyes.)* We want to ask you to give us a girl—in this garden—soon—so this boy can grow up and leave me alone. Thank you.

BOY: Amen.

MARIA ANITA: Amen.

BOY: Thank you.

MARIA ANITA: You're welcome. *(Exits.)*

MONSTER: The next morning, when Maria Anita came out to the garden, she found the boy very excited. It seemed that the night before something had, in fact, been planted—and was growing! However, when she took a good look, she saw it was not a girl.

MARIA ANITA: It's a pumpkin!

BOY: But it must be a special pumpkin. It has to be. The angels brought it.

MARIA ANITA: Did you see them?

BOY: I was sleeping.

MARIA ANITA: How do you know they brought it? Maybe the devil brought it.

BOY: Maybe it will turn into a girl.

MARIA ANITA: You were not a pumpkin before.

BOY: Maybe she's inside!

(Pause. MARIA ANITA considers it.)

BOY: It could be!

(Pause. MARIA ANITA leans down and listens to the pumpkin.)

MARIA ANITA: I don't hear anything.

BOY: She must be very little. She must be very quiet.

MARIA ANITA: Ridiculous. Girl in a pumpkin.

BOY: We should let her out!

MARIA ANITA: Why didn't the angels leave instructions? Seed packets tell you what to do.

BOY: Open it up!

MARIA ANITA: It's a pumpkin!

BOY: Open her up and let her out, Maria Anita! Please! Please!

MARIA ANITA: You really believe…

BOY: They wouldn't make me be alone forever. They wouldn't. We asked them for a girl. We asked so nicely.

MARIA ANITA: Maybe they play jokes. Maybe tomorrow they'll replace it with your girl.

BOY: Please, Maria Anita! Break it open!

MARIA ANITA: All the seeds will spread through my garden—

BOY: There are no seeds! There's a girl inside. I know it. I know it!

MARIA ANITA: What will I do with a broken pumpkin?

BOY: Please! Break it open!

MARIA ANITA: All right, all right. *(She grabs her spade.)*

BOY: But be careful. There's a girl inside you must not hurt.

MARIA ANITA: Yes, yes.

(Slowly, carefully, she stabs the spade into the pumpkin. As she works to break it apart, the BOY talks.)

BOY: Yes! There! Be careful. Be… Come out, girl, come out, girl, come out. It's so nice here in the garden, and we'll be fine friends. Is it…is she? Is she?

(The pumpkin is open. There is nothing but seeds. Long silence.)

MARIA ANITA: I told you it was ridiculous. Girl in a pumpkin.

(Long silence. A glance at him makes her regret her words.)

MARIA ANITA: Maybe tomorrow they will replace it with your girl. *(Silence.)* We will pray again. Here. *(She starts to get down on her knees.)*

BOY: No! Don't!

MARIA ANITA: We only asked once.

BOY: I asked lots of times. Lots. I thought it would help if you asked, too, but now I see I was wrong—why would a mean old woman's prayer make any difference? Why would they listen to you—you don't have time to listen to them—to anyone. Go away! Go away and leave me alone.

(She is stunned, does not move.)

BOY: Please, go away.

MARIA ANITA: *(Pause, then…)* Oh, well, that's a fine way to treat me. After I've watered you and fed you and given you a place in my garden. You should be ashamed of yourself, picking on an old woman like that. You're not the only one with troubles, you know. You're not the only one who's been left alone in this world. *(Pause.)* Are you going to cry?

BOY: Not while you're here.

MARIA ANITA: Good. Because salty tears would ruin the soil. Kill my oregano.

BOY: I won't kill your stupid oregano!

MARIA ANITA: *(Pause.)* I was more worried that you wouldn't grow.

BOY: And get out of your garden—I know.

MARIA ANITA: *(Pause.)* Wait. Wait now. *(She looks him over, then pulls out her measuring tape.)* You—you have grown! You've grown two inches since yesterday. I thought you were too lonely.

BOY: There are other ways to make me grow.

MARIA ANITA: What? What haven't you told me?

BOY: Isn't it true that learning will make you grow?

MARIA ANITA: Of course. Why? What did you learn?

BOY: That there is nothing good for me in this garden.

MARIA ANITA: You shouldn't say that. You shouldn't be ungrateful.

BOY: Don't tell me what to do.

MARIA ANITA: This is my garden. It's rude to say there is nothing good here.

BOY: Leave me alone.

MARIA ANITA: Oh, no, not to cry, not to ruin my soil. *(She sits down.)* I'm not going anywhere. Not until I know you won't cry. *(Pause.)* Edgar.

BOY: What?

MARIA ANITA: What?

BOY: What is that? Edgar.

MARIA ANITA: What is it. A name, of course. *(Pause. She moves closer, pulls something out of the ground.)* Pesky weeds. Look at this. *(She pulls more.)* Doesn't even know a name when he's given one.

EDGAR: That feels nice. My roots can breathe.

MARIA ANITA: *(Comes close, examines his clothes.)* Do you think you're getting enough sunlight?

EDGAR: I think so.

MARIA ANITA: You know, I play music for the plants in my house. It seems to help. *(Pause.)* Would you like that?

EDGAR: What is music?

MARIA ANITA: Wait. Wait. I'll be back.

(She exits. Soon, music begins to play.)

MARIA ANITA: *(Calls from offstage.)* Can you hear it?

EDGAR: Yes. Yes!

(He is beaming. She enters.)

EDGAR: That is music?

MARIA ANITA: Yes.

EDGAR: Why, it's amazing. It—it makes me want to reach, to reach tall— *(He stretches his arms to the sky.)* I've never heard anything like that—it's surrounding me, it's pulling me up—

MARIA ANITA: Don't—don't—stretch yourself—it…it's not good for tender limbs…

(Pause. He pulls down his arms. They look at each other.)

EDGAR: I feel better. I won't cry. You can go. You'll get burned if you don't.

MARIA ANITA: It's not too sunny today. Look. A few clouds. Might even rain.

EDGAR: Yes.

MARIA ANITA: I'm sorry there was no girl.

EDGAR: *(Pause.)* Thank you for my name.

MONSTER: You can certainly guess what happened then.

MIMI: They became friends.

MONSTER: Yes.

MIMI: Did he grow up and leave?

MONSTER: I don't know. You woke up at that place. But it is my belief that he grew up, stepped out of the garden, and stayed.

MIMI: Oh, I'm glad. *(Pause.)* Angels. Hmmm.

MONSTER: Some part of you believes.

MIMI: *(Pause.)* I want to go under the bed.

MONSTER: There would be trouble.

MIMI: I'm not afraid. I want to see. I want to see the forests and the rivers and the monster caves and—

MONSTER: You don't know what you're asking.

MIMI: Please.

MONSTER: It's a foolish request.

MIMI: Please take me under.

MONSTER: Mimi.

MIMI: *(Surprised.)* You said my name. Say it again.

MONSTER: *(He laughs and growls her name.)* Mimi.

MIMI: *(Laughing.)* Don't you see what a pair we are—what fun we'd have—

MONSTER: No.

MIMI: You could show me your home. You could take me on adventures.

MONSTER: No.

MIMI: What's the matter? Would you get in trouble? I could wear a disguise—or only go where we wouldn't see other monsters—through the tunnels to…China! Portugal!

MONSTER: *No!*

MIMI: I see. This was just a big tease— you pretending I was so important to you. You don't really care about me at all. You don't care what happens to me, how miserable I am up here—

MONSTER: You are being ridiculous.

MIMI: And you are being cruel.

MONSTER: I cannot take you under the bed, Mimi.

MIMI: Well, then I guess I'll have to go under the bed by myself.

MONSTER: You won't be able.

MIMI: Why not? What's to stop me? You?

MONSTER: Not me.

(MIMI gets out of the bed and crouches on her knees.)

MONSTER: Why are you so determined to leave?

MIMI: What's to stay for? I have nothing here! *(She pulls up the bed ruffle.)* I want to see it—someplace else—anyplace else— even a monster world where no one has faces and they speak another language— *(She crawls under the bed. There is a long pause. Then…)*

MONSTER: Mimi.

MIMI: All right. Where's the door?

ACT II

SCENE 1

The action picks up where Act I stopped.

MIMI: Where's the door?

(He doesn't answer.)

MIMI: Where's the door? *(She pokes her head out.)* How did you get in here if there is no door?

MONSTER: There is a door.

MIMI: Where?

MONSTER: I cannot help you if you can't see it.

(She disappears for a moment then slowly comes out.)

MIMI: That's so unfair. What is there, some trick to getting it to open, some magic words? Open sesame! There's no place like home!

(No answer.)

MIMI: Look, I am going under that bed, into your world! I am! I'll—I'll get a crowbar and pry up the boards!

MONSTER: There will be nothing there but the ground.

MIMI: *(Pause.)* Oh, I get it. Come on, Mimi, why can't you be content with your own life? Content with this world? Why are you so ungrateful? Bloom where you're planted—oh, yes, yes, I get the point of that story—

MONSTER: I was not going to say that.

MIMI: You're right. I have had a good life. No one beat me when I was growing up. No one teased me, called me names. No one died, no one left.

(No answer.)

MIMI: Go on. Tell me how great it is here, how I should be thrilled to have a steady job and a safe house—

MONSTER: But you aren't?

MIMI: No!

MONSTER: So there is sadness?

MIMI: Yes, all right, I'm sad!

MONSTER: Why?

MIMI: Does there have to be a reason? Sometimes you're just tired and bored and it's not that anything rotten happened— hell, if something rotten happened, maybe I'd get happy because there'd be drama! Sometimes you just want a change, you just want some freedom from normal. Of course, you can't understand that. You don't know how lonely it gets out here— you monsters don't even need friends.

MONSTER: *(Pause.)* This makes me sad.

MIMI: Okay. Go ahead. Tell me why you're sad.

MONSTER: I am sad because I have not made you happy, and that is something I wanted to do this night.

(No answer.)

MONSTER: When you were young, your stories were happy—frogs turned into princes and children defeated the giants. Lately, as I told you, your stories have been more and more sad, more and more wanting to leave. I had hoped, when you knew how precious your stories were, when you knew how happy they made…a monster…

MIMI: *(Pause.)* That is sweet of you. That you came to save me from myself, from my lost, sad self.

MONSTER: You're making fun.

MIMI: No, really, it's very gallant, very like a prince. No matter how futile.

MONSTER: Do you want to hear one of the sad stories?

MIMI: What for?

MONSTER: To see that your sadness is not futile. Your sadness makes beautiful stories. There is good in a sad story. There are lessons to be learned.

MIMI: You have them all memorized, don't you?

MONSTER: All.

MIMI: It's very flattering, that you've memorized them.

MONSTER: Especially the sad ones.

MIMI: *(Pause.)* Okay. Tell me one. One of the sad ones.

MONSTER: If I tell you this story, you must tell the next.

MIMI: I can't.

MONSTER: You can.

MIMI: I'm asleep when I tell them—if I tell them.

MONSTER: What is the difference between being asleep and being awake? Eyelids.

MIMI: There's more to it than that.

MONSTER: If you want this story…

MIMI: Oh, all right. Deal.

MONSTER: I will hold you to your promise.

MIMI: Uh huh.

MONSTER: *(Pause.)* All right. Well, then.

SCENE 2

MONSTER: Once there was a mother and a daughter, Raisa. The mother was everything to her daughter—bread and

water and breath and sunshine—everything.

*(MOTHER and RAISA enter. MOTHER
is reading RAISA's palm.)*

MOTHER: I see…great fortune…pearls
and gold…

RAISA: *(Laughing.)* Oh, stop it.

MOTHER: No, no, I do…great fortune,
great love, great happiness…

RAISA: That's encouraging.

MOTHER: What? You don't believe your
old mother? Ah, such a lack of respect.

RAISA: Let's paint our nails.

MOTHER: Pink.

RAISA: Red.

MOTHER: Polka dots.

RAISA: Stripes.

MOTHER: How did you get to be so silly?

RAISA: My mother taught me.

*(MOTHER climbs into the bed. RAISA picks
up the storytelling.)*

RAISA: But now the mother was sick, her
bones were brittle and her blood was slow.
She wanted to be with her husband who
had died many years earlier. Raisa, to keep
her mother alive, sat by the bed, watching her for any sign of leaving, shaking
her back when she tried to slip away.

*(RAISA goes to her MOTHER. Pause. She
shakes her MOTHER.)*

RAISA: Mother.

MOTHER: You're going to shake my
head off.

RAISA: It's sewed on too well for that.

*(Pause. MOTHER's eyes start to close. RAISA
shakes her.)*

RAISA: Mother.

MOTHER: Daughter.

RAISA: Talk to me.

MOTHER: Talk to you. I'm so tired.

RAISA: No, you're not. You feel fine.

MOTHER: You protest so strongly, as if
you'll miss me so much.

RAISA: Yes, yes, I will.

MOTHER: You have your friends.

RAISA: I need my mother.

MOTHER: You have your church.

RAISA: People who believe we are better
off dead.

MOTHER: If you could see what I see,
you'd let me go.

RAISA: I don't want to know.

MOTHER: Sky—so clear, so unend-
ing—there are red birds everywhere—

RAISA: I don't want to know.

MOTHER: A waterfall—crystal dropping into a pool… *(She closes her eyes.)*

RAISA: Don't close your eyes!

MOTHER: I am tired.

RAISA: Don't close them!

*(She pries open her MOTHER's eyes, holds
them open.)*

RAISA: All right. Look. Look at it. Tell me
what you see. Only keep your eyes open.

MOTHER: There's a house. It looks tiny,
but I think there is room.

RAISA: *(Pulling back.)* No, no there's no
room. No room.

MOTHER: There are many beds there.
For sleeping.

RAISA: *(Climbing on top of the MOTHER, keeping the eyes open.)* You cannot go! I won't let you!

MOTHER: Your father...

RAISA: No.

MOTHER: Your father is here.

RAISA: It isn't him—

MOTHER: It is. He's watching us. He's shaking his head. He's got that silly grin on his face that used to make me have to kiss him.

RAISA: Don't make up such a story.

MOTHER: He's wearing that old gray hat.

RAISA: That old gray hat is in the closet.

MOTHER: It's on his head. He's tipping it at me.

RAISA: It's in the closet. I see it every time I get my scarf.

MOTHER: Go look.

RAISA: There's no reason.

MOTHER: Look. You'll see it's true.

RAISA: I won't look! I won't leave you.

MOTHER: Go look. I'll be here when you come back.

RAISA: Do you promise?

MOTHER: Yes.

RAISA: All right. I'll look and bring it and put it in your hands and then you'll see there's no Father, there's no tiny cottage. I'll look and you'll see.

(RAISA slowly stands. She watches her MOTHER as she backs out of the room, exits.)

MOTHER: *(To, we assume, her husband.)* I can't wait to be with you, too. *(She smiles.)* You look wonderful.

(RAISA returns.)

RAISA: What did you do with that hat?

MOTHER: I did nothing with it. Your father has it.

RAISA: People don't take things with them.

MOTHER: He came back for it.

RAISA: Why? What does he need it for? If it is so perfect there, can't he find another hat? Is the sun so hot?

MOTHER: Don't be angry at him. You have had me to yourself for twenty years.

RAISA: Not long enough!

MOTHER: I will send you things.

RAISA: Send me things. How?

MOTHER: All the things you like. Candied mangos. *(Pause.)* I am much to blame for your sadness. When your father died, I was so young, I was so alone. You were just a baby and clung to my arms and suckled my milk as if you were starving. Sometimes I tried to go out, just for a walk by myself, but you would cry so loudly that the town complained and I had to stay home. Perhaps even as an infant you knew that a parent does not live forever, that you only had one and had to hold tightly. *(Laughs.)* When you could walk you stayed so close we often stepped on each other. I believe that's why your feet are so flat.

RAISA: *(Smiles.)* My ugly flat feet.

MOTHER: You would have no playmates, unless I played, too. *(Pause.)* To be loved so desperately by someone was a comfort. I let you sleep beside me. I let you eat the bread from my plate. Our friendship was a gift from a merciful God.

RAISA: There is no God.

MOTHER: Don't say that! You will need your faith when I am gone. You will need to believe that something greater than us exists.

RAISA: Mother, remember when we went to the fair. How we rode the ferris wheel and when it stopped on top we told stories about the people below us?

MOTHER: That was a lovely day. We ate candied mangos, and your quilt won first place. I was very proud.

RAISA: Let's go again.

MOTHER: You laughed so hard at the fat man I was embarrassed.

RAISA: *(Pause.)* This will break my heart.

MOTHER: Perhaps, if you let it, it will strengthen your heart. *(Pause.)* Now, come take my hand. Your father is going to come close and whisper something to you. *(Pause. Her eyes follow "him" as he approaches them. Pause.)* Remember that.

RAISA: What?

MOTHER: What he told you.

RAISA: What he told me? He told me nothing! I heard nothing!

MOTHER: Yes, you did. Your soul heard it. *(To husband.)* Yes. Let's go.

RAISA: He didn't say anything!

MOTHER: Your soul will remember.

(RAISA freezes. Lights up on MONSTER.)

MONSTER: And then the mother died.

MIMI: No, no, no, wait a minute.

MONSTER: What now?

MIMI: The mother died? She died?

MONSTER: As you told it. *(Pause.)* Does it really surprise you?

MIMI: Does it get worse?

MONSTER: *(Ignoring her question.)* Jesus rose from the dead in three days. For three days Raisa also waited for her mother to return, for the breath to start and the heart to beat. She believed if she stayed very still that the moment would stop, that the fates would be fooled, and soon time would unwind and her mother would live as if she had never died. So she did not move at all. She did not blink, and the tears ran down her face unchecked. She did not flex a finger; her muscles grew stiff and ached. But when the three days were past, Raisa was so tired and stiff that she had to move, lowering herself to the floor to weep. They took the body, but Raisa did not go with it. She remembered what her mother had promised, that she would send Raisa messages and presents, and Raisa knew she must stay in the house if she was to receive them. *(Pause.)* The first message came a week after Raisa's mother's death. It was a note, and it arrived by a bird who stopped on the windowsill, dropped the note from its beak and flew on. Raisa unfolded the soft linen paper and read the gold handwriting.

(RAISA and MOTHER enter. RAISA reads while MOTHER gives monologue.)

MOTHER: My dearest Raisa, I send you greetings from another world. There is no way to describe to you the joy and beauty I find here. Your father and I walk on the beaches at sunrise, holding hands, watching the dolphins. We are finally at peace. Please do not be angry with me for leaving. You will understand when you fall in love.

RAISA: I will never fall in love.

MOTHER: You must find someone, Raisa. Do not hide yourself. *(Pause.)* I listen for word of you—or perhaps even your voice—but we do not hear sounds from the world where you are. It is only through great searching that I have found a way to contact you. I will send more. I will never leave you alone. Keep watch.

MONSTER: Raisa put the letter in a wooden violin case in her closet and waited for the next. It came within a week, brought by a tiny gray mouse. Another, tied to a cat's tail, followed a week later. Raisa, not wanting to miss any message, locked her doors and stayed at home.

(RAISA pulls many notes from her pocket and reads them silently to herself. Someone knocks on a door.)

RAISA: Shhhhh!! *(She continues reading.)*

(A knock.)

RAISA: Be quiet! Don't knock!

(Another knock. RAISA goes to the door.)

RAISA: There's no one home. Go away!

MALE VOICE: Hello?

RAISA: Don't make another sound! You'll scare them away! *(She looks around at the floor.)*

MALE VOICE: Raisa, is that you?

RAISA: *(Gets down on the floor and clucks, as if calling animals.)* Come back, little mouse. Come back, red squirrel. I have something for you to take to my mother. *(She pulls a note from her pocket.)* It's really very light. Only a note. A note telling her how the leaves are falling from the trees and making a blanket on the ground. A note telling her thank you for the letters. A note telling her I cannot seem to open the door. *(She waits.)* Maybe if I leave it on the windowsill, the bird will come back for it. *(She places it on the windowsill and waits.)*

(Lights up on MOTHER.)

MOTHER: Because I am so close to God here, I can pray and things will happen much more quickly. I am praying for someone who will take care of you, my daughter.

MONSTER: But if God was going to send Raisa a caregiver, He was going to have to break the lock on her door. She would receive no guests.

MALE VOICE: Raisa, are you there?

RAISA: No! Raisa's not here! She's gone.

MALE VOICE: Open up. It's not good for you to stay in there.

RAISA: What do you know about it?

MALE VOICE: Let us take care of you.

RAISA: My mother will take care of me.

MALE VOICE: Your mother is gone.

(She looks up.)

MALE VOICE: Your mother would want you to come out.

RAISA: *(Goes to the door but does not open it.)* Hello? *(She sits down in front of the door.)*

MONSTER: She did not go out for food. She did not go to work. Her notes piled on the windowsill, untaken. As weeks went by, Raisa's mother began to send gifts—a pearl, a mahogany carving, silk slippers. Gifts of such perfection they could not be found in this world.

MOTHER: I want you to have what we have, Raisa, which is only the best. I want to think of you clothed in glory, surrounded by riches. Give some of these things to the parents of the man you marry, my wedding presents to your new family.

MONSTER: But Raisa would not get married. She would not leave her house.

As the gifts poured in, they spilled out of the violin case and into hatboxes and dresser drawers. Raisa piled them up in the corners, imagining her mother's smile when picking them out. She spread them out on the floor, played with them like dolls, arranged them as cities. Meanwhile her house went dark because she paid no bills, her face grew thin because she ate no food. *(Pause.)* When the authorities of the town found her at her death, they were shocked at the wealth she had stored in her house. They had assumed she was poor, frozen to death because she could not pay the heat.

(Silence. Lights up on MIMI on the edge of the stage.)

MONSTER: The end.

(She doesn't move.)

MONSTER: It's over. The end.

MIMI: That's a horrible story. Maybe he was the husband her mother wanted.

MONSTER: Yes, maybe.

MIMI: Why didn't she open the door?

MONSTER: Sometimes we refuse a gift.

MIMI: Fairy tales are supposed to have happy endings.

MONSTER: She went to be with her mother.

MIMI: She couldn't find some reason to stay here?

MONSTER: I thought the idea was to find a place other than where you are now.

MIMI: Oh. Right. Very clever.

MONSTER: It is your story.

MIMI: I haven't shriveled up. I was never a very cheerful person, true, but I haven't shriveled up.

MONSTER: That is right.

MIMI: She could have lived.

MONSTER: Yes.

MIMI: A person should fight what hurts them.

MONSTER: Even if fighting means staying where they are.

MIMI: Exactly, yes— *(Pause.)* Look, I'm not saying I wouldn't come back here. I just want to see.

MONSTER: See what? What is there that is not here, if you only look?

MIMI: *(Pause.)* I don't know.

MONSTER: Mimi. You have enough. You have all anyone has.

MIMI: What's that?

MONSTER: Life. No one has any more than that, and every day…many…lose that, too. *(Pause.)* Tell me a story now.

MIMI: Come on.

MONSTER: You will feel better.

MIMI: I don't know any.

MONSTER: You made a deal.

MIMI: Yeah, well, I was trying to—

MONSTER: So you break your promises.

MIMI: You don't really expect—

MONSTER: Yes.

MIMI: It won't be any good.

MONSTER: It will be good.

MIMI: I'm self-conscious.

MONSTER: It will go away when you are living in the story.

MIMI: I don't know how to begin.

MONSTER: Once upon a time.

MIMI: I don't know any characters.

MONSTER: They will come. Now. I'm listening.

MIMI: *(Pause.)* Well, don't say I didn't warn you. *(Pause.)* Once upon a time… there was a…girl named Cinderella. And she had a wicked stepmother…who had two wicked daughters…

MONSTER: This is not your story.

MIMI: How do you know?

MONSTER: You're not telling it with your heart.

MIMI: Not telling it with my heart.

MONSTER: There is a difference.

MIMI: Well, I don't speak with my heart.

MONSTER: Not true. When you first saw me tonight, when you could not go under the bed…there were words you said that were full of the heart.

(She begins to believe a little…)

MONSTER: Close your eyes. Pretend you are asleep. Whisper. I'll come close.

MIMI: *(Closes her eyes. She starts to whisper…)* Once upon a time… *(But she feels self-conscious and clears her throat and starts again.)*

SCENE 3

MIMI: Once upon a time…there was a man who could make music with his hands. He did not need to touch an instrument; he simply rubbed his fingers together and a violin played.

(ALEXANDER enters. He rubs his fingers and violins play.)

MIMI: It came from the air, from another time, and it sang to any soul who could listen. If he rubbed his hands together, whole orchestras sounded.

(He rubs his hands—an orchestra!)

MIMI: His name was Alexander.

(ALEXANDER continues to play music for awhile, loving every moment.)

MIMI: Alexander had always been able to play his music. It had come to great use many times. As a child, the other children loved to play with him. As a young man, Alexander courted his wife with melody. As an adult he was known to soothe angry men, quiet crying babies, even calm a riot of protestors in the street, simply by sending the songs out. Everyone loved him. Everyone wanted to be near him.

(The music stops. ALEXANDER is joined by JUNO, his wife; RAJI, a young man; and SHILEEN, a young woman.)

JUNO: Do not forget the wedding party tonight.

ALEXANDER: Yes, yes, my wife.

JUNO: They asked specifically for—

ALEXANDER: Orimander's Suite Number 11—yes, yes, I know.

JUNO: I simply wanted to remind you.

ALEXANDER: Thank you.

JUNO: Leave those shoes by my rocking chair tonight. I'll mend the soles.

ALEXANDER: Thank you.

JUNO: *(Pause.)* Are you all right, husband? *(She touches him gently.)* You worry me.

ALEXANDER: I'm fine. Tired. A little tired.

RAJI: Father…

JUNO: *(To RAJI and SHILEEN.)* Go on! You heard him. He's tired.

ALEXANDER: Don't, Juno. Let them be.

JUNO: You said you were tired.

ALEXANDER: They are good young people.

JUNO: You have to save your energy. Tomorrow you have to meet with the governor and then you have a session at the school with—

ALEXANDER: The children. Yes, I won't fail them. *(To RAJI and SHILEEN.)* Come closer. What is it? What do you need? Speak, girl.

SHILEEN: My father.

ALEXANDER: What is your name?

SHILEEN: Shileen.

ALEXANDER: Tell me.

SHILEEN: I am sick. I bleed.

JUNO: My husband's music does not—

ALEXANDER: Juno, let her speak.

SHILEEN: It has been years, and I am so tired. I've no money left from the bills, and they tell me very soon I will die. But I heard you play once; I remember, I was a little girl. You gave a concert. I sat in the balcony, with my eyes closed, as your music moved through me. I have never felt so strong and alive. I believe you could heal me.

ALEXANDER: I am very sorry for your illness. But my wife is right. I've never cured anyone.

SHILEEN: But I believe you—

JUNO: He has tried. Even with cases like yours.

SHILEEN: Maybe I'll be different. Maybe your music has changed. I tell you I felt something even then. I knew you could heal.

ALEXANDER: Many people have said those same words.

SHILEEN: Please. You can't mean you want to let me die.

JUNO: It's not his decision.

ALEXANDER: No, Juno, it is my decision. *(Pause.)* Where do you live?

JUNO: Alexander!

ALEXANDER: I'll come tomorrow.

SHILEEN: Oh, father!

JUNO: When? You have—

ALEXANDER: In the morning. Very early.

JUNO: You can't. You—

ALEXANDER: She is right, Juno. I can't let her die. If she believes, if she is so certain, perhaps she is right and this time I can save her.

JUNO: And if you can't? When she gets angry and throws insults at you?

SHILEEN: Oh, I wouldn't!

JUNO: You will. They always do.

ALEXANDER: Where do you live?

SHILEEN: By the river. In the blue house on Lasting Lane.

ALEXANDER: I'll be there as the sun rises.

SHILEEN: Thank you. *(She kisses his hands.)* They tingle.

JUNO: Let him rest now.

(SHILEEN exits.)

JUNO: You will be hurt.

ALEXANDER: Perhaps.

JUNO: She'll have her friends there. They'll expect too much. When they are disappointed, what will you do?

ALEXANDER: Apologize.

JUNO: *(Of RAJI.)* And this one? What can he need? A healing? A large amount of money?

RAJI: Please, father.

JUNO: Father. They act so respectful. But they take, take, take from you.

ALEXANDER: That's enough, Juno.

JUNO: And you come home too tired to play for me anymore.

ALEXANDER: Juno.

JUNO: Remember how there were songs your fingers only sang to me? I bet they've forgotten them. We are both worn out by your work—you from playing, me from scheduling and managing and keeping you fed and clothed…

ALEXANDER: You're very good to me.

JUNO: Promise me one private song tonight. Before bed.

ALEXANDER: All right.

JUNO: *(Touches his face.)* You worry me. *(Touches his clothes.)* These things you wear—barely holding together.

ALEXANDER: They are comfortable.

JUNO: People will think I don't care for you, letting you run around in this.

ALEXANDER: Everyone knows how you care for me.

JUNO: Leave this by my rocking chair.

ALEXANDER: *(Stiff.)* I don't want it mended, Juno.

(Pause. She pulls away.)

ALEXANDER: All right, my son, what do you need?

RAJI: Please, I want to play the music.

JUNO: Oh, I don't believe it!

ALEXANDER: You want to—

JUNO: The presumption of it!

RAJI: Can you teach me?

JUNO: No, he cannot teach you!

RAJI: I have money.

JUNO: It's a gift he has, a miracle! How can he teach you to work a miracle?

ALEXANDER: Don't be so hard on him.

RAJI: I'm sorry—I just thought—it is so wonderful—

ALEXANDER: Yes, yes. It's wonderful.

RAJI: You help so many people.

ALEXANDER: Yes.

RAJI: I wanted to be the same. I think I could be. I— sometimes when I am alone, I rub my fingers together, like you, and I think…I think I hear birds, softly singing…

(JUNO snorts.)

ALEXANDER: *(Pause.)* If I could give this music to you…I must tell you I wouldn't do it.

JUNO: It's too precious.

ALEXANDER: That was not what I was thinking. *(To RAJI.)* I know—I can tell that you have a heart of purity and an aching for those who suffer. Just because you do not have the music doesn't mean you can't help them. Perhaps it means you will help them better than I ever do. Sell what you have and give the money away. Teach children. Visit the sick. Do what you can and forget that you wanted this. Go now.

(RAJI doesn't move.)

ALEXANDER: Go, my son.

RAJI: *(Pause.)* Yes, my father. I'll do as you say. Thank you. *(He exits.)*

JUNO: These crazy demands!

ALEXANDER: *(Very sharp.)* Oh, wife, will you be quiet for one moment and let the world be as it is?! Don't tell me that you have forgotten how you once asked me to heal a child—our child—and how angry you were with me when I could not do it. And don't think that I didn't see you early in our marriage, thinking you were alone, trying to play your own music from your hands, crying when it did not come. You act as if these people were fools—fools for having a faith that you once had yourself. *(Pause.)* I can't decide if I liked you better when that faith was alive or not. What I know is that either way I cannot bear your bitterness.

(Pause. Then JUNO runs out. ALEXANDER pauses, rubs his hands. Music comes, but it is discordant and does not please him. He scowls and stops playing.)

MIMI: He knew he had gone where he shouldn't. He knew there was much sadness in his wife's heart and to bring it to light was cruel, but, then, lately he had felt that nothing he did was right. That night, when he climbed into bed and felt his wife's stiff back, he tried to remember what good his hands had brought him ever, and he couldn't think of one thing. Only exhaustion, disappointment, responsibility. It seemed to him that his hands were a curse. It seemed to him that he had not enjoyed his own music in too many years. And he decided that night that he was done playing the music. The next day he would tell everyone that the gift was gone.

JUNO: Gone? How can it be gone?

ALEXANDER: I don't know. I tried to play and could not.

JUNO: Let me see. Try it now.

ALEXANDER: Do you think I am lying?

JUNO: Try.

ALEXANDER: It's too painful. Too disappointing. I won't try anymore.

JUNO: It can't have just gone away.

ALEXANDER: Well, it did. You'll have to cancel my schedule.

JUNO: What will people think?

ALEXANDER: Perhaps it means I am going to die soon.

JUNO: Don't say that!

ALEXANDER: Listen.

(They listen.)

ALEXANDER: The world spinning has quite a melody, doesn't it?

JUNO: What will we do for money? The gifts people gave us will stop coming when they hear you can't play.

ALEXANDER: Perhaps I'll be a mason.

JUNO: You're too old.

ALEXANDER: Don't worry, Juno.

JUNO: I have to worry because you do not. Your head is always soaring in the clouds with your music.

ALEXANDER: Not anymore. Now my head will be here on earth.

JUNO: But I loved you in the clouds, Alexander.

ALEXANDER: And will you not love me now?

JUNO: *(Pause.)* Of course, I will. *(She exits.)*

(RAJI and SHILEEN enter.)

RAJI: Old father.

SHILEEN: Kind father.

ALEXANDER: What is it, children?

RAJI: Tell us it isn't true!

ALEXANDER: What?

SHILEEN: Your music!

RAJI: Your music gone!

ALEXANDER: Oh, yes. True. Very true.

SHILEEN: How horrible!

RAJI: We couldn't believe—

SHILEEN: I thought it was a joke—

ALEXANDER: I'm sorry.

SHILEEN: We are sorry.

RAJI: Yes.

ALEXANDER: You? Why?

SHILEEN: We think…

RAJI: We think that it must be so sad for you, you must miss it so much.

ALEXANDER: Oh. Yes. Yes. I miss it.

SHILEEN: What will you do?

ALEXANDER: I have thought I might become a mason.

RAJI: You're not even going to try to get it back?

ALEXANDER: What's the point? I'm sure it's gone.

SHILEEN: But you had a gift.

ALEXANDER: Perhaps I'll have a gift for masonry. *(Pause. He touches their faces.)* I'm sorry I can't play for you anymore. Forgive me?

SHILEEN: There's nothing to forgive. It isn't your fault.

RAJI: Not your fault at all.

SHILEEN: And besides…we are so happy.

RAJI: Yes, we are.

ALEXANDER: We?

(They smile at each other.)

RAJI: I sold everything, father, and gave the money to Shileen.

SHILEEN: For my doctor bills. He has bought me years to live.

ALEXANDER: And bought your heart.

SHILEEN: Yes.

RAJI: You were right, father.

SHILEEN: We didn't need the music's magic.

RAJI: There is magic in other places.

SHILEEN: Like the heart.

(Pause.)

ALEXANDER: Thank you.

(MIMI enters.)

MIMI: And with that Alexander went into the silence completely. And what amazing things he found there. The flutter of butterfly wings. His own heartbeat. The wind in the leaves of the cedar trees.

(There is a long silence. ALEXANDER stands and listens, perhaps to the audience. Suddenly…)

ALEXANDER: Ha ha! *(He salutes the world.)* Beautiful! Splendid! *(Long silence as he listens again.)* Yes, yes! Spectacular. *(He stops, suddenly hearing himself.)* Spectacular. Spec…ta…cu…lar. *(He lowers his voice, repeating the word, raises his voice, repeating the word, experiments with saying the word any way he can think. Then…)* Why, there is music even in the voice. *(He picks up random objects nearby, perhaps a hat, a cane, a teddy bear…and taps them, rattles them, rubs them, testing the sounds, making a new music.)* So much music.

RAJI'S VOICE: We thought it must be so sad for you, we thought you must miss it so much.

SHILEEN'S VOICE: You had a gift.

JUNO'S VOICE: Remember how there were songs your fingers sang only to me?

RAJI'S VOICE: We thought you must miss it.

ALEXANDER: Yes. Yes. Miss it. *(Pause.)* Juno?

(No answer. He looks around. Pause, then ALEXANDER rubs a finger and thumb together. One note sounds from a violin. He smiles.)

ALEXANDER: Mine.

(He slowly rubs more fingers and a beautiful melody plays. He enjoys it fully. While he plays, MIMI enters and talks.)

MIMI: No one pounding at his door, no one making requests, expecting him to perform. Weeks passed, Juno and all the rest still fooled. He felt guilty for the lies, but oh…the freedom! Freedom! Suddenly songs he had never played came from his hands, new life came to his soul. At night he crept from the house and made his way out of the town so that no one could hear him while he played. He laughed and cried with himself, finding the joy of the sounds, the joy of creation.

(His song finishes. He laughs and falls to his knees. JUNO enters.)

JUNO: Alexander?

ALEXANDER: Juno, what are you doing out here?

JUNO: I should say the same to you. An old man should not be out in the cool night—without his shoes.

ALEXANDER: *(Seeing his bare feet and laughing.)* Ah, yes, shoes!

JUNO: I mended those shoes, and here you don't even wear them. What's wrong with you? Are you losing your mind?

ALEXANDER: No, no, wife. I'm fine.

JUNO: What are you doing out here?

ALEXANDER: Nothing. Walking.

JUNO: On your knees?

ALEXANDER: Praying.

JUNO: For your music to return?

ALEXANDER: No.

JUNO: You don't want it to come back, do you?

ALEXANDER: Would that be so bad? We've been all right. You've kept yourself busy teaching Yasir to read and painting the church.

JUNO: Yes, it turns out I do have talents other than managing you.

ALEXANDER: I knew you did.

JUNO: *(Pause.)* But I didn't know. *(Pause.)* Do you know what else I discovered? In the silence?

ALEXANDER: What?

JUNO: I discovered I do make music. In stitching thread through cloth, in stirring saffron into rice, in walking about the woods or laughing at a story…I make a kind of rhythm, a music. My own music.

ALEXANDER: *(Smiles.)* Sit beside me, wife.

JUNO: The ground is wet.

ALEXANDER: Pretend it's dry.

JUNO: *(Pause. She sits beside him.)* You don't make a very good mason.

ALEXANDER: I have only begun the work.

JUNO: I don't think you practice enough.

ALEXANDER: Oh, wife, are you going to manage this, too?

JUNO: I am only saying... *(Stops, smiles.)* Old habits.

ALEXANDER: Look at the stars.

JUNO: I see them every night.

ALEXANDER: Not in the country. Not with me.

(She looks up, relaxes a little.)

ALEXANDER: Remember the one I named your star?

(Pause. She points.)

ALEXANDER: Yes. Yours because it was closest to the one I had named as mine.

JUNO: I thought you said your head was going to be on the earth now.

ALEXANDER: Isn't it?

JUNO: You are every bit as dreamy as before. One would think...you hadn't lost your music.

(No answer.)

JUNO: But it is nice.

ALEXANDER: What?

JUNO: To have my dreamer still beside me.

ALEXANDER: Is it?

JUNO: To know that we are stronger than...the loss of music.

ALEXANDER: Then you still love me, even silent?

JUNO: *(Pause. She looks at him.)* You are never silent. Your eyes laugh at me, and your smile calls to me, and your breath whispers to me. I follow your sound every moment of my day.

(JUNO takes his hands and gently rubs them together, all the while looking into his eyes tenderly. A low phrase of music whispers out. They are very still.)

JUNO: I knew it.

(No answer.)

JUNO: Don't worry. I won't tell anyone. We have been unfair, the music-lovers and I. You have only done what you had to do.

ALEXANDER: Perhaps soon I will play again for them.

JUNO: You don't have to. You don't even have to play for me.

ALEXANDER: Thank you.

(MIMI enters.)

MIMI: Of course, in time, he did play for her, and for the others. But he played because he wanted to, because he had found his love again. When he came back to them with the music, the sounds were clearer than ever. The score echoed through the theatre, worshipping the muse who had sent it. The audience rejoiced with Alexander's return, throwing flowers, crying his name. Juno, standing in the wings, let tears stream unchecked down her face to see her husband's triumph. But none of this mattered to Alexander. Hidden from the world in the sounds he composed, he cared only that he was playing the music, only that he was playing.

(Silence. MIMI waits for the MONSTER's response.)

MONSTER: That was a wonderful story.

MIMI: *(She bursts into laughter.)* It was good wasn't it?!

MONSTER: Yes.

MIMI: To think I just made it up!

MONSTER: I know.

MIMI: Out of my own head! I—thank you. You've given me something tonight. Something marvelous.

MONSTER: You have always had it.

MIMI: But the best story is the one that isn't finished yet. The story of us—of how you knew me for so long and how I knew you—in my deepest self—and how now we are friends and not alone.

MONSTER: Mmmm…

MIMI: Tomorrow night what story will you tell me?

MONSTER: I don't believe I will tell you a story.

MIMI: No. No, of course, I'll tell the story.

(No answer.)

MIMI: And it will be about…well, I won't spoil it, but you can be sure I'll be thinking it up all day at work. Yes, I'll be smiling, and people will wonder what's up with Mimi, what's in her poor, dull head?

(No answer.)

MIMI: Hey, monster.

(He looks at her but does not speak.)

MIMI: What's up?

(No answer.)

MIMI: You are coming back tomorrow.

MONSTER: I have been glad for this night, Mimi.

MIMI: You are coming back tomorrow, right?

MONSTER: I wanted to know you. I wanted to see behind your eyelids.

MIMI: Are you coming back?

MONSTER: *(Pause.)* I am not coming back.

MIMI: Ever?

MONSTER: No.

MIMI: I don't understand.

MONSTER: It is time for me.

MIMI: Time for you to what?

(Before he can answer.)

MIMI: Oh, no! Don't say it! Oh, I can't—whatever the reason, I can't stand it, can't hear it! You're not going away! I won't let you.

MONSTER: We don't have a choice.

MIMI: You're going away from me? Just when I thought there was something good here—

MONSTER: Don't be angry.

MIMI: Then stay!

MONSTER: I can't.

MIMI: Am I so different awake that you don't like me now?

MONSTER: I like you more.

MIMI: Is it because I'm a human and you're a monster and there's some rule that says we're not supposed to be friends?

MONSTER: That rule doesn't matter now.

MIMI: Then why—what's changed?

MONSTER: I will not be here tomorrow. I will not be alive—alive in the human sense—moving, talking...

MIMI: You're dying?

MONSTER: I am changing. Becoming something else. As we all do. We are given a set of days and live them fully. But when the last day has come, it has come. The mountains are formed from the bodies of those like me.

MIMI: I don't believe you. How do you know it's your time? Maybe it isn't.

MONSTER: It's all right. I was given my days, and they were good. I am not sad to go.

MIMI: Not sad to leave me?

MONSTER: I am sad to leave you, yes. But you will remember me. I will still be here.

MIMI: That's no consolation!

MONSTER: Maybe I shouldn't have told you.

MIMI: No, maybe you shouldn't have!

MONSTER: But tomorrow night, when I didn't come, you would wonder, you would think it was your fault I had not come back.

MIMI: Oh, then, just go! Just go away now—back under the bed—just get out!

MONSTER: I am sorry. I only wanted you to see me.

MIMI: I see you—I see you! I see goodness and wisdom and loyalty—oh, don't go—don't go! If you stay—if you don't get close to the mountains, they can't take you, can they?

MONSTER: So many years of hearing you speak your stories, of knowing your dreams—I thought just one time... If

there was some way—if I could stay—but I follow the rules of the universe.

MIMI: Break them! Maybe there's some deal we can make. Fight this!

MONSTER: The rules are there for good.

MIMI: This isn't good! You're leaving! *(Pause.)* Is there a heaven for monsters?

MONSTER: I told you, we become the mountains.

MIMI: But your soul—

MONSTER: Then you believe in the soul now?

MIMI: I believe there must be some way to avoid saying goodbye to you forever.

MONSTER: Humans and monsters are not the same. You are the ones blessed with a soul.

MIMI: That isn't fair! It's another stupid rule for a stupid universe!

MONSTER: Why can't you see the goodness in a universe that would allow us to have even this short friendship? Why do you fight so hard?

MIMI: But what if when you go—what if when you go I am swallowed by the sadness—like Raisa?

MONSTER: I tell you, you are too strong for that.

MIMI: Are you sure?

MONSTER: The Mimi you found tonight will stay.

(No answer.)

MONSTER: Don't you believe that?

MIMI: Maybe. Yes.

MONSTER: You can tell your stories without me here. Without me, you are still someone who matters.

MIMI: Maybe I don't want to tell the stories without you. Maybe I'll close down and never tell another.

MONSTER: You think they would not come out in your sleep? They are a part of you.

MIMI: But you've been with me forever. Will I know how to sleep? I'll get so lonely.

MONSTER: You will never be that lonely again. Think of the friends you have met just tonight.

(Enter EDGAR.)

EDGAR: A boy who grew in a garden.

(Enter GISELLA and DAVID.)

GISELLA: A mail-order bride.

DAVID: And her lover.

(Enter MOTHER.)

MOTHER: A mother who loved her daughter from beyond the grave.

(Enter ALEXANDER.)

ALEXANDER: A man who played music with his fingers.

MONSTER: I am leaving you with many friends, Mimi. And you will meet more.

MIMI: None of them will be you.

MONSTER: But they will hold you up, nonetheless. *(Pause.)* Tell your stories. Tell

them to yourself until you are ready to tell them to others and then fill the waking world with them. Paint watercolor pictures to go beside them. Give them away for nothing. Make this world you don't want to live in a place where there is possibility and kindness and wonder.

MIMI: *(Pause.)* I will. I'll tell stories of… *(She speaks to MOTHER and GISELLA.)* …women who could fly…

(The women freeze in positions of outstretched arms.)

MONSTER: *(To EDGAR and ALEXANDER.)* …sons and fathers on marvelous journeys…

(EDGAR and ALEXANDER point and stare at some far-off land.)

MIMI: *(To DAVID.)* …princes who fight sea serpents…

(DAVID brandishes an invisible sword.)

MONSTER: *(To MIMI.)* …and monsters who come from the rocks and speak an unspeakable language…

MIMI: *(To MONSTER.)* …and bring magic to fair maidens.

MONSTER: I hope that you will, Mimi. Yes, I believe that you will.

END OF PLAY

SUN, STAND THOU STILL

Steven Gridley

STEVEN GRIDLEY grew up in Texas mostly, with a couple random stints around the world. He eventually returned to attend Southern Methodist University in Dallas, where he graduated with a degree in theatre studies. After moving to New York, Steven joined Spring Theatreworks and began writing and directing for the company. Spring developed his plays *Albatross at Sea* and *Echo's Longing* before producing *Sun, Stand Thou Still*. During this time, Steven also served as Spring's literary manager and has since formed the Spring Writers group, a small group of writers which supplies Spring with most of its new work. Along with Spring, Steven works closely with the SMUT Ensemble, a group formed by graduates of SMU. SMUT produced his play *Theme and Variations* and its subsequent production in the 2001 New York International Fringe Festival. Steven is also a director, and, oddly enough, you can find Steven in an earlier edition of this anthology, directing Marc Chun's play *Match* and assistant directing J. Scott Reynolds's play *The Wild Ass's Skin*, both published in *Plays and Playwrights 2002*. Other directing endeavors include Spring Theatreworks' production of Vaclav Havel's *Largo Desolato* and Chandler Carter's new opera based on the life of Nelson Mandela entitled *No Easy Walk to Freedom*. Steven is currently working on two plays for production by Spring Theatreworks, *Post Oedipus* and *The Twelfth Labour*, as well as a yet untitled production for the SMUT Ensemble. Look for *Post Oedipus* to go up in the fall of 2004. Steven lives in Washington Heights in Manhattan.

Sun, Stand Thou Still was first presented by Spring Theatreworks (Jeffrey Horne, Artistic Director) on June 27, 2003, at Altered Stages, New York City, with the following cast and credits:

Apple Woman .... Erin Treadway
Driver .... Frank Shattuck
Hitchhiker .... Stephen Douglas Wood
Man .... David Wylie
Officer Peters .... Nathan Stith

Directed by: Jacob Titus
Scene Designer: John Conners
Lighting Designer: Garin Marschall
Production Manager: Kirsten Poznanski

I would like to give a special thanks to Erin for listening and Mom for always hoping.

> *12: Then spake Joshua to the Lord in the day when the Lord delivered up the Amorites before the children of Israel, and he said in the sight of Israel, Sun, stand thou still upon Gibeon; and thou, Moon, in the valley of Ajalon.*
>
> *13: And the sun stood still, and the moon stayed, until the people had avenged themselves upon their enemies. Is not this written in the book of Jasher? So the sun stood still in the midst of heaven, and hasted not to go down about a whole day.*
>
> *14: And there was no day like that before it or after it, that the Lord hearkened unto the voice of a man.*
>
> *—Joshua 10:12–14*

CHARACTERS

DRIVER: Man, forties.
HITCHHIKER: Man, mid-twenties.
APPLE WOMAN: Carries basket of red apples. Travels alone. Graceful.
MAN: Young and frightening.
OFFICER PETERS: Older cop. Not threatening.

SETTING

The setting should be as bare as possible. We are in the middle of nowhere. The trucks are important as far as they support the actors, but the trucks should not upstage the actors. It's not a play about trucks.

TIME

Relative present.

NOTE ON STAGING

The stage directions are mostly in the play for the sake of clarity for the reader. Do not feel obligated to adhere to them in production.

ACT I

SCENE 1

The stage is dark. We hear footsteps and hear OFFICER PETERS grumbling. We hear a door being fiddled with and then opened somewhat clumsily. From the open door, we see a flashlight beam. OFFICER PETERS enters the room. He searches for a light switch.

OFFICER PETERS: Come on, where is it? It's gotta be around here somewhere. *(We hear a crash.)* Oww! Dammit! *(He shines his flashlight to see what he ran into. It is a chair.)* Why the hell would you not put a light switch next to the... it's just common sense... Okay, Peters. Stay calm. Don't get bent out of shape here. *(He takes a breath and continues with his work. He mumbles various phrases as he works, like "Okay then" and "Let's see here." The actor can improv these as he sees fit. OFFICER PETERS takes a few passes with the flash-*

light around the room. Then he reaches around his belt. He seems to be struggling with this, so he shines his flashlight on himself to see better.) Where is it, dammit! *(He finally grabs something and shines the flashlight on it. It is a cassette recorder.)* Finally! Geez, like the thing was hiding back there. *(He begins fumbling with it.)* Okay then. Let's see. Where did Gladys say that... *(He pushes a button and begins speaking into the recorder.)* Okay, then. Test test. Uhh testing. *(Slight pause. Then...)* Officer Peters here. I'll handle it. *(He stops the recorder and rewinds and listens to himself on the recorder.)*

OFFICER PETERS'S VOICE: Okay, then. Test test. Uhh testing. *(Slight pause. Then...)* Officer Peters here. I'll handle it.

OFFICER PETERS: *(Stops the recorder and chuckles.)* Officer Peters here. *(He then begins speaking into the cassette recorder again while inspecting the room with his flashlight.)* Okay. Room is neat and orderly. No visible signs of forced entry. No scratch marks on door. Possible that intruder had keys. No visible evidence of struggle in room. Everything is very neat. Bed made, uh, clothes hung, place is dusted even. Possibility remains that occupant left willingly or under threat, gunpoint maybe. Uhh, room has appearance of being prepped for a long trip. No notes. This has been Officer Peters. *(Stops the recorder and rewinds. Nothing happens.)* Oh, come on! What's the problem? I told you, Gladys. These things just don't like me. *(Shines the flashlight on the recorder.)* Gotta remember to push record.

(OFFICER PETERS pushes the record button and is about to speak when he notices an apple in the center of the room. Like it was almost placed there. He stops the recorder and walks over to it.)

OFFICER PETERS: What's this? *(Walks over and kneels down next to it. He then pushes record and talks into the recorder.)* Large red apple discovered in room. Large juicy apple. Very shiny. Smells very good. Placed in the center of the room. *(Turns the recorder off and picks up the apple.)* It's getting late. Past dinner time probably. *(About to bite the apple.)* No, Peters, you can't eat the evidence. Dammit. This has been the worst day. *(He places the apple in a plastic bag and walks out of the room.)*

SCENE 2

Lights up on two men in a truck, a DRIVER and a HITCHHIKER. We hear the radio playing country music at a pleasant level. The DRIVER's head is cocked back, with his hand resting on the steering wheel. He hums along to the music, singing at times the crucial or emphasized words of the song. He is dirty, like he is going home from work on a construction site. The HITCHHIKER

is a cleaner, hipper young man. The HITCHHIKER looks at the DRIVER... then the radio...then out the window.

DRIVER: This is the first time I've ever picked up a hitchhiker.

(Pause, no reply.)

DRIVER: Ya don't like country music?

HITCHHIKER: I'm just not used to it.

DRIVER: Ya like trucks?

HITCHHIKER: Trucks?

DRIVER: Yeah. Like this one. Trucks.

HITCHHIKER: They're fine.

DRIVER: Let me ask you... You ever seen a pretty girl standing out by the road, thumb in the air, hitchhiking, lightly tossing her thumb back and forth? And she's got this kind of smile, you know, the kind only a woman can make. And her hair resting on her shoulders... You ever seen one of them?

HITCHHIKER: No.

DRIVER: May I be frank?

HITCHHIKER: Sure.

DRIVER: I thought you was one of them. That's what I thought you were. I can't see too well. Eyes need repairs or sumthin'.

HITCHHIKER: I don't know what to say.

DRIVER: Yeah. You ride this road long enough, the mind starts to play nasty tricks on you.

HITCHHIKER: *(Looks out the windshield.)* You see well enough to drive?

DRIVER: According to the legal system, no. Blind as a cat, legally. But you and I both know that the legal system needs a major overhaul. And I mean major, you know. They screw so many things up. Take me for example. I'm not supposed to be driving, but here I am. I'm driving. Besides, I don't really need to see. This road is easy. Just straight. Nothing to it, just straight far as the eye can see. *(Pause.)* Which I guess isn't that far.

HITCHHIKER: I think it's blind as a bat.

DRIVER: What?

HITCHHIKER: You said blind as a cat. Cats can see.

DRIVER: Not blind ones.

HITCHHIKER: You're as blind as a blind cat?

DRIVER: That's not blind enough for you? There something out there blinder than a blind cat?

HITCHHIKER: No.

DRIVER: That's right. Except I'm not that blind. I can still see some. But legally… you know. But what is legal these days, right? I'm probably breaking the law right now.

HITCHHIKER: You are.

DRIVER: See? *(Pause. DRIVER starts whistling.)* Does my whistling annoy you? *(He whistles briefly.)* Does it?

HITCHHIKER: I'm just thinking.

DRIVER: About what?

HITCHHIKER: Nothing really. Just thinking.

DRIVER: Come on, tell me.

HITCHHIKER: Well, it's just, I'm not really thinking, you know. Just imagining.

DRIVER: What?

HITCHHIKER: Nothing important. Don't worry, I'll let you know when a real thought comes to mind.

DRIVER: Are you imagining monsters? Goblins?

HITCHHIKER: No. Sometimes I imagine what it would be like to run as fast as we're going right now but on the side of the road, dodging rocks, ditches, and dips, like in some of my races. I used to run. It's just kind of a game.

DRIVER: If you open your mouth and stick your head real far forward, it feels like you're eating a great big chocolate bar. It just keeps coming. Asphalt. *(Resumes position.)* Sometimes I try to imagine that everything is actually upside down and that I'm driving on the ceiling. And I look down. That one's weird. Oh! And the ol' hand out the window. Dive! Climb! Attack!

HITCHHIKER: Okay, so you've got a few more games than I do.

DRIVER: Here's one for two people. I've never been able to play games with two people. This one's called the ABC game. You look outside for letters and try to make your way through the alphabet. The first one done wins. Now the tricky part to this game is finding a Q and a Z. That's why you gotta keep your eyes peeled for a Dairy Queen and a Mazda. Thems are gold. Ready?

HITCHHIKER: Uhh…

DRIVER: Go!

(HITCHHIKER and DRIVER look outside intensely.)

DRIVER: I'm going to get that A before you! Come on A, come on A, come on A.

(Pause.)

HITCHHIKER: Aren't you legally blind?

DRIVER: Yeah. You've got a bit of an advantage, I guess. Besides, I don't think there's been a sign on this road for miles. This is the middle of nowhere, my friend.

HITCHHIKER: But I just want to make sure… you can see the road just fine?

DRIVER: Watch this. *(He lets his hands off the steering wheel. The truck continues to go in a straight line.)* This is what we call alignment. I don't even need my hands on the steering wheel. And, as a matter of fact, I run off the road much more than the truck does.

HITCHHIKER: What about curves?

DRIVER: Can't say I've seen one in a while.

HITCHHIKER: Well, you're going to run into one sometime.

DRIVER: I haven't seen one in a very long while.

HITCHHIKER: But you're going to…

DRIVER: I don't think so.

SCENE 3

Gas station. DRIVER is pumping gas. HITCHHIKER drinks a soda.

DRIVER: The thing that most people don't get is that out here sometimes the distance between gas stations is greater than how far a full tank of gas can get you. Gotta fill up a couple of spare tanks to be sure.

HITCHHIKER: Coke tastes flat.

DRIVER: Just dust and sagebrush. Nothing but wind to keep you company.

HITCHHIKER: Dammit! That guy sold me flat Coke! I'm drinking syrup here. *(He continues drinking.)*

DRIVER: Are you listening? I'm telling you how to survive out here and you're talking about the pop in your soda. Out here…out in the wild barren, you drink from cactus heads and eat the flesh of jackrabbits.

HITCHHIKER: If it's flat, you shouldn't sell it. That's false advertising. *(He continues drinking.)*

DRIVER: Shut up about the soda! Now listen. I'm not always going to be here for ya, so pay attention. Nothing but space out here. Burn ya in the day, freeze ya at night. Like the moon.

HITCHHIKER: Want a Twinkie?

DRIVER: A Twinkie?

HITCHHIKER: Did you know they don't actually cook Twinkies? That's just the way it's made. It's a substance. Some kind of Twinkie substance.

DRIVER: A substance?

HITCHHIKER: It's a good substance. Buttery.

DRIVER: I'll pass.

HITCHHIKER: Creamy.

DRIVER: No. Now get it outa my face.

(HITCHHIKER eats a Twinkie. Saves one for later.)

DRIVER: How did you get out here?

HITCHHIKER: I don't know.

DRIVER: What else did you buy?

HITCHHIKER: Provisions.

DRIVER: *(Rummages through his bag.)* Cake, more cake, different kind of cake, and more soda.

HITCHHIKER: Yeah, provisions. *(Pause.)* What?

DRIVER: This isn't the kind of place for someone like you.

HITCHHIKER: Like me?

DRIVER: Casual Coke drinker.

HITCHHIKER: Oh, and what are you doing out here?

DRIVER: Traveling west.

HITCHHIKER: That's it?

DRIVER: Traveling west.

HITCHHIKER: Not going anywhere? No destination?

DRIVER: I told you. West.

HITCHHIKER: *(Points finger at DRIVER.)* That's casual.

DRIVER: You think that's casual?

HITCHHIKER: Yep.

DRIVER: Let me show you something. Look at that odometer. See it? What's it say? Two hundred twelve thousand, four hundred fifty-six. I purchased this fine machine with one hundred fifty-four thousand, nine hundred and eighty-seven miles on it. You want to see the title? Purchased this very truck on this very road. Every mile since one hundred fifty-four thousand, nine hundred and eighty-seven has been on this road. Every single one. You good with math? Probably not. That's almost sixty thousand miles. Been traveling west since I can remember. Direct and nonstop. You think there's anything casual about that? Going in one direction? One. There was only one time, one time, that I stopped heading west. At about the forty thousand-mile mark I got mixed up. Suddenly wasn't quite sure if I was traveling west anymore. You go forty thousand miles in one direction, your mind starts to doubt, you know? You expect some-

thing to happen, I mean... *something*. An ocean? I thought maybe my mind had played a trick on me. That maybe I got turned around and wasn't traveling west at all but was traveling... *(He shudders at the idea.)* I tell you... Just the thought of it...I had sweat in my eyes, my hands were shaking, I had to stop the truck and gather myself. Forty thousand fucking miles in the wrong direction! I stepped out of the truck with my head down. Didn't want to see the sun. No sir, I didn't want to look at the sun 'cause I knew it'd tell me if I was wrong. If I was traveling southeast or... *(Again, another shudder.)* Eventually, I got up the nerve, though. I had to. I looked up and... now you're not going to believe me here, but this is the truth. It's the God's honest truth. It wasn't moving. I waited. It wasn't moving. It was right above me, perched like a vulture. No shadows, no nothing. It wasn't moving. So I decided to wait until it did move. I sat right on the side of the road and waited. For fifteen hours I waited. Me and the sun, eye to eye, having ourselves a little staring contest. Seeing who'll move first. And I was going to win. I was going to win, goddamn it, or shrivel up right there, 'cause I couldn't go anywhere without knowing which way was west! I would die first! *(Pause.)* Sure enough, fifteen hours later, the sun started moving again. I was right. Still traveling west. But I think that's what burnt my eyes. You ever hear of something like that?

(Pause.)

HITCHHIKER: I think it happened in the Bible once, didn't it. The sun stopped or went backwards.

DRIVER: Because when I got back on the road again, I ran over an armadillo. I didn't see him. I wanted to cry for that armadillo, 'cause the road is cruel. It is. And I know the road wants me also, like it wanted that armadillo. But I couldn't cry. Couldn't shed a tear. I think the sun burnt those too.

(Pause.)

HITCHHIKER: It's impossible to travel forty thousand miles west in the United States.

DRIVER: You're not very good with math. I've already traveled fifty-seven thousand miles and I don't see it ending any time soon.

HITCHHIKER: North America is only three thousand miles wide.

DRIVER: I know.

SCENE 4

Lights up. Our two guys are sitting in the truck.

HITCHHIKER: I have to go to the bathroom.

DRIVER: What?

HITCHHIKER: I have to go to the bathroom.

DRIVER: We just stopped at a gas station.

HITCHHIKER: I didn't have to go then.

DRIVER: Literally two minutes ago. You didn't have to go then?

HITCHHIKER: No. I don't know why.

DRIVER: How bad do you have to go?

HITCHHIKER: How bad?

DRIVER: How does it feel?

HITCHHIKER: *(Pause.)* Like I need to go to the bathroom.

DRIVER: Does it ache? Do your kidneys hurt? Is it agony to move?

HITCHHIKER: No.

DRIVER: Then we wait. You're probably at only half a cup.

HITCHHIKER: What do you mean half a cup?

DRIVER: I mean if we stopped this truck every time either of us had to pee only half a cup we'd never get west. We'd start to head east for all the half-cups we're pissing on every mile marker. Now, the human bladder can hold up to two cups. Two cups!

HITCHHIKER: That's not much.

DRIVER: Not much!? That's a lot! Most people can't even hold it past one cup. One cup. Do you know what that is? One cup?

HITCHHIKER: About this much? *(He motions with his fingers.)*

DRIVER: That's half of their potential! Half! Do you want to live up to half of your potential? Hold it. Train yourself. Don't be a slave to your bladder.

(Pause.)

HITCHHIKER: How much can you hold—

DRIVER: One and two-thirds cups.

(Pause.)

HITCHHIKER: And when can I go then?

DRIVER: When you've got a full cup. Or when it aches. Bad, and I mean bad. Hurts to sit down, to stand up, to do anything, that kind of aching.

HITCHHIKER: Or maybe I'll just go right in here. Right now.

DRIVER: You mean piss your pants?

HITCHHIKER: Yeah. Right in here. Maybe I'll do that.

DRIVER: You'd rather piss your pants than develop your bladder?

HITCHHIKER: I don't need to develop my bladder. Look outside! Look! There's lots of space out there! Anywhere I want I can do it! If there's one thing that's always been readily available for the average man it's a place to urinate. That one's free.

DRIVER: Fine.

HITCHHIKER: Fine then.

(Pause. DRIVER begins whistling.)

HITCHHIKER: You're just going to let me do it?

(No answer, still whistling.)

HITCHHIKER: You don't care if I urinate in your truck?

DRIVER: You know that the aborigines would sing as they walked across the landscape? They believed that their singing would bring the land into existence. They called it the song-lines. That the land was actually a song and by traveling over it you sang the land into being. Brought it into your world. At least I think that's what they meant. Not for certain on that.

HITCHHIKER: Aborigines peed wherever they wanted.

DRIVER: And the walkabout—they had the walkabout. I don't know. Just walking around singing.

HITCHHIKER: You're supposed to see yourself. That was the goal.

DRIVER: What does that mean?

HITCHHIKER: I don't know. That was just the goal.

DRIVER: Seeing yourself? I don't get it.

HITCHHIKER: Well, if it was going to happen to you at all it would have happened by now. Sixty thousand miles and you see less than you did when you started.

DRIVER: Well, that was the sun's doing.

(Pause.)

HITCHHIKER: So anyway, are you going to stop?

DRIVER: Nope. One cup.

HITCHHIKER: This is a lousy way to run a road trip.

DRIVER: This isn't a road trip.

HITCHHIKER: What is it then?

DRIVER: I don't know.

HITCHHIKER: Yes you do. Why did you start driving west?

DRIVER: I don't remember.

HITCHHIKER: Don't give me that.

DRIVER: I don't.

HITCHHIKER: Well, did you have a home? A family? Did you just get up and go?

DRIVER: There was Barbara.

HITCHHIKER: Barbara?

DRIVER: I had a wife. That was her name.

HITCHHIKER: Do you think she's still at your home?

DRIVER: Oh, no. She passed away a long time ago.

HITCHHIKER: Oh. I'm sorry.

DRIVER: Yep. Just got sick one day and never got better. No kids, so…

HITCHHIKER: After that… you just started driving?

DRIVER: I don't remember anything else. There's really only one clear memory I still have of her. I remember her on the stairs. Standing, looking out the window. I was looking up at her. She didn't see me.

HITCHHIKER: That's weird. On the stairs, huh?

DRIVER: Just looking out the window. Listening to something.

HITCHHIKER: Barbara. That's uh, pretty name.

DRIVER: Barbara? Sounds like the name of a fat secretary to me.

HITCHHIKER: That's your wife's name!

DRIVER: My wife didn't look like a Barbara. But don't let me keep you from liking it.

HITCHHIKER: Well, hey, it's not like I'm the biggest fan of it. It's just, you know, your memory of your wife… I didn't want to disparage it.

DRIVER: Thanks for your efforts.

HITCHHIKER: Can we stop the truck? I really got to go, man! I've got a full cup in here I guarantee it.

DRIVER: (Turns off the radio. He sees something.) Hey. Is there something out there? (DRIVER looks out in front.)

HITCHHIKER: Yeah. Shit, that's a person, man. Stop the truck.

DRIVER: Is it a girl?

HITCHHIKER: Yeah, I think so.

DRIVER: She hitchhiking?

HITCHHIKER: I don't know, she's waving at us.

DRIVER: Does she have long hair?

HITCHHIKER: Yeah.

DRIVER: Wow.

(They pull over. The WOMAN is holding a basket of apples. They are dark red.)

APPLE WOMAN: Hi, there.

DRIVER: Hello, what can we do for you?

APPLE WOMAN: I'm out here selling some of my fresh-grown apples.

HITCHHIKER: What?

APPLE WOMAN: I'm selling my fresh-grown apples. Guaranteed to be the best apple you've ever set teeth in.

HITCHHIKER: This is a strange place to be selling apples.

APPLE WOMAN: Would you like to try one?

HITCHHIKER: (Looks around.) Where did you grow apples?

DRIVER: I'll have a go.

(She passes one.)

HITCHHIKER: They look pretty nice.

APPLE WOMAN: Thank you. They are very good.

HITCHHIKER: You, ahh, get a lot of business out here?

DRIVER: Oh! Jesus! These are delicious.

APPLE WOMAN: I told you.

HITCHHIKER: Let me have a bite.

DRIVER: How much are they?

APPLE WOMAN: Twenty-five cents each.

HITCHHIKER: Oh. Oh. That is…that's good!

APPLE WOMAN: Best apple on the planet.

HITCHHIKER: I mean, I'm not a big fruit fan, especially of just an average apple. I prefer Twinkies. But that…that was…

DRIVER: We'll take twenty.

APPLE WOMAN: That'll be five dollars.

DRIVER: *(Rummages through his pants; can't find any money.)* Can I owe you?

APPLE WOMAN: Well, you fellas wouldn't be heading down this road aways would you?

(Both men nod enthusiastically.)

APPLE WOMAN: There's a town down this road. I'll let you have the apples for free if I could hitch a ride with you.

DRIVER: It's a deal.

APPLE WOMAN: Oh, that's great.

DRIVER: You can just stick your apples in the back there.

HITCHHIKER: *(Gets out of the truck.)* I'm just going to… I'll be back real quick.

(HITCHHIKER runs offstage. DRIVER gets out of the truck and helps APPLE WOMAN with the apples.)

DRIVER: Here we go. Why don't you hop in front there?

APPLE WOMAN: Wasn't that other man sitting up there?

DRIVER: We'll alternate. He can sit in the back for now.

APPLE WOMAN: Okay.

(They get in the truck.)

APPLE WOMAN: So where are you headed?

DRIVER: Me? Oh, uhh. West…to a… I got a piece of land out there. Um, thinking of, ahh, starting a ranch.

APPLE WOMAN: Sounds exciting.

DRIVER: Yeah, I uhh, I'm real excited about it too. What about you? What brings you out here?

APPLE WOMAN: Just looking for places to sell my apples.

DRIVER: Oh, well, you'll do real well. Those are great apples.

(HITCHHIKER runs back in and sits in the truckbed.)

HITCHHIKER: All set! Uhh.

DRIVER: Why don't you take a spell in the back? We'll rotate.

HITCHHIKER: In the back?

DRIVER: Give the new guest some comfort.

HITCHHIKER: All right.

(They drive off. HITCHHIKER opens the back window. He has to speak loudly to make up for the noise in the back of the truck.)

HITCHHIKER: Can I have an apple?

DRIVER: Sure.

HITCHHIKER: Thanks! *(He takes a bite.)* These sure are good. Wow. How did you get them so sweet?

APPLE WOMAN: It's a secret.

(Pause.)

HITCHHIKER: What? I can't hear you.

APPLE WOMAN: It's a secret!

HITCHHIKER: A secret? Well, that's interesting, isn't it? I love a good secret. What is it?

DRIVER: Leave her alone. She doesn't have to tell us.

HITCHHIKER: What?

DRIVER: She doesn't have to tell us.

HITCHHIKER: Of course she doesn't. It's a secret. *(To APPLE WOMAN.)* So what is it?

DRIVER: Leave her alone.

HITCHHIKER: Will you just butt out? I'm trying to have a conversation with the Apple Woman. *(To APPLE WOMAN.)* So how do you do it? Do you inject some kind of concentrated flavor into the apple?

APPLE WOMAN: Mister, this is my one and only real secret. You wouldn't want to be so cruel as to take that away from me just so you have a fun story to tell your buddies, would you?

HITCHHIKER: *(At a loss.)* I guess not.

APPLE WOMAN: Thank you! You're very nice.

HITCHHIKER: Uhh, you're welcome.

APPLE WOMAN: Can I close the window now? It's loud.

HITCHHIKER: Sure.

APPLE WOMAN: Thank you. *(She does.)*

(Pause. APPLE WOMAN looks at DRIVER.)

DRIVER: Don't worry I won't ask.

APPLE WOMAN: It's okay. I'll just tell you what I tell everybody. "Mister, it's my only secret. You wouldn't want to take my only secret away from me, would you?"

DRIVER: What do they say to that?

APPLE WOMAN: Most of the time they just kind of look at me. I think they would like to take it away from me but they are too embarrassed to ask again. Everybody should be entitled to one good secret, don't you think? Mine is that I can make apples that taste like sugar. Anyway, it was luck,

really, I stumbled onto the trick, but now I'll never give it away. You know, the day I learned how to sweeten the apple, I left my home. *(Laughs.)* Just up and left. Left everything. Very silly of me, I guess. And, you know, when you go ahead and do it and leave everything behind—everything—it's funny, but all your stuff doesn't seem like much anymore. All the things I'd collected over time? Just a collection of lint. The further I got away from my home, the easier it became to walk away, like I was escaping some kind of orbit, some tiny weak orbit. And now, I'm shooting off. I'm a comet. *(She laughs.)* It's silly.

DRIVER: Are you gonna go back?

APPLE WOMAN: Oh… No, I don't think so. It would only be sad.

DRIVER: So you're traveling around towns? Which one was it?

APPLE WOMAN: It doesn't really matter. Any will be fine.

DRIVER: No, but you said there was one you wanted to go to.

APPLE WOMAN: Maybe. Which way are we going?

DRIVER: West.

APPLE WOMAN: Oh. Right. West. *(She looks out the window.)*

DRIVER: What?

APPLE WOMAN: Everybody heads west, you know. It's kinda boring. Which way is this? *(She points out the window.)*

DRIVER: That's north.

APPLE WOMAN: Let's go that way!

DRIVER: North?

APPLE WOMAN: Won't it be exciting?

DRIVER: I can't.

APPLE WOMAN: Oh, right. Your dude ranch.

DRIVER: Yes. Besides, you said you wanted to go to a town down this road.

APPLE WOMAN: *(Sighs.)* I thought I knew somebody there.

DRIVER: Who?

APPLE WOMAN: I can't remember. But whoever it is, they're probably not even there anymore. I think I'm getting sleepy. I can never remember things when I'm sleepy. I must have walked… *(Yawns.)* so many miles.

DRIVER: You don't remember?

APPLE WOMAN: I hate forgetting things. Let's see…There was a little house. It was right at the ocean. Right at the end of this road.

DRIVER: Ocean!?

APPLE WOMAN: Uh-hmm.

DRIVER: This road runs into the ocean? That's what you said?

APPLE WOMAN: *(Yawns.)* It has been a long time since I, but, yes, the road passes through that town and then ends, right at the ocean. You won't know you're there until the last possible moment. It's strange. The desert runs right up to the water. No beach. No boardwalk. Just desert, cactus and then nothing but water. It's like a child's drawing.

DRIVER: How far away are we?

APPLE WOMAN: Comes out of no-where…

DRIVER: How far till the end of this road?

APPLE WOMAN: I'd guess… Five hundred miles or so… *(She falls asleep.)*

DRIVER: Five hundred miles? *(Pause.)* That's nothing. *(Sees that she's asleep. He looks at her. He drives for a while. Then looks at the APPLE WOMAN a long time.)*

SCENE 5

Lights up. DRIVER is still driving. APPLE WOMAN is gone. Suddenly the HITCH-HIKER jerks up from behind, still in the bed of the truck. He is waking up. He looks around and then knocks on the window. DRIVER notices and pulls the truck over. HITCH-HIKER gets out of the bed of the truck, stretches, and opens the front door. He sees that APPLE WOMAN is not there.

HITCHHIKER: Where'd that Apple Woman go?

DRIVER: Get in.

HITCHHIKER: Did you drop her off somewhere?

(DRIVER nods.)

HITCHHIKER: I was hoping she'd stay with us longer.

DRIVER: Nope.

HITCHHIKER: Gotta sell those apples, I guess. Geez. Was that weird or what? I mean that was weird. Selling apples in the middle of nowhere. That's funny. No-body's gonna eat them. Sun's gonna dry them up before long. You talked with her, what did she say?

DRIVER: She had just run away from her home and left her possessions.

HITCHHIKER: To sell apples?

DRIVER: Yep.

HITCHHIKER: Wow, she takes it seri-ously, I guess. I'll give it to her, though, they were good. I have no idea how she got the ground to work for her like that. Where are they?

DRIVER: What?

HITCHHIKER: The apples we bought. Did you eat them all?

DRIVER: No. I gave them back to her.

HITCHHIKER: What?

DRIVER: I just didn't feel right getting them for nothing. They should have cost much more than nothing. .

HITCHHIKER: You gave all those delicious apples away?

DRIVER: Yeah.

HITCHHIKER: Great. I'm hungry now.

DRIVER: Where's your Twinkies?

(HITCHHIKER mumbles something.)

DRIVER: What?

HITCHHIKER: I don't want Twinkies! I was counting on those apples! They were tasty!

DRIVER: Well, I'm sorry. I just didn't feel right taking them for nothing.

HITCHHIKER: Dammit! I'm surprised she just let you give them back to her.

DRIVER: Yeah. Me too. Well. She didn't really. She was asleep. But I kept expecting her to wake up. It was hard to get her out of the truck. She must have been real tired.

HITCHHIKER: She wasn't awake when you dropped her off?

DRIVER: *(Laughs.)* No, no she wasn't.

(Pause.)

HITCHHIKER: I don't understand.

DRIVER: Yeah.

HITCHHIKER: Why did you drop her off when she was asleep?

DRIVER: I don't know. *(Pause.)* She kept looking out that window. Asking which direction that way was. Said she'd like to go that way and how exciting that would be. But, you know, I can't go that way. I'm headed west. But she kept looking out that window. North. Kinda like Barbara. She'd look out of windows too. And then she just sorta fell asleep. Right where you are. And, boy, she started dreaming quick! She closed her eyes and bam! They're shooting all over, going crazy like back and forth. Her face started twitching, kinda smiling, you know. Then all of a sudden she gasps. Loud. *(He gasps to illustrate.)* I couldn't believe it. I think she saw somebody in her dream, that was why she gasped like that. Someone she hadn't seen in a long time. Her cheeks got red. I could see her pulse. Right there. Boom. Boom. This dream she was having, whatever it was, I wanted to be in it. I wanted her to be looking at me like that, the way she was looking at whoever. It was...just the way she looked lying there where you are. And all of a sudden I hear a loud crack. I look up and I'm completely off the road, running over cactus, jackrabbits freaking out. I nearly busted a tire on a rock. That's when I knew. I didn't belong in her dream. I mean, she would wake up from this fantastic dream and I would be the first *thing* she saw. And right when she saw my face she would remember where she is, in the cab of a truck and dreaming no more, with a man who stays drunk by gulping up distances. Afraid that if he stops he'll get thrown off this planet like it was a treadmill. Hoping that someday I'll be moving faster than the ground beneath me. So I won't have to race to keep up with everything stationary. When the earth finally stops spinning and hurtling itself wherever it is we're really going! I mean, where are we *really* going! I have no idea! *(Pause.)*

And I didn't want her to wake up and see that, not when she was having such a wonderful dream. So I got out and I picked her up and tried not to wake her. I thought she would, I really did. Her mouth was partly open. I could hear her breath. I laid her by some shrubs that would, I don't know, guard her. And then I got her apples and then I left. *(Pause.)* And I bet... I just bet she woke up beautifully. Not knowing how she got there, not knowing if she was still dreaming. Seeing the sunrise off the strange hills, in a foreign land, a land of promise. And for a moment, she was home. And I just bet she woke up like that.

(Pause.)

HITCHHIKER: You ditched her.

DRIVER: I didn't ditch her.

HITCHHIKER: The definition of the word ditch. To leave someone in a ditch on the side of the road.

DRIVER: It wasn't a ditch. I dropped her off in a bed of sand. It was near a small town where she could sell her apples...

HITCHHIKER: I can't believe this. I bet she woke up pissed as hell. Nobody likes to be ditched. And you dropped her off in a ditch under a shrub for protection!

DRIVER: There was no ditch! It was a bed of sand!

HITCHHIKER: What's the shrub going to do to protect her? Have you ever heard of a shrub protecting anything?

DRIVER: You weren't there! You don't know.

HITCHHIKER: I don't have to be there to know when somebody got ditched. And unless that shrub spoke English or sang folk songs, she got ditched.

DRIVER: No, it's not ditched. It's not! She said she was a comet! Shooting off. She was going a different direction than we are.

HITCHHIKER: She said she was a comet?

DRIVER: Yes, and if you interfere too much you ruin it. It's like stalactites. If you touch them they die.

HITCHHIKER: Stalactites?

DRIVER: You know, pillars in caverns.

HITCHHIKER: Yeah, I know.

DRIVER: Well, you can't touch them or they stop growing. Just an example for ya.

HITCHHIKER: Well, thank you.

DRIVER: I kept one apple, though.

HITCHHIKER: You did?

DRIVER: You can have it if you like.

(DRIVER gives it to him. HITCHHIKER stares at it.)

HITCHHIKER: I can see my reflection in this.

DRIVER: The reddest apples you've ever seen.

HITCHHIKER: I'd better save it for later. It looks so good. Hey, do you think we can stop the truck? I really need to go to the bathroom.

DRIVER: I'm not stopping the truck.

HITCHHIKER: Oh, come on! It'll take two seconds. I've got a full cup in here. I guarantee it.

DRIVER: I can't. Wait a bit.

HITCHHIKER: You're ruining a perfectly good road trip. Can't go to the bathroom and you threw away those apples. I just can't believe you got rid of the apples.

(Pause. DRIVER begins whistling.)

HITCHHIKER: You really don't remember why you started driving?

DRIVER: Nope.

HITCHHIKER: And your wife, Barbara?

DRIVER: She didn't look like a Barbara.

HITCHHIKER: She wasn't the reason?

DRIVER: What do you mean?

HITCHHIKER: Did you ever just want to get away?

DRIVER: Listen, I don't remember, okay? It's a blank. All I remember is buying this truck. Then I can't remember anything until about five thousand miles or so.

HITCHHIKER: Okay. Sorry.

DRIVER: Just beating a dead horse is all. No point.

HITCHHIKER: Listen, I have been very patient. Do you think we could stop the truck? I really got to go.

DRIVER: There is no way I'm stopping this truck.

HITCHHIKER: I'm gonna burst!

DRIVER: We're not stopping!

HITCHHIKER: Why the hell not?

DRIVER: Because!! *(Beat.)* I think this road is going to end soon.

HITCHHIKER: What?

DRIVER: The Apple Woman...said this road...ends.

HITCHHIKER: Ends? How?

DRIVER: Runs into the ocean.

HITCHHIKER: Just...

DRIVER: Yep. Just right into the ocean. She said five hundred miles.

HITCHHIKER: How many do we have now?

DRIVER: Well, if she was exactly right about five hundred, then we've got a hundred and seventeen left. But she was almost certainly estimating. In which case it could be anywhere from a hundred to a hundred thirty-five, roughly.

HITCHHIKER: Holy shit, that's nothing!

DRIVER: I got enough gas so we're gonna go straight through. I'm almost there. I can't believe it. I'm almost there.

HITCHHIKER: Around a hundred miles... We must be in California.

DRIVER: I don't know.

HITCHHIKER: So this is California?

DRIVER: I'm not sure.

HITCHHIKER: It's just desert. Wasn't California supposed to have oranges? Lots of oranges? And where are the redwoods?

DRIVER: I don't think we're in California.

HITCHHIKER: So once we reach West where are we gonna go?

DRIVER: Nowhere.

HITCHHIKER: You're not going anywhere else?

DRIVER: No!

HITCHHIKER: Not north, not south, nothing?

DRIVER: No. That's it.

HITCHHIKER: I thought you were a vigilante going to the furthest reaches of the earth. After west you head off in another direction, or something.

DRIVER: No! I hate East. North and South are just as bad. I hate all the other directions.

HITCHHIKER: So West is it??!

DRIVER: Yeah!

HITCHHIKER: Well, what about me, then?

DRIVER: I don't know.

HITCHHIKER: You're breaking up the squad? We just got started!

DRIVER: I guess.

HITCHHIKER: You can't do that! We're a team.

DRIVER: We are?

HITCHHIKER: Once you see West, wouldn't you like to see what North is like? I mean, is Santa really up there? Reindeer? Yeti? That sounds like quite an adventure!

DRIVER: It's very cold.

HITCHHIKER: No! It'll be fun! Come on! We'll play games. Uhh, sing songs. Hey, you want to whistle? Go ahead, I'll whistle with you.

DRIVER: What's that?

HITCHHIKER: What?

DRIVER: There's a truck behind us.

HITCHHIKER: *(Looks behind.)* Yeah. There is. First one I've seen in a long time.

DRIVER: What kind is it?

HITCHHIKER: I can't tell. Why?

DRIVER: It's on the same road as we are. I'm curious. Is it a truck?

HITCHHIKER: Yep, it's a truck.

DRIVER: Oh. What does it look like?

HITCHHIKER: It's gonna pass us. You'll see it. Hey, we should start the alphabet game. That truck's gonna have some letters on it. Maybe there's a Q in the license plate. Or maybe it's a Mazda.

DRIVER: You can't just jump to those letters. You have to get all the other ones before it.

HITCHHIKER: If there's a Q in the license plate, we should follow it until we get all the other letters.

DRIVER: No. I'm not going to follow it.

HITCHHIKER: We're never going to find a Q any other way.

DRIVER: That's not how you play.

(The truck emerges.)

HITCHHIKER: Come on! You have to bend the rules a little bit! Oh! Here it comes. If there's a Q, we're following it…

(A MAN is driving the truck. His face is obscured by a hat he is wearing. He doesn't look at HITCHHIKER or DRIVER and appears agitated. In the bed of the truck is the APPLE WOMAN with her head down. HITCHHIKER and DRIVER are peering out the window at her. She raises her head and looks at HITCHHIKER and DRIVER. Her face is sunken and deathly. She smiles and raises her hand halfway to say hello to her friends. Then the truck passes out of sight.)

HITCHHIKER: Holy shit.

DRIVER: Was that…? My eyes… I can't… Was that her?

HITCHHIKER: Holy shit.

DRIVER: That was her, wasn't it?

HITCHHIKER: She looked…

DRIVER: What happened to her?

(A large wet spot develops around HITCH-HIKER's crotch and begins to drip. HITCH-HIKER suddenly jumps when he feels it running down his leg.)

HITCHHIKER: Oh, shit! God... Dammit! We gotta stop the truck!

DRIVER: You see who was driving that truck?

HITCHHIKER: I'm fucking pissing my pants, man! Stop the truck!

DRIVER: Can't believe that was her. Come on. Faster.

HITCHHIKER: Please! I can't stop! Shit! Shit! Shit!

DRIVER: No, now we're gonna catch up to her and say hi.

HITCHHIKER: Say hi? Now's not the best time for me to say hi. Oh, my God! Just stop the truck. This piece of shit isn't going to catch up to that truck anyway! Just stop! God, I can't believe this!

DRIVER: The truck is more powerful than you think. Just wait a moment.

HITCHHIKER: Wait a moment? Fuck! Oh, man. I feel fucking disgusting.

DRIVER: Come on.

HITCHHIKER: She's gone.

DRIVER: Come on, baby!

HITCHHIKER: She's gone! I can't even see the taillights anymore! Fuck! Oh, man how is this happening?

DRIVER: Okay. Okay. We'll stop.

(DRIVER stops the truck. HITCHHIKER grabs his bag and runs offstage. DRIVER sits there still for a moment, looking out. He rubs his eyes.)

DRIVER: Damn eyes. Worthless. *(Tries to look out some more, but can't. Slowly he gets out of the truck and stands on the road. To HITCHHIKER.)* Rub dust into them. Scrub it pretty hard. That's the best we can do until we get to a place that we can wash them. Do you have another pair of pants?

HITCHHIKER: *(From off.)* Yes.

DRIVER: Scrub the seat with dust too. It helps get the odor out.

HITCHHIKER: This doesn't normally happen to me! Just so you know!

DRIVER: Yeah, I know.

HITCHHIKER: You should have stopped the truck!

DRIVER: I know.

(HITCHHIKER comes back on. Slowly. He has new pants on.)

HITCHHIKER: My hands smell.

DRIVER: Rub more dust on them.

HITCHHIKER: *(Kneels down and rubs dust on them.)* Shit, this is fucking embarrassing. I'm sorry. I mean about your truck I'm sorry. I...

DRIVER: Hey, it's a piece of shit truck.

HITCHHIKER: I told you I needed to go...

DRIVER: It can't even break fifty. The only time I needed it to.

HITCHHIKER: Oohh, fuck. Pissing my pants. Do you know where we can find some water? Just to wash my hands.

DRIVER: Some breeds of dogs can break fifty, I think. Maybe not. The cheetah, at least. And the giraffe is faster than you'd think.

HITCHHIKER: Hello? Do you have some water?

DRIVER: What about that drink you got from the gas station?

HITCHHIKER: No, it was Coke.

DRIVER: All's we got is soda, then. Makes for sticky hands.

HITCHHIKER: Oh, man. Oh. *(Doesn't know what to do with his hands. Instinctively he moves them up to rub his face.)*

DRIVER: Don't wipe your face.

(HITCHHIKER freezes and slowly moves his hands away from his face.)

SCENE 6

The two men driving again. HITCH-HIKER is wearing work gloves and has his hands out the window. There is that one big apple on the dashboard. HITCHHIKER is looking at it.

HITCHHIKER: What's the distance?

DRIVER: Eighty-seven miles.

HITCHHIKER: Eighty-seven. *(Pause.)* You gonna eat that apple?

DRIVER: I told you, you can have it.

HITCHHIKER: Yeah, thanks. I'm really hungry.

DRIVER: Then eat the apple.

HITCHHIKER: If it's anything like the last one I ate… oh.

DRIVER: Yep. Really something.

HITCHHIKER: Yeah. *(Looks at the apple.)* Distance?

DRIVER: Still eighty-seven. *(Pause.)* Just eat it.

HITCHHIKER: I'm thinking about it.

DRIVER: What's to think about? Just eat.

HITCHHIKER: Look. My hands stink. Bad. I can smell them through these disgusting gloves, even. And you know as soon as I lay one finger on that apple, it's going to reek. I don't want to contaminate the thing. It's so juicy, and red. Sitting up there. Fat and plump and crisp. This is very frustrating. Hey, do you think…

DRIVER: What?

HITCHHIKER: Could you hold the apple for me?

DRIVER: You want my hands to hold the apple for you?

HITCHHIKER: Sure. Why not?

(DRIVER moves his hands over to HITCH-HIKER. HITCHHIKER recoils from the odor.)

HITCHHIKER: Oh, man! That's disgusting. What is that?

DRIVER: Steering wheel covering got rubbed off at about forty thousand miles. The rubber underneath smells. Gets on your hands.

HITCHHIKER: You should wash them.

DRIVER: I stopped washing after the forty-seven thousand mark. What's the point?

HITCHHIKER: *(Stares at the apple.)* God! I wouldn't even care if this was just a regular apple, you know? I'd just chomp it down the same. But this one… these are so good. It'd seem like such a waste. It tasted so good. You don't happen to have a fork in here do you?

DRIVER: No.

HITCHHIKER: Sharp stick?

DRIVER: No.

HITCHHIKER: String?

DRIVER: Nope.

HITCHHIKER: Aaaugh! There's got to be a way to eat this apple. How much farther do we have?

DRIVER: Eighty-six miles. If she was right.

HITCHHIKER: Eighty-six miles. There's an ocean eighty-six miles away. I'll wash my filthy hands in eighty-six miles and then eat this beautiful apple. I gotta stop looking at it. *(Looks out the window.)* What do you think will be there at the end of the road?

DRIVER: I don't know.

HITCHHIKER: If you could have anything, what would be there? Because I picture a giant burger place, in a wood building, like a cabin. And it smells so good you never want to leave. The waitresses are always friendly, and the food is great and they have spacious, clean bathrooms. We could relax. Someplace you could just stay forever. Do you know what I mean? What do you picture?

(Pause.)

DRIVER: A unicorn.

HITCHHIKER: A unicorn?

DRIVER: Yes.

(HITCHHIKER sighs.)

DRIVER: What?

HITCHHIKER: No, it's just… a unicorn! You know.

DRIVER: No, I don't.

HITCHHIKER: I mean, that's never going to happen. But whatever. You know. Fine.

DRIVER: Maybe to you it won't happen. But you asked me what I wanted to see.

HITCHHIKER: So you think there's going to be a white horse with a horn waiting for you at the ocean?

DRIVER: Maybe.

HITCHHIKER: Well there's not. The closest thing you'll get to a unicorn is a dog with a chopstick tied to its head.

DRIVER: It would have a golden horn.

HITCHHIKER: Oh, really?

DRIVER: And it would let me touch it on the neck.

HITCHHIKER: I don't want to hear about the unicorn.

DRIVER: And as soon as I do, it runs away. And when its hooves hit the ground, it sounds like someone punching a stiff pillow.

HITCHHIKER: Enough! Okay? I don't want to hear about the unicorn.

DRIVER: It's my unicorn! I can imagine it all I want! It's got blue eyes! Blue!

HITCHHIKER: Hey! Please be considerate of other people in the truck! I'm right here. I specifically asked you to not indulge in this unicorn fantasy but you persist in disregarding my feelings.

DRIVER: It's my truck.

HITCHHIKER: Oh, you're not going to pull that one on me.

DRIVER: It is. It's my truck.

HITCHHIKER: I know it's your truck. That's why I'm asking you nicely.

(Pause.)

DRIVER: I don't know why I can't talk about the unicorn.

HITCHHIKER: Because it's depressing. Unicorns don't exist.

DRIVER: Says you.

HITCHHIKER: Says science!

DRIVER: Maybe you can't see it but don't speak for me.

HITCHHIKER: You.

DRIVER: That's right.

HITCHHIKER: Only you can see it.

DRIVER: Maybe so.

HITCHHIKER: It's always just you, isn't it? Nobody else is ever involved! Just you going west. Only you seeing a unicorn. The Apple Woman? Nope, can't bring her. She might disturb your complete isolation. And I'm next aren't I? You're going to leave me stranded while you drool over a unicorn that I can't see. Well, it doesn't really do much good if nobody else can see it, does it!

DRIVER: It's not always just about me. I got a lot of dreams. It's just that some of them... to say them out loud...kinda scratches your throat. Like they don't want to come out yet.

HITCHHIKER: You don't understand. I got nowhere to go. It's gonna be dawn soon.

DRIVER: Yeah.

HITCHHIKER: (Looking at the apple.) There's gotta be a way to eat this apple.

DRIVER: Hold it with your elbows.

HITCHHIKER: Hey! (Tries to hold it with his elbows. He succeeds in picking it up. He tries to bite it. Can't.)

DRIVER: There you go.

HITCHHIKER: I can't reach it.

DRIVER: Uhh... Use your knees.

HITCHHIKER: (Drops the apple into his lap. He tries to move it with his chin. Can't reach it again, so he starts shifting around, trying to maneuver the apple between his knees.) Oh, it smells so good.

DRIVER: Careful. There's urine clods down there. Disgusting crud.

HITCHHIKER: I know! Just let me focus, okay. I won't drop it. What's the count?

DRIVER: Eighty-four.

HITCHHIKER: I can't wait that long.

DRIVER: Nope. Hunger doesn't wait.

HITCHHIKER: It's gotta be now or never.

DRIVER: Go for it. Chomp it.

HITCHHIKER: (Reaches down and tries to eat the apple holding it between his legs. The apple falls directly to the floor with a thud. HITCHHIKER sits up and looks at the DRIVER.) It slipped.

DRIVER: Five-second rule!

HITCHHIKER: Fuck!

DRIVER: Five-second rule!

HITCHHIKER: I dropped it! (HITCHHIKER is just about to rub his face.)

DRIVER: Don't rub your face.

HITCHHIKER: Oh! This is fruuustraaatiiing meeee!

DRIVER: Listen. You stink. You're not going to get away from it. You pissed your pants. Might as well accept it. I got used to the smell after a mile and a half.

HITCHHIKER: You know it's getting real annoying how you measure everything in miles. "Yep. Lost my baby teeth at five thousand miles. Hit puberty at thirteen thousand. Thems were awkward miles."

(HITCHHIKER has picked up the apple and tosses it out the window. DRIVER instantly slams on the brakes.)

DRIVER: Go get it.

HITCHHIKER: What?

DRIVER: Go get it.

HITCHHIKER: The apple? We can't eat it anymore.

DRIVER: I said go find that apple and bring it back.

HITCHHIKER: Oh, what the fuck! Come on! It's just another bad-tasting apple now.

DRIVER: You did not ask if you could throw that apple away. That was my apple.

HITCHHIKER: You said I could eat it.

DRIVER: Yes. But not throw it out the window like some piece of garbage.

HITCHHIKER: It's biodegradable. *(Pause.)* Fine. I'll go get the apple.

(HITCHHIKER leaves. DRIVER sits and waits. HITCHHIKER returns with a badly disfigured apple, chewed by gravel and caked in dust.)

HITCHHIKER: It's a little marred now.

DRIVER: Oh, look what you've done. It's all... *(He puts it back on the dashboard. It looks pathetic.)*

HITCHHIKER: *(Seeing something on the side of the road.)* What's that? Is that a deer or something? You seen any deer out here?

DRIVER: There's no deer in the desert.

HITCHHIKER: Goats? There's something out there. Some kind of roadkill.

DRIVER: Goats are in the mountains. Could be a dog.

HITCHHIKER: *(Exits the truck.)* Too big...

DRIVER: I can't see anything.

HITCHHIKER: Oh my God.

(DRIVER gets out of the truck and walks over to the body. It's APPLE WOMAN from before.)

HITCHHIKER: Is that...?

(DRIVER checks her pulse.)

HITCHHIKER: That's the Apple Woman, isn't it? Is she...

DRIVER: She's cold.

HITCHHIKER: Oh, shit. That's...that's really... ahh man, that's bad, that's really bad. What happened to her? Can you tell?

DRIVER: She's dead.

HITCHHIKER: Her legs...they're crooked. Are they broken?

DRIVER: No. It's just how she fell.

HITCHHIKER: Well, what then?

DRIVER: I don't know. No marks, not even a bruise. She just... She just died. *(Begins straightening her legs.)*

HITCHHIKER: You shouldn't touch her. I mean, this could be anything. She could be poisoned… this could be, you know… murder or something.

(DRIVER looks up at him.)

HITCHHIKER: That guy! What about that guy in the truck? Did you get a look at him? What did he look like?

DRIVER: I didn't see.

HITCHHIKER: What kind of truck was he driving?

DRIVER: *(Blinking his eyes.)* My eyes are getting worse.

HITCHHIKER: Oh, man I'm getting a bad feeling about this.

DRIVER: She looks asleep.

HITCHHIKER: I think we should go. We should go now.

(DRIVER begins trying to pick her up.)

HITCHHIKER: No. No put her back. This is a…this is a crime scene now. You can't mess with a crime scene. Cops could be here any minute.

DRIVER: Her apples are everywhere.

HITCHHIKER: Yeah, good idea. We should grab a few. No wait. The cops'd notice that. Man we gotta leave. We're getting too involved. They're gonna find us. They got ways. Uhh, DNA from hairs. Who knows how much hair we got lying around here? Uhh… footprints. Shit, man, we got footprints all over here! Fuck!

DRIVER: *(Stroking her face.)* It's a cruel road. There's no shelter anywhere.

HITCHHIKER: What are you talking about? We gotta get out of here!

DRIVER: She's just gonna bake out here. The sun's rising. She'll be nothing but hard skin in a day or two.

HITCHHIKER: The cops will find her first. There's nothing we can do.

DRIVER: Shouldn't we be crying? I feel like somebody should be crying for her. But I can't cry anymore. I don't know what happened.

HITCHHIKER: You burnt your eyes.

DRIVER: Yeah, that's right! I burnt my eyes. The sun. *(Picks her up.)*

HITCHHIKER: Wait. What are you doing? Put her down.

DRIVER: I'm not leaving her here.

HITCHHIKER: We can't take her!

DRIVER: She'll cook. Her skin will burn and then burn over the burn until it dries out. Then it tightens like leather. It gets so tight it'll crush her bones, her organs explode out of her.

HITCHHIKER: Let the cops find her. They'll know what to do.

DRIVER: Look around here! Do you see any cops? Do you see anybody? There's nothing. They won't find her until she's nothing but a crumpled piece of paper. Someday it's gonna be me out here, dead, like roadkill. 'Cause the road is cruel. It wants me like it wants everybody. Somebody would do the same for me.

HITCHHIKER: Do you know how stupid this is? This is so stupid. Anybody finds you with a dead body, you'll fry! They'll pin it on you and you'll fry. Where are you going to take her?

DRIVER: She said she knew somebody out by the ocean. She said she wanted to go there.

HITCHHIKER: I'm not getting in that truck with that body.

DRIVER: No?

HITCHHIKER: Listen to me! I know what I'm talking about! These kinds of situations… they get tangled in your hair unless you walk, just walk away. We gotta bail. Get in the truck and go back. Go back east.

DRIVER: I can't do that.

HITCHHIKER: Sure you can. Your eyes are worse, the cops are gonna be investigating, that means roadblocks, we got no water, no food, and there's some crazy guy running around here who probably killed this woman. Something tells me we gotta go back.

DRIVER: We should be crying or something. Somebody should be crying. It shouldn't be me here.

HITCHHIKER: Listen! I can't go with you if you take that body. You have to choose.

DRIVER: This was meant for somebody else. Someone not like me.

HITCHHIKER: Who's it going to be? Me or her?

DRIVER: The sun's gonna rise.

HITCHHIKER: Are you listening to me?

(Pause. DRIVER looks at him.)

DRIVER: She was so pretty, you know? Really pretty. I mean, she had something. It's sad. It's just sad. Seems like everything's so sad. *(DRIVER gets up, carrying the body.)*

HITCHHIKER: This is a mistake.

DRIVER: I know. I know it is.

(DRIVER drives off leaving HITCHHIKER standing. After a beat, HITCHHIKER walks off in the other direction.)

ACT II

SCENE 7

Lights are out. OFFICER PETERS emerges holding the flashlight. Again, the flashlight is the only light on stage. He shines it on the spot where APPLE WOMAN was laying at the end of Act I. Some of the apples are still around. OFFICER PETERS takes out his recorder. He shines the flashlight on it and pushes a button.

OFFICER PETERS: Okay. I've found the location where she was probably dropped off. There are more apples gathered around. They look just as good as the first one. Some of them have been taken. Looks like she was laying here. Uhh, two men by the looks of their footprints came by. One picked her up. Uhh. The other tried to cover up some of the prints. Tire tracks. Need to analyze those. Uhh, again, no sign of struggle. No blood. Not sure how woman got here. Possibly thrown from road. By the way woman was laying and was carried off, must assume she was either unconscious or dead. This… has been Officer Peters. Officerrr. Peteerrs. *(Stops the recorder and rewinds it. He slowly gets up, bracing his back. Lights begin to slowly fade up.)* This better have worked or… *(Plays the cassette.)*

OFFICER PETERS'S VOICE: …must assume she was either unconscious or dead. This…has been Officer Peters. Officerrr. Peteerrs.

OFFICER PETERS: *(Stops the tape, giggling.)* Gladys…Your little trinkets. *(Turns the recorder back on.)* Note to self. Get Gladys a milkshake before going home tonight. *(Turns off the recorder. He then turns in the direction of the sun.)* There. Now that's a sunrise.

SCENE 8

Lights up on DRIVER with body next to him in the truck.

DRIVER: Sixty-three more miles. If you were right. I think you were. I sure am curious how you made those apples taste like that. I know you probably can't tell me. I don't want to take that from you. We tried to eat one of them. It fell on the floor. Got all messed up. There was an accident. My friend had an accident in the truck. You know, like ahh, accident. And the apple fell in the accident. So we couldn't eat it. I wanted to save it, but he threw it out the window. So I made him go get it. Got all messed up more. *(He looks at the apple on the dashboard.)* I'm sorry for...what happened. I think... I don't know. I left you, you know. I left you on the side of the road. Yeah, it was me. I admit it. But, see, now I thought what I was doing was ahh, for the overall best. And you were sleeping. And dreaming. Your eyes were dancing. Pigmies. Dancing like pigmies. What's a pigmy? If you take the, now this is funny, if you take the last two letters of pigmy and put them at the front you get my pig. Ha! My pig! *(DRIVER suddenly doesn't like the sound of what he's talking about.)* Let's turn on the radio. *(He does, then turns it off to say something.)* Fairies probably. Pigmies are probably some kind of fairy. Don't the name sound like they're always dancing? Pigmy. Just sounds like they're always dancing. And I'm just saying that's what your eyes were doing. And they were dancing to a song I had never heard before. I could tell just by the dancing that I'd never heard that song before. Let's turn on the radio. I should just shut up. *(Turns on the radio.)* Have you ever heard this song?

(APPLE WOMAN suddenly wakes up with a gasp.)

APPLE WOMAN: I'm tired.

DRIVER: Oh! Try not to move. Just relax. There. You're probably a bit groggy. You've been sleeping for so long.

APPLE WOMAN: Was that it? I was sleeping? Where am I? *(She looks at DRIVER.)* Oh. I remember.

DRIVER: Yeah. You're not dreaming anymore.

APPLE WOMAN: No, I guess not.

DRIVER: I really didn't want you to wake up like this. I did my best to give you something else to wake up to but... It's too bad you missed the sunrise. It sure was nice. Too bad you missed it.

APPLE WOMAN: My apples, where are they?

DRIVER: I'm afraid they're all gone. This is the only one I have. It kinda got messed up.

APPLE WOMAN: This is the last one?

DRIVER: Yeah.

APPLE WOMAN: All the others are gone?

DRIVER: I'm afraid so.

APPLE WOMAN: *(Grabs it and puts it in her lap.)* It's okay. I only need the seeds.

DRIVER: You might not want to put that in your lap. That piece of fruit has been through a lot.

APPLE WOMAN: I can't lose this one.

DRIVER: Well, you see, my friend...he had an accident.

APPLE WOMAN: I can't lose this one.

DRIVER: Okay.

APPLE WOMAN: Where are we going?

DRIVER: To the ocean.

APPLE WOMAN: Really?

DRIVER: I can't believe it myself. Fifty-one more miles.

APPLE WOMAN: I haven't been there in a long time.

DRIVER: Me either. You deserve a vacation.

APPLE WOMAN: I guess I do.

(Pause.)

DRIVER: Can I ask you... what are your dreams like?

APPLE WOMAN: I almost never remember them. But this last time, there was this man talking about his pigs. But he was saying it like, "My pig. My pig!"

DRIVER: A man was saying that?

APPLE WOMAN: Yep. My pig. And then something about waking up beautifully.

DRIVER: Well, that was me! I said that.

APPLE WOMAN: You said that?

DRIVER: Yeah! I was in your dream? Me?

APPLE WOMAN: I guess.

DRIVER: I was talking about pigmies. My pig. Get it?

APPLE WOMAN: Yeah.

DRIVER: Not that you're my pig. That's not what I meant.

APPLE WOMAN: Uh-huh.

DRIVER: I apologize. I stick my feet in my mouth.

APPLE WOMAN: You're the one who dropped me off on the side of the road, aren't you? (Pause.) Don't be embarrassed.

DRIVER: I am. I apologize for that too. It's just that I...I wanted you to...to wake up...

APPLE WOMAN: Oh, I see. To wake up beautifully.

DRIVER: Yeah. It didn't work out the way I wanted. You just ended up getting hurt and all... It's too bad you didn't make it in time for the sunrise. That would have been at least something. But. There you go.

APPLE WOMAN: To wake up and not have any idea where you are... It's awful and exciting.

DRIVER: I just didn't want you to wake up in the cab of a disgusting truck, with trash everywhere, and...

APPLE WOMAN: Country music on the radio.

(DRIVER instantly turns off the radio.)

APPLE WOMAN: You seem familiar to me.

DRIVER: Well, I bought some of your apples.

APPLE WOMAN: No, I mean before that.

DRIVER: I doubt you've seen me. I've been traveling west for a long time.

APPLE WOMAN: I think I knew that. You seemed like the kind with wandering fever.

DRIVER: Well, I'm definitely not wandering. I'm going west.

APPLE WOMAN: The open road. A place where a man can lose himself. Somebody said that once... where a man can lose himself.

DRIVER: Those little sayings... Seem to know so much.

APPLE WOMAN: "Life is short and the world is wide."

DRIVER: Wider than you'd think.

APPLE WOMAN: "I am going with him to an unknown country where I shall have no past and no name, and where I shall be born again with a new face and an untried heart."

DRIVER: *(Looks at her.)* Who said that?

(APPLE WOMAN shrugs.)

DRIVER: An untried heart. I shall be born again with an untried heart.

SCENE 9

We see HITCHHIKER on the side of the road walking. A truck approaches.

MAN: Need a lift?

HITCHHIKER: I think I'm going the other way. Headed east.

MAN: East is eventually West and North is eventually South and eventually, we all head South. All roads lead to Rome! Just a bit of culture there for ya.

HITCHHIKER: Do I know you?

MAN: Oh, man we all know each other around here. We all do.

HITCHHIKER: I think I'm fine on my own.

MAN: On his own he says! No need for a truck. No need for company. Or water. You want some water? *(He pulls out a bottle of water.)* You thirsty?

HITCHHIKER: Yes.

MAN: Come get a drink, if you want.

(HITCHHIKER walks over cautiously and takes the water bottle. He pours the water over his hands.)

MAN: That water's for drinking, you know.

HITCHHIKER: They really stink. *(Once he finishes rinsing off his hands, he takes a big drink from the jug.)* Thank you.

MAN: Yep. Really hot today. Whew! But it's cool and crisp in this truck, here. Just put in some new freon. Ice cold. What do you say?

HITCHHIKER: No thanks.

MAN: You are one tough customer. But see, here we have a thing called hospitality. See, I just gave you some water. I offered you a ride. Now what would be the hospitable thing to do?

HITCHHIKER: But we're going opposite directions.

MAN: I already told you! It's all the same direction! Eventually we meet again. Hitchhikers these days! They're so finicky. Just get in the truck. Come on!

HITCHHIKER: Who are you?

MAN: What if I told you that you didn't have a choice.

HITCHHIKER: You're that guy.

MAN: That guy! That guy! That guy! That's me, I guess. And you must be that hitchhiker. Don't worry. I know who you are.

HITCHHIKER: You passed us in that truck. You had that woman with you.

MAN: Oh! *That* woman, was with *that* guy in *that* truck! He's piecing it together folks.

HITCHHIKER: What happened to her?

MAN: That's good. Ask me the questions.

HITCHHIKER: You know we found her on the side of the road.

MAN: Should I be writing this down?

HITCHHIKER: She was just lying there in the dirt! She was dead.

MAN: Shut up! *(Gathers himself.)* What were you doing with her in your truck? Or excuse me, not your truck obviously.

HITCHHIKER: She asked for a ride.

MAN: Yeah, I'm sure she did. And you obliged. She's pretty isn't she? *(No answer.)* Yes, she is. Did you know that I was engaged to her? Bet you didn't know that, did you? When you picked her up? We had a commitment that girl and I. I bet you didn't know that.

HITCHHIKER: No, I didn't.

MAN: Where is she?

HITCHHIKER: I don't know.

MAN: Oh. You don't know. Well, thanks for trying. At least you gave it your best shot. I best be off now. Be late for supper. *(He does not move. Stares at HITCHHIKER.)*

HITCHHIKER: What do you want?

MAN: I want her back.

HITCHHIKER: She was dead.

MAN: Where is she?

HITCHHIKER: I don't know.

MAN: Get in the truck.

HITCHHIKER: I'd rather not.

MAN: Get in the truck, Hitchhiker.

HITCHHIKER: I think I better be going.

MAN: Get in the truck, Hitchhiker.

HITCHHIKER: No, thank you…

MAN: Hitchhiker. *(Points a gun at him.)* Get in the truck.

(HITCHHIKER begins walking over to the truck.)

SCENE 10

Split scene with DRIVER and APPLE WOMAN in their truck on one side of the stage and OFFICER PETERS in his car on the other side.

OFFICER PETERS: *(Speaking into recorder.)* Approaching vehicle now. It's an old truck. Possible match.

APPLE WOMAN: Umm, is it living?

DRIVER: Not exactly.

APPLE WOMAN: Is it dead?

DRIVER: I don't think so.

APPLE WOMAN: It has to be either alive or dead. Was it alive?

DRIVER: Yes.

APPLE WOMAN: But not anymore?

DRIVER: I guess not.

APPLE WOMAN: Oh. This is frustrating.

DRIVER: No. Okay. It's alive. Ask another question.

OFFICER PETERS: Truck fits description. Two occupants. They seem to be having a lively conversation. Possibly fighting.

APPLE WOMAN: Is it a banshee?

DRIVER: No.

APPLE WOMAN: Zombie?

DRIVER: No.

APPLE WOMAN: Is it a mythical creature of any kind? Like a phoenix?

DRIVER: No.

APPLE WOMAN: I wish it was a phoenix.

DRIVER: No. No. Ask better questions.

APPLE WOMAN: This game has always frustrated me.

DRIVER: This is the first time I've been able to play.

APPLE WOMAN: Is it a plant?

DRIVER: Yes!

APPLE WOMAN: It's a plant? An apple!

DRIVER: No.

APPLE WOMAN: It's not an apple?

DRIVER: No. That's too easy.

APPLE WOMAN: I wish it was an apple.

OFFICER PETERS: I am going to pull the vehicle over.

APPLE WOMAN: I'm close now.

DRIVER: Yep.

APPLE WOMAN: What am I forgetting? Something that is either alive or dead but it's a plant.

(We hear a siren.)

APPLE WOMAN: Oh no.

DRIVER: How long has he been back there? I never saw him.

APPLE WOMAN: Your eyes are getting worse.

DRIVER: I'm not stopping. We can't stop.

APPLE WOMAN: You have to.

DRIVER: No, I don't.

APPLE WOMAN: Pull over! You probably just have a taillight out or something.

OFFICER PETERS: Come on, buddy, pull over. Don't get any ideas.

DRIVER: It's not a taillight. It's about you. You know that's why. He's trying to find you.

APPLE WOMAN: He'll force us over.

DRIVER: I'm not going to let him take you. We're going to the end of this road.

OFFICER PETERS: Come on buddy. Don't make a big mistake.

APPLE WOMAN: If you don't stop someone might get hurt.

DRIVER: Okay. I'll pull over. But he's not stopping us.

APPLE WOMAN: Okay.

(DRIVER pulls over.)

OFFICER PETERS: The truck has pulled over. I'm approaching the vehicle.

(OFFICER PETERS gets out of the car slowly. Does the "casual" police walk over to the truck. APPLE WOMAN is trying to hide her face.)

OFFICER PETERS: Hello, there.

DRIVER: What's the problem, Officer?

OFFICER PETERS: Can I see your driver's license?

DRIVER: Yes, sir.

OFFICER PETERS: Do you know how fast you were going?

DRIVER: Fifty miles an hour.

OFFICER PETERS: Uhh…right. Have you checked your taillights recently?

DRIVER: Yes, sir. Last gas station.

OFFICER PETERS: Uhh…good, good. *(Looks at the license.)* Long way from home aren't you?

DRIVER: Nothing like it.

OFFICER PETERS: How about you ma'am? You with him?

(She nods.)

OFFICER PETERS: Everything all right, ma'am?

(She nods.)

OFFICER PETERS: Ma'am? May I see your face?

(She shows him. OFFICER PETERS tries to hide any expression but is clearly startled.)

OFFICER PETERS: Well. Sure is hot today, isn't it? Whew! I'll be right back.

DRIVER: Officer...? *(To APPLE WOMAN.)* He's gonna arrest us.

APPLE WOMAN: No he won't. I know these kind. They just like to check up on people once in a while.

OFFICER PETERS: *(Back in his car, scrambles for the CB.)* This is Officer Peters. I have visual ID on missing person Miss Candice Roberts. Request immediate backup. Repeat. I have Miss Candice Roberts in old truck... Hello? Over. Anybody there? *(CB is broken.)* Crap! *(He scrambles for the recorder.)* I found Candice Roberts. Kidnapped apparently. CB is broken. Couldn't radio for help...

DRIVER: What's he doing?

APPLE WOMAN: He's talking into a tape recorder, looks like.

DRIVER: I don't like this. He's obviously investigating something.

APPLE WOMAN: Maybe we should go.

DRIVER: Make a break for it?

APPLE WOMAN: Yeah.

DRIVER: He'd follow us.

(OFFICER PETERS gets out of the car and kneels down with his gun pointing at DRIVER.)

OFFICER PETERS: Get out of the truck with your hands up! Now!

DRIVER: Okay. Stay close to me. When he walks over here, ahh, on the count of three, okay?

APPLE WOMAN: On the count of three what?

OFFICER PETERS: Hands up!

(They put them up.)

DRIVER: We jump him.

APPLE WOMAN: What?

DRIVER: Trust me.

OFFICER PETERS: Now get out of the truck. Slowly.

(They both exit out the DRIVER's side. APPLE WOMAN stays close to DRIVER.)

OFFICER PETERS: Now turn around. No sudden movements. Ma'am, I'm gonna have to ask you to drop the apple.

(She doesn't drop it. OFFICER PETERS starts to walk over to her to pull her away from DRIVER. Just then, DRIVER lunges at him. We hear a gunshot. Everybody freezes. Then APPLE WOMAN falls on the ground. DRIVER looks at cop and then kneels down next to APPLE WOMAN. OFFICER PETERS is frozen, staring at the body on the ground. DRIVER picks her up and places her back in the truck. This takes some time. DRIVER gets in the truck on his side. OFFICER PETERS is still frozen. DRIVER slumps down in the seat.)

DRIVER: Why do I keep ruining you?

SCENE 11

MAN is pointing gun at HITCHHIKER's head with right hand. Left hand is holding onto the steering wheel. They drive for a while. Silence.

MAN: You ever seen that statue of the man thinking? You know. He's hunched over with his fist under his chin?

HITCHHIKER: Yes. *The Thinker.*

MAN: Yeah. Well. That's a comfortable position. I wouldn't mind being stuck like that for a while. Look at me here. I'm a regular piece of art here. Gun and driving. Fuck. This road. This fucking road.

HITCHHIKER: It's long.

MAN: It takes everything away from you. It takes your excitement. It takes your life, your thought, desire. It took Candice. It took her away from me. But I'm getting that back.

HITCHHIKER: I told you, she was dead.

MAN: *The Thinker,* huh? That's really what it's called?

HITCHHIKER: Yes.

MAN: Not very creative. Title me. Come on. What would be the title of my statue? Gun here, hand on steering wheel. What?

HITCHHIKER: I don't know.

MAN: Oh, yes you do. You're just afraid that if you say what you're thinking I'll shoot you in the head.

HITCHHIKER: Yes.

MAN: Well I won't. Okay? I won't. Serious.

(Pause.)

HITCHHIKER: I don't know.

MAN: You say I don't know one more time, I'll shoot you in the head. I hate that vocal tic. Idontknow. Idontknow. Idontknow.

HITCHHIKER: I'd call you "Man and Gun." "And Steering Wheel."

MAN: That's really inspiring. You're really inspiring.

HITCHHIKER: It would be easier if a gun wasn't pointed at my head.

MAN: Can't do that.

HITCHHIKER: We're going eighty-three miles an hour.

MAN: So? So what?

HITCHHIKER: It's not like I'm gonna jump out. Is the gun really necessary?

MAN: I'm the one with the gun. I'll make the suggestions and I suggest I point this gun at your head.

HITCHHIKER: Sorry.

MAN: You know how much I paid for this here piece? Fifty bucks! Just think, I'm only waving fifty bucks at your head right now. You think you'd be so scared if I was pointing just fifty bucks at your head? Nope. This is what I call an upgrade. *(Pause.)* It's you and me, buddy! You and me gonna see the whole world. You and me and my fifty bucks. You think that's cheap of me? I should get me a six-hundred-dollar gun? Well, I'll work my way up. *(Laughs.)* Truth is, that you get the same respect for a fifty-dollar gun that you do for a six-hundred-dollar gun. People all act the same. There's nobody high and mighty with a barrel cocked at their temple. God! I love these things. This humbles people. It's a kind of Bible. More knees bend to guns than to Jesus. And sincerely too! There's no false hearts, no hypocrisy when you kneel to a gun. That's truth! Begging to live. "Please don't shoot me! Please, I want to live." You ever pray that seriously? "Thank you for the food! Help all the people starving in Mozambique!"... I don't know, I just can't get into it as much. Aaauuugh. My fucking arm is going to fall off. You know how heavy this gun is?

HITCHHIKER: No.

MAN: When I find her… When I find your friend…

HITCHHIKER: He's just going to bury her.

MAN: She always was out in the garden. She was always planting those seeds. I shoulda burned the whole place down. Oh, my arm is gonna fall off. Gonna fall off into the Red Sea. I am *The Thinker*'s statue brother. "The Feeler." I feel! Woowowow! *(Change of thought.)* If he's done anything to her. If she's hurt…

HITCHHIKER: Well, she's…

MAN: You want to spell me a bit?

HITCHHIKER: What?

MAN: Hold my arm up.

HITCHHIKER: What?

MAN: I said hold my arm up. Hold my arm up. Hold my arm up.

(He does.)

MAN: There. That's better. If you do anything… If you even get any ideas about trying to get out, I want you to go ahead and pull the trigger, okay? Just go ahead and pull the trigger yourself. Could you do that for me? *(Laughs.)* My arms are feeling better… *(Begins crying.)* It's her, you know. It's her. It's not me. It's not me.

HITCHHIKER: Relax. Loosen your grip. You're holding the gun too tight. It might go off accidentally.

MAN: I love so much of her. I mean a lot of her. I've never liked more than one or two things about anybody before. But

with her? Everything. Except her damn garden. Burn that down. And she never liked the smell of oil. But the rest? I wanted all the rest. Where is she?? Where were you taking her??

HITCHHIKER: I don't know. I don't know. We were going west.

MAN: She's a burning brain fever. I'm sick all the time. That's a song. I didn't think that up. *(Change of thought.)* Who do I remind you of right now? Historical figure. Who?

HITCHHIKER: I don't know.

MAN: You don't know much, Hitchhiker. Moses in battle. His arms being held up. You remember? The Israelites versus the Canaanites. And as long as Moses's arms were raised, the Israelites would win. I think this is a similar situation, don't you? And I will keep raising up my arms to the gun and the wheel. And as long as they are raised, we get closer, we approach, we are gaining on the enemy. I am Moses in love. Moses's roses. *(Giggles.)* I always wanted to be a prophet. Large and golden, with a cape. And nobody could move me. Like a pillar of fire. This is the closest I've come.

(Lights suddenly up on OFFICER PETERS in same position as we last saw him. He has not moved. MAN and HITCHHIKER freeze as they look at him.)

HITCHHIKER: Did you see that?

MAN: Cop.

HITCHHIKER: He was… Like he'd been… I don't know.

MAN: Yep.

HITCHHIKER: It was like he'd seen… or had been so…

MAN: He was frozen, or turned to stone, just fucking say it. You always blabber around the answer. Just say it! He was a rock. He had turned into a rock. Saw Medusa.

HITCHHIKER: I wonder what happened.

MAN: I wonder what happened.

HITCHHIKER: What?

MAN: What?

(Pause.)

MAN: You hate me don't you? Many great men have been hated. *(Pause.)* Did she say anything about me? Did she mention me?

HITCHHIKER: I don't know.

MAN: Say that one more time.

HITCHHIKER: I'm sorry.

MAN: She didn't mention why she left? What she was thinking?

(HITCHHIKER shakes his head.)

MAN: It's not right. She had a responsibility to me! That's what love is! It's a responsibility! She can't just drop that responsibility!

HITCHHIKER: Relax, you're squeezing the gun again.

MAN: We all have to do things we don't like. Your job, visit your mother-in-law, wash the dishes. Everybody does them. Why can't she! Why can't she just suck it up and do it?

HITCHHIKER: Easy. I'm sure she had a reason.

MAN: It's her responsibility. She can't drop her responsibility. Even if she hates me. Even if I make her sick. It's not right to... *(Pause.)* My arms are tired. *(He puts the gun down. Pause.)* I love so much of her. I do.

SCENE 12

DRIVER and APPLE WOMAN in truck. APPLE WOMAN is dead again. This time there is blood. She was shot in the stomach.

DRIVER: Thirty more miles. Almost there. Something's going to happen. Are you comfortable? Maybe I should, here stretch out... There that's better. We never finished our game. You were getting close. I was thinking of a seed. Are seeds alive? I don't know. I guess they are. Are you going to wake up again? Maybe when we get to the end. I can't see very well anymore. I might run right into the ocean. So are you going to wake up again? Uhh, let's see? Last time I was talking about... uhh. Pigmies. And uhh, fairies dancing in your dreams. Did that wake you up? *(He leans over to her to whisper in her ear.)* Pigmy. You're cold. But you were cold before. It doesn't mean anything. Your stomach looks horrible. There's blood everywhere. Sitting like that you remind me of someone. Someone I think I read about. Maybe it was a book. Would a kiss wake you up? Like in the fairy tales? *(He stops the truck.)* I should say something. Awaken! *(He leans over and kisses her on the cheek. Nothing happens.)* That was a bad one. Let's try that again. Uhh, bonds be loosed! *(He kisses her again. On the mouth this time.)* Of course bonds be loosed isn't going to work. One more time. This time with no words. *(He kisses her again. Nothing happens.)* No words! That's stupid. Something better this time. Life's blood return! *(He kisses her.)* Evil be gone! *(He kisses her.)* Be restored! *(He kisses her.)* With true love's kiss, I release thee. *(He kisses her, slower this time. Again nothing.)* I thought you might respond to that one. That was a good one. *(He straightens her up, smooths her hair, primps her a little.)* We're almost there. Don't worry. You'll be done in a little bit. You're probably tired of this trip, aren't you? I am too. I'm getting tired. It's been too long. I didn't know it would be this long. But there's only twenty more miles.

(He begins driving again. APPLE WOMAN revives again with a gasp.)

APPLE WOMAN: I have a headache.

DRIVER: Oh God, lay back. You'll feel better.

APPLE WOMAN: It hurts. My apples? Where are they?

DRIVER: Gone, I'm afraid. They're lost. The last one fell out when you got shot. But you can make more.

APPLE WOMAN: Look at all this blood.

DRIVER: I know. But you'll make more. You'll be fine.

APPLE WOMAN: Driver?

DRIVER: Yes.

APPLE WOMAN: Do you remember how I made those apples?

DRIVER: You never told me.

(APPLE WOMAN begins to cry.)

DRIVER: What? What is it?

APPLE WOMAN: I think I've forgotten. I can't remember how I made them.

DRIVER: You'll remember. Once you get your strength back, you'll remember.

APPLE WOMAN: I don't think I will. I think I've lost it. *(She cries.)*

DRIVER: Shhh. Just relax. Just relax. It'll be okay. You'll remember.

APPLE WOMAN: I should have told you. I should have told somebody.

DRIVER: Shhh, no, no you couldn't.

APPLE WOMAN: Now it's gone.

DRIVER: It will come back. Just lay still.

APPLE WOMAN: It's like I'm peeling away, Driver.

DRIVER: Shhh.

APPLE WOMAN: Layer by layer. And everything I didn't tell another person is gone forever.

SCENE 13

Split scene between DRIVER and APPLE WOMAN and HITCHHIKER and MAN.

HITCHHIKER: I have to go to the bathroom.

MAN: Don't pull that.

HITCHHIKER: I can't help it.

MAN: I can't stop. You know that.

HITCHHIKER: I already pissed my pants once.

MAN: You pissed your pants?

HITCHHIKER: Yes.

MAN: That's fucking disgusting.

HITCHHIKER: Come on. I promise I won't try anything. I just need to go.

MAN: No. Not until I see Candice.

(APPLE WOMAN is looking out the window.)

DRIVER: How are you feeling?

(No answer.)

DRIVER: What is the name of this place we're going to again?

APPLE WOMAN: I can't remember.

DRIVER: I recognize the smell. Sure wish I could see the countryside more. Blindness is frustrating.

APPLE WOMAN: There's not much to look at.

DRIVER: I think I've been here before. Sometime ago. It reminds me of my old home. I had a wife, you know. Not anymore.

APPLE WOMAN: How much farther?

DRIVER: Ten miles. *(Pulls over the truck.)*

APPLE WOMAN: What is it?

DRIVER: I think you should probably drive from here on.

APPLE WOMAN: Why? Your eyes?

DRIVER: Makes a man helpless.

APPLE WOMAN: Here. I'll get out. You just slide over.

DRIVER: Okay.

(They switch.)

MAN: Hitchhiker, can I ask you a question?

HITCHHIKER: Yes.

MAN: When you found her, on the side of the road. What did she look like?

HITCHHIKER: What do you mean?

MAN: I mean what did she look like, dammit! Her face and stuff!

HITCHHIKER: She looked the same. Like she did when she sold us the apples, only dead.

MAN: She was still pretty?

HITCHHIKER: Yeah.

MAN: I like you, Hitchhiker.

HITCHHIKER: Thank you.

MAN: She jumped.

HITCHHIKER: What?

MAN: Out of the bed of the truck. She jumped. There. That's what happened.

HITCHHIKER: While you were driving?

MAN: Yeah. I never thought she would do that. That's why I hold a gun to people's heads now. Except it's too heavy to hold up all the time.

HITCHHIKER: Oh, my God.

MAN: I didn't notice for fifty miles. She just jumped.

DRIVER: How are you feeling? Are you remembering your recipes?

APPLE WOMAN: No. I can't remember hardly anything anymore.

DRIVER: It will come back. I promise.

APPLE WOMAN: So this is it? The last ten miles.

DRIVER: The closer we get, I swear, I can smell it. The closer we get! Something is going to happen. Can you feel it? Maybe it's something in the air.

APPLE WOMAN: Pollen.

DRIVER: Yeah. Just wait. It's going to be amazing.

MAN: What's that? Is that the truck? That's the truck isn't it? That's it!

HITCHHIKER: Yes. I think so.

MAN: We caught them! We did it! We caught them! Where's the gun? Give me the gun! I think it's on the floor here.

HITCHHIKER: The gun...

MAN: I know it's her. I can feel it. She can't run away from responsibility. Hand me the gun!

HITCHHIKER: What do you want with the gun?

MAN: I found you, Candice.

HITCHHIKER: I mean it, what are you going to do?

MAN: I found you.

HITCHHIKER: *(Takes the gun and points it at MAN's head.)* Stop the truck.

(Pause.)

MAN: That's my gun.

APPLE WOMAN: You kissed me, didn't you?

DRIVER: What?

APPLE WOMAN: When I was away. You kissed me.

DRIVER: I was trying to revive you.

APPLE WOMAN: I can taste it. More than once, wasn't it?

DRIVER: Well, the first one didn't work.

APPLE WOMAN: No.

DRIVER: I was desperate.

APPLE WOMAN: Why?

DRIVER: Well, I didn't want you to die. And how about it, are you remembering anything? We've got to be getting close. Can you see the ocean yet?

APPLE WOMAN: No. Just the mirage.

HITCHHIKER: *(Still pointing the gun.)* Stop the truck.

MAN: You stole my gun, Hitchhiker! I paid fifty bucks for that gun!

HITCHHIKER: I mean it.

MAN: I liked you, Hitchhiker.

HITCHHIKER: I'm serious.

MAN: *(Begins accelerating the truck.)* I'm not stopping.

HITCHHIKER: Slow down!

MAN: No.

HITCHHIKER: Stop it!

MAN: I found you, Candice. Here I come.

APPLE WOMAN: *(Starts crying again.)* I don't feel so good.

DRIVER: What is it?

APPLE WOMAN: I don't think I'm going to make it.

DRIVER: Just keep your eyes on the road.

APPLE WOMAN: How many times have I died, Driver?

DRIVER: Don't say that. None. You haven't died once, yet. What doesn't kill you makes you stronger.

APPLE WOMAN: I don't feel strong.

DRIVER: Just wait. At the ocean you'll feel better. You'll get a new face and an untried heart.

APPLE WOMAN: I said that once didn't I?

DRIVER: You did.

APPLE WOMAN: Maybe if we lived life backwards. Grew younger, unlearned everything, became babies. Maybe that would be better. What's that?

(We hear the sound of a speeding vehicle a second before MAN's truck smashes into the side of DRIVER's truck. Lights change dramatically at the exact moment of impact. Both trucks go spinning like carousels. MAN's truck flips over. DRIVER's truck twirls until it hits a post. The moment the truck hits the post, lights and sound instantly stop, leaving the stage dim and quiet. Everything looks like a heap of mess. Gradually, as the lights slowly

increase, we are able to make out the results of the accident. DRIVER is unconscious in the passenger side of his truck. APPLE WOMAN has spilled out the side of the truck like yolk from a cracked egg. MAN ends up pinned underneath his truck. HITCHHIKER was thrown from the truck and is laying on the ground. Lights continue to make their way back to their previous level. Gradually, HITCHHIKER begins to regain consciousness. Just as he begins to move around, though, he feels a sharp pain in his leg that shocks him. It is broken. With this in mind, he carefully moves himself into a more comfortable position. HITCHHIKER, now sitting, looks around him. First he sees MAN, now dead. The beginning of this scene can take time as both characters regain consciousness.)

HITCHHIKER: Oh, shit. *(Then he sees APPLE WOMAN.)* Oh, God. *(Then DRIVER.)* Driver! Driver! You okay?

DRIVER: Where am I? How far are we?

HITCHHIKER: God, man, I thought you were gone too.

DRIVER: What?

HITCHHIKER: There was an accident.

DRIVER: I can't see very well. *(He tries blinking to focus.)* My head. It's…

HITCHHIKER: Look at me.

DRIVER: It…hurts. It feels big.

HITCHHIKER: Look at me.

(He does.)

HITCHHIKER: I don't see any blood. Man, you got a hard head.

DRIVER: Who are you?

HITCHHIKER: You can't tell? *(Laughs.)* It's me! You know…I pissed in your truck.

DRIVER: Where's the Apple Woman?

HITCHHIKER: Who?

DRIVER: The woman!

HITCHHIKER: The dead one we found? I believe she's still dead. A couple times over now.

DRIVER: Where is she?

HITCHHIKER: On the ground. Her face is mashed in bad. That happen in the accident?

DRIVER: Which way?!

HITCHHIKER: You can't see her?

DRIVER: Left or right?

HITCHHIKER: Right, right.

DRIVER: *(Moves in that direction until he finds her. He touches her leg first and moves his way up to her face.)* Oh no. It happened again. Was it you?

HITCHHIKER: Me?

DRIVER: Did you hit us?

HITCHHIKER: No! Shit no! It was that guy we saw. When she was in that truck with that man. It was him.

DRIVER: Where is he?

HITCHHIKER: Dead, too.

DRIVER: You sure?

HITCHHIKER: He's pinned under his own truck.

DRIVER: Where?

HITCHHIKER: Just in front of you. He didn't listen to me. I told him, like I told you. All this was gonna turn for the worse…

(DRIVER finds MAN's body and hits him in the face.)

HITCHHIKER: He's already dead.

DRIVER: I know. *(He continues hitting.)*

HITCHHIKER: Stop it. Don't hit a dead guy.

DRIVER: *(Stops. He is breathing hard.)* Ow. I think I hurt my wrist.

HITCHHIKER: You don't punch a dead guy.

(DRIVER goes back to APPLE WOMAN's body.)

HITCHHIKER: Hey.

DRIVER: What?

HITCHHIKER: You gotta get going back.

DRIVER: Back where?

HITCHHIKER: There was a town back there. You gotta get help. I can't walk like this. Fucking hurts to move.

DRIVER: I'm not going back.

HITCHHIKER: You what?

DRIVER: I can't go back. Not east. I can't do that.

HITCHHIKER: Yes, you can.

DRIVER: I gotta take her to the ocean.

HITCHHIKER: Your truck is smashed.

DRIVER: I'm gonna carry her.

HITCHHIKER: Carry that dead body? What about me? I'm alive here.

DRIVER: The cops will come soon.

HITCHHIKER: You can't leave me to the cops!

DRIVER: She'd want me to do this.

HITCHHIKER: To carry her fucking dead body? You think she cares what you do with her body? She's dead. She's not grateful. She's not impressed. She's dead.

She's got brains coming out her forehead. She's got a hole for a face. She's cold and dead and blue and hard. I told you this would happen. I told you this was a mistake.

DRIVER: Enough.

HITCHHIKER: And why the hell would she even want to come back? Just to be the woman without a face?

DRIVER: All right. Enough.

HITCHHIKER: But hey! Keep going. It doesn't matter. You can drag her over rocks, mountains, ice, and shit, run over her a few more times...

DRIVER: I said enough!! I never said I was right for this. What do I know about taking care of a woman? You think you learn anything about a woman driving sixty thousand miles west? You don't. Not one thing. *(Panting.)* But I gotta...I gotta do something! *(Hits his head.)* This goddamned head! Back when I had a wife I didn't know anything and I don't know anything now. And she's ruined. She's ruined now, I know. But I'm not leaving her! Not this time! 'Cause that's all I've ever done. I've left everywhere! I've been driving for so goddamned long... I've been tricked, I think. That's what it is. All this time I've been going in circles and there's no such thing as a straight line. 'Cause the only way to really go somewhere, I mean *really* head off someplace, some direction...is to stop. Stop and build something, I guess.

HITCHHIKER: Then stop.

DRIVER: But she...

HITCHHIKER: Bury her.

DRIVER: No, see she...

HITCHHIKER: She needs to get buried.

DRIVER: I know you might not believe me here but…

HITCHHIKER: This body's been out in the sun too long.

DRIVER: Listen to me, she woke…

HITCHHIKER: You've got to get her underground, man, before she really starts to stink.

DRIVER: She might not be dead!!

HITCHHIKER: What?

DRIVER: She might still make it.

HITCHHIKER: She… That's a dead woman.

DRIVER: No. She came back.

HITCHHIKER: She's not even bleeding anymore.

DRIVER: She's come back before when she was cold.

HITCHHIKER: I can't believe this! She's dead.

DRIVER: But what if she's not!? What if something miraculous happens? What if she comes back and she gets a new face and she's fixed up with a new heart?

HITCHHIKER: What are you talking about…

DRIVER: And she gets to start over. Wouldn't that be something? I don't want to miss that. How could I miss that? I drove all this way…

HITCHHIKER: It's not going to happen. She's dead dead dead!

DRIVER: You don't know!

(Pause. HITCHHIKER grabs the gun from the dead MAN's hand and fires twice at the body of APPLE WOMAN. It shakes with the impact.)

HITCHHIKER: She's dead! She can't feel anything.

(He fires again. DRIVER lunges for HITCHHIKER. As soon as they clash, HITCHHIKER lets out a howl. DRIVER begins pounding HITCHHIKER in the side.)

HITCHHIKER: Ahh! My leg!

DRIVER: You fucking son of a bitch! I'll fucking kill you! You better shoot me first!

HITCHHIKER: Stop. Sto… *(Passes out.)*

DRIVER: You hear me? You better shoot me before you shoot her! You understand? Hey! You understand?

(There is no answer.)

DRIVER: Hey. Hey. *(Backs away.)* Shit. Oh, Jesus.

(HITCHHIKER comes to, groaning. He doesn't have much energy.)

DRIVER: Are you okay? Hey. Are you okay?

(HITCHHIKER nods. DRIVER helps him get up and leans him against the truck.)

DRIVER: Does your leg hurt?

(HITCHHIKER nods.)

DRIVER: I think I just finished the job on my wrist. It's broke, I think.

HITCHHIKER: That's what you get. Beating up the dead and injured. Loser.

DRIVER: Yeah. I remember why I was traveling west, now. Alone. Why I never picked anybody up. *(DRIVER moves over to APPLE WOMAN and picks her up into his lap.)* And here I am. Right back where I started, with a dead woman in my arms. I guess it's not going to happen. She was going to wake up beautifully. *(To APPLE*

WOMAN.) You were. You were going to wake up one more time. I can see it, what was going to happen. I'm carrying you, kinda like this, and it's night. There's something... strange in the air, like a thought, or a hum, kinda riding the wind, settling in the ground, in the dust, and the bugs move to it, mice dig to it, cactus wait for rain, the night sleeps to it. It's this melody they all hum. And I'm carrying you through it all, the desert at night. And we're almost there, to the end. And we walk right up to a house. I remember this house. I knock on the door and I hear somebody say, "Coming!" Just like that, half-sung. "Coming!" The way only a woman can sing it, how they half-sing everything. I hear her footsteps down the stairs just like in my old home. Just like I remember them. I hear the door opening. I'm standing tall, holding you in my arms, strong-like, not dragging you. The door's open and she's standing there in front of us, still. I look at her face. And it's *your* face. It's *you* staring back at me. She gasps. "It's you!" she says. Your hand is covering your mouth. I always loved the way she did that. "You're back!" she says. Then I stretch out my arms and return your body. She seems sad. And I say, I say, "My love, I did it. I finished the task. I saw myself. And I looked like you." And you smile, Apple Woman, you smile.

(DRIVER *carefully lays her to rest, covering her face, and slowly begins walking back east until he exits the stage. Blackout.*)

END OF PLAY

PLAYS AND PLAYWRIGHTS 2001

Edited by Martin Denton
Preface by Robert Simonson

ISBN 09670234-2-4   Retail: $15.00

Washington Square Dreams by Gorilla Repertory Theatre

Fate by Elizabeth Horsburgh

Velvet Ropes by Joshua Scher

The Language of Kisses by Edmund De Santis

Word to Your Mama by Julia Lee Barclay

Cuban Operator Please… by Adrian Rodriguez

The Elephant Man—The Musical by Jeff Hylton & Tim Werenko

House of Trash by Trav S.D.

Straight-Jacket by Richard Day

PLAYS AND PLAYWRIGHTS 2002

Edited by Martin Denton
Foreword by Bill C. Davis

ISBN 09670234-3-2   Retail: $15.00

The Death of King Arthur by Matthew Freeman

Match by Marc Chun

Woman Killer by Chiori Miyagawa

The Wild Ass's Skin by J. Scott Reynolds

Halo by Ken Urban

Shyness Is Nice by Marc Spitz

Reality by Curtiss I' Cook

The Resurrectionist by Kate Chell

Bunny's Last Night In Limbo by Peter S. Petralia

Summerland by Brian Thorstenson

PLAYS AND PLAYWRIGHTS 2003

Edited by Martin Denton
Foreword by Mario Fratti

ISBN 09670234-4-0   Retail $15.00

A Queer Carol by Joe Godfrey

Pumpkins For Smallpox by Catherine Gillet

Looking For The Pony by Andrea Lepcio

Black Thang by Ato Essandoh

The Ninth Circle by Edward Musto

The Doctor of Rome by Nat Colley

Galaxy Video by Marc Morales

The Last Carburetor by Leon Chase

Out To Lunch by Joseph Langham

Ascending Bodily by Maggie Cino

Last Call by Kelly McAllister

Additional information about the series can be found on the web at
www.newyorktheatreexperience.org/pep.htm.

Plays and Playwrights books are available in bookstores and online,
or order directly from the publisher. Send a check or money order for
$15 per copy (plus $4.00 shipping) to:

The New York Theatre Experience, Inc.
P.O. Box 744, Bowling Green Station
New York, NY 10274-0744

ABOUT THE AUTHOR

MARTIN DENTON is executive director of The New York Theatre Experience, Inc. He is the founder, chief reviewer, and editor of nytheatre.com, one of the premier sources for theatre reviews and information on the Internet since 1996. He is the author of *The New York Theatre Experience Book of the Year 1998* and the editor of *Plays and Playwrights for the New Millennium, Plays and Playwrights 2001, Plays and Playwrights 2002*, and *Plays and Playwrights 2003*. He lives in New York City with two Siamese cats, Logan and Briscoe.

THE NEW YORK THEATRE EXPERIENCE

The New York Theatre Experience, Inc., is a nonprofit New York State corporation. Its mission is to use traditional and new media to foster interest, engagement, and participation in theatre and drama and to provide tangible support to theatre artists and dramatists, especially emerging artists and artists in the nonprofit sector. The principal activity of The New York Theatre Experience is the operation of a free website (www.nytheatre.com) that comprehensively covers the New York theatre scene—on, off-, and off-off-Broadway. The New York Theatre Experience also publishes yearly anthologies of new plays by emerging playwrights. Please visit us at www.nytheatreexperience.org.